BLOOMSBURY
THEATRE GUIDE

BLOOMSBURY THEATRE GUIDE

Trevor R. Griffiths and Carole Woddis

BLOOMSBURY

DEDICATION

FOR GAY CLIFFORD

First published 1988

Bloomsbury Publishing Limited, 2 Soho Square, London W1V 5DE

All photographs © Donald Cooper, except Brook, Charabanc, Errol John, LIFT © Sarah Ainslie. We gratefully acknowledge the photographers' help and co-operation.

British Library Cataloguing in Publication Data

Griffiths, Trevor R.
Bloomsbury theatre guide.
1. Theatre
I. Title II. Woddis, Carole
792

ISBN 0 7475 0091 6

Designed by Anita Plank

Typeset by Alexander Typesetting, Inc., Indianapolis, IN

Printed in Great Britain by Butler & Tanner Limited, Frome & London

CONTENTS

INTRODUCTION

This is a theatre reference book with a difference because it concentrates on the writers, the plays and the companies you are actually likely to be able to see in the theatre now, rather than those who get into theatre reference books because they have always been in theatre reference books, even though no one has done their plays for the last hundred years. Its other unique feature is a cross-referencing system that allows you to find other plays or authors who have tackled similar topics, share similar interests or offer marked contrasts to the one you started with; and when you look at those further entries you will find more cross-references that can lead you on a sometimes surprising journey of discovery that will give added enjoyment to your appreciation of theatre.

We hope the result is a work that communicates some of the enthusiasm and pleasure all of us who contributed to the book have had from our theatre-going, and that it is a useful guide to the contemporary theatre scene. Theatre, after all, is to be enjoyed, whether that means something to stretch the imaginative and intellectual sinews or escapism; and it always reflects the society in which it takes place, for good or ill, directly or indirectly, positively or negatively, and so offers a way of taking the temperature of a nation.

In making our choices of entries for this book we were aware that we would appear to be privileging dramatists and plays over the other vital aspects of the production process. In fact, we share the dramatist Bryony Lavery's view that 'a play is a wonderfully nutty fruit cake . . . made up of the script, the directors, actors, audience, technicians . . . it's what happens the night we were all there for the performance', but we also know that what gets handed down as theatre, what gets remembered, is often to do with what gets published; if it's not printed it doesn't exist.

When we talk about our cultural heritage, the 'our' tends to refer to white middle-class heterosexual men; the female voice and women's experience of life, like those of black, Asian and gay communities and people with disabilities, is under-represented. Within the limitations of space and the need to span the range of international theatre, we have tried to do a little to redress that balance. Our choices are inevitably subjective—particularly as regards very new writers and companies of promise and we have not included writers who work mainly for television—but part of the fun for us was to try to pick out those who would make a lasting contribution, as well as those whose reputations are secure; and remember that no matter how fringe or minority some of our choices may appear today, and how idiosyncratic the juxtaposition of the tried and established with the burgeoning talents may seem, the unknowns of today may be the Harold Pinters, Caryl Churchills and Hanif Kureishis of tommorrow, because film and television feed off the theatre. Live theatre, with all the challenges of entertaining an audience who are actually there with you sharing the same space, is the place where playwrights go to serve their apprenticeship and to renew their spirits (if not their bank balances).

Trevor R. Griffiths
Carole Woddis

May 1988

HOW TO USE THIS BOOK

The book is divided into an alphabetical list of over 300 main entries (which cover individual dramatists, some theatre companies, areas of theatre such as Pantomime and important directors/theorists) and an index of play titles, theatres, companies, theatre people and topics such as 'Theatre of the Absurd'.

You can look up an individual in the main alphabetical list and use that as your starting point, or you can start with a dramatist's name or a play title and look it up in the index which will tell you where that name or title appears in the book, either in a main entry or in a cross reference from another entry. A ▷ in front of a dramatist's or company's name indicates that they have their own main entry.

Each main entry for an individual writer follows a standard format with a list of plays, discussion of the writer and a list of cross-references. For most writers there is also a key play selected by the contributor for more detailed treatment and for a few major writers there may be more than one key play. We have tried to make the dates of plays as accurate as possible but in some cases there is uncertainty about the exact order of composition and/or production of plays: the dates given are, wherever possible, those of the first public appearances of plays whether in production or in print or in some cases, particularly living playwrights, when written. In the case of writers' dates of birth and death there are also some areas of uncertainty (and some living writers, or their agents, have been unwilling to release information); wherever there is doubt we have reflected it in the use of c by the doubtful date. We have not tried to include all the plays written by each writer or a comprehensive list of film, television, radio, translation and adaptation, or other writing credits but we have tried to draw attention to those that form a significant part of a writer's output. Similarly we have not aimed to be inclusive in our coverage of awards won by writers. In the case of foreign language plays we have tried to include familiar English titles where these exist and literal translations where they don't. We have also tried to track down alternative titles and revised versions of plays going under different titles wherever possible, but a glance at the entry for John Byrne will show the scope of the problem.

The authors would be grateful if any corrections to matters of fact and suggestions for inclusions in future editions were sent to them care of the publishers.

ABBENSETTS, Michael [1938–]
Guyanaian dramatist, now living in the USA

Plays include :

***Sweet Talk* (1973), *Alterations* (1978), *Samba* (1980), *In the Mood* (1981), *The Dark Horse* (1981), *El Dorado* (1983), *Outlaw* (1983)**

Television includes:

***The Museum Attendant* (1973), *Inner City Blues* (1975), *Crime and Passion* (1976), *Black Christmas* (1977), *Roadrunner* (1977), *Easy Money* (1982)**

Michael Abbensetts was the first Caribbean writer to have a television series in Britain with *Empire Road* (1978). Before that he had already had success with *Sweet Talk*, *Alterations*, a television play *The Museum Attendant* and radio plays. The secret of Abbensetts' success was his ability to write situation comedies whose characters and human predicaments struck a common chord, and where colour was not the predominant theme. They appeared therefore to have a universal appeal. However, under the comic, often genially satirical veneer, they reveal bitter legacies of colonialism and emigration as seen through the frustrations, aspirations, and tragedies of the ordinary British black-man-in-the-street. He deals with marital problems (*Sweet Talk*), and the price to pay for ambition (*Alterations*), with the pathos of individuals who have seen better days (*Samba*), and with those who fought for the 'mother country' (*In the Mood*).

With the increasing sense of black consciousness in Britain, Abbensetts' gentle humour is less in favour now, but he continues to write successfully in the USA and *Sweet Talk*, Abbensetts' most popular play, has been produced in Nigeria (The World Black Arts Festival; 1977), New York, Kenya, Canada, and throughout the Caribbean.

TRY THESE:
▷Mustapha Matura, ▷Edgar White, ▷Derek Walcott, particularly for examining painful personal legacies of colonialism; ▷Hanif Kureishi and ▷Mustapha Matura for 'mother country' disillusionment; ▷Trevor Rhone for a similar use of sit-com; ▷Tunde Ikoli, ▷Caryl Phillips, and Felix Cross and David Simon's *Blues for Railton* have all focused on the British black experience; for American equivalents, see Samm-Art Williams and ▷Negro Ensemble Company.

ABBOTT, George [1887–]
American writer and director/producer of musicals

Plays and musicals include:

***Three Men on a Horse* (with John Cecil Holm; 1935), *On Your Toes* (with Rodgers and Hart; 1936), *The Boys from Syracuse* (based on Shakespeare's *Comedy of Errors*; 1938), *Beat the Band* (with George Marion Jr; 1942), *Where's Charley* (1948), *A Tree Grows in Brooklyn* (with Betsy Smith; 1951), *The Pajama Game* (with Richard Bissell; 1954), *Damn Yankees* (with Douglas Wallop; 1955), and *Fiorello* (with Jerome Weidman; 1959)**

Author and co-author of over fifty plays and musicals, and a legendary director and producer, if anyone sums up the Broadway musical in its hey-day, they say George Abbott. Like a eulogy to the great American dream, an evening with Abbott paid homage to the vivacity of the entrepreneurial spirit; it was ebullient, full of slick one-liners and showbiz razzmatazz, and put together with brilliant efficiency. Like all good farceurs, Abbott spins his plays and musicals on the corniest of plots – in *Damn Yankees*, it's a losing baseball team; in *Three Men on a Horse*, it's a natural gift for winning. But likes all good farceurs, there's often a twist – *Damn Yankees*

TRY THESE:
Frank Loesser's *Guys and Dolls* for its similarly colourful array of gamblers and low-life characters; ▷Brecht's *Schweik in the Second World War* for its triumph of the 'little man'; ▷Kaufman and ▷Hart for more celebrations of the amiable eccentric; see also musicals.

also has a touch of the Faustian knot thrown in (the baseball fan sells his soul to the devil in exchange for footballing skills), whilst *The Pajama Game* may be about boy meets girl but she's a shop steward and he's the management stooge out to stop her from earning a few cents more an hour. Like all the best farces, a good moral message gets stirred in along with the humour.

Abbott was also responsible for producing and directing some of Broadway's greatest classics, such as *Pal Joey*, *Call Me Madam*, and *On Your Toes*. All these seem endurably buoyant and have been more successfully revived in the West End in recent years than his own shows, with Sian Phillips huskily recalling Dietrich in *Pal Joey* and prima ballerina Natalia Markova outshining even the elasticated Tim Flavin in *On Your Toes*. *Call Me Madam* was indelibly marked as Noële Gordon's last major public show before her death. On the other hand, *The Boys from Syracuse* bombed on its last outing in London. Abbott's 1920s period piece *Broadway*, directed on Broadway by the author in 1987, also failed to make the time trip. Perhaps his greatest achievement to date, at 100 plus is simply staying alive.

Three Men on a Horse

Three Men on a Horse, a happy mix of farce, parable and sentiment, is a classic of its kind, with its downtrodden copy-writer, who also happens to have a way of predicting horse-race winners, plus a large supporting cast of kind-hearted gamblers, brassy blonde, long-suffering but loyal wife (and the inevitable butt of comedy, the dragon mother-in-law). *Three Men on a Horse* cleverly ridicules the American obsession for winning, turning it equally into a celebration of warm-hearted moral decency and the triumph of the downtrodden little man over the system. It was captured with spirit and affection in Jonathan Lynn's 1987 ▷ National Theatre revival – not least in Geoffrey Hutchings' innocent-at-large and Gemma Craven's tart-with-a-heart.

ADAMOV, Arthur [1908–1970]

French dramatist

Plays include:

> ***La Parodie* (*The Parody*; 1950), *La Grande et la Petite Manoeuvre* (*The Large and the Small Manoeuvre*; 1950), *Le Professeur Taranne* (*Professor Taranne*; 1953), *Le Ping-Pong* (*Ping-Pong*; 1955), *Paolo Paoli* (1957), *Printemps 71* (*Spring of 71*; 1962), *Sainte Europe* (*Holy Europe*; 1966), *Off Limits* (1968)**

Adamov's plays are most often put on by amateur and college groups, and they usually try the short and Kafkaesque dream play *Professor Taranne*; but there are more interesting possibilities in his later plays. His father was a Russian refugee, and he himself made a precarious literary living in Paris in the 1920s and 1930s, when he was a friend of ▷ Artaud and linked with the Surrealists, and did not start writing plays until his forties. His 1950s plays are dream-like and obsessional, dealing with his urges to suicide, fear of impotence, and general masochism, and his name then tended to be bracketed with those of ▷ Beckett and ▷ Ionesco; however, there are signs of his later political interests in *Ping-Pong*, in which two men spend their lives developing a better electric pin-table, a heavy-handed symbol for capitalism in general.

With the coming of the Algerian War he turned to political plays, notably *Paolo Paoli*, which uses the trade in ostrich feathers and rare butterflies to make anti-capitalist points about the *Belle Époque*. In the 1960s he wrote plays on the Paris Commune and on apartheid, a satire on de Gaulle's France, and an interesting and complex full-length play set in the USA at the time of the Vietnam War. *Off Limits* is built around a series of parties where the middle-aged drink and the young take dope, each scene interrupted by games or agit-prop sketches. This would be worth trying in English, though expensive, as would Planchon's collage of his work, *A.A. Théâtres d'Adamov*.

TRY THESE:
▷Strindberg for the early dream plays; ▷Ionesco for writing as a liberation from personal neurosis; ▷Brecht for the later political plays; ▷Trevor Griffiths' *The Party* for another party at a time of political strife; ▷Megan Terry's *Viet Rock*, for an anti-Vietnam American satire; also ▷Jean-Claude Van Itallie's *America Hurrah* for more anti-US satire.

ADAPTATIONS AND ADAPTERS

The tradition of translating/adapting/reworking plays by

other authors in other languages is almost as old as the theatre itself – witness the 'identical twins' plot that is found (inter alia) in Plautus, the *commedia dell'arte*, ▷ Goldoni, ▷ Dario Fo, and ▷ Shakespeare (twice). However, the more proprietorial attitude to literary works of the last two centuries has meant that modern translations of contemporary plays have been attempts to make the work of foreign authors accessible to a public which cannot understand them in the original rather than springboards for something fresh – though the frequency with which works are described as 'adaptations' and the tendency to share the task of translation between two people, one of whom can understand the original and one of whom can write plays, makes one wonder about the fidelity of the English versions.

Attempts to put novels on the stage (as opposed to the Shakespearean habit of taking his plots where he could find them) date back to the Victorian era, when they were primarily 'the play of the book', mostly run up by the resident hack for an audience unaccustomed to reading for pleasure; this market vanished with the rise of the cinema. (*Ben Hur*, for instance, started as a novel and was made into a very successful melodrama before it became a film.) In recent years, however, there have been a remarkable number of adaptations of novels, 'classic' and otherwise, aimed at an audience of much greater sophistication than their Victorian predecessors. The earliest (and one of the longest) was probably the Science Fiction Theatre of Liverpool's *Illuminatus*, which opened the Cottesloe in 1977; the paradigm the ▷ RSC's *The Life and Adventures of Nicholas Nickleby*, adapted by ▷ David Edgar in 1979; the most disastrous was ▷ Mike Alfreds' *The Wandering Jew*, at the ▷ National Theatre in 1987 (the melodramatic acting style was carefully worked out, but the plot wasn't up to it); and the culmination of this tendency is surely ▷ Peter Brook's *The Mahabharata*, which manages to contain a massive Indian epic within nine hours of superb narrative theatre. Shorter and more manageable adaptations of novels have included those by ▷ Shared Experience, including Evelyn Waugh's *A Handful of Dust* (1982) and Zola's *Nana* (1987); ▷ Brian Friel's version of Turgenev's *Fathers and Sons* (1987), and ▷ Christopher Hampton's superb transmutation of Laclos' *Les Liaisons Dangereuses* (1985). These adaptations seem to meet a basic need for story-telling that is not satisfied by most modern playwrights. They are sometimes produced as a collective effort by a writer and a company; they tend to be long, and to move between narration and impersonation, because of the amount of plot which has to be got in; staged non-illusionistically, because the original author set his/her scenes with no eye to dramatic practicability; full of bravura acting and furious doubling, for the same reason; and, at their best, very exciting indeed.

Aside from these adaptations from novels, there have been a growing number of translations, free and otherwise, from foreign plays in recent years: plays by ▷ Racine, ▷ Schiller, ▷ Lessing, and other authors previously thought untranslatable and/or unactable have been successfully presented, and added to the well-known stock of ▷ Ibsen and ▷ Chekhov (though Michael Meyer's reliable ▷ Ibsen and ▷ Strindberg translations are put on somewhere in most years, eg in 1985 *Little Eyolf* appeared at the Lyric, Hammersmith, and *Peer Gynt* at The Place; in 1986 *Creditors* was at the Almeida and *A Dream Play* at the King's Head). A number of translators' names recur frequently: Tony Harrison became well-known for his brilliant translation and updating of *The Misanthrope* in 1973, and his later translations and adaptations for the ▷ National Theatre – *Phaedra Britannica* (1975, set in British India), *The Oresteia* (1981), and *The Mysteries* (presented all together at the Lyceum in 1985) – have been equally successful. He has a fine line in knotty, colloquial verse ('Batter, batter the doom-drum, but believe there'll be better' went his Anglo-Saxon line in *The Oresteia*, where the ▷ RSC's *The Greeks* had the more mellifluous 'Cry sorrow, sorrow, but let the good prevail'); and he happily engages with the most 'un-

Belinda Davison as ***Nana*** in Shared Experience's 1987 production of the same name, adapted from Zola's novel by Olwen Wymark, directed by Jane Gibson and Sue Lefton.

translatable' authors. The same is true of Robert David Macdonald, who has been prepared to tackle, generally for the ▷ Glasgow Citizens' Theatre, ▷ Racine's *Phedra*, ▷ Lorca's *The House of Bernarda Alba*, ▷ Schnitzler's *Intermezzo*, and ▷ Goethe's *Faust* (both parts), usually working from the original, which is by no means true of most translators; he has also joined the novel-adapters with such unlikely authors as Proust. ▷ Mike Alfreds, beside his adaptations of novels, has directed his own workmanlike translations of many plays, mostly for ▷ Shared Experience, including ▷ Chekhov's *The Seagull*, *Three Sisters*, and *The Cherry Orchard*, ▷ Schnitzler's *La Ronde*, and *The Comedy Without a Title* (from Ruzzante); Christopher Hampton has translated ▷ Horváth for the ▷ National Theatre (*Tales from the Vienna Woods*, 1977, and *Don Juan Comes Back from the War*, 1978); and Adrian Mitchell has translated ▷ Calderón (*The Mayor of Zalamea*, ▷ National Theatre 1981, and *Life's a Dream*, ▷ RSC 1984), as well as ▷ Gogol's *The Government Inspector* (▷ National 1985). One should also mention John Fowles, ▷ Dusty Hughes, and ▷ John Mortimer's speakable versions of ▷ Feydeau, (notably *A Little Hotel on the Side*, National 1984); the list of works now made available is long and encouraging, and currently nothing looks impossible. However, one could wish that more of these plays would enter the repertoire, rather than being done once only to acclamation and then forgotten again.

ADSHEAD, Kay [1954–]

British dramatist

Plays include:

***Thatcher's Women* (1987)**

Like ▷ Sharman Macdonald's *When I Was a Girl I Used to Scream and Shout*, *Thatcher's Women* is a first play by actress/writer, Kay Adshead. Manchester-born Adshead's acting credits include the ▷ National Theatre, the Royal Court, as well as Cathy in a television adaptation of *Wuthering Heights* and a ▷ Mike Leigh 'Play for Today', *Kiss of Death* – a fact which is perhaps relevant when looking at *Thatcher's Women* (presented by ▷ Paines Plough and directed by Pip Broughton), which shows definite traces of television influences in its story of a northern middle-aged wife, pushed reluctantly south and on to the game by her husband's unemployment. One of a rash of plays on similar topics of economic policies impinging on private lives, Adshead's spirited if uneven play – a kind of School in Unsentimental Education or How I Learned to Stop Feeling and Just Play The Game – hops about wildly in tone and style; resilient humour one moment, strained metaphor the next.

Jumpy but promising, Adshead's career – juggling new baby with Royal Court commission and spells of acting – is indicative of the present generation of playwrights, for whom several directions look possible.

TRY THESE:
Julia Schofield's *Love on the Plastic* and ▷Peter Terson's *Strippers* make similar links between unemployment and female exploitation; for contrast see *Stars in the Morning Sky* by Alexander Galin, a more melodramatic view of prostitutes; ▷Debbie Horsfield for a contemporary northern ambience; see also ▷Paines Plough for other new writers.

AESCHYLUS [c 525–456 BC]

wrote the earliest surviving Greek tragedies

Plays include:

***The Persians* (472 BC), *The Seven Against Thebes* (469 BC), *The Oresteian Trilogy* (458 BC), *The Suppliant Women*, *Prometheus Bound* (dates unknown)**

Aeschylus is credited with two of the major innovations in Greek drama: the introduction of a second actor (which made possible dialogue that did not involve the chorus, thus opening the way for greater dramatic flexibility); and the reduction in size (and therefore importance) of the chorus. *The Persians* is particularly interesting for presenting the recent defeat of the Persians at the Battle of Marathon, from a sympathetic viewpoint.

Aeschylus' tenuous hold on the current repertory derives almost entirely from *The Oresteian Trilogy*, the only complete

TRY THESE:
▷Aristophanes, ▷Euripides, Menander and ▷Sophocles wrote the other surviving Greek plays; ▷T. S. Eliot's *The Family Reunion* updates the Orestes myth to 1930s England and ▷Eugene O'Neill's *Mourning Becomes Electra* updates it to New England.

Peter Hall's masked all male production of Tony Harrison's version of Aeschylus' ***The Oresteia***, at the National Theatre, 1981.

trilogy to survive from the Classical Greek theatre. It tells the story of the royal house of Atreus in which crime breeds crime over the generations until the goddess Athene intervenes to substitute reconcilation and justice for the blind process of revenge. Peter Hall directed a memorable all-male version for the ▷ National Theatre in 1981, adapted by Tony Harrison, which is likely to be the basis of future English-language productions.

AGE EXCHANGE,

British touring theatre company

Age Exchange, the brainchild of director Pam Schweitzer is a company aimed specifically at older people with shows based largely on the actual experiences and memories of pensioners. As musical entertainments, enjoyable on several levels, they are performed in community centres, old people's homes, clubs, hospitals etc, by groups of young professional actors and musicians with a minimum of props; they sometimes have the feel of a small end-of-the-pier concert party, and none the worse for that. One moment exuberantly light-hearted (somewhere along the line there is bound to be a singalong of some good old classics) they can also be quite remarkably moving as pieces of theatre, recalling moments of personal tragedy to do with loss of husbands and brothers in the war, or the hardships of the 1920s Depression, or some small individual detail of life, immediately recognisable to all of the audience.

On another level, by sharing past experiences, this kind of 'reminiscence' theatre is thought to help restore identity to pensioners who may have become shut off from their present life. In fact, this kind of oral history is not new. Community and left-wing companies in the 1970s such as Covent Garden Community Theatre or Red Ladder made great use of the actual spoken experiences of ordinary people in their work and ▷ Charabanc, the Belfast company, have built several of their shows largely round recorded interviews.

Likewise, Schweitzer's shows have been built directly around recorded memories and reminiscences of pensioners. *The Time of Our Lives*, for example, recalled outings, dancing, going to the cinema and other memories of courting in the 1920s and 1930s; *Can We Afford the Doctor?* recalled what it was like being ill before the NHS; and *A Place to Stay* helped pensioners from ethnic groups to remember what it has been like living in Britain and growing old here. Though nostalgic, the shows have also had a campaigning tinge: *Return of the Good Old Days* and *Just Deserts* were both aimed to help pensioners' campaigns and to look at how they have been treated over the years whilst *What Did You Do in the War Mum?* specifically concentrated on the contributions by women in World Wars I and II.

Such has been the success of this reminiscence work that it has now spawned an associated industry, with an Age Exchange Resource Centre open five days a week in south London and a collection of books of each show with edited highlights and photographs.

TRY THESE:
Bedside Manners is another theatre company performing to pensioners; *Falklands Sound/ Voces de Malvinas*, edited by ▷Louise Page used actual material from recorded interviews as did Peter Cox's *The Garden of England* about mining communities and the miners' strike of 1984; Greg Cullen's *Taken Out* was based on recorded interviews; much of Peter Cheeseman's work at stoke-on-Trent has used local oral history, as does much community theare and ▷Ann Jellicoe's work.

ALBEE, Edward [1928–]

American dramatist

Plays include:

***The Zoo Story* (1959), *The Death of Bessie Smith* (1960), *The Sandbox* (1960), *Fam and Yam* (1961), *The American Dream* (1961), *Who's Afraid of Virginia Woolf?* (1962), *Tiny Alice* (1964), *A Delicate Balance* (1966), *Box and Quotations from Chairman Mao Tse-Tung* (1968), *All Over* (1971), *Seascape* (1975), *Counting the Ways* (1976), *Listening* (1976), *The Lady from Dubuque* (1980), *The Man Who Had Three Arms* (1983)**

The adopted grandson of Edward Franklin Albee, a vaudeville theatre owner and manager, Albee consolidated the initial

TRY THESE:
▷Ibsen, ▷Lillian Hellman's *The Children's Hour*, ▷Enid Bagnold's *The Chalk Garden* for closely knit dramas centring on disruptions in family life through the revelation of guilty secrets; ▷Arthur Miller and ▷Tennessee Williams for investigations

success of *The Zoo Story*, in which two men struggle for control of a park bench, with his most popular play *Who's Afraid of Virginia Woolf?*. His later plays have been less universally successful, though *A Delicate Balance*, a somewhat Pinteresque use of drawing room comedy as a metaphor for life, was more readily accepted – probably because of its more realistic surface – than such works as *Seascape*, in which a couple confront two humanoid creatures on a beach, or *The Man Who Had Three Arms*, a tale of a man whose early reputation established him as a freak.

of the American Dream.

Who's Afraid of Virginia Woolf?
A campus play in which a childless middle-aged married couple play sado-masochistic games with a younger couple, *Who's Afraid of Virginia Woolf?* is a searing study of the power of fantasy to both sustain and wreck people's emotional lives. Always attractive to mature actors (Richard Burton and Elizabeth Taylor played the leads in the 1966 film version), the play remains popular with audiences and with managements who appreciate its use of only one set and four actors for financial as well as artistic reasons.

ALFREDS, Mike [1934–]
British adapter, director

TRY THESE:
▷David Edgar, ▷Timberlake Wertenbaker, ▷Michelene Wandor as adapters; ▷Ken Campbell for a similar though more anarchic tradition of adaptation; see also ▷Adaptations and Adapters, ▷Shared Experience.

Plays directed for ▷ Shared Experience include:

> ***Three Sisters* (1980), *Cymbeline* (1980), *The Seagull* (1981), *The Merchant of Venice* (1981), *La Ronde* (1982), *False Admissions* and *Successful Strategies* (by ▷ Marivaux; 1983), *The Comedy Without a Title* (by Ruzzante; 1983); *Marriage* (by ▷ Gogol; 1984); and adaptations of *The Arabian Nights* (1975–7); *Bleak House* (1977–78); and *A Handful of Dust* (1982)**

Long before ▷ David Edgar's adaptation of *Nicholas Nickleby* for the ▷ RSC, the art of adapting novels and producing them as vivid ensemble stage pieces had been steadily continuing under Mike Alfreds' direction for ▷ Shared Experience. London-born Alfreds, who trained in the USA at Carnegie Mellon, and also spent five years in Israel as a director/lecturer, founded Shared Experience in 1975. He pioneered a form of working in which old texts took on new theatrical form, pared down but keeping a strong narrative line, using few props, and relying on the speed, and dramatic and physical skills of a core of performers to play dozens of characters.

Alfreds' adaptations of Charles Dickens' *Bleak House* and Evelyn Waugh's *A Handful of Dust* were particular early successes. He transferred to the ▷ National Theatre to direct *The Cherry Orchard* successfully for the Ian McKellen/Edward Petherbridge group, but his time there has been marred by the sudden withdrawal from the repertory in January 1988 of the five-hour Goldoni trilogy *Countrymania*, reputedly because of poor bookings. How much this also had to do with the lukewarm response to Alfreds' technically impressive but equally lengthy *The Wandering Jew*, adapted by ▷ Michelene Wandor from Eugène Sue's nineteenth-century novel is hard to say. With its cast of seventeen playing over fifty characters, Alfreds' approach to this epic tale of Machiavellian evil and contrasting virtue epitomised the best of his method of working – a galvanic inventiveness, superbly energised and filled-out performances (particularly from such Alfreds regulars as Paola Dionosotti and the extraordinary and under-rated Philip Voss – but still left audiences a little unsure how to react to the production's melodramatic excesses. As a director, Alfreds is much in demand abroad. Hopefully, Britain will not have lost him for too long.

Other adapters who have been involved with ▷ Shared Experience include ▷ Timberlake Wertenbaker (whose English translations of the ▷ Marivaux plays exquisitely caught the mannered artifice and brittle sarcasm of the originals), Fidelis Morgan and Giles Havergal (adaptation of Samuel Richardson's *Pamela*) and Olwen Wymark whose adaptation of Zola's *Nana* directed by Sue Lefton and Jane Gibson steadily grew in performance, deservedly earning a West End run. Havergal also adapted Elizabeth Bowen's *The Heat of the Day* with Felicity Browne.

ALRAWI, Karim [1953–]

Anglo-Egyptian dramatist

Plays include:

***Aliens* (1980), *Before Dawn* (1981), *Sink the Pink* (1982), *Migrations* (1982), *Divide and Rule* (1983), *In Self Defence* (1983), *Fire in the Lake* (1985–87), *A Colder Climate* (1986), *A Child in the Heart* (1987)**

Alrawi was one of only a few dramatists in the early 1980s writing about the effects of racism (others were ▷ Hanif Kureishi and ▷ Tunde Ikoli) from a non-Caribbean point of view. Brought up in Egypt (he can remember the bombing of Suez), Alrawi came to live in Britain at the age of fourteen, in Hackney, and has never forgotten the sense of dislocation the move produced in him or the racial prejudice he experienced in English schools. His plays have always, one way or another, looked with some anger and political awareness at the experience of being an immigrant in this country, often from the vantage point of living in the East End. *Migrations* (an Arts Council John Whiting award winner, and a reworking of the earlier lunchtime *Before Dawn*) looks at issues of religion and culture, integration and local authority corruption, through the eyes of an old Jewish stall holder in Brick Lane, his young Pakistani assistant and the dilemmas of the assistant's sister. *A Colder Climate* is a more subtle, bold attempt to comment on Thatcher's Britain, showing racism and National Front attitudes filtering through into the behaviour of a group of contemporary East End characters, but it suffered in a Royal Court production that seemed unusually ill-prepared. Reviews have not always been kind to Alrawi but he remains a dramatist of flair and passionate commitment. Now a member of ▷ Joint Stock's newly constituted management team, he has also been writer-in-residence at the Royal Court and the Theatre Royal Stratford East. His latest play for ▷ Joint Stock, *A Child in the Heart*, typically pulls no punches in its indictment of Third World cultural exploitation by the West, and particularly the dubious motivations behind charity-giving, Third World child fostering, and inter-cultural marriage. In many senses, there is an almost Old Testament feeling about it in its ultimate insistence on sticking to Tribe, in keeping with Alrawi's consistent investigation of cultural identity and what it means.

TRY THESE:
▷Hanif Kureishi's *Borderline* for images of National Frontism and Asian girls in conflict with their traditional culture; ▷Harwant Bains' *The Fighting Kite* for British Asians caught between two cultures; for images of the East End, ▷Tony Marchant's *The Lucky Ones*; Jonathan Falla's *Topokana Martyr's Day* also deals with the questionable motivations of Western charity-giving, in the Third World.

AMERICAN THEATRES

'Why doesn't America have a National Theatre?' envious Yanks ask upon arrival in London, a capital which in effect has two such institutions (the ▷ National Theatre and the ▷ RSC). The prevailing wisdom goes that it is the network of non-profit regional theatres spread across the fifty states whose collective repertories together constitute that national theatre. According to the Theatre Communications Group in New York, there are over 300 such theatres whose stability seems reasonably assured in an era of precarious private sector funding and government support that pales (believe it or not) next to Britain's.

Many of the best-known producing theatres (ie venues that initiate their own work as opposed to receiving plays from outside), are in New York, although the hegemony of the East Coast has been challenged of late by cultural capitals like Chicago, San Diego, and Los Angeles. Some theatres are associated with certain writers (Charles Fuller and Samm-Art Williams with the ▷ Negro Ensemble Company in New York; ▷ August Wilson with the Yale Repertory Theatre in New Haven, Connecticut); others with certain styles (▷ Wisdom Bridge and Steppenwolf in Chicago, with their high-energy kineticism); still others with both (New York's Playwrights' Horizons, with their brightly designed yet thematically disturbing plays about family angst). The non-profit theatre in America may depend for its repertoire too heavily on Broadway (a hit Broadway revival, like John Guare's *House of Blue Leaves*, tends to dominate Theatre Communications Group members' line-ups the following year), but it's still the principal outlet for serious, challenging work – and for work in the classics – free from the commercial pressures of Broadway.

TRY THESE:
▷Wisdom Bridge, ▷Steppenwolf, and the ▷Negro Ensemble Company for troupes seen in London; ▷Wendy Wasserstein, ▷Christopher Durang, ▷Albert Innaurato for playwrights associated with a particular venue; ▷Megan Terry for The Omaha Magic Theatre.

ANOUILH, Jean [1910–1987]
French dramatist

Plays include:
***Le Bal de Voleurs* (*Thieves' Carnival*; 1932), *La Sauvage* (*The Restless Heart*; 1934), *L'Eocadia* (*Time Remembered*; 1940), *Le Rendezvous de Senlis* (*Dinner with the Family*; 1941), *Eurydice* (*Point of Departure*; 1941), *Antigone* (1942), *Medée* (*Medea*; 1946), *Roméo et Jeanette* (*Romeo and Jeanette*; 1946), *L'Invitation au Château* (*Ring Round the Moon*; 1947), *Ardèle ou La Marguerite* (*Ardèle: The Cry of the Peacock*; 1948), *La Répétition ou L'Amour Puni* (*The Rehearsal*; 1950), *La Valse des Toréadors* (*Waltz of the Toreadors*; 1952), *L'Alouette* (*The Lark*; 1953), *Pauvre Bitos ou le Dîner de Têtes* (*Poor Bitos or the Masked Diner*; 1956), *L'Honneur de Dieu* (*Becket*; 1959)**

Anouilh's popularity and influence were at their height in the immediate post-war period, and most of his fifty or so plays have been produced in Britain. Known for his exquisite craftsmanship, in later years his work appeared to take on a whimsical tone. But in a theatre career that spanned over half a century, his opus covered a wide range: from the controversial *Antigone*, written against a background of the German occupation (some saw it as an apologia for the Nazis, others as a statement against them), to *Number One*, a self-pitying portrait about the ageing playwright facing up to solitude and old age. Anouilh himself categorised his plays into *pièces roses* (rosy, such as *Dinner with the Family* or *Time Remembered*), *pièces noires* (dark, which include the three Greek-based tragedies, *Eurydice* or *Point of Departure*, *Antigone*, and *Medea*, as well as *Romeo and Jeanette*), *pièces brillantes* (sparkling, such as *Ring Round the Moon*), *pièces grinçantes* (grating, such as *Ardèle* or *Waltz of the Toreadors*), and *pièces costumées* (costume or historical plays such as *Becket*, or *The Lark* (about St Joan). Never regarded as a 'political' writer, Anouilh's plays seem haunted by certain private and obsessive concerns; the corruption of innocence, the pain of human existence, its ugliness and compromise, (the incompatibility of happiness with purity), the clash between the inner and outer worlds, the conflict between past and present, and later in life, loneliness. Above all, as Harold Hobson put it, talking about *Antigone*, there was bitterness and regret at the contrast between 'what life could be and what life was'.

Anouilh's early plays, however, show the bitterness leavened by laughter and strongly influenced by the form and gloss of ▷ Marivaux (for example, *The School for Fathers*, or the Pirandellian play-within-a-play, *The Rehearsal*), where behind brilliant comic dialogue you can detect a typical Anouilh confrontation between purity and the artifice of the aristocratic world. Again, in *Ring Round the Moon*, Anouilh's crippled old lady exploiting her power by re-arranging the lives of those around her is yet another veneer for the playing out of a deeper battle between power and money on the one hand, and poverty and purity on the other.

Anouilh's heroines or heroes frequently sacrifice themselves for a nobler cause; Becket and Joan in *The Lark* are both martyrs to their faith and purity, a theme re-enacted not only in *Antigone* but also by Orpheus and Eurydice, Romeo and Jeanette, and even Medea. *Poor Bitos* on the other hand, about the humiliation of a smug communist deputy at a party where the guests are dressed in Revolutionary costume, is also seen by some as Anouilh's self-portrait etched in self-disgust.

With his fall from fashion, it is easy to forget the impression Anouilh earlier made on British theatre, with successful London productions including *Antigone* (1949), directed by Laurence Olivier with Vivien Leigh, *Ring Round the Moon* (1950) directed by ▷ Peter Brook with Paul Scofield, *The Lark* (1955)) with Dorothy Tutin, and the ▷ RSC's 1960 production of *Becket*, with Christopher Plummer and Eric Porter. Though unpopular in the present climate, time will no doubt resurrect Anouilh in the eyes of a new generation of theatre-goers.

Antigone
Antigone follows ▷ Sophocles but is typically Anouilh in its heroine's option for the purity of death rather than the muckiness

TRY THESE:
▷Sophocles' *Antigone* for the original; The Living Theatre also did a version of *Antigone*; Sartre's *Les Mouches* was another war-time play subversively attacking the Vichy regime; ▷George Bernard Shaw for another treatment of *St Joan*; ▷Terence Rattigan for other personal pains treated with similar skill.

and compromise of life. Sophocles' version dices with the conflict between secular and divine law (another, more modern and interesting reading could see it as a re-assertion of the female and instinctual over man-made law). Anouilh's Antigone is not so much the victim of an unjust law as in Sophocles (who prevents her from burying her brother; she commits suicide when she is punished for attempting to do so) as a martyr to purity. Creon argues with her and, unlike Sophocles' Creon who is thoroughly guilt-stricken for the trail of tragedies his decisions have provoked, Anouilh's Creon is a thoroughly modern pragmatist who puts duty – upholding the security of the state – above personal emotion. To what extent Anouilh sympathises with Creon's response remains a question for conjecture.

ARBUZOV, Aleksei Nicolaevich [1908–]
Russian dramatist, actor and director

Plays include:
Tanya (1939), _It Happened in Irkutsk_ (1959), _The Promise_ (also known as _My Poor Marat_; 1965), _Tales of Old Arbat_ (1970), _An Old Fashioned Comedy_ (also known as _Do You Turn Somersaults?_; 1978)

A prolific playwright who ranges from 'Brechtian' techniques to the sentimental, melodramatic and near vaudeville, Arbuzov's first big success was *Tanya*. His most popular play in the USSR is probably *It Happened in Irkutsk*, a personal drama set against the construction of a power station in Siberia, using a Brechtian chorus, but in the West he is best known for *The Promise*, (a 1966 Oxford Playhouse production by Frank Hauser, with Judi Dench, Ian McShane and Ian McKellen, had subsequent successful runs in London and New York). Like many of his plays it spans a long period, presenting the interaction of a woman and two men – would-be doctor, poet and bridge-builder – in Leningrad in 1942, at the time of post-war reconstruction (1946) and post-Stalin (1959) in the same Leningrad flat. Though the development of their romantic relationships is somewhat predictable it is the most tightly written of his plays.

TRY THESE:
▷Hugh Whitemore's *The Best of Friends* for an affectionate look at English friendships over a long time span; ▷Robert Holman's *Today* for contrasting views of English idealism pre- and post-war; ▷Barry Collins' *The Strongest Man in The World* for a personal drama set ostensibly in the Soviet community; see also ▷Chekhov and ▷Brecht for contrast.

ARCHER, Robyn [1948–]
Australian writer, singer, cabaret performer

Plays include:
The Pack of Women (1981), _A Star is Torn_ (with Rodney Fisher; 1982), _Cut and Thrust_ (1986)

Iconoclast, feminist and charismatic performer, Archer is best known to theatre audiences in Britain for her cabaret shows (at the Drill Hall in London), and most of all for her success with the one-woman show *A Star is Torn*. Co-authored with Rodney Fisher, and premiered originally in Australia 1979, this musical celebration of legendary torch song singers such as Judy Garland, Edith Piaf, Janis Joplin, Billie Holliday and Marie Lloyd is something of an antidote to the apparently never-ending appetite for feeding off tragic female stars (recent subjects for musicals include Jean Seberg and Billie Holliday). For Archer, for whom sexual politics, ▷ Brecht and Berlin-style political ▷ cabaret of the 1930s are major influences, the show (which opened at Stratford East's Theatre Royal before moving on to the West End) was not just an opportunity for another nostalgic, emotional wallow in tragic female-stars-as-victims (they all died young), but a critical reassessment that saw them as talented women, exploited like women anywhere who have to contend with the prejudices facing those who dare to step outside the prescribed boundaries of their sex. Some critics liked this approach and the wry humour that went with it; others were more scathing, but all agreed that it confirmed Archer's amazing musical range and versatility (she has one of the most thrillingly rich voices on the musical stage). *The Pack of Women* and *Cut and Thrust*, by contrast, were both more outright cabaret, mixing prose, poetry and song, and augmented by a clutch of equally talented international musicians and performers. Over-long, they nonetheless remind us that the art of the political cabaret has a

TRY THESE:
▷Pam Gems' *Piaf*; for contrast, solo performer ▷Rose English; see also ▷Cabaret.

potential still untapped – and more needed than ever – in the present day, despite the renaissance in alternative cabaret.

Identified in Australia at one time as 'Adelaide's answer to Janis Joplin', Archer's shows are at their strongest in their musical content – always a mix ranging through rock, blues and jazz – when her voice comes into its own. At their best, her lyrics match the strength of her vocals, satirising domestic and public sexism, singing of women's issues (menstruation, love between women) with an uncompromising, cheeky *joie de vivre*. But her concerns are global, and the art of the political cabaret, as she says, is not just a series of short thirty-second items but the way they are placed, 'enabling one piece to inform and illuminate what goes before and after it'.

In Australia, Archer has also written children's shows (and a children's book, *Mrs Bottle Burps*; 1983), several musical shows including *Songs from Sideshow Alley* (1980) about the relationship of two women, the death of the sideshow and the rise of the pinball machine; and political cabaret for street theatre.

ARDEN, John [1930–]
English dramatist and collaborator with ▷ Margaretta D'Arcy

Plays by John Arden include:
***All Fall Down* (1955), *The Waters of Babylon* (1957), *Live Like Pigs* (1958), *Serjeant Musgrave's Dance* (1959), *The Happy Haven* (1960), *The Business of Good Government* (1960), *Ironhand* (1963), *The Workhouse Donkey* (1964), *Armstrong's Last Goodnight* (1964), *Ars Longa, Vita Brevis* (1965), *Left Handed Liberty* (1965), *The Royal Pardon or, The Soldier Who Became an Actor* (1966), *The True History of Squire Jonathan and His Unfortunate Treasure* (1968), *The Hero Rises Up* (1968), *Harold Muggins is a Martyr* (1968), *The Ballygombeen Bequest* (1972), *The Island of the Mighty* (1972), *The Non-Stop Connolly Show* (1975). He has also translated *Fidelio* (1965), *The Soldiers Tale* (1968),**

Plays written in collaboration with ▷ Margaretta D'Arcy:
***The Happy Haven* (1960), *Ars Longa, Vita Brevis* (1965), *The Royal Pardon or, The Soldier Who Became an Actor* (1966), *The Hero Rises Up* (1968), *Harold Muggins is a Martyr* (1968), *The Ballygombeen Bequest* (1972), *The Island of the Mighty* (1972)**

For plays written by ▷ Margaretta D'Arcy with John Arden see her entry.

Radio includes:
***The Life of Man* (1955), *The Dying Cowboy* (1961), *The Bagman* (1970), *Keep Those People Moving* (1972), *Pearl* (1978), *To Put It Frankly* (1979), *Gentleman Don Quixote De La Mancha* (1980), *Garland for a Hoar Head* (1982), *The Old Man Sleeps Alone* (1982), *Whose is The Kingdom* (1988)**

Television includes:
***Soldier, Soldier* (1960), *Wet Fish* (1961), *Sean O'Casey: A TV Portrait* (1972)**

Barnsley born, a student of architecture and, in his own words, 'a product of English public schools and three years as a conscript in Scotland', Arden began writing plays at university. Considered one of the most influential political playwrights of his generation, Arden's output has been indelibly influenced by his meeting with ▷ Margaretta D'Arcy in 1955. As he himself has written: 'D'Arcy is Irish and began her career in Dublin in the small experimental theatres that flourished there in the same period, where there was a much keener sense of the political implications of the drama than could be found in this country.'

Most of Arden's major stage plays appeared in a ten-year period from the late 1950s to the late 1960s, ceasing abruptly after a famous if painful furore over the ▷ RSC's handling of *The Island of the Mighty,* when Arden declared he would never write again for the stage. Instead both his and D'Arcy's work over the past ten years has been more or less devoted to radio, culminat-

TRY THESE:
▷Peter Barnes for similar epic treatments of historical subjects; ▷John Osborne's *A Patriot for Me* for another army play with echoes of male sexual fear of women (also *Look Back in Anger*); for contrasting treatment of a national hero (*The Hero Rises Up* which debunks Nelson), see ▷Terence Rattigan's *Bequest to the Nation*; for a different handling of local small town corruption, see ▷Gogol's *The Government Inspector*, ▷Peter Flannery's *Our Friends in the North*; see also ▷Community Theatre.

ing in *Whose is the Kingdom*, the 1988 epic nine-part BBC radio series on a theme which has run through several of his plays – early Christianity. Always a moralist, Arden's dissenting voice has increasingly swung away from the earlier anarchic detachment where there are no heroes (even the so-called pacificism of *Serjeant Musgrave's Dance* is hotly disputed by some commentators, who feel it is difficult to decide which side Arden's sympathies are on), through political activism to revolutionary socialism by the late 1970s. Others, however, argue that the seeds of Arden the revolutionary were implicit from the beginning, particularly in the fact that the plays were usually sparked off by historical and contemporary political events. *Armstrong's Last Goodnight*, for example, though set in sixteenth-century Scotland, was inspired by the Congo War in the mid-1960s, and intended as an analagous, moral parable on the subject of violence. Written in Lowland verse, it emerged as a rumbustious, sardonic study in *realpolitik*, opposing the urbane politician (Lindsay) with the highland rebel, Johnny Armstrong.

Arden, from the beginning, rejected naturalism and though his plays were *about* social, political and economic issues – small town corruption (*The Workhouse Donkey*), the welfare state (*Live Like Pigs*), violence and militarism (*Serjeant Musgrave's Dance*) – his use of bold, imagistic techniques – epics, parables, sometimes grotesque comedy – and the fact that they have an obvious polemical intent, inevitably led to Arden being compared with ▷ Brecht, an influence he has always denied. Yet other observers, playing the influence game, detect a kinship with ▷ Ben Jonson and ▷ Aristophanes in such plays as *The Workhouse Donkey*. In any event, as Catherine Itzin has pointed out, as Arden became more politicised post-1968: 'the history of Arden and D'Arcy as co-dramatists. . .was not so much what they wrote, but what happened to what they wrote.' Arden/D'Arcy's work, with its increasingly anti-English, pro-Irish and community stance – *The Hero Rises Up* is an anti-heroic view of Nelson; *The Ballygombeen Bequest*, an attack on absentee landlordism in Ireland; *The Non-Stop Connolly Show*, a pro-Irish Republican epic which, according to Arden's biographer, Albert Hunt, should be regarded as a masterpiece – has come under increasing censorship. To the overall impoverishment of British theatre, their work remains outside the mainstream.

Serjeant Musgrave's Dance

Serjeant Musgrave's Dance is still the play most often revived. Set in a bleak mining town in northern England in the 1880s, a small group of soldiers invade a village ostensibly on a recruiting drive. But the men are deserters, and their leader, Serjeant Musgrave, who has become fanatically anti-war, is as terrifying in his religious zeal as the evil against which he inveighs: he demands the death of twenty-five local townspeople to match the death of a local boy who died in a colonial war and who was the trigger, in reprisal, for the death of five men. A male-oriented play, where women are seen either as whores (sexual and dangerous) or mothers (asexual and comforting), it seems hard in retrospect to see it as anything other than a passionately pacifist, anti-imperialist play.

ARDREY, Robert [1908–]

American scientist and dramatist

Plays include:

***Thunder Rock* (1939), *Jeb* (1946), *Shadow of Heroes* (1958)**

Probably best known today for his scientific theory of 'the territorial imperative', Ardrey worked for most of his career as a dramatist. His place in the current repertory depends entirely on *Thunder Rock*, which receives occasional starry revivals – the most recent being a television vehicle for actor Charles Dance. The play, first staged at the beginning of World War II, is an atmospheric allegorical piece in which a lighthouse keeper's encounters with the spirits of shipwrecked travellers rekindle his fighting spirit. *Jeb*, an investigation of the operations of racism in the American South, was uncomfortably enough in advance of its time to be commercially unsuccessful.

TRY THESE:
▷Pirandello's *Six Characters in Search of an Author* for its use of 'unfinished' characters; ▷David Edgar's *Maydays* deals with the Hungarian uprising which is the subject of *Shadow of Heroes*.

ARISTOPHANES [c 450–385 BC]
Greek comic dramatist

Surviving plays:
***The Acharnians* (425 BC), *The Knights* (424 BC), *The Clouds* (423 BC), *The Wasps* (422 BC), *Peace* (421 BC), *The Birds* (414 BC), *Lysistrata* (411 BC), *The Thesmophoriazousae* (410 BC; sometimes called *Women at the Festival* or *The Poet and the Women* or *Women at the Thesmophoria*), *The Frogs* (405 BC), *Ecclesiazousae* (392 BC; sometimes called *Women in Parliament*), *Plutus* (388 BC; also called *Wealth*).**

Aristophanes' plays, the only surviving representatives of Greek Old Comedy, are infrequently performed in the contemporary professional theatre, probably because their blend of topical satire, punning and lyricism poses major difficulties for translators, while the need for a chorus poses economic difficulties. *Lysistrata* has attracted a number of productions because of its concentration on sexual politics, although it is far from a feminist play. When it is produced, the warring Athenians and Spartans are often translated into the American Civil War period or presented as English and Scots.

TRY THESE:
▷Aeschylus, ▷Euripides, ▷Sophocles for Greek tragic drama; Plautus and Terence for Roman comedy; Theatre Workshop's *Oh What a Lovely War* for a play blending popular forms; see also ▷Community Theatre.

ARNOTT, Peter [1962–]
British dramatist

Plays include:
***The Boxer Benny Lynch* (1985), *White Rose* (1986)**

Arnott, a Cambridge English graduate who has worked in ▷ community theatre in Scotland, made the transition from non-professional theatre with *The Boxer Benny Lynch* (Glasgow Mayfest). His *White Rose*, an elegant account in somewhat Brechtian style of the career of a female Russian fighter pilot in World War II, was staged by the Traverse and seen in London at the Almeida.

TRY THESE:
▷Arbuzov's *The Promise* is another three-hander set in Russia in World War II; ▷Terence Rattigan's *Flare Path* and ▷Willis Hall's *The Long and the Short and the Tall* are other noteworthy World War II plays but their tone is very different and male-centred.

ARRABAL, Fernando [1932–]
Spanish dramatist born in Spanish Morocco, who writes in French

Plays include:
***Les Deux Bourreaux* (*The Two Executioners*; 1958), *Le Cimetière des Voitures* (*The Vehicle Graveyard*; 1964), *Fando et Lis* (*Fando and Lis*; 1964), *L'Architecte et l'Empereur d'Assyrie* (*The Architect and the Emperor of Assyria*; 1967), *Et ils Passerent des Menottes aux Fleurs* (*And They Put Handcuffs on the Flowers*; 1969)**

Arrabal's plays reflect his nightmarish childhood, during which his father mysteriously disappeared from prison at the beginning of the Spanish Civil War and his mother tried to behave as though his father had never existed. Unresolved difficulties over this, plus a strict Spanish Catholic upbringing, have led to a number of sado-masochistic plays filled with disturbing images of torture, suffering, blasphemy and eroticism, often involving members of the same family, at which one is horrified to find oneself laughing. Arrabal's Théâtre Panique takes the Theatre of Cruelty label over-literally! Directors with a strong visual sense, such as Victor García and ▷ Charles Marowitz, have responded with enthusiasm to these dramatisations of private fantasies. García directed *The Architect and the Emperor of Assyria* (translated by Jean-Norman Benedetti) for the ▷ National Theatre in 1971; it was played with some brio by Jim Dale and Anthony Hopkins as two men stranded on a desert island, playing a series of games, exchanging roles of master and slave, mother and child, victim and executioner, until finally one eats the other. The play owes something to ▷ Artaud and ▷ Beckett, but also to Lewis Carroll, whom Arrabal greatly admires. Marowitz produced *And They Put Handcuffs on the Flowers* at the Open Space in 1973, but none of Arrabal's other plays has appeared in Britain recently.

TRY THESE:
▷Artaud, with whom his name was often associated in the 1960s; ▷Pirandello for role-swopping; ▷Genet for role-playing; ▷Derek Walcott's *Pantomime* is a variation on the master/slave theme.

ARTAUD, Antonin [1896–1948]

French actor, director, theorist

Works include:

Jet de Sang (play; 1925, _Jet of Blood_), _La Coquille et le Clergyman_ (filmscript; 1927, _The Seashell and the Clergyman_), _Les Cenci_ (1935; _The Cenci_), _Le Théâtre et son Double_ (1938; _The Theatre and its Double_, incorporating his _First_ and _Second Manifestos of the Theatre of Cruelty_, 1931–35)

It is possible, but misleading, to regard Artaud as the archetypal mad genius. He was badly affected by meningitis when young, spent much of his life struggling against an addiction to drugs, and much of the rest in lunatic asylums. He is also one of the most important and seminal theatrical thinkers of the century, with a considerable (but disputed) influence on a wide variety of authors and especially directors, and was, incidentally, a very powerful actor. His principal theoretical work, *Le Théâtre et son Double*, influenced by his partial understanding of performances of Cambodian and Balinese dance, recommended a 'total theatre' that would use sound, light, gesture, and visual image rather than relying on the written or even the spoken word, to disturb fundamentally the imagination and subconscious of audience and actors alike; it has in different ways influenced Barrault, ▷ Peter Brook, ▷ Charles Marowitz, Grotowski, ▷ Adamov, ▷ Arrabal, ▷ Genet, Pip Simmons, Julian Beck, and the Open Theatre – partly because it is full of memorable but somewhat gnomic pronouncements which one can interpret to suit one's own inclinations (eg 'We are not free, and the sky can still fall on our heads; and the theatre exists to remind us of this fact').

Artaud worked as an actor with Georges Dullin and in films (he can be seen to mesmeric effect as a monk in Dreyer's film *La Passion de Jeanne d'Arc*, and as Marat in Abel Gance's *Napoléon*); he was expelled from André Breton's Surrealist movement for being inadequately committed to Communism; his actual stage output is small, though he mounted four productions with the Théâtre Alfred Jarry, 1927–9, including Vitrac's *Victor* and ▷ Strindberg's *The Dream Play*, and in 1935 he put on his own version of *The Cenci* at the Folies Wagram, with little success. He also wrote the filmscript for the Surrealist film *La Coquille et le Clergyman*.

Artaud's life is sometimes treated as myth (as with ▷ Dylan Thomas and Marie Lloyd) and used as matter for plays, such as ▷ Marowitz's *Artaud at Rodez*, Open Space 1975, with a fine haunted performance from Clive Merrison. The most recent of these is *The Asylum of Antonin Artaud*, by Mike Downey and Dennis Akers at the Gate in 1986, which dwelt on the drug-induced madness rather than the 'illuminated genius' (▷ Peter Brook's phrase).

TRY THESE:
▷Peter Weiss for a dramatist and La Mama for a group influenced by Artaud's ideas; ▷Performance Art for attempts to realise the idea of total theatre; ▷Claudel for impossible stage directions (*The Satin Slipper*, etc); see also ▷Expressionism for a non-illusionistic approach to theatre.

Jet of Blood

The text is less than four pages long, but manages to touch on many obsessions – Artaud's and our own. It would be very un-Artaudian to describe the plot, but the following stage directions give the flavour:

'The Whore bites God's wrist. An immense jet of blood shoots across the stage, and we can see the Priest making the sign of the cross during a flash of lightning that lasts longer than the others.'

'An army of scorpions comes out from under the Nurse's dress and swarms over her sex, which swells up and bursts, becoming glassy and shining like the sun. The Young Man and the Whore flee.'

Nonetheless, it was included in the ▷ Peter Brook ▷ Charles Marowitz Theatre of Cruelty season at LAMDA in 1964, and student groups attempt it from time to time.

ASIAN THEATRE IN BRITAIN

Asian theatre in Britain is like an iceberg – while relatively few groups are visible from the white mainstream, a significant amount goes on in the privacy of separate language groups. At the last public gathering – for the Alternative Festival of India in 1982 – work on display came from groups working in Malayalam,

TRY THESE:
For more plays reflecting experiences of being British and Asian, see ▷Karim Alrawi, ▷Harwant Bains and Farrukh

Tamil, Bengali, Hindi/Urdu, Punjabi, Gujarati and English, with another in the wings in Marathi. Although it is hard to be categorical across the board, there have been noises of disquiet from some areas of the movement: Gujarati theatre (a busy movement when it was imported from East Africa) has questioned its own tendency to turn back to India for its material – a fact, it has been suggested, that connects with the decline in interest among the young born or largely brought up in Britain.

Secondly it should be realised that much of what is really 'Asian theatre' goes, in Britain, by another name. The great Indian sourcebook of performance, the second-century Bharata Natya Shastra, does not make the kinds of distinction between theatre, mime and dance that the West does. Indian dancers are accomplished mime artists and the Academy of Indian Dance's 1986 *Return of Spring* was based on a script (by Dr Sita Narasimhan), spoken by a traditional narrator figure.

The English language theatre, recognised by Western eyes as bona fide 'theatre', is a recent growth with few locally derived works to its name. Dilip Hiro's *To Anchor a Cloud*, a sumptuous costume drama in the mid-1950s, was one of few to give the increasing body of Asian actors and actresses a vehicle. ▷ Hanif Kureishi's *Outskirts* and *Borderline* were the first major works to base themselves firmly in the life of British Asians today and they share, with other developments in the field, highly political roots. His characters exist in a 1980s limbo, without a history and with a future that has to be determined by their own fighting qualities.

▷ Tara Arts Group, started in 1977 in reaction to the racial murder of Gurdip Singh Chaggar, was formed by young Asians from different community backgrounds. Its early devised plays were crisply agit-prop – of racism at school, hypocrisy at home – and its themes were derived directly from the realities of the Asian experience and covered issues like old age and mental disturbance. Increasingly Tara has come to see form as vital and has set out to create a distinctive style that takes in traditional Indian dramaturgy, rejects the Western watertight compartments, and creates a fusion between Indian classics and modern concerns.

Slough Asian Theatre Company and Hounslow Arts Co-operative also arose as a deliberate challenge to the status quo. A more constant development (the Slough company is no more), Raj Patel's British Asian Theatre has aimed for a middle course between professional mainstream venues and street concerns, using scripted plays rather than improvisation for productions like *Ahmed, the Wonderful Oriental Gentleman*, *Anarkali* and *My Name is Ghalib*. The Asian Theatre Co-operative set out to provide highly professional theatre, but though their productions of plays by Farrukh Dhondy and H.O. Nazareth have been done with flair, their track record has not managed to be as steady a development as Asian theatre needs.

Dhondy; see also ▷Community Theatre; ▷Peter Brook's production of the Mahabharata has popularised an Indian classic for Western audiences; see also ▷Tara Arts.

AUDEN, W. H. (Wystan Hugh) [1907–72]
British poet, dramatist and critic

ISHERWOOD, Christopher (William Bradshaw) [1904–86]
British novelist, dramatist and screenwriter

Joint plays include:

***The Dog Beneath the Skin; or, Where is Francis?* (1936), *The Ascent of F6* (1937), *On the Frontier* (1938).**

Auden:

***The Dance of Death* (1933) and libretti for the operas *The Rake's Progress* (1951; Stravinsky), *Elegy for Young Lovers* (1961) and *The Bassarids* (1966) (both Henze)**

Isherwood:

adaptations of ▷ Shaw's *Little Black Girl in Search of God* and (with Don Bachardy) his own novel *A Meeting by the River*

TRY THESE:
▷Brecht, who compared these plays with ▷Aristophanes, for his influence; for other modern verse drama, ▷T. S. Eliot, ▷Chrisopher Fry, Ronald Duncan; for socialist plays in the epic tradition, ▷Edward Bond, ▷Trevor Griffiths ▷David Edgar, ▷Howard Barker, ▷Howard Brenton, ▷Caryl Churchill, ▷Bernard Kops, ▷David Rudkin, Henry

Although both produced theatre work independently, their best known plays are the jointly written verse dramas of the 1930s. *I Am a Camera* and the musical *Cabaret* are based on Isherwood's Berlin stories but are not his dramatisations.

Left-wing intellectuals from elitist Oxbridge backgrounds, Auden and Isherwood were politicised by the Depression, the Spanish Civil War and by living in Germany. All their joint work, and Auden's *Dance of Death*, set out to attack capitalist power and bourgeois values; *Ascent of F6*, with its protagonist clearly modelled on T.E. Lawrence, added elements of mysticism as well. Their style is not naturalistic and suggests strong Brechtian influence. Despite the evident homosexual content in some of both men's other work, these verse dramas do not explore such themes.

Livings; also ▷Terry Johnson's under-rated *Cries from the Mammal House* for a disenchanted view of the contemporary male using an animal metaphor; ▷Alfred Jarry for a similarly eclectic dramaturgy.

The Dog Beneath the Skin
This is a morality in verse which makes use of a chorus, song and dance, masks, cabaret, and a Master of Ceremonies to present the life of a man-sized dog as it passes from owner to owner through a society peopled with caricatures – a general, financier, churchman, etc. Savagely satirical in its time, it may seem naive when set against contemporary polemics.

AYCKBOURN, Alan [1939–]
British dramatist/director

Plays include:
***Mr Whatnot* (1963), *Relatively Speaking* (1967), *How the Other Half Loves* (1969), *Time and Time Again* (1972), *Absurd Person Singular* (1972), *The Norman Conquests* (comprising: *Table Manners, Round and Round the Garden, Living Together*; 1973), *Absent Friends* (1974), *Confusions* (1974), *Bedroom Farce* (1975), *Just Between Ourselves* (1976), *Joking Apart* (1979), *Ten Times Table* (1977), *Sisterly Feelings* (1979), *Taking Steps* (1980), *Suburban Strains* (1981), *Season's Greetings* (1982), *Way Upstream* (1982), *It Could Be Any of Us* (1982), *Making Tracks* (1983), *Intimate Exchanges* (1984), *A Chorus of Disapproval* (1985), *Woman in Mind* (1985), *A Small Family Business* (1987)**

TRY THESE:
Brian Rix, Ray Cooney as two of the most celebrated exponents of contemporary farce, the conventions of which Ayckbourn liberally exploits; ▷Michael Frayn's *Noises Off* as one of the funniest and cleverest examples of theatrical sleight-of-hand; ▷Feydeau is a French nineteenth-century equivalent, and perhaps some of ▷Labiche; ▷De Filippo is a European equivalent; ▷Tom Stoppard as another juggler of theatrical conventions.

Ayckbourn is now one of Britain's most commercially successful playwrights, with regular West End and repertory productions, frequent televisations, and commissions both as writer and director at the ▷ National Theatre. He has written over thirty plays to date, but says of himself that he is a 'director who writes, rather than a writer who directs'.

After starting his theatrical career as an actor and stage-manager with Donald Wolfit's company, he moved to Stephen Joseph's Studio Theatre Company in the early 1960s, where he began directing and writing with Joseph's encouragement. Many of his most successful plays began at Scarborough, where he was Artistic Director of the Library Theatre and where he would produce a new play annually for their repertory season. Many of these transferred to London, but he continued to base his work in Scarborough long after he had become the toast of the West End.

A superb theatrical craftsman, his plays are often constructed around a tour de force of staging: *The Norman Conquests* is a trilogy of plays, each of which stands on its own, and presents the same events from the garden, sitting room and dining room; *How the Other Half Loves*, *Absurd Person Singular* and *Bedroom Farce* each present more than one household on stage simultaneously; *Way Upstream* launched a riverboat onto the ▷ National Theatre stage; *Sisterly Feelings* offers alternative versions for the central section of the play. His plays have their roots in the tradition of farce rather than in experimental theatre, an allegiance confirmed by the staging of *Intimate Exchanges* by Ray Cooney's Theatre of Comedy company. He has, however, stretched the boundaries of comedy and farce as his work has developed; increasingly, the comings and goings of married couples are injected with a note of black comedy, and social groups are fraught with suggestions of the darker arenas of human interchange. The social niceties of the tea party in *Absent Friends* are disrupted by the inability of the participants to cope with the idea of death, and in *Just Between Ourselves* and *Woman in Mind*, what begins as the familiar comic theme of a sterile marriage transforms into tragedy as the wife descends into catatonia and breakdown. One (male) critic has hailed Ayckbourn as the best contemporary feminist playwright for *Woman in Mind*; while this is clearly arguable, Ayckbourn is one of the sharpest observers in theatre of contemporary suburban values. Ayckbourn's success might be accounted for in that his work is challenging, but within strict limits; his subject matter has tended to be middle-class values and lifestyle under threat (but not too much), while his dramatic form plays with theatrical convention but is always firmly rooted in the familiar structures of farce and West End comedy.

Ayckbourn was appointed director of one of the ▷ National Theatre's companies under Sir Peter Hall's policy, and with his group of actors (perhaps most notably Michael Gambon) he has produced some memorable productions; his own *A Small Family Business*, ▷ Arthur Miller's *A View from the Bridge*, and ▷ John Ford's *'Tis Pity She's a Whore*.

Bedroom Farce

First produced at Scarborough, *Bedroom Farce* was the first of Ayckbourn's plays to be produced at the ▷ National Theatre. As in many of his plays, it deals with simultaneous stories, presenting four couples whose dramas interweave around the house-warming party of Malcolm and Kate. Three of the households are on stage, and the action moves from bedroom to bedroom; sometimes all three are presented at once. The potential for farce is explored in the shifts in the occupancy of the bedrooms, but the bedroom of one couple, whose relationship is on the verge of collapse, is a significant absence in the play – an absence which constructs an awareness of the bleakness that underlies the comedy.

BABE, Thomas [1941–]
American dramatist

Plays include:
***Kid Champion* (1974), *Mojo Candy* (1975), *Rebel Women* (1976), *Billy Irish* (1977), *Great Solo Tour* (1977), *A Prayer For My Daughter* (1977), *Fathers and Sons* (1978), *Taken in Marriage* (1979), *Salt Lake City Skyline* (1980), *Kathleen* (1980), *Buried Inside Extra* (1983)**

Buffalo-born and Harvard-educated, and one of America's toughest, most independent playwrights, Babe has yet to achieve the recognition he deserves. 'I've never gotten a prize and I don't expect one, but I would love to be able to continue to work,' he has said. Associated with Joe Papp's Public Theatre off-Broadway, where many of his plays began, he is interested both in revisionist treatments of history (*Fathers and Sons* and *Salt Lake City Skyline* are about Wild Bill Hickok and union organiser Joe Hill, respectively) and in closer-to-home, more domestic themes. In *A Prayer For My Daughter*, arguably his best-known work, a Sergeant Kelly ignores the suicidal telephone calls of his own daughter to concentrate on the young murder suspect, Jimmy, whom he starts treating as a kind of aberrant 'daughter'. *Taken in Marriage*, which brings a quintet of women together in a New Hampshire church hall to attend a marriage rehearsal fraught with domestic volatility, and *Buried Inside Extra*, a play about journalists which inaugurated the Royal Court's exchange with the Public, are best seen as vehicles for actors, who tend to rip into Babe's roles with abandon.

TRY THESE:
▷Arthur Kopit's *Indians* and much of ▷Sam Shepard and ▷Romulus Linney for iconoclastic views both of history and of the American West; ▷Hecht and McArthur's *The Front Page*, Stephen Wakelam's *Deadlines*, and ▷David Hare and ▷Howard Brenton's *Pravda* for alternative dramatic treatments of journalism.

BAGNOLD, Enid (Lady Roderick Jones) [1884–1981]
British novelist and dramatist

Plays include:
***The Chalk Garden* (1955)**

Books include:
***National Velvet* (1935)**

Author of *National Velvet* (filmed in 1944 with Elizabeth Taylor) and numerous other successful novels, *The Chalk Garden* was the most successful of her original plays. A typical 'Haymarket play' of the 1950s, when the Theatre Royal was the showcase for star-studded (in this case Edith Evans and Peggy Ashcroft) middle-class theatre with its heart in the right place, it is well tailored, well characterised and with only sufficient undermining of entrenched attitudes to make the audience feel already more enlightened than the characters, as the governess, who brings life to the household and garden of eccentric Mrs St Maugham, is exposed as a convicted murderess.

TRY THESE:
▷N.C. Hunter, ▷Dodie Smith, ▷William Douglas Home for plays of a similar type; ▷Lillian Hellman's *The Children's Hour* for another play of aomestic revelation; also Ibsen for plays of family revelation.

BAINS, Harwant [1963–]
British dramatist

Plays include:
***The Fighting Kite* (1987), *Blood* (1988)**

TRY THESE:
▷Hanif Kureishi's *Borderline* and *Outskirts* for an earlier handling of racial

Bains has been hailed as a possible successor to ▷ Hanif Kureishi, much to his irritation ('Just because I've got a brown face and write plays. . .') but it's hard, for the moment, to avoid the inevitable comparison. Southall based, and son of Indian parents, Bains' first staged play, *The Fighting Kite*, was presented at Stratford East's Theatre Royal and shows a new British Asian voice taking up some of the subjects the young Kureishi and, to some extent, ▷ Karim Alrawi, explored in the early 1980s, in particular racial violence and the subject of retaliation. *The Fighting Kite*, a sprawling, episodic account of a racial attack in Southall, fails to provide more than stereotyped cut-outs of National Front skinheads and their racial hatred, but is subtle and sensitive in its handling of emotions and the response of its young Asians to their cultural identity and alienation (feeling neither 'English' nor accepted back on the Indian subcontinent). Bains has also now been taken up by the Royal Court and *Blood*, commissioned by them, is said to mark a significant progress in his development as a playwright.

violence; ▷Karim Alrawi's *A Colder Climate* for another view of East End racial tension; see also ▷David Edgar's *Destiny* for a bold attempt to pinpoint the rise of post-war British fascism; Farrukh Dhondy's *Vigilantes* for another exploration of the problems of immigrant cultural identity (within the first generation British Bangladeshi community); for Afro-Caribbean equivalents see Edgar White's *The Nine Night*, ▷Caryl Phillips' *Strange Fruit*; for a female view of being young, black and British see ▷Jackie Rudet's *Money to Live*.

BALDWIN, James [1924–87]

American dramatist

Plays include:

***Blues For Mr Charlie* (1964), *The Amen Corner* (1965), *A Deed From the King of Spain* (1974)**

James Baldwin's theatrical reputation rests on his two early plays, both of which struck a lasting chord at their New York debuts, and one of which (*The Amen Corner*) made London history in March 1987 as the first-ever all-black non-musical British production to open in the West End (where, sadly, it losts its £150,000 investment). In *Blues For Mr Charlie,* Baldwin told an unforgettable tale of racial poison based on a true story – a white jury's acquittal, in 1955, of two white men who murdered black Chicagoan, Emmett Till, in Mississippi. In *The Amen Corner*, which was performed briefly at Howard University in 1955, and opened on Broadway in 1965, Baldwin drew on his own background as the son of a Harlem minister to depict the crumbling domestic life and fading religiosity of Sister Margaret Alexander, the censorious pastor of a 'storefront' Harlem church. An avowed homosexual, perhaps best-known for his novels, the expatriate Baldwin, who spent much of his later life in France, was a vociferous champion of civil liberties and of both sexual and racial equality. Interestingly, however, in an interview before his death, he played down the importance of race in his plays, saying with customary wryness: '*The Amen Corner* is not about black people or white people. It's about the people in the play.'

TRY THESE:
▷Amiri Baraka for a raised temperature level, inherited in the 1980s by George C. Wolfe (*The Colored Museum*, which takes satiric aim at Baldwin's dramatic style); ▷August Wilson for detonating treatments of racism, especially *Ma Rainey's Black Bottom*; ▷Lorraine Hansberry's *A Raisin in the Sun* for an early view of America's black community confronting racism; Kalamu Ya Salaam's *Black Love Song No 1* for another contemporary satirical swipe at American black stereotypes, produced under the white yoke.

BARAKA, Amiri (Leroi Jones) [1934–]

American dramatist

Plays include:

A Good Girl is Hard to Fine* (1958), *Dante* (1961), *Dutchman* (1964), *The Baptism* (1964), *The Slave* (1964), *The Toilet* (1964), *Jello* (1965), *Experimental Death Unit No 1* (1965), *A Black Mass* (1966), *Slave Ship: A Historical Pageant* (1967), *Madheart* (1967), *Arm Yourself or Harm Yourself!* (1967), *Great Goodness of Life (A Coon Show)* (1967), *Home on the Range* (1968), *Resurrection in Life* (1969), *Junkies Are Full of (SHH. . .)* (1970), *Bloodrites* (1970), *A Recent Ceiling* (1973), *The New Ark's a Moverin'* (1974), *Sidnee Poet Heroical* or *If

TRY THESE:
▷Lorca and ▷Strindberg (especially *Miss Julie*) for often explosive theatrical rituals; ▷Miguel Pinero's *Short Eyes* and ▷David Rabe's *Streamers* as 1970s equivalents to *The Toilet*, in which constricted environments

***in Danger of Suit, the Kit Poet Heroical* (1975), *S-1* (1976), *The Motion of History* (1977)**

Probably the first black theatrical radical to come to prominence in the 1960s, Baraka is legendary for breaking wide open the conventional realism of such black writers as ▷ James Baldwin and ▷ Lorraine Hansberry in favour of a more coruscating and explosive kind of theatre, and one which helped give a centrality to black playwriting in America which it thankfully still enjoys today. 'The black artist's role in America is to aid the destruction of America as he knows it,' wrote Baraka, who changed his name in 1968 when he converted from the Christian to the Muslim faith. His best plays were early – *Dutchman*, in which Clay, a black man, and Lola, a white woman, enact a mating game of attraction and rage on a subway platform, and *The Toilet*, a tapestry of festering bigotry brought to the boil, set in a high school lavatory.

heighten racial tension; George C. Wolfe's *The Colored Museum,* Kalamu Ya Salaam's *Black Love Song No 1* and ▷Ntozake Shange's *Spell No 7* for equivalent rage, 1980s-style; ▷August Wilson, Richard Wesley, Samm-Art Williams for somewhat gentler chronicles of racism and the black experience; for British equivalents, see ▷Barry Reckord; ▷Mustapha Matura, ▷Caryl Phillips; ▷Barrie Keeffe's *Sus*, and Gabriel Gbadamosi's *No Blacks, No Irish* show racism and prejudice in 1950s England.

BARKER, Howard [1946–]

British dramatist

Plays include:

***Cheek* (1970), *No One Was Saved* (1970), *Alpha Alpha* (1972), *Claw* (1975), *Stripwell* (1975), *That Good Between Us* (1977), *Fair Slaughter* (1977), *The Hang of the Gaol* (1978), *The Love of a Good Man* (1978), *The Loud Boy's Life* (1980), *No End of Blame* (1981), *The Poor Man's Friend* (1982), *Victory* (1983), *A Passion in Six Days* (1983), *Crimes in Hot Countries* (1983), *The Power of the Dog* (1984), *The Castle* (1985), *Downchild* (1985), *Women Beware Women* (reworking of ▷ Middleton's play; 1986), *The Possibilities* (1988), *The Last Supper* (1988)**

One of a generation of British dramatists deeply concerned with political and social issues, Barker has never received the degree of critical acclaim given to some of his contemporaries, probably because his interest in the psychopathology of capitalism and patriarchy leads him to deal in much of his work with the grotesque and the distorted, often in highly scatalogical language. His plays firmly eschew naturalism in favour of an incisive and theatrically inventive cartoon-like style which juxtaposes private desires with public postures and aims for psychological and sociopolitical truth rather than the texture of everyday life. He works, then, in a tradition which aligns him with the social criticism of ▷ John Gay and ▷ Brecht, with whom he shares a crucial perception of the apparent identity of interest between criminal and politician and the inherent corruptions of capitalism. As he sees it, 'the working-class criminals in my plays are victims of a phoney individualism, seduced into aping the ideals and goals of the ruling class and squandering their real talents in the process'. The 'criminal' strand in his work is well represented by, for example, *Alpha Alpha* (a study of two brother patterned on the Kray twins), *Claw* (in which the hero acts as procurer for the Home Secretary) and *Stripwell*, with its judge faced both with the criminal activities of his son and a man he sentenced returning for revenge.

Barker is a history graduate and many of his plays also pursue an interest in historical moments and their lessons for the present. *Victory*, subtitled punningly 'Choices in Reaction', a fine example of this second strand, deals with the aftermath of the Restoration of Charles II, mixing historical and stereotypical characters in an extraordinary evocation of the collapse of the ideals of the Commonwealth. The play is notable for a brilliant explanation of the nature and contradictions of capitalism involving

TRY THESE:

▷Howard Brenton shares many of Barker's preoccupations and much of his approach to writing for the theatre; ▷David Edgar has also tackled similar issues, particularly in *Destiny* (fascism and Labour reactions to it) and *Maydays* (opposition to totalitarian impulses); ▷Peter Flannery has looked at corruption and the Labour party in *Our Friends in the North*; ▷Ibsen's *The Master Builder* also uses architecture metaphorically; ▷Peter Barnes uses an inventive rhetorical style reminiscent of Barker, particularly in *Leonardo's Last Supper*; ▷Timberlake Wertenbaker's *The Grace of Mary Traverse* explores capitalism and the present through the past; ▷Pam Gems, ▷Caryl Churchill, ▷Deborah Levy and, to some extent, ▷Aphra Behn in her time, have all explored the relationships of gender and power to capitalism.

Charles himself, a banker called Hambro, Nell Gwynne, the skull of the parliamentarian Bradshaw, and a large store of gold.

A third significant strand is concerned with specifically Labour party themes, as in *The Loud Boy's Life*, *Downchild* and *A Passion in Six Days* (a dramatic cantata about a Labour Party conference). His most recent works are *The Possibilities*, a set of short plays investigating conflicts between self preservation and humanitarian impulses across time and place, and *The Last Supper*, about a messianic figure.

The Castle

The Castle is an extraordinary meditation on issues of gender, power, rational and emotional knowledge, war and peace, in which a returning Crusader confronts the peaceful female community established by his wife in his absence. The battle lines, both medieval and contemporary, are drawn between creativity and destruction in confrontations and dialogue that are brilliantly imagined and draw to the full on Barker's ability to write with a poetic density of language, comic as well as tragic, which uses everyday idiom as much as architectural imagery to create an extraordinarily flexible language. In Nick Hamm's original ▷ RSC production there were superb performances from Penny Downie as the fecund matriarch, Harriet Walter as her lesbian lover, Ian McDiarmid as the returning Crusader and Paul Freeman as his castle building architect.

BARNES, Peter [1931–]

British dramatist

Plays include:

***The Time of the Barracudas* (1963), *Sclerosis* (1965), *The Ruling Class* (1968), *Leonardo's Last Supper* (1969), *Lulu* (from Wedekind; 1970), *The Bewitched* (1974), *Frontiers of Farce* (adaptations from Feydeau and Wedekind; 1976), *Noonday Demons* (1977), *Laughter* (1978), *Red Noses* (1985)**

Films include:

***The White Flags* (1959), *Breakout* (1959), *The Professionals* (1960), *Off-Beat* (1961), *The Man with a Feather in his Hat* (1961), *Ring of Spies* (with Frank Lauder; 1963), *Not with My Wife You Don't* (1966), *The Ruling Class* (1972)**

In the published text of *The Ruling Class* Barnes declared his aim was 'to create by means of soliloquy, rhetoric, formalised ritual, slapstick, song and dances, a comic theatre of contrasting moods and opposites, where everything is simultaneously tragic and ridiculous'. On its first production *The Ruling Class* was hailed as 'a pivotal play' by critic Ronald Bryden, and Harold Hobson placed it on a level with *Waiting for Godot*, *Look Back in Anger* and *The Birthday Party* but Barnes' later work has been less rapturously received. A passionate attack on Toryism, class and privilege, *The Ruling Class* presents a rampaging madman who inherits an earldom and believes he is God. It shows his return to 'sanity', confirmed when he makes a pro-hanging and pro-flogging speech to his cobwebbed fellow peers in the House of Lords.

Barnes' early one-act play *Sclerosis* dealt with British torture of an EOKA suspect in Cyprus but Barnes generally confronts wider political issues, emulating the broad scale, richness of character and theatricality of ▷ Ben Jonson, though eschewing his bourgeois values. He has also 'adapted' a number of Jacobean plays, including Jonson's *The Alchemist, The Silent Woman, Bartholomew Fair, Eastward Ho* and *The Devil is an Ass* (in which nearly half of the material is new). Other adaptations include ▷ Feydeau farces; *Laughter* opens with a custard pie slammed in the face of an author and the vitality of music hall humour jostles, sometimes uncomfortably, with the harsh cruelties which Barnes depicts to make emotive attacks on the use of power by the State, the Church and big business. Barnes has also directed some of his own plays.

Red Noses

Written in 1978, *Red Noses* took seven years to be produced by

TRY THESE:
▷Edward Bond, (especially *We Come to the River*); ▷Steven Berkoff for outrage; ▷Alan Bennett for satire; ▷David Hare and ▷Howard Brenton's *Pravda*, ▷Peter Nichols' *The National Health*, and *Privates on Parade* for contemporary satires on an epic scale; ▷Nick Dear for historical debunking; ▷John Whiting's *The Devils* and ▷Robert Bolt's *A Man For All Seasons* for treatments of historical aberrations without the satire.

the ▷ RSC and was Barnes' first play in London after a gap of seventeen years, evidence of how uncomfortable some can feel about his work. *Red Noses*, set in France at the time of the Black Death, is populated by roaming bands of guilt-ridden flagellants, 'Ravens' who smear bits of infected corpses on the doors of the rich and 'Flotties', red-nosed comics who confront disease with laughter – almost every critic compared them to a medieval ENSA. They are tolerated by the Church because they keep the people cheerful, but when the plague abates and their performances begin to become subversive they are ruthlessly squashed. Some critics found a one-legged dancer and a blind juggler – their leader Flote describes them as 'the triumph of hope over experience' – and a pope who cracked 'I'm giving up hope for Lent' too much to take. Barnes is not a polemicist and, though the bold and epic scale of the play gives marvellous opportunities to performers, its characters' hope that 'every jest should be a small revolution' is not answered.

BARRIE, (Sir) James Matthew [1860–1937]
British dramatist and novelist

Plays include:
***Ibsen's Ghost* (1891; one-act), *Walker, London* (1892), *The Professor's Love Story* (1894), *The Little Minister* (1897), *Quality Street* (1902), *The Admirable Crichton* (1902), *Peter Pan* (1904), *What Every Woman Knows* (1908), *The Twelve Pound Look* (1910; one-act), *Dear Brutus* (1917), *The Truth About the Russian Dancers* (1920; one-act), *Mary Rose* (1920), *Shall We Join the Ladies?* (1922; one-act), *The Boy David* (1936)**

Barrie, born of a poor Scottish family, went South after leaving Edinburgh University. He started his career as a journalist, then struck gold with the novel of *The Little Minister* in 1891 and wrote prolifically and very successfully through the Edwardian era and beyond. Although Dorothy Tutin added an edge to the whimsical sexism in a recent West End revival of *What Every Woman Knows*, and the equally whimsical toing and froing of the classes in *The Admirable Crichton* surfaces from time to time, in recent years *Peter Pan* has been the only one of Barrie's many plays to be revived regularly. It was staged by the ▷ RSC from 1982–4, and turned into a musical at the Aldwych in 1985. His one-act plays, such as *Ibsen's Ghost*, *The Twelve Pound Look*, and the tantalising first act of the thriller, *Shall We Join the Ladies?* are more effective than the full-length ones and well worth reviving. *Mary Rose*, however, with its odd mixture of whimsy, innocence, fantasy, and slightly sinister unquiet spirit, has had a sudden resurgence, and was both revived (at Greenwich) and given a television production in 1987.

Peter Pan
The plot centres on Peter Pan (the Boy Who Never Grew Up), who flies off to the Never Never Land with the Darling children (Wendy, John and Michael), leaving their father to take refuge in the dog kennel. After defeating the Pirates, they return to Bloomsbury with the Lost Boys, leaving Peter to forget all that has happened and wait for the next generation of Darlings. Although the years when Peter was played by one long-legged young actress after another have gone, and she has been replaced by the likes of Miles Anderson and Stephen Moore, the play is still a Freudian's delight and must have bewildered a great many children over the years. Captain Hook, however, remains one of the great bravura parts (Donald Wolfit played it in 1953).

TRY THESE:
▷G.B. Shaw for class issues in *The Admirable Crichton*; ▷Joe Corrie offers a rather different Scottish sensibility; the use in *Mary Rose* of a ghostly spirit has parallels, from ▷T.S. Eliot in *Family Reunion* to ▷Louise Page's *Salonika*, though none treat it with the almost touching feyness of Barrie.

BARRY, Philip [1896–1949]
American dramatist

Plays include:
A Punch for Judy* (1921), *You and I* (1923), *The Youngest* (1924), *In a Garden* (1925), *White Wings* (1925), *John* (1927), *Paris Bound* (1927), *Cock Robin* (with Elmer Rice; 1928), *Holiday* (1928), *Hotel Universe* (1930), *Tomorrow and Tomorrow* (1931), *The Animal Kingdom

TRY THESE:
▷Noël Coward for a British equivalent to Barry's deceptive dark domestic frivolity, specifically *Private Lives* as a play about divorcés getting back together; ▷George

***(1932), The Joyous Season* (1934), *Bright Star* (1935), *Spring Dance* (1936), *Here Come the Clowns* (1938), *The Philadelphia Story* (1939), *Liberty Jones* (1941), *Without Love* (1942), *Foolish Notion* (1945), *My Name is Aquilon* (1949), *Second Threshold* (completed posthumously by Robert Sherwood; 1951)**

Born in Rochester, New York, Barry defined a kind of American comedy of manners which the British find in ▷ Noël Coward. Educated at Yale and Harvard, he wrote about the sophisticated set of which he was a part, but not without healthy criticism of upper-class complacency and snobbery. His two best-known plays make his bemused contempt clear, even as they introduce the so-called 'Barry girl', a clear-headed, no-nonsense rich kid who is more on the ball than her posh surroundings might suggest. In *Holiday*, the self-made Johnny Case becomes engaged to the heiress Julia Seton only to find he has more in common with her younger sister Linda, who shares his desire for a 'holiday' from rampant materialistic pursuits. In *The Philadelphia Story*, later made into the stage and screen musical *High Society*, the moneyed divorcée Tracy Lord forsakes the dour stiff she's supposed to marry for a man defined more by his personality than his social position. Not all Barry's plays treat the mores of the well-heeled: *John* was a Biblical tragedy; *Cock Robin*, written with Elmer Rice, a comic mystery; and *Liberty Jones*, an allegory. But he remains best-known for his social satire on the swells among whom he moved so easily.

Kaufman for comparable sophistication; ▷Tina Howe and A.R. Gurney for modern chroniclers of American class; also ▷Neil Simon; ▷Alan Ayckbourn for another British equivalent.

BEAUMARCHAIS, Pierre Augustin Caron de [1732–99]

French dramatist

Plays include:

***Eugénie* (1767), *Les Deux Amis* (*The Two Friends*; (1770), *Le Barbier de Séville* (*The Barber of Seville*; 1775), *Le Mariage de Figaro* (*The Marriage of Figaro*; 1784), *Tarare* (1787), *La Mère Coupable* (*The Guilty Mother*; 1792)**

As well as being a dramatist, Beaumarchais was a watchmaker, musician, financier, courtier, pamphleteer, gun-runner and secret agent, in all of which he achieved some distinction but no lasting success. He wrote two very good plays (*The Barber of Seville* and its sequel *The Marriage of Figaro*) which might be more often performed in English had they not also been the bases of two superlative operas. The first has a plot that can be described in a few lines – old guardian, young ward, young nobleman in disguise, clever servant to help him – the second would need several pages to describe, and combines non-stop comic invention with sharp social satire. *The Marriage of Figaro* is possibly unique in being a successful sequel; there is a third in the series, *The Guilty Mother*, which has a strange combination of elevated moral tone and prurient plot (the Almavivas have come to live in France because of the Revolution, and like to be known as Citoyen and Citoyenne; the hero finds that he is the illegitimate son of the Countess and Chérubin, the latter having been killed in the wars, and so he can marry the Count's illegitimate daughter by the gardener's daughter). There was going to be a fourth episode of this increasingly depressing story, but Beaumarchais died first.

TRY THESE:
▷Marivaux for eighteenth-century French comedy (though their language and approach are very different, Marivaux being a natural miniaturist and Beaumarchais a poster artist); ▷Feydeau for the complications of plot in *The Marriage of Figaro*; ▷von Horvath for updating and development in *Figaro Gets a Divorce*.

BEAUMONT, Francis [1584/5–1616]

English Renaissance dramatist, collaborator with ▷ John Fletcher

Plays include:

***The Knight of the Burning Pestle* (1607), *Philaster* (with Fletcher; pre 1610), *The Maid's Tragedy* (with Fletcher; pre 1611)**

Although Beaumont is traditionally associated with Fletcher, his place in the contemporary repertory rests largely on his own *The Knight of the Burning Pestle*. A lively blend of satire at the expense of middle-brow taste, this uses plays within plays, popular songs, apparent interruptions from the audience,

TRY THESE:
▷Dekker's *Shoemaker's Holiday*, ▷Heywood's *Fair Maid of the West* and *Four Prentices of London* (the prime object of Beaumont's parody) are more complimentary to citizen taste than ▷Middleton's *A Chaste Maid*, which shares more of

romance and melodrama in a heady mixture which has maintained its appeal because the tastes and attitudes it confronts are easily recognisable today. It is not surprising that it attracted Michael Bogdanov, a director with a penchant for the freewheeling, who staged the last major revival, for the ▷ RSC in 1981. There was something of a Beaumont and ▷ Fletcher revival at that time with successful productions of *The Maid's Tragedy*, a love, honour and duty tragedy, by both the ▷ Glasgow Citizens' and the ▷ RSC, but there has been little recent interest in Beaumont.

Beaumont's standpoint; ▷Ben Jonson's *Bartholomew Fair* and ▷Shakespeare's *The Merry Wives of Windsor* also offer portraits of the middle classes from this period; there are many plays about theatre companies and interrupted performances including ▷Sheridan's *The Critic*, ▷Pirandello's *Six Characters in Search of an Author* and Tom Stoppard's *The Real Inspector Hound.*

BECKETT, Samuel [1906–]

Irish/French dramatist and novelist

Plays include:

***Waiting for Godot* (1953), *Endgame* (1957), *All That Fall* (1957), *Act Without Words I* (1957), *Krapp's Last Tape* (1958), *Embers* (1959), *Act Without Words II* (1959), *Happy Days* (1961), *Words and Music* (1962), *Cascando* (1963), *Play* (1963), *Eh Joe* (1966), *Come and Go* (1966), *Breath* (1969), *Not I* (1972), *That Time* (1976), *Footfalls* (1976), *Ghost Trio* (1976), *. . .But the Clouds. . .* (1977), *A Piece of Monologue* (1980), *Ohio Impromptu* (1981), *Rockaby* (1980), *Quad* (1982), *Catastrophe* (1982), *Nacht und Träume* (1983), *What Where* (1983)**

Beckett is probably the greatest living playwright; he was awarded the Nobel Prize for Literature in 1969. Born in Ireland of Anglo-Irish parents, he went to Paris in the late 1920s where he worked for a while as secretary to James Joyce and later as a lecturer in English. In 1938 he settled in Paris, where he now lives and works, writing both in French and English and translating his own work into English. He was active in the French Resistance during World War II, although this political activity is something he resolutely does not speak about.

Martin Esslin has claimed Beckett as the figure who brought Absurdism to public attention, but Beckett himself does not accept that characterisation, nor can his considerable output and the range of his experiments in drama be neatly categorised. Beckett himself has consistently refused to explain his work, continuing to direct and to produce drama that defies easy definition. Existentalism, Christian allegory and nihilism have all been employed as theoretical accounts of Beckett's work, but he has said only, 'I meant what I said'. To reduce the stark and complex imagery and language of Beckett's work to a single 'meaning' would be to diminish their power.

Beckett began writing as a critic; his first published work was a piece on *Finnegan's Wake*, written at Joyce's request. In 1931 he produced a study of Proust, he then wrote verse, short fiction and novels and turned to drama, he says, for 'relaxation'. *Waiting for Godot* arrived in England at a period in which there was a growing interest and awareness of non-realist forms of drama and of the innovations of European theatre. A play in which two tramp-clown figures wait for Godot, who never arrives, it was greeted with both mystification and acclaim. Beckett has denied that it is a Christian allegory; it is a firmly aetheist play.

Beckett's work is full of powerful images which are not referred to or explained, often images of human immobility: in *Play*, the three voices are trapped in jars; Winnie of *Happy Days* is gradually buried up to her neck in sand; in *Endgame*, one of the characters cannot walk, another cannot sit. These images

TRY THESE:

▷Brecht saw *Waiting for Godot* and hated it, believing it to be indicative of Western decadence. ▷Ionesco and ▷Genet were seen with Beckett to represent a European 'Theatre of the Absurd'; ▷Stoppard's *Rosencrantz and Guildenstern are Dead* clearly owes a great deal to Beckett's *Waiting for Godot*; ▷Harold Pinter has clearly been influenced by Beckett; for contrast on the master/servant relationship, see ▷Derek Walcott's *Pantomime*, in the context of the Robinson Crusoe/Man Friday relationship.

Billie Whitelaw, one of the leading exponents of Samuel Beckett's work, as the immobilised Winnie in his own production of his ***Happy Days***, Royal Court, 1979.

can be seen as metaphors for inescapable traps; in Beckett's plays, as in Sartre's *Huis Clos*, there is literally no way out.

Beckett's plays have become increasingly minimalist, and have explored the limits of the dramatic form. In *Acts Without Words* he produced the works with no verbal language, only sounds, and in a television piece in which actors silently moved around a floor diagram, he raised the question of what a 'play' is; at what point does drama cease to be drama and become dance or mime? He has also written a number of monologues, most memorably for women: in *Not I*, *Rockaby*, and *Footfalls*, which was written for Billie Whitelaw. The setting, timing and direction of a Beckett play are as integral as the text; his stage directions are extremely precise. In *Footfalls* the character is described as 'compulsively pacing', but the footfalls are not arbitrary, they are minutely scripted: 'starting with right foot (r) from Right (R) to left (L). . .'. Beckett places enormous demands upon the performer, but Whitelaw says, I think if that is what he's written, that is what he wants. And I think it's up to anyone who's actually doing his work to follow that as faithfully as they can'.

Despite the difficulty of much of Beckett's work, he is not as obscure as he is often thought; his plays are full of comic invention and punning. He has a fascination with clowning (his one film, *Film*, 1965, was made with Buster Keaton): *Waiting for Godot* employs comic routines which are worthy of Laurel and Hardy; Max Wall was a thoroughly appropriate performer for *Krapp's Last Tape* and *Endgame*, in recent revivals for Beckett's eightieth birthday; whilst John Alderton, another well-known comedy actor, starred with Alec McCowen in the ▷ National's 1987 revival of *Waiting for Godot*.

Endgame

The four characters of *Endgame* exist in a bare white set, with only a small window. Two of them are locked in a symbiotic relationship: Clov cannot sit, Hamm, blind and impotent, cannot stand; they hate, but need each other, in a pairing that echoes the master/servant relationship of Pozzo and Lucky in *Waiting for Godot*. The senile Nell and Nagg are encased in dustbins, their concerns only the immediately physical. In a bitter image of a marriage, unable to reach one another but to scratch, Nagg wistfully reminisces about the erotic (a theme also explored in *Krapp's Last Tape*). The claustrophobic world of the play is never specified, the world outside the room only available through the telescope through which Clov sees a barren landscape. Written in 1958, with nuclear war felt as a very real threat, one possibility is that this is a post-holocaust world. The only clue Beckett has offered is his reply to an actor that 'the play doesn't happen only in one person's mind'. The play is full of theatrical references: Clov and Hamm evoke Caliban and Prospero in ▷ Shakespeare's *Tempest*; Hamm (who often sounds Shakespearean) is a reference to 'ham' acting (and to Hamlet?); at one point Clov turns his telescope directly onto the audience and reports: 'I see a multitude in transports of joy'.

Not I

Not I is a stunning visual theatrical effect; the short play is performed on a darkened stage on which only a shadowy draped figure and a spotlighted mouth are visible. The draped figure moves slightly during the course of the play, while the mouth babbles a fragmented and pain-filled discourse. Actress Billie Whitelaw has described the experience as 'falling backwards into Hell, emitting cries'. It is enormously demanding for an actress – when Whitelaw was confronted with the script she told Beckett: 'You've finally done it, you've written the unlearnable and you've written the unplayable'. When she asked Beckett if the character was dead he responded 'Let's just say you're not quite there'.

BEHAN, Brendan [1923–64]
Irish playwright, journalist, house-painter, and alcoholic

Plays include:
***The Quare Fellow* (1954), *An Gaill* (reworked as *The Hostage*; 1958), *Richard's Cork Leg* (1972)**

TRY THESE:
For plays on Irish politics, see ▷Sean O'Casey, ▷Brian Friel, Frank McGuinness, ▷Seamus Finnegan; ▷Genet's *The*

Books include:
Borstal Boy (1958), Confessions of an Irish Rebel (1965)

A member of the IRA at fourteen, sent to Borstal for three years, sentenced at nineteen to fourteen years jail for political offences and attempted murder, Behan drew on his own life for his autobiographical books *Borstal Boy* and *Confessions of an Irish Rebel* and early radio plays which Alan Simpson adapted for the Pike Theatre Club, Dublin. His first stage play *The Quare Fellow*, set in a prison on the eve of an execution, was 'developed' by ▷ Joan Littlewood for a new version presented by Theatre Workshop (1956) and in the West End, and had an important effect on attitudes to imprisonment and capital punishment. *An Gaill*, commissioned by the Irish language society Gael Linn, and reworked by Theatre Workshop as *The Hostage*, presents a picaresque set of characters in a brothel used as an IRA safe house where a British soldier is held prisoner. Much of its success was due to the Workshop's style of songs, repartee and audience confrontation. *Richard's Cork Leg*, a political comedy about fascism, was left unfinished and completed by Alan Simpson in 1972.

Behan's own curtain speeches, colourful behaviour and alcoholic interviews attracted as much media attention as his plays. He claimed: 'I'm not a postman . . . I don't deliver messages.' However, although *The Hostage* is very funny, and Behan himself described *The Quare Fellow* as a comedy-drama, both plays have a great deal to say to their audiences and the Theatre Workshop productions affected British attitudes both to the topics discussed and to ways of presenting theatre.

Balcony for a rather different use of a brothel setting; for plays on prison brutality, ▷Wisdom Bridge's *In the Belly of the Beast* and, for a female view, ▷Clean Break.

BEHN, Aphra [1640–1689]
English dramatist and novelist

Plays include:
***The Forced Marriage* (1670), *The Rover* (1677), *The Lucky Chance* (1686), *The Feign'd Curtizans; or a Night's Intrigue* (1678), *The Roundheads; or The Good Old Cause* (1681), *The City-Heiress; or Sir Timothy Treat-All* (1682), *The Emperor of the Moon* (1687)**

The first woman to earn her living by the pen, Aphra Behn was renowned both for her wit and her prolific output. In her lifetime she was one of the most frequently performed playwrights, comparable with ▷ Dryden, ▷ Wycherley (four plays produced) or ▷ Congreve (six in his lifetime) and actually left behind eighteen separate plays, as well as novels and some poetry anthologies. An early champion of a woman's right to free expression – Virginia Woolf suggested that 'all women together ought to let flowers fall upon the tomb of Aphra Behn. . .for it was she who earned them the right to speak their minds' – she was consistently vilified by male critics for daring to write as bawdily as they did. After the opening of *The Lucky Chance* an accusation of indecency brought from her a typically robust plea to be accorded the same freedom to write as that enjoyed by men. Her plays deal with subjects familiar to Restoration audiences fattened on a diet of elegant debauchery; double standards in high places; sexual intrigue; and cuckoldry. She wrote tragi-comedies, historical comedies, political lampoons and, with the *commedia dell-arte* based *The Emperor of the Moon*, is credited with a forerunner to the English ▷ pantomime.

After two-and-a-half centuries of neglect, Behn is beginning to enjoy a small renaissance: *The Lucky Chance* was revived by the Women's Playhouse Trust (1981) and *The Rover* (1986) by the ▷ RSC. Modern audiences enjoy her plays particularly for their good humour and energy, whilst recognising her early feminist claims for equality in relationships between the sexes. A night with Behn is still a good night out and her plays have as much to offer as those of her better known male contemporaries.

TRY THESE:
Other Restoration playwrights such as ▷Congreve, ▷Etherege, ▷Wycherley, ▷Farquhar, ▷Vanbrugh; ▷Edward Bond's *Restoration* and ▷ Caryl Churchill's *Serious Money* for modern similarities; also ▷Timberlake Wertenbaker's *The Grace of Mary Traverse* as a feminist model in an historical setting (eighteenth-century) striking out for independence and a similar concern for women in their social context.

BENNETT, Alan [1934–]
British dramatist and actor

TRY THESE:
John Dighton's *The*

Aphra Behn's ***The Lucky Chance***, successfully revived by Jules Wright for The Women's Playhouse Trust at the Royal Court in 1984 after some 250 years of neglect. Front left: Alan Rickman, front right, Paul Bacon; rear, left to right, Christopher Fairbank, Harriet Walter, Jonathan Adams.

Plays include:
***Forty Years On* (1968), *Getting On* (1971), *Habeas Corpus* (1973), *The Old Country* (1977), *Enjoy* (1980), *Kafka's Dick* (1986)**

Films include:
***A Private Function* (1985), *Prick Up Your Ears* (1986)**

Television includes:
***A Day Out* (1972), *Sunset Across the Bay* (1975), *A Little Outing* (1977), *A Visit from Miss Protheroe* (1978), *Me, I'm Afraid of Virginia Woolf* (1978), *Doris and Doreen* (1978), *The Old Crowd* (1979), *Afternoon Off* (1979), *One Fine Day* (1979), *All Day on the Sands* (1979), *A Woman of No Importance* (1982), *Intensive Care* (1982), *An Englishman Abroad,* (1983), *The Insurance Man* (1986), *Talking Heads* (1988)**

Bennett first attracted attention as a writer and performer in revue on the Edinburgh Fringe, especially with *On the Fringe* with Jonathan Miller, Dudley Moore and Peter Cook which had long runs in London and New York. *Forty Years On* seemed to please everyone, a 'good night out' and a clever satire with songs which analyses Britain in the twentieth century via a revue put on by a boarding school (much of it began life as pastiches of literary and other styles). *The Old Country*, a cerebral discussion of national identity through the image of a British defector living in the USSR, made more demands on audiences. *Enjoy* so subverted West End expectations of Bennett as entertainer that it was a commercial flop and *Kafka's Dick*, in which Kafka, his parents and his publisher materialise in the suburban home of a would-be biographer, found appreciative audiences among Royal Court literati but failed to transfer to the West End.

Bennett is a very funny writer, adept at using the techniques of farce and music hall, especially in *Habeas Corpus*, but, while he will find humour in the predicament of cancer patients, geriatrics, Jewish mothers, social workers' cases or homosexual spies, his characters are not butts for laughter. His own comment on one of his television creations that, 'by the end. . .you understand why she is like that and you sympathise with her', is true of them all. He has an uncannily accurate ear for the richness of real speech, evident most recently in his six-part television monologue series, *Talking Heads*. *The Old Crowd* and *The Insurance Man* have explored techniques outside the apparent naturalism of most of his other television plays.

As well as appearing in revue, Bennett has brought the same observation to his performances as an actor as he brings to his writing.

Happiest Days of Our Lives for broad satire on the English public school system; also ▷Simon Gray's *Butley*, ▷Christopher Hampton's *The Philanthropist*; ▷Peter Nichols, and ▷Joe Orton for satirists of social mores; also ▷Michael Wilcox's *Lent* for linking the school play with homosexuality.

Enjoy

Enjoy manages to be illuminating about class values, town planners, the generation gap, sexual politics, and fashionable sociology in a play that continually suprises. An ageing working-class couple in the North of England, living in a house due for demolition, and due for removal to a new estate, are visited by an apparently female social worker who, the audience does not realise, is actually their son in drag. Proud of their children, they try to play it his way, and they also boast of their prostitute daughter: 'She's exceptional. You won't find girls like her on every street corner.' This is not Bennett being the naughty boy out to shock – though that element is present – here he wants to deliver a much more profound shock to the complacency of those who react to him only as an entertainer.

BERKOFF, Steven [1937–]

British actor and dramatist

Plays and adaptations include:
***The Penal Colony* (1968), *Metamorphosis* (1969), *The Trial* (1970), *Agamemnon* (1973), *The Fall of the House of Usher* (1974), *East* (1975), *Greek* (1979), *The Murder of Jesus Christ* (1980), *Decadence* (1981), *One Man* (1982), *West* (1983)**

Berkoff is as widely known as a performer as he is a writer. He

TRY THESE:
▷Alan Bennett's *Kafka's Dick* is a wildly imaginative, but very Bennett-like play on fame and literature, in which Kafka is omnipresent; ▷Lindsay Kemp, though entirely different, is as

studied mime in Paris with the École Jacques Le Coq, an emphasis very evident in his performances and plays, which rely as much for their impact on movement as on language. After working in repertory theatre Berkoff went on to found the London Theatre Group, where he began to direct and to develop adaptations from literature into theatre. Kafka and Edgar Allan Poe were favoured authors for this treatment, which often involved Expressionistic sets and acting style. The London Theatre Group also developed a version of ▷ Aeschylus' *Agamemnon*, and Greek tragedy became an informing principle of Berkoff's own writing. His first original play was *East*, produced at the ▷ Edinburgh Festival and then at the ▷ National Theatre's Cottesloe, which used a juxtaposition of street language with high tragedy and blank verse to produce a vitriolic and abrasive account of East End life. *Greek* employed the Oedipus myth to polemicise about mothers, marriage and women. *West* rewrote the Beowolf legend into a scabrous attack on the British upper classes and was (ironically) a great success in the West End.

Most recently Berkoff's strange and dangerous theatrical presence has been lent to James Bond and Beverley Hills Cop films and to a sherry advertisement.

idiosyncratic and unique in his performance style; ▷Jim Cartwright's *Road* uses language as explosively; the Capek brothers' *Insect Play* is another insect-infected metaphor for society.

Metamorphosis

Metamorphosis was the most successful of the London Theatre Group's productions. Kafka's tale of a young man who wakes up to discover he has been transformed into a beetle becomes a sustained scream of rage against the constraints of conventional society in Berkoff's hands. First performed with Berkoff at the Round House in 1969, *Metamorphosis*, which is highly stylised using acrobatics and mime to powerful effect, toured extensively in Britain and overseas. The play was revived (with another performer, Tim Roth, as the young man, and with Berkoff in the role of the father) at London's Mermaid Theatre in 1986, and is now, as a spectacular showcase for an actor, a regular feature of the ▷ Edinburgh Festival.

BERLINER ENSEMBLE

East German theatre company, founded by Bertolt Brecht

In 1948 Brecht returned to Berlin, attracted by the promise of funding for his own company from the government of the GDR, and created the Ensemble at the Deutsches Theater, presenting *Mother Courage and her Children* in January 1949. Here he was provided with the resources to mount definitive productions of some of his own plays, though many of the Ensemble's productions of his work date from after his death in 1956. Nevertheless, they form the most direct link with the methods which he adopted, a practical demonstration of his stagecraft rather than his theory. In 1954 the Ensemble moved to the Theater am Schiffbauerdamm which then became its home.

Following Brecht's death the 296 strong company (including sixty actors) was headed by his widow Helene Weigel, and on her death in 1971 by Ruth Berghaus. Although, for a time, it appeared to have become a little stereotyped and unimaginative, under its current director Manfred Wekwerth it is again producing exciting work, expanding its repertory beyond that of a Brecht museum and restaging his plays in new productions.

The Ensemble has made a number of overseas visits. Its first to Britain in 1956 had a major effect on British theatre: both the techniques used in the productions and the ensemble playing of the company inspired many directors who applied the lessons learned to their own work. In the 1970s, many small British left-wing companies aspired to running as ensembles; so too American groups like the Open Theatre and the Wooster Group. However, various reasons – limited funding particularly – have prohibited the survival of long-term ensembles, with the exception perhaps of the Wooster Group.

TRY THESE:
Few British or American companies have managed to operate as ensembles, but the influence of the Berliner Ensemble has been widespread, particularly on the ▷RSC and the Royal Court and in the practice of many directors such as Bill Gaskill at the ▷RSC in the 1960s (his *Caucasian Chalk Circle*, and *Cymbeline*); see also the ▷Wooster Group, ▷Brecht.

BERNARD, Jean-Jacques [1888–1972]

French dramatist

TRY THESE:
▷Chekhov, ▷Harold

Plays include:

***Le Voyage à Deux* (*Travel for Two*; 1909), *La Joie de Sacrifice* (*The Joy of Sacrifice*; 1911), *La Maison Epargnée* (*The House Saved*; 1919), *Le Feu Qui Reprend Mal* (*The Sinking Fire*; 1921), *Martine* (1922), *L'Invitation au Voyage* (*Invitation to the Journey*; 1924), *Le Printemps des Autres* (*Other People's Springtime*; 1924), *Denise Marette* (1925), *L'Ame en Peine* (*The Lost Soul*; 1926), *Le Secret d'Arvers* (*The Secret of Arvers*; 1926), *Le Roy de Malousie* (*The King of Malousie*; 1928), *La Louise* (*Our Louise*; 1930), *A La Recherche des Coeurs* (*Searching for Hearts*; 1931), *Les Soeurs Guedonec* (*The Guedonec Sisters*; 1931), *Jeanne de Pantin* (1933), *Nationale 6* (*Highway No 6*; 1935), *Deux Hommes* (*Two Men*; 1937), *Le Jardinier d'Ispahan* (*The Gardener of Ispahan*; 1939)**

Writing just prior to the generation of ▷ Cocteau, Genet, and ▷ Giraudoux, Bernard is the best-known examplar of the 'theatre of the inexpressible', a French school of writers including Denys Amiel and Charles Vildnac in which it's our unspoken dialogue that resonates, not the words themselves ('subtext', as acting teachers might put it). Bernard brought this theory to bear in a variety of plays from which *Martine* stands out, primarily because of Peter Hall's 1985 production at the ▷ National Theatre. Telling of the peasant girl Martine's misplaced attraction for a callow upper-class journalist, Julien, the play proceeds inevitably to its sad ending, as Martine's passivity hardens into a tacit acknowledgment of perpetual rejection (see Claude Goretta's film *The Lacemaker* for a contemporary update on this theme). *Nationale 6* tells a similar story whereby an ordinary provincial girl is done in by an overactive imagination, and in *Les Soeurs Guedonec*, two spinsters pass a miserable holiday in complete silence, accompanied by three loud orphan children.

Pinter, and ▷Samuel Beckett for transmuting the 'inexpressible' into art rather than just an end in and of itself; equally, ▷Robert Holman and ▷Marguerite Duras for the 'inexpressible' recall of past emotions; for treatments of class clashing, see ▷Chekhov's *Three Sisters*.

BETTI, Ugo [1892–1953]
Italian dramatist and judge

Plays produced in translation include:

***Il Paese delle Vacanze* (*Summertime*; 1942), *L'Aurola Bruciata* (*The Burnt Flowerbed*; 1942), *Curruzione al Palasso di Giustizia* (*Corruption in the Palace of Justice*, also translated for radio as *The Sacred Seals*; 1949), *La Regina e gli Insorti* (*The Queen and the Rebels*; 1951)**

Some Italian critics considered Betti's later plays even better than those of ▷ Pirandello, whose influence is evident in his work. Betti's themes are moral and in the wider sense, religious: his translator Henry Reed suggested that his major theme was 'man's fatal disregard of God'. Carefully plotted and well-constructed in a conventional way, his plays tend to be set in rather unlocalised symbolic settings, though the dialogue is naturalistic. His interest is in the personal and ethical problems of his protagonists rather than any political dialectic: the rebels in *The Queen and the Rebels* or the contending powers in *The Burnt Flowerbed*, for instance, are abstractions without identifiable ideologies. His concerns in these plays are the sacrifice by which a prostitute saves the live of a worthless queen and so herself gains 'queenly' virtues, and a similar self-sacrifice intended to destroy the cynicism of a former politician.

TRY THESE:
▷Genet's *The Balcony*; ▷Pirandello; ▷Barry Collins' *Judgement* for moral enquiry; ▷Anouilh, Montherlant, ▷Giraudoux similarly for ethical discussions.

BILL, Stephen [1948–]
British dramatist

Plays include:

***Girl Talk* (1977), *The Old Order* (1979), *The Final Wave* (1979), *Piggy Back Riders* (1981), *The Bottom Drawer* (1982), *Naked in the Bull Ring* (1985), *Over the Bar* (1985), *Crossing the Line* (1987), *Curtains* (1987)**

Relatively unrecognised nationally until the success of *Curtains*, which won three awards when it was produced at the Hampstead Theatre in 1987, Stephen Bill has a solid record of

TRY THESE:
▷Alan Bleasdale and ▷Willy Russell use Liverpudlian settings and ▷John Byrne uses Glaswegian settings in similar ways to Bill's use of Birmingham; ▷Sophocles' *Oedipus* for family reunions that go wrong;

regional successes, including *The Old Order*, for which he won the 1979 John Whiting Award. Set in Birmingham, *Curtains*, an acutely observed savage comedy about a family birthday celebration which turns into a wake, presents an everyday situation of a family's attitudes to the problems of ageing and to euthanasia in terms which are memorably comic as well as horrific. It is a well-crafted, almost old-fashioned play which uses the familiar devices of the family gathering and the unexpected return of the prodigal to unlock themes and to analyse the roots of situations. However, its sombre material is unlikely to make it a popular favourite, as the shortness of its West End run sadly indicates.

contemporary dramatists who share some of Bill's preoccupations are ▷Alan Ayckbourn, ▷Joe Orton and ▷Marsha Norman (*Night Mother*); other contemporary dramatists from Birmingham are ▷Alan Drury and ▷David Rudkin.

BLACK THEATRE

TRY THESE:
for other black writers not mentioned here see ▷James Baldwin, ▷Amiri Baraka, ▷August Wilson.

Black theatre in Britain has usually lumped together writers from both Afro-Caribbean and Asian cultures. Representatives of both sit on the ▷ Black Theatre Forum but in line with their own recognition of their cultural differences, this entry refers in the main to Afro-Caribbean writers. For more on the British Asian perspective, see under ▷ Asian Theatre, ▷ Tara Arts, and individual writers such as ▷ Hanif Kureishi and ▷ Karim Alrawi.

There are over thirty black Afro-Caribbean companies in Britain operating with a variety of styles, scale and focus and reflecting the diversity of the black experience in Britain today. Not all black writers necessarily wish to write about being black, though the musicals of Felix Cross at London's Albany (like *Blues for Railton*), ▷ Edgar White's *The Nine Night* and Dennis Scott's *Echo in the Bone* exemplify a stream of black writing engaged in self-examination of Caribbean roots, particularly through ritual. On the other hand, Umoja's production of James Saunders' *Alas Poor Fred* or ▷ Tunde Ikoli's double-bill for ▷ Foco Novo, *Banged Up* show that black theatre is equally interested in exploring timeless themes about personal relationships. The policies of ▷ Temba's Alby James, who revived *Romeo and Juliet* in 1988 in a Latin American/Caribbean setting is indicative of a feeling that black theatre now rejects the ghettoised consciousness into which it was forced in the early years. Alby James, for example, wants to see a company like ▷ Temba attracting the kind of middle-class audiences that go to see ▷ Alan Ayckbourn's work and addressing itself to English classics through a black perspective, as well as exploring the black experience.

Up until 1982, Black Theatre in Britain was more or less dominated by male writers; ▷ Errol John's *Moon on a Rainbow Shawl* (1956, revived in 1988, directed by Maya Angelou) was the first black play to win a drama award and was subsequently followed by a steady stream of writers including ▷ Barry Reckord, ▷ Mustapha Matura, Farrukh Dhondy, ▷ Tunde Ikoli, ▷ Caryl Phillips, whose plays (as Fay Rodrigues has noted in her introduction to the *Alternative Theatre Guide*, 1985–86) amounted to a *theatre of protest*: against apartheid, the racism of British society, imperialism, police brutality and economic exploitation.

However, ▷ Michael Abbensetts's *Sweet Talk* (1973) opened up a different, more light-hearted vein, dealing with domestic and family problems, which led to the first black television sitcom, *Empire Road* (1978–79). Jamaican writers like ▷ Trevor Rhone, and some of the plays of ▷ Derek Walcott and ▷ Edgar White have continued to mine a strong comic seam in their work.

Since 1982, black theatre too has begun to reflect a different set of pre-occupations – sexism, violence against women, young women's aspirations – with the emergence of young women writers spearheaded by the Royal Court's Young Black Writers festival, the outreach programme for young women at the Albany (as well as its Second Wave festival for young women writers), and the Theatre of Black Women. However, it was Black Theatre Co-op who presented ▷ Jacqueline Rudet's first play and ▷ Temba who produced her second. ▷ Jackie

Kay's *Chiaroscuro* was the product of encouragement from ▷ Theatre of Black Women and a reading at ▷ Gay Sweatshop's GS × 10 workshop festival. Paulette Randall emerged, like the founders of ▷ Theatre of Black Women, Bernadine Evaristo and Patricia Hilaire from the Royal Court's Young Black Writers festival and her *Fishing* formed part of the first Black Theatre Season at the Arts Theatre at the end of 1984. More recently some of the work of black American women writers has happily arrived in Britain with Black Theatre Co-op's fine revival of ▷ Lorraine Hansberry's 1950s classic *A Raisin in the Sun* and the Women's Playhouse Trust's premiere of ▷ Ntozake Shange's *Spell No 7* (her long-running Broadway hit *for colored girls who have considered suicide when the rainbow is enuf* was seen in Britain in 1983 but would be well worth reviving).

Black theatre in Britain has also been enlivened by visits from many black theatre companies from South Africa, and neighbouring black states whose anti-apartheid productions have combined agit-prop with tremendous vitality, vigour, and humour, with the Market Theatre of Johannesburg's diversity of styles – from the plays of ▷ Fugard to Percy Mtwa, M'ongeni Ngema and Barney Simon's *Woza Albert* and *Sizwe Bansi is Dead* with John Kani and Winston Ntshona – adding a further dimension. Women's groups have also visited like the South African Vusisizwe Players' *You Strike the Woman, You Strike the Rock*, Saira Essa's *You Can't Stop the Revolution*, the Jamaican Sistren collective and the extraordinary *Poppie Nongena*. Nigerians ▷ Wole Solinyka and Yemi Ajibade have also brought a wholly different flavour of the black experience to theatre audiences. Like so much else in current British theatre, black theatre is now at a crossroads, financially and artistically. With dwindling support from public funds, and the abolition of the Greater London Council, black theatre is facing a harder struggle than ever to survive – it still has no arts centre to call its own. There is no Keskidee Centre or Factory as in the 1970s where many of the directors, performers and writers of today's established black theatrical community gathered – ▷ Edgar White, Amadu Maddy, Rufus Collins, Malcolm Fredericks, Yvonne Brewster, Anton Phillips, T Bone Wilson, Carmen Munroe, Linton Kwesi Johnson and many more). The Roundhouse remains stillborn, and it is left increasingly to either the ▷ Black Theatre Forum or individual energies – such as the indefatigable Yvonne Brewster – to keep the light shining. What will be black theatre's future direction and inspiration? Will it keep its anti-apartheid resistance (such as in a young group, Double Edge's revival of Miashe Maponya's *And the Poet Died* about Steve Biko) or examination of African roots (as in Mfundi Vundla's *A Visitor to the Veldt*)? Will it find new areas such as rap and British identity as in ▷ Black Theatre Co-op's *Slipping into Darkness* and Benjamin Zephaniah's *Job Rocking*? Will it settle its soul in Rasta, and the Caribbean heritage, or like Temba's Alby James search for more integration, with plays about the black experience merging into the repertory? More white companies are joining ▷ Foco Novo (who have led the field) ▷ Joint Stock and ReSisters in including plays about race and identity as a matter of course. Perhaps this will be the new direction.

BLACK THEATRE CO-OPERATIVE (BTC),
British theatre company

Key productions include:

Welcome Home Jacko **(by ▷ Mustapha Matura; 1979),** ***Mama Dragon*** **(by Farrukh Dhondy; 1980),** ***One Rule*** **(by ▷ Mustapha Matura; 1981),** ***Trojans*** **(by Farrukh Dhondy; 1982),** ***Trinity*** **(by ▷ Edgar White; 1982),** ***Fingers Only*** **(by Yemi Ajibade; 1982),** ***The Nine Night*** **(by Edgar White; 1983),** ***Nevis Mountain Dew*** **(by Steve Carter; 1983),** ***The Tooth***

TRY THESE:
▷Mustapha Matura, ▷Edgar White, ▷Sam Shepard, ▷Jacqueline Rudet, ▷Lorraine Hansberry, ▷Alfred Fagon; ▷Black Theatre; ▷Temba.

of Crime **(by ▷ Sam Shepard; 1983),** ***No Place to be Nice*** **(by Frank McField; 1984),** ***Redemption Song*** **(by ▷ Edgar White; 1984),** ***Money to Live*** **(by ▷ Jacqueline Rudet; 1984),** ***A Raisin in the Sun*** **(by ▷ Lorraine Hansberry; 1985),** ***Ritual*** **(by ▷ Edgar White; 1985),** ***Waiting for Hannibal*** **(by ▷ Yemi Ajibade; 1986),** ***11 Josephine House*** **(by Alfred Fagon; 1987),** ***The Cocoa Party*** **(by Ruth Dunlap Bartlett; 1987),** ***Slipping into Darkness*** **(by Jamal Ali; 1987)**

One of the most dynamic of the black theatre companies, and, like ▷ Temba, a focus for new black writing, BTC was founded in 1979 by ▷ Mustapha Matura and Charlie Hanson to give opportunities to black writers, directors, musicians, technicians in a way that they had previously been unable to enjoy in other aspects of British theatre, and to serve the needs essentially of black audiences. In the early 1980s, BTC's work achieved the kind of buzz and thrill, despite limited funds and no permanent home or even office, that companies hope for but sometimes never achieve, culminating only four years after the group came together in being asked to create the Channel 4 series *No Problem*, followed in the following year with a request to stage a New Year's television special, *Party at the Palace* (this later became a stage version).

Built around a core of performers that included Victor Romero Evans, Janet Kay, Malcolm Fredericks, Bert Caesar, Trevor Laird, Gordon Case, Judith Jacobs, Chris Tummings and Shope Shodeinde with director Charlie Hanson, BTC productions have created a style that has a lot to do with exuberance, trust, some shrewd choices and some risk-taking.

▷ Mustapha Matura's *Welcome Home Jacko* set the tone with its youth club setting, Rasta ideals, and four unemployed youngsters, encouraged to take on the system but handled with humour. Farrakh Dhondy's equally successful *Mama Dragon*, about opposing political views on a black community newspaper, confirmed the company's growing popularity, and with it a burgeoning archetype – the young, male, disaffected youth. It was followed with more plays by Matura and Dhondy, but one of the other staples of BTC at that time was ▷ Edgar White. BTC premiered four of White's plays with varying degrees of success – *Trinity, The Nine Night, Redemption Song* and *Ritual* – and they also introduced the work of Nigerian ▷ Yemi Ajibade with his comedy *Fingers Only* about a group of pickpockets in a small town near Lagos, and his rather less successful, and ambitious historical drama *Waiting for Hannibal*.

Early BTC plays were performed in London's short-lived but important black community centre, The Factory, also at Riverside and later at the Theatre Royal, Stratford East, as well as touring nationally and overseas (*Welcome Home Jacko*, and *Mama Dragon* both toured in Europe, Dhondy's *Shapesters* visited the Third World Theatre Festival in Korea in 1981, and the revival of *Welcome Home Jacko* went to New York to the 'Britain Salutes New York Festival' in 1983).

Other company successes have been ▷ Sam Shepard's *Tooth of Crime* in which Victor Romero played the ageing style leader Hoss, and a first-rate revival of Lorraine Hansberry's *A Raisin' in the Sun* with memorable performances from Carmen Munroe's steadfast matriarch and Ella Wilder as her daughter-in-law. Since then the company seems to have undergone a bit of artistic 'burn-out' and slightly lost its impetus, a fact which may be partly due to the departure of Charlie Hanson, and partly financial. However, Jamal Ali's *Slipping into Darkness*, a rapping solo of anger and disaffection may indicate a revival of fortunes.

BLACK THEATRE FORUM

As the term implies, a talking shop (set up by the Greater London Council) in which fifteen different companies can argue, debate and generally work to find what Yvonne Brewster, a leading light of the black theatre community, calls 'a black aesthetic'. Companies participating at the time of writing (April 1988) include: Saas, Double Edge, ▷ Black Theatre Co-operative, ▷ Temba, ▷ Tara Arts, British Asian Theatre, Asian Thea-

TRY THESE:
See ▷Temba, ▷Black Theatre Co-operative, ▷Theatre of Black Women, ▷Asian Theatre, ▷Tara Arts.

tre Coop, Afra-Sax, ▷ Theatre of Black Women, L'Ouverture, Talawa, Hi-Time, Ten and Africa Players.

Currently funded by Greater London Arts (but for who knows how much longer in the present financial climate), each company pursues a slightly different focus. Thus Double Edge, a Rastafarian company, are interested in productions exploring the British Rasta Afro-Ethiopian experience; *L'Ouverture* are a Theatre in Education company interested in Caribbean roots; Talawa are interested in the importance of ritual in the black Caribbean experience. Similarly, the Asian companies also reflect varying preoccupations and interests.

Perhaps as important at this point in the development of Britain's multi-racial society is the discussion the Forum are now engaging in, with some courage, as to whether, given the differing cultural and historical backgrounds of Asian and Afro-Caribbean, it is still appropriate for all to be lumped together under 'black'. Out of this discussion will no doubt come future directions.

BLEASDALE, Alan [1946–]

British dramatist

Plays include:

***The Party's Over* (1975), *Down the Dock Road* (1976), *It's a Madhouse* (1976), *Should Old Acquaintance. . .* (1976), *No More Sitting on the Old School Bench* (1977), *Pimples* (1978), *Crackers* (1978), *Having a Ball* (1981), *Are You Lonesome Tonight?* (1985), *Love is a Many-Splendoured Thing* (1986)**

Films include:

***No Surrender* (1985)**

Television includes:

Two successful mini-series, *The Boys From the Blackstuff* (1983) and *The Monocled Mutineer* (1986), as well as *Scully* (1984), adapted from his long-standing radio series

TRY THESE:
▷Willy Russell as the other pre-eminent Liverpudlian writer, and Jim Hitchmough as a promising newcomer; ▷Hanif Kureishi as an urban realist with a comparable sense of humour; ▷Joe Orton for black comedy.

A Merseyside writer who – up until 1985 – had developed a strong reputation without ever having been seen in the West End, Alan Bleasdale is a gritty comic satirist who has reached his widest theatre audience with what is, paradoxically, his most earnest work: *Are You Lonesome Tonight?*, an overtly hagiographic musical about Elvis Presley that aims to set the record straight about a musical legend Bleasdale thinks has been vilified. Set on the last day of the King's life before drugs and booze did him in at forty-two in 1977, the musical is an unabashedly sentimental picture of a bloated talent looking back sardonically on his younger self, before he allowed himself to be mercilessly corrupted by managers, promoters and the press. Earlier stage plays of note include *It's a Madhouse*, set in a psychiatric hospital in the northwest of England, and *Having a Ball*, about four men awaiting surgery in a vasectomy clinic. In addition, Bleasdale has written memorably for other media: Peter Smith's 1985 film *No Surrender* had a strong Bleasdale script about rival factions in a Liverpool nightclub where the tensions mirror those in Northern Ireland. His TV writing has also tapped the psychic pulse of Britain today, in series like *Scully* (about a feckless young Liverpudlian), *Boys From the Blackstuff* (a howl of rage against unemployment, set in Liverpool, that nonetheless caught a national feeling) and *The Monocled Mutineer* (a parable of powerlessness in Thatcher's Britain).

BLOOD GROUP

Key productions include:

***Barricade of Flowers* (1981-2), *Dirt* (1982–3), *Cold Wars* (1984), *Clam* (1985), *Nature* (1985)**

TRY THESE:
Women's groups such as Burnt Bridges and Tessa Schneideman's Loose Change; mime-oriented, groups such as Théâtre de

A small but influential visual performance oriented women's experimantal touring group, founded by Anna Furse with Suzy

Gilmour in 1980, Blood Group's work is an attempt to construct a form of 'total theatre', which combines mime, with dance, video with music to create a new stage vocabulary – often non-verbal – of striking, reverberating images.

Distinguished by its inventiveness and humour, Blood Group has looked at slave mentalities in *Barricades of Flowers* inspired by ▷ Genet's *The Maids*; dealt with pornography and sex and other topics such as the examination of women as performers, 'good' women and 'bad' women, 'clean' money and 'dirty' in *Dirt*, and explored nuclear holocaust through parallels with the 'nuclear family' and parent/child relationships, again non-verbally and with great potency, in *Cold Wars*. *Clam*, with a typically witty, pungent text by ▷ Deborah Levy was another contemplation of nuclear war, along with sexual politics and the possibilities of peace, using two actors. Blood Group's *Nature* on the other hand used a company of thirty woman to look at gender, drag and sexual mores through its adaptation of Virginia Woolf's ambiguous *Orlando*.

Complicité, whose work has the comic bite of the best of ▷Alan Bennett-type observation of the minutiae of middle-class mores combined with superb physical skills; other performance art groups such as Impact, Lumiere and Son have taken combinations of text, video, music score, physical movement to an even more extended point; for themes of pornography and sex, see ▷Sarah Daniels' *Masterpieces*; for themes of nuclear holocaust, see ▷Deborah Levy's *Pax*, ▷Noël Greig's *Poppies*; demolition of the nuclear family ranges far and wide – from ▷Eugene O'Neill's *Long Day's Journey into Night* to ▷Alan Ayckbourn, particularly *Absent Friends*; see also ▷Performance Art.

BOLT, Robert [1924–]

British dramatist and screenwriter

Plays include:

The Critic and the Heart (1957), _Flowering Cherry_ (1957), _A Man for All Seasons_ (radio version 1954; staged 1960), _The Tiger and the Horse_ (1960), _Gentle Jack_ (1963), _The Thwarting of Baron Bolligrew_ (for children; 1965), _Vivat! Vivat Regina!_ (1970), _State of Revolution_ (1977)

Films include:

Lawrence of Arabia (1962), _Doctor Zhivago_ (1965), _A Man for All Seasons_ (1966), _Ryan's Daughter_ (1970), _Lady Caroline Lamb_ (director and writer; 1972)

A school teacher who began writing plays for children and then for radio, Bolt modelled *The Critic and the Heart* on ▷ Maugham's *The Circle*, while *Flowering Cherry*, his first popular success, was greeted as Chekhovian by contemporary critics. Its picture of an insurance salesman living among his own illusions has an edge of non-naturalism which contrasts with its largely conventional structure; Ralph Richardson's eccentric performance had much to do with the play's original success. Bolt has continued to essay a variety of styles. Critics saw the influence of ▷ Brecht in *A Man for All Seasons* (it was staged four years after the ▷ Berliner Ensemble's London season), but the device of a chorus figure, the Common Man, weaving in and out of the action, owes much more to the techniques of radio, for which it was originally written. However, when interviewed in 1961, Bolt declared: 'Brecht is the writer I would most wish to resemble'. *Gentle Jack* made a gesture towards ritual theatre, drawing parallels between pagan folklore and capitalist mores, and he

TRY THESE:
▷Brecht, ▷Peter Shaffer ▷David Edgar, ▷David Hare and ▷Howard Brenton for historical epics; ▷Peter Barnes for a debunking of history; for plays on anti-nuclear issues, ▷Nick Darke's *The Body*, ▷Brian Clark's *The Petition, and* ▷Lanford Wilson's *Angels Fall*; and ▷Stephen Lowe for a number of plays with an anti-war theme.

Maggie Steed and Ann Mitchell in Edward Bond's ***War Play Three***, the final play in Bond's war plays trilogy at the RSC's The Pit, 1985, directed by Bond with Nick Hamm.

originally proposed that *Vivat! Vivat Regina!* should be given an *Oh What a Lovely War!*, pier-end-style presentation. *Vivat!* was intended to provide a meaty role for his wife, Sarah Miles, as Mary Queen of Scots, but he overwrote the part and the more sparsely written Elizabeth I is dominant in performance. *State of Revolution*, written for the ▷ National Theatre, is his most ambitious theatre work in its attempt to present a political dialectic rather than a personal story but its hagiographic portrayal of Lenin against a complex revolutionary background does not come off as well as his Tudor portraits. His films have been more successful in handling epic themes.

Bolt's involvement in CND and membership of the Committee of 100 are reflected in *The Tiger and the Horse*, in which an academic wife has to decide whether to sign an anti-bomb petition although doing so will jeopardise her husband's elevation to Vice Chancellor of his university.

A Man for All Seasons

A Man for All Seasons presents the conflict between Sir Thomas More and Henry VIII, and the title role gave Paul Scofield a triumph in both play and film. Here, most clearly, is the thread that runs right through Bolt's work of personal integrity, responsibility and the use of power. The human element holds the play together without need to explore religious or political polemics. As in *Vivat!* actors and director are offered chances to create striking theatre and the play has proved a durable favourite.

BOND, Edward [1934–]

British dramatist

Plays include:

***The Pope's Wedding* (1962), *Saved* (1965), *Narrow Road to the Deep North* (1968), *Early Morning* (1968), *Black Mass* (1970), *Passion* (1971), *Lear* (1972), *The Sea* (1973), *Bingo: Scenes of Money and Death* (1973), *The Fool: Scenes of Bread and Love* (1975), *Stone* (1976), *The Bundle* (1978), *The Woman* (1978), *The Worlds* (1979), *Restoration* (1981), *Summer* (1982), *The War Plays* (1985)**

Adaptations include:

***Three Sisters* (from Chekhov; 1967), *Spring Awakening* (from Wedekind; 1974), *The White Devil* (from Webster; 1976)**

Films include:

***Blow-Up* (1967), *Laughter in the Dark* (from Nabokov; 1969), *The Lady of Monza* (1970), *Walkabout* (from James Vance Marshall; 1971)**

Bond, one of the most radical of playwrights, has been called 'the most important and controversial dramatist writing in Britain today'. Notorious for a scene in *Saved* in which a baby is stoned to death, he has consistently written from a Marxist perspective, and argues that the shock of such violent images is necessary to represent the violence that is done to people by capitalism.

Born in London, Bond left school at fourteen, worked in factories and offices, writing plays in his spare time, and sent them to the Royal Court. Keith Johnstone invited him to become a member of the Writer's Group led by himself and William Gaskill; *The Pope's Wedding* was produced at the Royal Court as a Sunday Night performance. Bond's next play *Saved*, developed with the Writer's group, was instrumental in ridding British theatre of the censorship of the Lord Chamberlain. The Court staged it under club conditions to avoid the cuts imposed by the Lord Chamberlain, but nonetheless, summonses were issued. The company was finally fined only £50, and achieved a moral victory in demonstrating that club conditions did not offer any protection from censorship. In 1968, The Theatres Act abolished the powers of the Lord Chamberlain, and *Saved* and *Narrow Road to the Deep North* were toured throughout Europe under the auspices of the British Council.

Many of Bond's plays offer radical rereadings of historical events, texts and figures that are commonly held as a source of national pride; *Bingo* confronts the dying and unheroic

TRY THESE:

The Pope's Wedding was first staged on the set of ▷Beckett's *Happy Days*, and the pile of sand became a contributory factor to the final image of Scobey; ▷Ann Jellicoe, ▷Maureen Duffy, ▷John Arden and ▷Arnold Wesker were also members of the Writer's Group with Bond; Bond has cited ▷Joint Stock as 'the kind of theatre I want'; Artaud was an important influence on Bond; ▷Brecht is a strong influence and *The Narrow Road to the Deep North* and its companion play *The Bundle* use an oriental setting in ways reminiscent of *The Caucasian Chalk Circle* and *The Good Person of Sezchuan*; *The Woman* is a rereading of the Trojan wars more familiar in ▷Euripides' *The Trojan Women*, ▷Shakespeare's *Troilus and Cressida* or ▷Giraudoux' *The Trojan War Will Not Take Place*; *Restoration* is a rereading of Restoration comedy. Bond himself has drawn attention to the Oedipal elements in *Saved* (see ▷Sophocles).

▷ Shakespeare and ▷ Ben Jonson, *The Fool* is about the 'peasant poet' John Clare. Bond has described his reworking of ▷ Shakespeare's *King Lear* in *Lear* as 'an attack on Stalinism, as seen as a danger to Western revolution, and on bourgeois culture as expressed in Shakespeare's *Lear*'. He has consistently spoken out for political causes; *Black Mass* was written for the Anti-Apartheid movement; *Stone* for Gay Sweatshop; *Passion* was commissioned by CND and performed on the grandstand at Alexandra Park Racecourse.

A recent revival of his early work at the Royal Court gave *The Pope's Wedding* its first full production, (it had previously been seen only in a club performance). The season confirmed Bond as a writer of savage power, with a command of language and poetic imagery that went beyond the shocking.

Bond refers to his drama as 'a Rational Theatre'. According to Bond: 'Theatre is an event about life and takes place in life. It is an experience about experience. . .The routes of communication between spectator and stage run both ways'.

In 1979 Bond cast his play *The Worlds* with a non-professional cast of young people, members of the Activists Youth Theatre Club, part of the Court's Young People's Theatre Scheme; it was a demonstration of his commitment to his principle that: 'New writing needs new acting, new directing and new audiences'.

Saved

Saved is a difficult play to watch; dealing with a community of young people in South London it charts their desperate and violent lives. Its first performance at the Royal Court provoked extreme, and extremely polarised, reactions. The *Daily Telegraph* critic reported 'cold disgust' and horror at the scene in which a group of young men stone a baby to death (and was not alone in his reaction), while other critics and writers greeted the power of Bond's writing and imagery with acclaim. It is not only that scene which makes the play so harrowing; in one section, the baby wails unrelentingly while no one on stage responds to its cries, and the audience is made to physically experience the frustration and apathy of the play's characters.

BOUCICAULT, Dionysus Larner [1820–96]

Irish actor and dramatist

Plays include:

***London Assurance* (1841), *The Vampire* (1852), *The Corsican Brothers* (1852), *The Poor of New York* (1857), *The Octoroon* (1859), *The Colleen Bawn* (1860), *Arrah-na-Pogue* (1864) and *The Shaughraun* (1874)**

Greatly admired as an actor in Britain and the USA, Boucicault was a wide-ranging and prolific dramatist who wrote nearly 150 original plays and adaptations, operettas, pantomimes and melodramas (including sixteen plays in one year). The flood was aided by reworking to suit new audiences: *The Streets of London* and *The Streets of Liverpool* are almost identical to *The Poor of New York*. Many of his plays offer opportunities for spectacle: the burning of a Mississippi steamer in *The Octoroon*, or, in *Arrah-na-Pogue*, the whole scene sinking slowly as the hero climbs an ivy-clad turret to seize the villain and hurl him to his death. Though melodramas like *The Vampire* follow the pattern for the genre, his work shows careful construction and keen observation. *The Octoroon* was probably the first play in which an American black slave was treated seriously and the social themes which often attracted him prefigured later dramas about the common people. His Irish plays, such as *The Shaughraun*, provided fine vehicles for himself but, though he fought to establish copyright for dramatists in the USA and was the first to receive a royalty instead of a flat fee, he died an impoverished teacher of acting in New York.

His plays continue to be revived fairly regularly in Ireland and occasionally elsewhere: in 1975 an ▷ RSC production of *London Assurance*, with Judi Dench, found great success; a musical version of *The Streets of London*, transferred from Stratford East to Her Majesty's, was modestly successful in

TRY THESE:
Phantom of the Opera offers many of the attractions that delighted Boucicault's nineteenth-century audiences; *London Assurance* shows resemblances to the plays of ▷Goldsmith and ▷Sheridan (as well as another ▷RSC revival, John O'Keefe's *Wild Oats*), and through them to ▷Congreve and other Restoration comic dramatists; Boucicault's concern with Irish politics marks him out as an ancestor of ▷Sean O'Casey and ▷Brian Friel.

1980; and *The Shaughraun* was revived at the ▷ National Theatre in 1988.

London Assurance
London Assurance presents the courtship by a young gentleman, who is heavily in debt, of a cynical country beauty. She is at first happy at the idea of marriage to an old man who will provide her with a secure income, until she falls in love with his son. A witty piece which owes a great debt to earlier comedies of manners, its characters are sharply drawn, and a plot which turns upon a father not recognising his disguised son is acceptable within a structure that includes some farce-like devices. Donald Sinden, who played in the ▷ RSC revival, considered this play the equal of ▷ Wilde's *The Importance of Being Earnest*.

BRECHT, Bertolt [1898–1956]

German dramatist, poet, theatrical innovator and theoretician

Plays include:

***Baal* (1918; performed 1923), *Drums in the Night* (1922), *In the Jungle of Cities* (1923), *Edward II* (1924; with Lion Feuchtwanger), *The Elephant Calf* (c 1924–5), *Man is Man* (1926), *The Threepenny Opera* (1928; with music by Kurt Weill, from ▷ John Gay's *The Beggar's Opera*), *Happy End* (1929, with Elisabeth Hauptmann and music by Weill), *He who says Yes* and *He who says No* (1930), *The Measures Taken* (1930), *The Exception and the Rule* (1930), *The Rise and Fall of the City of Mahagonny* (1930; with music by Weill), *The Mother* (1932; from Gorki), *St Joan of the Stockyards* (1932), *The Seven Deadly Sins* (1933; with Weill, also known as *Anna Anna*), *Senora Carrar's Rifles* (1937; based on ▷ Synge's *Riders to the Sea*), *Fear and Misery of the Third Reich* (1938; also known as *The Private Life of the Master Race*), *Mother Courage and Her Children* (1941), *The Resistible Rise of Arturo Ui* (1941), *The Life of Galileo* (1943), *The Good Person of Sezchuan* (1943), *Schweik in the Second World War* (1943), *The Caucasian Chalk Circle* (1945), *Mr Puntila and His Servant Matti* (1948), *The Days of the Commune* (1949), *The Tutor* (1950; from Jacob Lenz)**

Brecht is one of the most influential (if often unacknowledged) figures in contemporary culture. He has affected a generation of socialist playwrights, his principles have informed contemporary film theory, a whole genre of 'agit-prop' theatre productions and companies, and his 'alienation effects' are now almost fashionable practice in stage, television and film.

Brecht's history is bound up in the rise of fascism in Germany. He was born in Augsburg and in 1918 was drafted to serve at Augsburg military hospital, an experience which gave him a lifelong commitment to pacifism. Through drama criticism, he became involved in the theatre, and his first plays were very much influenced by Expressionism. *Baal*, the life of a poet, prefigures his later work in its deliberately shocking effects. Brecht went on to become part of a group of radical intellectuals in the theatre and cultural life of Berlin, becoming increasingly involved with Marxist theory, and beginning to develop an aesthetic practice that integrated with his politics, and which was bound up with the social and economic conditions of the period. He became very much part of the European avant-garde, exchanging ideas with the Formalist group in Russia.

During the 1920s Brecht developed a collaboration with Kurt Weill, which gave rise to the musical productions of *The Threepenny Opera*, *The Seven Deadly Sins* and *The Rise and Fall of the City of Mahagonny* (produced in the year the German economy crashed, and which presents a society in which *anything* can be had for money). These plays were much influenced by the Berlin cabaret of the 1920s and early 1930s, and Brecht felt that the theatre should be a place in which audiences could smoke, drink and relax, the better to take up the points of the play for discussion.

In 1932 Brecht was on the Nazis' list of banned writers, and in 1933, the year in which Hitler came to power, he fled to Denmark the day after the Reichstag fire. The Danes refused to hand

TRY THESE:
▷Edward Bond has called his own theatrical project 'Rational Theatre', in homage to Brecht's 'Theatre of Reason'; *Tales from Hollywood* ▷Günther Grass' *The Plebeians Rehearse the Uprising* and Nigel Gearing's *Berlin Days, Hollywood Nights* include Brecht among their characters; ▷Shaw, ▷Pirandello, ▷Galsworthy, ▷Eugene O'Neill and ▷Strindberg were among the dramatists banned by the Nazis; ▷Howard Barker, ▷Howard Brenton, ▷David Edgar, ▷Trevor Griffiths, and ▷John McGrath are among dramatists who have inherited Brechtian principles of theatre; among contemporary plays on the question of child custody are ▷Gay Sweatshop's *Care and Control* and ▷Sarah Daniels' *Neaptide*; ▷Caryl Churchill's *Serious Money* has similarities to Brecht and Weill's analyses of capitalism in *Mahagonny* and *The Threepenny Opera*; *Edward II* is taken from ▷Marlowe and Brecht was generally impressed by ▷Shakespeare; *St Joan of the Stockyards* and *Simone Marchard* are treatments of a St Joan figure to be contrasted with ▷Shaw's *St Joan* and ▷Anouilh's *The Lark*; *Happy End* has remarkable similarities to the much later

Judi Dench as Mother Courage in Bertolt Brecht's ***Mother Courage and Her Children*** in Howard Davies' 1984 RSC production of Hanif Kureishi's version at the Barbican.

Brecht over to the German authorities, but when Germany invaded Denmark, Brecht escaped to Finland. The events of the rise of fascism are charted in the ironically allegorical *The Rise and Fall of Arturo Ui*, in which Brecht made an analogy between the rise of Nazism and Chicago gangsters. He spent the years of the war in exile in Hollywood, where he wrote the script for the film, *Hangmen Also Die*. In 1947, after an appearance before the House of Representatives' Committee of Un-American Activities, Brecht moved to Switzerland, and in 1949 he returned to East Germany, to take up an offer of his own theatre and extensive subsidy, founding the ▷ Berliner Ensemble, on his own principles of political theatre. On his death it was taken over by his widow, Helene Weigel.

In his plays, Brecht often turned to fable and to history, to construct 'Parables' for the theatre, offering radical re-readings of familiar texts. When accused of plagiarism, Brecht's reply was ▷ 'Shakespeare was a thief', not an unreasonable analogy.

Brecht wrote forty plays altogether, which can roughly be divided into three groups (although there are elements of each phase in most of his plays): the early Expressionist plays and the musical pieces he devised with Weill; the Lehrstücke (or 'Learning pieces') and Parable plays; and his 'Epic theatre'.

In *The Messingkauf Dialogues* (one of his many writings on theatre) Brecht sets out his principles for a 'Theatre of Reason' (also known as epic theatre), in which acting, direction, set design, and all aspects of theatrical production were organised to produce a dramatic effect which challenged the audience and which implicated them in the dramatic events. Central to Brechtian theory is the 'Verfremdung' effect (often mistakenly translated as 'alienation effect', 'distancing' is closer) which refers to devices in staging, acting, music and direction which encourage the spectator to avoid cathartic identification. Songs which comment on the action of the play, placards which describe the context, direct address to the audience, open set changes all demonstrate the theatre as a place of work. Acting too becomes a means of distancing. Brecht was thoroughly opposed to Stanislavski's Method of acting the 'truth' of a character.

Brecht's achievement was to demonstrate his principles in the theatricality of his plays, their politics become something which the audience experiences and is given space to think about and to debate. Few have achieved such a stimulating and actively engaging political theatrical practice since it is hard to produce work which combines dialectical toughness, humour and theatricality in the way that Brecht usually did. Brecht's politics are integral to the structure and form of his drama, his plays are structured around a dialectical principle, between scene and scene, between audience and stage, and between theatrical event and political practice. A Brechtian theatre practice should never be static, but respond to contemporary political events, and engage the audience in a challenge to 'common sense' modes of perception. For example, in *The Good Person of Sezchuan* and *The Caucasian Chalk Circle* the difficulties of behaving humanely are dramatised in, respectively, a woman who has to invent a male protector (actually herself in disguise) to fend off claims on her, and a woman who asserts the claims of nurture over biological motherhood.

The Measures Taken

One of the 'Lehrstücke', it begins with a group of members of a Communist cell, who admit to the audience and to the party leaders that they have killed one of their members by throwing him into a limepit. The killing seems to be an indefensible act of violence, and the appearance of the comrade in flashbacks as the play proceeds only confirms the suspicion that there can be no justification for his death; he is an active and committed member of the group. But as the play progresses backwards through the events that led to his killing, the reasons become clear. His 'individualism' threatened to destroy the work of the group, and to bring about a bloody massacre, that would have cost many more lives than his own. The play is very much part of a debate within the Left about the place of violent action in revolutionary politics, about individualism and leadership and it is a fine example of a didactic theatre.

Mother Courage and her Children

This play belongs to the 'epic' period of Brecht's work. Although

▷musical *Guys and Dolls*; the ▷Glasgow Citizens' has been one of the most consistent champions of Brecht in the British theatre; Manfred Karge, whose *Man to Man* was presented at the Traverse (1987) and then The Royal Court (1988), worked with Brecht at the ▷Berliner Ensemble; see also ▷Berliner Ensemble, and ▷cabaret.

it is often taken as a study of the struggle of a resilient woman and her family and her doughty survival in a period of war (The Thirty Years' War), the play is structured specifically not to be seen as the study of a single individual, but as parable and metaphor. Mother Courage is a small business woman, who struggles with her cart to scrimp a living for her daughter, the dumb Kattrin, and her sons. Over the course of the play she is confronted with decisions which become increasingly complex, and more overtly political. Mother Courage resolutely asserts that she is not interested in politics, only the survival and care of her family but the consequence is that she loses them all. Her fate is not a simple one; the play makes it quite clear that other decisions could have averted the events of Mother Courage's tragedy. Brecht once said: 'We must be able to lose ourselves in the agony and at the same time not to. Our actual emotion will come from recognising and feeling the double process.' This double process is at work in *Mother Courage*: while her situation is undoubtedly moving, the play constantly points to the events and system which have placed her there, and to her own collusion in that system. The play is intercut with songs at the moments at which Mother Courage is required to take action, which point to the far reaching implications of individual acts. The play has a stunning alienation effect at the moment when Kattrin, silent for the entire play, creates its most violent and loudest noise. In a moment in which she has to make a political choice between saving other lives or her own, she alerts the villagers who are about to be destroyed by banging on a drum.

BRENTON, Howard [1942–]

British dramatist

Plays include:

***Gum and Goo* (1969), *Heads* (1969), *The Education of Skinny Spew* (1969), *Revenge* (1969), *Christie in Love* (1969), *Wesley* (1970), *Fruit* (1970), *Lay By* (1971; with ▷ Brian Clark, ▷ Trevor Griffiths, ▷ David Hare, ▷ Stephen Poliakoff, Hugh Stoddart, ▷ Snoo Wilson), *Scott of the Antarctic* (1971), *Hitler Dances* (1972), *England's Ireland* (1972; with Tony Bicât, ▷ Brian Clark, ▷ David Edgar, Francis Fuchs, ▷ David Hare, ▷ Snoo Wilson), *A Fart for Europe* (1973; with ▷ David Edgar), *Magnificence* (1973), *Brassneck* (1973; with ▷ David Hare), *The Churchill Play* (1974), *Weapons of Happiness* (1976), *Epsom Downs* (1977), *Deeds* (1978; with ▷ Ken Campbell, ▷ Trevor Griffiths, ▷ David Hare), *Sore Throats* (1979), *A Short Sharp Shock* (1980; with Tony Howard), *The Romans in Britain* (1980), *Thirteenth Night* (1981), *The Genius* (1983), *Sleeping Policemen* (1983; with ▷ Tunde Ikoli), *Bloody Poetry* (1984), *Pravda* (1985; with ▷ David Hare), *Greenland* (1988)**

Although he has achieved recognition as one of Britain's leading dramatists with plays produced by the ▷ National Theatre, ▷ RSC and even a Royal Court season in 1988 which included revivals of *Bloody Poetry* and *Sore Throats* as well as the premiere of *Greenland*, Brenton remains an independent figure willing to continue working on the fringe which first nourished him as much as within the established theatre. His is an uncomfortable talent, with a particular capacity for anatomising the unhealthy state of Britain today and exhuming the uncomfortable truths about the past that people would rather forget in ways that antagonise the Establishment, from his anti Enoch Powell version of *Measure for Measure* at Exeter in 1972, through the presentation of the ghost of Airey Neave in *A Short Sharp Shock*, to the major row over *The Romans in Britain*, where moral uproar over the simulated anal rape of a Druid led to a prosecution which was ultimately abandoned. It was probably more than coincidental that *Romans* says some rather uncomfortable things about imperialism, including the present situation in Northern Ireland, since there was considerable resistance throughout the 1970s to theatrical treatments of the Irish question. A committed socialist, Brenton tackles his themes with a cartoon-like ferocity and humour which has not diminished since his early fringe days with the Combination and Portable Theatre. Brenton's work is consistently engaged

TRY THESE:
Brenton has collaborated more extensively than most dramatists, most notably with ▷David Hare; ▷Howard Barker shares his socialist preoccupations and anti-naturalistic approach; ▷David Edgar and ▷Trevor Griffiths are other leading British socialist writers; ▷Ben Jonson's *Bartholomew Fair* also takes the nation's temperature on a holiday, ▷Peter Nichols' *The National Health* does the same through an institution; ▷Ann Jellicoe's *Shelley* and Liz Lochhead's *Blood and Ice* also tackle the Shelleys, as does the women's company, Tattycoram's *The Very Tragical History of Mary Shelley* – a completely biased and anti-Shelley piece; also ▷Doug Lucie's *Progress* for an attempt to build a new society, flawed by old sexisms.

with topical issues and immediate concerns, as in *Wesley*, written to be performed in a Methodist chapel or *Scott of the Antarctic*, performed on an ice rink. But even in his most topical plays there is an abiding concern with making people aware of the underlying nature of their situation, what represses them and what sustains them, and encouraging them to change things for the better. Brenton has written on the criminalisation and corruption of society, from his early *Revenge* through to *Pravda*, and on the difficulties of effecting change, from the gesture politics of *Magnificence* to the nuclear politics of *The Genius*, in which two mathematicians try to evade the forces that would turn their discoveries to destructive use. In *Epsom Downs* Brenton and the ▷ Joint Stock Theatre Group take the temperature of Britain on Derby Day 1977 in a kaleidoscopically inventive re-creation and interrogation of the contradictions of that event with the ghost of the suffragette Emily Davison attempting to persuade a modern woman to try to slash the picture as she did when she ran out in front of the king's horse in the 1913 Derby. The play is comically incisive in its presentation of contradictions and in its interweaving of threads within the apparently haphazard events of Derby Day.

Bloody Poetry

Bloody Poetry, commissioned by the touring company ▷ Foco Novo of which Brenton is a board member, grapples with sexual and other politics, the role of the artist and the need to make revolutions in the heart and mind as much as in the body politic. Byron, ▷ Shelley, Mary Shelley and Claire Clairemont reach out for a model of existence which is beyond their grasp, at great cost to themselves and to their families. Brenton has described this as a utopian play, which has led some critics to castigate him for his male characters' sexism, but he is actually concerned with the forces, sexism included, which militate against the creation of utopia. Other forces also stand in the way: some people refused to see the play because it had 'bloody' in the title, others because of the presence of 'poetry'!

BREUER, Lee [1940–]

American avant-garde director

Breuer-staged Maboue Mines productions include:

***The Red Horse Animation* (1971), *The B-Beaver Animation* (1974), *The Lost Ones* (1975), *The Shaggy Dog Animation* (1977), *Prelude to Death in Venice* (1978), *It's a Man's World* (1984)**

Other stagings include:

***Lulu* at the American Repertory Theatre in Cambridge, Massachusetts; *The Tempest* for Joe Papp in New York's Central Park; and *Gospel at Colonus* in Brooklyn and on Broadway**

Although he has directed widely on his own, Lee Breuer remains associated first off with the avant-garde collective known as Mabou Mines, a 1969 offshoot of New York's La Mama founded by Breuer, with William Raymond, Ruth Maleczech, and JoAnne Akalaitis. Based in New York, the company takes its name from an abandoned Nova Scotia coal mine, and its aesthetic draws on patterns of allusion and of visual and aural repetition (animals abound) to devise a nonlinear, often highly technological theatre. Breuer spent part of the 1960s in Berlin and Poland, and his work can have the dissociative, potentially alienating effect common to the European avant-garde. In *The Lost Ones*, for example, the audience is asked to remove their shoes before being led into a cylindrical environment filled with toy binoculars; a man is seen revealing 200 flesh-coloured people from train sets, and before the end of the forty-five-minute piece, he and a woman are both naked against the back wall. His solo stagings have been controversial, and few critics admired his 1982 *The Tempest* for the New York Shakespeare Festival, which surrounded Raul Julia's Prospero with a punk Caliban, a skittish, female Ariel, and the villains done up – Jonathan Miller-style – as mafiosi. More successful was his *Gospel at Colonus*, a sung gospel version

TRY THESE:
▷Samuel Beckett for redefining the range of theatrical possibility; ▷Robert Wilson, ▷The Wooster Group, ▷Spalding Gray for other pre-eminent figures in the American avant-garde; Impact Theatre, Jan Fabre for English and Continental comparisons.

of the Greek tragedy, which moved to Broadway's Lunt-Fontanne Theatre in March 1988 for a brief run.

Prelude to Death in Venice
Images of Dracula and a Vampire bat are seen while the music of Bach plays on in a mixed-media experience that draws on such disparate sources as Thomas Mann, ▷ Beckett, and the New York Police Department. A character, Bill, manipulates a dummy called John, who is suspended between two telephone poles; while tapes of various voices are heard, images appear and disappear in a fragmentary yet deliberate style that toys with form and meaning. For some, the absence of character and motivation in this sort of theatre dehumanises; for others, Breuer's brand of dramatic poetry excites through its embrace of a range of effects most theatres shut out.

BRIDIE, James (Osborne Henry Mavor) [1888–1951]
British doctor and dramatist

Plays include:

***The Sunlight Sonata* (as Mary Henderson; 1928), *The Anatomist* (1930), *Tobias and the Angel* (1930), *Jonah and the Whale* (1932), *A Sleeping Clergyman* (1933), *Colonel Wotherspoon* (1934), *Mary Read* (1934), *The Black Eye* (1935), *Storm in a Teacup* (adapted from Bruno Frank; 1936), *Susannah and the Elders* (1937), *The King of Nowhere* (1938), *What They Say* (1941), *Mr Bolfry* (1943), *It Depends What You Know* (1944), *The Forrigan Reel* (1944), *Daphne Laureola* (1949), *Mr Gillie* (1950), *The Baikie Charivari* (1952), *Meeting at Night* (1954)**

Born in Scotland, Bridie's plays range from biblical and hagiographic tales, to a play based on the Edinburgh body-snatchers Burke and Hare (*The Anatomist*), to the episodic history of an eighteenth-century woman pirate (*Mary Read*). His characters have occasioned many virtuoso performances and launched a number of actors into stardom. *Dr Bolfry*, one of his most successful plays, tells how the Devil visits a Scots minister in the shape of another clergyman. Together they form an alliance against non-believers, but when they meet later as antagonists the issue is undecided. The minister returns home thinking himself triumphant, only to see the Devil's umbrella rise and stalk slowly from his house. *A Sleeping Clergyman*, is a study of heredity through three generations, which shows that though 'evil' may persist through seduction, blackmail and murder, 'good' can reappear just when the world most needs it – in this case medical genius. *Daphne Laureola* was one of Edith Evans' greatest successes and also gave Peter Finch his first big opportunity. Although it tends to be individual performances in Bridie's plays that people remember, rather than the plays themselves, they are still occasionally revived, particularly in Scotland.

Bridie was a co-founder of the Glasgow Citizen's Theatre, as well as instrumental in establishing the Royal Scottish Academy of Music (now the Academy of Music and Drama).

TRY THESE:
▷Christopher Fry for similar treatments of religious themes; ▷Chekhov as another dramatist who brought his doctor's observation of character to his work; ▷Steve Gooch's *The Women-Pirates Ann Bonney and Mary Read*; ▷J. M. Barrie, as a Scottish contemporary; ▷Lillian Hellman for discussions of moral values; ▷Mary O'Malley's *Talk of The Devil* and ▷Dekker, ▷Ford and ▷Rowley's *The Witch of Edmonton*, ▷Václav Havel's *Temptation* for devilish visitations; see also ▷Kaufman and Hart, ▷George Abbott for more American equivalents.

BRIGHOUSE, Harold [1882–1958]
British dramatist

Plays include:

***Dealing in Futures* (1910), *Lonesome Like* (one-act; 1911), *Graft* (originally entitled *The Polygon*; 1912), *Garside's Career* (1914), *Hobson's Choice* (1915), *Zack* (1916)**

Part of the ▷ 'Manchester School' of playwrights Brighouse wrote and produced some seventy plays, mostly realistic and set in Lancashire. The most well-known of these is *Hobson's Choice*, a play 'built like an iron girder' (Michael Billington), whose heroine, the strong-minded and down-to-earth Maggie Hobson, thirty years old and thought 'past the marrying age', sees a suitable husband in the shy but talented boot-maker Willie Mossop, marries him out of hand (he not having much say in the matter), and with him takes over the town's boot-making business from her

TRY THESE:
Brighouse's work was mainly premiered at Manchester's Gaiety Theatre where he was part of the ▷'Manchester School'; see ▷Stanley Houghton for another 'Manchester School' playwright.

heavy father. The play is frequently revived, most recently at the Lyric Hammersmith in 1981, with Arthur Lowe and Julia McKenzie, and at the Haymarket in 1982, with Penelope Keith as Maggie. Brighouse's comedy *Zack* has been played twice in ten years at the Royal Exchange, Manchester (1976 and 1986), with some success; and several of his one-act plays, such as *Lonesome Like*, would easily bear revival if anyone did one-act plays any more.

BROOK, Peter [1925–]

British director and theorist

TRY THESE:
▷Brecht and ▷Stanislavski were other major dramatic theorists of the twentieth century.

Books include:

The Empty Space **(1968),** ***The Shifting Point*** **(collected writings, 1988)**

Peter Brook is probably the most influential director Britain has ever produced, though there was never a more international one, and much of his work has appeared outside the country. Many of his productions have become legendary and his book *The Empty Space* rapidly became a set text for many theatre workers, with its crucial distinctions between 'rough' and 'holy' theatre. He has often been regarded as a theatrical guru and by any standards, he has been a key figure in exploring and developing the possibilities of drama. In 1968 he wrote 'I can take any empty space and call it a bare stage', and he has pursued this idea all over the world in a career which has spanned forty years of productions of theatre and opera, from the West End to Persepolis to disused quarries in Australia to African villages that had never before seen a theatre company.

Brook was born in London of Russian parents, and directed his first (amateur) production (▷ Marlowe's *Dr Faustus*) in 1942, before going to Oxford University. In 1946 he directed *Love's Labour's Lost* at Stratford, thus beginning a connection that lasted for more than twenty years. He also directed plays and operas in the West End, including Strauss' *Salome* (with designs by Dali) for Covent Garden in 1949, and plays by Sartre, ▷ Anouilh, ▷ Arthur Miller, and Genet, in London and Paris. In 1962 he was appointed a co-director (with Peter Hall and Michael Saint-Denis) of the newly-named ▷ Royal Shakespeare Company; and there throughout the 1960s he developed a range of experimental and innovative work, including his setting-up with ▷ Charles Marowitz of a group to work on ▷ Artaud's ideas. This culminated in the 'Theatre of Cruelty' season at LAMDA in 1964, where they staged Artaud's unstageable play *Jet of Blood* and ▷ Marowitz's first *Hamlet* collage, discovered the young Glenda Jackson, and prepared the way for the exciting production of ▷ Peter Weiss' *Marat/Sade*. In 1966 Brook devised with the ▷ RSC the controversial *US*, a bitter attack on American involvement in Vietnam and British government support for it, and his only 'political' work; Kenneth Tynan was probably right to say that Brook's political sense was naïve. His 1970 production of *A Midsummer Night's Dream* is among the most celebrated and discussed of Shakespearean productions: staged on a bare white box set, it used acrobatics, juggling and magic tricks in a joyous response to the play's challenges. The emphasis on visual spectacle was very much the direction that Brook's later work was to take.

In 1970 he left the British theatre and established an International Centre of Theatre Research in Paris to work out his ideas of a theatre laboratory on Grotowski's lines, 'to explore the sources of theatrical expression – language, movement, sound and space'. He extracted grants from the Ford, Anderson and Gulbenkian Foundations, gathered an international company of actors dedicated to his way of working, and proceeded to experiment with Kathakali dance techniques, circus skills, masks, and a general exploration of dramatic forms, in an attempt to work out an 'international theatre language' that would transcend Western theatre conventions. In 1972 the company took a play, *Orghast*, written in an invented language by Ted Hughes, to Persepolis, subsidised by the Shah, and established a policy of international touring. They also toured parts of Africa, performing spontaneous improvisations to village audiences, and then developed a play based on a Persian story, *Conference of the Birds*, which was performed to aboriginal audiences in Australia, to festival audiences in France, and across the Sahara desert. In 1974

Peter Brook's, ***The Mahabharata***, with (top) Sotigui Kouyate and (bottom) Miriam Goldschmidt; at Glasgow's Old Transport Museum, April 1988.

the French Ministry of Culture took over the funding and the company moved to a long-disused and slightly ruinous operetta house in an immigrant quarter of Paris, the Bouffes du Nord, and began to put on plays for more conventional audiences –though not necessarily conventional plays. They have included *The Ik* based on Colin Turnbull's account of an African tribe which had to change its life-style and thus lost most of its humanity, and a pared-down version of Bizet's *Carmen* with three separate casts.

The culmination of his work at the Centre so far has been the dramatisation, with Jean-Claude Carrière, of the Hindu epic *The Mahabharata* in a cycle of three plays lasting nearly ten hours, using a very multi-racial cast, many of them old Brook hands. It was set originally in a quarry near Avignon, the main features of which have now been reproduced (at considerable expense) from Australia to Glasgow. He used a cast of twenty-four to represent forty-five characters, omitted much of the theology, and was left with a great story superbly told with great economy of means (if not of money – the entire cast was sent to India for a month just before the opening). Although all the acting is fairly physical, there is no other attempt to impose a uniform style; instead, national differences are exploited. The semi-comic strong man, Bhima, is played with enormous exuberance by the Senegalese Mamadou Dioume, while Yoshi Oida (who trained as a Noh actor) makes Drona, the tutor in the arts of war, a very Japanese master of the martial arts. There are occasional unforgettable stage pictures, generally achieved very simply, with coloured floor mats and cloths, water, fire, and mime – two of the most powerful images are produced with nothing more than a bottle of petrol and a taper, producing a ring of fire within which Duryodhana can see what Arjuna is doing in the Himalayas, and a large jar full of something red, as Drona pours blood over his head and accepts death. By now it seems that Brook's mastery has reached the level of the truly great stylist –the man who makes it look easy.

BUBBLE THEATRE COMPANY

(now called the LONDON BUBBLE)

TRY THESE:
▷Community Theatre; ▷Mikron offer an interesting variant on local touring.

The Bubble Theatre Company was founded in 1972, with the encouragement of the Greater London Arts Association, to bring popular but professional entertainment to areas within London which had no permanent theatre building. To this end it performs in specially designed tents, adaptable and easy to transport, and holding up to 250 people. It opened with a successful production, *The Blitz Show*, which aimed to re-create the atmosphere of an impromptu war-time concert party, and was at once booked by twenty boroughs. The show was compiled by the company and its artistic director Glen Walford (later of the Everyman, Liverpool).

Over the years, under a series of directors, the company developed some reputation both with compiled shows and with standard plays such as Brecht's *The Caucasian Chalk Circle*, but had no clear ideology except a commitment to popular theatre. The current artistic director, Peter Rowe, has in the last few years changed the emphasis in various ways. The company now covers a smaller area of London, but with longer and more frequent visits, and Rowe has added a community arts work specialist unit with trained workshop leaders, with the aim of encouraging the community to participate more and to devise their own shows. Their current 'statement of artistic policy' keeps the original aims of working with people who do not normally have access to theatre, and of encouraging them to develop theatre skills, but adds that of challenging 'racism, sexism and other forms of prejudice and bigotry'; and their preferred way of working is described as 'to create a popular form which is bold and bright, fast and physical, open and accessible'.

Though the company's shows are rarely reviewed in the national newspapers, they are always covered by London's listings magazines, *City Limits* and *Time Out*, and they have attracted a steady stream of well-known writers such as ▷ Tunde Ikoli (*Duckin'n'Divin'*, 1984) and Bryony Lavery (*The*

Headless Body, 1987). They also offer children's shows, late night reviews, and street theatre, using clown, pantomime and music hall techniques, song and dance, to raise community awareness and political consciousness. Their surroundings in summer often resemble a small fair, with refreshments and beer tent; in winter they have to move indoors, but they continue their activities at a lesser tempo.

BÜCHNER, Georg [1813–1837]
German dramatist

Plays include:
Danton's Death (1835), _Leonce and Lena_ (1836), _Woyzeck_ (1836)

The son of a doctor, Büchner was educated at the Universities of Strasburg and Giessen, studying medicine. There he was strongly influenced by the revolutionary 'Young Germany' movement, but developed his own political philosophy which turned its back on the educated classes, placing its hopes instead with the peasantry. After his involvement with an abortive attempt to overthrow the government of the state of Hesse in 1834, he withdrew from revolutionary politics. He wrote *Danton's Death* in 1835 and the following year became a lecturer in Anatomy at the University of Zürich. He worked on *Woyzeck* that year, drawing on the details of a controversial court-case. He died of typhoid fever in 1837, with *Woyzeck* still not in a completed form. Although his plays were not performed until many years after his death, Büchner is one of the major influences in contemporary world drama. Somehow he managed to foreshadow many of the great theatrical movements of the twentieth century: epic theatre, Surrealism, Expressionism, and the Theatre of the Absurd. The sense of history as a major force dominates his work, as does society as the destroyer of the individual. His principal characters struggle unsuccessfully to communicate their feelings until they recognise their helplessness and incomprehension in the face of the forces that destroy them.

Woyzeck
The central character, Woyzeck, is a repressed and oppressed soldier, crushed by his social superiors, goaded by his mistress, tormented by his own sense of guilt. Although the play was never put into a final form by Büchner, each of its scenes is remarkably powerful, and cumulatively they create an overpowering atmosphere of alienation and bleakness. Woyzeck ultimately perishes, but in highly ambiguous circumstances which deliberately confuse suicide and accident. *Woyzeck* is a regular staple of the fringe and student productions.

TRY THESE:
Kafka's *Metamorphosis* and *The Trial* for a sense of the individual being crushed, ▷George Abbott's *Three Men on a Horse* for an American, more light-hearted treatment of the little man at the mercy of external forces; ▷Eugene O'Neill for another stream of writing of individuals crushed by social forces, also ▷Arthur Miller's *Death of a Salesman*; Büchner was much influenced by ▷Shakespeare; his plays in turn influenced such apparently opposed figures as ▷Artaud and ▷Brecht; ▷Mnouchkine's *1789* is *the* French Revolution play; see also ▷Pam Gems' adaptation of Stanislawa Przybyszewska's *The Danton Affair* which itself was highly influenced by *Danton's Death*; see also ▷Peter Weiss' *Marat/Sade*.

BULGAKOV, Mikhail Afanasievich [1891–1940]
Russian novelist, journalist and dramatist

Plays include:
The Days of the Turbins (a dramatisation of his novel _The White Guard_; 1926), _The Crimson Island_ (1927), _Dead Souls_ (from Gogol; 1928), _Molière_ (1936), _Don Quixote_ (1940), _The Last Days of Pushkin_ (published 1943)

Novels include:
The White Guard (published 1925; full version 1966), _Black Snow_ (written 1936–37; published 1965)

Born in Kiev, Bulgakov qualified as a doctor, and became a professional writer in 1919. He wrote a novel *The White Guard* about the horrors of the civil war in Kiev, which was unusually sympathetic to the White side. He was asked by Pavel Markov, the Moscow Arts Theatre's new dramaturg, to turn it into a play. At first delighted, Bulgakov was soon disconcerted by the cutting and reshaping required to suit the company, and the changing of the title and the ending to suit the censor (the Bolsheviks are welcomed to the strains of the Internationale). However, he valued the experience for teaching him stagecraft, and he went on to write thirteen more plays and to become arguably the most

TRY THESE:
▷Stanislavski for getting Bulgakov started as a playwright, and for his depiction in *Black Snow*; ▷Arbuzov, ▷Gorki, ▷Mayakovsky for other well known Soviet dramatists; ▷Molière for his own plays; ▷David Pownall's *Master Class*, for a musical variation, with Shostakovich, and Prokofiev, on the theme of state control and artistic freedom; also tackled in ▷Tom Stoppard's *Every Good Boy Deserves Favour.*

important Soviet playwright of the period. His theatrical career was blighted by his *Molière*, in which the contemporary relevance of references to the frustrations of the artist controlled by the State were only too obvious. After four years in rehearsal, it was taken off after less than a week. But Bulgakov had his revenge in the very thinly disguised, very unkind, and very funny accounts of the Moscow Arts Theatre and of ▷ Stanislavski's system, in his novel *Black Snow*. The best section of the book is perhaps the instruction to the author to write-in older roles (his play has no character over twenty-eight, but the company includes nobody under fifty). *The White Guard*, produced by the ▷ RSC in 1979, is perhaps his best-known play in Britain; but *The Crimson Island*, an effective satire on both political censorship and the acting profession (and duly banned in 1927), appeared at the enterprising Gate Theatre Club in 1981, and Lou Stein also directed *Molière* at the Latchmere in 1983, the same year that Anthony Sher appeared in it with some success at the Pit.

BYRNE, John [1940–]
British dramatist

Plays include:

***Writer's Cramp* (1977), *The Slab Boys* (1978; also known as *Paisley Patterns*), *Cuttin' a Rug* (1979; originally *The Loveliest Night of the Year*, also performed on radio as *The Staffie* and as *Threads*), *Normal Service* (1979), *Still Life* (1982)**

Now widely known to television audiences after the success of his series *Tutti Frutti*, Scottish-born John Byrne has been delighting theatre audiences in Scotland, England and the USA for years with his ironic observations on literary pretension (in *Writer's Cramp*) and everyday working life in *The Slab Boys* trilogy, which starts with adolescence in *The Slab Boys* itself, takes us through the staff dance in *Cuttin' a Rug*, and ends in the cemetery in *Still Life*. Byrne trained at the Glasgow School of Art and his work reveals in its different moods both a painter's eye for detailed observation and a cartoonist's gift for caricature; the interest tends to be less in plot and more in the presentation of memorable characters.

TRY THESE:
▷Harold Pinter's *No Man's Land* and ▷Michael Hastings' *Tom and Viv* offer contrasting views of the literary world; ▷Doug Lucie's view of an advertising agency in *Fashion* makes an interesting comparison with the television station of *Normal Service*; ▷Arnold Wesker's *Trilogy* is probably the best known modern set of linked plays; ▷Iain Heggie, one of the newest Scottish voices for robust Glaswegian dialect.

CABARET

In the Weimar Germany of the 1930s, there was a cabaret tradition of popular songs and political sketches which was very influential for contemporary European theatre. It had a marked impact on the work of ▷ Brecht, who advocated that people should eat and drink while watching his plays. Kurt Weill, with whom he collaborated, was also much influenced by contemporary cabaret song: *The Threepenny Opera*, *The Rise and Fall of the City of Mahogonny* and *The Seven Deadly Sins* all owe a great deal to cabaret.

The origins of contemporary cabaret in Britain can be seen in ▷ music hall in which audiences could drink while watching songs and sketches. At one end of the spectrum, through the 1930s, 1940s, and 1950s, it was associated with night-clubs, a certain degree of glamour and sophistication, with performers from Josephine Baker to Elizabeth Welch and Shirley Bassey making their reputations as much through the night-club circuits of Paris and London as through theatres or music concerts.

Things began to change round about the 1960s with the appearance of the Cambridge Footlights team of Peter Cook, Jonathan Miller, Dudley Moore and Alan Bennett. Not only was their *Beyond the Fringe* an out-and-out theatre success, leading on to the weekly television series, *That Was The Week That Was* but the Establishment, set up by amongst others, Cook and Ned Sherrin opened in Greek Street in Soho. A late night cabaret club, it placed satire back on the map and went on to spawn such further outcrops and televisual raves as the Monty Python team (another set of Footlights alumni including Michael Palin, Terry Jones, John Cleese, Terry Gilliam, Eric Idle, and Graham Chapman), and The Goodies, (Graeme Garden, Bill Oddie and Tim Brooke-Taylor), as well as playing host to such American exponents of bitter satire as Lenny Bruce and Mort Sahl.

Cabaret in Britain is now more or less synonymous with 'alternative cabaret', a phenomenon that came up out of the 1970s with two Soho venues called the Comedy Store (based on a New York model) and The Comic Strip and has produced its own crop of stars such as Rik Mayall, Nigel Planer, Alexei Sayle, French and Saunders and Ben Elton, all of whom have subsequently moved into television. 'Alternative cabaret' started out by being, as with the satire of the 1960s, relentlessly anti-establishment, and as tasteless as they could get away with. That remains, although there is a feeling that too many artists these days, with one eye on seduction into television, produce too much material that audiences/television researchers *want* to hear, rather than sharp, intrusive, intelligent criticism. Sexual politics, the Royal Family, and Thatcher are the current staples – topicality is still the essence of good satire.

There is an ever-increasing 'alternative cabaret' circuit, mostly made up of pubs (Jongleurs in Battersea even have their own television show), but also some clubs and the welcome revival of the Hackney Empire which combines the best of variety, ▷ music hall and alternative cabaret in its line-up. Today's cabaret stars like the best of theatre – the likes of Simon Fanshawe, Jenny Lecoat, Arnold Brown, Jeremy Hardy,

TRY THESE:
▷Pub/café theatre; for other cabaret performers see ▷Robyn Archer, ▷Women in Theatre; see also ▷Performance Art, ▷Lesbian Theatre.

Kit Hollerbach, Hattie Hayridge, John Hegley, Helen Lederer – and a newer crop including Sharon Landau, and Harry Enfield (another big television name whose 'loadsamoney' catchphrase has now entered daily usage and sums up a whole ethos of greed in today's Britain), hold a jagged but truthful mirror up to nature – their weapons, irony, satire, exaggeration, and humour in various proportions of gentleness or brutality. Some cabaret performers like John Sessions who specialises in impersonations have gone on to fuller stage performances; his *Napoleon*, a superb, one-man tour-de-farce moved from Riverside into the West End. Others, like the very popular women's trio, Fascinating Aida, are sophisticated songsters, whose style is reminiscent of the 1960s duo Flanders and Swann with a 1980s feminist bite. And of course, there is the incomparable Victoria Wood who has raised cabaret/comedy sketches to the level of high, but extremely popular, art. Cabaret can also embrace the newer form of 'dub' poets, such as Benjamin Zephaniah and Seething Wells whose rap poetry is a million miles away from the solemn discourses of traditional poetry recitals. The form has become very popular over the past four to five years and attracted a growing following of young supporters. Cabaret continues to be big business; the number of cabaret artists has steadily increased at the Edinburgh fringe, (one of the big awards now of the Edinburgh fringe is the Perrier Cabaret award-winner and runners-up who then transfer to London after the festival for a season at the Donmar), Glasgow Mayfest and even the biennial York festival. But cabaret performers, like today's pop stars have also acquired political and social consciences and are frequently to be seen lending their support to a variety of charity performances or benefits on issues ranging from the environment to the Third World, from Nicaragua to AIDS.

CALDERÓN DE LA BARCA, Pedro [1600–81]

Spanish dramatist

Plays include:

***La dama duende* (*The Phantom Lady*; 1629), *El príncipe constante* (*The Constant Prince*; 1629), *La vida es sueño* (*Life is a Dream*; 1635), *El médico de su honra* (*The Physician of his Honour*; 1635), *El alcalde de Zalamea* (*The Mayor of Zalamea*; 1643), *El gran teatro del mundo* (*The Great Theatre of the World*; 1645)**

Calderón is the most polished Spanish dramatist of the Golden Age; less prolific than ▷ Lope de Vega, he borrowed freely from his predecessors, tightened up the plots and characterisation, and added a peculiarly intense line in passionate conflicts with often shocking outcomes. He studied for the priesthood, but soon took up duelling, women, and poetry; his first known play was staged at the Spanish Court when he was twenty-three, and after that his output was considerable. He claimed to have written about 120 secular plays, eighty *autos sacramentales* (the Spanish form of morality play, performed on great church occasions) in his later and more pious years, and twenty minor pieces. He is also credited with the invention of the *zarzuela*, the classic Spanish musical form. His range covers cloak-and-sword plays, historical plays, honour-and-jealousy plays, comedies of manners, and the famous *Life is a Dream*, commonly thought his masterpiece, and well revived by the ▷ RSC in 1984. This is a complex and unusual play about the Polish Crown Prince Sigismondo, prophesied to grow up a monster of cruelty and therefore hidden away in a tower in a wood by his father, and his gradual education and emergence as a wise ruler. The plot incorporates philosophical discussion of reason versus natural impulses and free will defeating superstitious prophecy.

Calderón's plays have never been very popular in Britain, but seem to be catching on in the 1980s. *The Great Theatre of the World*, an *auto sacramental*, was given a colourful and inventive production by the Medieval Players in 1984. Nobody, though, has

TRY THESE:
▷Lope de Vega, the earlier master playwright of the Spanish Golden Age, and source for some of Calderón's best known plays; von Hofmannsthal and Max Reinhardt for an updating of *The Great Theatre of the World*; Grotowski for his version of *The Constant Prince*; rape is handled very differently in Eve Lewis' *Ficky Stingers*; there is also an off-stage rape in *Last Summer in Chulimsk* by the modern Soviet playwright Alexander Vampilov, presented at Riverside Studios by the Cambridge Theatre Company in 1987.

recently tried *The Physician of his Honour*, his most notorious 'honour' play, in which a husband has his wife's blood drained on the mere suspicion of adultery, and the King not merely commends his action but offers our hero another bride.

The Mayor of Zalamea
This is Calderón's best known play; like *The Physician of his Honour*, it is based on an earlier work attributed to ▷ Lope de Vega. It was a masterpiece as played by Michael Bryant in Adrian Mitchell's translation at the ▷ National Theatre in 1981. It is the story of a Spanish peasant whose daughter is raped by an aristocratic captain, and who then becomes the Mayor and sentences the captain to a garrotting – all are agreed that the captain deserved it and that justice was done, but of course the girl still ends up in a nunnery.

CAMPBELL, Ken [1941–]
British director, dramatist and actor

TRY THESE:
▷Snoo Wilson, ▷N.F. Simpson, ▷Jarry and ▷Ionesco share something of Campbell's anarchic surreal inventiveness; amongst other writers for children are ▷Bryony Lavery, David Wood, Penny Casdagli, Stephen Wyatt, and pre-eminently David Holman.

Plays include:

> ***Old King Cole* (1969), *Jack Shepherd* (1969; also known as *Anything You Say Will Be Twisted*), *Bendigo* (1974; with Dave Hill and Andy Andrews), *The Great Caper* (1974), *Walking Like Geoffrey* (1975; with Hill and Andrews), *Skungpoonery* (1975), *School For Clowns* (1975), *Illuminatus* (1977), *Deeds* (1978; with ▷ Howard Brenton, ▷ David Hare, ▷ Trevor Griffiths), *The Hitch-hikers Guide To The Galaxy* (1979), *The Third Policeman* (1980), *War With The Newts* (1981)**

After training as an actor at RADA, Ken Campbell soon turned to writing and directing. His directorial debut – organising the shallow end for the Summer Water Show at Bournemouth Baths – heralded a brilliant career as Britain's champion of anarchic fun. With his own company, Ken Campbell's Roadshow, his work was toured to bars and theatres throughout the country with a uniquely eccentric entertainment of staggering inventiveness coupled with red-noses and ferret-down-the-trousers interludes. Gleefully iconoclastic, Campbell recognised no boundaries, taking on the challenge of the *Illuminatus* books and triumphantly portraying Howard the talking dolphin as an operatic tenor. In *War With The Newts* the hilarity included a newt family called Olivia Newt, and John. In Michael Coveney's words, Campbell is 'a master of the ebulliently childish caper' who reaches for any and every theatrical device without regard to consistency or convention, demanding that the audience keep up with the crazed inventiveness on the stage. As a result he is overwhelmingly popular. One critic warned against the dangers of swamping a story with good humour and 'dropping our standards as cheerfully as our trousers', but concluded that, with Ken Campbell, this attitude was taken seriously: 'incident-packed, joke-packed economic writing is very difficult, and Ken Campbell has mastered it completely'.

Old King Cole
As it is almost impossible to do justice to the more anarchic of Campbell's scripts, it is perhaps best to look at this children's entertainment. It seems to spring directly from the imagination of an eight-year old. Hard-up, inventive genius Faz and his likeable but dim-witted assistant Twoo are approached by the weedy Baron Wadd, who asks Faz to ensure that Wadd wins the hand of Princess Daphne in a sporting competition against handsome, superbly fit, boring Cyril. Faz attempts to fix the events at the competition, but not even his outrageous trickery can defeat Wadd's weediness and incompetence. In a last-ditch effort to win the Princess, Cyril is put out of action – by dropping a ton-weight on him – and employing Faz's spectacular magic. All seems to be well, but Princess Daphne has other ideas, and runs off with Twoo. Wadd becomes Faz's new assistant, and they all live happily ever after. It is a minor masterpiece of cartoonery, mad invention and childlike glee.

CAPEK, Karel [1890–1938]
Czech novelist and dramatist

TRY THESE:
▷Brecht, particularly

Plays include:
***The Robber* (1920), *R.U.R.* (1921), *The Power and the Glory* (1937), *Mother* (1938); and with his brother Josef, *The Insect Play* (1922), *The Makropoulus Secret* (1922), *Adam with Creator* (1927)**

A socialist and pacifist, Capek's second play *R.U.R.* (Rossum's Universal Robots) gave the world the word 'robot' and offered a protest against the dehumanising elements of mechanisation and industrial capitalism. Its final moments, when two advanced robots (androids as we would now call them) have emotions of love and sacrifice, with the suggestion that humans have a second chance in this new Adam and Eve, have been frequently copied, although Czechs consider Capek's last anti-fascist plays his best. *The Mother*, produced only months before Hitler marched into Czechoslovakia, shows a small nation invaded by a fascist state, provoking civil war. The mother, already a soldier's widow, has a pilot son killed in an aircrash, two other sons – one fascist, one communist – die in a feud, and she sees her last son, an anti-violence poet, go off to fight. Capek's love of freedom was in the end stronger than his pacifism but he died soon after, three months before his brother was taken off to Belsen by the Nazis.

The Insect Play
John Gielgud who played the Chief Butterfly in the British premiere, declared this was a part almost certain to ruin the reputation of an actor, but Capek's expressionist vision of human greed, violence and self-interest presented through parallel behaviour in the insect world can still be disturbingly effective. When the insects' physical characteristics are used to highlight their human counterparts, (a myriad faceted mirror set, like an insect's eye, was used in the most recent London production by Miroslav Machacek) the play has the harsh reality of a Steve Bell cartoon. The presentation of this parallel world and its tramp observer – the only human character – has precursors in fabulists from Aesop to Swift but its bite is closer to that of ▷ Brecht and less easy to sweeten.

Mother Courage, *The Threepenny Opera*; ▷Galsworthy, ▷Edgar and ▷Shaw for presentations of industrial relations; adaptations of George Orwell's *Animal Farm*, ▷W. H. Auden's *On the Frontier*, ▷Tom McGrath's *Animal*, Terry Johnson's *Cries From the Mammal House* and ▷Steven Berkoff's adaptation of Kafka's *Metamorphosis* for beast fables; ▷Alan Bennett's *Kafka's Dick* for a similar use of disturbing and fabulous metaphor.

CARROLL, Paul Vincent [1900–68]
Irish dramatist

Plays include:
***Things that are Caesar's* (1932), *Shadow and Substance* (1937), *The Whole Steed* (1938), *The Wise have not Spoken* (1944)**

All Carroll's plays involve a priest and most suggest an indictment of a repressive and reactionary Church and its effect on Irish life – though his is an accusing Catholic voice. Typical is *Shadow and Substance*, about a servant girl who has miraculous visions of St Brigid. It centres on a bitter feud between a proud and snobbish Canon and an anti-clerical schoolmaster, which leads to the girl's death in the same manner as the saint. *The Wise have not Spoken* was thought by many to be a better play, not least because it widens the issues. This time the priest is unfrocked; suspended for championing workers' rights. He and a Communist crippled in the Spanish Civil War offer different remedies for the injustices they both hate. All this is set against a background of hereditary insanity, sexual guilt and desertion, in a farm about to be seized by the bailiffs. Carroll often strains credulity and tends to state his case repetitiously – do not look to him for the reasoned arguments of ▷ Shaw. Rather than the richness of peasant Irish speech, his dialogue tends to over-poeticise and he is thin on leavening humour.

TRY THESE:
Graham Greene for treatments of Catholicism; for images of Ireland, ▷Brendan Behan's prison and brothel, ▷Sean O'Casey's tenements, ▷Friel's hedgeschool (in *Translations*), and ▷Yeats' personifications; ▷J.M. Synge's *Playboy of the Western World* for richness of dialect; Tom Murphy's *Conversations on a Homecoming*, also ▷Charabanc and ▷Seamus Finnegan for similar expressions of anti-Catholicism from an Ulster perspective.

CARTWRIGHT, Jim [1958–]
British dramatist

Plays include:
***Road* (1986)**

Television includes:
***Road* (1987)**

TRY THESE:
▷J.M. Synge's *Playboy of the Western World* and ▷Iain Heggie's *A Wholly Healthy Glasgow* for boldness of dialect; ▷ Thornton

Films include:
***Vroom* (1988)**

Bolton-born Cartwright was just one of the great unemployed before he wrote his first play, which has been called one of the most exciting plays of the decade and picked up four awards in 1986 – the George Devine Award, the British Theatre Association Award for Best New Play, Plays and Players Award for Best New Play and the Samuel Beckett Award. First staged at the Royal Court's Theatre Upstairs, Cartwright's raw, grim account of unemployment seen through the eyes of a narrator, Scully, and the inhabitants of a Lancashire street broke on an unsuspecting public with the force of a hurricane. Its impact was increased by Simon Curtis' promenade production, which brought audiences face to face with women, young and old; a couple who starve themselves to death in bed; a middle-aged man's lyrical memories of the 1950s; close sexual encounters of an abortive kind between a woman and a drunken soldier; and finally a young foursome whose terminal chant epitomises the general states of pent-up anger and frustration. Revived twice within a year in the Royal Court's main house, *Road* seems certain to be regarded as a seminal, bitter portrait of Thatcher's other Britain – despite its structural shortcomings as a series of loosely connected vignettes, its element of self-pitying, undiluted misery, the characters' lack of resistance, and the fact that, as Ros Asquith noted in *The Observer*, in this '*Under Milk Wood* for the Great Unemployed, men talk ideas, women only sex'. For Cartwright, who makes no claims to great erudition (he says he has only read three books in his life), his thoughts are 'demons in the brain – Mr Poverty, Mr Unemployment, Mr Injustice: Man, when I hit that old paper, and the play leaps out like a toad then I'm purged'.

Wilder's *Our Town*, ▷Dylan Thomas's *Under Milk Wood* for a specific sense of place; ▷John Osborne's *Look Back in Anger* for a similar 1950s burst of national vitriol; see also ▷Promenade Performances.

CHAPMAN, George [c 1560–1634]
English Renaissance dramatist and poet

Plays include:
***Monsieur D'Olive* (1604), *Bussy D'Ambois* (1604), *Eastward Ho!* (with ▷ Jonson and ▷ Marston; 1605), *The Widow's Tears* (pre 1609), *The Revenge of Bussy D'Ambois* (c 1610), *The Wars of Caesar and Pompey* (c 1613)**

A friend of and collaborator with ▷ Ben Jonson, Chapman pursued the career of a professional writer with sufficient assiduity to serve a prison term for overstepping the mark in his criticism of the Scots and James VI and I in *Eastward Ho!* He is probably best known now for his poetry rather than his seldom performed plays, and his densely philosophical and erudite approach to writing may go some way to explain the discrepancy between his academic (traditionally high) and theatrical (virtually non-existent) reputations. Jonathan Miller's 1988 Old Vic production of *Bussy D'Ambois*, a revenge tragedy in the familiar Renaissance mode, is unlikely to herald a Chapman revival but it would be good to see its sequel *The Revenge of Bussy D'Ambois* (proof that the Renaissance theatre knew how to cash in on success as much as Hollywood does!). Chapman's comedies seem even less likely to be revived than his tragedies but *Monsieur D'Olive* with its weird mixture of elements, including a character who keeps his dead wife's body sitting in a chair because he hasn't come to terms with death, might be a good outside bet for an adventurous company.

TRY THESE:
Most Renaissance dramatists used revenge plots and malcontent figures – ▷Shakespeare's *Hamlet* is the most famous example of both, but ▷Kyd's *The Spanish Tragedy* started the vogue for revenge and there are notable examples in ▷Ford, ▷Middleton, ▷Tourneur and ▷Webster; ▷Red Shift's *In the Image of the Beast*, a 'Science Fiction Revenge Tragedy', draws on *Bussy D'Ambois* to tell a chilling tale of a spaceman wreaking an awful revenge on those who abandoned him adrift in a spaceship.

CHARABANC
Northern Irish touring company

Key productions include:
***Lay Up Your Ends* (1984), *Oul Delf and False Teeth* (1984), *Now You're Talkin* (1985), *Gold in the Streets* (1986), *The Girls in the Big Picture* (1986), *Somewhere Over The Balcony* (1987)**

Charabanc is a versatile, ebullient, mainly female, Belfast-based company whose energy and humour have endeared them to audiences throughout Ireland and in London (built up

TRY THESE:
For oral history, from which plays are then scripted see ▷Age Exchange, ▷Gay Sweatshop, ▷Joint Stock, ▷Ann Jellicoe; for the vernacular and exploration of a Catholic rural community see ▷J.M. Synge's *Playboy of*

Carol Scanlan in the Belfast-based Charabanc company's production of ***Somewhere Over The Balcony***, by Marie Jones, directed by Peter Sheridan at the Drill Hall Arts Centre, September 1987.

through regular annual visits to London's Drill Hall Arts Centre.) Hallmarks of their work are the scripts, usually devised from local research and written by company and founder member Marie Jones, and the vivid detail and characterisation of their performances. As they are a touring company, their productions too make the most out of the minimum: the set for their first show *Lay Up Your Ends* about the 1911 Belfast mill girls was a simple use of scaffolding and placards. Most of their productions (several directed by Pam Brighton) use a naturalistic format though their latest, *Somewhere Over The Balcony*, directed by Peter Sheridan experiments with a more surrealistic treatment. Subjects have ranged from the disillusionment of Labour politics post World War II (*Oul Delf and False Teeth*), through the complexities of reconciliation between Protestant and Catholic in *Now You're Talkin'*, emigration (*Gold in the Streets*), rural social patterns and pressures (*The Girls in the Big Picture*) and in *Somewhere Over The Balcony*, the effects of the British Army presence and institutionalised violence on residents of Belfast's notorious Catholic high rise block, the Divis Flats.

Like many playwrights and companies coming out of Belfast, Charabanc's work takes a non-sectarian stance and the company contains both Protestant and Catholic members. The strength of their productions lies in their ability to reveal social networks and loyalties even if, as some commentators complain, they lack a deeper sense of political analysis. However, Charabanc remain one of the most entertaining companies to emerge out of Northern Ireland and can boast a clutch of performers such as Marie Jones, Eleanor Methven, Carol Scanlan, all of whom are founder members of the company, whose flair, warmth and flexibility have made them popular, not just throughout Ireland and the UK, but overseas in the USSR and the USA.

the Western World; also ▷Field Day for another contemporary Irish theatre company; for other playwrights writing on the subject of Northern Ireland, see ▷Ann Devlin, ▷Seamus Finnegan, ▷Ron Hutchinson, ▷Thomas Kilroy, Frank McGuinness, ▷Christina Reid, Nell McCafferty, Allan Cubitt.

CHEEK BY JOWL

British touring theatre company

Cheek by Jowl, one of Britain's leading touring companies, was founded in 1981 by Declan Donnellan and his designer and colleague Nick Ormerod. An Arts Council drama officer saw the young Donnellan's potential and they started with a small Arts Council grant, which has been steadily, but not greatly, increased. They have a company of eight or nine young and not very well-known players at a time, and they tour 'classics' on a relentless schedule, receiving a guaranteed sum from the box office at each venue. They say they have performed in 200 towns, usually staying for a week or so at a time, all over England, and also in Europe and further afield (eg South America). For the last few years they have appeared in London for several weeks each year, usually at the Donmar Warehouse, and have usually sold out. They prepare and tour an average of two plays a year: they started with ▷ Wycherley's *The Country Wife*, and have done a good deal of ▷ Shakespeare, but also an adaptation of Thackeray's *Vanity Fair* (in the ▷ Shared Experience manner), ▷ Etherege's *The Man of Mode*, and the British premières (more or less) of ▷ Racine's *Andromache* and ▷ Corneille's *The Cid*. In 1988 they are putting on ▷ Ostrovsky's *A Family Affair*; and for 1989 they are contemplating *The Tempest*, ▷ Lope de Vega's *Fuente Ovejuna*, and ▷ Sophocles' *Philoctetes*.

A Cheek by Jowl production treats the play as though it was written last week, and plays it with great economy of means plus constant inventiveness, visual clarity, and apparent simplicity of style. The sets are usually minimal, often just chairs and a floorcloth as in *The Cid*, or a white floor and coloured backcloth, as for *A Midsummer Night's Dream*; the costumes tend to be modern; there is a good deal of doubling of parts, sometimes cross-gender, and Donnellan coaxes fine ensemble acting from his teams. They show up best in small studio spaces, where they can effectively put across powerful pas-

TRY THESE:
Actors Touring Company, ▷Shared Experience and the Medieval Players for ensemble work in classical revivals that often breathe ebullient new life into old chestnuts; ▷Berliner Ensemble for a European ensemble company.

sions (as with *The Cid* and *Andromache*) or reduce audiences to helpless laughter, as in *A Midsummer Night's Dream*'s Pyramus play, put on by a three-person team of mechanicals, the Reverend Bottom, his spinsterly helper Miss Quince, and an uncontrollable and intense Ms Flute doing Brook-type exercises. This production also had a finely observed Theseus clearly but affectionately based on Prince Charles. There is a cheerful theatricality and subversion about their productions.

CHEKHOV, Anton [1860–1904]
Russian dramatist

Plays include:

***On the High Road* (1884), *Ivanov* (1887), *The Bear* (1888), *The Wood Demon* (1889), *The Wedding* (1890), *Platonov* (c1890; not produced until the 1920s), *The Seagull* (1896), *Uncle Vanya* (1899), *The Proposal* (1899), *Three Sisters* (1901), *The Cherry Orchard* (1904)**

Chekhov is a master at depicting groups, charting the nuances of dialogue and character with extraordinary sensitivity and subtlety. Many of his plays deal with temporary communities that are coming to an end; their elegiac qualities seem to foreshadow events in Russia with remarkable prescience.

Born the son of a grocer and the grandson of a serf, and brought up in a small port town on the Sea of Azov, he went to the University of Moscow to train as a doctor in 1879. On graduation, he practised medicine in Moscow and wrote for the *St Petersburg Gazette*. His first full-length plays, *Ivanov* and *The Wood Demon*, were unsuccessful. In 1890 Chekhov travelled through Russia and Siberia as a medical practioner, the first of many such journeys, in order to assist peasants. He then settled on a small estate outside Moscow, where he attempted to be an enlightened landlord and provided medical care and schooling for the peasants in the area, experience which is central to *Uncle Vanya* and *The Cherry Orchard*.

After the failure of the first production of *The Seagull* Chekhov swore that he would never have another play produced. However, ▷ Stanislavski persuaded him to revive *The Seagull* for production by the Moscow Arts Theatre. Stanislavski gave it a very careful production, employing his methods of acting and direction, and the play was recognised as an important new drama. In a speech given to the writer Constantine in the play, Chekhov offers a damning critique of the contemporary conventions of naturalist theatre: 'I regard the stage of today as mere routine and prejudice. . .We must have new formulas. That's what we want.'

Uncle Vanya, a reworking of *The Wood Demon*, followed *The Seagull*, quite successfully, although *Three Sisters*, again produced at the Moscow Arts Theatre, was not well received. In 1904, after the first production of *The Cherry Orchard*, Chekhov suffered two heart attacks and died in the German spa town of Badenweiler, just as he was beginning to be recognised internationally as a major dramatist. In the notebooks of the period of the *Three Sisters* Chekhov wrote: 'We struggle to change life so that those who come after us might be happy, but those who come after us will say as usual, it was better before, life now is worse than it used to be.' Chekhov's plays stand as powerful statements which attest to the fact that things were *never* better, and that hope for the future matters more than anything.

Three Sisters

This is a study of three sisters, locked in a small military town, watching their lives drift past. The constant refrain of the play is the cry of the youngest sister Irina, 'Let us go to Moscow', but as the play progresses, even she, the youngest and therefore most hopeful, comes to realise that they will never leave, and that even if they *did* reach Moscow, they would bring themselves and all their frustrations with them. Each of the sisters suffers the frustration of her hopes: Olga, the eldest has given up all hope of children; the most sensual of the sisters, Masha, is trapped in a sterile marriage and loses the lover who promises her romance; Irina never achieves her ambition to see Moscow. The

TRY THESE:
Chekhov said, '▷Ibsen is my favourite author', and claimed *The Wild Duck* as his favourite play; ▷Michael Frayn's *Wild Honey* is a version of *Platonov*; ▷Brian Friel has adapted *The Cherry Orchard* to an Irish setting, Michael Picardie's *The Cape Orchard* applied it to South Africa, and ▷Trevor Griffith's version stressed its politics; ▷Mustapha Matura has transferred *Three Sisters* to Trinidad in his *Trinidad Sisters*; ▷G.B. Shaw claimed *Heartbreak House* was Chekhovian; ▷N.C. Hunter was routinely compared to Chekhov.

Ian McKellen as Platonov in, ***Wild Honey***, Michael Frayn's adaptation of Chekhov's ***Platonov***, directed by Christopher Morahan, National Theatre, 1984.

men who come within the orbit of the sisters also suffer from unfulfilled hopes and ambitions: the sisters' brother Andrey ends the play married to a vulgar woman; the Doctor has not sustained the commitment and conviction with which he entered medicine; Vershinin, the glamorous commander, has hopes for a 'beautiful life' in another two centuries. None of the characters can achieve contentment, with the exception of Andrey's wife, Natasha, whose dreams are only of material comforts. The play ends with the three sisters standing alone, their youth and romance leaving with the soldiers. Olga reaffirms the importance of their lives in a final and wistful speech: 'We shall be forgotten – our faces, our voices, even how many of us there were. But our sufferings will turn to joy for those who live after us.' The experience of the audience watching the play is such as to reaffirm its slender hopes, the act of watching the *Three Sisters* confirms that they have indeed not been forgotten.

CHRISTIE, Agatha (Mary Clarissa) [1890–1976]

British author of detective stories and dramatist

Plays include:

***Black Coffee* (1930), *Ten Little Niggers* (also known as *Ten Little Indians*; 1943), *Appointment with Death* (1945), *Murder on the Nile* (1945), *The Hollow* (1951), *The Mousetrap* (1952), *Witness for the Prosecution* (1953), *The Spider's Web* (1954), *Towards Zero* (with Gerald Verner; 1956), *Verdict* (1958), *The Unexpected Guest* (1958), *Go Back for Murder* (1960), *The Rule of Three* (1962), *Fiddlers Three* (1971), *Akhnaton* (published 1973)**

Writer of the longest running play ever (*The Mousetrap*, now in its thirty-sixth year), Christie excels at telling a story. Though her characters verge upon the stereotypical, they have firm roots in the backgrounds of the middle-class audiences which have flocked to see her plays, giving them opportunities to identify with the characters and vicariously enjoy the excitement of involvement with murder and mayhem. However, her characters are not mere cyphers and she sometimes uses them to voice ideas that reveal a strong concern for the problems in relationships. As in many of her novels, the revelation of 'who-done-it' is often not over-clearly signalled in the plot and comes as a surprise.

Several of Christie's detective stories have been adapted for the stage by other writers and they have been made into a number of feature films, though only recently adapted for television.

TRY THESE:
▷Thrillers; ▷Alan Ayckbourn for similar plot manipulations; ▷J. B. Priestley's *An Inspector Calls* for the use of a detective plot to make a moral point; ▷Tom Stoppard's *The Real Inspector Hound* for a parody of the genre; ▷Anthony Shaffer's *Sleuth* is more psychologically oriented.

Ten Little Niggers/Ten Little Indians

Ten Little Niggers (retitled in various ways as *Ten Little Indians* or *And Then There Were None* to try to avoid racial offence) has been revived several times, and is popular with amateur dramatic societies. In one of Christie's more mechanical plots, a group of people, each revealed later as having possibly been responsible for a death, are invited to a house party on an island and there, in ways to match the rhyme of the play's title, they are themselves murdered, one by one. The denouement hinges on a theatrical trick that the audience cannot be expected to guess so that the plot is more that of a thriller than a detective story. The character unveiling and the tension created can be effective even when the mechanism of the plot is known.

CHURCHILL, Caryl [1938–]

British dramatist

Plays include:

***Owners* (1972), *Objections to Sex and Violence* (1975), *Light Shining in Buckinghamshire* (1976), *Vinegar Tom* (1976), *Cloud Nine* (1979), *Three More Sleepless Nights* (1980), *Top Girls* (1982), *Fen* (1983), *Softcops* (1984), *A Mouthful of Birds* (1986; with ▷ David Lan, *Serious Money* (1987)**

Churchill has gradually established herself as Britain's leading woman dramatist with a series of vibrant and inventive plays,

TRY THESE:
Many of Churchill's plays were first staged by Max Stafford-Clark for ▷Joint Stock or the Royal Court; ▷Sarah Daniels' *Byrthrite* is another play about seventeenth-century women; ▷Edward Bond's mixture of 'historical' and

Gary Oldman (centre) in Caryl Churchill's hit ***Serious Money***, directed by Max Stafford-Clark, Royal Court, 1987.

almost all of which have been presented by ▷ Joint Stock or the Royal Court, and she is now virtually as successful in New York as she is in Britain. In many ways she has been in an ideal position to chart the contradictions of the developing position of bourgeois women under the impact of feminism because of her own experience. After writing extensively for radio, which is traditionally more accommodating to female writers, and juggling with the demands of her husband's career and of child care, Churchill moved into theatre in the early 1970s, writing initially as an individual but eventually learning different ways of working as a result of her collective ventures with ▷ Monstrous Regiment and particularly ▷ Joint Stock. This move into collective creation reflects a significant challenge to traditional ways of organising theatre, which themselves reflect traditional divisions of labour in society.

Inevitably, Churchill has tackled many of the fashionable themes of British political and feminist theatre in the 1970s, including witches (*Vinegar Tom*), terrorism (*Objections. . .*), and seventeenth-century revolutionary sects (*Light Shining. . .*), as well as more unusual topics such as the nature of ideology and repression in the all male *Softcops*, inspired by a reading of the French theorist Michel Foucault. Her work has been particularly asociated with treatments of sexual politics, especially in *Cloud Nine* (in which the links between patriarchy and colonisation are mercilessly and wittily exposed) and *Top Girls*, a study of a 'successful' career woman. She has always been keenly aware of the socio-political dimension of oppression, which affects men as well as women, as in *Fen*, her study of the quiet horrors of rural life (notable for a stunning central performance from Jennie Stoller), and in the earlier urban landscape of *Owners*. Churchill uses time shifts, uneven ageing (the characters in *Cloud Nine* are twenty-five years older in part two than they were in part one, but one hundred years has passed), cross race and cross gender casting, doubling, pastiche Victorian light verse and also rhyming couplets, as part of a strategy of upsetting and destabilising conventional assumptions about both drama and life itself. Sometimes the sprightliness of her writing, the accuracy of her observation, and her unwillingness to be overly didactic can lead to reactions which call her effectiveness as a social critic into question: some people interpreted *Top Girls* as a hymn in praise of its central character and the runaway success of her exposé of the financial markets, *Serious Money*, owed much to its popularity with the very people it satirised, who flocked to see it both at the Royal Court and in the West End.

invented characters in *Early Morning* ran into some of the same problems with critics as *Top Girls*; among the women dramatists to emerge since Churchill and ▷Pam Gems are ▷Timberlake Wertenbaker, ▷Julia Kearsley, ▷Bryony Lavery, ▷Berta Freistadt, ▷Debbie Horsfield, ▷Ayshe Raif, Liz Lochhead, ▷Jacqui Shapiro, ▷Jackie Rudet, Heidi Thomas, Charlotte Keatley; see also ▷New Writing and ▷Women in Theatre.

Top Girls

The play begins with a gathering of women from different periods and cultures to celebrate the promotion of Marlene, the central character, within the Top Girls employment agency. The choice of relatively unfamiliar historical characters reminds us of the way that women's histories have been submerged by traditional male-dominated approaches to history. It also brings us into a critical relationship with Marlene's story from the very beginning, forcing us to supply many of the connections between the first scene and the more 'normal' narrative that follows in which the women who played party guests reappear as contemporary women. In the first scene Marlene is apparently emancipated from the traps and entanglements of family and children that have constrained the others but much of the rest of the play is concerned with destabilising this privileged position by trapping audiences into semi-agreement with her and then encouraging them to see her putative success in a far wider context in which she is just as much a victim of the system. The play is both enormously funny and chilling in its brilliantly observed presentations of the everyday contradictions of life. Churchill, like ▷ Brecht, suggests that what we need is a new way of seeing if we are to understand and confront the pressures the characters in *Top Girls* fail to grasp.

CIXOUS, Hélène [1937–]

French radical feminist and dramatist

Plays include:

Portrait de Dora* (*Portrait of Dora*; 1976), *La Prise de l'École de Madhubaï* (*The Capture of the Madhubaï School*; 1983), *L'Histoire Terrible Mais Inachevée de

TRY THESE:

▷Marguerite Duras, with whom she seems to have very little in common, but they were both born

***Norodom Sihanouk, Roi du Cambodge* (*The Terrible But Unfinished Story of Norodom Sihanouk, King of Cambodia*; 1985), *L'Indiade* (*The Indiad*; 1987)**

Born in Algeria, Hélène Cixous teaches at the University of Paris VIII where she runs the Centre de Recherche en Études Féminines (Research Centre for Women's Studies) and publishes formidable theoretical works on feminism. Since 1967 she has also published novels, short stories, and essays, and she made a tentative entry into playwriting in 1976, when Simone Benmussa produced her *Portrait de Dora* at the Théâtre d'Orsay. After an experiment with an opera libretto (*Le Nom d'Edipe*, Avignon Festical 1978) she had some success with *La Prise de l'Ecole de Madhubaï* at the Petit Odéon in 1983, where most of the set in the tiny theatre was taken up with a banyan tree, and most of the play was a discussion on social responsibility and individual rights between a female bandit and a friendly prime minister with an umbrella. Since then, Cixous has been engaged in a rewarding partnership with ▷ Ariane Mnouchkine and the Théâtre du Soleil, for whom and with whom she has researched and written two substantial and successful historical plays, one on the history of Cambodia and one on the partition of British India.

in French colonies and they have both written about what was formerly French Indo-China; see also ▷Mnouchkine and the Théâtre du Soleil.

CLARK, Brian [1932–]
British dramatist

Plays include:
***Lay By* (1971; with ▷ Trevor Griffiths, ▷ David Hare, ▷ Stephen Poliakoff, Hugh Stoddart, ▷ Snoo Wilson), *England's Ireland* (1972; with Tony Bicât, ▷ David Edgar, Francis Fuchs, ▷ David Hare, ▷ Snoo Wilson), *Truth or Dare* (1972), *Campion's Interview* (1976), *Whose Life is it Anyway* (1978), *Post Mortem* (1978), *Can You Hear me at the Back* (1979), *Switching in the Afternoon; or, As the Screw Turns* (1980), *The Petition* (1986)**

Television includes:
***Whose Life is it Anyway* (1972), *Telford's Change* (1979)**

Originally a collaborator with younger left-wing dramatists such as ▷ David Hare on plays for the anti-establishment Portable Theatre Company, Clark did not pursue consciously political theatre. The 1972 television version of his best-known play *Whose Life is it Anyway* was written in the same period and is more typical. In it an accident victim, paralysed from the neck down, fights for the right to die. It provides the opportunity for a virtuoso central performance, seized by Tom Conti on stage and in the subsequent film as a springboard to star status, but little opportunity for non-verbal theatre. Clark not only argues his case but writes elegantly and entertainingly, with an excellent feel for the mores and preoccupations of the English middle class. The problems of the mid-life male, professionally and domestically, are explored in *Can You Hear me at the Back*, and especially in the television series *Telford's Change*, both of which provide sensitive portraits that will assure the troubled professional that he (rather than she) is not alone – but do not look to Clark for the political critique his earliest work might seem to promise. In *The Petition* Clark is persuasive if predictable in his mainstream treatment of the anti-nuclear issue through discussions between a general and his quintessentially 'decent' middle-class wife, but the impact is fatally undermined by the melodramatic device of her political consciousness being made coincidental with the revelation that she is dying of cancer.

TRY THESE:
For hospital, illness, and disability plays of various kinds see ▷Peter Nichols' *The National Health*, ▷Tom Kempinski's *Duet for One*, ▷Louise Page's *Tissue*, ▷Phil Young's *Crystal Clear*, ▷Mark Medoff's *Children of a Lesser God*, ▷Bernard Pomerance's *The Elephant Man*, ▷Graeae Theatre Company; ▷Jean-Claude Van Itallie's *The Traveller* creates a language to describe aphasia; ▷Beckett's *Happy Days* offers another version of immobility; for anti-nuclear issues see ▷Nick Darke's *The Body*, ▷David Edgar's *Maydays*, ▷Sarah Daniels' *The Devil's Gateway*, ▷Edward Bond's *War Plays*, ▷Howard Barker's *The Passion*, ▷Howard Brenton's *The Genius*.

CLAUDEL, Paul [1868–1955]
French dramatic poet and diplomatist

Plays include:
***Tête d'Or* (*Golden Head*; published 1890, produced 1924), *Partage de Midi* (*Break of Noon;* published 1906, produced 1948), *L'Otage* (*The Hostage*; 1911), *L'Annonce Faite à Marie* (*The Tidings Brought to Mary*; 1912), *Le Soulier de Satin* (*The Satin Slipper*; published 1929,**

TRY THESE:
▷Jean Giraudoux for poetic French drama, though on less apocalyptic subjects; Charles Peguy's *Le Mystère de la Charité de Jeanne d'Arc* (*The Mystery of the Charity*

produced 1943), *Le Livre de Christophe Colomb* (*The Book of Christopher Columbus*; 1930)

Claudel's plays, with their characteristic long psalm-like verse line, were largely written in the first quarter of the century, and many were not intended for production under the prevailing stage conditions. They took on a new lease of life in the 1940s and 50s when Jean-Louis Barrault persuaded the author to let him put on the painfully autobiographical *Break of Noon* (*Partage de Midi*), and to turn the 'unplayable' six-hour-long *The Satin Slipper* (*Le Soulier de Satin*), with its themes of sin and salvation and the destinies of civilisations, into a colourful piece of 'total theatre'. They have not recently been tried in English translation, though Edith Craig produced *The Tidings Brought to Mary* (*L'Annonçe Faite à Marie*) in 1916, and had a success with Sybil Thorndike in *The Hostage* (*L'Otage*) in 1919. However, as part of Peter Daubeny's World Theatre Seasons, Barrault brought over and acted in *Le Livre de Christophe Colomb* in 1956, *Le Soulier de Satin* in 1965, and *Partage de Midi* in 1968 and was received most respectfully. However, it would take a bold director to try *The Satin Slipper* in English.

of Joan of Arc) for similar treatments of Catholic themes; ▷Mary O'Malley's *Once a Catholic* for a very different view of Catholic upbringing.

CLEAN BREAK

Touring company formed by women ex-prisoners

Plays include:

Ephemera **(1979),** ***Question of Habit*** **(1979),** ***Under Eros*** **(1979),** ***Killers*** **(1980–81),** ***In and Out*** **(1980–81),** ***Avenues*** **(1982–83),** ***Time and Other Thieves*** **(1982–83),** ***The Good Life*** **(1984),** ***Decade*** **(1984),** ***The Easter Egg*** **(1985),** ***The Sin Eaters*** **(1986),** ***Treading on My Tale*** **(1986; television version 1988),** ***Voices from Prison*** **(with the ▷ RSC; 1987),** ***Te Awa i Tahutu*** **(*****The River that Ran Away*****; 1988)**

An agit-prop theatre company started in 1978 by two former prisoners, ▷ Jacqueline Holborough and Jenny Hicks, in Askham Grange Prison in response to initiatives from the then prison governor to hold theatre workshops, Clean Break is a women's collective which has established a firm reputation for authentic drama about women and prison, challenging popular stereotypes of the criminal woman. If you want to know what the emotional effects of prison are really like, what the institutionalisation process does to people – not just prisoners but all of those involved, prison officers as well as family and friends – Clean Break is an eye-opener. Their work can be crude, but though rough-edged (the productions are always scripted by ex-prisoners, sometimes with the help of professional directors and performers such as Ann Mitchell and Maggie Ford), it has a compulsive, emotional power. As well as a theatre company, Clean Break is also a resource centre and support network for ex-prisoners; it has provided material for television programmes on women's prison experiences and it works to offer training skills to help re-integrate offenders into the community. Indeed, Clean Break's very existence is a constant reminder that drama can have a socially constructive application as well as being a source of entertainment. Apart from performances for the public (which always include an end-of-performance discussion as an integral part of the work), the company also visits colleges, community centres, and psychiatric units and keeps in contact with prison authorities, as part of a policy to help break down barriers.

Clean Break's repertory has covered a wide range of subjects – from *Ephemera*, a twenty-minute sketch speculating on how plants feel (isolated? like housewives trapped in their homes?), to self-analysis and cultural identity (*The River that Ran Away*), lesbianism, mother and daughter relationships, terrorism and maximum security wings (*Question of Habit*, *Killers* and *The Sin Eaters*), and, especially, how women come to find themselves in prison (*Avenues* and *The Garden Girls*). In 1987, Ann Mitchell directed an eminently revivable large-scale programme of poetry written by women in prison, performed by

TRY THESE:

Plays by women about prison are rare – Sheila Dewey's 1987 fringe production, *Out of Sight*, tells the true story of a young girl remanded in Holloway's psychiatric wing for non-payment of a taxi fare, who later killed herself; Kate Phelps' 1978 play *Confinement* was an early investigation of women in prison; for accounts of male prison life, see ▷Brendan Behan, ▷Wisdom Bridge Theatre Company, and ▷Tom McGrath and ▷Jimmy Boyle's *The Hard Man*; for the relationship between women, mental illness and custodial treatments, see ▷Melissa Murray's *Body-cell*, ▷Tony Craze's *Shona*, ▷David Edgar's *Mary Barnes*; see also ▷Jacqueline Holborough.

Clean Break and women members of the ▷ RSC at the Barbican, which for breadth of experience, compassion and beauty, would be hard to surpass.

Writers who have worked with Clean Break include Chris Tchaikovsky (*The Easter Egg*), Jenny Hicks (*In and Out*, in collaboration with Eva Mottley; *Question of Habit*, with ▷ Jacqueline Holborough and Ros Davies), Gilli Mebarek (*Treading on My Tale*), and Rena Owen (*The River that Ran Away*).

COCTEAU, Jean [1889–1963]

French avant-garde poet, film-maker and dramatist.

Plays include:

***Les Mariés de la Tour Eiffel* (*The Wedding on the Eiffel Tower*; 1924), *Orphée* (1927), *Antigone* (1928), *La Voix Humaine* (*The Human Voice*; 1930), *La Machine infernale* (*The Infernal Machine*; 1934), *Les Chevaliers de la Table Ronde* (*The Nights of the Round Table*; 1937), *Les Parents terribles* (*The Terrible Parents*; 1938), *L'Aigle a deux têtes* (*The Eagle Has Two Heads*; 1946)**

Cocteau was a permanent avant-gardist in the 1920s and 30s (or, to put it another way, the ultimate in trendy chic); his talents included poetry, drawing, film and playmaking, and he had a considerable vogue in England after World War II, but he has not been popular with the next generation. However, there are signs of a revival, which may grow as the period flavour becomes clearer; in 1984 *Orphée* was revived at London's Upstream Theatre, and Susannah York translated and performed the bravura piece for solo actress and telephone, *The Human Voice*, at the Gate; and in 1986 Simon Callow produced Maggie Smith in his own fine high camp version of *The Infernal Machine*, Cocteau's variation on the Oedipus story.

TRY THESE:
▷Anouilh, ▷Gide, ▷Giraudoux, and ▷Sartre for using modernised Greek plays and legends to comment on contemporary French affairs.

COLLINS, Barry [1941–]

British dramatist

Plays include:

***And Was Jerusalem Builded Here* (1972), *Beauty and the Beast* (1973), *Judgement* (1974), *The Strongest Man in the World* (1978), *Toads* (1979), *The Ice Chimney* (1980), *Atonement* (1987)**

Halifax based writer, one-time provincial journalist, and director of northern avant-garde studio theatre, Collins writes of monumental themes – human beings at the extremes of experience, in the grip of personal and social tragedy. Often, though not always, his focus is a northern one; nineteenth-century poverty and struggle in the Luddite riots in West Yorkshire (*And Was Jerusalem Builded Here*); Maurice Wilson the eccentric Yorkshireman who tried to climb Everest (*The Ice Chimney*); the television play *Witches of Pendle* set in seventeenth-century Lancaster, or the satirical swipe at Soviet obsession with creating sporting champions, *The Strongest Man in the World*, (described by Bernard Levin as 'a Great Passion Play'), written in a northern dialect.

Collins is, however, probably best known for his dramatic monologue *Judgement* – a horrific tale of cannibalism based on a real war-time incident when seven Russian soldiers were left for sixty days without food, and recounted by one of the two remaining survivors. Described by critic Steve Grant as having the 'hypnotic rhetoric of a John Donne sermon, the moral intensity of a Conrad novel and finely observed lyric detail of a Louis MacNeice poem', Collins' two-and-a-half-hour tour de force has provoked magnificent performances from its interpreters, first Peter O'Toole (1974), then memorably Colin Blakely (1975, 1976), and Ben Kingsley (1977). By now a much travelled piece (it has been seen in over twenty countries), this cool, clinical investigation into the moral and philosophical laws of human degradation, survival and the nature of guilt and sanity conjures with themes Collins has continued to re-address though perhaps nowhere else with so much control. *Atonement*, his most recent stage

TRY THESE:
For another monologue dealing with extremism, see Alan Drury's *The Man Himself*; for three-handed images of destructive love, see ▷Strindberg's *Creditors*; ▷Sam Shepard's *Fool for Love* depicts a similar scene between a brother and sister, ▷David Rudkin's *Ashes* the sterility of a marriage; see also ▷Botho Strauss' *The Tourist Guide* for the obsessive destructiveness of sexual love (between an older man and younger woman).

play, grapples bravely with the nature of guilt and the symbiotic destructiveness of obsessive love but fails to draw us successfully into its world.

COMMUNITY THEATRE

TRY THESE:
▷Joan Littlewood; ▷Ann Jellicoe; ▷Gay Sweatshop, ▷Age Exchange, ▷Bubble Theatre Company, ▷Charabanc, ▷Clean Break as examples of community theatre.

Community theatre can mean practically all things to all people, from performances in small community venues such as halls or old people's homes, to large-scale open-door spectaculars as developed by John Fox for Welfare State or its off-spring, IOU. And if ▷ David Edgar's definition of community theatre as something which addresses 'communities of ideas' means anything, then companies that particularly aim to address the gay, the black, or the women's communities, or, in times of strike, striking communities, could all be said to be part of community theatre.

Many playwrights have become involved with community theatre at one level or another. In the 1960s and 1970s, it was seen as part of the drive to re-enfranchise great swathes of the British non-theatre-going public and to engage head-on with the political issues of the day, from property development to racism. Companies as diverse as ▷ 7:84, Covent Garden Community Theatre, Red Ladder, Roland Muldoon and CAST, North West Spanner, Belt & Braces, Portable, and ▷ Monstrous Regiment (to name but a few) were all part of the movement to take theatre out of theatre buildings and bring it to 'the people' – a time, too, when 'agit-prop' and 'street theatre' became the buzz words and popular mode of performance.

▷ Margaretta D'Arcy and ▷ John Arden have been involved with community theatre since the early 1970s (particularly with the Galway Theatre Workshop), producing plays mostly on community/political themes. Peter Cheeseman at Stoke-on-Trent evolved a whole tradition of drama-documentaries based on the local community. Recently, ▷ Ann Jellicoe's work in the southwest with the Colway Trust has sparked something of a revival. The 'community play', which she has helped pioneer, can involve hundreds of local people in researching their local history and performing in the subsequent play, frequently scripted by a professional. *Entertaining Strangers* at the ▷ National Theatre, scripted by ▷ David Edgar, and focusing on two local protagonists, a fundamentalist preacher and an entrepreneurial female brewery owner, started out in Dorchester, Dorset, as a Colway Trust project, as did ▷ Nick Darke's *Ting Tang Mine*, set in Cornwall. But for ▷ Jellicoe, as indeed probably for most of those now working in community theatre, its essence is in participation, a shared sense of excitement between professional theatre workers and non-professonals alike in 'building a work of art in the community'. Several London fringe venues first started off as campaigning or touring community theatre groups, such as The Albany (originally The Combination at Brighton), The Tricycle (originally Wakefield Tricycle), and Freeform, who were invited into Chat's Palace for a Christmas show and stayed two or three years.

Community theatre and its aims remain diverse: Solent People's Theatre's last shows in the Southampton and Hampshire area, have included youth work, Theatre in Education, a Christmas show, and a children's show specially for those with hearing disabilities; Theatre Foundry's, in the West Midlands, have included a play about a local women's factory strike in 1910 as well as new plays by Les Smith and David Holman; Reminiscence theatre, created by Pam Schweitzer, centres on the memories of older generations; and ▷ Gay Sweatshop continues to serve the needs of the gay community as well as trying to reach mixed audiences with plays written from a gay perspective. Whatever their shape, the work of all these disparate groups addresses 'communities of ideas'.

CONGREVE, William [1670–1729]
English dramatist

Plays include:
***The Old Bachelor* (1693), *The Double-Dealer* (1693), *Love for Love* (1695), *The Mourning Bride* (1697), *The Way of the World* (1700)**

English born and Irish educated, Congreve lived a fashionable life (his mistresses included the actress Anne Bracegirdle and the Duchess of Marlborough), indulged in some unsuccessful theatrical management, and wrote three comedies which are still staged. Although the satirical edge of Congreve's work is less sharp than ▷ Wycherley's, public taste had changed sufficiently to make both *The Double-Dealer* and *The Way of the World* less successful with their original audiences than they have been since. *The Mourning Bride* is a tragedy but the other plays deal with the usual characters and issues of the period's comedy: arranged marriages and pretended marriages; the conflict between country and town values; lust and romance; rakes and fops and heiresses and mistresses; comic intrigues and revenges; age and youth and money and lack of it. Yet within this conventional material which is beautifully organised and wittily presented, the most interesting feature is Congreve's treatment of the romantic figures: in *The Double-Dealer, Love for Love*, and *The Way of the World* there are men and women who move towards a marriage based on mutual respect rather than money. The attitude to marriage is wary but ultimately positive, as in the so-called 'proviso scene' in *The Way of the World* where Millamant and Mirabelle lay down the ground rules of their marriage even as far as discussing how to bring up their children!

TRY THESE:
Other Restoration comic writers, such as ▷Aphra Behn, ▷Etherege and ▷Wycherley; other writers of comedy of manners, such as ▷Goldsmith, ▷Molière, ▷Sheridan, ▷Oscar Wilde, ▷Noël Coward, and ▷Doug Lucie; ▷Edward Bond's *Restoration* uses conventions and themes derived from the practice of Restoration writers to make modern points.

CORNEILLE, Pierre [1606–84]
French dramatist

Plays include:
***Mélite* (1629), *Clitandre* (1631), *L'Illusion Comique* (*The Illusion* or *The Comic Illusion*; 1636), *Le Cid* (*The Cid*; 1636–7), *Horace* (1640), *Cinna* (1640), *Polyeucte* (1641), *Rodugune* (1644–5), *Oedipe* (*Oedipus*; 1659), *Tite et Bérénice* (*Titus and Berenice*; 1670), *Suréna* (1674)**

Corneille was a lawyer from Rouen; his early plays were comedies or tragi-comedies, but after the success of *Le Cid* he settled down to write heroic tragedies, somewhat in the Spanish manner, with strong-willed heroes and heroines in impossible situations, with which they cope, whatever it costs them. He suffered from being the first major French dramatist to try and keep the neo-Aristotelian rules – the three unities of time, place and action. Unlike Racine, he usually had too much plot for the requisite twenty-four hours, and was much discouraged by the resulting criticism.

Corneille's tragedies have not often been produced in English since they were translated in the seventeenth century by the Matchless Orinda (Katherine Philips). But recently (1987) ▷ Cheek by Jowl had a success with a terrific modern dress, unrhetorical but intensely acted version of *Le Cid. L'Illusion Comique* which has a magician, a Spanish braggart called Matamore, a play within a play within a play, and characters who appear to die, and are then revealed as a company of actors sharing out the takings, would seem to offer further potential for ▷ Cheek by Jowl's 'Wunderkind', Declan Donnellan.

TRY THESE:
▷Racine for seventeenth-century French drama and for keeping to the neo-Aristotelian rules better; ▷Calderón for the influence of Spanish ideas of family honour.

The Cid (*Le Cid*)
This is the archetypal 'Love against Honour' play. Rodrigue (the Cid) loves Chimène, but has to kill her father in a duel because the latter has insulted his (Rodrigue's) father; Chimène loves Rodrigue, but has to demand his life from the King because he has killed her father. Happily, the King needs to keep Rodrigue alive to beat the Moors, and persuades Chimène to avow her love by telling her Rodrigue is dead. The play is called a tragi-comedy, but no one seems quite sure whether this is a happy ending or not. The language is elevated and the statements of all concerned excessively noble. Surprisingly, the effect can be very

powerful, especially with a flamboyant hero played by the likes of the young Gérard Philipe.

CORRIE, Joe [1894–1968]

British dramatist

Plays include:

***In Time o'Strife* (1927), *Martha* (1935), *Hewers of Coal* (1937)**

Although Corrie was an admirer of Sean O'Casey and they were both self-educated former manual labourers (Corrie was a miner), unlike O'Casey Corrie remained in his native Scotland for most of his life and wrote most successfully about Scottish mining. His commitment to writing one-act plays for groups within the Scottish Community Drama Association means that much of his work is unlikely to be staged professionally outside Scotland in the current theatrical climate. Amongst his best one-act plays are *Hewers of Coal*, the archetypal pit disaster play which presents the interaction between a small group of men trapped below ground as they wait for rescue; and *Martha*, which occupies the same kind of territory as ▷ J.M. Barrie's *Mary Rose*, in this case the ghostly return of a mother's lost son from World War I, in a more robust way. Corrie's greatest play, *In Time o'Strife*, chronicles the last days of the post-General Strike miners' lockout in a small Scottish village. The ▷ 7:84 Theatre Company's revival in 1982 showed that the play's concentrated naturalistic virtues have stood the test of time, and the political issues remain as relevant now as they did in the 1920s. Although Corrie is sometimes sentimental, his sentiment is grounded in a genuine understanding and compassion for his characters and their predicaments, and it goes along with an unsentimental analysis of the responsibilities for those predicaments. The mine owners never appear in *In Time o'Strife* and many of its virtues stem from its willingness *not* to try to see both sides of the question.

TRY THESE:
▷Sean O'Casey, particularly *The Plough and the Stars* for a play showing a working-class community under the strain of great political upheaval and *The Silver Tassie* for the impact of war on a community; Scottish playwright Ena Lamont Stewart's *Men Should Weep* for another example of a 1920s Scottish community under strain; ▷Synge's *The Riders to the Sea* for the impact of sons' deaths on a mother in a peasant community; ▷7.84 Scotland as a Scottish group touring politically concerned plays in Scotland; ▷Galsworthy's *Strife* for a presentation of strikes from within a more established theatre.

COWARD, Noël [1899–1973]

British dramatist

Plays include:

***The Young Idea* (1921), *The Vortex* (1924), *Fallen Angels* (1925), *Hay Fever* (1925), *Easy Virtue* (1926), *Semi-Monde* (written 1926, performed 1977), *Bitter Sweet* (1929), *Private Lives* (1930), *Cavalcade* (1931), *Design For Living* (1933), *Tonight At 8.30* (1936), *Operette* (1938), *Blithe Spirit* (1941), *Present Laughter* (1943), *This Happy Breed* (1943), *Relative Values* (1951), *Quadrille* (1952), *Nude With Violin* (1956), *Waiting In the Wings* (1960), *Sail Away* (1961), *Suite In Three Keys* (1965)**

Screenplays include:

***In Which We Serve* (1942), *Brief Encounter* (1945)**

Whether you see him as the doyen of bitchery or the ultimate connoisseur of camp, or if you find various moral tales peeking out from behind his characters' poor and pricelessly funny manners, Noël Coward remains this century's supreme wit, a playwright in a direct line from ▷ Congreve through to ▷ Sheridan, ▷ Oscar Wilde and ▷ Joe Orton (Millamant's 'I Love To Give Pain', from *The Way of the World*, could serve as the subtext for Coward creations). The consummate man of the theatre himself, theatrical folk figure heavily in Coward's plays, whether it's the matriarchal actress, Judith Bliss, in *Hay Fever* or the preening comedian Garry Essendine in *Present Laughter*, who admits, 'I'm always acting.' Non-actors in his plays act, too: the hypertheatrical Madam Arcati in *Blithe Spirit*, the polyglot houseboy Sebastien in *Nude With Violin*. For Coward, as for ▷ Wilde, acting equals artifice equals disguise, and the tension in his work often comes from the effort required to sustain a pose without which his characters, and their egos, dry up. Coward's plays may come adorned with comic frills that continue to entice, but he is as serious and penetrating a dramatist as Britain has known this

TRY THESE:
▷Oscar Wilde, especially *The Importance of Being Earnest*, for effortlessly funny repartee; ▷Joe Orton for epigrammatic similarities in tone, and ▷Philip Barry for the American equivalent; ▷Neil Simon for inferior variants on similar ideas; ▷N.F. Simpson's *One Way Pendulum*, and ▷Alan Ayckbourn for more middle-class versions of the comic cruelties of English eccentrics; ▷Edward Albee's *Who's Afraid of Virginia Woolf?* for a more scabrous treatment of guests.

century. He was also an accomplished lyricist and cabaret performer.

Hay Fever
Last seen in the West End in 1983 (with Penelope Keith), and on Broadway in 1985 (with Rosemary Harris), *Hay Fever* is an anarchic precursor of 'get the guest' in ▷ Edward Albee's *Who's Afraid of Virginia Woolf* – Coward's eccentric Bliss family invites guests to their home in Cookham only to drive them away again through their own accumulated eccentricities. The play both revels in, and comments on, the English fondness for ill-mannered artifice, and at its best – the visiting 'drearies' skulk away as the family carries obliviously on over breakfast – it can be a deliriously funny experience. As usual with Coward, a critique is implied: the Blisses may be lethally exciting with their fondness for games and poses, but their mores also serve to isolate them; they are fundamentally alone.

Private Lives
Written by Coward for himself and Gertrude Lawrence to act, *Private Lives*, is one of the simplest, yet most subtle of comedies, and one can take pleasure in the perfect rhythms of its language: 'Don't quibble, Sybil' and 'very flat Norfolk' have both entered history books. Two divorcés, Amanda and Elyot, bump into one another on their second honeymoons only to end up ditching their new spouses, Victor and Sibyl, and absconding to Paris. Typically for Coward, elegant repartee hides hideous manners, and the characters are both aware of – and blind to – their own ruthlessness. It was last seen in 1982 on Broadway in a critically reviled but financially sucessful production co-starring Elizabeth Taylor and Richard Burton; recent London versions have paired Maggie Smith and Robert Stephens (in 1970) and Maria Aitken and Michael Jayston (in 1980).

CRAZE, Tony [1944–]
British dramatist

Plays include:
***The Love You Take* (1981), *Kaleidoscope* (1981), *Confrontations* (1981), *Shona* (1983), *Living With Your Enemies* (1985), *Angelus* (1987), *Going West* (1988)**

Craze, a former journalist and screen writer (trained at the London Film School), has been both script and workshop adviser at the Soho Poly, which has staged his major plays. His plays pack a powerfully cumulative, emotional punch (though his dialogue can be irritatingly cryptic), showing individuals not only at logger-heads within the family but also as victims of blighted dreams which reflect the way society has failed them. *Living with Your Enemies*, for example, relates a mother's lost opportunities, sacrificed in bringing up her children, back to her post-war youth and the promise offered in the glimmerings of the Welfare State. The flawed but explosive *Angelus* is a three-hander in which the spectre of a Jimmy Porter figure for the 1980s is resurrected in Mick, bully boy, drugs dealer, and sinner seeking redemption. With its desperate spiritual yearnings, *Angelus* indicated Craze as something more than simply an adherent of the raw 'slice of life school' of drama. Champion of the underdog, as in *Shona* (the first winner of the Verity Bargate new playwriting award) – a terse, painful blast against modern psychiatric practices told through the story and ultimate lobotomisation of a young twenty-eight-year old schizophrenic – Craze is also a writer with a romantic's ambivalence towards women: part aggressive (mothers come in for a particular bashing), part protective (Ruth, the redemptive character in *Angelus* is seen both as a madonna-like creature of goodness and as the embodiment of Mick's aspirations to a new life in the USA). If he has yet to find a unified style, Craze is a voice of honest compassion and insight into the area where dreams turn into anger, despair and ferocious frustration.

TRY THESE:
Johnnie Quarrell, Mick Mahoney's *When Your Bottle's Gone in SE1* and ▷Tony Marchant's *The Lucky Ones* for contemporary angst in the working class; for other images of insanity, see ▷Melissa Murray's *The Admission*, ▷David Edgar's *Mary Barnes*, ▷David Mercer's *In Two Minds*; for equivalent images of generational conflict between mothers and offspring, see ▷Julia Kearsley, ▷Louise Page, ▷Ayshe Raif, ▷Caryl Phillips' *Strange Fruit* for generational differences in terms of the black community; ▷Stephen Lowe's *Touched* for more images of women's pleasures and pains in the 1940s; ▷John Osborne's *Look Back in Anger* for the original Jimmy Porter.

DANIELS, Sarah [1957–]

British dramatist

Plays include:

***Ripen Our Darkness* (1981), *Masterpieces* (1983), *The Devil's Gateway* (1983), *Neaptide* (1984), *Byrthrite* (1987)**

A spirited, anarchically funny, angry young writer, Daniels is also one of the most controversial British female playwrights, and the only radical lesbian feminist to have made it into the mainstream. She first came to prominence as part of the 'new wave' of young women writers in the early 1980s with *Ripen Our Darkness* – a play famous for the line 'Dear David, your dinner and my head are in the oven' – premiered, like *Byrthrite*, at the Royal Court Upstairs (which also presented *Masterpieces* after its Royal Manchester Exchange opening). Her attacks on patriarchy involve the rebellion of mothers (*Ripen Our Darkness* and *The Devil's Gateway*) and the discussion of lesbian custody of children in *Neaptide* (originally commissioned by Liverpool Playhouse). *Byrthrite* is a warning shot across the bows for women about the possible consequences of modern genetic engineering and reproductive techniques and is linked to a familiar theme of the persecution of the old 'wise women' of the seventeenth century (though by no means treated in familiar fashion, and, in its high-camp, historical setting, a breakaway from Daniels' usual quasi-naturalism).

Needless to say, Daniels' plays and her expression of unpalatable truths (especially if you are a man) have invoked, in their turn, vitriolically hostile reviews from critics (mostly but not exclusively male), particularly over *Masterpieces* and *Byrthrite*. But Daniels' early protagonists are recognisable suburban wives and mothers rebelling – wittily – against their roles as general moppers-up after men and the male value system that has put them there. In Daniels' world, the personal becomes graphically political. Despite the outcries, Daniels won the George Devine Award in 1982 for *Neaptide*.

Masterpieces

This is an uncompromisingly didactic play that makes a direct link between the seemingly innocuous dinner table misogynist joke – 'a little harmless fun,' says one of the male characters – and male violence against women, as in *Ripen Our Darkness* and *The Devil's Gateway*. It is a tale of growing awareness, focused on Rowena, a social worker, (the archetypal Daniel's heroine) who gradually moves from naivety to anger, from passivity to action and wholesale rejection of the man-made world in which she lives and to which she has, in the past, given tacit acceptance. The play has an irrefutable emotional force about it and has deservedly already come to be regarded as a feminist classic, even if some find its philosophical link questionable.

TRY THESE:
For a contrasting male treatment of pornography, see ▷Doug Lucie's *Progress*; ▷Gay Sweatshop's *Care and Control* for an earlier treatment of lesbian custody; ▷Caryl Churchill's *Vinegar Tom* and ▷Dekker, ▷Ford and ▷Rowley's *The Witch of Edmonton* for witches; ▷Joe Orton for a similarly anarchic approach to wit (juxtaposing the surreal with the ordinary); ▷Bryony Lavery for a similar adventurer using wit to attack the bastions of patriarchy; ▷Aphra Behn for a seventeenth-century feminist equivalent; see also ▷Lesbian Theatre; Alison Lyssa's *Pinball* for an Australian lesbian mother custody case; ▷Shakespeare's *The Winter's Tale* uses the same Demeter myth as *Neaptide*.

D'ARCY, Margaretta

Irish dramatist and long-time collaborator with ▷ John Arden

TRY THESE:
For more voices of

John Wilson and David Benedict in Noël Greig's ***Poppies***, directed by Philip Osment, presented by Gay Sweatshop at the Drill Hall, 1985.

Bernard Strother, Patti Love and Kathryn Pogson in Jules Wright's 1983 Royal Court production of ***Masterpieces*** by Sarah Daniels.

Plays written in collaboration with John Arden include:
***200 Years of Labour History* (1971), *The Non-Stop Connolly Show* (1975), *The Little Gray Home in the West* (1978), *Vandaleur's Folly* (1978)**

See ▷ John Arden for his plays written in collaboration with D'Arcy.

D'Arcy started her career in Dublin in small experimental theatres. She then went to London where she acted in club theatres and at the Hornchurch Rep, one of the first regional companies to be local-authority funded. Her involvement with ▷ community theatre stems from these early experiences, and much of her writing has been community-orientated. There are also several pieces written collectively, especially with Galway Theatre Workshop and with Galway Women's Voice Group, exploring a feminist interpretation of classical theatre. She has collaborated with Muswell Hill Street Theatre on *My Old Man's a Tory, Little Red Riding Hood and Granny Welfare* (1971); and with Corrandulla, Galway, *The Devil and the Parish Pump* (1974). Other pieces (some readings) include: *A Pinprick of History* (1977), *West of Ireland Women Speak* (1978), and *Trial and Prison Experience of the Countess Markievicz* (1979).

women in prison, see ▷Clean Break; for more on community theatre, see ▷Ann Jellicoe and community theatre; for contrasting voices of women from a Northern Ireland perspective, see ▷Charabanc; for women and Irish history, a new, young women's Irish company, Trouble and Strife, in *Now and at the Hour of Our Death*.

DARKE, Nick [1949–]
British dramatist

Plays include:
***Never Say Rabbit In A Boat* (1978), *Landmarks* (1979), *A Tickle On the River's Back* (1979), *Say Your Prayers* (1980), *The Catch* (1980), *High Water* (1980), *The Body* (1983), *The Oven Glove Murders* (1986), *The Dead Monkey* (1986), *Ting Tang Mine* (1987)**

An erstwhile actor, Cornish-born Darke is a prolific dramatist who has yet to write a play that can be endorsed without reservation. Some of his plays draw on the terrain of his upbringing, but his psychological grasp often falls short of his geographical one, and his writing becomes more earnest and pedantic the further it strays from his own roots. In *The Body*, an eccentric West Country community must contend with the presence of an American airforce base in one of those plays about the bomb that shows what poor art can come out of good politics. In *Ting Tang Mine*, orginally staged as a Cornish community play in 1984 under the title *The Earth Turned Inside Out*, the fate of two rival mining communities becomes an unconvincing parable of Thatcherite avarice. Greed's relationship to the screen gets the treatment in *The Oven Glove Murders*, set in the Soho offices of Absolutsky films, and Californian morality comes under the cudgel in *The Dead Monkey*, about a childless West Coast couple whose relationship has been kept alive for fifteen years by the now-dead simian of the title. Like many of Darke's plays, the topic is interesting, the style derivative. For a writer who's produced so much, this playwright has yet to find his true voice.

TRY THESE:
▷Charles Wood (especially *Has 'Washington' Legs?* and *Veterans*) for theatrical looks at film world life styles; ▷J.M. Synge (especially *Playboy of the Western World*) for *Ting Tang Mine* – like portraits of a community reacting to its errant son; ▷Sam Shepard, ▷Edward Albee, and ▷David Rabe for a kind of American absurdism which Darke seems to want to capture for himself; ▷Brian Clark's *The Petition*, ▷Sarah Daniels' *The Devil's Gateway*, ▷David Edgar's *Maydays* for other plays about American airforce bases (both Greenham) in Britain; see also ▷Ann Jellicoe, ▷Community Theatre.

DE ANGELIS, April [1960–]
British dramatist

Plays include:
***Breathless* (1986), *Wanderlust* (1988), *Women in Law* (1988)**

Radio includes:
***Visitants* (1988)**

One-time actress, who has worked with ▷ Monstrous Regiment, ReSisters and Lumiere and Son, April De Angelis is fast becoming the mistress of theatre noir. *Breathless*, an award winner in

TRY THESE:
▷Deborah Levy for a similar kind of verve and imaginative drive; see Siren's *PULP* and Don Hale's *Every Black Day* for the use of pulp thrillers à la Philip Marlowe; ▷Graeae have done a version of Frankenstein; Annie Griffin directed an

the 1987 Second Wave Young Women's writing festival at the Albany propelled her into prominence. A short, gothically atmospheric drama written with verve, wit and very contemporary consciousness about women and science, it rehashed the old Frankenstein myth and the stereotypical helpless Victorian heroine, with a contrasting pair of drooping mistress and obsessive maid, beavering away in the dungeons amongst the test tubes, frustrated at not being taken seriously as scientists. *Women in Law* carries on in something of the same vein. It uses a gothic setting, a thriller convention, unfortunately now becoming something of a cliché in women's theatre circles, and another, even more extravagant variant of *la châtelaine enchainé* (this one owes more than a little to a demented kind of Bette Davis/Miss Faversham) who is, again, a scientist manqué, pining for a lost career as a marine biologist. Commissioned by the ReSisters theatre company (she is currently their writer-in-residence), the play was ostensibly written to back up ideas about women and violence and the way they are treated in law, and though the polemic was laudable, the play suffered from its obvious brief. *Wanderlust*, created through the Oval House women writers' workshop, and given a reading at Wordplay '88 (jointly organised by the Playwrights Co-operative and New Playwrights' Trust), was 'straining at the leash' to get on to a real stage according to one reviewer. The play is also set in the nineteenth century, and this time De Angelis' wilder shores and tongue-in-cheek imagination takes on the Great Man myth of David Livingstone, to make some serious points about colonialism in Africa. Definitely a name to watch.

irreverent version of the story, *The Very Tragical History of Mary Shelley*, which gives an unflattering view of Shelley the husband; for other plays on women, violence and the law, see ▷Clean Break, ▷Sarah Daniels; ▷Kay Adshead, ▷Julia Schofield and ▷Sharman Macdonald are other new actress-dramatists.

DEAR, Nick [1955–]
British dramatist

Plays include:
***The Perfect Alibi* (1980), *Temptation* (1984), *The Bed* (1986), *The Art of Success* (1986); adaptations include *A Family Affair* (1988; from Ostrovsky's *The Bankrupt*, 1850)**

The Portsmouth-born playwright Nick Dear came to attention in 1986–7 with his play *The Art of Success*, an ▷ RSC entry that earned him an Olivier Award nomination for the Most Promising Newcomer in Theatre. Set during the eighteenth-century epoch of William Hogarth, the satirical draughtsman, the play is purposefully revisionist and anachronisitic in order to make a retroactive point about opportunism and lust, with Walpole as the Mrs Thatcher of his time facing off against the similarly Thatcherite entrepreneurial Hogarth. The play compresses ten years into one night and takes various liberties with personal and political history; still, there's no denying the Jonsonian vigour of Dear's scatology-laden language. His follow-up play *A Family Affair* — an Ostrovsky adaptation for ▷ Cheek By Jowl – has a similarly contemporary bent in its depiction of a society both goaded on, and paralysed, by matters financial.

TRY THESE:
▷Edward Bond's *Bingo* and Peter Shaffer's *Amadeus* for analogous debunkings of historical greats; ▷Ben Jonson and, of Dear's contemporaries, ▷Howard Barker for a similar robustness of language.

DE FILIPPO, Eduardo [1900–]
Italian actor, poet, dramatist

Plays include:
***Oh These Ghosts!* (1946), *Filumena* (1946), *Inner Voices* (translated by ▷ N.F. Simpson; 1948), *Fear Number One* (1950), *My Darling and My Love* (1955), *Saturday, Sunday, Monday* (translated by ▷ Keith Waterhouse and ▷ Willis Hall; 1959), *Ducking Out* (translated by Mike Stott; 1982)**

De Filippo has written more than fifty plays although surprisingly few have been performed in Britain. Born into a family of actors (one of three illegitimate children), De Filippo began his career by touring with the famous Scarpetta acting company before founding a company with his brother Peppino and sister Titina. Based on his experience as an actor, and his early days writing comedy and musical sketches, his later Neapolitan comedies are nothing if not supremely actable, distinguished by their craftsmanship and a Pirandellian involvement with the fine line between illusion

TRY THESE:
▷Alan Ayckbourn for scenes from family life (especially *The Norman Conquests* for Christmas British-style, and *Way Upstream* for the darkest Ayckbourn to date; ▷Stephen Bill's *Curtains* for the joys (or otherwise) of families; ▷Pirandello, ▷Dario Fo and ▷Franca Rame are the other regularly performed Italian dramatists.

and reality. However, three of the most recent productions in Britain have been more concrete examples of De Filippo's comedies in which the virtues of family life, in all their eccentric and extravagant glory, rule supreme. And, as in ▷ Ayckbourn's plays (the British equivalent par excellence at chronicling the tragicomedy of family life) the comic impetus comes from the recognisable ordinariness of domestic life, crashing up against the unexpected, the surreal, or the inappropriate emotional overreaction.

The challenge in translating De Filippo's particular but universal Neapolitan temperament has succeeded with spectacular success in at least two cases. Adopting an Italianate approach, Zefferelli's productions of *Saturday, Sunday, Monday* and *Filumena* succeeded, against the odds, in transmitting to British audiences the heightened emotion of families locked in the communal rituals of Sunday lunch on the one hand, and affection, albeit illegitimate, on the other. Mike Stott's relocation of the working-class Neapolitan family in *Ducking Out* to a council flat in west Lancashire was less successful and, some observers felt, sat oddly with the Christmas and Catholic rituals required. Nonetheless, most agreed that this grimmer than usual family portrait, with its kleptomaniac son, neurotic daughter, long-suffering mother, homosexual uncle, and presiding (if ultimately ineffective) paterfamilias, stroke-ridden and reduced to monosyllabic platitudes, once again showed De Filippo achieving a remarkable balance between laughter and pathos.

Less successful was the elusive *Inner Voices* (revived at the ▷ National Theatre in 1983), which, despite the presence of the late and much lamented Ralph Richardson as the man who dreams a murder and precipitates a wave of paranoia, could best be summed up in the memorable words of *City Limits* critic Ros Asquith as 'actors and a set in search of a play'.

Saturday, Sunday, Monday

The quintessential De Filippo, in which the warring factions of an extended family – squabbling off-spring, eccentric relatives, a paranoid husband, opportunistic friends, and lumbering maid – somehow live, love, eat, fight, and become reconciled, presided over by the inevitable matriarch (a magisterial Joan Plowright as Rosa in the ▷ National Theatre's 1973 production).

Filumena

Paternity and female subterfuge form the lynch-pins of this comedy in which a woman, the mistress for twenty-five years of a wealthy businessman, hoodwinks him into marriage with her when he threatens to marry a younger woman, by refusing to disclose which of her three illegitimate sons is by him. Again with Joan Plowright in command at the ▷ National in 1977, *Filumena* tells us as much about male pride as it does about female deviousness. Once more, it is De Filippo's skill in creating characters of sympathy as well as pomposity that makes these Neapolitans so accessible to British audiences.

DEKKER, Thomas [c 1572–1632]

English Renaissance dramatist and pamphleteer

Plays include: ***The Shoemaker's Holiday* (1599), *Sir Thomas Wyatt* (with ▷ Heywood [?] and ▷ Webster; pre-1607), *The Honest Whore* (with ▷ Middleton; 1604), *The Roaring Girl* (with ▷ Middleton; 1610), *The Virgin Martyr* (with Massinger; 1624), *The Witch of Edmonton* (with ▷ Ford and ▷ Rowley; 1621)**

A rather shadowy figure who seems to have earned his living as a kind of house dramatist cum play doctor (▷ Jonson, who satirised him in *The Poetaster*, called him a 'dresser of plays') and pamphleteer, Dekker was imprisoned on more than one occasion for the debt that dogged him throughout his life. He seems to have spent much of his life producing collaborative work in whatever style was needed by the theatre manager Philip Henslowe. His work camed back into theatrical fashion in the 1980s with productions of the plays discussed below by the ▷ RSC and the ▷ National Theatre. This may reflect a more widespread awareness that co-authored works are not necessarily incoherent and inferior and may partly stem from the growth

TRY THESE:
Dekker's collaborators, ▷Ford, ▷Heywood, ▷Massinger, ▷Middleton, ▷Rowley and ▷Webster; ▷Auden and ▷Isherwood, ▷Brenton and ▷Hare, ▷Hecht and ▷MacArthur are examples of successful twentieth-century partnerships; among other contemporary writers who have also collaborated successfully are ▷Tunde Ikoli (with ▷Howard Brenton),

of collaboration elsewhere in the theatre at that time. Dekker's own dramatic work is generally genial, compassionate, London-centred and populist as in *The Shoemaker's Holiday* with its Dick Whittington-like tale of a cobbler who rises to become Lord Mayor of London while a disguised young nobleman woos and wins the daughter of the current Lord Mayor and receives the king's pardon for doing so. *The Roaring Girl* is particularly interesting since its portrait of a woman who scandalises contemporary society by wearing men's clothing and indulging in typical male pursuits like smoking and brawling is based on a real person, Mary Frith, who herself sat on stage to watch an early performance of the play. Dekker is also credited with the sympathetic portrayal of the witch in *The Witch of Edmonton*.

▷Caryl Churchill (with ▷David Lan), ▷David Edgar (with Susan Todd), ▷Trevor Griffiths (with ▷Brenton, ▷Clark, ▷Hare, ▷Poliakoff, Hugh Stoddart and ▷Snoo Wilson on *Lay By* and with ▷Brenton, ▷Ken Campbell and ▷Hare on *Deeds*); for another real-life portrait of a woman stepping outside her womanly needs, see ▷Timberlake Wertenbaker's account of intrepid traveller, Isabelle Ebhardt, in *New Anatomies*; ▷Aphra Behn for other prototype feminists.

DELANEY, Shelagh [1939–]

British dramatist

Plays include:

A Taste of Honey (1958), _The Lion in Love_ (1960), _The House That Jack Built_ (1978)

Films include:

A Taste of Honey (1962), _The White Bus_ (for Lindsay Anderson; 1966), _Charley Bubbles_ (1968), _Dance With a Stranger_ (1985), _A Winter House_ (from _Snowblind_ by Cherry Smith; 1986), _Love Lessons_ (from the book by Joan Wyndham; 1987)

Television includes:

Did Your Nanny Come From Bergen (1970), _St Martin's Summer_ (1974), _The House That Jack Built_ (1977), _Find Me First_ (1979)

Radio includes:

So Does the Nightingale (1980), _Don't Worry About Matilda_ (1983)

Delaney's main stage claim to fame is based on *A Taste of Honey*, the play she wrote at nineteen. Born in Salford, this one-time salesgirl, cinema usherette and photographer's lab assistant who left school at sixteen, wrote what has come to be regarded as one of the definitive plays of the 1950s. *A Taste of Honey*, her first play, was accepted by ▷ Joan Littlewood's Theatre Workshop, was filmed (with Rita Tushingham as Jo), was hailed in New York (in 1961 and again twenty years later), and is constantly revived in the repertory in Britain. Delaney's second play, *The Lion in Love*, about a disturbed and unhappy family, again took a mother and daughter – Kit and Peg this time – as its focal point, but its more symbolic treatment found less favour, and some thought it was swamped by Littlewood's Theatre Workshop production. The play is seldom revived, although its style, themes, and sensitivities prefigure the work of such contemporary dramatists as ▷ Ayshe Raif and ▷ Julia Kearsley. A revival giving us a chance to 'compare and contrast' would be fascinating.

Delaney has written many screenplays, notably *Charley Bubbles* (starring Albert Finney) and the highly acclaimed *Dance With a Stranger* about the last woman to be hanged in Britain, Ruth Ellis.

TRY THESE:

See ▷Ann Jellicoe's *The Sport of My Mad Mother* for a bold, non-realistic treatment of the mother image; ▷Keith Waterhouse and ▷Willis Hall's *Billy Liar* for the theme of transposing grim reality into dreams; ▷Sharman Macdonald for comparable but different images almost twenty years later of mother/ daughter in conflict, also ▷Julia Kearsley and ▷Louise Page; ▷John Osborne's *Look Back in Anger* for a contrasting treatment and male view of pregnancy; ▷Ibsen's *Hedda Gabler* for another image of reluctant pregnancy; for more warring families, see ▷De Filippo's *Ducking Out*.

A Taste of Honey

In many senses, this is a play that breaks with its time's conventions about motherhood and female sexuality in its portrait of Jo, the young working-class, reluctant mother-to-be and anti-heroine. In another sense it is very much of its time, the late 1950s, in that it celebrates a working-class approach, at once unsentimental and free of moral judgments in so far as illegitimacy, racial inter-marriage, or homosexuality are concerned. With its female centred focus, and final opting for a life without men, it is a play that predates the concerns of later feminist writers – the optimism and the vulnerabilities, as well as the strengths of women – by well over a decade. However, despite its apparent affiliation to the realistic school of 'kitchen sink' drama and, no doubt, revivals along such lines, its original production by Littlewood made sure that audiences were not let off the hook as she confronted them with the challenges and the responsibilities raised by the sexual politics of the play.

DE VEGA CARPIO, Lope Félix [1562–1635]
Spanish dramatist

Plays include:
***Fuenteovejuna* (*The Sheep Well*; (1612), *The Simple Lady* (1613), *The King is the Best Judge* (c 1620), *Punishment without Revenge* (1631)**

Lope de Vega claimed to have written an amazing total of 1500 plays, of which about 480 survive (mostly in manuscript). He also wrote (inter alia) three novels and 3000 sonnets, married twice, had some seven major love affairs, and sailed with the Spanish Armada. He fixed and developed the form of the Spanish *comedia*, attacking the pseudo-Aristotelian unities and freely mixing comedy and tragedy (and indeed pastoral and historical as well). His plays are well constructed, more inclined to entertaining action than subtle characterisation (most of his work was done at speed to satisfy the demands of theatre directors), and often deal with questions of family honour and paternal authority (of which he is in favour). The large remaining stock of his plays could well yield something revivable, though perhaps not many of the plays where private executions are condoned in the cause of restoring a wife's honour. The best of these is probably *The King is the Best Judge*, in which the king, disguised as a mayor, obliges a nobleman to marry a village girl he has abducted, has him beheaded and then grants her half of his estate and gives her back to her young lover – a satisfying solution on both a personal and a civic level. ▷ John Osborne adapted *La Fianza Satisfecha* as *A Bond Honoured* for the ▷ National Theatre in 1966, but the only play one is at all likely to see at present is some version of *Fuenteovejuna*.

Fuenteovejuna
This play is unusual in that the people of the village become a collective protagonist. The overlord snatches the mayor's daughter Laurencia from her wedding and imprisons the groom, but she escapes and incites the townspeople to behead him. The whole village, even under torture, declare that 'Fuenteovejuna did it', and finally King Ferdinand collectively pardons them for the justice of the act and reunites the lovers. The play is popular with progressive political groups, but some of the honour-and-revenge plays would give them more trouble.

TRY THESE:
▷Calderon, who borrowed plots from Lope de Vega and refined his plays; ▷Aeschylus' *The Persians*, for another collective protagonist; ▷Steve Gooch for an adaptation of *Fuenteovejuna*; Adrian Mitchell's adaptation of Robert Browning's *The Pied Piper* presents a township from which the children want to escape; *Heads Held High*, written by Alan 'Brookside' McDonald, music by Lindisfarne member Alan Hull, is a piece of popular music-theatre inspired by the Jarrow March of 1936, in which a sense of community is a vital ingredient; as it is in Howard Goodall's *The Hired Man*, based on the book by Melvyn Bragg; and the *Larkrise to Candleford* trilogy, by Flora Thompson, adapted by Keith Dewhurst for the ▷National Theatre.

DEVLIN, Ann [1951–]
Northern Irish dramatist

Play include:
***Ourselves Alone* (1985)**

Television includes:
***A Woman Calling* (1984), *The Long March* (1984), *Naming the Names* (1987), *The Venus De Milo Instead* (1987)**

Devlin's theatrical reputation rests at the moment, like one or two other contemporaries, on one stage play, *Ourselves Alone*, which in one year won both the George Devine and Susan Smith Blackburn awards, although she had already won the 1984 Samuel Beckett award for her two television plays, *A Woman*

TRY THESE:
▷Christina Reid's *Tea in a China Cup* and ▷Charabanc for Belfast plays with a specifically women-centred focus; ▷Daniel Mornin's *Kate* and *Built on Sand* for showing the effects on women of the troubles; ▷Seamus Finnegan for a more stylised, many-faceted exploration of

Calling and *The Long March*, and is also a published short story writer.

Ourselves Alone, originally commissioned by the Liverpool Playhouse, opened as a co-production at the Royal Court in 1985 and was soon revived. A warm, toughly plotted, political thriller, set in the aftermath of the 1981 Hunger Strikes, it's an honest attempt to show, as so many others have before and no doubt will again, the tragic nature of entrenched views and attitudes. As such, its central focus is less the pros and cons of Republicanism (some have felt in fact it is a dig against it) than a foray into the arena of sexual politics, in the attempts of three sisters to escape their stifling familial and political bonds. But does it reinforce certain stereotypes about the male chauvinism of Irish men, and is her portrait of women unduly pessimistic (one reacts by escaping to England, the other, a former IRA supporter, settles down to blissful maternity)? Whichever way you fall on this one, this telling-it-how-it-is picture has already found its own level of popularity and has seen productions as far apart as Chicago and Hamburg's prestigious Schauspielhaus.

religious and political loyalties; ▷Ron Hutchinson's *Rat in the Skull* for a different variant; ▷Sean O'Casey's *Plough and the Stars* for similar concerns; and, of course for three sisters of a very different kind, but in a no less stifling environment, see ▷Chekhov's *Three Sisters*.

DRUID
Galway based Irish theatre company

Druid, formed in Galway in 1975 by its current artistic director Garry Hynes, actress Marie Mullen and Mick Lally, has survived against the odds to become a leading force in contemporary theatre, with regular tours to London and recognition in Australia and the USA. The company's first production, logically enough in view of their location and the tourist trade, was ▷ J.M. Synge's *Playboy of the Western World*, though they opened ▷ Brian Friel's *The Loves of Cass Maguire* and Kevin Laffan's *It's A Two Foot Six Inches Above the Ground World* (a daring choice since it is about a Catholic family and contraception) in the same week. The production styles and the choice of plays remain eclectic, since the company has now clearly taken on one of the traditional functions of a major regional or national theatre in providing a varied international repertory. Their productions include European classics such as ▷ Büchner's *Woyzeck*, ▷ Dario Fo's *Accidental Death of an Anarchist* and ▷ Ibsen's *A Doll's House*; Irish works such as ▷ Boucicault's *The Shaughraun,* ▷ Yeats' *King Oedipus* and ▷ Beckett's *Endgame*; American ▷ Sam Shepard's *Geography of a Horse Dreamer*, and even Frederick Knott's repertory warhorse *Dial M for Murder*. They have also staged new Irish writers such as Tom Murphy and Frank McGuinness and resurrected M.J. Malloy's forgotten 1952 play about emigration, *Wood of the Whispering.*

TRY THESE:
▷Lady Gregory and the Abbey Theatre for the effective beginnings of a professional Irish theatre; ▷Field Day for another contemporary Irish theatre company; 7:84 have latterly championed some neglected dramatists; for American equivalents see ▷Wisdom Bridge and ▷Steppenwolf companies; see also ▷Charabanc for a Northern Irish company.

DRURY, Alan [1949–]
British dramatist

Plays include:

***Asides* (1974), *The Man Himself* (1975), *Sparrowfall* (1976), *Communion* (1976), *Change of Mind* (1977), *An Empty Desk* (1979), *An Honourable Man* (1980), *Nasty Stories* (1982), *The Dean's Tale* (1983), *Mr Hyde* (1984), *Little Brown Jug* (1985)**

Drury has written some forty works for radio, television, stage and cinema, been a script editor for BBC television, resident dramatist at the York Theatre Royal and the Royal Court, and literary manager at the Hampstead Theatre. His work ranges from monologues to ▷ pantomime, and his subjects have included many aspects of sexual politics, attitudes to the National Front (the monologue *The Man Himself*), the psychopathology of murderers, contemporary (*Sparrowfall*) and Victorian corruption (*Mr Hyde*), but he has yet to find a secure niche in the current repertory and his greatest success has been with his translation of Molière's *The Hypochondriac* (▷ National Theatre, 1981).

TRY THESE:
▷Peter Flannery's *Our Friends in the North* for contemporary corruption; ▷Christopher Hampton's *Treats* covers similar ground to *Asides*; ▷Lillian Hellman's *The Children's Hour*, like *An Honourable Man*, deals with accusations of sexual impropriety against a teacher; ▷Tony Marchant's *The Attractions* is a modern, gothic thriller about violence; see ▷Barry Collins' *Judgement* and *The Ice Chimney* for monologues of

comparable intensity to *The Man Himself.*

DRYDEN, John [1631–1700]

English dramatist, poet and critic

Plays include:

***The Indian Queen* (with Sir Robert Howard; 1664), *The Indian Emperor* (1665), *The Tempest* (with Sir William Davenant; 1667), *Tyrannic Love* (1669), *The Conquest of Granada* (in two parts; 1670 and 1671), *Marriage à la Mode* (1672), *Aureng-Zebe* (1675), *All for Love* (1677), *Oedipus* (with Nathaniel Lee; 1678), *Troilus and Cressida* (1678)**

Dryden, one of the great literary figures of his age, wrote singly or in collaboration, nearly thirty plays but the only one of his plays to be staged regularly is *All for Love.* It is a treatment of the Antony and Cleopatra story, which is usually compared unfavourably with ▷ Shakespeare's play by those who assume, wrongly, that because Dryden adapted *The Tempest* he did the same to *Antony and Cleopatra.* The fact that the very occasional productions of Dryden's *Tempest* demonstrate that it is a good acting play tend to be forgotten in routine denunciations of the depravity of even daring to adapt the Bard. Something similar happens with *All for Love*, which tends to get castigated for not achieving the epic grandeur and flexibility of ▷ Shakespeare's play; in fact it is a far more concentrated and domestic work dealing with the theme in terms of a love/honour conflict of the kind beloved of Restoration tragedy.

TRY THESE:
▷G.B. Shaw's *Caesar and Cleopatra* is another treatment of the Cleopatra story which, like *All for Love*, is sometimes staged in repertory with ▷Shakespeare's *Antony and Cleopatra*; ▷Otway's *Venice Preserv'd* is the only other tragedy from the period still staged regularly.

DUFFY, Maureen [1933–]

British novelist, poet and dramatist

Plays include:

***The Lay Off* (1962), *The Silk Room* (1966), *Rites* (1969), *Solo* (1970), *Old Tyme* (1970), *A Nightingale in Bloomsbury Square* (1973)**

Radio includes:

***Only Goodnight* (1981)**

Television includes:

***Josie* (1961)**

A foremost novelist, lesbian and feminist, whose dramatic output has been small but significant, Duffy is a writer of rich imagination and plunderer of classical mythologies, 'pitched between fantasy and realism' (Frank Marcus). Her main dramatic claim to fame resides in the pioneering *Rites*, presented as part of a ▷ National Theatre workshop evening. Set in a ladies public lavatory and loosely based on ▷ Euripides' *The Bacchae*, *Rites*, with its collection of women, can be seen as a precursor of ▷ Nell Dunn's *Steaming.* But it is considerably more audacious in its mix of classical and modern ritual (a latter-day chorus inveighing against daily frustrations) and violence (the murder of a transvestite lesbian). It is a brave and questioning play that prefigures many of the concerns of female playwrights of the past decade about language, territory, gender and making the personal public and political. *Solo* and *Old Tyme* are other studies based on the mythological characters of Narcissus and Uranus respectively. *A Nightingale in Bloomsbury Square*, by contrast, is more of a bio-drama-cum-monologue around the figure of Virginia Woolf, nudged on by Vita Sackville-West and Freud.

TRY THESE:
▷Sharman Macdonald's *When I Was a Girl I Used to Scream and Shout* for another example of female privacy made public; innumerable subsequent plays by writers like ▷Caryl Churchill, ▷Pam Gems, and ▷Sarah Daniels, and women's groups like Scarlet Harlets, with women at the centre of the action.

DUMAS, Alexandre (fils) [1824–95]

French dramatist and novelist

Plays include:

***La Dame aux Camélias* (variously translated as *The Lady of the Camellias*, *Heartsease*, but most often as *Camille*; 1851), *Le Demi-Monde* (1855), *Le Fils Naturel* (*The Natural Son*; 1858), *Francillon* (1857)**

TRY THESE:
▷Zola's *Nana* rings the changes on the courtesan theme; ▷Pinero for the 'woman with a past' in *The Second Mrs Tanqueray*; ▷G.B.

In general, Dumas fils' worthy studies of contemporary problems of the bourgeois family have survived much less well on stage than have adaptations of the yarns of his reprobate father (*The Three Musketeers*, *The Count of Monte Cristo*, etc). However, his first play, *La Dame aux Camélias*, remains one of the most potent myths of the present day, and there is often a version running somewhere in London (even though it is generally the opera version *La Traviata*). Modern permutations of *La Dame aux Camélias* include ▷ Terence Rattigan's *Variation on a Theme*, and references in ▷ Tennessee Williams; and it is interesting that the two most recent London versions have been by women writers, both of whom have re-assessed Camille in terms of her relationship to society and the values of the times. ▷ Pam Gems' *Camille* (▷ RSC Stratford 1984, London 1985) made most of the characters a good deal less high-minded (especially Alfred's father, who becomes improbably wicked instead of improbably noble) and stressed the power of money as the driving force in society, while still giving Frances Barber the chance not to leave a dry eye in the house. Nancy Sweet's thrilling ▷ Brechtian *Camille* (Old Red Lion, 1987) turned the play into a rehearsal directed by a tyrannical Dumas, who made the real-life Alphonsine (Marguerite) and others re-enact his version of their lives; she tries and fails to escape by tearing down the blood-smeared curtains of the set. This version deserves a wider audience.

Shaw for an attack on this kind of play in *Mrs Warren's Profession*; ▷Tennessee Williams for echoes of the theme in *A Streetcar Named Desire* and *Camino Real*; ▷Pam Gems for feminist re-assessments of other mythical/legendary figures such as Piaf, Queen Christina.

DUNBAR, Andrea [1965–]

British dramatist

Plays include:

***The Arbor* (1980), *Rita Sue and Bob Too* (1981), *Shirley* (1986)**

Andrea Dunbar sent *The Arbor*, her first play, written at the age of fifteen, to the Royal Court Young Writer's Festival. It was produced at the Theatre Upstairs in March 1980 and transferred to the main stage in an expanded version. It is a bleak study of life on a council estate in Bradford, of the violence and deprivation of family life in the midst of urban decay. Sex offers the only pleasure, and that is seen to lead to abuse and pregnancy. Dunbar was seen to mark a return to the Royal Court's heyday of finding and championing work by working-class writers.

Brought up on a council estate on the outskirts of Bradford, Dunbar has never left it. *Rita Sue and Bob Too* followed a year after *The Arbor*, as a companion piece to it, but her next play, commissioned from the Court, took five years to arrive. Her plays have presented a stark account of the frustrations and impoverishment of economic deprivation, and she writes with a remarkable ear for nuances of language. *Shirley*, in its unsentimental non-moralising attitude to its heroines – Shirley and her mother – is like *A Taste of Honey* for the 1980s.

The film *Rita Sue and Bob Too* was developed from the play of the same name and incorporated sections from *The Arbor*. It was filmed on the council estate where Dunbar lives, and provoked the same kind of critical controversy as her plays: does Dunbar offer a patronising and unnecessarily bleak account of working-class life, or is that how it is? Andrea Dunbar remains unimpressed and continues to live in Bradford with her children.

TRY THESE:
▷Shelagh Delaney's *A Taste of Honey* for obvious echoes; ▷Arnold Wesker for affinities with the gritty social realism of family life; ▷Jim Cartwright's *Road*, ▷Christina Reid's *Joyriders*, ▷Julia Kearsley and ▷Ayshe Raif are other like-minded contemporaries.

DUNN, Nell [1936–]

British novelist and dramatist

Plays include:

***I Want* (with Adrian Henry, 1972; staged 1982), *Steaming* (1981), *The Little Heroine* (1988)**

Television includes:

***Up the Junction* (1963), *Every Breath You Take* (1988)**

Films include:

Poor Cow

Novelist, and stage and television writer, London-born Dunn made her name in 1963 with the award-winning television play

TRY THESE:
▷Maureen Duffy's *Rites* and ▷Sharman Macdonald's *When I Was a Girl I Used to Scream and Shout* for other pictures of female intimacies unveiled; ▷Pam Gems' *Dusa, Fish, Stas and Vi* for women under pressure finding support in each other; ▷Clean Break's *The*

Up the Junction, a gritty tale of down-and-out urban life that summed up a whole era. She followed that up with *Poor Cow*, subsequently filmed by Ken Loach.

Dunn has continued to explore the female situation with sympathy. Her most famous stage play, *Steaming* (which started out at the Theatre Royal, Stratford before transferring to the West End and being filmed), was hailed on both sides of the sexual politics divide as a popular breakthrough. However, directed by Roger Smith with an eye definitely on the satirical, this apparent celebration of female solidarity, set in a public Turkish bath threatened with closure, posed more problems about voyeurism and the male gaze than it answered, and could be seen as a more populist successor to ▷ Maureen Duffy's *Rites* without the moral clout. Dunn's most recent stage play, *The Little Heroine*, staged by the Southampton Nuffield Theatre, is another variation on exploring the vulnerabilities – and strengths – of women, this time through the example of a young heroin junkie and her successful kicking of the habit. *Every Breath You Take*, screened by Granada television in 1988, was another exploration of a woman under pressure, a single mother whose son is discovered to have diabetes.

River That Ran Away is a powerful prison-based portrait of a heroin addict's rehabilitation through therapy; ▷C.P. Taylor's *Withdrawal Symptoms* takes withdrawal from heroin and from Empire together, in a fine study of the personal and the political.

DURANG, Christopher [1949–]

American dramatist and actor

Plays include:

***I Don't Generally Like Poetry But Have You Read 'Trees'* (with ▷ Albert Innaurato; 1972), *The Mitzi Gaynor Story, or Gyp* (1973), *The Idiots Karamazov* (1974), *Death Comes to us All, Mary Agnes* (1975), *When Dinah Shore Ruled the Earth* (with ▷ Wendy Wasserstein; 1975), *Das Lusitania Songspiel* (with Sigourney Weaver; 1976), *The Vietnamization of New Jersey* (1977), *A History of the American Film* (1978), *Sister Mary Ignatius Explains It All For You/The Actor's Nightmare* (1979), *Beyond Therapy* (1981), *Titanic* (1983), *The Baby and the Bathwater* (1983), *The Marriage of Bette and Boo* (1985), *Laughing Wild* (1987)**

Films include:

***Beyond Therapy* (1987)**

Whether you regard him as the quintessential American 'diaper dramatist' – Benedict Nightingale's term for what he sees as the terminal self-absorption of Durang and his literary peers – or as a tough-minded satirist lashing out at his Catholic upbringing, the sweet-faced Durang is an idiosyncratic absurdist who writes deceptively fast, bright-eyed plays about dark and furious subjects. His earlier works were primarily parodies and often written in collaboration with fellow Yale Drama School graduates ▷ Wendy Wasserstein, ▷ Albert Innaurato, and the actress Sigourney Weaver (who starred in *Alien*). On his own, he wrote the zany comic circus *A History of the American Film*, in which a variety of actors play screen icons from Cagney and Bogie to – most memorably – Tony Perkins in *Psycho*. More recently, the tone has darkened. In *Sister Mary Ignatius Explains It All For You*, his best-known, longest-running play, four former students of an authoritarian nun return to her classroom to exact revenge for her wrong-headed instruction. *The Baby and the Bathwater* and *The Marriage of Bette and Boo* (a son's episodic narration of his parents' horrific marriage) are blackly and anarchically humorous depictions of families in crisis.

As an actor, Durang has appeared in several of his plays including the two most recent ones.

TRY THESE:
▷Mary O'Malley's *Once A Catholic* for contrasting take-offs of Catholic dogma; ▷Wendy Wasserstein, ▷Ted Tally, ▷Albert Innaurato for other Playwrights' Horizons-schooled authors fuelled by familial disorder; ▷Jules Feiffer's *Grown Ups* for locating that domestic intersection where home and hatred meet, also ▷Tony Craze's *Atonement*; ▷De Filippo's *Ducking Out*; see also ▷Alan Ayckbourn for recent anatomies of families.

DURAS, Marguerite [1904–]

French novelist, dramatist and writer of screenplays

Plays include:

***Le Square* (*The Square*; 1965), *La Musica* (1965), *Les Eaux et les Forêts* (*The Waters and the Forests*; 1965), *Le Shaga* (1967), *L'Amante anglaise* (*A Place Without Doors*, or *The Lovers of Viorne*; (1968), *Suzanna Adler* (1971), *India Song* (1973; commissioned by the**

TRY THESE:
▷Hélène Cixous, who was also born in a French colony, and who writes about what was formerly French Indo-China, but with quite different intent;

▷ National Theatre but not performed), *L'Eden-Cinéma* (*Eden Cinema*; 1977), *Savannah Bay* (1984)

Screenplays include:
***Hiroshima mon amour* (1960)**

Marguerite Duras was born near Saigon in what was then French Indo-China; her recollections of these childhood years have been used for her novel *Le Barrage Contre le Pacifique* (*The Sea Wall*; 1950), her play *Eden Cinema*, and her autobiographical novel *L'Amant* (*The Lover*; 1984). She is known primarily as a novelist (and won the 1984 Goncourt prize), but her novels transfer well to radio, stage or screen, and it is characteristic of her methods to rework material into different forms and to try to break down the boundaries between media. Her first play, *The Square*, was taken from her novel of the same name; *A Place Without Doors* is the second version of a play about a horrifying real-life murder, and she turned it into a novel as well, treating the story from a different point of view each time; *Vera Baxter* has as complicated a history, and became a film at one stage. Most of her characters are women, and they suffer; they are often in love, about to take leave of their lovers, or abandoned by them. The plays are not linear, but unfold gradually like petals and the dialogue is full of hesitations, pauses, fragments of memory, ellipses, and the sudden recollection of violent or painful events. The story is not explained, sometimes there is only a stream of discourse, with questions left about motives or ideas or even identity. Duras is concerned with the processes of the artist's own mind rather than those of society, and with problems of language, rather than ideas or a story line.

▷Beckett for the recurring theme of the nature of memory; Alain Robbe-Grillet and Nathalie Sarraute for moving freely between novel, play and film.

Savannah Bay
This ninety-minute two-handed Proustian play was written for Madeleine Renaud, who played an ageing actress visited each day by a girl who may be her grandchild, and with whom she reconstructs the story of her daughter Savannah, who met a lover, gave birth, and later drowned in Savannah Bay in Siam. Both characters obsessively relive this story and gradually unfold it in a dream-like and elliptical text, with recurring images of two lovers on a white rock; it has strong resemblances to *Eden Cinema*, where again there is a piecing together of memories by an old and a young woman. It was beautifully produced in Britain by ▷ Foco Novo in 1988, with the main theme echoed by the black mirror-glass floor, rocks, and white gauzy curtains.

DÜRRENMATT, Friedrich [1921–]
Swiss dramatist

Plays include:
***It Is Written* (1947), *The Blind Man* (1948), *Romulus the Great* (1949), *The Marriage of Mr Mississippi* (1952), *An Angel Comes To Babylon* (1953), *The Visit* (1956), *The Physicists* (1962), *The Meteor* (1966), *King John* (1968), *Play Strindberg* (1969)**

The son of a Protestant clergyman, Dürrenmatt was brought up amidst a highly educated, creative, and distinguished family and their friends. After studying at the Universities of Bern and Zurich, he decided to commit himself full-time to writing. Since his first successful play, *It Is Written*, in 1947, he has become one of the leading dramatists in the German language, achieved a world-wide fame, and been recognised as one of the world's leading dramatic theorists. Clearly influenced by the pre-war German Expressionists and conspicuously by ▷ Brecht, Dürrenmatt's particular gift is a brilliant sense of theatricality allied to an acute perception of the moral dilemmas of the contemporary world. Unlike Brecht, Dürrenmatt's gripping plots and fascinating characters, his ability to chill in the midst of grotesque comedy, the clarity with which he raises great issues of personal and public morality, lead not towards an argument for hopeful political change, but towards despair. Although his characters frequently achieve a transcending dignity and even heroism, they do so in a world which renders individual action and sacrifice irrelevant. Although much of his work is built on the form of classical Greek tragedy, this sense of individual irrelevance denies the possibility

TRY THESE:
For Expressionist influences on his style, ▷Wedekind, Toller and Kaiser; for political themes and epic theatre see ▷Brecht; for a comparison with other German contemporary writing, see ▷Max Frisch.

of catharsis. To Dürrenmatt, the human condition is unchangeable and meaningless, and best examined through sardonic comedy. Believing that art is most effective 'where it is least suspected', his plays – despite the depth of thought and feeling which they contain –are above all else thoroughly gripping and entertaining. *The Visit* was the subject of a famous production by the Lunts on Broadway in the '50s and subsequently brought to London in 1960; *The Physicists* was revived by The RSC at the Aldwych also in the early 1960s.

The Visit

The ageing millionairess Claire Zachanassian returns to her economically depressed home town, raising local expectations of a substantial act of charity. However, the millionairess is bent on vengeance on the man who wronged her many years before, the town's most honoured citizen, Alfred Ill. Finding that she was pregnant by him, he denied that the child was his and bribed two men to assert that she was no better than a prostitute, with the result that she left the town destitute and in disgrace. Since that time she has diligently whored and married her way to a fortune, and the price she demands for the town to share her wealth is the death of Alfred Ill. At first the townspeople express shock and disdain for such a proposal, but the power of money is already demonstrated by the presence in the old woman's retinue of the two perjurers from her trial, tracked down, blinded and castrated by her, and forced to work as her servants. Soon the townsfolk – including Alfred's own family – are buying luxuries on credit. They then discover that Claire Zachanassian owns the local factories, and has closed them deliberately to achieve her ends. Alfred abandons the struggle to save himself and is strangled by the townspeople during a celebration of the town's new wealth. The old woman gives her money to the town, and is cheered on her departure.

DYER, Charles (Raymond) [1928–]

British dramatist, actor and director

Plays include:

***Clubs Are Sometimes Trumps* (written as C. Raymond Dyer; 1948) *Rattle of a Simple Man* (1962), *Staircase* (1966)**

Dyer's first play, *Clubs Are Sometimes Trumps*, was followed by nine more (all as C. Raymond Dyer) before *Rattle of a Simple Man* brought critical and commercial acclaim. His practical experience in the theatre shows in efficient, well-constructed plays that are commercially viable with small casts and simple sets, but his quality lies in the vitality and richness of his writing, the sensitivity with which he presents his characters and the subjects which he has tackled. His major plays, *Rattle of a Simple Man* (about a prostitute and a football fan) and *Staircase*, handle subjects and characters rarely treated in theatre – *Staircase*, was extensively cut by the Lord Chamberlain's Office – and centre on dependence and our attempt to escape loneliness. This is not a theatre of action but of need. In his characters Dyer shows the audience their own inadequacies and fears; but while stripping away self-illusion he also offers hope and a lot of laughs.

As an actor, Dyer made his debut at Crewe in ▷ Terence Rattigan's *While the Sun Shines*. He has worked widely, mainly in the provinces, ranging from ▷ Shakespeare to tours of *Worm's Eye View* and *Dry Rot*.

TRY THESE:
▷Genet, ▷Harvey Fierstein, ▷Larry Kramer, and ▷Martin Sherman for treatments of male homosexual relationships; for instance two-handed relationships, see ▷Manuel Puig and Tom Kempinski; ▷Pam Gems's transvestite farce *Aunt Mary* for images of the seemingly outrageous, expressing questions about society's conventional images of gender; ▷Joe Orton for a heightened sense of shock to overturn conventional attitudes; see also ▷Gay Sweatshop.

Staircase

This two-hander set in a Brixton barber's shop presents the mutual dependence of two middle-aged homosexuals: Harry, a totally bald barber, and Charlie, the ex-actor who he had picked up in a tea-shop years before and who faces a summons after being caught cross-dressing by police raiding a club. Charlie Dyer (the character carries the author's name) has created a more successful fantasy life, peopled by characters who are all anagrams of his own name, to cover a period he spent in jail on a sex charge and clings to the fact that he was once married and fathered a child. Harry is self-disgusted by his baldness and the physical side of life. The characters fascinate and repel at the same time. They are marvellous opportunities for actors, totally convincing yet offering a parallel of the struggle in any relationship. Dyer's work is totally unsentimental. At the end of the published text Dyer suggests that Harry, perhaps even the summons, perhaps all we have seen exist only in Charlie's imagination.

EDGAR, David [1948–]
British dramatist

Plays include:
***Two Kinds of Angel* (1970), *State of Emergency* (1972), *Rent, or Caught in the Act* (1972), *A Fart for Europe* (with ▷ Howard Brenton; 1973), *Operation Iska* (1973), *Dick Deterred* (1974), *Saigon Rose* (1976), *Blood Sports* (1976), *Destiny* (1976), *Wreckers* (1977), *Our Own People* (1977), *Mary Barnes* (1979), *Teendreams* (with Susan Todd; 1979), *Maydays* (1983), *Entertaining Strangers* (1985; revised version 1987), *That Summer* (1987)**

Adaptations include:
***The Life and Adventures of Nicholas Nickleby* (1980)**

Screenplays include:
***Lady Jane* (1986)**

One of the most radical dramatists in British theatre, Edgar has written for both radical touring companies and for the establishment theatres of the ▷ National Theatre and the ▷ RSC. He is active in socialist debates on theatre and culture, often appearing on platforms at conferences, and has written regularly for a number of journals, including *The New Statesman*, *New Socialist* and *Marxism Today*. He has been particularly active in anti-racist politics, both *Our Own People* and *Destiny* are studies in the racism of British life, and he has written essays for the Institute of Race Relations and for the anti-fascist journal, *Searchlight*.

Born in Birmingham, of a theatrical family, Edgar read Drama at Manchester University. After working as a journalist in Bradford, he took up full time writing in 1972 when he became a fellow in creative writing at Leeds Polytechnic. He became a Resident Playwright at Birmingham Rep in 1974, and in 1979 undertook a year's fellowship in the USA for the British Council.

Much of Edgar's early work was written for political theatre groups and for touring and repertory theatres outside London; *Wreckers* was written for ▷ 7:84, *Teendreams* for ▷ Monstrous Regiment. These plays often take up topical campaigns and political events. *Dick Deterred* was written in response to Nixon's part in Watergate, *A Fart for Europe* was written as an anti-EEC polemic at the time of Britain's entry into the EEC.

Unlike ▷ Trevor Griffiths, Edgar has chosen to base his intervention as a socialist dramatist in the theatre, believing that television is an isolating experience, while theatre has to be experienced in a collective audience. *Maydays*, an epic account of Britain from 1956 to the present, one of Edgar's major works, was produced by the ▷ RSC as one of the first new plays to be produced on the main stage at the Barbican, and established an important precedent. Edgar has said that the complicated set, which includes a moving train and a gate at Greenham Common was written in as a strategy, so that the play technically had to be put on at the main stage at the Barbican and could not be relegated to the small Pit Theatre, where new writing invariably ended up.

Edgar's greatest success, *The Life and Adventures of Nicholas Nickleby* was developed over a long period with the cast, who

TRY THESE:
▷Caryl Churchill employs a similar juxtaposition of past and present to that of *Destiny* in *Cloud Nine*; ▷Brecht is the effective originator of the dialectical theatre practised by ▷Howard Brenton, Edgar, ▷Edward Bond, ▷Trevor Griffiths and ▷John McGrath; see also ▷Adaptations; *That Summer* is about the 1984 miners' strike as is Peter Cox's *Garden of England* and Cordelia Ditton and Maggie Ford's *About Face*; *Saigon Rose's* treatment of venereal disease anticipates AIDS plays such as ▷Larry Kramer's *The Normal Heart*; *Mary Barnes'* treatment of schizophrenia links it with ▷Tom Stoppard's *Every Good Boy Deserves Favour* and ▷Heathcote Williams' *AC/DC* though their approaches are very different; ▷Tony Craze's *Shona* is another study of schizophrenia; ▷David Mercer's *In Two Minds*, and Charlotte Perkins Gilman's *The Yellow Wallpaper* are two further studies of women and madness; ▷Karim Alrawi's *A Child in the Heart* is a contemporary exploration of racism and National Front allegiances in the East End.

Tim Piggott-Smith, Morris dancers and members of the audience, in Peter Hall's promenade production of David Edgar's ***Entertaining Strangers***, National Theatre, 1987. The original version of the play had been staged by Ann Jellicoe's Colway Theatre Trust in 1985.

thoroughly researched (David Threlfall, who played Smike, studied the symptoms of rickets) and devised the play with Edgar. The result was a collaborative project and a conviction in the performances and production that is rarely seen in mainstream theatre. More recently, Edgar was invited by ▷ Ann Jellicoe to collaborate in a theatre community project in Dorset: *Entertaining Strangers* was based on research into the history of Dorchester, and devised by and for the local community. It was then given a production in revised form at the ▷ National Theatre with professional actors. Edgar has said: 'I think revolutionary ideas are hard, you have to struggle to find a way of presenting extremely complex, difficult, precise ideas'.

Destiny
Destiny was the play which established Edgar as a major dramatist, and which took him to mainstream and critical recognition. It was the first of his plays to be produced by the ▷ RSC, at The Other Place, and was so well received that it transferred to their then home, the Aldwych. The play is an analysis of fascism and racism in British culture, through its links with the imperialist past, and in the response to immigration in the 1970s. It employs a juxtaposition of a contemporary and politician at the moment of a by-election with soldiers of 1947 discussing the independence of India. In the contemporary scenes, *Destiny* explores the relation of parliamentary politics to fascist groups, and also the way in which immigration becomes a scapegoat for the problems of British society. The juxtaposition, however, establishes the historical context for the roots of British facism. The play was written as a response to the rise in National Front activity in the mid-1970s, a period in which the Anti-Nazi League (which Edgar was involved with) was a central campaign for the Left. The play acts as a warning about the conditions that give rise to totalitarianism, and draws an analogy with the position of the Jews in Germany; Adolf Hitler appears at the end, to give a warning.

EDINBURGH FESTIVAL

The Edinburgh Festival is now the biggest and best arts festival in Britain: last year it fielded over a thousand different shows. As the Fringe Festival brochure has put it: 'in all its guises and in all its forms there is nothing quite like it anywhere else in the world'. The Edinburgh Festival is actually two festivals, the official 'International Festival of Music and Drama', instituted in 1947, and the Fringe, which began in 1949. Held annually during the three weeks from mid-August to September, it is now almost a trade fair for the theatre profession; an essential forum for new writers, performers and companies. Many of Britain's literary managers, agents, and artistic directors scour the Festival each year for new talent; and many productions offered in the winter seasons at theatres all over the country will have originated at the Edinburgh Festival.

The Official Festival was initiated by the opera impresario, Rudolph Bing, then general manager of Glyndebourne, and has since imported international theatre, opera, dance companies and orchestras, and new work from British companies. ▷ T.S. Eliot, ▷ Sean O'Casey and ▷ Ionesco are among the playwrights to have had premieres of new plays at the main Festival. Under the directorship of Frank Dunlop, recent Festivals have had international themes; 1986 was an 'entente cordiale' between Britain and France, 1988 focuses on the Arts of Italy (with some sponsorship from the Italian Consulate). The Official Festival now provides one of the best opportunities to see world theatre; recent memorable Festival imports have included *Miss Julie* directed by Ingmar Bergman, *Medea* and *Macbeth* from the Japanese Ninagawa company (which were all taken up by the ▷ National Theatre for production in London) and a revival of Victor Garcia's production of *Yerma* (last seen at Daubeney's World Theatre Season) from the Nuria Espert company.

The Fringe Festival grew up spontaneously in response to the official festival, and now outnumbers it in the range of productions it offers. There is no qualification for entry in the Fringe Festival, and amateur, student and professional companies battle it out for their share of the audience. The streets of Edinburgh during the Festival are full of white-faced clowns, spear carriers, mimes and street theatre. Any group or individual can take a show to the Fringe, the only requirements are

TRY THESE:
▷Cabaret for the many cabaret acts who start out as Edinburgh fringe try-outs (Beyond the Fringe is probably the most famous, Fascinating Aida one of the most recent to put themselves on the map through their fringe run); ▷Tom Stoppard, ▷Ionesco, ▷Trevor Griffiths and ▷David Edgar have all had new plays premiered at the Edinburgh Festival; ▷Beckett had a retrospective; fringe theatre got its name from the Edinburgh Festival in referring to productions which were on the fringes of the official festival; see also ▷one person shows, for their proliferation in recent years; see ▷LIFT for another festival.

an entry in the Fringe broch1s a
stage, from pubs to church halls, schools and art galleries.

Over the past ten years the Fringe has become increasingly professionalised, often rivalling the Official Festival in the quality and innovation of its productions. Fringe Festival awards, which are offered weekly and help to attract audiences to the otherwise hidden away and unnoticed, are now also matched by the very up-market Perrier awards given at the end of the Festival and specifically aimed at ▷ cabaret performers (usually followed up by a London Perrier award winners season at the Donmar Warehouse).

However, costs have also soared along with the increasing professionalisation so whilst venues like the Traverse and particularly William Burdett Coutts' running of the Assembly Rooms (practically a mini-festival in its own right with the emphasis on the up-market end of the fringe) have deservedly flourished, the spontaneous but under funded small company or student group end of the fringe is having a harder time staying in the market. The Official Festival continues to receive financial support from the Scottish Arts Council and Edinburgh City Council.

Edinburgh too is now also rivalled by Glasgow's Mayfest held to coincide with local May Day celebrations. Quite different in emphasis, Mayfest is an entirely local initiative – it emerged out of an alliance between the local TUC, the Labour-run council and two directors of the Scottish Wildcat company – and is a vibrant mix of the indigenous (professional Scottish companies such as Wildcat, ▷ 7:84 Scotland, the Glasgow Citizens') and the community with the international. Mayfest was the first UK venue to host Whoopi Goldberg, cabaret turned film star of *The Color Purple* fame.

ELIOT, T.S. (Thomas Stearns) [1888–1965]

Anglo-American poetic dramatist

Plays include:

***Sweeney Agonistes* (1926), *The Rock* (1934), *Murder in the Cathedral* (1935), *The Family Reunion* (1939), *The Cocktail Party* (1949), *The Confidential Clerk* (1953), *The Elder Statesman* (1958)**

One of the great poets of the twentieth century, Eliot led a mid-century revival of verse drama, which ultimately failed because it assumed that the 'poetic' in the theatre was a function of the text rather than the whole theatrical process. The most innovative of his plays is *Sweeney Agonistes*, an unfinished piece which has proved very effective in performance, with its jazz rhythms and dialogue which anticipates the early ▷ Pinter. *Murder in the Cathedral* is probably the most successful of the plays because the historical subject sanctions the use of non-naturalistic dialogue, but the verse of *The Family Reunion* is probably the most flexible of the completed plays. *The Cocktail Party* tends to be given star productions from time to time but it already shows the pernicious effect on his work of Eliot's decision to adapt contemporary theatrical forms: there is an uneasy match between the poetic impulse and the drawing-room form which becomes more pronounced in his last two plays, which are (justly) seldom revived. The success of the musical *Cats*, based on his *Old Possum's Book of Practical Cats*, indicates another route which might have led Eliot, an admirer of the music-hall, to find the popular audience he craved.

TRY THESE:
▷Aeschylus, ▷Euripides, ▷Sophocles, who provided models for Eliot's plays, generally in terms of the use of the chorus, and specifically in respect of particular plots; medieval drama, particularly *Everyman*, for the inspiration for *Murder in the Cathedral*; ▷Harold Pinter for his approach to dialogue similar to *Sweeney Agonistes*; ▷Community Theatre for plays in similar form to *The Rock*; ▷Christopher Fry for contemporary verse dramas.

ELLIS, Michael J. [mid-1950s–]

British dramatist

Plays include:

***A Temporary Rupture* (1983), *Starliner 2001, a Soap Odyssey* (1984), *Chameleon* (1985)**

An East-ender of Jamaican parents, Ellis picked up various writing awards whilst still at school. *Chameleon*, the play with which he is most associated at present, was toured for a year by ▷ Temba to enthusiastic houses, despite a lukewarm reception from reviewers (who don't get it right every time, as theatre history happily shows). It is easy to see why there was the discrep-

TRY THESE:
▷Tony Marchant's *The Lucky Ones* is also an office-based saga of young folk and contrasting attitudes to 'making it'; Earl Lovelace's *The Hardware Store* is another cautionary tale connecting capitalism and the black community;

ancy, however: Ellis' office-bound two-hander is not especially sophisticated, but it is unusually satirical about its leading character, the awful, social-climbing Benjamin, and it is a brave and subversive tale against buying into the system, and the dangers of ignorance. *A Temporary Rupture* carries on in like vein as a sprightly dig at the macho insensitivity of young black males, with a jilted girlfriend getting her own back on the returning former lover and father of her child. Both plays would certainly repay further viewing.

Nigel Moffatt is a young contemporary black voice; for contrasting styles see ▷Edgar White and ▷Derek Walcott; for other black dramatists writing about being black in Britain, see ▷Mustapha Matura, ▷Caryl Phillips, ▷Tunde Ikoli and ▷Barry Reckord; see also ▷Temba.

ENGLISH, Rose [1950–]

British dramatist and performer

Plays include:

***Plato's Chair* (1983), *The Beloved* (1985), *Thee Thy Thou Thine* (1986), *Moses* (1987)**

Rose English, ex-art student and solo performer extraordinaire, has been described as 'the doyenne of the subtle, the ambiguous and the comic' (Naseem Khan), and as a performer directed as if 'by a choreographer specialising in ballets performed by pelicans' (Ros Asquith). Defying theatrical wisdom she has worked with dogs and children (who, in *Moses*, almost stole the show but had competition from a large four-poster bed, a small boat, and a Jack Russell performing with insouciant aplomb as though to the manner born). Rose English has the mischief of a child let loose in a circus, and the same wonder; she is the spirit of Bloomsbury translated to the pedestrian 1980s, a philosophical butterfly, with the curiosity of Isadora Duncan and the grace of Anna Pavlova. That she is unique is undisputable and that she was *born*, to English parentage, an army father and a posh mother (her words), is equally not in dispute. Playing with the notions of the infinite, the nature of reality, the wonder of illusion, hopefulness, and the quirky uneasy relationship between audience and performer, her 'plays' or performances have been forays into unknown waters that have left her audiences either outraged (stamping out claiming to have had more entertainment from a bus ticket) or demented with delight. Either you love her or you hate her, but Rose English is a pure original, an English eccentric not afraid to disarm and disorientate. Prior to her theatre career, she was a luminary of the performance art circuit, performing in places as diverse as Swiss Cottage's Adelaide Pool, Sherwood Forest, the Serpentine Gallery in London, and the Southampton Horse Show, often with avant-gardist Jacky Lansley and Sally Potter director (of *The Gold Diggers*).

TRY THESE:
For solo performers, see ▷Cabaret; Barry Humphries for audience engagement (a more patronising user, however, of the get-the-guest routine); Ken Campbell and The People Show for their own brands of sustained anarchy and mix of circus, music hall and pantomime conventions; women's groups with visual arts roots, such as Anna Furse and ▷Blood Group, or Tessa Schneideman's Three Women Mime, and Jacky Lansley and Fergus Early's experimental dance at X6; Annie Griffin, another solo performer with performance art antecedents, who also writes and devises her own shows, brings a similar, though different, iconoclastic wit to her work; also Ben Keaton, another minimalist; see also ▷Performance Art.

ENGLISH STAGE COMPANY (at the Royal Court)

Beginning as a way of finding a London home for productions from the Tor and Torridge Festival, the ESC was the idea of playwright Ronald Duncan, who involved businessmen Neville Blond and Greville Pike and theatre manager Oscar Lewenstein. To run it they invited actor-director George Devine (previously associated with the Young Vic School and company) and Tony Richardson (then a television director) who earlier in the 1950s had themselves tried to start a company to present the kind of plays not put on by West End managements. After proposals for other theatres fell through, they acquired a lease for the Royal Court, Sloane Square, and in 1956 opened with *The Mulberry Bush*, commissioned from novelist Angus Wilson. Duncan, himself a poet, had originally thought of this as a home for verse drama, but although the company has always been a champion of new writing this was not one of Devine's interests. The plays presented subsequently have included

TRY THESE:
Among the companies and venues particularly associated with new writing are ▷Theatre of Black Women, ▷Foco Novo, ▷Paines Plough, ▷Joint Stock, the Bush and the Tricycle; see also ▷New Writing.

many by writers politically far to the left of Duncan; members of the new company were soon carrying its banner in early demonstrations against nuclear warfare. The third production of the new company, presented within five weeks of opening, was ▷ John Osborne's *Look Back in Anger*, which had an immediate impact on British audiences and theatre workers, difficult to imagine today, and was closely linked to the general exasperation of young people at the time of Suez and the Hungarian rising.

Although the company has staged some classic revivals, it has mainly been an important venue for new writing, introducing to London, and sometimes to the world, such dramatists as ▷ Arnold Wesker, ▷ John Arden, ▷ Ann Jellicoe, ▷ David Storey, ▷ Edward Bond, ▷ Charles Wood, ▷ Christopher Hampton, ▷ Howard Barker, ▷ Howard Brenton, ▷ David Hare, ▷ N.F. Simpson, ▷ Harold Pinter and ▷ Michael Hastings, and presenting such overseas writers as ▷ Brecht, ▷ Beckett, Sartre, ▷ Ionesco and ▷ Sam Shepard. Although the company is no longer unique in producing new work, the growth of opportunities for new writers owes much to its existence.

It was the English Stage Company which encouraged leading actors to take the risk of appearing in the 'new drama', with Peggy Ashcroft in ▷ Brecht's *The Good Person of Sezchuan*, Laurence Olivier in ▷ John Osborne's *The Entertainer* (1957) and John Gielgud and Ralph Richardson in ▷ David Storey's *Home* (1970). It also established such directors as William Gaskill, Lindsay Anderson, John Dexter and Peter Gill. After Devine, Bill Gaskill took over the running of the company (1965–77), followed by Oscar Lewenstein, Nicholas Wright and Robert Kidd, Stuart Burge and, since 1979, Max Stafford-Clark.

The company played an important role in the fight against stage censorship, turning itself into a club for the presentation of ▷ Osborne's *A Patriot for Me* because of its homosexual theme, and standing up against heavy criticism over plays such as ▷ Edward Bond's *Saved*, although Jim Allen's *Perdition* was cancelled in 1987 before it opened, after a fierce onslaught from outside the theatre and disquiet from the Board (it eventually appeared elsewhere in 1988).

In 1969 the old rehearsal room at the top of the theatre, reclaimed from use as a night club, was opened as the Theatre Upstairs to provide a home for visiting fringe companies and the company's own more experimental work. Productions have ranged from ▷ Richard O'Brien's *The Rocky Horror Show* (1973) to ▷ Jim Cartwright's *Road* (1986). This intimate, adaptable space is now an important national venue which has premiered new plays by many of today's leading dramatists including ▷ Sarah Daniels, ▷ Timberlake Wertenbaker, Daniel Mornin, ▷ Louise Page, Nick Ward, ▷ Hanif Kureishi and ▷ Sue Townsend. The theatre also runs a Young People's Theatre Scheme, not only encouraging playgoing among the young but also offering them opportunities for workshops and productions of their scripts which have produced a whole new crop of writers, particularly among young black women.

The fact that the Royal Court no longer stands alone as a theatre for new writing is a measure of its success in its aims, but recognition of the artistic and critical importance of the Royal Court's activities has been a hard-won victory, and even that achievement is insufficient to guarantee financial stability. As a consequence the company not only enters into more co-production arrangements with regional theatres, but also survives thanks to a generous exchange deal with New Yorker Joe Papp, some of whose Public Theatre productions are exchanged with those of the Royal Court.

ETHEREGE, George [1634–91]

English Restoration dramatist

Plays include:

***The Comical Revenge: or, Love in a Tub* (1664), *She Would If She Could* (1668), *The Man of Mode* (1676)**

Etherege has some claims to have invented what we now call Restoration Comedy in his plays, which present fashionable,

TRY THESE:
Other Restoration comic writers such as ▷Aphra Behn, ▷William Congreve and ▷William Wycherley; other writers of comedy of manners, such as

witty, amoral characters engaged in a round of sexual intrigues in a recognisable version of contemporary London society. His own life could have been a model for one of his characters: his actress mistress, Elizabeth Barry, also had a liaison with the Earl of Rochester (identified as the original of Dorimant in *The Man of Mode*); his outrageous behaviour as ambassador in Regensburg scandalised the inhabitants and he ended his career by joining James II in exile in Paris where he died.

The contemporary canvas is broadest in *The Comical Revenge*, where the humiliation of a venereally diseased French valet at the hands of English female servants gives the play its title, and contrasts with three other plots, including a rather more 'heroic' one largely conducted in rhyming couplets. Etherege, like other Restoration dramatists, is much more open about women's sexuality than dramatists of many other periods, though his view can be inferred, not unfairly, from the title of his second play, *She Would If She Could*. As with ▷ William Wycherley, the difficulty is knowing where celebration of a society ends and criticism of it begins. Particularly in *The Man of Mode*, the only one of his plays to appear regularly in the modern repertory, the absence of an obvious authorial point of view and explicit moral judgments leads to contradictory evaluations of the characters and of the play. Clearly Sir Flopling Flutter, the man of mode of the title, is a comic butt because of his ridiculous pretensions to be fashionable but the energetic protagonist Dorimant's dealings with various potential and actual mistresses and wives are much more open to scrutiny. This can be regarded either as masterly ambiguity or as poor dramatic technique.

▷Goldsmith, ▷Sheridan, ▷Oscar Wilde, ▷Noël Coward, ▷Doug Lucie; ▷Edward Bond's *Restoration* uses conventions and themes derived from the practice of Restoration writers to make modern points.

EURIPIDES [484–406/7 BC]

Greek tragic dramatist

Surviving plays include:

***Alcestis* (438 BC), *Medea* (431 BC), *The Children of Heracles* (c 429 BC), *Hippolytus* (428 BC), *Hecuba* (c 425 BC), *The Suppliant Women* (c 420 BC), *Andromache* (c 419 BC), *Heracles* (c 416 BC), *The Trojan Women* (415 BC), *Electra* (413 BC), *Helen* (412 BC), *Iphigenia in Tauris* (c 411 BC), *Ion* (c 411 BC), *Orestes* (408 BC), *The Phoenician Women* (c 408 BC), *The Bacchae* (produced c 405 BC), *Iphigenia in Aulis* (405 BC), *Cyclops* (date unknown); *Rhesus* is also attributed to Euripides**

Euripides wrote over ninety plays during a long career but was less immediately popular than his contemporary, ▷ Sophocles. His subjects are those of the other Athenian tragic dramatists – stories of the gods and heroes, particularly those relating to the Trojan wars –but his treatment of them is more domestic and more sceptical, almost realistic and sociological rather than religious and philosophical. It was probably this aspect of his work, together with his penchant for experiments in form, that made him a controversial figure. His subsequent reputation was high, but his plays are still as elusive on the modern stage as those of the other Greek dramatists. *The Bacchae*, a very powerful treatment of the relationship between the Apollonian and the Dionysiac impulses, has been influential on various experimental theatres in the twentieth century (eg the Performance Group's *Dionysus in 69*) but the most recent large-scale staging was John Barton and Kenneth Cavander's ▷ RSC production, *The Greeks,* which used seven of Euripides' plays in its marathon cycle of the Trojan wars. This kind of approach, in which the audience is immersed in the subject matter for a large part of a day, appears to be the best hope for Greek drama in the contemporary theatre, and the popularity of marathon stagings of ▷ medieval drama, Dickens, ▷ Shakespeare's history plays and *The Mahabharata* (by ▷ Peter Brook) could encourage a revival of Greek drama.

TRY THESE:
▷Aeschylus and ▷Sophocles wrote the other surviving Greek tragedies; see ▷Artaud for a theory of theatre with close connections to *The Bacchae*; ▷T.S. Eliot, ▷Giraudoux, ▷O'Neill and ▷Soyinka (*The Bacchae of Euripides*) are among modern playwrights who have tackled themes drawn from Greek drama; ▷Caryl Churchill and ▷David Lan collaborated on the recent *Mouthful of Birds* derived from *The Bacchae*.

EVELING, (Harry) Stanley [1925–]

British dramatist

Plays include:

Come and Be Killed* (1967), *The Strange Case of Martin

TRY THESE:
▷Ionesco for Absurdist influence; ▷John Mortimer (*The Dock Brief*) for

***Richter* (1967), *The Lunatic, The Secret Sportsman, and the Woman Next Door* (1968), *Dear Janet Rosenberg, Dear Mr Kooning* (1969), *Mister* (1970), *Caravaggio, Buddy* (1972)**

Stanley Eveling was born in Newcastle-upon-Tyne and went from a working-class background to degrees in both English and Philosophy at the University of Durham. Since 1960 he has lectured in moral philosophy at the University of Edinburgh (where he is now Reader) and has also written plays with a characteristic mixture of moral questioning and wry or Surrealist humour, in which the sexes often disastrously fail to understand each other. His characters tend to be in extreme states of mind, and in his later plays often suicidal, but a sardonic humour continues throughout. Many of his plays were first performed at Edinburgh's Traverse theatre, and Charles Marowitz put on *Come and Be Killed* (Eveling's most painfully naturalistic play, dealing with abortion) and *The Lunatic...* at the Open Space in 1968, but his only real West End success has been *Dear Janet Rosenberg, Dear Mr Kooning*, in which a fifty-year-old novelist and a young female fan start a correspondence and then a relationship, competitively improvising a narrative version of it for the audience.

characters acting out fantasies, as in *Mister*; Mario Vargas Llosa's *Kathie and the Hippopotamus* and ▷Harold Pinter's *Old Times* for uncertain pasts.

EXPRESSIONISM

Expressionism as a historical phenomenon is mainly associated with Germany and the first quarter of the twentieth century, but Expressionist influence is widespread in twentieth-century drama and theatre, in terms of both production style and subject matter. Although it is notoriously hard to pin down exactly what people mean by Expressionism, its most common feature is a reaction against current versions of realism. There tends to be a concentration on the individual standing out against the dehumanising tendencies of modern civilisation, especially in relation to the horrors of World War I. This can lead both to a stress on the importance of fighting capitalism (as the prime example of dehumanisation) and to a cult of the individual (which in turn leads to worship of the super hero), although (curiously) the characters in Expressionist plays tend to be types rather than individuals. Expressionist staging is characteristically symbolic, dealing more with the landscapes of the unconscious, dreams and nightmares, than with the everyday. ▷ Büchner, whose works were 'discovered' in the late nineteenth century, ▷ Wedekind in (*Spring Awakening* and *The Lulu Plays*), and the ▷ Strindberg of such plays as *The Road to Damascus* and *Easter* are often regarded as major precursors of Expressionism.

Relatively few German Expressionist plays are now staged professionally, although there is the occasional oddity such as the ▷ Glasgow Citizens' staging of Karl Kraus's mammoth *The Last Days of Mankind*, ▷ C.P. Taylor's adaptation of Carl Sternheim's *Schippel* (which surfaced in the West End with Harry Secombe, under the title of *Plumber's Progress*), ▷ Michelene Wandor's reworking of Ernst Toller's *The Blind Goddess*, or Ballet Rambert's adaptation of Oscar Kokoschka's *Murderer Hope of Womankind*. Expressionist influence is much more widespread, particularly in terms of approaches to staging and playwriting, often mediated through ▷ Brecht's epic theatre, in a general refusal to be confined to reproducing surface realities of everyday life and a willingness to search for theatrical means of showing underlying causes. Nancy Duguid's 1980 production of ▷ Noël Greig's *Angels Descend on Paris* was praised for its Expressionistic verve and visual tableaux, and Pip Broughton's 1987 production of *Berlin Days, Hollywood Nights* also used Expressionistic techniques to great effect.

The major German dramatists associated with the movement are George Kaiser (1878–1945) and Ernst Toller (1893–1939). Kaiser, whose plays include *From Morning to Midnight* (1912) and *The Burghers of Calais* (1914); the *Gas* trilogy (1917–1920), has fared less well in recent British productions than has Toller. Kaiser's *Flight to Venice* (about Georges Sand and Alfred De

TRY THESE:
Adaptations of Franz Kafka's novels usually stress their Expressionist elements; among the many dramatists influenced by Expressionism are ▷Eugene O'Neill, Elmer Rice, ▷Tennessee Williams, ▷Sean O'Casey, the ▷Capek brothers and ▷Mayakovsky; Peter Stein's version of O'Neill's *The Hairy Ape*, brought to the ▷National Theatre in 1987, is probably the most monumental expression of Expressionist theatre to have been seen in Britain for years; for contemporary Expressionistic approaches see ▷Red Shift and ▷Steven Berkoff.

Musset) at the Gate in 1986, and Sue Dunderdale's production of *From Morning to Midnight* at the Soho Poly in 1987, were both received politely as mildly interesting historical curiosities but there was little sense of excitement. Toller's plays, which include *Transfiguration* (1918), *Masses and Men* (1920), *The Machine Wreckers* (1922), *Hinkemann* (1923), *Hoppla! We're Alive* (1927), manifest both his pacifism (a result of his experiences at the front during World War I) and his hatred of the effects of industrial capitalism on the workers. Their very heightened language can be emotionally bludgeoning, and the tone can be virtually hysterical, but there are compensations. *Hinkemann*, staged at the Old Red Lion by The Group in 1988, shows the unemployment, moral degradation and impotence of the working class in 1920s Germany through the story of Hinkemann who, castrated by a battle wound, joins a circus to find work biting the heads off rats, while his wife is seduced by his best friend. ▷ The Glasgow Citizens' also staged *The Machine Wreckers* in 1985.

FAGON, Alfred [1937–86]

Plays include:

***11 Josephine House* (1972), *Death of a Black Man* (1975), *Four Hundred Pounds* (1983), *Lonely Cowboy* (1985)**

Jamaican born Fagon went to Britain in 1955, worked on the railways and served in the army before emerging as a professional actor and dramatist in the 1970s. He died while out jogging and, before any of his friends found out, was buried anonymously because the police believed he was a vagrant. As his subsequent *Times* obituary put it, 'his plays take as their theme the relationship between the cultures of the English and Caribbean peoples, their friendships and conflicts'. This theme is characteristically treated in the form of a comedy of manners with an underlying seriousness as in *11 Josephine House* with its black family trying to adjust to the temptations of English life, particularly in the form of the white woman who causes the black preacher's fall from grace. In *Four Hundred Pounds* TeeCee's sudden refusal to pot the black in a snooker game on ideological grounds loses him and his more pragmatic gambling partner that sum of money, and in *Lonely Cowboy* a couple's attempt to start a café leads first to comedy and then tragedy as the values of a world they try to ban from their café reassert themselves.

TRY THESE:
11 Josephine House has affinities with ▷Molière's *Tartuffe* and ▷Baldwin's *Amen Corner*; Fagon's work offers interesting points of comparison with that of other British black writers such as ▷Michael Ellis, ▷Mustapha Matura, ▷Tunde Ikoli, and ▷Caryl Phillips; ▷Michael Abbensetts and ▷Trevor Rhone also handle racial conflicts through humour.

FAIRBANKS, Tasha [1948–]

British dramatist

Plays include:

***Sidewalk* (1976), *Wedlocked* (1978), *Fruit of the Earth* (1979), *Lucy and the Steel Queen* (1979), *Mama's Gone a-Hunting* (1980), *Curfew* (1981), *From the Divine* (1983), *Now Wash Your Hands, Please* (1984), *PULP* (1985), *Ties* (1985), *Fixed Deal* (1986), *Up For Demolition* (1987), *Hotel Destiny* (1987), *A Private View* (for Graeae; 1988)**

Television includes:

***My Blue-Eyed Son* (1979), *Army of the Night* (1981)**

Radio includes:

***Salt of the Earth* (1980)**

The versatile Fairbanks, (she plays saxophone, is a ventriloquist and has won a Plays & Players award for Best New Actress) is co-founder of Siren, the ebullient radical feminist/lesbian theatre company, as well as playwright. Despite a prolific turnover – from a spoof Philip Marlowe thriller (*PULP*), to sci-fi fantasies on male violence, militarism, and separatism (Siren's *Mama's Gone a-Hunting*, *From the Divine* and *Curfew*), – she has never quite broken into the mainstream (though she has written for the BBC). Few lesbian playwrights (or admitted ones) have. At her worst, Fairbanks' scripts can be over-dense and heavy-handed (*A Private View* on the subject of disability is a case in point) and in need of firm editing, perhaps because, as with much work on the fringe, her scripts are often the result of a collaborative process of workshops and improvisations with the companies concerned. At her best, along with Siren's subversive invention,

TRY THESE:
▷Anne Caulfield's *Cowboys* for ▷Red Shift and ▷Bryony Lavery's *Calamity* for a different kind of reassessment of the Western myth; the American group Split Britches offer even more entertaining radical departures; see also ▷lesbian theatre. For other post-Falklands explorations, see ▷Tony Marchant's *Coming Home*; ▷Noël Greig's *Poppies* for another gay perspective on militarism; for a case of double identity, see ▷Tom Stoppard generally and ▷Alan Bennett's *The Old Country*.

Fairbanks' scripts are like imaginative Molotov cocktails, launched into the arena of sexual politics with energy and humour. *From the Divine* used the hysteria of the Falklands to explore ideas about war, machismo, power, and female stereotypes through a 1940s ENSA concert party setting, a Master of Ceremonies, a ventriloquist's dummy and a 'bolshie angel in a plastic mac'. *PULP*, a lesbian thriller on the theme of double identities combined glamour with sleaze in its parody of the femme fatale images of the Hollywood 1950s, alongside issues of betrayal, deceit, McCarthyism and espionage. *Up for Demolition*, on the other hand, set in a derelict house which a local women's group are trying to turn into a knitting co-op, is rather more in line with predictable radical feminist agit-prop, but takes an interestingly socio-historical approach to the way oppression gets passed on, and, by introducing links with the past, suggests how the past can help to make changes in the future. Her latest piece for Siren, a lesbian Western, *Hotel Destiny*, however, was less constructive though it still found some rib-tickling ways of injecting old Western clichés with alternative new lesbian life. *From the Divine*, *PULP* and *Hotel Destiny* have all been warmly received when they have toured, showing there is an ever-increasing demand nationwide for such alternative images.

FARCE/LIGHT COMEDY

Farce is both the more popular and the more intellectually respectable of these two forms, at least since Eric Bentley and the other theorists got at it. It is also, with ▷ musicals and ▷ thrillers, one of the current mainstays of the commercial theatre. The reasons for its popularity may throw a disturbing light on the modern world, especially if one believes the theorists about its subversive qualities and its role in satisfying our unspoken urges. However, what is certainly true is that farce is the most technically difficult of all dramatic forms. Even ▷ Ben Travers needed the ferocious criticism of Tom Walls to produce his classics, and the history of the stage is littered with the ruins of those who ignored Garrick's aphorism that, 'Comedy, sir, is a serious business'. Bamber Gascoigne's attempt to outdo ▷ Feydeau (*Big in Brazil*, Old Vic, 1984) proved that you could have an excellent cast and good ideas, use all Feydeau's tricks, and still not be very funny.

The most successful school of postwar British farce began at the Whitehall Theatre. Brian Rix started acting with the Donald Wolfit company in 1942 (which may be significant of something) and after the war he founded his own company, Rix Theatrical Productions. In 1950 he put on Colin Morris' *Reluctant Heroes*, which ran for four years; its success led to a series of long-running plays which became known as 'Whitehall farces', including John Chapman's *Dry Rot* (1954) and *Simple Spymen* (1958), Ray Cooney's *One for the Pot* (1961) and *Chase Me, Comrade!* (1964). The company later moved to the Garrick with a less successful series of farces, including Ray Cooney and Tony Hilton's *Stand By Your Bedouin* (1967). Rix played leading roles in most of these plays with amiable gusto, and many of them became widely known through being televised. He is a Trustee of Ray Cooney's Theatre of Comedy Company, which hands on the torch of harmless (more or less) British farce, though it has also played ▷ Ayckbourn and ▷ Orton.

Ray Cooney appeared in *Dry Rot* and *Simple Spymen* at the Whitehall, then wrote for them (with Tony Hilton) his first play, *One for the Pot*, a classic farce with Brian Rix playing four brothers, and also *Chase Me, Comrade!*, about a defecting Russian ballet dancer, also played by Brian Rix. Other successful farces followed, three written with John Chapman, *Not Now, Darling* (Strand, 1967), *Move Over, Mrs Markham* (Vaudeville, 1969), and *There Goes the Bride* (Criterion, 1974), and one with Gene Stone, *Why not Stay for Breakfast?* (Apollo, 1973), all in the genteel British line of cheerful suggestive sex rather than the manic and more explicit style of ▷ Feydeau or ▷ Orton, and guaranteed to please the coach parties. He formed the

TRY THESE:
For theatrical writing using elements of farce ▷Peter Barnes, ▷Alan Bennett, ▷Dario Fo, ▷Michael Frayn, ▷W.S. Gilbert, ▷Goldoni, ▷Ronald Harwood, ▷Hecht and McArthur, ▷N.C. Hunter, ▷Ionesco, ▷Jarry, ▷Jonson, ▷Kaufman and Hart, ▷Labiche, ▷Mike Leigh, ▷Doug Lucie, ▷Nestroy, ▷Ostrovsky, ▷Pinero, ▷Terence Rattigan, ▷Peter Shaffer, ▷Tom Stoppard, and ▷Oscar Wilde.

'Theatre of Comedy' Company in 1983, cannily bringing in Thelma Holt as his administrator, to run both the Shaftesbury and the Ambassadors'; they put on his own plays, *Run for Your Wife!* (1983, still running in 1988) and *Two Into One* (1984), with great success, and in spite of the occasional flop (such as *An Italian Straw Hat* in 1986) they have done well, bringing in a wide public to efficient, slick, and very funny shows with reliable actors of the quality of Maureen Lipman, Richard Briers, Paul Eddington, and Leonard Rossiter.

Farce does seem to appeal to something basic in human nature, and looks like lasting as long as the theatre. Light comedy, on the other hand, comes and goes, and at the moment seems to have gone, dying with the society in which you did wear evening dress in the dress circle, the world of the matinée idol and the actress with 'charm'. Although the term is Victorian – such delightful works as O'Keefe's *Wild Oats* and ▷ Boucicault's *London Assurance* were probably thought of as 'light comedies' – the genre reached its peak in the first thirty or forty years of this century, from Henry Arthur Jones to ▷ Noël Coward by way of ▷ Maugham and Frederick Lonsdale. Its major features are an absence of strong emotion, an unquestioning acceptance of its audience's values, an air of rather conscious sophistication, and some very good parts for the sort of player who looks well in evening dress and can handle epigrams. Most of ▷ Coward still revives well, and some of ▷ Maugham, but Lonsdale on the whole does not – for instance, *Canaries Sometimes Sing* (Albery, 1987) was found to have dated badly.

It is perhaps to be regretted that the world has changed, and that the playgoer who wants an undemanding evening out has nowhere to go except farces, thrillers and revivals – even modern musicals tend to have a 'message' – but there is no point in pretending that it is not so.

FARQUHAR, George [1678–1707]

Irish dramatist

Plays include:

***Love and a Bottle* (1698), *The Constant Couple, or A Trip to the Jubilee* (1699), *Sir Harry Wildair, being a sequel to The Constant Couple* (1701), *The Inconstant, or The Way to Win Him* (1702), *The Twin Rivals* (1702), *The Stage Coach* (1704), *The Recruiting Officer* (1706), *The Beaux' Stratagem* (1707)**

Farquhar left Trinity College, Dublin, to become an actor but gave up the boards when he injured his opponent in the duel at the end of ▷ Dryden's *The Indian Emperor* and took to writing. He married a woman he mistakenly believed to be an heiress and died in poverty aged only 29.

His writing is witty and stylish, and rather warmer than that of ▷ Congreve and ▷ Wycherley who precede him. The later plays are more closely drawn from life with a very positive attitude to the situation of women in his society. In *The Constant Couple* he created the role of Harry Wildair, a kind-hearted rake, which became a celebrated breeches part for Peg Woffington and other actresses for many years, but he is now best known for his two last plays *The Recruiting Officer* and *The Beaux' Stratagem*. Set in Lichfield, the latter shows two London beaux seeking country marriages to restore their fortunes, one posing as his own elder brother, the other as his servant. It makes a case for divorce on the grounds of incompatability and, in introducing Lady Bountiful, added an expression to the English language.

TRY THESE:
▷Aphra Behn, ▷Congreve, ▷Etherege, ▷Vanbrugh and ▷Wycherley for other 'Restoration' dramatists; ▷Goldsmith and ▷Sheridan wrote within broadly similar conventions; ▷Noël Coward, ▷Oscar Wilde, ▷Doug Lucie, ▷Mike Leigh and ▷Alan Ayckbourn for more contemporary comedy of manners.

The Recruiting Officer

Set in Shropshire, where Sgt Kite is recruiting Silvia, the daughter of a local Justice, enlists, disguised as a man, so that she can be near her lover. An outstanding production by Bill Gaskill, in the ▷ National Theatre's opening season at the Old Vic in 1963 (partly influenced by ▷ Brecht's adaptation *Trumpets and Drums*), emphasised the clarity of Farquhar's presentation of his divided society and its power structures so that the affected mannerisms which had previously tended to suffice for 'Restoration style' began to lose their foothold in contemporary productions.

FEIFFER, Jules [1929–]

American dramatist

Plays include:

***The Explainers* (1961), *Crawling Arnold* (1961), *The World of Jules Feiffer* (1962), *Little Murders* (1967), *The Unexpurgated Memories of Bernard Mergendeiler* (1967), *Feiffer's People* (1968), *God Bless* (1968), *The White House Murder Case* (1970), *Munro* (1971), *Watergate Classics* (1973), *Knock Knock* (1976), *Hold Me* (1977), *Grown Ups* (1981), *A Think Piece* (1982)**

Films include:

***Little Murders* (1971), *Carnal Knowledge* (1971), *Popeye* (1980)**

'It's murder out there,' says the beleaguered father of the Newquist clan in Jules Feiffer's *Little Murders*, but in the New York landscape of this writer's plays it's often murder inside, as well. For although the Bronx-born Feiffer is capable of great belly laughs and a wise, often self-mockingly existential humour, his strengths lie in his relentless chroniclings of violence, both domestic and social. In *Little Murders*, the urban decay outdoors comes to roost inside the family, with a household on the verge of anarchy reduced to taking potshots at passers-by out of the window. His later, *Grown Ups* recalls no writer more than ▷ Strindberg, in its depiction of an affluent New York family spiralling into emotional chaos. Occasionally, he misses his target: *A Think Piece*, his 1982 play about the dreary domestic routine of one Betty Castle, is too vaguely self-pitying to have much impact. As a long-time cartoonist for *The Village Voice*, Feiffer is equally well-known for his sketch plays (*Feiffer's People*, *Hold Me*), the best moments of which have the subversive punch of a good drawing, and his political satire (*Watergate Classics*, a spoof of the Nixon years). His plays have, not surprisingly, fared better off-Broadway than on, and *Little Murders* is in the history books as the first American play the ▷ RSC ever performed (in 1969).

TRY THESE:
▷Strindberg, ▷Edward Albee for households on the boil; ▷Murray Schisgal's *An American Millionaire* for a Feifferesque black farce about violence and affluence; ▷Neil Simon for more sanitised versions of New York angst; ▷Christopher Durang and early ▷Arthur Kopit (especially *Oh Dad Poor Dad*) for comparably deranged families.

FEYDEAU, Georges [1862–1921]

French dramatist

Plays include:

***Tailleur pour Dames* (*The Ladies' Tailor*; 1886), *Champignol malgré lui* (*Champignol in spite of himself*; 1892), *L'Hôtel du Libre-Echange* (*Hotel Paradiso* or *A Little Hotel on the Side*; 1894), *Un Fil à la patte* (*Cat Among the Pigeons* or *Get Out of my Hair*; 1894), *Le Dindon* (*Ruling the Roost* or *Sauce for the Goose*; 1896), *La Dame de chez Maxim* (*The Lady from Maxim's*; 1899), *La Puce à L'Oreille* (*A Flea in Her Ear*; 1907), *Occupe-toi d'Amelie* (*Look After Lulu*; 1908), *Feula Mère de Madame* (*My Late Mother-in-law*; 1908), *Léonie est en Avance* (*Any Minute Now*; 1911), *Hortense a Dit: 'Je m'en fous'* (*Hortense Said 'Stuff it'*; 1916)**

Feydeau's middle period plays are the archetype of French farce. The principal characters are Parisian bourgeois, their major driving force is extra-connubial lust, and the basic source of the humour is their ever more desperate attempts to avoid being found out. Although no respectable married woman is ever seduced by her husband's best friend, it is not for want of trying on either side. The plots seem to have been constructed by a mad watchmaker, but the status quo is always restored at the end. His later one-act plays (after he left his wife) are more misanthropic, more loosely constructed, and need more careful production; the recent ▷ RSC attempt to make one play of three of these *Scenes from a Marriage*, 1986) misfired badly. (The three plays included were *Hortense said 'Stuff it'*, *Any Minute Now*, and *My Late Mother-in-law*.) However, *The Lady from Maxim's*

TRY THESE:
▷Labiche for nineteenth-century French farce; ▷Joe Orton for the occasional casual cruelty of the humour (eg the man with no roof to his mouth, the character with bad breath, the comic foreigners); perhaps the contemporary English equivalent is Ray Cooney's farces, also invariably focused on extra-marital lust.

and *A Little Hotel on the Side*, both adapted by John Mortimer, did well at the ▷ National Theatre in 1977 and 1984, and the Orange Tree production of *Sauce for the Goose* in 1986 showed how effectively the full-length plays can be produced in a small space without elaborate scenery.

A Little Hotel on the Side
It would be a waste of time to detail the whole plot of this farce, but in Act Two (set in the eponymous hotel) the attempt of M Pinglet (a building contractor) to spend the night with Mme Paillardin is frustrated by the presence in the hotel of their friend M Mathieu and his four daughters, M Paillardin (an architect, there as an officer of the court, who quite reasonably believes M Mathieu's daughters to be ghosts), M Pinglet's nephew and the maid Victoire (who alone get what they came for), the hotel manager's habit of drilling holes in the wall to admire what is going on, and a final visit from the Vice Squad.

FIELD DAY
Northern Irish theatre company

Field Day was formed by the dramatist ▷ Brian Friel and the actor Stephen Rea in Derry in 1980. As well as being a theatre company Field Day is a forum for debate and analysis of current political and cultural issues in Ireland through the medium of pamphlets, books and a large-scale anthology of Irish literature; its other directors are Seamus Deane, David Hammond, Seamus Heaney and Tom Paulin. Field Day's opening production was ▷ Friel's hugely successful *Translations* and they have also staged his *The Communication Cord*, Frank McGuinness's *The Carthaginians* and ▷ Athol Fugard's *Boesman and Lena*. Among their adaptations are Friel's version of Chekhov's *The Cherry Orchard*, Paulin's *The Riot Act* (a version of ▷ Sophocles' *Antigone*) and Derek Mahon's *High Time* (a version of ▷ Molière's *École des maris*). Among their most recent productions are ▷ Thomas Kilroy's *Double Cross*, on the themes of national identity, role playing and betrayal as manifested in an imaginative re-creation of the lives of two Irishmen, William Joyce (notorious as 'Lord Haw-Haw') and Brendan Bracken (the confidant of Winston Churchill); and ▷ Stewart Parker's *Pentecost*, an O'Caseyish piece about the sterility of the Northern Ireland situation, set in Belfast during the Ulster Workers' Strike of 1974.

TRY THESE:
▷Druid and ▷Charabanc offer contrasting approaches to Irish theatre; 7:84 are the nearest thing in British touring theatre; ▷Tom Stoppard's *Hapgood* plays with the notion of opposites in ways reminiscent of *Double Cross*; see also ▷Brian Friel.

FIERSTEIN, Harvey [1954–]
American dramatist

Plays include:
In Search of the Cobra Jewels (1973), _Freaky Pussy_ (1982), _Flatbush Tosca_ (1982), _Torch Song Trilogy_ (1982), _Spookhouse_ (1984), _Safe Sex_ (1987); also the libretto for _La Cage Aux Folles_ (1983)

The son of a handkerchief manufacturer, this throaty American writer/actor found sudden fame when his off-off-Broadway trio of plays about gay life in New York City, *Torch Song Trilogy*, won two 1982 Tony Awards following their move to Broadway. This success prompted predictable cries that Fierstein had sold out (the plays are, for example, noticeably lacking in physical passion), and it was hard not to concur when his slick and superficial libretto for the musical *La Cage Aux Folles* won him another Tony the following year. His subsequent plays have been disastrously received in New York; *Spookhouse*, seen off-Broadway in 1984 and at Hampstead in 1987, failed to convince in its Paul Zindel-like tale of a harridan mother living in Coney Island, and his 1987 trio, *Safe Sex* — his first overtly post-AIDS drama – closed on Broadway after a scant two weeks. Still, at his best (as in the mother/son scenes that close *Torch Song*), Fierstein writes winningly emotional dialogue that neither glosses over the complexities of homosexual feeling nor indulges them in a way that would ghettoise his audience. If his model for gay relationships is disconcertingly heterosexual, that's because he sees people as

TRY THESE:
▷Larry Kramer (*The Normal Heart*) and William M. Hoffman (*As Is*) are two other contemporary gay American writers whose works have reached a broad audience, but Fierstein writes less polemically than either; also Neil Bell, ▷Martin Sherman as dramatists who write frankly about gay life and issues; for British equivalents, see ▷Gay Sweatshop, ▷Noël Greig, ▷Drew Griffiths.

bound by common emotion, not divided by issues of sexual preference. As an actor Fierstein has appeared both in his own plays and in ▷ Sidney Lumet's film *Garbo Talks* (1984).

FINNEGAN, Seamus [1949–]
Northern Irish dramatist

Plays include:
***Laws of God* (1978), *Paddy and Britannia* (1979), *I Am a Bomb* (1979), *Victims* (1979), *Act of Union* (1980), *Herself Alone* (1981), *Soldiers* (1981), *James Joyce and the Israelites* (1982), *Loyal Willy* (1982), *The Little People* (1982), *Tout* (1984), *North* (1984), *Beyond a Joke* (1984), *Mary's Men* (1984), *Bringing It Home* (1984), *Gombeen* (1985), *The Spanish Play* (1986), *The German Connection* (1986), *Ghetto* (1987), *The Murphy Girls* (1988)**

Radio includes:
***The Cemetery of Europe* (1988)**

Films include:
***The German Connection* (1988)**

Belfast-born, Catholic-bred, a former teacher (at the Jewish Free School in London) and political activist (for the now almost moribund socialist Civil Rights movement), Finnegan has become one of the most prolific but under-rated of contemporary commentators on Northern Ireland – his output in the past decade (all directed by Julia Pascal, and mostly for her own company on the fringe circuit) amounts to a magnum opus on its historical complexities and contradictions. Ambitious in his wide-ranging themes, Finnegan has moved from the early monologues of outrage (*I Am a Bomb* and *Victims*) through the complexities of the situation (*Act of Union*, *Soldiers* and *North*) to exploration of loyalties and principles on an epic scale in *The War Trilogy* which spans the Spanish Civil War (*The Spanish Play*), the Holocaust in Europe (*The German Connection*) and Israel (the radio play *The Cemetery of Europe*). Finnegan's plays exploring the complexities of Catholicism and Protestantism in Northern Ireland are notable for their non-sectarian, even ironical detachment, and for their concern, like James Joyce, with the Jewish Belfast links (*James Joyce and the Israelites*, *The War Trilogy*) and increasingly strike away from seeing Ireland and the North in isolation but rather as part of a larger, global universality. Finnegan is equally capable of providing dramatic cameos on a smaller, more domestic canvas such as in *Mary's Men*, a poignant portrait of lost dreams among Belfast's down-and-outers. Like many playwrights writing about war, Finnegan sees the real culprit as the British establishment; the British squaddie as much a victim as the Belfast mother mourning her schoolboy son killed by a squaddie.

Resident in London since 1974, Finnegan has yet to see any of his plays performed anywhere in Ireland, North or South. Some enterprising producer in Britain would do well to organise a major revival, particularly of *The War Trilogy* – something which may be prompted once Chariot Film's movie version of *The German Connection* confirms Finnegan's quality.

TRY THESE:
▷Charabanc's *Somewhere over the Balcony* and ▷Daniel Mornin's *Kate* for another view of the madness of living under constant army surveillance; for soldiers and barrack room scenes of British squaddies, see ▷Tony Marchant's *Coming Home*, Greg Cullen's *Taken Out*; for contrast, other contemporary Northern Irish playwrights: ▷Christina Reid, ▷Ann Devlin, ▷Thomas Kilroy, Martin Lynch, Frank McGuinness, ▷Stewart Parker, Allan Cubitt.

Act of Union
Produced in 1980 at the Soho Poly, this was the first play seen in London to deal with the current situation in Northern Ireland and, in true Finnegan style, to do so through the eyes of contrasting Belfast inhabitants. Embroidered with mordant humour, it introduced a distinctive voice of tragi-comedy into a situation of despair, at the same time making a trenchant plea to leave North and South to sort things out for themselves.

FLANNERY, Peter [1951–]
British dramatist

Plays include:
Heartbreak Hotel* (1975), *Last Resort* (1976), *Savage Amusement* (1978), *The Boy's Own Story* (1978), *The

TRY THESE:
▷Howard Brenton and ▷David Hare's *Brassneck* and *Pravda*, ▷Peter Barnes' *The Ruling*

***Adventures of Awful Knawful* (1979), *Jungle Music* (1979), *Our Friends in the North* (1982), *Heavy Days* (1982), *Silence on My Radio* (1983)**

Television includes:
***Kissing Goodbye* (1980), *Radical Chambers* (1988)**

Flannery, a Manchester University drama graduate, has had most of his work staged by the Manchester based Contact Theatre Company or the ▷ RSC, for whom he was resident dramatist in 1979–80 and for whom he is completing a commission. Much of his work includes songs, often by fellow Manchester student Mick Ford, and he has been particularly concerned with problems of despair and urban decay in *Savage Amusement* and *Jungle Music*. His best known work is *Our Friends in the North* which won the John Whiting Award for its vivid and trenchant recreation of some of the interlocking strands of corruption in British life between 1964 and 1979, from faulty high rise blocks and bent policemen to Rhodesian sanctions-busting. It has all the virtues of a thriller and reserves its anger for the Labour politicians who wasted their golden opportunity. Perhaps it seemed a little long in performance, but then there was a lot of material to be considered; an updated version would be far more chilling and would presumably be even longer!

Class, ▷Howard Barker's *A Passion in Six Days* and *Stripwell* are among the many contemporary British plays that deal with politics, corruption and the establishment; ▷Thomas Otway's *Venice Preserv'd*, ▷John Gay's *The Beggar's Opera*, ▷Shaw's *Widower's Houses*, ▷Granville Barker's *Waste* are examples from the seventeenth, eighteenth, nineteenth and early twentieth centuries; for 'bent' policeman see ▷G.F. Newman's *Operation Bad Apple*, ▷Nigel Williams' *WCPC*, ▷Joe Orton's *Loot*; ▷Caryl Churchill's *Serious Money* offers a satirical view of some aspects of current City scandals.

FLETCHER, John [1579–1625]
English Renaissance dramatist, collaborator with ▷ Francis Beaumont, ▷ Philip Massinger and ▷ William Shakespeare

Plays include:
***The Woman's Prize* (with ▷ Beaumont; after 1604), Philaster (with ▷ Beaumont; pre 1610), *The Maid's Tragedy* (with ▷ Beaumont; pre 1611), *A King and No King* (with ▷ Beaumont; 1611), *Henry VIII* (with ▷ Shakespeare; 1613), *The Two Noble Kinsmen* (with ▷ Shakespeare; 1613), *The Custom of the Country* (with ▷ Massinger; c 1619)**

Son of a clergyman who eventually died in poverty despite having been Bishop of London, Fletcher was a prolific and popular dramatist who succeeded ▷ Shakespeare as resident dramatist with the King's Men. His current theatrical reputation rests almost entirely on his collaborations with Shakespeare and *The Maid's Tragedy*, though he wrote many comedies of manners which might repay attention as precursors of Restoration comedy and he also wrote *The Woman's Prize*; *or The Tamer Tamed*, a revivable sequel to *Taming of the Shrew*, in which Petruchio gets his just deserts at the hands of his second wife. *Henry VIII* is a celebratory epic of the birth of Protestant England in which Henry is presented rather more favourably and seriously than he tends to be in our contemporary picture of him. It uses non-naturalistic dramatic devices in a way that ▷ Brecht would have admired. The two gentlemen who meet at major events throughout the play and remind each other and the audience of the historical context are particularly endearing if you like that kind of approach to dramatic writing (and particularly irritating if you like tightly controlled causality and plausability).

The Two Noble Kinsmen
The Two Noble Kinsmen is a fascinating study of conflict between honour and love. Derived from Chaucer, in which Palamon and Arcite, the kinsmen of the title, imprisoned by Theseus, vie for the love of Hippolyta's sister Emilia. In the subplot the gaoler's daughter who loves Palamon goes mad for love and is subsequently cured by the attentions of her former suitor disguised as Palamon. The whole effect is truly tragi-comic with many possibilities of death and disaster but virtually everything turns out well for everybody in the end, except for Arcite who

TRY THESE:
Theseus figures in ▷Euripides' *The Suppliant Women* and *Hippolytus* (which deals with the Phaedra story later dramatised by ▷Racine, in which Hippolytus dies in a similar way to Arcite); ▷Shakespeare uses Theseus and Hippolyta in *A Midsummer Night's Dream*; the substitution of one beloved for another which figures in *The Two Noble Kinsmen*, ▷Shakespeare's *Two Gentlemen of Verona*, *Measure for Measure* and *All's Well that Ends Well*, has sinister parallels in the substitution of one woman for another in a man's bed in ▷Middleton's *The Changeling*; ▷Bolt's *A Man for All Seasons* offers a different interpretation of Henry VIII to that of ▷Fletcher and ▷Shakespeare; ▷Shakespeare's other history plays cover the period from *King John* to *Henry VI*.

wins the contest for Emilia but is killed accidentally, thus leaving the way clear for Palamon to marry Emilia. Quite what Emilia makes of this last minute substitution is not clear. The 1986 ▷ RSC revival showed that the play can hold its own; what it needs now is regular revivals so that we can gauge its true strengths.

FO, Dario [1926–]

Italian political performer, dramatist and manager

Plays include:

***Stealing a Foot Makes you Lucky in Love* (1961), *Mistero Buffo* (1969), *Accidental Death of an Anarchist* (1970), *Can't Pay? Won't Pay!* (1974), *Female Parts* (with Franca Rame; 1977), *Trumpets and Raspberries* (1981), *Elizabeth* (1984) *The Open Couple* (with Franca Rame; 1986–7)**

TRY THESE:
▷Franca Rame, Fo's wife and long-time collaborator; ▷John McGrath for the mixture of comedy and politics, and also ▷John Arden's *Non-Stop Connolly Show*; Plautus, ▷Goldoni and ▷Shakespeare et al for plays about doubles.

Dario Fo is one of the funniest performers alive, especially in his solo piece, *Mistero Buffo*, which he has performed (in Italian, but it really doesn't matter) all over the world. His peculiar strutting walk, leaning backwards as he goes, and his expressive features and shark-like smile, are inimitable. He has also written forty or so plays, which have made him in recent years the most widely performed dramatist in the world, and he has upset successive Italian governments considerably. His combination of popular farce and savage political comment is unique and very effective.

Fo's father was a socialist railway worker and amateur actor. He himself started in the Italian theatre in Milan in the 1950s, with revue sketches, radio comedy and songs, and some early farces with the Fo-Rame Company (founded with his wife ▷ Franca Rame) from 1959 to 1968. They are very competent (*Stealing a Foot Makes you Lucky in Love* surfaced at the ▷ Edinburgh Festival in 1983), but have no great political content except for a general dislike of authority. He had a good deal of commercial success in Italy in the 1960s, but his political commitment grew, until in 1968 he and his wife left the bourgeois theatre to set up a co-operative group called the Compagnia Nuova Scena, where he first performed his bravura solo act *Mistero Buffo*. This is a free-wheeling act, partly written in *grammelot*, an invented language which he declares was made up by medieval strolling players to avoid political censorship, and in which he satirises the Catholic Church, politicians, big business, repressive laws, and generally presents the irrepressible underdog, improvising freely as he goes. (Fo miming the Pope kissing babies is the sort of thing that makes you laugh until your ribs hurt.) He has been developing and changing this act for the last twenty years.

In 1970 he founded a new company, La Comune, a theatrical collective, which worked as a ▷ community theatre in a working-class suburb of Milan; here his work became overtly political and revolutionary. In December of the same year the company put on 'a grotesque farce about a tragic farce', *Accidental Death of an Anarchist*.

Later Fo plays that have appeared in Britain include *Can't Pay? Won't Pay!* (Criterion, 1981), a well structured farce about civil disobedience in the face of high prices, that became a little cosy in the English production; a too-short season of the maestro in *Mistero Buffo* at Riverside Studios in 1983; *Trumpets and Raspberries* (Palace Theatre, Watford, and Phoenix, 1984), which makes hilarious use of the 'double' joke, as the Fiat boss, Agnelli, is saved in an attempted assassination by a Fiat worker, but given the worker's features by mistake in plastic surgery; and the misconceived *Elizabeth* (Half Moon, 1986), which showed that Fo should stay with his own cultural and historical assumptions – still, there was a lovely piece of *grammelot* in the middle of it. Some of the plays devised with and for ▷ Franca Rame, *Female Parts*, have also been put on at the Cottesloe with Yvonne Bryceland in 1981 and 1983 as *One Woman Plays*, and Rame herself appeared in *It's All Bed, Board & Church* at Riverside in 1983.

Accidental Death of an Anarchist

This play was based on the death of Guiseppe Pinelli, an anarchist railway worker who had 'accidentally' fallen from a Milan police station window during interrogation about planting bombs.

Fo himself played the part of the 'Maniac' who infiltrates police headquarters and shows the unlikeliness of the police story; the mode is farcical, but the content profoundly disturbing. The show was changed nightly through its run, as more facts about the Pinelli affair emerged. It was produced in London by Belt and Braces at the Half Moon in 1979, and subsequently transferred to Wyndham's in 1980; it had a great commercial success, but probably lost them their Arts Council grant.

FOCO NOVO

British touring theatre company

Foco Novo, founded in 1972 by David Aukin, ▷ Bernard Pomerance, and its artistic director Roland Rees, is committed to touring new writing and new versions of contemporary classics. The company takes its name, which means 'new focus', from ▷ Pomerance's play about a CIA agent captured by urban guerillas which they staged in and around a garage in Kentish Town. The company has produced plays by established writers like ▷ Howard Brenton, ▷ Mustapha Matura and ▷ C.P. Taylor, encouraged newer writers such as ▷ Tunde Ikoli, Michael Picardie and Nigel Gearing, and staged memorable versions of classics by ▷ Brecht, ▷ Büchner, ▷ Genet and ▷ Gorki. The company has also toured community venues with smaller-scale shows specifically generated with those communities in mind and moved into music theatre with Mike and Kate Westbrook's *The Ass*, from D.H. Lawrence. The company's greatest success was probably ▷ Pomerance's *The Elephant Man,* which Rees restaged at the ▷ National Theatre with some of the original cast, including David Schofield and Jennie Stoller, but their most recent production of ▷ Marguerite Duras' *Savannah Bay*, brilliantly directed by Sue Todd, was acclaimed as a triumph at a time when the company's future was in doubt as a result of a reduction in Arts Council subsidy. Throughout its existence Foco Novo has usually succeeded in matching high production values to challenging scripts; the success of *The Elephant Man* and ▷ Brenton's *Bloody Poetry* (revived by the Royal Court in 1988), the long-term encouragement of ▷ Tunde Ikoli and the apparent re-establishment of ▷ Duras as a theatrical force in Britain are obvious achievements, but equally important is the opportunity for unestablished writers to receive serious and full-scale production of their early work.

TRY THESE:
Bristol Express, ▷Women's Theatre Group, ▷Monstrous Regiment, ▷Paines Plough, and ▷Joint Stock are other touring companies committed to new work; the Royal Court is a venue committed to ▷New Writing.

FORD, John [1586–c 1640]

English Renaissance dramatist

Plays include:

***The Witch of Edmonton* (1621, with Dekker and Rowley), *Perkin Warbeck* (c 1622–32), *The Broken Heart* (c 1629), *'Tis Pity She's a Whore* (c 1632)**

Ford had a legal training at the Middle Temple but may not have practised law. He made his theatrical debut with *The Witch of Edmonton*, collaborated in five plays and wrote another eight by himself. Because *'Tis Pity She's a Whore* deals sensitively and not unsympathetically with incest, Ford has been subject to high moral condemnation and treated as the prime representative of the alleged decadence of the drama of the reign of Charles I. He, ▷ Middleton and ▷ Massinger are, in fact, the latest of the pre-Civil War dramatists to be staged on anything like a regular basis in the contemporary theatre, and there can be no denying the sensational quality of *'Tis Pity* in view of such moments as Giovanni's entrance with the heart of his sister Annabella on the point of his dagger. Nevertheless, it is a play well within the Renaissance tradition of scrutinising limits and defying convention which still attracts modern audiences. *Perkin Warbeck*, a very late example of the chronicle play fashionable in the Elizabethan period, is a fascinating study of role-playing with its protagonist, who claims to be the son of Edward IV, choosing to be executed rather than admit his imposture.

TRY THESE:
Ford was clearly heavily influenced by ▷Shakespeare in both *'Tis Pity She's a Whore* (aspects of *Romeo and Juliet*) and *Perkin Warbeck* (particularly the *Henry VI* plays and *Richard III*, which deal with the historical events preceding the action of Ford's play); ▷Middleton's *Women Beware Women* has an incest plot which is thought to have influenced Ford's treatment; incest is also a main theme in ▷Shelley's, and ▷Artaud's, *The Cenci*; ▷Barry Reckord's *X* also uses incest as a main theme; ▷Tom Stoppard's *The Real Thing* uses *'Tis Pity*

as one of its intertexts; ▷Pirandello's *Henry IV* (which is not about the English king) is a significant modern play about the construction of identity.

FRANCESCHILD, Donna [1954–]
American dramatist

Plays include:
***The Cleaning Lady* (1977), *Soap Opera* (1979), *Diaries* (1979), *Mutiny on the M1* (1980), *Tap Dance on a Telephone Line* (1981), *The Pickpocket* (1981, *Songs for Stray Cats and Other Living Creatures* (1985), *Rebel* (1986)**

Playwright/songwriter and a native of California, Donna Franceschild has lived in Britain since 1976. She was writer-in-residence with the Cambridge Theatre Company in 1980, and at Glasgow University in 1983. But she has mostly made a name for herself as the composer of ▷ musicals several of which have had work as their main focus. *Tap Dance on a Telephone Line* actually reflected Franceschild's own experiences as an operator in a downtown LA telephone exchange and scored some neat points about the slave-driving, productivity-obsessed atmosphere which reduces one member to attempted suicide, and leads ultimately to a 'wild-cat' strike. But most likely for revival is ▷ Paines Plough's commissioned *Songs for Stray Cats and Other Living Creatures* which also had some acerbic things to say on behalf of its five characters working in a musical equipment warehouse in Glasgow, all of whom had taken a battering from life in one way or another. *Rebel*, presented at the Albany in London, was a bold attempt to update another of life's victims, the 1950s James Dean, to contemporary London, complete with simulated car smash (one of the triumphs of the evening), police brutality, drugs, and an all pervasive ugliness, that didn't quite come off but boasted some splendid pastiche doo-wap 1950s rock 'n' roll. *Mutiny on the M1*, predating ▷ John Byrne's 1987 smash television hit *Tutti Frutti* by at least seven years, has been perhaps her most ambitious work to date. Performed by the Combination at the Albany, it included twenty-two songs, two bands (one playing live, one playing the band-within-the-play) in this everyday story of rock business life, set in a broken-down van on the M1, crammed with archetypal rock music 'characters' – seedy manager, clashing personalities, flying egos, drugs, stress, and various assorted hangers-on.

TRY THESE:
▷John Byrne, not just for *Tutti Frutti* but also *The Slab Boys* for Glaswegian work setting; also ▷Tony Marchant's *The Lucky Ones*, ▷Arnold Wesker's *The Kitchen*, Robert Tressell's *Ragged Trousered Philanthropists* and ▷David Storey's *The Contractor* are all centred round the work-place; for rock musicians see ▷Barrie Keeffe's *Bastard Angel*, ▷David Hare's *Teeth 'n' Smiles* ▷Willy Russell's *John, Paul, George, Ringo. . .and Bert*; Scotland's Wildcat Theatre Company specialise in rock musical treatment of contemporary issues.

FRAYN, Michael [1933–]
British dramatist, novelist, journalist and translator

Plays include:
***The Two of Us* (comprising *Black and Silver, The New Quixote, Mr Foot, Chinamen*; 1970), *The Sandboy* (1971), *Alphabetical Order* (1975), *Donkey's Years* (1976), *Clouds* (1976), *Balmoral* (1978; retitled *Liberty Hall*), *Make and Break* (1980), *Noises Off* (1982), *Benefactors* (1984)**

Films include:
***Clockwise* (1986)**

Novels include:
***The Tin Men* (1965), *The Russian Interpreter* (1966), *Towards the End of the Morning* (1967), *A Very Private Life* (1968), *Sweet Dreams* (1973)**

Born in the London suburbs, Frayn co-scripted the 1957 Cambridge University Footlights revue 'Zounds', on graduating worked as a reporter for *The Guardian*, and was a regular columnist for *The Observer* until 1968, a period during which he

TRY THESE:
▷Farce for Ray Cooney and Brian Rix; whose farces provide the bones of the play within the play of *Noises Off*; ▷Chekhov and ▷Anouilh, whom Frayn has adapted and translated, and with whom he clearly feels an affinity; ▷Feydeau is *the* classic French farceur; ▷Tom Stoppard and ▷Alan Ayckbourn, like Frayn, use the conventions of farce innovatively.

wrote four of his novels. He still contributes occasional articles and wrote an award-winning series on Cuba. *Clouds* is about the experience of journalists in Cuba. His first professional production was *The Two of Us*, a group of four plays, in which Lynn Redgrave and Richard Briers played a range of characters.

Frayn's plays are often comic, but the comedy is very edgy and sometimes even, as in *Noises Off*, manic. Many of them explore behaviour within the constraints and frames of institutions; *Alphabetical Order* is set in the library of a provincial newspaper, *Donkey's Years* at an Oxford college reunion, *Make and Break* is about a businessman's experience of an international trade fair. His film script for *Clockwise* is about the host of trials and tribulations that thwart the journey of a headmaster (played by John Cleese) to a conference.

In a television interview, Frayn acknowledged that the tragicomedy of his plays was something that he associated with ▷ Chekhov, and in recent years, Frayn has proved himself a sensitive and intelligent translator of Chekhov. Of *Three Sisters* he has said: 'It is about the irony of hopes. . .the way life mocks them', a sentiment that applies to his own work too.

Noises Off

Of all Frayn's work, *Noises Off* has been the most successful. It is at one level an extraordinarily well-crafted farce, at another, a play about the hopes and frustrations of a group of actors as they tour the provinces with the farce, 'Nothing On'. 'Nothing On' is a play-within-a-play, complete with a programme that lists the cast biographies of the characters. The first act opens on a traditional farce set, with the stock character of a cleaning woman, although this is soon interrupted by the interventions of a director, and the cleaning lady emerges as an actress rehearsing for the first night of the farce. The second act turns the set around, and the audience is confronted with the backstage events during a performance of 'Nothing On'. In the third act, the backstage relationships between the actors, stage management and director, after long months of touring, invade the performance of the play to chaotic effect. *Noises Off* is a brilliant parody of a particular kind of farce, of certain kinds of actors, and of theatrical conventions.

FREISTADT, Berta [1942–]

British dramatist

Plays include:

***Chicken Licken* (1981), *Keely's Mother* (1981), *Poor Silly Bad* (1982), *The Burning Time* (1983), *Woman with a Shovel* (1983), *A Fine Undertaking* (1984), *The Life and Death of Laura Normill* (1986)**

Berta Freistadt is one of the many unsung, unheralded talents of the fringe circuit. Writing since the age of ten, she has been working in and around the theatre as actor/teacher/director most of her life. Her plays take up where many leave off and challenge the most comfortable and established of ideas from a feminist, often lesbian feminist, perspective, with a dark, surreal sense of humour that knows no bounds, and happily mixes absurdism with realism, and an overall sense of positivism.

Her targets have ranged from the domestic to the grave; chauvinist fathers who stick their daughters into hen coops because they want sons (*Chicken Licken*); possessive mothers who brandish six foot knives and forks over their daughters because they want to eat them (*Keely's Mother*); echoes of Evelyn Waugh's *The Loved One* thoroughly turned about in a lesbian farce set in a funeral parlour in *A Fine Undertaking*. If male domination and independence from mothers are key themes in her earlier plays, they crop up again in two of her most provocative pieces. *Woman with a Shovel*, commissioned for the ▷ Fo/Rame week at the Riverside Studios in 1983, is a highly dramatic monologue that culminates in a woman turning her pent-up wrath on men with unusual violence. Performed by Maggie Ford with beautifully paced subtlety, its spine-chilling ending is all the more shocking for its slow, unassuming build-up. *Poor Silly Bad*, on the other hand, explores independence from a different angle, that of the old. It is a funny, sensitive portrayal of three women, and particularly of the old woman Dot living alone and trying to

TRY THESE:

▷Franca Rame's collection of monologues, *Female Parts*, also details female domestic and sexual oppressions; Siren's *Curfew* engages with a separatist culture as does *The Burning Time*; Americans ▷Susan Yankowitz and Adrienne Kennedy have also used grotesque and sometimes violent images to put over feminist ideas; ▷Joe Orton for a similar glee in humour of the macabre and outrageous; American group, Split Britches' *Dress Suits To Hire* is an exuberantly provocative treatment of lesbianism and male domination (expressed by a performer simply by the constant, suggestive use of a white-gloved hand); *A Question of Silence*

preserve some degree of dignity and choice in her own death. Set alongside her growing relationship with a young woman tearaway, it is one of the few recent plays to try to successfully bridge the generation gap and show youth the importance of old age.

Lately, Freistadt has looked beyond the present: the post-holocaust *The Burning Time* renews the domestic theme (quoting Engels about the modern family being based on slavery) and confronts survivors of the past with representatives of the new. A plea to change the old systems of domination, *City Limits*' Lyn Gardner called it 'one of the most exciting, risky and provocative shows in town'. Perhaps the Great Reviewer in the sky might make a similar comment on her latest escapade, *The Life and Death of Laura Normill*, where a lesbian is waiting at the Pearly Gates to see whether Himself or Satan (a woman of course) will claim her for their own!

by the Dutch film-maker Marleen Gorris has been controversial because of its dress-shop act of violence committed by a group of ordinary women at the end of their tether.

FRIEL, Brian [1929–]
Northern Irish dramatist

Plays include:

***This Doubtful Paradise* (1959), *The Enemy Within* (1962), *Philadelphia, Here I Come!* (1965), *The Loves of Cass McGuire* (1967), *Lovers* (1968), *Crystal and Fox* (1970), *The Gentle Island* (1971), *Freedom of the City* (1973), *Volunteers* (1975), *Living Quarters* (1977), *Aristocrats* (1979), *Faith Healer* (1979), *Translations* (1981), *Three Sisters* (from ▷ Chekhov; 1981), *The Communication Cord* (1982), *Fathers and Sons* (from ▷ Turgenev; 1987)**

Friel, born in Derry, is probably both the best-known and the best contemporary Irish dramatist. His work is naturally much preoccupied with the current political situation in Ireland in the broadest terms, particularly with the pressures that contribute to the intractability of that situation, the difficulty of rational responses to the legacy of hundreds of years of hostility and mistrust, communities divided by religion and language and the search for a way out of the impasse. There is a strong emphasis on the theme of exile which reflects one traditional escape route from the economic and political ills of Ireland; in *Philadelphia, Here I Come!* the escape is to America, in *The Gentle Island* it is to Glasgow. The renewed violence and gradual breakdown of the political situation after 1968 is reflected in such plays as *The Freedom of the City* and *The Volunteers* which deal directly with aspects of 'the Troubles', but Friel is also concerned with the wider problems of communication and identity. He may not be a particularly daring dramatist in terms of formal experimentation but he makes effective use of splitting a character into public and private selves in *Philadelphia* and of the contrast between the judicial inquiry which 'establishes' that the civil rights marchers were terrorists in *The Freedom of the City* and their innocent behaviour in the flashbacks that show what led up to their deaths. In *The Faith Healer* three characters speak four forty-minute monologues in a hauntingly written multi-viewpoint drama which again draws on the themes of exile and return and the pains of both.

Translations

Translations, the first play staged by ▷ Field Day, the company Friel co-founded with the actor Stephen Rea, is a very fine parable of the current situation in Northern Ireland which also teases out some of its cultural roots. The play is set in 1830s Donegal, in a world where tramps can read Homer in the original but not ▷ Shakespeare, a world doomed to vanish under the assault of state education (in English) and the Royal Engineers' Survey of Ireland. Earnest English subalterns and unhappy Irishmen try to produce English equivalents of Irish placenames in an act of cultural appropriation which remakes Ireland in the image of England. The English Lieutenant Yolland and the Irish woman Maire (who have no common language at all) fall in love, but the barriers of others' suspicion are too great for them to surmount and the play ends in muddle, confusion and destruction. Although the issues are serious and the allegorical applications clear, Friel handles events with a light touch and there is much gentle comedy at the expense of the two lovers failing to communicate –

TRY THESE:
For images of rural Irish life see Synge, particularly *Playboy of the Western World* for parallels with *The Gentle Island*; ▷Sean O'Casey is the great dramatist of an earlier period of political strife in Ireland; among contemporary dramatists writing about Ireland are ▷Christina Reid, ▷Seamus Finnegan, ▷Stewart Parker, ▷Bill Morrison, and Allan Cubitt's *Winter Darkness*, which also has language as one of its main concerns; other notable plays with tribunal settings are ▷Brecht's *The Measures Taken*, ▷John Osborne's *Inadmissable Evidence* and ▷David Edgar's *Our Own People*; Robert Patrick's *Kennedy's Children* intercuts monologues in a powerful re-creation of the mood of 1960s USA; ▷Harold Pinter's *Old Times* deals with differing recollections of events in ways reminiscent of *The Faith Healer*; ▷Peter Nichols' *Passion Play* is a memorable example of the use of two actors to play the public and personal faces of one character; see also ▷Field Day; for another variation on the theme of colonialism, Derek Walcott's *Pantomime*.

they both actually speak English in the play but neither understands the other – and at the expense of linguistic failures in general.

FRISCH, Max [1911–]
Swiss dramatist and novelist

Plays include:
***Now You Can Sing* (1946), *Santa Cruz* (1947), *The Great Wall of China* (1947; revised 1955), *When the War was Over* (1949), *Oederland* (1951; revised 1961), *The Fire Raisers* (1958), *The Fury of Philip Hotz* (1958), *Andorra* (1961), *Don Juan, or The Love of Geometry* (1962)**

Born in Zurich, Frisch did not complete his doctoral studies in philosophy because of lack of money, and took up journalism, travelling through Greece and the Balkans as a freelance. He went back to university to study as an architect, and produced his first building and his first novel in 1943. He worked simultaneously as a writer and an architect for ten years but then went to live in Rome as a full-time writer. Frisch was an influential figure in bringing new European drama and its ideas to a British theatre that was dominated by the social realism of 'The Angry Young Men'. Edna O'Brien has described him as a 'European brain that is as witty as it is adult'.

The Fire Raisers
This is a key text for the Theatre of the Absurd, and the most 'absurdist' of Frisch's plays. Its performance at the Royal Court in 1961 was central to the British awareness of new forms of European and non-realist drama. A black comedy and a cautionary tale, the play is subtitled (with a nod at ▷ Brecht) 'A didactic play without a moral'. Throughout the play a chorus of firemen acts to extend the individual history of Biedermann to a wider political allegory. Biedermann, the central figure of the play is A Bourgeois (the translation of his German name), who constantly protests his status as 'a good citizen'. Two strangers appear in his house and lodge in the attic, without any protest from Biedermann, where they prepare to raise a fire. The play has an afterpiece in which the devil appears; Biedermann is still protesting his innocence and good citizenship in the face of hell fire. It becomes clear that the fire, and Biedermann's lack of resistance, is a parable for the way in which 'good citizens' can collude with the forces of tyranny. It thus refers to the position of those intellectuals in Germany who did nothing to resist the rise of fascism, but also to any political context in which 'good citizens' refuse to question.

TRY THESE:
Sartre's *The Condemned of Altona*, ▷Genet's *The Blacks*, and *The Fire Raisers* all had their first London productions in 1961, and were significant in bringing an awareness of European theatre to Britain; Frisch was influenced by ▷Brecht – *The Fire Raisers* in its political allegory clearly owes a lot to Brechtian principles; ▷Ionesco and ▷Beckett were the other main figures in the so-called 'theatre of the absurd'; C.P. Taylor's *Good* is another treatment of the contribution of 'good citizens' to the rise of fascism; Adrian Mitchell's deservedly much-acclaimed adaptation of *The Pied Piper* poses more fascinating questions about 'good citizenry', and is a highly effective utopian allegory.

FRY, Christopher [1907–]
British dramatist and director

Plays include:
***The Boy with a Cart: Cushman, Saint of Sussex* (1938), *A Phoenix too Frequent* (1946), *The Firstborn* (1948), *The Lady's Not for Burning* (1948), *Thor, With Angels* (1948), *Venus Observed* (1950), *A Sleep of Prisoners* (1951), *The Dark Is Light Enough: A Winter Comedy* (1954), *Curtmantle* (1961), *A Yard of Sun: A Summer Comedy* (1970)**

Films include:
***Ben Hur* (1959), *Barabbas* (1962), *The Bible* (1966)**

Involved in amateur theatre while a teacher and on the staff of Dr Bernardo's, before becoming a professional director at Oxford Playhouse, Fry's early writing included revue material, lyrics and pageants. He is a Quaker, whose compassion is reflected in all his work – several plays use biblical material or religious and ethical conflicts and he wrote the screenplays for a number of movie bible-epics. He uses words like a skater giving dazzling displays of speed and balance, and his witty verbal dexterity is something you either love or loathe. His plotting is not very strong, but neither is it important. He has written that 'progress is the growth of vision: the increased perception of what makes for

TRY THESE:
▷John Whiting for the same combination of verbal skill and comedy with a deep undercurrent; ▷T. S. Eliot and ▷Anouilh are among other dramatists handling the Becket-Henry II theme of *Curtmantle*; Ronald Duncan (who shared the Mercury season), Maxwell Anderson, ▷W. H. Auden for other verse drama; ▷James Bridie for religious drama; ▷Barry Collins' *Judgement* for contrasting prison setting with soldiers; see also ▷Adaptations and Adapters.

life and what makes for death. I have tried, not always successfully, to find a way for comedy to say something of this, since comedy is an essential part of man's understanding.'

Fry's first metropolitan success came in a season of verse drama at London's Mercury Theatre (now closed) with the one-act play *A Phoenix too Frequent*, a retelling of Petronius' story of the widow of Ephesus, with the addition of the idea that being useful after death is a kind of resurrection. Fame came with *The Lady's Not for Burning*, especially its second production with John Gielgud (1949), although few people, including the director, seemed to respond to the dark undercurrent of bitterness and war-weary disenchantment that permeates the play below its springtime charm. The later seasonal pieces more clearly show their sombre colours through the surface glitter. His most direct statement is *A Sleep of Prisoners* in which four soldiers, prisoners in a church, each dream the others into enactments of Old Testament conflicts.

A brilliant translation of ▷ Anouilh's *L'Invitation au château* as *Ring Round the Moon* was the first of a number of translations/adaptations which include *Tiger at the Gates* and other plays by ▷ Giraudoux, ▷ Anouilh's *The Lark* and ▷ Ibsen's *Peer Gynt*.

FUGARD, Athol [1932–]

South African dramatist

Plays:

***No Good Friday* (1959), *Nongogo* (1960), *Blood Knot* (1961), *People Are Living There* (1968), *Hello and Goodbye* (1965), *Boesman and Lena* (1969), *Statements After an Arrest Under the Immorality Act* (1972), *Sizwe Bansi is Dead* and *The Island* (with John Kani and Winston Ntshona, 1973), *Dimetos* (1975), *A Lesson From Aloes* (1978), 'Master Harold' . . . and the Boys (1982), *The Road to Mecca* (1984), *A Place With the Pigs* (1987)**

Films include:

***Boesman and Lena* (1972), *The Guest at Steenkampskraal* (1977), *Marigolds in August* (1979)**

The leading South African playwright of his generation, Athol Fugard has been a major influence in creating an understanding of the black and the 'coloured' person's situations in South Africa. He is to drama what writers like Alan Paton and Nadine Gordimer are to fiction and essays – clear-eyed white chroniclers of apartheid and its ills, who remain bound in what is, to co-opt the title of a Fugard play, a tortured and complex 'blood knot' with a homeland they both love and hate.

Born to an Irish father and a Dutch mother, Fugard began his reputation with the 1961 play *Blood Knot*, which was first performed secretly in a Johannesburg attic because of its mixed-race cast, and which was staged twenty-five years later much more publicly in an acclaimed 'anniversary revival' on Broadway, with Fugard and his original co-star, Zakes Mokae. Interested in dramatically distilled situations, often with very few characters, Fugard has been linked with a writer he expressly admires – ▷ Samuel Beckett – particularly because of *Boesman and Lena*, a play about two coloured outcasts inhabiting a plaintive Beckettian void. After collaborations with the black actors John Kani and Winston Ntshona, Fugard reached into his childhood to write the piercingly autobiographical *'Master Harold'. . .and the Boys*, and into real-life situations, either experienced first-hand or read about in the newspapers, to write *The Road to Mecca* and *A Place With the Pigs* (suggested by a report of a Red Army deserter who hid in a pigsty for over forty years). If his writing is marred by anything it is an excessive fondness for metaphors which are sometimes used gracefully – the ballroom dancing in *'Master Harold'*, the detritus in *Hello and Goodbye* – and often overemphatically – the resilient aloes plant in *A Lesson From Aloes*, the 'pigsty' of Pavel's soul in *A Place With the Pigs*. Still, at his best, Fugard's overwhelming humanity redeems everything. You may quarrel with individual moments from his plays, indeed with individual plays, but the strength of the playwright's searching and generous vision ultimately silences all argument.

Fugard has also made many appearances as an actor

TRY THESE:
Market Theatre of Johannesburg and Barney Simon as the initiators of multi-racial and anti-apartheid plays; for other treatments of apartheid by white South Africans see ▷Nicholas Wright ▷Ronald Harwood, ▷David Lan, Michael Picardie, Yana Stajno's *Salt River*, and Peter Speyer's *Old Year's Eve*; ▷David Edgar's *The Jail Diary of Albie Sachs*; also ▷Michael Abbensetts, ▷Mustapha Matura, ▷Edgar White and ▷Derek Walcott for comparable Caribbean treatments of racism in Britain; productions from black South African companies, including those focusing on women's responses, such as 'Poppie Nongena' (from the Market Theatre), Vusisizwe Players' *You Strike the Woman You Strike the Rock*, Upstairs Theatre Company, Durban's *You Can't Stop The Revolution*; ▷Tina Howe, ▷Neil Simon and ▷Hugh Leonard for the formation of the artist; ▷Tennessee Williams for a similar use of metaphor; new South African writer Mfundi Vundla's *A Visitor to the Veldt* and ▷August

including *Meetings With Remarkable Men*, *Gandhi*, and *The Killing Fields*.

Boesman and Lena
The most Beckettian of Fugard's plays and – like most of his works, few of which have more than three characters – an intimate, small-scale piece on vast themes. Two abject castaway coloureds make their way across the mud flats of South Africa's River Swartkops, in what the playwright calls in his notebooks 'a poem of destruction'. They are a comical and pitiable pair – the talkative fidget, Lena, chattering into the void in an effort to stave off madness, and her brutalising Boesman. An elderly, near-mute black, Outa, appears at the campsite, but the emphasis is on the title characters – two living embodiments of 'white man's rubbish', who like ▷ Beckett's tramps, are bound ever more closely through their mutual teasing and torment.

'Master Harold' . . . and the Boys
In a Port Elizabeth tea room one rainy afternoon, a young boy commits a reprehensible act which will haunt him the rest of his life. Such is the bare-bones background to Fugard's most intensely autobiographical play, whose 1982 world premiere at New Haven's Yale Repertory Theater remains the high point of a fruitful and happy relationship between Fugard and the venue. Fugard wrote the play to honour his childhood servant, Sam Semela, whom the young Fugard once cruelly humiliated as Hally does in the play; as an act of atonement, it's a piercingly magnanimous gesture. As an act of playwriting, the work has a devastating simplicity and force which pull you through its ninety minutes (without interval) from a beginning steeped in good cheer and high spirits to a conclusion that leaves you stunned. As Hally turns on the two black servants, Sam and Willie, whom he has loved as surrogates for the alcoholic father he loathes, Fugard shows the sources of racism in self-loathing, in an inward despair so profound it can only lash out and wound. A shapely and graceful piece of writing, the play makes a restorative theatrical experience out of spiritual depletion.

Wilson's *Jo Turner's Come and Gone* for forging a link between black America and black South Africa.

GALSWORTHY, John [1867–1933]
British novelist and dramatist

Plays include: ***The Silver Box* (1906), *Strife* (1909), *Justice* (1910), *The Skin Game* (1920), *Loyalties* (1922), *Escape* (1926), *Exiled* (1929)**

Galsworthy practised for a time as a barrister, but then set out methodically to learn to write fiction; after ten years' hard work he hit the jackpot with *A Man of Property* (1906). By contrast his first play *The Silver Box*, written for the Court Theatre, was an immediate success, though it now seems an over-schematic treatment of the theme of 'one law for the rich and another for the poor'. He wrote twenty-six more plays, many of which did well; they tend to be well-made sub-Ibsen problem plays, with mild social criticism, not-too-stereotypical characters, a strong narrative line, a touch of melodrama, and upper-middle class settings; these qualities made them the mainstay of Saturday Night Theatre for many years, but only a few now hold the stage.

One that would be worthy reviving is *Justice*, which Galsworthy meant as a demonstration that society tends to destroy its weaker members, and which was unusual in having a direct effect on the law – the silent scene with the prisoner in solitary confinement seems to have persuaded Winston Churchill that the practice should be reformed forthwith.

Strife

This over-symmetrical but well crafted strike play, in which the old Chairman of the Board and the strike leader both suffer from the long strike, and are both repudiated when agreement is reached on the same terms as were offered at the start, carries a powerful punch on stage.

Galsworthy meant the play not to take sides, and the cases for capital and labour are both strongly made, but his anti-extremist conclusions are too obviously underlined. The casting of Andrew Cruickshank versus Michael Bryant made the ▷ National Theatre production of 1978 very effective; an extra resonance was added by the theatre's long dispute with its stage staff which was running at the same time.

TRY THESE:
▷Ibsen for well-crafted plays with a 'social message'; ▷Shaw for similar concerns, but Galsworthy lacks Shaw's experiments in structure; ▷Granville Barker for superficially similar plays, but with a looser structure, and more interesting experiments with character-drawing; for contemporary examples of plays about strikes, see Peter Cox's *The Garden of England*, *About Face* by Cordelia Dutton and Maggie Ford and ▷David Edgar's *That Summer*, all responses to the miners' strike of 1984; Stephen Wakelam's *Deadlines* is about journalism and the miners' strike.

GARRICK, David [1717–1779]
British actor-manager and dramatist

Plays include:

***Miss in her Teens* (1747), *The Clandestine Marriage* (with George Colman the Elder; 1766), *The Irish Widow* (1772), *Bon Ton; or, High Lift Above Stairs* (1775)**

Garrick may have been the greatest actor-manager in the history of the British stage, but as a dramatist he was no more than a very competent hack. Beside a number of farces, he collaborated with George Colman the Elder on *The Clandestine Marriage*, which is revived from time to time (most recently in 1984 as the first production of Anthony Quayle's touring company Compass). It is an amiable farcical comedy with a reliably well-worn plot, involving a new-rich bourgeois trying to buy his two daughters into marriages with the minor aristocracy. The fun

TRY THESE:
▷Sheridan, ▷Goldsmith for more original eighteenth-century comedies; ▷Aphra Behn, ▷Congreve, ▷Etherege, ▷Jonson, ▷Wycherley for earlier treatments of this theme.

arises because the younger daughter is already secretly married to her father's clerk and is also fancied by both the aged and lecherous Lord Ogleby (the best part in the play) and his son; the satirical possibilities of this marriage market are on the whole fudged, and of course all are reconciled at the end.

GATTI, Armand [1924–]
Italian director, dramatist and film-maker, who has worked mainly in France

Plays include:
***La deuxième existence du camp de Tatenberg* (*The Second Existence of the Tatenberg Camp*; 1962), *La vie imaginaire de l'eboueur Auguste Geai* (*The Imaginary Life of the Streetsweeper Auguste Geai*; 1962), *Chant public devant deux chaises électriques* (*Public Song in Front of Two Electric Chairs*; 1966), *V comme Vietnam* (*V as in Vietnam*; 1967), *Les treize soleils de la rue Saint-Blaise* (*The Thirteen Suns of the rue Saint-Blaise*); 1968), *La passion du Général Franco* (*The Passion of General Franco*; banned until 1976)**

Gatti was born into a poor immigrant family in Monaco, and spent part of World War II in a German labour camp; the concentration camp theme recurs in several of his plays (eg *La deuxième existence du camp de Tatenberg*, where the second existence of the camp is in the minds of those who survived it). He is an engagingly optimistic and energetic character, who truly believes that theatre can change the world. He wrote a number of plays on political themes during the 1960s, influenced by ▷ Adamov and Planchon (and of course ▷ Brecht), but often showing a fragmentation of character and of reality (eg his semi-autobiographical play, *La vie imaginaire de l'eboueur Auguste Geai*, shows his father at five different ages, played by five different actors, sometimes all on stage at once, and in seven possible different spaces on stage). These 1960s plays, on subjects such as the Chinese Civil War, the execution of Sacco and Vanzetti, and the Vietnam War, had considerable success all over France. Gatti gradually came to believe that the audience should participate in the production rather than merely consume it and since the mid-1970s he and a troupe of faithful followers have devoted themselves to the production of community plays and films on politically sensitive themes and often in politically sensitive areas, such as Londonderry in 1984, to which he was invited by ▷ John Arden, and where his film *The Writing on the Wall* (*Nous etions tous des noms d'arbres*; 1985) used Catholic teenagers to play Protestant characters and vice versa. Unlike ▷ Ann Jellicoe, he deals with contemporary events, and aims to stir up the community rather than to reconcile it; his results are less artistically finished than hers, and he provokes more local hostility, but his activities seem to have no less of a liberating effect on the participants.

TRY THESE:
▷Ann Jellicoe for plays involving the community; ▷Brecht for his views on the ability of plays and role-playing to change lives (though Gatti styles himself an anarchist rather than a Marxist); see also ▷Community Theatre.

GAY, John [1685–1732]
English poet and dramatist

Plays include:
***The Beggar's Opera* (1728), *Polly* (published; 1729)**

A friend of Jonathan Swift and Alexander Pope, Gay wrote a number of comedies and the libretto to Handel's *Acis and Galatea* but is remembered largely for *The Beggar's Opera*, a send up of the eighteenth-century fashion for Italian opera and a satire on the Prime Minister Sir Robert Walpole and his administration. It takes a great number of popular songs and folk tunes, provides them with new words and sets them in a tale of thieves, whores and highwaymen, which, in turn, mirrors the corruption of contemporary society. Its first production achieved the then longest run on the London stage. The play's popularity continues but its satire is less personal now and it survives more for its lively action and memorable tunes. *Polly*, a sequel which carries heroine Polly Peachum to the West Indies, failed to pass the censorship imposed by Walpole and it was seven years before it could be staged. Gay lost most of

TRY THESE:
▷Brecht's *Threepenny Opera* reworked the story of *The Beggar's Opera*, adding a more consciously political polemic and replacing the songs with new biting lyrics to music by Kurt Weill; ▷Nick Dear's *The Art of Success* presents the introduction of Walpole's Licensing Act as an allegory for modern censorship; see Frank Loesser's *Guys and Dolls* for a more sentimental musical approach to thieves and rascals;

his profits in South Sea Bubble speculation and died only four years after his great success.

for satires on political corruption, see ▷Barrie Keeffe, ▷Mrozek, and for a blander attempt, John Wells' *Anyone for Dennis.*

GAY SWEATSHOP

British theatre company

Key productions include:

Mister X (by Roger Baker and ▷ Drew Griffiths; 1975), *Any Woman Can* (by Jill Posener; 1976), *The Fork* (by Ian Brown; 1976), *Randy Robinson's Unsuitable Relationship* (by Andrew Davies; 1976), *Stone* (by ▷ Edward Bond; 1976), *Indiscreet* (by Roger Baker and ▷ Drew Griffiths; 1976), *The Jingle Ball* (by ▷ Drew Griffiths and the company; 1976), *Care and Control* (devised by the company, scripted by ▷ Michelene Wandor; 1977), *As Time Goes By* (by ▷ Noël Greig and ▷ Drew Griffiths; 1977), *Iceberg* (devised by the company; 1978), *The Dear Love of Comrades* (by ▷ Noël Greig; 1979), *I Like Me Like This* (by Sharon Nassauer and Angela Stewart Park; 1979), *Blood Green* (by ▷ Noël Greig and Angela Stewart Park; 1980), *Poppies* (by ▷ Noël Greig; 1983), *Telling Tales* (by Philip Osment; 1984), *Raising the Wreck* (by Sue Frumin; 1985), *Gay Sweatshop Times Ten Festival* (1985), *Gay Sweatshop Times Twelve Festival* (1987)

The first and still Britain's only professional gay company, co-founded in 1975 by ▷ Drew Griffiths and Gerald Chapman, was formed out of the Gay Liberation Movement of the USA. (It actually arose out the season of gay plays organised by Ed Berman at the Almost Free during 1975 in the more liberalised and financially expanding climate of the 1970s; male homosexuality had only been decriminalised in 1967.)

As a touring company, Gay Sweatshop have always attracted audiences beyond the 'gay' constituency, and have played in colleges, universities and clubs as well as theatres. Their plays have largely been about being gay but have also constantly addressed wider social and political issues, to do with history, prejudice, class, race and disability, in a variety of styles and techniques, often highly experimental.

Mister X and *Any Woman Can* however, the first two plays, were supreme examples of 'coming out' plays. Consciousness raising exercises in one sense, and perhaps crude in their use of personalised accounts, dialogue and monologue to show processes of change, they both made an enormous impact.

Another early piece was *Care and Control* about lesbian mothers and custody, initiated by Nancy Duguid with Kate Crutchley, and joined later by Mary Moore and Kate Phelps. Using the style of drama-documentary made popular by Peter Cheeseman and scripted by ▷ Michelene Wandor, it was based on actual court cases, tapes, and months of combined company work using improvisations. Both in its working methods and its content, it was reflective of the company and its approach in which personal politics and the method of work – in this case working collectively as a feminist ethic and lesbian politics – were creatively entwined. Two of Gay Sweatshop's other early successes were by Noël Greig who, as a director remained with the company for over ten years and whose work for the company can hardly be over-estimated: *As Time Goes By* co-written by ▷ Greig and ▷ Griffiths showed gay repression in three different periods, Victorian England, Nazi Germany and modern America. From this influential production came *The Dear Love of Comrades* by ▷ Greig (songs by Alex Harding). An all-male piece, directed by Nancy Duguid, about the nineteenth-century Utopian socialist Edward Carpenter, it engaged both with the politics of sexual repression, class (Carpenter's three lovers were all working-class), and the early roots of the Labour Party. Written in 1979, and showing Labour's distancing from questions of sexuality for reasons of vote-catching palatability, the play, from a 1988 perspective, seems eerily pertinent today.

Other successes have been *Poppies* by ▷ Noël Greig; *More*

TRY THESE:
▷Drew Griffiths, ▷Noël Greig, ▷Michelene Wandor, ▷Jackie Kay; see also Lesbian Theatre, Women in Theatre; ▷Sarah Daniels' *Neaptide* was a later treatment of lesbian mothers and custody.

by Maro Green and Caroline Griffin, a highly physical and original treatment using music-hall elements, of the subject of 'hidden' disabilities – agrophobia and anorexia; Sue Frumin's *Raising the Wreck* about women's history; the recent *Compromised Immunity* (1985/6) by Andy Kirby, one of the early plays to deal with AIDS and responses to it realistically and again with humour; and Philip Osment's gentle and humane *This Island's Mine* (1986/7), which recalls *Mister X* in its style of working and biographical approach about the inter-connecting lives of several people living in one house. Partly prompted by financial problems, two festivals of workshops and rehearsed readings, Gay Sweatshop Times Ten and Gay Sweatshop Times Twelve have also been remarkably successful in bringing forward new work. GS × 10 had new pieces by ▷ Tasha Fairbanks (*Ties*); ▷ Michelene Wandor (*Meet My Mother*); and new writers Diane Biondo (*Hitting Home*); and Nicolle Freni (*Lifelines*), ▷ Jackie Kay's *Chiaroscuro* also emerged from a reading at GS × 10. GS × 12 introduced Philip Osment's *This Island's Mine*, ▷ Jackie Kay's *Twice Over*, and Martin Patrick's *Where To Now?*

Despite changes to the law affecting local authority promotion of homosexuality in the arts, Gay Sweatshop are still forging ahead in new directions with a season planned by designer/director Kate Owen for 1989 in multi-media forms, bringing together a range of artists – poets, visual artists, musicians, choreographers, video makers as well as playwrights.

GAY THEATRE

TRY THESE:
▷Harvey Fierstein; ▷Drew Griffiths; ▷Noël Greig; ▷Martin Sherman; ▷Gay Sweatshop; ▷Lesbian Theatre; ▷Cabaret.

Openly gay theatre is perhaps a phenomenon of the last twenty years. Granted there have always been areas of theatre given to a degree of cross-sexual adventure, from ▷ Shakespeare's female roles played by boys, to the uniquely British pantomime traditions of slapping-thighed Principal Boys played by women, and Ugly Sisters played by men, but it is only since the beginning of Gay Sweatshop in 1975 that homosexual love has been openly presented on the professional stage in Britain. Since then, there has been a steady increase that has shown gay theatre moving out from the underground circuit into the mainstream – at least in so far as gay *male* plays are concerned. Gay is here used in the generic sense, though strictly speaking these days, gay is usually taken to mean a reference to men, gay women nearly always referred to as lesbian; for more on specifically ▷ lesbian theatre, see separate entry.

Gay theatre has steadily grown since the decriminalisation of male homosexuality in 1967, and the influence of the Women's and Gay Liberation Movements. However, ▷ Gay Sweatshop's *Mister X* in 1975 could be said to have played a fairly influential role with a line that can be traced from the success of its trail-blazing first tour to the Broadway successes of ▷ Harvey Fierstein's *Torch Song Trilogy*, ▷ Larry Kramer's *The Normal Heart* etc. From the success of *Mister X* came a season of gay plays the following year at the ICA (see under ▷ Drew Griffiths and ▷ Noël Greig), followed by *As Time Goes By*, co-written by Griffiths and Greig – a seminal play which spawned *The Dear Love of Comrades*, and ▷ Martin Sherman's *Bent*, which by its success in Britain, and on Broadway showed the demand and audience for plays on gay subjects.

But whilst such plays about male homosexuals became acceptable (even as television fodder, both the soap-operas *Brookside* and *East Enders* have seen fit to introduce credible homosexual characters), lesbians are notable by their absence on main stage, television soaps or whatever, with one or two rare exceptions (▷ Sarah Daniels' *Neaptide* is one of them).

There have been as many different styles and directions as there have been individuals, for one thing gay theatre has tried to show is that there is no one stereotype of a gay man or lesbian; nor any one mode of expressing it, be it agit-prop, or 'coming out' exercises, examinations of social and political forces in the creation of sexual identity, investigations into lesbian custody, off-the-wall comedy of Parker & Klein, cultural debunking à la Donna & Kebab, stand-up comics such as Simon Fanshawe or the wilder shores of satire/drag epitomised by Bloolips. Much of all of this takes place in the smaller fringe theatres, pub, club and college circuits, and the few lesbian and gay centres, on little or no money. London's Lesbian and Gay Centre for the past couple of years has also played host to a fair range of entertainers and plays in its basement theatre. However, such activity and steady liberalisation of attitudes seems increasingly in jeopardy, given the increasing homophobia now enshrined in Section 28 of the Local Government Bill prohibiting local authorities from giving any financial aid to any activity seen to be promoting homosexuality. As the onus is all on the 'intention' of the local authority, and how that can be interpreted in law, the effect of the legislation has been to create widespread uncertainty. Whilst it is difficult to predict its long-term effects, companies like ▷ Gay Sweatshop are obviously in immediate danger of suspension from withdrawal of financial support (GS tour in many venues directly or indirectly funded by local authorities) as are YPT (Young People's Theatre) whose work may often deal with topics of sexuality. The biggest danger, however, as voiced by many performers, playwrights and directors is the more insidious form of self-censorship that will begin to creep in. To what extent it will have affected the theatrical landscape in twelve months time is anyone's guess.

GELBER, Jack [1932–]
American dramatist

Plays include:
The Connection (1959), _The Apple_ (1961), _Square in the Eye_ (1965), _The Cuban Thing_ (1968), _Sleep_ (1972), _Barbary Shore_ (1974), _Farmyard_ (1975), _Jack Gelber's New Play: Rehearsal_ (1976)

'I have no theory of the theatre to proclaim,' Jack Gelber once announced, but the Chicago-born playwright nonetheless remains associated with the breakdown of the fourth wall and a freer, looser theatrical style in keeping with the improvisatory off-Broadway climate in which he was spawned. Gelber got his start with New York's Living Theatre, who performed what remains his best-known work, *The Connection*, a piece about drug addiction featuring its own play-within-a-play. Celebrated both for its bold realism and its seeming formlessness, *The Connection* opened to general pans ('oh man! what junk!' cried one critic), but time has bolstered its reputation as a frontrunner of the drama of the dispossessed that ▷ Miguel Pinero, ▷ Sam Shepard and ▷ Lanford Wilson (in *Balm in Gilead*) would go on to write. None of his plays has garnered equal attention, although their subjects range from scientists in a sleep lab (*Sleep*) to an overtly theatrical piece about the nature of the theatre (*Jack Gelber's New Play: Rehearsal*) in which a play is cast, developed, and then cancelled. Since 1972, Gelber has been devoting the bulk of his energies to teaching as a Professor of English at Brooklyn College in New York City.

TRY THESE:
▷Pirandello, ▷Sam Shepard for theatrical gamesmanship and plays about theatricality; ▷Lanford Wilson's *Balm in Gilead* for loose, improvisatory and powerful treatments of New York low-lifers in an all-night coffee shop; ▷Miguel Pinero's *Short Eyes*, ▷Nell Dunn's most recent play, *The Little Heroine* and the documentary-like *The Concept* for plays about addicts; ▷José Triana, ▷Howard Sackler's *Goodbye, Fidel* for Cuba-related works.

GEMS, Jonathan [1953–]
British dramatist

Plays include:
The Tax Exile (1979), _The Paranormalist_ (1981), _Naked Robots_ (1983), _Susan's Breasts_ (1985)

The oldest of four children of playwright ▷ Pam Gems (*Piaf, Camille*) Jonathan Gems has developed a reputation in just four plays as the chronicler of the New Bohemianism. Having trained as a stage manager, following stints farming in Scotland and working in a fish cannery in America, Gems made his mark with *The Tax Exile*, a social farce whose characters include a traitorous lesbian and a blue-haired punkette. In his next play, *The Paranormalist*, a household of eccentrics, headed by the selfish mother Barbara, conspire to despatch the ageing grandfather, the paranormalist of the title. In *Naked Robots*, the characters are two squatters in love: the twenty-four year-old waitress and

TRY THESE:
▷Hanif Kureishi and ▷Doug Lucie for plays about 'the way we live now'.

would-be pop singer Dana and her Mombasa-born fashion-designer boyfriend, Nudy. *Susan's Breasts*, predictably, made headlines for its title, not for the play itself – a half-written parable about our loveless age in which the flat-chested Susan develops breasts once she develops a relationship. Is Gems 'the Neil Simon of the punk generation', as one critic has remarked? His mother puts it this way: 'He encapsulates the nihilism, the anarchic humour, of his group.' He has subsequently turned his hand more to film scripts and whether he's a fully-fledged playwright remains to be seen.

GEMS, Pam [1925–]

British dramatist

Plays include:

***Betty's Wonderful Christmas* (1972), *My Warren & After Birthday* (1973), *The Amiable Courtship of Miz Venus & Wild Bill* (1973), *Sarah B Divine* (1973), *Piaf* (1973; not produced till 1978), *Go West Young Woman* (1974), *Dusa, Fish, Stas and Vi* (1975, originally called *Dead Fish*), *The Project* (1976; expanded and re-titled *Loving Women*; 1984), *Guinevere* (1976), *The Rivers and Forests* (1976; from Marguerite Duras), *My Name is Rosa Luxemburg* (1976), *Franz in April* (1977), *Queen Christina* (1977), *Ladybird, Ladybird* (1979), *Sandra* (1979), *Uncle Vanya* (1979; from ▷ Chekhov), *A Doll's House* (1980; from Ibsen), *The Treat* (1982), *Aunt Mary* (1982), *Camille* (1984), *The Danton Affair* (1986; from Stanislawa Przybyszewska)**

Television includes:

***Builder by Trade* (1961), *We Never Do What They Want* (1979)**

Socialist realist, mother of four, Gems is one of the few women playwrights to span two generations. Rooted in a working-class consciousness with a racy, pungent turn of phrase, she did not, in fact, take up writing full-time till after forty, though she had written scripts for radio and television whilst also bringing up her children and had been involved with the early feminism of the 1970s. More than any other writer, she consistently explores the dilemmas and specificity of what it is to be female in a world still largely dominated by men. Her best known play *Piaf* (her first full-length work, written in 1973, but not staged until 1978), which started out at the ▷ RSC's Other Place studio theatre and ended up triumphant on Broadway, was a typically earthy – some called it rude – debunking of the myth surrounding the Little Sparrow. Piaf's battle to overcome the pressures of fame, alcohol and drugs is also the story, warts and all, of a gritty, working-class woman searching for economic and sexual independence – a treatment Gems served up also on *Camille*, which stripped Dumas's original of its sentimentality to show the high price of love in a money-regulated market. *Dusa, Fish, Stas and Vi*, the play that put Gems on the map, is a reiteration of these pressures, worked out through four young women of the 'post-pill' generation, a theme which consistently intrigued Gems, a pre- and war-time young mother. Gender too is at the heart of the epic *Queen Christina*, (the first play by a woman to be staged at the ▷ RSC's Other Place), which juggles with the contradictions of gender stereotyping and choices (Queen Christina was brought up as a man but longs in the end to give birth; Gems calls it her 'uterine' play), and the less successful transvestite farce, *Aunt Mary*. *The Danton Affair*, another epic, but based on the manuscript of Stanislawa Przybyszewska, unusually for Gems centres on two male protagonists, and stands rather as an implicit homage by Gems to the almost forgotten creativity of the young Polish woman writer.

TRY THESE:
For a comparison of women as stereotypically bitchy, see Clare Booth Luce's *The Women*; for contemporary women, see ▷Caryl Churchill's *Top Girls*, ▷Jacqueline Holborough's *Dreams of San Francisco*; for male characters being bitchy and unsupportive see ▷Harold Pinter's *No Man's Land*; Nancy Sweet's excellent free adaptation of *Camille* for the fringe group, London Actor's Workshop, directed by Catherine Carnie; ▷Robyn Archer for more 'alternative' images of female stars as victims.

Dusa, Fish, Stas and Vi

Dusa, Fish, Stas and Vi is a pioneering work in the sense of its depiction of women struggling towards self-fulfilment, confronted with problems of sexuality, (anorexia, rejected love), child-rearing (the children have been taken by a former husband) and survival (one character, a physio by day is a high-earning prostitute by night) yet still supportive of each other. Deservedly, it remains a favourite staple of regional repertory.

GENET, Jean [1910–1986]
French novelist, poet and dramatist

Plays include:
***Les Bonnes* (*The Maids*; 1946), *Haute Surveillance* (*Deathwatch*; 1949), *Le Balcon* (*The Balcony*; 1956), *Les Nègres* (*The Blacks*; 1959), *Les Paravents* (*The Screens*; 1961)**

A delinquent and thief who spent much of his first thirty years in reformatory or gaol, where he began to write. He was released from a life-sentence on the plea of ▷ Jean-Paul Sartre and other French existentialist luminaries who recognised his prodigious talent. Even those repelled by the subject matter of his books, in which he presents the violence and vice of criminals and prostitutes as a mixture of luminous beauty and masturbatory fantasy, can be reached by his plays which act as a mirror to the 'normal' world in which he sees true vice and corruption. The tough dream objects and fantasising homosexuals of his novels and his romantic obsession with homosexuality give place to more accessible portraits of men outside society in the prisoner relationships of *Deathwatch* and to more abstracted studies of private and public expliotation and interdependence in *The Balcony* and *The Blacks*. His theatre is often ritualistic and abstracted, its form sometimes echoing Catholical liturgy. Cross-casting, both sexual and racial is intended in *The Maids* and *The Blacks*. *The Screens* echoes the Algerian struggle for independence but the other plays offer a more general criticism of society, playing on the prejudices of the audience to intensify their effect. As well as fiction and autobiographical works, Genet also wrote three screenplays and a ballet scenario.

The Balcony
Set in a brothel where representatives of establishment power groups – church, police, etc – act out their fantasies while a revolution brews outside, *The Balcony* turns a mirror on society which it sees as a whorehouse. Its images, drawn from the conventional repertoire of the pornographer, are not used to titillate but to show how people wilfully preserve the sham of conventional society and power structures. It offers a challenge to directors and to audiences to convey and comprehend the twists and turns of its ideas and provides an opportunity for an Artaudian theatricality, although the 1987 RSC production did little to enhance its reputation.

TRY THESE:
▷Peter Weiss, whose *Marat/Sade* uses a madhouse for its charades and demands similar virtuoso staging; John Herbert's *Fortune and Men's Eyes* and ▷Manuel Puig's *Kiss of the Spider Woman* also show homosexuals in prison; ▷Lindsay Kemp for his work based on Genet; Joint Stock and ▷Caryl Churchill for the use of cross-casting; ▷Brendan Behan for alternative treatments of prison life and the brothel setting; ▷Wendy Kesselman's *My Sister in This House* for feminist treatment of the real-life incident at Le Mans that gave rise to *The Maids*.

GILBERT, (Sir) William Schwenck [1836–1911]
English librettist, dramatist and director

Plays include:
***The Palace of Truth* (1870), *Pygmalion and Galatea* (1871), *Dan'l Druce, Blacksmith* (1876), *Engaged* (1877), *Rosencrantz and Guildenstern* (1891)**

Savoy Operas (with music by Sir Arthur Sullivan) include:
***Thespis* (1871), *Trial by Jury* (1875), *HMS Pinafore* (1878), *The Pirates of Penzance* (1879), *Patience* (1881), *Iolanthe* (1882), *Princess Ida* (1884), *The Mikado* (1885), *Ruddigore* (1887), *The Yeoman of the Guard* (1888), *The Gondoliers* (1889), *Utopia Limited* (1893), *The Grand Duke* (1896)**

Although Gilbert's real claim to fame must be as the librettist half of Gilbert and Sullivan, he was also a considerable (and at times rather sour) dramatist in his own right, ranging from burlesque-extravaganza to comedy to straight melodrama.

Engaged
This comedy shows to a high degree the fundamental Gilbertian discrepancy between the characters' noble speeches and their actual intentions; the humble but warm-hearted Scottish peasants whom we find exchanging highly moral platitudes as the

TRY THESE:
▷Oscar Wilde for similarities to *Engaged* in *The Importance of Being Earnest*; ▷Tom Stoppard for variations on the adventures of Rosencrantz and Guildenstern; ▷Joe Orton for the deadpan delivery of preposterous sentiments.

curtain rises rapidly prove to be an updated version of Cornish wreckers – they derail trains so that they can rob the passengers; and under the many romantic protestations of true love (Cheviot Hill, the hero, manages to become engaged to three women at once) lies simple arithmetic (in pounds, shillings and pence). It reads very well, but never seems to work as well on stage as it does on the page; however, it is revived with reasonable frequency, eg at the ▷ National Theatre in 1975, and at the Arts Theatre in 1983.

In the operas too, things are seldom what they seem; the highest principles are applied in a way which somehow produces the most material benefit, as with Pooh-Bah's readiness to humble his family pride for the smallest of bribes; this combines happily with the Carrollian logic of a world in which (for example) all problems are resolved by the mere insertion of a 'not' in a royal decree (*Iolanthe*). It is probably significant that, though Strauss and Lehar and even Offenbach travel well, Gilbert and Sullivan opera is put on only by the English-speaking.

Since the operas came out of copyright, and left the dead hand of D'Oyly Carte historicism, there have been some interesting productions: for instance the *Black Mikado* (1975), Joe Papp's exuberant production of *The Pirates of Penzance* at Drury Lane in 1982, and Ned Sherrin's sharply satirical updates during the last stand of the G.L.C. *The Ratepayer's Iolanthe* (1984) and *The Metropolitan Mikado* (1985).

GILL, Peter [1939–]

British actor, director and dramatist

Plays include:

***The Sleeper's Den* (1966), *A Provincial Life* (from ▷ Chekhov; 1966), *Over Gardens Out* (1969), *Small Change* (1976), *Kick for Touch* (1983), *As I Lay Dying* (after William Faulkner; 1985) *In the Blue* (1985), *Mean Tears* (1987)**

Welshman Gill began his theatrical career as an actor, but has been largely known as a director since he attracted attention with a sensitive and very naturalistic production of D.H. Lawrence's *A Collier's Saturday Night* (1965) at the Royal Court. An associate director at the Royal Court (1970–72) and Director of Riverside Studios (1976–80) he then joined the ▷ National Theatre where, since 1984, he has been director of the Studio, running experimental workshops for performers and developing new work with writers, as well as directing for the main auditoria. The Lawrence productions for which he is best known demonstrated his creation of authentic atmospheres and relationships. Not all his work has been so naturalistic, whether classical revivals – especially ▷ Chekhov – or new plays.

Of his own plays *The Sleeper's Den* is a naturalistic study of a poverty-stricken housewife pressured into breakdown by the indifference and demands of her family, but later plays have been more abstracted. *Over Gardens Out*, with its two misunderstood boys driven to violence, is more of an impressionistic emotional battle in both past and present. Gill has directed all his own plays.

Mean Tears

This is an episodic presentation of a painful and hopelessly ill-balanced affair between a vaguely academic or literary figure and his younger bisexual love object, seen not so much as a story line, although there is a sequence to the events shown, but in terms of anguish and emotion. Gill's own production, set on a steep rake with no furniture and no scenic indication of locations, was the antithesis of his detailed recreations of working-class life in the Lawrence plays but matched the lack of background given in the text. Anyone who has found themselves trapped in a relationship where the love object seems totally egocentric bad news will confirm its emotional truth; frustration and confusion blocking out the rest of life. Like a sonnet, the play is seemingly slight but with resonance.

TRY THESE:
For the painful distance between speech and silence in personal relationships, see ▷Harold Pinter, ▷Marguerite Duras, ▷Sam Shepard, ▷David Mamet, also, of course, ▷Chekhov and ▷Beckett; other contemporaries charting the parameters of personal pain in relationships are ▷Julia Kearsley, ▷Ayshe Raif, ▷Barry Collins, ▷Alan Ayckbourn, David Spencer (Verity Bargate award winner with *Releevo*); see also ▷The National Theatre.

GIRAUDOUX, Jean [1882–1944]

French dramatist

TRY THESE:
▷Claudel for poetic

Plays include:

***Siegfried* (1928), *Amphitryon 38* (1929), *Intermezzo* (1933), *La Guerre de Troie n'aura pas lieu* (*Tiger at the Gates* or *The Trojan War will not Take Place*; 1935), *Electre* (*Electra*; 1937), *Ondine* (1939), *Sodome et Gomorrhe* (*Sodom and Gomorrah*; 1943), *La Folle de Chaillot* (*The Madwoman of Chaillot*; 1945), *Pour Lucrèce* (*Duel of Angels*; 1953)**

Giraudoux was a diplomat until 1940, writing carefully wrought novels and short stories on the side. He was forty-six when the actor/director Louis Jouvet urged him to try adapting his novel *Siegried et le Limousin*, the story of a Frenchman brought up as a German who has to choose between his nationalities. The great success of his plays in the 1930s was largely due to the continued partnership with Jouvet, whose inventive staging and superb acting combined with Giraudoux's verbal glitter to cover any deficiencies in the dramatic action. Several of the plays show the fashionable 1930s French interest in updating Greek myth; the most successful of these was *La Guerre de Troie n'aura pas lieu*, into which he put all his strong conviction that the French and the Germans were not natural enemies. World War II came as a particular catastrophe to Giraudoux; it is poignant that on the outbreak of war he was set to run French propaganda, as an unlikely rival to Dr Goebbels.

When *Amphitryon 38* (not really the thirty-eighth version, but at least the sixth), was successfuly revived by the ▷ National Theatre in 1971, with Geraldine McEwan, its witty artificiality and clever paradoxes seemed full of charm, but when they revived ▷ Christopher Fry's translation of *The Trojan War will not Take Place* in 1983, it seemed wordy, precious and static. In 1955 Kenneth Tynan had called the play the 'highest peak in the mountain-range of modern French theatre', but either the fashion has moved against Giraudoux (as against Fry), or else one just needs the right production. ▷ Glasgow Citizens' might be able to make the play look a masterpiece again.

rhetoric; ▷Anouilh, Gide, ▷Cocteau, and later Sartre for relating classical legends or Greek play themes to contemporary French concerns; ▷Caryl Churchill and ▷David Lan's *A Mouthful of Birds*, is based on ▷Euripides' Greek classic, *The Bacchae*, as is ▷Maureen Duffy's *Rites*.

GLASGOW CITIZENS' THEATRE

The Glasgow Citizens' is arguably the most successful remaining repertory theatre in the British Isles, both artistically and economically speaking. It was run by ▷ James Bridie from its foundation in 1943 until his death in 1951, with a policy of encouraging new Scottish plays; this remained the policy until Giles Havergal took over in 1969, since when he and the writer and translator Robert David Macdonald and the designer and director Philip Prowse have worked as a team to turn it into an internationally known theatre with a very strong personal style. Their strength lies in their excitingly staged reinterpretations of classical plays from most European countries, full of striking stage images; but they still manage to retain a loyal young local audience in the Glasgow, partly by very careful accounting and by keeping the prices low. The contrast between the stark exterior and bleak surroundings of the theatre, and the refurbished scarlet, gold and black opulence of the interior, is deliberate and typical.

The range of plays presented at the Citizens' is wide and international: several plays each by ▷ Brecht, ▷ Shaw, ▷ Genet, ▷ Coward, ▷ O'Casey, ▷ Massinger and ▷ Goldoni have been put on in recent years, but also big difficult meaty plays like ▷ Seneca's *Thyestes* (set in tribal Kenya), ▷ Goethe's *Torquato Tasso*, ▷ Marlowe's *The Massacre at Paris*, Sartre's *Altona*, ▷ Toller's *The Machine Wreckers*, and long rich adaptations like *A Waste of Time* (from Proust, adapted by Macdonald, with Havergal as Baron Charlus), and *The Last Days of Mankind* (from Karl Kraus, with Havergal as Kraus) which managed to fill the Edinburgh Assembly Hall with clouds of smoke and the ruins of Europe. They are from time to time reproached for not putting on many new Scottish plays, with the exception of Macdonald's *Chinchilla*; but they do very good traditional pantomimes at Christmas. Their productions

TRY THESE:
Strehler, Peter Stein, Chéreau, and other visually-oriented European directors, who have more in common with Havergal and Prowse than most British directors; ▷Tony Harrison for actable verse translations; ▷Peter Brook's *Oedipus* for another attempt to show that ▷Seneca is not unstageable; Anthony Vivis who has also made a habit of translating modern European classics (particularly German) eg Fassbinder's *The Bitter Tears of Petra von Kant* excellently revived at the Latchmere fringe theatre in London in 1987, and Manfred Karge's *Man to Man* with Tilda Swinton.

are not always entirely successful, and are quite often controversial, but rarely boring.

They have made many successful visits to European and indeed South American theatre festivals, where the broad visual style goes down well; but efforts to bring Citizen's productions to London were puzzlingly unsuccessful for some years (eg *Summit Conference*, a meeting between Eva Braun and Clara Petacci, written by Macdonald and directed and designed by Prowse, did not do well in 1982 in spite of Glenda Jackson and Georgina Hale). However they successfully brought three plays to the Greenwich Theatre in 1984 with their own actors (*The Way of the World*, *The Seagull*, and *The White Devil*), and in recent years the triumvirate have been involved in many London ventures, severally and together; and the power of the heightened physicality of typical Citizens' acting has brought London success to Mike Gwilym, Gerard Murphy, Suzanne Bertish, and Jonathan Hyde. Macdonald has translated *Phedra*, directed and designed by Prowse 1984, with Glenda Jackson; Schnitzler's *Intermezzo* at Greenwich in 1985; *The House of Bernarda Alba* at Hammersmith in 1986; and *Faust* (both parts) in 1988. Havergal directed Ena Lamont Stewart's *Men Should Weep* for 7:84 Scotland, seen at Stratford East in 1983, and, with Fidelis Morgan, made a version of Samuel Richardson's *Pamela* for Shared Experience in 1985. Prowse, after directing and designing *The Seagull* and *The White Devil* in the Greenwich season in 1985, directed *The Duchess of Malfi* for the ▷ National Theatre in 1986, and in the same year a fine version of *The Orphan* at Greenwich. Clearly the London theatre is catching up with Glasgow at last.

GLASPELL, Susan [1882–1948]
American dramatist

Plays include:

***Suppressed Desires* (1915, with George Cram Cook), *Trifles* (1916), *The Outside* (1917), *Bernice* (1919), *Inheritors* (1921), *The Verge* (1921), *Alison's House* (1930)**

Glaspell, a founder of the influential Provincetown Players with her husband George Cram Cook and ▷ Eugene O'Neill, played an important part in establishing the serious American theatre but the majority of her plays are now neglected. *Trifles*, an acute account of different understandings of the nature of events and motivations on the basis of gender, is finely observed but too short to be readily revived professionally. *Inheritors*, a well crafted longer play which examines the corruption of the pioneering spirit and the American Dream, would repay revival for the light it sheds on the historic roots of many contemporary American attitudes. *The Verge*, with its heroine on the point of a breakthrough into either madness or understanding anticipates the hothouse atmosphere of ▷ Tennessee Williams. *Bernice* and *Alison's House* (based on Emily Dickinson's life) share the device of an offstage female protagonist with *Trifles*; an economical way of suggesting the absences which can constitute the notion of 'woman'. *Alison's House* was revived in London in 1983 by the briefly flourishing women's group, Mrs Worthington's Daughters.

TRY THESE:
Glaspell's work links with many strands of American playwriting, particularly the work of ▷Eugene O'Neill and ▷Tennessee Williams; there is also a ▷Strindbergian quality in her analysis of the ways marriage can work, although her conclusions unsurprisingly differ from his; the contrast between a desire for immolation and a desire for life in *The Outside* anticipates ▷Beckett; Noël Greig takes up similar themes in *Poppies*, as does Megan Terry in *Approaching Simone*.

GODBER, John [1956–]
British playwright and director

Plays include:

***Toys of Age* (1978; with Richard Lewis, *Up 'N' Under*, (1984), *Bouncers* (1985), *Shakers* (1986; with Jane Thornton, *Blood Sweat and Tears* (1986), *Cramp* (1986), *Putting on the Ritz* (1987), *Teechers* (1987)**

The son of a miner, Godber began writing short stories for Radio Sheffield at the age of sixteen, trained as a teacher in Wakefield and taught for five years, while doing postgraduate work in drama at the University of Leeds. At twenty-two he co-wrote

TRY THESE:
▷David Storey's *The Changing Room*, ▷David Williamson's *The Club*, ▷Louise Page's *Golden Girls*, ▷Claire Luckham's *Trafford Tanzi*, ▷Howard Sackler's *The Great White Hope* for plays with sport as a central element; ▷Willy

Toys of Age with Richard Lewis, which was filmed for television, and then began to contribute to the television series *Crown Court*, *Grange Hill* and *Brookside*. He has continued to move fruitfully between theatre and television – *Blood Sweat and Tears* was televised in 1986 and *Putting on The Ritz* was adapted from his six-part television series *The Ritz* (1987) – but he is most closely associated with the Hull Truck Theatre Co, of which he has been artistic director since 1984. Godber has said: 'I think the theatre should be exciting. It should involve action. . .at Hull Truck we're trying to break down the barriers. . .' His involvement with Hull Truck is an expression of his commitment to a theatre outside London, and opposition to the enshrining of 'theatre' at the ▷ National Theatre and the ▷ RSC and much of his work has extensive tours with Hull Truck. His project is what he calls a 'genuinely serious popular theatre. . .a situation in which ordinary people: plumbers, bricklayers, shop assistants, miners, shepherds, doctors, dentists, professors . . . go to the theatre for a shared experience'.

Most of his plays are social comedies which take place in public arenas and are generally concerned with what Godber has called 'working class leisure activities'; *Up 'N' Under* and *Cramp* (which is about a body-builder, and has music by Tom Robinson) both take a sport as their central device. They are intensely physical pieces of theatre, drawing heavily on caricature for effect. *Bouncers* and *Putting on the Ritz* are set in discos.

Russell's *Stags and Hens* is *the* disco play; ▷Steven Berkoff for another form of highly physical theatre; ▷Nigel Williams' *Class Enemy* for a classroom play.

Up 'N' Under

Up 'N' Under won the Laurence Olivier Comedy of the Year award for 1984. Rugby League becomes a means of exploring the contradictions of macho and the energy and resources devoted to the game also become a powerful image of resources that have gone to waste in contemporary Britain (body building is used similarly in *Cramp*). Godber is himself a rugby player, and says that a lot of the play came directly out of his own experience of the game. The play toured with Hull Truck for two years, won a Fringe First Award at the ▷ Edinburgh Festival, and was the first of Godber's plays to reach the West End.

GOETHE, Johann Wolfgang von [1749–1832]

German dramatist and poet

Plays include:

Götz von Berlichingen (1773), Clavigo (1774), Stella (1775), Egmont (1788, produced 1796), Iphigenia in Tauris (1779, second (verse) version 1787), Torquato Tasso (1789, produced 1807), Faust Part I (published 1808), Faust Part II (published posthumously 1833)

Goethe studied in Leipzig, like the young Faust, and like him studied alchemy and forbidden subjects. His first play, *Götz von Berlichingen*, was written in what he hoped was a Shakespearean manner, under the eager influence of Herder; the result is the story of an honourable robber knight in revolt against tyrannical rulers, and a very untidy construction. *Clavigo* is a curiosity, presenting a heightened version of ▷ Beaumarchais' real-life journey to Spain to avenge his sister's seduction and abandonment by a Spaniard; the subject of *Egmont* is the revolt of the Netherlands against Spain, and again the hero is shown as a noble and honourable humanist who goes to his death as a fighter against tyranny. Goethe began the play just before accepting an invitation to Weimar, where he inadvertently stayed for the rest of his life, becoming Finance Minister and Lord High everything else. He managed the Court Theatre from 1791 until 1817, when he was displaced by an actress who had the advantage of being the Grand Duke's mistress. From a literary point of view, his reign was a golden age – besides his own plays, he put on most of ▷ Schiller's – but as a director he was less successful, finding it difficult to get on with the less intelligent actors, and tending to drill them. In a two-year absence in Italy he wrote *Iphigenia in Tauris* (from ▷ Euripides) and *Torquato Tasso*, a study of a poetic hero with emotional difficulties which were not unlike his own. His last play, the two parts of *Faust*, was written over a long period, and is usually regarded as unactable, though from time to time somebody is rash enough to try to scale its

TRY THESE:

▷Schiller for eighteenth-century German drama; ▷Marlowe for *Dr Faustus*, ▷Havel for *Temptation*; Berlioz and Gounod are among opera composers who used the Faust theme; ▷Ibsen's *Peer Gynt* has Faustian redemptive overtones; Andrew May, the editor in ▷David Hare and ▷Howard Brenton's *Pravda*, like Alfred Bagley in their earlier *Brassneck*, makes a Faustian bargain; Helen of Troy, who figures in both Goethe's and ▷Marlowe's treatments of the Faust story also figures in ▷Shakespeare's *Troilus and Cressida*, ▷Euripides' *Trojan Women*, *Helen*, *Orestes* and ▷Giraudoux's *The Trojan War Will Not Take Place*; *Iphigenia*

Simon Callow (centre) and company in the first major production this century of Goethe's ***Faust*** (Parts 1 & 2), directed by David Freeman in Robert David Macdonald's adaptation at the Lyric, Hammersmith, 1988.

dizzying heights, especially with shortened versions of Part I. Though his less demanding and more actable plays are regularly performed in Germany, they rarely appear in Britain.

Faust (I and II)
The story of the scholar tempted by the devil to barter his soul for the things of this world was already well-known, but Goethe turned it into a vast poem on the destiny of man, and his Faust is redeemed at the end (which led George Steiner to call it 'sublime melodrama'). The style of the play shifts from broad farce to high tragedy and most stages in between without warning, changing verse forms as it goes. There have been many attempts to put it on in English, usually making much of the Gretchen episode – Mephistopheles was one of Irving's favourite parts, in a very tame version of Part I by W.G. Willis, and the latest Robert David Macdonald's fine 1988 version at the Lyric, Hammersmith, with Simon Callow outstanding as Faust, is the most complete so far. This exuberant production (by David Freeman of Opera Factory) was staged with a mere twelve acrobatic actors, and managed to hold the balance between spectacle and poetry with great inventiveness, using a great overarching iron bridge on which the actors climbed and swung, a moving glass bubble to enclose the artificially created Homunculus in Part II, and a splendid show of cascades and watertanks for the mystical union of Homunculus and the sea-nymph Galatea, besides fire, smoke, and a wide variety of musical instruments.

in Tauris is a reworking of ▷Euripides' play of the same name; ▷Edward Bond's *The Fool* (about John Clare) and ▷Howard Brenton's *Bloody Poetry* (about the Shelleys and Byron) are other plays about poets to contrast with Goethe's treatment of Tasso.

GOGOL, Nikolai Vasilevich [1809–52]
Russian novelist and dramatist

Plays include:
***The Government Inspector* (1836), *Marriage* (1842), *The Gamblers* (1842)**

Gogol worked as a civil servant, took a course in painting, tried to become an actor and lectured on medieval history – failing at them all – before he achieved success with two volumes of Ukrainian tales in 1831–32. He is best known for his novel *Dead Souls* (of which he destroyed a second volume shortly before his death) and the comedy *The Government Inspector* of which he wrote: 'I decided to collect everything that was evil in Russia, all the injustices committed in places where justice is most of all expected of man –and laugh it off.' Its humour found an instant response and aroused considerable anger which for a time drove Gogol from Russia. *Dead Souls* was dramatised by ▷ Bulgakov and a production by ▷ Stanislavski joined the repertoire of the Moscow Arts Theatre in 1928.

The Government Inspector
A satire on official corruption in a small provincial town where an impecunious imposter is mistaken for a government official making an inspection, *The Government Inspector* introduced a grotesque farcical realism to the Russian theatre. Its frequent revivals show how little the basic satire dates and the name part has provided a vehicle for some outstanding interpretations, notably Paul Scofield's for the ▷ RSC, and for comedians such as Tony Hancock and Rik Mayall.

TRY THESE:
▷Dario Fo for similar broad satire of petty officials; ▷Peter Flannery's *Our Friends In The North* for local government corruption; ▷Barry Collins' *The Strongest Man in the World* as a modern equivalent; ▷Barrie Keeffe's many social satires; ▷Ibsen's *Pillars of Society* for Norwegian hypocrisy and corruption in high places.

GOLDONI, Carlo [1707–93]
Italian dramatist

Plays include:
***Belisario* (1734), *The Servant of Two Masters* (1746), *Mine Hostess* (also known as *Mirandolina*; 1753), *Il Campiello* (1756), *The Mania for the Country, The Adventure in the Country* and *The Return from the Country* (a trilogy; 1761), *The Fan* (1763)**

Goldoni wrote his first play at eleven and ran away with some travelling players at fourteen. He practised law for a short time before a tragi-comedy, *Belisario*, was accepted for performance in 1734 and he became the playwright of the Teatro San Samuele in Venice. For thirty years he tried to change the pattern of Venetian theatre before accepting the post of director of the

TRY THESE:
▷Beaumarchais' *Marriage of Figaro* for its treatment of servant and master relationships; ▷Molière, writing in a more formal style, is more savage in exposing bourgeois and aristocratic hypocrisies; for dramatists in the Goldoni tradition, ▷Eduardo De Filippo and ▷Dario Fo.

Comédie Italienne in Paris. He remained in Paris until his death. He wrote about 200 plays in Italian or French, the majority of them comedies.

Productions of Goldoni's plays have too often been conceived in *commedia dell'arte* style when, in fact, Goldoni's intention was to replace the improvised and now debased *commedia* with scripted plays which would reflect and comment on contemporary society. But he did not want to lose his audience – he had to wean them gradually. He considered that, 'the secret of the art of writing comedy is to cling to nature and never leave her' and, because his comedy is rooted in the way people behave rather than political satire, much of it is as relevant today, for though society has changed, his characters are still recognisable in a modern form. His comedies are mainly of middle-class life and they become increasingly sharp and critical. There is no 'typical' Goldoni play. *The Servant of Two Masters* comes early in his campaign of reform and still retains much of the structure of *commedia* with its fast moving farce. The development to a new form is gradual, reaching a peak with the last plays written in Venice. Despite the ponderousness of a 1987 ▷ National Theatre production – occasioned largely by trying to cram three plays into one evening – an earlier Glasgow Citizen's production to a different adaptation seems to have had much more bite; the trilogy of plays about 'Countrymania' shows clever plotting, and a witty dissection of character that spares no one.

GOLDSMITH, Oliver [1730–74]

Irish dramatist and man of letters

Plays include:

***The Good-Natured Man* (1768), *She Stoops to Conquer* (1773)**

Goldsmith appears to have been an attractively indigent figure in fashionable London society who, as well as earning the friendship of Dr Johnson, amongst other notables, wrote one play, one poem and one novel that have stood the test of time (*She Stoops to Conquer*, 'The Deserted Village' and *The Vicar of Wakefield*). Few eighteenth-century dramatists find a regular place in the twentieth-century repertory but *She Stoops to Conquer*, a genial comedy of manners, owes much of its continuing popularity to its combination of the sentimental and the satirical. The central character, Kate Hardcastle, uses great skill to expose the contemporary double standard of sexual morality and force the otherwise eligible Charles Marlow to come to terms with his own sexism. These characters are surrounded by foils, each with a prevailing character trait which allows actors considerable scope for comic invention.

TRY THESE:
▷Sheridan is the only other late eighteenth-century British dramatist whose work is regularly performed; the Restoration dramatists ▷Aphra Behn, ▷William Congreve, ▷George Etherege, ▷William Wycherley offer more robust treatments of similar themes; Kate herself refers to similarities between ▷Farquhar's *Beaux' Stratagem* and the play she exists in, and her name points to *The Taming of the Shrew*, in which the situation is reversed.

GOOCH, Steve [1945–]

British dramatist and translator

Plays include:

***Will Wat, If Not, Wat Will?* (1972), *Female Transport* (1973), *The Motor Show* (1974; with Paul Thompson), *Strike '26* (1975), *Back-Street Romeo* (1977), *The Woman Pirates Ann Bonney and Mary Read* (1978), *Future Perfect* (1980), *Landmark* (1980, revised version of *Our Land, Our Lives*, 1976), *Fast One* (1982), *What Brothers Are For* (1983), *Taking Liberties* (1984), *Star Turns* (1987)**

Keenly interested in ▷ community theatre, Gooch has pursued an interest in the labour movement, class and gender issues which has not brought him great recognition, despite his capacity to find genuinely interesting subjects such as the Peasants' Revolt of 1381 in *Will Wat*, nineteenth-century transportation of women convicts from Britain to Australia in *Female Transport* or late eighteenth-century mock elections involving Samuel Foote and John Wilkes in *Taking Liberties*. Even his treatment of the potentially fascinating story of Ann Bonney and Mary Read in *The Woman Pirates* failed to convince in an

TRY THESE:
▷Arnold Wesker's *Caritas* is also set at the time of the Peasants' Revolt; ▷James Bridie also wrote on *Mary Read*; see ▷Ann Jellicoe and ▷community theatre; see also ▷Howard Barker, ▷Howard Brenton, ▷David Edgar, ▷Trevor Griffiths, ▷David Hare for other, more successful, contemporary British socialist dramatists; ▷Ted Whitehead's *Old Flames* for another party where the male guest is

ill-received and short-lived ▷ RSC production and his most recent work *Star Turns*, in which three women invite men representing all the star signs to a party where they will act out the ways the planets influence them but only one turns up, did not meet with great success. His translations have been more consistently successful than his own original work: his version of ▷ Brecht's *The Mother* is the standard one in the British theatre and he has also translated Harald Mueller's (*Big Wolf*, 1972, *Rosie*, 1977, *Flotsam*, 1982), Fassbinder's (*Cock-Artist*, 1974), Martin Walser's (*Säntis*, 1980) and ▷ Franz Xaver Kroetz's (*Home Work*, 1982). His 1982 version of ▷ Lope de Vega's *Fuenteovejuna*, in which a village defeats a local tyrant through collective action, was an apt combination of Gooch's own political interests and his talent for adaptation, and *What Brothers Are For* was based on the Roman dramatist Terence's *The Brothers*.

outnumbered; ▷Caryl Churchill, ▷Pam Gems, and Timberlake Wertenbaker, for women's treatments of gender issues in both contemporary and historical contexts; also ▷Bryony Lavery for *Calamity*, re-examining pioneer women of the Wild West.

GORKI, Maxim (Alexei Maximovitch Peshkov)
[1868–1936]
Russian dramatist

Plays include:

***The Philistines* (1901), *The Lower Depths* (1902), *Summer Folk* (1904), *Children of the Sun* (1905), *Enemies* (1906), *Vassa Shelesnova* (1910)**

One of the great Russian dramatists, despite writing only a few major plays, Gorki's importance stems from his success as a dramatist both under the Czar and after the Revolution. His obvious feeling for the down-trodden underclass of Czarist Russia and his enormous status after the Revolution – he was the first president of the Soviet Writers' Union – won him at least the outward approval of Stalin, and he used his position to champion literary culture and to protect other writers from the censor and the secret police.

An orphan at the age of eleven, he worked through his adolescence and youth at every kind of ill-paid, temporary work. He learned to read while employed on a river steamer, turned to writing, and found literary success in 1895 with his story *Chalkash*. He became active in politics, befriended Tolstoy and ▷ Chekhov, and left the country after the failure of the 1905 Revolution. He returned to Russia in 1913, and became a champion of the Bolshevik Revolution. He developed the theory of 'Socialist Realism' which was soon distorted by Stalin's requirement for exclusively positive images of Soviet life. He died of TB in 1936, a death later laid at the door of a supposed Trotskyist plot 'uncovered' during the show-trials of Stalin's enemies.

An implacable enemy of the wealthy and the intellectual in pre-revolutionary society, who are invariably depicted as weak and ineffectual, his sympathy for the poor and the oppressed is powerful and sincere. Although in his time the realism of his portrayals of poverty was unprecedented, they transcended mere documentation by the author's obvious compassion for suffering and anger against its causes. The plays suffer frequently from Gorki's tendency to moralise and preach, a flaw he himself despaired of.

TRY THESE:
Gorki is a character in Dusty Hughes' *Futurists*; ▷Tunde Ikoli produced a memorable adaptation of *The Lower Depths*; ▷David Pownall's *Master Class* investigates the whole issue of socialist realism in the context of music; ▷Chekohov and ▷Mayakovsky were Russian contemporaries of Gorki; the visionary who briefly transforms lives is a notable figure in ▷Eugene O'Neill's *The Iceman Cometh* and ▷Ibsen's *The Wild Duck*. ▷Gregory Motton is a young, contemporary playwright who has certain affinities with Gorki in his compassion for lost dreams in his 1980s down-and-outs.

The Lower Depths
Set in a squalid slum-property in Moscow, run by the brutal, insensitive Kostilyov, the play portrays the miserable lives of the misfits and failures who are obliged to live there. Among the assorted poverty-stricken characters are the thief Vaska, Kostilyov's wife Vasilissa, her good sister Natasha, a ruined nobleman, a failed actor, and an ex-convict. An old man called Luka arrives, no better off than the others but inspired by an ideal of worthiness in everyone. For a short time his influence transforms the others. The actor becomes convinced that he can fight his alcohol-addiction and return to the stage, and Vaska decides to reform his ways, and leave with Natasha for a better life. The jealous Vasilissa overhears and with her husband attacks Natasha. A general fight ensues, in the course of which Vaska kills Kostilyov. In the aftermath of this disaster Luka vanishes. The ex-convict declares his faith in the old man's idealism, but the actor is crushed by depression and kills himself.

GRAEAE

British theatre company

Key productions include:

Sideshow (devised by Richard Tomlinson and the company; 1980), _3D_ (devised by Richard Tomlinson and the company; 1981), _Not Much to Ask_ (by Patsy Rodenburg; 1983), _Casting Out_ (by Nigel Jamieson; 1983), _Cocktail Cabaret_ (devised by the company; 1984), _Frankenstein_ (adapted by Geoff Parker; 1984), _Practically Perfect_ (by Ashley Grey; 1985), _Working Hearts_ (by ▷ Noël Greig; 1986), _Equality Street_ (devised by Ashley Grey and Geoff Armstrong; 1987), _A Private View_ (by ▷ Tasha Fairbanks; 1987)

Graeae, Britains major professional company of disabled performers, takes its name from the three mythological sisters who shared one eye and one tooth. Since its inception in 1980, Graeae has taken the subject of disability by the scruff of the neck and shaken up a good number of preconceptions previously existing about physical disability being any kind of handicap to theatrical invention, humour or pure enjoyment. Formed by Richard Tomlinson and Nabil Shaban who met whilst at college in Coventry, the company have toured nationally and internationally with great success.

The secret of this success lies in the nature and construction of the material, (often, though not always, devised with company members from their own experiences and given dramatic shape by a director and writer) and its defiant spirit. The shows have also revealed a wealth of talent, particularly in such performers as Nabil Shaban and Hamish Macdonald. The chair-bound Shaban in particular, an actor of extraordinary depth and comic skill, brought a wicked irony to his portrayal of Haile Selassie in Michael Hastings' *The Emperor* at the Royal Court.

Graeae's first show, *Sideshow*, gave a foretaste of what was to come with its story of fairground freaks who rebel, and their work has continued to give the lie to stereotypes of disability, of passivity or helplessness or tendencies to indulge in self pity. Their shows exude energy, shown for example in the exuberance of *Cocktail Cabaret*, whilst their adaptation of Mary Shelley's *Frankenstein* poignantly underlined the similarities between Frankenstein's feelings of isolation and general attitudes towards disability.

As well as their main productions Graeae also now have a Theatre in Education wing – *Practically Perfect* and *Equality Street* were both TIE productions – which tours schools with equal success. If Graeae is about anything, it is about re-educating public attitudes in the most entertaining way possible.

TRY THESE:
▷Phil Young's *Crystal Clear* and ▷Mark Medoff's *Children of a Lesser God* do the same for blindness and deafness; Maro Green and Caroline Griffin's *More* looked at hidden disabilities (agrophobia and anorexia); ▷Bernard Pomerance's *The Elephant Man* is another treatment of disability; Liz Lochhead's *Blood and Ice* is another look at Mary Shelley; SHAPE are an organisation specifically set up to co-ordinate access to the arts for groups with disabilities or special needs; Strathcona, a performing company of people with mental handicaps, is also highly regarded.

GRANVILLE BARKER, Harley [1877–1946]

British director, dramatist, actor and theorist

Plays include:

The Marrying of Anne Leete (written 1899; produced 1902), _The Voysey Inheritance_ (1905), _Waste_ (1907), _The Madras House_ (1910), _The Secret Life_ (written 1919–22; published 1923; produced 1988), _His Majesty_ (written 1928; not produced)

After ▷ Shaw, Granville Barker is perhaps the most important figure in the renaissance of English drama in the 1900s, and certainly one of the most intelligent. He was an excellent actor who worked with William Poel, and played ▷ Ibsen and Shaw parts for the Stage Society. He cut his director's teeth on the then fashionable Maeterlinck, and from 1904 to 1907, with John E. Vedrenne, managed the Court Theatre (now the Royal Court), where with an efficient ensemble company he produced contemporary European drama, Gilbert Murray's translations of ▷ Euripides, and new British plays, above all those of Shaw, in short runs of two or three weeks. They lost money, but their

TRY THESE:
▷Ibsen for problem plays and ▷Shaw for argument plays – Granville Barker often seems a cross between the two; for more well-crafted, family dramas with moral intent; ▷Lillian Hellman, much of ▷Terence Rattigan and, perhaps surprisingly, some of ▷Noël Coward; see also ▷John Galsworthy.

influence was seminal. Most of his plays were written for the Court; between 1912 and 1914 he directed some important productions of Shakespeare; but after his second marriage he virtually gave up the live stage and turned to writing and translation.

As a dramatist, he is most often bracketed with ▷ Galsworthy (and both are generally cross-referenced to Shaw), but his plays are livelier and less well-made than ▷ Galsworthy's, and he is better at putting argument on stage – though less funny – than Shaw. All his major plays except *The Voysey Inheritance* have received careful productions by the ▷ RSC or the ▷ National Theatre in recent years, and one of his final unperformed plays, *The Secret Life*, dealing with the perhaps autobiographical theme of public versus private life, was reverently resurrected at the Orange Tree, Richmond in 1988. His early play *The Marrying of Anne Leete* was found unconventional, elliptical, and somewhat ambiguous in 1902, and the ▷ RSC production in 1975 produced much the same reactions. *The Madras House* (▷ National Theatre 1977), directed by Bill Gaskill, was revealed as a very rich play: its structure seems loose at first – Barker is capable of creating the six carefully differentiated unmarried Huxtable girls in Act I and then abandoning them altogether – but the theme of the role of women in society holds it together, and it was one of the first productions to show the potential of the Olivier stage, in Hayden Griffin's lovely sets. *The Voysey Inheritance* is a good, dependable, well-crafted play, which generates considerable suspense, and the dreadful Voysey family are a fine collection of well-rounded upper-middle class characters, all visibly related. *Waste*, about the ruin of a politician through a casual affair which leads to abortion and death was written in 1907, banned by the censor, rewritten in 1926, and then almost unperformed until its quality was shown by the ▷ RSC revival in 1985. It is very well constructed, with a modern resonance to the abortion arguments and some fine long suspenseful scenes of political and personal argument.

GRASS, Günter [1927–]

West German novelist and dramatist

Plays include:

Onkel, Onkel (Mister, Mister; 1958), Die Bösen Köche (The Wicked Cooks; 1961), Die Plebejer proben den Aufstand (The Plebeians Rehearse the Uprising; 1965, produced 1966), Davor (Beforehand; 1969)

Socialist writer Grass was born in Danzig, and spent some time after the war in Paris, but now lives in West Berlin; he experimented with short Absurdist plays, stage design, poetry, and sculpture before making a hit with his novel *Die Blechtrommel* (*The Tin Drum*) in 1959. His most successful play internationally has been *The Plebeians Rehearse the Uprising*, an interesting metatheatrical piece. It is set in the Berliner Ensemble on 17 June 1953, when the East German workers demonstrated against demands for higher productivity; the boss is (unhistorically) rehearsing the plebeians' uprising against Coriolanus, when a group of construction workers breaks in to ask for a statement of his support. He refuses to give it, seeing the senselessness of this unplanned action, but he also refuses to denounce the uprising when asked by the authorities; and he continues the rehearsal, making the real workers participate, recording their voices and studying their reactions to improve his play. The situation is not treated naturalistically – parts are in verse – and there are touches of Expressionism; and it is far from being a simple attack on ▷ Brecht. It was performed with some success by the ▷ RSC at the Aldwych in 1970, directed by David Jones.

TRY THESE:
▷Brecht; ▷Hochhüth for German 1960s 'documentary' drama, but Grass has fewer pretensions and a sense of humour; ▷Trevor Griffiths' *The Party* for the relationship between rhetoric and political involvement, similarly ▷Bulgakov's *Molière*.

GRAY, Simon [1936–]

British dramatist and novelist

Plays include:

***Wise Child* (1967), *Dutch Uncle* (1969), *Butley* (1971), *Spoiled* (1971), *Otherwise Engaged* (1975), *The Rear Column* (1978), *Close of Play* (1979), *Stagestruck* (1979), *Quartermaine's Terms* (1981), *The Common Pursuit* (1984; revised version 1988), *Melon* (1987)**

TRY THESE:
▷Alan Bennett for wit with more compassion; ▷Tom Stoppard for wordplay with more intellect; ▷Christopher Hampton's *Philanthropist* offers a

Gray is a university lecturer and novelist whose plays often involve academics and people in publishing. His usually articulate characters are witty and often outrageous, so that audiences react to even his more macabre themes as comedies and have given him greater popular success than his rough handling by critics would suggest. Most of his plays present at least one homosexual character, though only in *Butley* and *Spoiled* (in which a schoolteacher with a pregnant wife teaches a pupil at home and becomes increasingly involved with him) is a homosexual relationship central to the play. Leading characters are often egocentric, sharp-tongued misfits, badly in need of a psychiatrist (*Melon* is a study of one such character's breakdown). Many of Gray's plays deal with sexual fetishism: *Wise Child* features transvestism, though the cross-dresser in fact turns out to be a crook in disguise; *Dutch Uncle* has a masochist seeking the attentions of a policeman by trying to murder his own wife; and in several plays characters indulge in sado-masochistic games. Such situations are usually exploited for laughs, though in *The Rear Column*, set in the Victorian Congo, sadism and cannibalism are used more seriously to show the degradation of the whites.

Several of Gray's plays were first seen on television and his screenplays include, for television, *After Pilkington* (1987) and, for cinema, *A Month in the Country* (1987) a gentle and understated script, quite different from the 'cleverness' of his stage plays.

Butley

Butley has a typical Gray protagonist, a bitchy university lecturer with a marriage in collapse, who drives away not only his wife but her replacement, the ex-student, now colleague, with whom he shares office and home. The savage tongue which makes him so offensive is also what provides much of the audience's fun. But if they enjoy seeing his selfishness get its comeuppance there is also a release for some of their own frustrations in seeing the characters find such vitriolic language for all those rows that happen in any highly stressed relationship. Gray is often too busy scoring points for the serious content of his plays to show but his exposure of our own selfishness and failure can be caustic and accessible to those prepared to think while they laugh.

different view of an academic; ▷Mike Leigh and ▷Alan Ayckbourn are as vituperative about middle-class mores, ▷Doug Lucie as vicious about contemporary media men.

GRAY, Spalding [1942–]

American playwright and monologist

Plays include:

Sex and Death to the Age 14 (1979), _Booze, Cars, and College Girls_ (1979), _A Personal History of the American Theatre_ (1980), _Points of Interest_ (1980), _In Search of the Monkey Girl_ (1981), _India (and After)_ (1982), _Interviewing the Audience_ (1982), _Swimming to Cambodia_ (1984), _Terrors of Pleasure_ (1986); he adapted _Rivkala's Ring_ (from ▷ Chekhov's _The Witch_, part of anthology _Orchards_ (1986)

Films include:

Swimming to Cambodia, writer and star; as an actor Gray has appeared in _The Killing Fields_ (1984), _True Stories_ (1986)

An integral part of the off-Broadway movement since the 1960s, Spalding Gray began his career as a member of the Performance Group, which later became the ▷ Wooster Group, before launching his successful solo career as a monologist. A self-described 'poetic journalist', Gray transmutes his daily life into detailed analyses of experience, in which any event – from his nervous breakdown in India in 1976 to his trip to the Tennessee State Fair in 1981 – is material ripe for comic, often acidic, investigation. In the 1986 compendium play *Orchards*, in which seven playwrights adapted ▷ Chekov short stories, Gray contrived a piece about an author who gets a Chekhov story in the mail, thereby prompting all manner of free association. Actual people figure prominently in his narratives, from ▷ Athol Fugard and Roland Joffe – his colleagues in the film *The Killing Fields* who pop up in *Swimming to Cambodia* — to his longtime girlfriend Renée Shafransky, whose joint renovation of a house in the Catskills is the impetus for *Terrors of Pleasure*. Allusions to sex and drugs

TRY THESE:
Gray's one-man assault on comic chaos is echoed by other American monologists/ comedians, including Whoopi Goldberg, Eric Bogosian, and Lily Tomlin.

abound in Gray's work, and at his best, his writing – and his delivery – provide a kind of erotic, hallucinogenic rush. Some find Gray nothing more than a particularly successful narcissist; others may see him as a profound human commentator who is the check on our age that men like Swift and Pope were on their's.

Swimming to Cambodia

Told in two parts, Gray's monologue – which was filmed in 1987 by Jonathan Demme (*Something Wild*) – was inspired by his experience playing the aide to the American ambassador in Roland Joffe's 1985 film *The Killing Fields.* With no props but a microphone, a glass of water, and several maps of Cambodia behind him, Gray charts a terrifyingly funny journey to the human heart of darkness in which the making of a film about genocide acts as a catalyst for ruminations on sex, death, human compassion and human destruction. One remarkable section recounts the fact that LA extras had to be flown to Asia to play Cambodian refugees, since Pol Pot had killed off all the real ones. In a voice capable of sustaining hypnotic waves of discourse, Gray's monologue combines keen-eyed analysis with profound irony.

GREGORY, (Lady) Isabella Augusta [1852–1932)

Irish theatre manager and dramatist

Plays include:

***Twenty-Five* (1903), *Spreading the News* (1904), *The White Cockade* (1905), *The Rising of the Moon* (1907), *The Workhouse Ward* (1908)**

Lady Gregory was an energetic Protestant landowner from Galway, who took to the theatre in middle age; after three years of experiment in Dublin with the Irish Literary Theatre (1899–1901), in the company of ▷ W.B. Yeats, Edward Martyn, and George Moore, and then with the Fay brothers' company, she helped to found the Abbey Theatre in 1904, and was involved in its management almost until her death in 1932. She did not start writing plays until she was fifty, but thereafter wrote around forty, mostly one-act farces, but also more pretentious (and thus less revivable) plays about Irish history, and such ventures as translations of ▷ Molière into the Galway dialect. She is probably more important for her management role than for her workmanlike plays; however her farcical comedies, such as *Spreading the News*, make a lively attempt to render Irish peasant speech patterns, and the plots crack along.

TRY THESE:
▷Yeats and ▷Synge for serious attempts to use the Irish dialect in the theatre; ▷Brian Friel's *Translations* bemoans the destruction of native Gaelic by imposed English.

GREIG, Noël [1944–]

British dramatist

Plays include:

***Bring Back The Cat* (1975), *Men* (1976), *As Time Goes By* (1977), *Heroes* (1977), *The Dear Love of Comrades* (1979), *Angels Descend on Paris* (1980), *Blood Green* (1980), *Hard Times for Our Times* (1982), *The Death of Christopher Marlowe* (1983), *Poppies* (1983), *Rainbow's Ending* (1984), *Spinning a Yarn* (1984), *Do We Ever See Grace?* (1985), *Best of Friends* (1985), *Working Hearts* (1986), *Laughter from the Other Side* (1986), *Whispers in the Dark* (1987), *Dusty Dreamtime* (1987), *Broken Armour* (1988), *Plague of Innocence* (1988)**

Television includes:

***Only Connect* (with ▷ Drew Griffiths; 1979)**

An extraordinarily prolific gay playwright whose work, still undervalued after twenty years, has covered an amazingly wide range and whose associations as writer/director with various groups in itself reflects some of the major theatrical trends of the past two decades. He was co-founder of The Combination, one of the first fringe groups to emphasise group work and improvisation and flexible working spaces; director at the Almost Free, scene of the first gay season of plays put on by Ed Berman; writer/director with the Bradford community based company The General Will;

TRY THESE:
▷Louise Page's *Salonika*, ▷Stephen Lowe's *Seachange*, ▷Greg Cullen's *Taken Out* all introduce corpses into plays which have a common war theme; ▷Jacqui Shapiro's *Winter in the Morning* takes a group of young Jews and shows their responses to Nazism and the Warsaw Ghetto; see also ▷Community Theatre; see also ▷Drew Griffiths; ▷Gay Sweatshop; ▷Gay Theatre.

Jonathan Pryce as Gethin Price performing his act, in Richard Eyre's original Nottingham Playhouse production of Trevor Griffiths' brilliant dissection of comedy and politics ***Comedians***, later seen at the Old Vic.

director with ▷ Gay Sweatshop from 1977–87 and writer-in-residence with Theatre Centre.

A writer of sensitivity and political consciousness, consistently exploring the points at which sexuality and social and political forces touch, his early work shows an interest too in exploring its historical roots, making connections with the present, and linking the personal with the public. *Men*, for example, deals particularly with socialism's inability to extend its ideology into personal, gay politics, through the story of a Bradford shop steward and his male lover. Probably Greig's best known play is *Poppies* which was presented by ▷ Gay Sweatshop and has also been produced in Germany and Australia. His earlier plays for ▷ Gay Sweatshop, *As Time Goes By* tracing gay repression through three different time periods, co-written with ▷ Drew Griffiths, and *The Dear Love of Comrades* have also been highly influential and performed abroad, in the USA and Australia. Another important, highly complex working out of repression and its responses was *Angels Descend on Paris* commissioned by The Combination at the Albany in London. Presented almost as an operetta, this six-character epic, threading its way from Nazi Berlin to Paris drew on Jacobean tragedy and the story of Bluebeard to explore the responses of people under pressure, as well as sexual identity, role playing, and opportunism. Not to everyone's liking, Nancy Duguid's ingeniously expressionistic production and Paul Dart's white-walled set impressed many more and surely deserves another outing.

Greig's most recent plays have however been aimed specifically at young people, TIE (theatre in education) and YPT (Young People's Theatre) groups. *Best of Friends*, (an adaptation of Dickens' *Hard Times*) *Dusty Dreamtime* and *Plague of Innocence* are all plays commissioned and written for YPT's, the latter dealing with AIDS. *Laughter from the Other Side*, *Whispers in the Dark*, *Broken Armour* are all plays written for Theatre Centre (which works in schools). Rattling good yarns on one level, these modern myths also deal with such contemporary issues as cultural suppression (*Whispers*), imperialism and sexuality. In *Laughter* and in *Best of Friends* sexuality, Thatcherism, and Greenham Common, are pulled together with typical ingenuity by Greig.

Poppies

Poppies is an anti-militaristic and anti-nuclear play and is indicative of both the best and the worst of Greig's style. Set on Hampstead's Parliament Hill where two middle-aged men, Sammy and Snow, are having a picnic, it utilises a favourite Greig technique, mixing past with present, poetry with polemics as ex-lovers come to life and matters of pacifism and the nature of masculinity are aired. A symbolic piece, it drew on images of mothers sticking photos of their own children on the wire fencing at Greenham Common air force base which Greig admitted had captured his imagination: 'I've always been preoccupied with the idea we shouldn't divorce our lives from history'. Though Nicholas de Jongh in the *Guardian* accused the play of being an incompatible mixture of styles, Jim Hiley in *City Limits* hailed its arrival as 'unflashy, intricately thoughtful and often elliptical . . . very much the product of gay consciousness' but thought that it contradicted common criticism of gay theatre 'by looking out from the ghetto and addressing itself with wit and sometimes brilliance to the biggest questions of the day'.

GRIFFITHS, Drew [1947–84]

British dramatist

Plays include:

***Mister X* (with Roger Baker; 1975), *Indiscreet* (with Roger Baker; 1976), *The Jingle Ball* (1976), *As Time Goes By* (with ▷ Noël Greig; 1977)**

Director, playwright and founder member with Gerald Chapman of ▷ Gay Sweatshop in 1975, Griffiths is a seminal figure in the history of gay political theatre in Britain. Remembered also as a devastating performer, and raised in the tradition of northern vaudeville and music hall, his final entrance in *Mister X* as a T-shirt and jeans drag queen (complete with feather boa) turned laughter to frozen chill. The first British gay play to challenge internalised self-oppression and assert gay pride, by implication,

TRY THESE:
▷Noël Greig; ▷Gay Sweatshop; ▷Lesbian Theatre; see also Jackie Kay's *Twice Over* as another gay play dealing with honesty in all relationships; for laughter with a sting in the tail, see ▷Trevor Griffiths' *The Comedians*, ▷John Osborne's *The Entertainer*, all of ▷Joe Orton, ▷Mike

Mister X's style set a precedent whose influence can be traced along a line of gay plays from *La Cage aux folles* on Broadway to Philip Osment's *This Island's Mine*. Equally influential and innovating is *As Time Goes By* co-authored with ▷ Noël Greig, whose historical perspective is everywhere apparent. An exploration of gay repression, it drew on three periods in history – Victorian England (▷ Oscar Wilde's trial and after), Nazi Germany in the 1930s and America 1969 with the beginning of the Gay Liberation Movement in the Stonewall Riots of that year. Again a pivotal play because of the way it draws together personal and political strands, (and the number of plays it subsequently spawned including ▷ Martin Sherman's *Bent*), its subject, sadly, could hardly be more relevant in the light of the enshrining of homophobia in current legislation, and it calls out for revival. *The Jingle Ball*, produced at Christmas 1976 was a spoof pantomime on Cinderella, gleefully following a natural line of work with the usual male Ugly Sisters, (but oh so aware of their sexual transposition and the traditionally weak ▷ pantomime jokes at the expense of gays) and a female Principal Boy whose love for Cinders was unequivocally lesbian.

Griffiths went on to write further plays for television and radio about gay relationships such as a comedy set in a gay disco over a straight pub, *The Only One South of the River*. What they all had in common was a basic love and a concern to show gay people with dignity and not a little humour.

Leigh's *Abigail's Party* and a good deal of ▷Alan Ayckbourn particularly *Absent Friends*; see also American comedians such as Lenny Bruce, Eric Bogosian; Cheryl Moch's *The Real True Story of Cinderella* is a spoof, all lesbian Cinderella; see also ▷Cabaret.

Mister X

Based on a pamphlet, *With Downcast Gays* by David Hutter and Andrew Hodges this is a cathartic 'coming out' play that made an enormous impact on audiences, gay and straight, wherever it went. Written in revue form – as though a personalised biography of the cast, with six sections telling different experiences and a gradually changing consciousness about being gay – the production used minimal props (chairs, a table and a tape recorder) in order to tour anywhere. It did, for over a year, (along with ▷ Gay Sweatshop's other 'coming out' play, Jill Posener's *Any Woman Can*) in pubs, clubs, the Mickery Theatre in Amsterdam, even Dublin. Times may have changed and so too some of the targets of homophobia in *Mister X*, but its radical use of laughter in breaking down stereotypes and overall humanitarian stance make it an interesting subject for reconsideration and revival, sadly without the inimitable performance of Griffiths himself.

GRIFFITHS, Trevor [1935–]

British dramatist

Plays include:

***The Wages of Thin* (1969), *Occupations* (1970), *Apricots* (1971), *Thermidor* (1971), *Lay By* (with Howard Brenton, ▷ Brian Clark, ▷ David Hare, ▷ Stephen Poliakoff, Hugh Stoddart, ▷ Snoo Wilson; 1971), *Sam, Sam* (1972), *The Party* (1973), *Comedians* (1975), *Deeds* (1978; with ▷ Howard Brenton, ▷ Ken Campbell and ▷ David Hare), *Oi for England* (1982), *Real Dreams* (1986)**

Griffiths is among the most important of contemporary socialist writers, and a central figure in the debate about the role of the dramatist in a capitalist culture. An unequivocal revolutionary Marxist, his work constantly questions which forms and which medium are most appropriate to a socialist theatre practice.

Born in Manchester Trevor Griffiths was of the first generation to reap the consequences of the 1944 Education Act and was the first of his family to go to grammar school and university. His first play *Sam, Sam* is a semi-autobiographical tale about two brothers, one of whom moves socially upward while the other is trapped by the class position of the family. Griffiths became a teacher, lecturer and an education officer for the BBC; his first full length play *Occupations* (a study of Gramsci) was taken up by the ▷ RSC, while his one-act plays *Apricots* and *Thermidor* were produced by the socialist company ▷ 7:84. *The Party* takes the form of a political debate among representatives from left-wing groups at the moment of May 1968; it was produced at the ▷ National Theatre with Laurence Olivier (rather improbably) in

TRY THESE:
▷David Hare, ▷Howard Brenton and ▷Howard Barker are among the 'political' dramatists of Griffiths' generation; ▷Tony Marchant's *Lazy Days Ltd* contrasts the opposing attitudes to life brothers, as does ▷Caryl Phillips' *Strange Fruit* and ▷Tunde Ikoli's *Scrape Off the Black*; Drew Griffiths and Roger Baker's *Mister X* uses comedy to subvert homophobic attitudes and was directly influenced by *Comedians*; ▷David Edgar's Marxist commitment is shared with Griffiths, and both have engaged in the debate about the best form for socialist drama throughout

the role of the Trotskyist John Tagg, and was revived again in a television version in the Spring of 1988 when its 'talking heads' political intellectualism suddenly seemed dated.

Griffiths very much sees his role as a writer as interventionist; he says 'my sort of writing is about impact and penetration' and the productions of *Occupations* and *The Party* on the stages of the Establishment theatres of the ▷ National and ▷ RSC were very much part of this. Griffiths' concern is to make socialist ideas accessible, and to make cultural forms part of a broader political struggle.

Griffiths has often chosen to work in television rather than the theatre in order to achieve the widest possible audience; he has adapted many of his plays for television, has contributed episodes to popular series (such as *Dr Finlay's Casebook*), and adapted novels (including D.H. Lawrence's *Sons and Lovers*) for television. His television series *Bill Brand* took the form of a socialist soap-opera, in its account of a Labour MP, whose career encompassed a range of socialist debates. His film work includes major contributions to the script of Warren Beatty's *Reds*, and *Fatherland* (1986). Griffiths has said: 'I chose to work in those modes because I have to work with the popular imagination. . .I am not interested in talking to thirty-eight university graduates in a cellar in Soho'.

Comedians
A study of the nature of comedy, it works both as a scabrous attack on the racist and sexist humour which passes for comedy in British popular culture, and as an exploration of the radical potential of comedy. The play begins in the classroom where an old comedian (originally, and appropriately, played by Jimmy Jewel) is training a group of stand-up comics. The group is made up of a docker, a milkman, an insurance agent, a labourer, a night club owner and a van-driver; for them all, success as a comedian is an escape route from the tediousness of their work; in the second act, the group perform at a bingo club for an agent who may supply the means. While desperate ambition fires most of the group to come out with a spate of cracks against the blacks, Pakistanis, Jews and women, the youngest member dumps his prepared act and in a stunning alienation effect, turns directly to the audience with a corruscating speech of class hatred. The final act of the play returns to the classroom, where pupil and teacher debate the private and public possibilities of comedy. The play's theatrical practice of challenging the basis of what it is possible to laugh at can be very unsettling for an audience.

their writing careers; ▷Margaretta D'Arcy and ▷John Arden have also engaged in the debate but have turned instead to ▷community-based theatre; ▷John McGrath has remained with ▷7:84; see also ▷Cabaret.

HALL, Willis and WATERHOUSE, Keith [1929–] and [1929–]
British dramatists

Joint plays include:
***Billy Liar* (1960), *Celebration: The Wedding and the Funeral* (1961), *England, Our England* (revue; 1962), *All Things Bright and Beautiful* (1962), *Say Who You Are* (1965), *The Card* (musical from Arnold Bennett's novel; 1973), and adaptations of ▷ Eduardo De Filippo's *Saturday, Sunday, Monday* (1973) and *Filumena* (1977)**

Yorkshiremen from Leeds, these dramatists have worked both independently and together and are best known for their well-constructed, accurately observed studies of north-country life, frequently showing their characters' attempt to escape – actually or in fantasy – from their surroundings. However, one of their biggest commercial successes, *Say Who You Are*, is a farce set in Knightsbridge and other major successes have been *Saturday, Sunday, Monday* and *Filumena*, both adaptations of Neopolitan plays by ▷ Eduardo De Filippo.

Hall had already had productions – especially *The Long and the Short and the Tall* (1958), a moving play about a trapped group of soldiers and their Japanese prisoner in Malaya – and Waterhouse had published novels before their collaboration on the stage version of his *Billy Liar*. Both separately and together they have produced a number of screenplays (including *The Long and the Short and the Tall* (1961), *Whistle down the Wind* (1961), *A Kind of Loving* (1963) *Billy Liar* (1963)), radio and television plays and series, and revue material.

There is no typical Hall and Waterhouse play as far as subject matter is concerned. What you can expect is assured handling of naturalistic details, fresh and original writing in a sound structure and at least one role that is a gift to the actor.

TRY THESE:
▷J. B. Priestley for earlier and middle-class Yorkshire comedies; ▷Alan Bennett for similar accurate depiction of Yorkshire life, though often less naturalistic in structure (especially *Worm's Eye View*); ▷David Storey for similar naturalistic portrayals of northern and working-class life in the 1960s and early 1970s; ▷R. C. Sherriff's *Journey's End*, ▷Terence Rattigan's *Flarepath* and ▷Arnold Wesker's *Chips with Everything* for some of the many different views of conscript life.

HAMPTON, Christopher [1946–]
British dramatist

Plays include:
***When Did You Last See My Mother?* (1964), *Total Eclipse* (1968), *The Philanthropist* (1970), *Savages* (1973), *Treats* (1976), *After Mercer* (1980), *Tales from Hollywood* (1982)**

Translations and adaptations include:
***Marya* (from Babel; 1967), *Uncle Vanya* (1970), *Signed and Sealed* (from ▷ Feydeau; 1976), *Hedda Gabler* (from ▷ Ibsen; 1970), *A Doll's House* (from ▷ Ibsen; 1970), *Ghosts* (from ▷ Ibsen; 1978), *The Wild Duck* (from ▷ Ibsen; 1979), *Tales from the Vienna Woods* (from ▷ Horvath; 1979), *The Portage to San Cristobal of A.H.* (from the novel by George Steiner; 1982), *Tartuffe* (from ▷ Molière; 1983), *Les Liaisons Dangereuses* (from Laclos; 1985)**

Films include:
A Doll's House* (1973), *Tales from the Vienna Woods

TRY THESE:
▷Brecht appears as a character in *Tales from Hollywood*; the treatment of sexual politics in *Les Liaisons Dangereuses* and *Treats* makes an interesting comparison – to ▷Ted Whitehead and ▷Strindberg; the eighteenth century setting of *Liaisons* is reminiscent of the world of Restoration comedy; see also ▷adaptations; ▷Terry Johnson is another male playwright whose work is informed by feminism,

Lindsay Duncan in Christopher Hampton's stunning adaptation of Laclos' epistolary novel ***Les Liaisons Dangereuses***, directed for the RSC by Howard Davies in 1985.

(1979), *The Honorary Consul* (from Graham Greene; 1983), *The Good Father* (1986)

Born in the Azores, Hampton was educated at public school and went to Oxford University to study French and German (which he has put to use in his many translations of French and German literature into drama) in 1963. The Oxford University Dramatic Society put on his first play (written when he was eighteen) *When Did You Last See My Mother?*, about two school leavers. It was taken up by the Royal Court and produced there as a Sunday night performance when Hampton was still an undergraduate. It was directed by Robert Kidd, who directed all of Hampton's plays at the Court, in line with their policy of matching writers and directors. In 1966 it transferred to the West End and Hampton was the youngest dramatist in living memory to have a West End production.

On leaving Oxford, Hampton became the first Resident Dramatist at the Court and supervised their script department. Hampton has said: 'At Oxford I learned to enjoy myself – but it was the Royal Court which gave me an education.' The Court produced *Total Eclipse*, a play about Verlaine which Hampton had written as a student and then *The Philanthropist*, written while Hampton was Resident Dramatist. This became, as Hampton puts it, 'disgracefully successful, so much so that I've always felt I left under something of a cloud'.

In the early 1970s Hampton translated and adapted a number of ▷ Ibsen's most important plays. In the period of the women's movement he was much affected by *The Doll's House*, and became preoccupied with questions of feminism and gender which he explored in *Treats*, and which have continued to inform his writing. His adaptation of *Les Liaisons Dangereuses* (from Laclos' epistolary novel) is not only a skilled dramatisation of a great French novel, but also a very contemporary study of sexual power struggles and exploitation.

as is ▷Stephen Lowe; ▷Tony Marchant is a contemporary male playwright who came to prominence while still in his early twenties; ▷Louise Page is an equivalent female dramatist.

The Philanthropist

The Philanthropist was the play which made Hampton a truly 'commercial' playwright. Subtitled 'a bourgeois comedy' the play focuses on the ironically named philanthropist, an academic, whose most apt line is: 'I'm a man of conviction – I think'. The title is a sideways nod at Molière's *Le Misanthrope*, of which it is something of an inversion. The play initially appears as an apparently conventional comedy, with wit and wisecracks flying in a bourgeois intellectual setting. But, in the first scene, an undergraduate (playwright) shoots himself, and introduces a dark edge to the comedy. The literary jokes and wit transmute into a bleak desperation. Over the course of the play, Philip, the philanthropist, demonstrates his ineffectuality, and thereby the sterility of the conventions by which he (and, by implication, the conventional form of this kind of play) work. In attempting not to do any harm, he actually wreaks havoc.

HANDKE, Peter [1942–]

Austrian dramatist

Plays include:

***Offending the Audience* (1966), *Prophecy and Self-Accusation* (1966), *Cries For Help* (1967), *Kaspar* (1969), *My Foot My Tutor* (1969), *Quodlibet* (1970), *The Ride Across Lake Constance* (1971), *They Are Dying Out* (1974), *A Sorrow Beyond Dreams* (1977)**

TRY THESE:
▷Ionesco, for word-games and the attempt to construct the world by the use of language; ▷Tom Stoppard for different kinds of word games; ▷Kroetz for a similar obsession with speech and communication; ▷Brian Friel's *Translations* for language as the symbol of cultural freedom.

Obsessed with the problems of language and communication Handke constantly challenges preconceptions of theatrical form, style and content. Having achieved some attention – some would say notoriety – with *Offending the Audience*, a title which seemed all too accurate a description of the piece, he proved himself a writer of serious intent with *Kaspar*. Here Handke takes the story of Kaspar Hauser, who lived without speech in total isolation until he was a full-grown adult, to illustrate his thesis that language defines personality and locks each of us within its patterns of cliché and custom. His later work continues to explore this 'crisis of language' theme.

Offending the Audience

Conspicuously lacking conventional plot or character, this

'Sprechstück' or 'speech-piece' presents four speakers of any age or sex who take an hour to work up to a climax of insults to the audience, deploying elaborate, structured sequences, often contradicting themselves, subverting all possible responses.

HANSBERRY, Lorraine [1930–1965]

American dramatist

Plays include:

***A Raisin in the Sun* (1959), *The Sign in Sidney Brustein's Window* (1964); and finished posthumously by her former husband, Robert Nemiroff, *To Be Young, Gifted and Black* (1969), *Les Blancs* (1970)**

Like ▷ O'Casey and ▷ Delaney, Hansberry transformed the grim world around her into something touched with gold dust. Both *The Sign in Sidney Brustein's Window* and *A Raisin in the Sun* deal in a kind of idealism, in rising above adversity. But it is the latter play that is regarded now as a cornerstone in the development of black theatre – a powerful, poignant protest against racial injustice and white bigotry, that still works today despite its somewhat solid naturalism and contradictory values (working-class aspiring to white middle-class values). As the recent Tricycle revival proved, there is enough still in the warm-hearted characterisations of the downside Chicago family – chauffeur Walter Lee with his dreams of a liquor store and his battle for self-respect, his put-upon wife Ruth, young son, sister-in-law and, above all, the dominating figure of Momma (a painfully honourable performance in the Tricycle version from Carmen Munroe) – to draw audiences inexorably into their world and, what's more, emerge moved, and even humbled by the experience. Far more than any outright agit-prop, *A Raisin in the Sun* is still inspirational theatre, showing how a black working-class family, even in the face of racism and hostility and their own struggles against the fast buck ethos, can retain dignity and pride. A big success (it ran for two years on Broadway, and won the New York Critics' Circle award for 1959), Hansberry's compassionate and gently humorous family saga was far ahead of its time and still strikes a common chord with current issues of racism and sexism. Tragically, Hansberry died of cancer at the age of thirty-four and it was she who inspired the song Nina Simone took from the posthumously finished *To Be Young, Gifted and Black*.

TRY THESE:
▷James Baldwin's *Amen Corner* for comparable style but more bitter analysis of his black community; ▷Robert Ardrey's *Jeb* for a white liberal approach to American racism; ▷Tennessee Williams and ▷Arthur Miller for contemporary white American treatments of the family; ▷Caryl Phillips' *Strange Fruit* for a more pessimistic black British view; ▷Ntozake Shange for contrast with black women's writing, thirty years on; Adrienne Kennedy is another black American whose style of grotesque imagery is in contrast to Hansberry.

HARE, David [1947–]

British dramatist and director

Plays include:

***Slag* (1970, *Lay By* (with ▷ Howard Brenton, ▷ Brian Clark, ▷ Trevor Griffiths, ▷ Stephen Poliakoff, Hugh Stoddart, ▷ Snoo Wilson; 1971), *England's Ireland* (with Tony Bicât, ▷ Brenton, ▷ Clark, ▷ David Edgar, Francis Fuchs, ▷ Wilson; 1972), *The Great Exhibition* (1972), *Brassneck* (with ▷ Brenton; 1973), *Knuckle* (1974), *Teeth'n'Smiles* (1975), *Fanshen* (1976), *Plenty* (1978), *A Map of the World* (1983), *Pravda* (with Brenton; 1985) *The Bay at Nice* (1986), *Wrecked Eggs* (1986)**

Hare came to prominence in the 1970s as one of a breed of committed socialist writers who included ▷ Howard Barker, ▷ Howard Brenton, ▷ David Edgar, ▷ Snoo Wilson and ▷ Trevor Griffiths. He founded Portable Theatre with the dramatist Tony Bicât in 1968 and the still vibrant ▷ Joint Stock company with William Gaskill and Max Stafford-Clark in 1974. He has also been literary manager and resident dramatist at the Royal Court Theatre and currently runs one of the companies at the ▷ National Theatre. Hare has also carved out a singular niche in television with his television films, *Licking Hitler* (1978), *Dreams of Leaving* (1980) and *Saigon – Year of the Cat* (1983), which subtly modified traditional television techniques.

Hare has described himself in recent years as a 'commentator' on the ills of contemporary capitalism. His plays still reflect a highly charged political consciousness but recent work – such as *The Bay at Nice*, *Wrecked Eggs* and the film *Wetherby* – mark a

TRY THESE:
For *Fanshen* see ▷Joint Stock; *Caucasian Chalk Circle* and other works by ▷Bertolt Brecht and *Narrow Road to the Deep North*, *The Bundle* and other works by ▷Edward Bond, like *Fanshen*, use epic style and geographical or spatially distanced settings; for plays about the impact of World War II see ▷Terence Rattigan's *The Deep Blue Sea*, Ian McEwan's *The Imitation Game*, ▷Stephen Lowe's *Touched*; for plays related to *Pravda*, see ▷Ben Jonson, particularly *Bartholomew Fair* and *The Devil is an Ass*, for his violently

return to a predominant interest in the topography of personal relationships.

Pravda
Pravda, probably Hare's most popular play to date, was written, like *Brassneck*, in collaboration with ▷ Howard Brenton (an intermittent partnership that began in the days of Portable Theatre). Both are exuberantly comic political satires on an epic scale. Much of *Pravda*'s popularity in performance was due to its coincidental topicality with real-life press dealings involving Rupert Murdoch and Robert Maxwell, as well as a lethally comic central performance from Anthony Hopkins as Lambert Le Roux, the energetically ruthless, reptilian newspaper magnate. Despite its popularity, *Pravda* confirmed a general unease among female critics about Hare's handling of female characterisation. As in *Plenty*, the leading female character carries the play's moral force, but remains an unreal, one-dimensional figure, on the periphery of the main action – more of a cipher than a fully-rounded character.

Plenty
Plenty attempts to use the story of the mental disintegration of its heroine, a former Resistance worker, to reflect the collapse of British post-war ideals, part of Hare's continuing preoccupation with wartime and immediate post-war England. The use of 'flashback' techniques is characteristic, giving historical depth and context to Hare's analysis of what he sees as decay in contemporary Western society particularly amongst the middle classes (a technique also used in *Wetherby*, Hare's first full-length feature film, which he wrote and directed in 1985). In *Plenty* audiences have tended to focus on the heroine's neuroticism but Hare insists on the importance of the social context to which she responds. The film version, starring Meryl Streep, released in 1986, abandons some of the narrative complexity and specifically British detail of the play.

entertaining attacks on capitalism; see ▷Marlowe's *Dr Faustus* for the interplay between a dupe and a satanic figure which parallels the relationship between the ineffectual editor Andrew May and Le Roux in *Pravda*; see ▷Michael Frayn and ▷Hecht and McArthur for newspaper plays; ▷Peter Nichols' *The National Health*, ▷Brenton's *Epsom Downs*, ▷Trevor Griffiths' *Comedians* for plays which treat the state of Britain through a national institution; for rock ▷musicals taking the temperature of a nation in similar fashion to *Teeth'n'Smiles* see ▷Barrie Keeffe's *Bastard Angel*.

HART, Moss

see KAUFMAN, George S.

HARWOOD, Ronald [1934–]
British novelist and dramatist

Plays include:
***Country Matters* (1969), *A Family* (1978), *The Dresser* (1980), *After the Lions* (1982), *Tramway Road* (1984), *Interpreters* (1985), *The Deliberate Death of a Polish Priest* (1985), *J.J. Farr* (1987)**

Born in South Africa, Harwood left to attend RADA in London and then joined Sir Donald Wolfit's Shakespeare Company as actor and dresser to this last of the old-style actor-managers. He continued as an actor until 1959, but in 1960 he had a play produced on television and published his first novel in 1961. He has had more success as a screenwriter than in the theatre. His subjects have been varied and his work is difficult to categorise in any medium, though you can expect well characterised parts for actors and a strong sense of theatre. *J.J. Farr*, about the loss of religious faith, offers acting opportunities, but found little favour with critics and, to date, *The Dresser* remains his only totally successful play.

The Dresser
Inspired by, though not a portrait of, Wolfit and his company, *The Dresser* is Harwood's only popular success. The play is set on tour in the provinces in the middle of World War II, as the actor-manager gets through his last performance of *King Lear*, and anyone with memories of that kind of theatre will recognise the authenticity with which he has captured it. Though the plot is not based on actual incidents, and it is set before Harwood knew Wolfit's company, his involvement with the material seems to have given this play a completeness lacking in his other stage works which never quite catch fire as this one does.

TRY THESE:
▷John Osborne's *The Entertainer* for a study of life on the variety circuit; ▷J.B. Priestley's *The Good Companions* and ▷Noël Coward's *Hay Fever* for other portraits of a life in theatre; ▷Trevor Griffiths' *Comedians* for a more barbed view; *42nd Street*, *Chorus Line*, *Mame* and a whole bandwagon of American musicals for the tears and bliss of showbiz; Graham Greene for plays about loss of faith.

Stefan Kalipha, Hepburn Graham, Ben Onwukwe and, foreground, Nabil Shaban, in Jonathan Miller's production of Michael Hastings's ***The Emperor***, Royal Court, 1987.

HASTINGS, Michael [1938–]
British dramatist

Plays include:
***Don't Destroy Me* (1956), *Yes – and After* (1957), *The World's Baby* (1964), *Lee Harvey Oswald* (1966), *The Cutting of the Cloth* (1973), *For the West* (1977), *Gloo Joo* (1978), *Full Frontal* (1979), *Carnival War a Go Hot* (1979), *Midnite at the Starlite* (1980; televised as *Midnight at the Starlite*), *Tom and Viv* (1984), *The Emperor* (1986)**

Hastings began his theatrical career as a trainee actor and writer at the Royal Court, where he is now Literary Manager. Born in London, his first play, *Don't Destroy Me*, an exploration of a Jewish household in Brixton, was produced when he was only eighteen and working as a tailor's apprentice. His second play, *Yes – And After*, was produced as a Royal Court Sunday night show, a series of productions 'without decor' initiated by George Devine to provide opportunities for new writers and directors. *The World's Baby* was also a Sunday night performance, with Vanessa Redgrave as the central character, a woman whom the play follows over twenty years, but it was never given a full-scale production. *The Silence of Lee Harvey Oswald*, produced at the Hampstead Theatre Club, is an example of what was known at the time as 'Theatre of Fact', a sort of documentary account of Oswald's life up to the point of Kennedy's assassination. *For the West* was staged at the Royal Court Theatre Upstairs, and was the first Royal Court play to transfer to the ▷ National Theatre. *Gloo Joo*, a study of a West Indian's experience of London, was produced at the Hampstead Theatre Club and went on to transfer to the West End. *The Emperor*, a controversial account of Emperor Haile Selassie (there were protests outside from Ethiopians and Rastafarians), was a subtle if quirky study of power and its acolyte tendencies. Hastings has a fascination with the possibilities of biography (he has published biographies of Rupert Brooke and Richard Burton), and has said: 'in all theatre all biography is fiction and some fiction is autobiography'. A number of his plays have been televised, including *For the West*, *Gloo Joo*, and *Midnight at the Starlite*, a comedy about ballroom dancing.

Tom and Viv
Probably Hastings' most successful play, *Tom and Viv* pursues his concern with the theatrical possibilities of biography in a study of the fraught marriage between ▷ T.S. Eliot and his first wife, Vivienne Haigh-Wood (originally played by Julie Covington). Vivienne ended her life in a mental hospital, and the play explores her mental fragility, her tortuous relationship with Eliot, and the contemporary British upper-class culture which produced Vivienne. The play is ultimately quite unsympathetic to Eliot and his role in their relationship. *Tom and Viv* was produced in America after a successful Royal Court run under the auspices of Joe Papp, and has been one of the most successful of the exchanges between the Royal Court and Joe Papp's theatre in New York.

TRY THESE:
▷Derek Walcott's *O Babylon* for other views of Haile Selassie; ▷Edgar White, ▷Michael Abbensetts, ▷Mustapha Matura and ▷Caryl Phillips for contrasting views of West Indians in London; ▷Barrie Keeffe's *King of England*; for other plays about poets and their domestic lives, see ▷Howard Brenton's *Bloody Poetry* and Liz Lochhead's *Fire and Ice*; also ▷Hugh Whitemore's portrait of the poet Stevie Smith, *Stevie*, ▷Susan Glaspell's *Alison's House* based on Emily Dickinson; and ▷Bond's *Bingo*.

HAVEL, Václav [1936–]
Czech dramatist and dissident

Plays include:
***The Garden Party* (1963), *The Memorandum* (1965), *The Increased Difficulty of Concentration* (1968), *Audience*, *Private View* and *Protest* (three short plays, 1975), *Largo Desolato* (1984), *Temptation* (1985)**

Havel has not been able to see any of his own plays since 1969 (except for a video of *Temptation* smuggled in by the ▷ RSC), and they are not published openly in Czechoslovakia, though they have been widely performed in the West. He wanted to study drama at university, but because of his 'bourgeois' family background he was forced to start as a stagehand; he then worked as a lighting technician and later became dramaturg at the avant-garde Prague Theatre on the Balustrade, for which he began to write plays in the 1960s. Havel's early plays were classified as absurdist, and *The Memorandum* showed one of his

TRY THESE:
▷Beckett, for *Catastrophe*, possibly the nearest he has ever come to making a political statement; ▷Mrozek, for Eastern European plays using 'absurdist' techniques to show political desperation; ▷Tom Stoppard (Ken Tynan was the first to link these two Czechs and to see Stoppard's potential political streak); ▷Arthur Miller's *The Archbishop's Ceiling*

recurring themes: life in an organisation where mechanical clichés and deformation of language conceal the fact that nothing actually gets done, and employees are always watching their backs. In 1968 he left the Theatre on the Balustrade, and he was effectively excluded from live theatre after the Soviet invasion of that year. He was imprisoned in 1979 for his involvement in VONS (the Committee for the Defence of the Unjustly Prosecuted), and ▷ Samuel Beckett wrote *Catastrophe* for him during this imprisonment. When released in 1983 Havel wrote the short play *Mistake* as a response; both were shown at the Barbican as *Thoughtcrimes* in 1984. *Largo Desolato* shows a dissident scholar reduced to near-nervous breakdown by the impossibility of living up to his reputation as a symbol of resistance and is an allegory of the artist's relationship to society; ▷ Tom Stoppard translated it for the New Vic, Bristol, in 1986, and the Orange Tree picked it up in 1987. Havel continues to write plays, perhaps as a safety valve, and apparently much faster since his imprisonment; and he refuses to leave his country.

Temptation
This is another satire on organisational hierarchies and yesmen, but based on the Faust story. It has a broader satirical sweep than his earlier plays, showing multiple layers of fear, disloyalty and double-cross. Dr Foustka, who wishes to study forbidden knowledge, is tempted to ever meaner betrayals by a Mephistophelean figure with smelly feet, who turns out to be a spy for the Director of his Institute; all is revealed at a wild Walpurgisnacht fancy dress party. The play was produced, to some acclaim, at the ▷ RSC's Other Place in 1987 and the Barbican in 1988; the RSC had to book a special call to Havel to give him news of its success.

for East European dissidents; ▷Goethe and ▷Marlowe for treatment of the Faust story; ▷Timberlake Wertenbaker's *The Grace of Mary Traverse* has Faustian resonances.

HAVERGAL, Giles

see GLASGOW CITIZENS' THEATRE

HAYES, Catherine [1949–]
British dramatist

Plays include:
***Little Sandra* (1976), *Not Waving* (1983), *Skirmishes* (1982), *Long Time Gone* (1986)**

When she was younger, Catherine Hayes wanted to be a detective. Instead she became a French teacher, and it was only when she saw ▷ Alan Bleasdale's advertisement for new writers for the Liverpool Playhouse that she decided to turn her hand to plays rather than novel writing. One thing led to another: she was commissioned, after the one-act *Merseyside Miscellany*, to write a full-length play and became writer-in-residence at the Playhouse. *Skirmishes* is the play that brought her into the public eye; essentially a two-hander (it won *Drama* magazine's Most Promising Playwright award for 1982), *Skirmishes* casts an unsentimental eye on the subject of mother/daughter and sibling relationships. Round a dying mother's bed, a bitter, if witty, war of verbal and emotional attrition is let loose as two sisters give vent to long-stored up resentments and misunderstandings. Hayes' drama is a searing, yet compassionate analysis, confronting painful truths about death, love, and the awful taboos to do with duty. Further revelations of female self-doubt and vulnerability are also behind *Not Waving*, which charts the crumbling fortunes of a female cabaret comic, brought on by ill-health, failing confidence (she can't get the audience to laugh any more) and a break-up with her manager.

Although *Skirmishes* has been performed all over the world, from Manhattan's Theatre Club in New York, to Australia, Japan and Germany, Hayes still regards herself as a French teacher first and as a writer second. She dislikes the over-subjectivity of writing: 'you explore what's within rather than what's outside yourself, and that's wrong.' A writer who 'hears' her plays rather than visualising them in her head, she sums up the feelings of a good many playwrights when she says of rehearsals: 'they make you realize what a vast difference there is between writing a play and putting on a production.' But she continues to enjoy writing,

TRY THESE:
▷Marsha Norman's *'Night Mother* takes an equally painful view of the symbiotic mother/daughter relationship; ▷Sharman Macdonald, ▷Julia Kearsley, ▷Ayshe Raif and ▷Louise Page are other contemporary playwrights who have dealt with equal realism about mothers and daughters; ▷Shelagh Delaney's *A Taste of Honey* and ▷Ann Jellicoe's *The Sport of My Mad Mother* were more extended treatments, one realistic, the other surreal; ▷Stephen Bill's *Curtains* also dealt with family pressures around a dying mother; Honor Moore's *Mourning Pictures* is a free verse treatment of a dying mother and her daughter (see ▷Monstrous Regiment); ▷Michel Tremblay's *Johnny*

has had further commissions, and, with its small cast and universal theme, *Skirmishes* is likely to be in the repertory for some to come.

Mangano and His Astonishing Dogs has a cabaret club setting for its two downward spiralling performers; ▷John Osborne's *The Entertainer* and ▷Trevor Griffiths' *Comedians* are more extended explorations into the nature of comedy as prop and social weapon; ▷Peter Nichols' *A Day in the Death of Joe Egg* for comparable humour.

HECHT, Ben [1894–1964]

MacARTHUR, Charles [1895–1956]
American dramatists

Plays include:
***The Front Page* (1928), *Twentieth Century* (1932), *Jumbo* (1935; book for the musical), *Ladies and Gentlemen* (1939), *Swan Song* (1946)**

A team who found success together writing screenplays, and also on their own, Hecht and MacArthur helped define a style of boisterous, cheerfully anarchic comedy which is definably American in its determined avoidance of anything genteel or refined. The duo are bestknown for two plays, *The Front Page* and *Twentieth Century*, both of which became films – or, in the case of the former, several films. Each is a kind of courtship comedy. In *Front Page*, an editor tries to lure his star reporter away from his fiancée by extolling the passion of journalism over that of romance. In *Twentieth Century*, which became a hit Broadway and West End musical in the late 1970s, an egomaniacal Broadway producer makes a young shopgirl a star, and when she makes moves to leave him, he spends a lengthy train journey trying to win her back. (Howard Hawks' 1934 movie version, with Carole Lombard and John Barrymore, is a comedy classic.) *Ladies and Gentlemen*, a romantic thriller set during a trial, was MacArthur's attempt to concoct a vehicle for his wife, Helen Hayes. The two found less success as collaborators in later plays.

The Front Page
A perennial favourite for revivals (most recently in London at the Old Vic in 1972 and in New York at the Lincoln Centre in 1986), this gregarious tale of Chicago newspapermen in the 1920s has spawned three films, one musical (the 1982 *Windy City*) and any number of spiritual children, from ▷ Thomas Babe's *Buried Inside Extra* to, in their own more politicised way, British works like ▷ Hare and ▷ Brenton's *Pravda* and Stephen Wakelam's *Deadlines*. Politics were not upmost in Hecht and MacArthur's minds as they spun a rapid-fire yarn about a scheming editor's attempts to keep his star reporter, Hildy Johnson, from succumbing to the enticements of love; but in its subplots about corruption in the sheriff's office and its often blistering portrait of male camaraderie, the play can seem surprisingly biting and contemporary.

TRY THESE:
▷Thomas Babe's *Buried Inside Extra*, ▷Hare and Brenton's *Pravda*, Stephen Wakelam's *Deadlines*; ▷George Abbott's *Broadway* and ▷Kaufman and Hart for similarly large-scale, rumbustious American works; and ▷David Mamet (especially *Glengarry Glen Ross*) for capturing both the brio and the venality that go with careerism.

HEGGIE, Iain [1953–]
British dramatist

Plays include:
***Politics in the Park* (1986), *A Wholly Healthy Glasgow* (1987), *American Bagpipes* (1988)**

Television includes:
A Wholly Healthy Glasgow (1988)

One-time PT instructor, drama teacher, and member of the

TRY THESE:
▷Jim Cartwright's *Road* for a similarly dynamic use of language; ▷John Byrne's *The Slab Boys Trilogy* for a similarly volatile if more socialist view of Glasgow working life; ▷David Mamet's

Royal Court's writing group, Glasgow-born Heggie went on to take the theatre world by storm with his first full-length play *A Wholly Healthy Glasgow*. Awarded a special prize in the first Mobil Playwriting competition in 1985, *A Wholly Healthy Glasgow* was taken up by Manchester's Royal Exchange, toured the ▷ Edinburgh Festival and came down to the Royal Court trailing clouds of glory in February 1988 (being televised at about the same time). Hailed as Glasgow's answer to ▷ David Mamet, Heggie's dialogue, steeped in Glaswegian, is the driving force of his work. Set in a health club, the play has been seen by some as a metaphor of modern-day survival; nearly all have agreed that, in the words of *The Observer*'s critic, Michael Ratcliffe, it is 'one of the funniest plays of the last few years'. However, in a post-AIDS climate, it is also fair to say that its libidinous gay character, with eyes set on 'a bit of nookie every fifteen seconds', must now also be viewed as something of an anachronism and, as a limp-wristed gay stereotype, albeit racy in his dialogue, may date badly. Heggie's earlier play, *Politics in the Park*, has also been produced, at the Liverpool Playhouse, and the Traverse in Edinburgh, whilst *American Bagpipes*, a suburban comedy about family disintegration commissioned whilst he was writer-in-residence and produced by the Royal Exchange, confirms Heggie's distinctive voice. *Wilma of Scotland*, a Royal Court commission, is the next play in the pipe line.

Glengarry Glen Ross for an American equivalent of small-time capitalism.

HELLMAN, Lillian [1905–1984]

American dramatist, screenwriter, journalist

Plays include:

The Children's Hour (1934), _Days to Come_ (1936), _The Little Foxes_ (1939), _Watch on the Rhine_ (1941), _The Searching Wind_ (1944), _Another Part of the Forest_ (1946), _Montserrat_ (1949), _Regina_ (1949), _The Autumn Garden_ (1951), _The Lark_ (1955; adapted from Anouilh), _Candide_ (musical; 1956), _Toys in the Attic_ (1960), _My Mother, My Father and Me_ (1963; adapted from Burt Blechman's novel, _How Much?_)

Screenplays include:

The Dark Angel with Mordaunt Shairp (1935), _These Three_ (1936), _Dead End_ (1937), _The Little Foxes_, with others (1941), _Watch on the Rhine_ with Dashiell Hammett (1943), _The North Star_ (1943), _The Searching Wind_ (1946), _The Children's Hour_, with John Michael Hayes (1961), _The Chase_ (1966)

Controversial playwright and long-time companion of thriller writer Dashiel Hammett, Hellman's pithy and pungent wit are typical of the Dorothy Parker period (she was a close personal friend). To audiences now, however, Hellman is probably more associated with screenwriting (Bette Davis's portrayal of Regina in the 1941 film of *The Little Foxes* remains a classic) and autobiography (memoirs like *Scoundrel Time*, *Pentimento*, *An Unfinished Woman*) rather than the theatre. Her plays have not been seen much in England since the 1950s, the most recent being the ▷ National Theatre's 1980 production of *Watch on the Rhine*, directed by Mike Okrent.

By modern standards, her plays are shamelessly melodramatic but they are also tightly constructed and highly moral, and they ruthlessly expose money as the most corrosive of agents, particularly in the family. Hellman's malign protagonists often have the best of the fray (and afford golden opportunities for actresses of the swinging 'bitch' type), but she uses them to show human perversity and the destructive power of evil on human relationships. Her world of decaying aristocrats and the upwardly mobile middle-classes is frequently a world of moral bankruptcy. Throughout her plays there is, too, a consistent concern to voice uncomfortable emotional truths as well as socio-political issues (her stand against the House Un-American Activities Committee of Senator McCarthy in 1952 is legendary if still disputed): in *Toys in the Attic*, her Southern portrait of a man dominated by two sisters, it is the injuries people inflict on each other in the name of security and love; in *Watch on the Rhine*, it is American non-interventionism, the spectre of fascism and the holocaust. Several of her plays have women in central roles, but

TRY THESE:
▷Jonson for characters as embodiments of moral evil; ▷Tennessee Williams for many of the plays' Southern setting (especially *Toys in the Attic*); for other female 'villains', see ▷Ibsen's *Hedda Gabler*, ▷Racine's *Phèdre*, and ▷Euripides' *Medea*; for dramas of family life, see ▷Alan Ayckbourn; for a contrasting contemporary treatment of plays on an anti-fascist theme, see Maxwell Andersen; see ▷Chekhov for family sagas of tight narrative, leisurely discussion and high moral intent.

by contemporary feminist standards they lack any radical re-assessment – rather, reinforcing certain female stereotypes. In *The Little Foxes*, the women are hard and narcissistic; in *The Children's Hour*, unhappily lesbian or emotionally dependent on men in *Toys in the Attic*. William Luce's biographical play based on Hellman, *Lillian*, produced in New York and in London (1985) with Frances de la Tour as Hellman proved that, posthumously, Hellman remains as controversial a figure as ever.

The Children's Hour
First produced in 1934, this is probably one of her best known and certainly most successful plays. Audaciously, for its time, it tackles the taboo subject of lesbianism, although the real subject of the play is considered to be the destructiveness of innuendo and rumour. Predictably, the tale is a tragic one: one of the teachers is accused by a revengeful pupil of having an 'unnatural' relationship with a colleague and commits suicide. Hellman's achievement is to show the consequences of the pupil's 'little lie' and, perhaps inadvertently, the consequences of society's intolerance towards lesbianism.

The Little Foxes
Set in the South at the turn of the century, this is a typically Hellmanesque tale of greed running riot in a family. Regina, the epitome of hard-hearted rapacity (a forbear of Joan Collins' Alexis of *Dynasty*, no doubt!), is prepared to sacrifice all for money – she lets her husband die in front of her eyes and double-crosses her brothers to get her hands on a share of the profits from the factory they want to build in the town. Such melodrama has become the meat and drink of American television soap opera but clearly for Hellman, there was a moral point to be made. Such goings on may bring material wealth, Regina is triumphant, but at the cost of the loss of her daughter's love and a lonely old age. Capitalism corrupts, and for women, absolutely, but as archetypal female villains go, Regina remains without peer!

HENLEY, Beth [1952–]
American dramatist

Plays include:
***Crimes of the Heart* (1980), *The Wake of Jamey Foster* (1981), *The Miss Firecracker Contest* (1982), *The Lucky Spot* (1987), *The Debutante's Ball* (1988)**

Films include:
***Nobody's Fool* (1986), *Crimes of the Heart* (1986), *The Miss Firecracker Contest* (1988)**

Born in Jackson, Mississippi, in Mark Twain territory, Beth Henley restores the all too frequently lacking Southern voice to an American playwriting industry dominated either by hyper-urban New York/East Coast angst or mimetic pieces about LA blankness. *Crimes of the Heart*, her Pulitzer Prize-winning debut play, introduced Henley's cheerfully gothic tone to audiences undeterred by her obvious indebtedness to Eudora Welty and Flannery O'Connor, Southern compatriots whose cockeyed logic and unexpected compassion she shares. Set five years after Hurricane Camille, *Crimes of the Heart* generates a comic hurricane of its own, as the three McGrath sisters make their peace with a world that never quite seems quick-witted enough for them. Henley's style, at its worst, can cloy – in the Broadway flop, *The Wake of Jamey Foster*, the comic grotesquerie is wearying, and the whole play seems all too trivial. Directors need to be on guard; her tone is elusive and, mishandled, it can come across as pseudo-lyrical bathos. But she gives juicy roles to actors, particularly women, and her genuinely theatrical energy and wit are most apparent when offset against the infuriating facetiousness of her followers (Robert Harling's *Steel Magnolias*, for example).

TRY THESE:
▷Kaufman and Hart for families bound by their own peculiar logic (the fireworks in *The Miss Firecracker Contest* seem to echo those in *You Can't Take it With You*); Clare Booth Luce for contrastingly staid see-saws between bitchery and 'meaning'.

HEYWOOD, Thomas [1574–1641]
English Renaissance dramatist

Plays include:
A Woman Killed with Kindness* (1603), *The Fair Maid of

TRY THESE:
Heywood's treatment of adultery in *A Woman Killed with Kindness*, with its

***the West* (pre 1610; published 1630), *The English Traveller* (published 1633)**

Heywood's current theatrical status depends largely on the ▷ RSC's romping 1986 conflation of his two-part *The Fair Maid of the West*, treated by Trevor Nunn as 'a comical/tragical adventure entertainment celebrating the birth of a nation', and on memories of a 1971 ▷ National Theatre production of *A Woman Killed with Kindness*. Heywood was a prolific writer and sometime actor who claimed to have contributed to over 200 plays, of which some twenty survive. He wrote in just about every genre and style available to him but, despite the success of the RSC's *The Fair Maid of the West*, *A Woman Killed with Kindness*, with its realistic treatment of domestic strife in a bourgeois context, is more likely to be revived. It is particularly interesting for the husband forgiving his adulterous wife and her lover rather than pursuing revenge.

realistic treatment of domestic strife, contrasts strikingly with ▷Shakespeare's in *Othello*; *The Fair Maid of the West* is one of many Renaissance plays to use the so-called substitute bed mate trick which occurs most notably in ▷Middleton's *The Changeling* as well as ▷Shakespeare's *All's Well That Ends Well* and *Measure for Measure*.

HILL, Errol [1921–]
Trinidadian dramatist and academic

Plays include:
***Brittle and the City Fathers* (1948; later known as *Oily Portraits*), *Square Peg* (1949), *The Ping-Pong* (radio 1950; staged 1953), *Dilemma* (1953), *Broken Melody* (1954), *Wey-Wey* (1957), *Strictly Matrimony* (1959), *Man Better Man* (1960; originally 1957), *Dimanche Gras Carnival Show* (1963), *Whistling Charlie and the Monster* (1964), *Dance Bongo* (1965)**

Hill's plays are seldom seen in Britain, but he is a major figure in the creation of a West Indian theatre through his work as writer, director, actor, editor of play anthologies, author of the standard work *The Trinidad Carnival* and academic (he has held posts in the West Indies, Nigeria and the USA). His aim, in his own words, has been 'to treat aspects of Caribbean folk life, drawing on speech idioms and rhythms, music and dance, and to evolve a form of drama and theatre most nearly representative of Caribbean life and art'. He draws on folklore associated with the calypso and carnival traditions in *Man Better Man*, which he selected to represent him in his own edition of three Caribbean plays (*Plays for Today*, Longman, 1985), with its obeah man brought in to help a young lover to win his bride in a duel with the village stick-fighting ('calinda') champion. The original version was written in prose and had no music, but in its current form it uses calypso verse and music in a comic form which celebrates aspects of folk culture that have survived despite colonial rule.

TRY THESE:
▷Mustapha Matura as a Trinadadian-born dramatist who shares many of Hill's interests, particularly in carnival in *Play Mas* and in folk culture in *Meetings*; ▷Synge's *Playboy of the Western World* (and Matura's reworking of it as *Playboy of the West Indies*) for one of the classic celebrations and interrogations of folk culture in drama; ▷Derek Walcott as the pre-eminent Caribbean dramatist who also shows Hill's concern for a rich theatrical language expressing the Caribbean culture as fully as possible; John Constable's *Black Mas* for a white writer's treatment of carnival; Felix Cross' musicals *Blues for Railton* and *Mass Carib* also celebrate pre-colonial, pre-Christian Caribbean cultures in music.

HOCHHÜTH, Rolf [1931–]
West German dramatist

Plays include:
***The Representative* (1963), *Soldiers* (1967), *Guerillas* (1970), *The Midwife* (1972)**

Hochhüth spent some years as a reader with a publishing firm, potentially a useful training for writing 'documentary' dramas. He has had some international success as a dramatist, largely because of the controversial nature of his best known plays.

The Representative
This was his first play, in five acts and in free verse; Piscator used it to open the new Freie Volksbühne in 1963, to immediate international controversy. It showed Pope Pius XII as failing to do anything to prevent the Holocaust because he was more con-

TRY THESE:
Piscator, for more effective documentary theatre in the 1920s; Heinar Kipphardt's *In the Matter of J. Robert Oppenheimer* (1964), ▷Peter Weiss's *The Investigation* (1965), and ▷Peter Brook's *US*, for more effective documentary theatre in the 1960s; ▷John Arden and Peter Cheeseman at Stoke-on-Trent, for other

cerned about the spread of Communism and the state of the Church's finances. Hochhüth suffers from being unable to make up his mind whether the great moments of history are caused by individual decisions or by economic and social forces; and the verse did not help the documentary side of the play either. It was put on by the ▷ RSC at the Aldwych in 1963, in Robert David Macdonald's translation, and revived by the Glasgow Citizens' in 1986, when it was given a respectful reception, though found to look its age.

Soldiers

In *Soldiers*, matters were somewhat improved by the use of 'rhythmic prose' for the play-within-the-play, but the subject caused as much controversy; it deals with Churchill's 1943 decision on saturation bombing of Dresden and other German cities, and he is also accused of conniving at the assassination of the Polish leader, Sikorski. The picture of Churchill is more sympathetic than that of the Pope, but the attempt to put on *Soldiers* at the ▷ National Theatre in 1967 led to a burst of patriotic objection that did nothing for the positions of either Olivier or Ken Tynan. It was produced at the New Theatre in 1968, after the Lord Chamberlain's powers had been removed, but did not run for long (partly because the pilot of Sikorski's plane successfully sued for libel). Hochhüth has never really repeated the *succès de scandale* of these two plays, though in *Guerillas* he still seems to think that American society could be changed by disposing of a small number of industrialists.

British equivalents; in the USA, the ▷Wooster Group, for a more experimental, highly charged mode of documentary; Brenton's *The Churchill Play* for an equally controversial portrait of the statesman.

HOLBOROUGH, Jacqueline [1949–]

British dramatist and co-founder (with Jennifer Hicks) of ▷ Clean Break

Plays include:

***A Question of Habit* (1979), *Killers* (1980), *Avenues* (1981–82), *Fallacies* (1983), *Decade* (1984), *The Sin Eaters* (1986), *The Garden Girls* (1985), *Dreams of San Francisco* (1987)**

Television includes:

***Sex and Violence in Womens' Prisons* (1983), *Time and Other Thieves* (1983), *Women of Durham Jail* (1984), *Killers* (1984)**

Born in Birmingham, Holborough was an actress before finding herself in prison – and high security for a while – as the result of placing an advertisement in the paper and subsequently being charged for conspiracy with people she didn't even know. Her early plays, mostly naturalistic in style, were devised with Jenny Hicks and members of the women prisoners' company, ▷ Clean Break; centring around the prison experience, they challenge traditional images of the 'criminal woman' as sexually aggressive or hysterical victims. Holborough has a very specific 'tone' – partly humorous, partly realistic. Her great distinction is to create characters with recognisably sympathetic, three-dimensional lives (her lesbian character in *The Garden Girls* was a case in point), but her sharp wit, much more prominent in her most recent play *Dreams of San Francisco*, may also indicate a budding sit-com writer, as well as the acknowledged prison chronicler. In her earlier plays in which her sympathies are decidely anti-state and pro-individual, prisoners and 'screws' are nonetheless presented as equal victims of institutional violence (as in the two-hander *The Sin Eaters* about IRA bomb suspect Judith Ward and her treatment in Durham prison's notorious H-block). *The Garden Girls*, Holborough's first full-length play, produced at London's Bush Theatre, is a classic (if overlong) and rare depiction of institutional, class and group pressures on a cross section of women, as well as an eloquent demythologising of the 'criminal woman'. It shows the varying ways women end up in prison – often because of men or simply because they have infringed some social code of how women ought to behave. But it may well be that Holborough's potential as a social satirist, revealed in the climax of *Dreams of San Francisco*, a ferociously ironic comment on the material opportunitism of late 1980s feminism, may come more to the fore.

TRY THESE:

▷Caryl Churchill's *Top Girls* and *Serious Money* for other images of contemporary opportunism; ▷Melissa Murray's *Body-cell* for another treatment of the effect of solitary confinement; ▷Brendan Behan's *The Hostage* for an earlier expression of penal life; ▷Pam Gems' *Dusa, Fish, Stas and Vi* for another treatment of women inter-acting; ▷Dario Fo and ▷Franca Rame's *Ulrike Meinhof* for an extraordinary portrait of woman as terrorist.

HOLMAN, Robert [1952–]
British dramatist

Plays include:
***Coal* (1973), *The Natural Cause* (1974), *Outside the Whale* (1976), *German Skerries* (1977), *Mucking Out* (1978), *Other Worlds* (1983), *Today* (1984), *The Overgrown Path* (1985), *Making Noise Quietly* (1986), *Across Oka* (1988), and adapted ▷ Mrozek's *Emigrés* (1976)**

Television includes:
***Mucking Out* (adapted from his play; 1978), *Chance of a Lifetime* (1980), *Summer's Awakening* (1983), *This is History Gran* (1986)**

At a time when too many playwrights seem content to score ideological points off their characters, Holman is to be commended for his droll, compassionate voice in a series of plays that movingly examine both the stresses and the bliss of intimacy amongst people of varying backgrounds and nationalities and at different times (*Other Worlds* is set during the Napoleonic era). Born in North Yorkshire, the son of a farm manager and a teacher, Holman moved to London at nineteen and spent two-and-a-half years working in the newsagent's on Paddington Station; perhaps his immersion in the world gives his plays their peculiar realism, but few writers chart human truths so perceptively, particularly the truths that accompany sudden intimacy. 'I always think you can hear silence,' a character comments in his play *The Overgrown Path*, and that's what Holman does, he keeps time with the human dialogues that go unspoken but are, nonetheless, felt. A resident playwright at the ▷ National Theatre from 1977–9, Holman regularly crops up in London's subsidised fringe – memorably, in 1986, in *Making Noise Quietly*, a trio of plays about relationships that flourish and flail under the strains of gender and class. Written in a temperate, considered mode, its title sums up what Holman has been doing to date: making noise quietly – and invaluably.

Today
A probing treatment of English idealism between the wars, this episodic play tells of Victor Ellison, the musically-gifted son of a Yorkshire joiner, who flirts with men during his days at Cambridge, with Socialism in the anti-fascist crusade of the Spanish Civil War, and with religious conversion in his Barcelona-based courtship of a British nun who ends up becoming his wife. Set alongside this spiritual development is an array of characters written with the deft, swift insight and immediate empathy one associates with the best British mini-series. This is that rare play where one admires the leading figure yet wants to know as much as possible about the supporting characters (whether it's a Marxist ventriloquist or a German male prostitute) as soon as they are introduced.

TRY THESE:
▷Michael Frayn's *Benefactors* for discussions of English idealism; ▷Louise Page (especially *Salonika*) for often elliptical domestic conflict; American writers such as ▷Tina Howe and ▷Lanford Wilson for clear, non-judgmental views of character.

HOME, William Douglas [1912–]
British actor and dramatist

Plays include:
***Now Barabbas. . .* (1947), *The Chiltern Hundreds* (*Yes M'Lord* in USA; 1947), *The Thistle and the Rose* (1949), *The Reluctant Debutante* (1955), *Betzi* (1964), *The Queen's Highland Servant* (1967), *The Kingfisher* (1977), *After the Ball is Over* (1985)**

An actor who appeared in many of his own plays, and whose experience shows in their careful construction, Home was rejected by the 'angries' of the late 1950s as an irrelevant writer of upper-class and well-made plays. Many of his more than forty plays are set in the world of lords and debutantes but, though deftly worked by his keen comic skills, they are firmly rooted in observation – and the plots are often developed from real life. *The Chiltern Hundreds*, for example, was suggested by the political activities of his father's butler, and *The Reluctant Peer* was linked to his Prime Minister brother's resignation of his title. Subjects range from a chronicle play of events leading to the Battle

TRY THESE:
▷Sheridan for similar comedies of an earlier time; ▷Genet, John Herbert's *Fortune and Men's Eyes* and ▷Brendan Behan's *The Quare Fellow* for death-cell dramas; ▷Alan Ayckbourn for Home-like treatment of the middle and lower-middle classes; ▷Noël Coward for more bitter observation of the British 'country house' set; Ray Cooney and ▷Ben Travers for blander versions.

of Flodden Field (*The Thistle and the Rose*) to the occupation of the Channel Islands, Napoleon's last love affair (*Betzi*), and a serious look at marriage in *Lloyd George Knew My Father* and *The Secretary Bird*, though they are also enjoyable comedies which make no great demands on their audiences. His early play *Now Barabbas. . .*, a study of life in a prison, from the arrival of a condemned murderer to his execution, plumbed much greater depths than his later work, including what was then a very daring treatment of a homosexual friendship.

Home writes about the people he knows and, though it is the carriage trade that will recognise themselves, he is not a Tory propagandist – their behaviour, prejudices and eccentricities are the butt of his humour which relies more upon elegant construction and skilful timing than dazzling wit.

HOPKINS, John [1931–]

British dramatist

Plays include:

***This Story of Yours* (1968), *Find Your Way Home* (1970), *Economic Necessity* (1973), *Next of Kin* (1974), *Losing Time* (1979)**

Television includes:

***Z-Cars* (1962–3), *Talking to a Stranger* (1966)**

Hopkins is best known for the creation of BBC-TV's *Z-Cars* (of which he wrote fifty-three episodes), a police series which changed the way in which the force was presented. His stage plays have been as strong as his television work. In *This Story of Yours*, a self-loathing detective in a bad marriage, with a job that both repels and fascinates him, beats a suspected child rapist to death. *Find Your Way Home* shows the relationship between a young occasional male prostitute and a married man who leaves his wife to live with him. Hopkins paints a bleak picture of the homosexual scene and of the difficulties they face, uncompromising and unsentimental, but it is as much about the difficulties of making any relationship as about homosexuality. Hopkins' dramas are strong meat, firmly rooted in contemporary experience, and confronting both private and public problems.

In addition to the creation of *Z-Cars*, Hopkins has written numerous other television plays; the four-part *Talking to a Stranger* which presents four overlapping views of a day in the life of a family culminating in the mother's suicide, was greeted by *The Observer* as 'the first authentic piece directly written for television'.

TRY THESE:
Michael Wilcox (*Rents*), ▷Peter Gill (*Mean Tears*), ▷Martin Sherman (*Bent*), and ▷Hugh Whitemore's *Breaking the Code* for other plays about the difficulty of homosexual relationships; G. F. Newman's *Operation Bad Apple*, Vince Foxall's *Pork Pies* for plays on 'bent' police; see also ▷Gay Sweatshop.

HORSFIELD, Debbie [1955–]

British dramatist

Plays include:

***Out on the Floor* (1981), *Away From it All* (1982), *All You Deserve* (1983); trilogy comprising *Red Devils, True Dare Kiss* and *Command or Promise* (1983); *Touch and Go* (1984; now known as *Revelations*)**

Radio includes:

Arrangements (1981)

Television includes:

Out on the Floor (1983)

One of the 'second wave' of young women writers who emerged in the early 1980s, Manchester-born Horsfield really came to prominence with *Red Devils*, the naturalistic saga of four female Manchester United supporters. She has written plays on computer dating (*Touch and Go*), northern discos (*Out on the Floor*), and more youthful dilemmas (*All You Deserve*), but the football trilogy remains her *pièce de resistance* at present. Like ▷ Alan Bleasdale's television winner *The Boys from the Black Stuff*, the three plays have a compulsive drive (like good soap-opera) as they follow the progress of four friends, through early adulthood, work and personal crises, often conflict-ridden but held together by loyalty and a shared obsession for Manchester United football team – Horsfield's own particular passion. *Red Devils* was reworked from an earlier play, *In the*

TRY THESE:
▷Sarah Daniels and ▷Ayshe Raif are other writers to emerge in the early 1980s; Victoria Wood's humour springs from the same northern roots; ▷Sharman Macdonald for female adolescent badinage; ▷Willy Russell's *Educating Rita* seems like a forerunner to *Touch and Go* and his *Stags and Hens* exploits a disco setting, as does ▷John Godber's *The Ritz*; ▷Louise Page's *Golden Girls* is a different look at young women, individually and in a group, at the competitive end of sport; ▷Pam Gems'

Blood, which was written in just two weeks and staged at the ▷ Edinburgh Festival whilst she was still at Newcastle University. It won her the Thames Television award, an attachment to the Liverpool Playhouse, and a commission to make it into a trilogy with *True Dare Kiss* and *Command or Promise*. *True Dare Kiss* also won the Thames award for best play in 1983, and both that and *Command or Promise* were shortlisted for the George Devine award. Two plays were performed as part of the ▷ National Theatre's short season of new plays at the Cottesloe in 1985, when some critics found them repetitious, soap-operish (in the bad sense) and sentimental, and one male reviewer even commented that it was unfair to men. Most agreed her great strength was her ear for dialogue – like a sort of Julie Walters on speed. Michael Billington has even dubbed her the funniest woman dramatist since ▷ Shelagh Delaney. Certainly, there is the same youthful energy, gritty turn of phrase and spikey humour, but Horsfield also reflects a quarter of a century in which feminism, unemployment, the increasing north/south divide, television and the consumerist society have changed perceptions.

Dusa, Fish, Stas and Vi for another young quartet coming to terms with womanhood; ▷Charles Dyer's *Rattle of a Simple Man* deals with a soccer fan from the North hitting the Big City; ▷Peter Terson's *Zigger-Zagger* is the definitive football supporters play; for an equivalent male trilogy, see ▷John Byrne's *The Slab Boys*.

Red Devils

Red Devils is the story of four young teenagers; Alice, Nita, Beth and Phil, their ambition to get to Wembley to see their team in the Cup Final, and the outcome when they actually achieve it. But the other half of the equation is the exploration of the idea of friendship, what binds four such disparate characters together, and the development of each – nascent punk Beth's incipient racism towards Nita and her better-heeled, Asian background (her father is a doctor), Alice who is going with Kev and wants to settle down; and Phil, who wants to get on. Her ultimate return to her roots, as a fledgling journalist in the final part of the third play forms the real heart of the play. There is plenty of aggro (these women are not exempt from showing the same sort of feelings as male football supporters), but throughout it all runs a solid thread of kinship, and the play is enormous fun. As Horsfield has said in reply to criticisms: 'It was not my intention to turn my characters into mouthpieces or agit-prop caricatures; I am aware only of recording what it was like for four young women growing up in Manchester in the 1980s.'

HORVÁTH, Ödön Joseph von [1901–1938]

German dramatist

Plays include:

***Italienische Nacht* (*Italian Night*; 1931), *Geschichten aus dem Wiener Wald* (*Tales from the Vienna Woods*; 1931), *Kasimir und Karoline* (*Casimir and Caroline*; 1932), *Figaro Lässt sich Schieden* (*Figaro Gets a Divorce*; 1937), *Don Juan Kommt aus dem Krieg* (*Don Juan Comes Back from the War*; produced 1952)**

Horváth, like ▷ Aeschylus and ▷ Molière, tends to be anecdotally remembered for the way he died; he was killed in the Champs Elysées when a tree struck by lightning fell on him, leaving several plays, novels and film scenarios unfinished. His plays were banned when the Nazis came to power, then neglected in Germany until the 1950s, and were almost unknown in Britain until the successful productions of *Tales from the Vienna Woods* at the ▷ National Theatre in 1977 and of *Don Juan Comes Back from the War* in 1978. His peculiar mixture of disdainful criticism of bourgeois capitalist greed and hypocrisy, sharp ironic observation of lower-middle-class stupidity, and melancholy resignation may stem partly from his background. He was born in Fiume (now Rijeka in Yugoslavia, but then a part of the Austro-Hungarian Empire) of an aristocratic Hungarian-speaking family and spent much of his life on the move – first because his father was a diplomat, then in search of artistic success, and finally in exile from the Nazis. *Tales from the Vienna Woods* is a hard and cynical picture of the lower middle classes, with a strong story-line; *Figaro Gets a Divorce* is set some years after *The Marriage of Figaro* and gets its effects by unexpectedly putting ▷ Beaumarchais' characters into a detailed social context; *Don Juan Comes Back from the War* is a very sardonic play, showing Don Juan as a modern disillusioned war veteran.

▷ Christopher Hampton, who translated both Horváth plays for the National Theatre productions, also anachronistically included him in *Tales from Hollywood* (1983) as part of the German

TRY THESE:

▷Franz Xaver Kroetz for the further development of the 'Volksstück', or plays dealing with lower class life; ▷Brecht for contemporary attacks on the capitalist system, though Horváth tends to despair rather than recommending positive action; the Mexican company, Compania Divas, presented an iconoclastic and controversial all-female version of Don Giovanni (*Donna Giovanni*) in the 1987 ▷LIFT; ▷Chekhov's *Platonov*, re-worked and retitled *Wild Honey* in ▷Michael Frayn's adaptation, was also known as *Don Juan in the Russian Manner*.

community in exile; Horváth did in fact mean to join them towards the end of his life.

HOUGHTON, Stanley [1881–1913]
British dramatist

Plays include:
The Dear Departed **(one-act; 1908),** ***Independent Means*** **(1909),** ***The Younger Generation*** **(1910),** ***Hindle Wakes*** **(1912)**

Part of the ▷ 'Manchester School' of playwrights, Houghton wrote all his successful plays for the Gaiety Theatre in Manchester, before dying untimely young. *Hindle Wakes*, the most controversial at the time and the most frequently revived (though not recently in the West End), is the story of the independent-minded mill-hand Fanny Hawthorn, who is unrepentant after spending a weekend in Llandudno with the mill-owner's son, and turns down his offer of marriage. It is an effective mixture of the comic and the serious, with strong feminist overtones and a *Doll's House*-type ending that nowadays leaves us asking a number of awkward questions about contraception and her possibilities of future employment.

TRY THESE:
▷Manchester School; see also ▷Harold Brighouse for another 'Manchester School' playwright.

HOWE, Tina [1937–]
American dramatist

Plays include:
The Nest **(1969),** ***Museum*** **(1977),** ***The Art of Dining*** **(1979),** ***Painting Churches*** **(1983),** ***Coastal Disturbances*** **(1986)**

A born New Yorker, Tina Howe has established herself as a leading American playwright on the basis of a scant five plays, particularly the most recent two. *Museum* and *The Art of Dining* are both clever but a bit arch, and much more beholden to her expressed idols – absurdists like ▷ Ionesco and ▷ Pirandello – than her emotionally and thematically wider-ranging recent work. In *Painting Churches,* her major achievement to date, Howe writes about a portrait painter called Mags, whose efforts to capture her parents on canvas bring to the fore her own problems of artistic expression and self-identification: her quest for the perfect painting becomes bound up with her quest for a perfect life. The parents, an elderly couple in Beacon Hill, Massachusetts, preparing to move to a retirement home on the Coast, might – in lesser hands – have been easily lampooned caricatures, but Howe sees all three characters with the objective empathy of a true artist. In *Coastal Disturbances*, set on a Nantucket beach at the end of a long and dreary summer, Howe gives us three generations of lovers embarking on mutual self-discovery amidst the shifting tides both of the sea and of human passion.

TRY THESE:
▷Chekhov for his mixture of compassion, irony, and the tendency of people to dramatise themselves; ▷Lanford Wilson, ▷August Wilson, and ▷Athol Fugard (see his *Road to Mecca*, another play about the formation of an artist) for their breadth of emotional generosity; ▷Philip Barry and, later, A.R. Gurney for ruefully comic views of the American upper-class; see also ▷David Hare's *Wrecked Eggs* for an Englishman's view of East Coast sensibilities; ▷Neil Simon, ▷Hugh Leonard for treatments about the formation of an artist.

HUGHES, Dusty [1947–]
British dramatist

Plays include:
Commitments **(1980),** ***Heaven and Hell*** **(1981),** ***Molière*** **(adapted from ▷ Bulgakov; 1982),** ***Bad Language*** **(1983),** ***Philistines*** **(adapted from Gorki; 1985),** ***Futurists*** **(1986),** ***Jenkins' Ear*** **(1987)**

Born in Lincolnshire and educated at Cambridge, Hughes has shown an impressive ability to leap between various periods and styles in a scant four plays and two ▷ RSC adaptations from Russian. At one point the theatre editor of the London listings magazine *Time Out* and then the artistic director of the Bush Theatre, Hughes came to attention with his play about English Trotskyites, *Commitments*, and consolidated his somewhat wry, acidic point-of-view with the bitterly funny *Bad Language*, about university disaffection amongst the Cambridge ranks. *Futurists*, galvanically staged by Richard Eyre at the ▷ National Theatre, remains his major achieve-

TRY THESE:
▷Doug Lucie, ▷Simon Gray for *Bad Language*-like depictions of Oxbridge; ▷Bernard Pomerance's *Foco Novo*, Donald Freed's *The Quartered Man*, ▷Manuel Puig's *Kiss of the Spider Woman*, Richard Nelson's *Principia Scriptoriae*; for plays about Latin America ▷C.P. Taylor's *Allergy* and ▷Christopher Hampton's *Philanthropist* are

ment to date. Set in a Petrograd café in 1921, the play charts, with exhilarating theatricality, a literary movement whose fate was contrastingly bleak. In the process, Hughes explores the paradox of twentieth-century Russia; the century ushered in by ▷ Chekhov and ▷ Gorki (a passage from *The Cherry Orchard* begins the play) gave way to the Cheka and Stalin despite the belief of one futurist poet, Osip Mandelstam, that 'poetry is a plough [that] turns time upside down'. After this risk-taking, Hughes' *Jenkins' Ear*, set in a 'small central American country north of Nicaragua', was all too prosaic and jumbled, the best of political intentions notwithstanding.

other contemporary university plays.

HUNTER, N.C. (Norman Charles) [1908–71]

British dramatist

Plays include:

***All Rights Reserved* (1935), *A Party for Christmas* (1938), *Waters of the Moon* (1951), *A Day by the Sea* (1953), *A Touch of the Sun* (1958), *The Tulip Tree* (1962)**

Beginning as a writer of light comedies, Hunter turned to plays of atmosphere and character, such as *Waters of the Moon* and *A Day by the Sea*, which the H.M. Tennent management presented with star casts at the Theatre Royal, Haymarket. Hailed by some critics of the time as 'English Chekhov', they do not seem quite so impressive today, although a recent revival at Chichester of *Waters of the Moon* still found it according to one critic, 'a play of gentle melancholy, rich in humour'.

TRY THESE:
▷Chekhov, with whom Hunter was routinely compared (to his disadvantage); ▷Enid Bagnold as another dramatist of the period; ▷Eugene O'Neill's *The Iceman Cometh* and *Long Day's Journey into Night* and ▷Agatha Christie's *Ten Little Niggers/Ten Little Indians* for plays in which isolated groups learn home truths as in *Waters of the Moon*.

HUTCHINSON, Ron [1946–]

Irish dramatist

Plays include:

***Says I, Says He* (1978), *Eejits* (1978), *Anchorman* (1978), *Christmas of a Nobody* (1979), *The Irish Play* (1980), *Risky City* (1981), *Into Europe* (1981), *The Dillen* (1983), *Rat in the Skull* (1984), *Babbit: a Marriage* (1987; a musical adaptation of Sinclair Lewis' novel)**

The fact that Hutchinson, writer in residence with the ▷ RSC in 1978–9, is now writing film scripts in Los Angeles might surprise those for whom he is best known as the author of two plays about Britain and Ireland (*The Irish Play* and *Rat in the Skull*) but might seem logical to those who know him as the writer of the television series *Bird of Prey* and *Connie*. Although Hutchinson's work also encompasses the highly successful Stratford-set promenade production *The Dillen*, which used both the Other Place and locations within Stratford, *Rat in the Skull* is probably the best of his plays. It's a fine study of the convoluted, almost incestuous, relationship between a Protestant RUC police officer and a Catholic terrorist suspect played out in a London police station populated with English policemen who want to keep their noses clean. Deceptively simple in its style, with many virtual monologues to the audience, the play never settles for an easy answer in its analysis of the interplay of personal and political motives and perspectives that lead to the intractability of the situation.

TRY THESE:
▷Promenade Performances and ▷Community Theatre for analogues of *The Dillen*; Hector MacMillan's *The Sash* for Orangemen in Glasgow; ▷Brian Friel, ▷Stewart Parker, Peter Sheridan, ▷Margaretta D'Arcy and ▷John Arden, Martin Lynch, ▷Seamus Finnegan, ▷Bill Morrison, ▷Daniel Mornin, Frank McGuinness and ▷Christina Reid are among the contemporary Irish writers who have dramatised the situation in Northern Ireland; ▷Brendan Behan and ▷Sean O'Casey did the same for earlier periods; ▷Howard Barker, ▷Howard Brenton and ▷David Rudkin offer perspectives from the mainlaind; G. F. Newman's *Operation Bad Apple*, Vince Foxall's *Pork Pies* and ▷Nigel Williams' *WCPC* are contemporary studies of the police.

IBSEN, Henrik [1828–1906]
Norwegian dramatist

Plays include:

***Catalina* (1850), *Lady Inger of Ostraat* (1854), *The Feast at Solhaug* (1856), *The Vikings at Helgeland* (1858), *Love's Comedy* (1862), *The Pretenders* (1863), *Brand* (1866), *Peer Gynt* (1867), *Emperor and Galilean* (1873), *Pillars of Society* (1877), *A Doll's House* (1879), *Ghosts* (1881), *An Enemy of the People* (1882), *The Wild Duck* (1884), *Rosmersholm* (1886), *The Lady from the Sea* (1888), *Hedda Gabler* (1890), *The Master Builder* (1892), *Little Eyolf* (1894), *John Gabriel Borkman* (1896), *When We Dead Awaken* (1899)**

Ibsen's influence on European and American drama has been enormous; he has been described as 'the father of modern theatre'. According to Rebecca West (who took her name from the heroine of *Rosmersholm*), expressing the feelings of many who felt the impact of the first productions of Ibsen in London: 'Ibsen converted me to the belief that it is ideas which make the world go round'.

Most of his early plays were traditional historical dramas, very much influenced by the German theatre of Hebbel and ▷ Schiller. They were unsuccessfully produced at the theatre in Bergen, where Ibsen worked as an assistant to the director, Ole Bull. After the theatre went bankrupt, Ibsen moved to Oslo where his satirical verse drama *Love's Comedy* was produced successfully. He travelled to Italy and Germany, living for two years in Rome where he wrote *Brand*. Never really intended for stage production it is often performed in an abridged version because of staging problems. However, *Brand* established Ibsen's reputation in Norway and across Europe and led to the awarding of a state pension, which left him free from financial worry and able to devote himself to writing. He spent most of the rest of his life in Italy and Germany. *Peer Gynt*, the last of Ibsen's verse dramas, is a fairy-tale fantasy which challenged traditional dramatic forms, It uses fantasy to explore fantasy and dream, and to investigate motivation and will through a young man's quest. From this point on Ibsen's plays were written in prose, and attempted, as Ibsen wrote to his publisher 'the very much more difficult art of writing the genuine, plain language spoken in real life'.

The plays which follow *Peer Gynt* are the beginnings of Ibsen's development of a naturalist drama and a refusal of traditional forms of theatre. Of his play *Emperor and Galilean* Ibsen wrote: 'The illusion I wished to produce was that of reality'. *Pillars of Society*, *A Doll's House* and *Ghosts* mark a decision to write about contemporary life: they are claustrophobic studies of small town parochial life, and of the conflicts, hypocrisies and destruction that families and small groups inflict on one another. These begin to develop a form of characterisation and action in which the emphasis is not on action, but on psychological complexity.

In Ibsen's later plays these dramatic techniques move close to symbolism. *The Wild Duck* and *Hedda Gabler* extend the symbolic elements that are already apparent in *A Doll's House* and *Ghosts*, and in *Rosmersholm* he moved to a thoroughly psychological drama.

While Ibsen is seen as the great Naturalist dramatist, Ibsen himself was careful to distinguish his work from Zola's naturalism, he

TRY THESE:
▷G.B. Shaw was powerfully influenced by Ibsen, and wrote a defence of him in *The Quintessence of Ibsenism*; ▷Strindberg was well aware of Ibsen's work, and, although he would have denied it, much influenced by him; ▷Christopher Hampton has translated much of Ibsen, and was very affected by Ibsen's studies of gender relations which inspired him to write *Treats*; ▷John Osborne's *Look Back in Anger* could be regarded as a reworking of *A Doll's House*; ▷Sarah Daniels' *Ripen Our Darkness* is a modern-day version of the rebellious wife, striking out for independence; ▷Trevor Rhone's *Two Can Play* goes two-thirds of the way down the line only to cop out at the end; ▷Franca Rame's *A Woman Alone* is another study of a woman pushed to extremes, as is ▷Berta Freistadt's *Woman with a Shovel*; images of women striving for independence run deep in much of women's writing, from ▷Shelagh Delaney's *A Taste of Honey* through ▷Pam Gems (eg *Piaf* or *Queen Christina*) to Carol Bunyan's *Waving* (1988) for ▷Monstrous Regiment, Frances McNeil's young single-mother

Vanessa Redgrave and Adrian Dunbar in Ibsen's ***Ghosts***, directed by David Thacker, Young Vic, 1986.

once said: Zola 'descends into the sewer to bathe in it; I to cleanse it'.

A Doll's House
The play was greeted with shock on its first production; both its style and subject matter were seen as radical and subversive. The play's form was technically innovative, in its use of contemporary and simple language and dress. Written in Rome when Ibsen was fifty-one, the play became a topic of international debate. Pamphlets and books were written about it, sermons and public debates held about it, and the text sold out within a month of its first printing. Feminism was a central issue in Norway at the time, and for Ibsen himself; his wife, Susannah, was an outspoken feminist, and the Norwegian novelist Camilla Collett had taken him to task about the representation of woman in his earlier plays. The play was based on an actual incident, but unlike Nora who boldly leaves the 'doll's house', the real woman ended her life in an insane asylum. In the notes for the play Ibsen writes: 'There are two kinds of moral laws, two kinds of conscience; one for men and one quite different for women. In practical life, woman is judged by masculine law, as though she weren't a woman but a man. A woman cannot be herself in modern society. It is an exclusively male society, with laws made by men.' *A Doll's House* is the study of the marriage of Nora and Torvald. In the first act, Nora is childlike, singing and taking pleasure in domesticity and her child. Her husband refers to her as a 'skylark', a 'squirrel', but the charm of their relationship takes on an uneasy edge as Nora has to beg for money from him, and her economic dependency becomes brutally clear. Nora attempts to enter into an economic transaction on her own, as she confides to her friend, the dying Dr Rank. But the money-lender blackmails her, and she comes to recognise her own dependence and gullibility. She dances an impassioned tarantella, an expression of her as yet unspoken rage and frustration. In the final scene of the play, Nora confronts Torvald with her own realisation that she has moved from her father's doll's house into yet another, and that she must leave both him and her child to find her own independence. The play ends with the door slamming behind her. According to one critic: 'With the slamming of the door behind Nora, the theatres of Europe woke up.'

attaining self-respect and identity through becoming a Muslim in *Jehad*, or the ebullient spirit that informs most of ▷Bryony Lavery's work.

IKOLI, Tunde [1955–]
British dramatist

Plays include:
***Short Sleeves in Summer* (1974), *On the Out* (1977), *Scrape off the Black* (1977), *Sink or Swim* (1981), *Wall of Blue* (1982, part of *Breach of the Peace*), *Sleeping Policemen* (with ▷ Howard Brenton; 1983), *Duckin'n'Divin'* (1984), *Week In Week Out* (1985), *Soul Night* (1985), *The Lower Depths* (from ▷ Gorki; 1986), *Please and Thank You* (1986; as a double bill with *Soul Night* under the title *Banged Up*)**

One of Britain's leading black dramatists, Ikoli has had a long and fruitful relationship with ▷ Foco Novo, whose artistic director Roland Rees has directed many of his works. Ikoli, born in the East End to a Nigerian father and a Cornish mother, was encouraged to involve himself in drama by a social worker, wrote and co-directed *Tunde's Film* at the age of eighteen, became an assistant director at the Royal Court (working on *Play Mas* amongst others), worked on the film of *In Celebration* and became a professional writer. Perhaps his non-Caribbean background helps Ikoli to look beyond the stereotypes of black writing in Britain, to investigate the realities of survival in a world which is increasingly hostile to those who have been identified as losers, be they black or white. Perhaps this comes over most clearly in *Please and Thank You* where a nervous, newly appointed, black, well-educated social worker finds his first client, a white, poorly-educated woman, about to put her head in the oven, and in *The Lower Depths* where his long

TRY THESE:
The brothers' reunion in *Scrape Off the Black* has been compared to ▷Eugene O'Neill's *Long Day's Journey Into Night*; ▷Caryl Phillips' *Strange Fruit* also fiercely centres on two brothers, also ▷Tony Marchant's *Lazy Days Ltd*; ▷Mustapha Matura is another black dramatist to rework the classics; ▷Jacqueline Rudet and ▷Jackie Kay are among a new generation of black women dramatists; ▷Jim Cartwright's *Road* has also been compared to *Under Milk Wood* for the 1980s.

admiration of Gorki is put to use to show the persistence of the attitudes and situations of the original in the new/old world of Thatcherism. Ikoli's collaboration with ▷ Brenton on *Sleeping Policemen* was highly unusual since, after a workshop period, each wrote his own play and they were then intercut to form what Michael Billington called 'a radicalised, phantasmagoric *Under Milk Wood*'. Like many young writers, Ikoli has largely been forced by the current funding situation in the arts to write for smaller casts than he would wish, and at the time of writing a major reworking of *The Tempest* is unproduced due to lack of funds.

INGE, William [1913–73]

American dramatist

Plays include:

***Come Back Little Sheba* (1950), *Picnic* (1953), *Bus Stop* (1955), *The Dark at the Top of the Stairs* (1957), *A Loss of Roses* (1959), *Natural Affection* (1962), *Where's Daddy?* (1966), *Summer Brave* (1973)**

Films include:

***Splendor in the Grass* (1961), which features Inge in a bit part as a minister**

TRY THESE:
▷Tennessee Williams, a friend of Inge's, for small-town despair and dashed hopes; ▷Mark Medoff, Ed Graczyk for more recent plays set off the beaten American track.

The son of a travelling salesman, Inge had his heyday in the 1950s when he wrote four Broadway hits back-to-back, several of which were made into well-known films, particularly *Bus Stop*, with Marilyn Monroe. Chronicles of small-town America, Inge's plays can seem dated today in their rather obvious symbolism and bald Freudian psychology, but he can paint a poignant image of desolation – as in *Come Back Little Sheba*, in which the lost dog Sheba functions as an image of the child the central couple, Doc and Lola Delaney, will never have. A homosexual, Inge wrote often about sexual magnetism, comically, in *Bus Stop*, between a Montana braggart and a nightclub singer, and, more seriously, in *Picnic*, in which the sexually attractive drifter Hal galvanises a Kansas community.

INNAURATO, Albert [1948–]

American dramatist

Plays include:

***Urlicht* (1971), *The Transfiguration of Benno Blimpie* (1973), *Gemini* (1976), *Earth Worms* (1977), *Ulysses in Traction* (1977), *Passione* (1980), *Coming of Age in SoHo* (1985), *Magda and Callas* (1988), *Gus and Al* (1988) and, in collaboration with ▷ Christopher Durang, *I Don't Generally Like Poetry But Have You Read 'Trees'* (1972), *The Life Story of Mitzi Gaynor, or Gyp* (1973), *The Idiots Karamazov* (1974)**

TRY THESE:
▷Christopher Durang, his erstwhile collaborator, for writing with an often manic tilt; ▷Kaufman and Hart for great scenes of familial hurlyburly; ▷Harvey Fierstein for gay dilemmas treated with an absence of handwringing; ▷De Filippo's *Saturday, Sunday, Monday* for other scenes of gastronomic mayhem.

Is he a South Philadelphian ▷ Shaw, as a New York critic once suggested, or a voyeur with a gleeful interest in the grotesque? Whatever one's individual slant, opinions on Innaurato are unlikely to be neutral, since his highly emotional, Italianate writing – ▷ Christopher Durang meets Lina Wertmuller – tends to elicit equally emotional responses. At his best, his plays, and their images, are frighteningly immediate and powerful, as in his early *The Transfiguration of Benno Blimpie*, in which the obese, unattractive Benno gorges himself to death. Food is central to his greatest success, *Gemini*, which lasted four years on Broadway largely due to a TV commercial emphasising the relevance of pasta. Set on the twenty-first birthday of a sexually and socially confused Harvard undergraduate, the comedy is loud, rude, and psychologically insightful, in Innaurato's typical blend. His follow-up Broadway show, *Passione*, was better on character than on overall concept (a circus fat lady's, diatribe against the grapefruit diet still reverberates), a problem that also beset *Coming of Age in SoHo*.

IONESCO, Eugène [1912–]
French dramatist, born in Rumania

Plays include:
***La cantatrice chauve* (*The Bald Prima Donna* or *The Bald Soprano*; 1950), *La Leçon* (*The Lesson*; 1951), *Les Chaises* (*The Chairs*; 1952), *Victimes du devoir* (*Victims of Duty*; 1953), *Amédée ou comment s'en débarasser* (*Amédée or How to Get Rid of It*; 1954), *L'Impromptu de l'Alma ou Le caméléon du berger* (*Improvisation or The Shepherd's Chameleon*; 1956), *Le nouveau locataire* (*The New Tenant*; 1957), *Tueur sans gages* (*The Killer*; 1959), *Rhinocéros* (*Rhinoceros*; 1960), *Le roi se meurt* (*Exit the King*; 1962), *La soif et la faim* (*Hunger and Thirst*; 1966), *Macbeth* (1966), *Voyages chez les morts* (*Journey Among the Dead*; 1982)**

Ionesco was born in Rumania, spent his childhood in France and his student days in Bucharest, and then settled in Paris in his twenties; this may have led to some of his questioning of identity. His short (and probably best) plays, *The Bald Prima Donna*, *The Lesson*, and *The Chairs*, became popular all over the world in the 1950s, but as he became more acceptable to the establishment his plays grew longer and lost some of their power to please and shock. His combination of inexhaustible and often hilarious linguistic invention with brooding despair in the face of death and contingency still has a good deal of force. What remains in the memory is a number of highly treatrical images; the rhinoceros, typifying the thick-skinned man of immovable conviction; the vast dead body in the next room haunting the pair in *Amédée*, that may or may not symbolise their former love; the girl killed by the word 'knife' in *The Lesson*; the stage filled with expectant empty chairs, addressed in vain by a dumb orator, in *The Chairs*; and the man in a bare room in *The New Tenant*, gradually engulfed by furniture, and the final turning off of the light – a simple but nightmarish metaphor for life.

Ionesco wrote a certain amount of dramatic theory, besides two plays about the act of playwriting (*Improvisation* and *Victims of Duty*) and in 1958 he engaged in a lively controversy with Kenneth Tynan in *The Observer* (later published in *Notes and Counternotes*, 1962), about the necessity for plays to be rooted in reality and to engage with society. Ionesco declared himself against (and free from) any political ideology: 'No political system can deliver us from the pain of living, from our fear of death, our thirst for the absolute'.

There were many Ionesco productions in Britain in the great days when Olivier and Barrault both played Berenger in *Rhinoceros*, but in recent years he has largely been confined to amateur and student groups, which keep happily rediscovering the short plays. However in 1983 Christopher Fettes directed *Exit the King* at the Lyric Studio; and *The Bald Prima Donna* did well at the Almeida in 1985, linked in an unlikely double bill with ▷ Sean O'Casey's *Bedtime Story*. His most recent play, *Journeys among the Dead*, was performed at Riverside Studios in 1987, but this semi-autobiographical Freudian dream journey among dead friends and relatives was on the whole found to be self-indulgent and badly shaped. Michael Billington wrote with some asperity: 'This play both suggests that the Absurdist movement led straight up a theatrical cul de sac and that a drama almost entirely cut off from social reality is one without purpose'. Clearly at the moment Tynan has the best of the argument.

Ionesco himself was also seen at Riverside Studios in 1983 in one of the strangest productions ever put on the London stage – Simone Benmussa's production (in French) of Virginia Woolf's *Freshwater*, a private but quite funny Bloomsbury joke, in which he played Alfred Lord Tennyson, his wife was the maid, Nathalie Sarraute the butler, and ▷ Snoo Wilson a porpoise.

The Bald Prima Donna
This short 'anti-play' epitomises the 'Theatre of the Absurd' in that it tries to reject all established theatrical conventions: it has no linear plot, proceeding instead by a series of disparate 'ten-minute takes'; its characters are interchangeable (indeed at the end of the play the Martins begin it again with the Smiths' dialogue); and the attempts at communication gradually disintegrate from cliché to reworded proverb to meaningless

TRY THESE:
▷Tom Stoppard, who borrowed from *The Bald Prima Donna* the device of the clock that struck at random, and used it in *Travesties*; ▷N.F. Simpson for verbal invention and logical paradoxes, though without the desperation; ▷Cocteau's film *Le Testament d'Orphée* (*The Testament of Orphée*) for a similar retrospective to *Journey among the Dead*.

syllables. It is less nightmarish than *The Lesson* or *The Chairs*, but it has considerable staying power; it has been playing at the unfortunate Théâtre de la Huchette in Paris for longer than *The Mousetrap*.

ISHERWOOD, Christopher

see AUDEN, W. H.

JARRY, Alfred [1873–1907]
French dramatist

Plays include:

***Ubu Roi* (*King Ubu*; 1896), *Ubu Enchaîné* (*Ubu in Chains*; 1900), *Ubu sur le Butte* (*Ubu on the Butte*; published 1906), *Ubu Cocu* (*Ubu the Cuckold*; published 1944)**

For a play that ran for only two nights when it first appeared, and could barely be heard at the first of these performances, *King Ubu* has had a considerable afterlife. Jarry's first version was written with other schoolfriends as a puppet play when he was fifteen, satirising an unpopular physics master, who then became a caricature of the greedy and cowardly French bourgeoisie. It shows a schoolboy's cruelty, love of lavatory jokes, and parody of ▷ Shakespeare, French Romantic drama, and Rabelais, besides a joyous taste for inventing words. When staged at the Théâtre de l'Oeuvre in 1896, it almost caused a riot, and it has been popular ever since – the Surrealists loved it, Apollinaire and ▷ Ionesco acknowledged its influence, and someone is always putting it on again, with varying emphases, though not yet at the Comédie Française or the ▷ National Theatre. Jean Vilar put on a conflation of *King Ubu* and *Ubu in Chains*, with songs from *Ubu on the Butte*, at the Théâtre National Populaire in 1957; Barrault nearly bankrupted himself with a collage of Jarry's work, *Jarry sur la Butte*, in 1970. The nearest to an establishment production has been ▷ Peter Brook's minimalist version at the Bouffes du Nord in 1977 which replaced the traditional fat figure of Ubu by the very tall Andreas Katsoulas and used very simple props – bricks, cable drums, silvered rubber balls, a bearskin rug – in a highly imaginative way. The play is clearly not yet so familiar as to be felt entirely safe.

The most recent British productions have been by the Actors Touring Company: *Ubu the Vandalist*, a lively variation of *King Ubu* in 1983, made Ubu a small energetic man with Groucho Marx spectacles and false nose, and added an extra political resonance to the fight between the small, Chaplin-like actor playing the Polish army and the Russians – armoured figures who entered on a darkened stage like the Teutonic Knights from *Alexander Nevsky*. *Ubu and the Clowns* in 1985, a version of *Ubu in Chains* at Brentford's Waterman's Arts Centre, unfortunately merely confirmed that this play has only one good joke (the army who all, systematically and in unison, disobey orders).

TRY THESE:
Apollinaire, for the Surrealist *Breasts of Tiresias*; ▷Ionesco, for wordplay and subversive invention. ▷Ken Campbell, ▷Joe Orton, ▷Tom Stoppard, ▷N.F. Simpson for subversive intention in the British theatre; ▷Arthur Kopit for something similar in America.

JELLICOE, (Patricia) Ann [1927–]
British dramatist, director and teacher

Plays include:

***The Sport of My Mad Mother* (1958), *The Knack* (1961), *Shelley; or, The Idealist* (1965), *The Rising Generation* (1967), *The Giveaway* (1968), *You'll Never Guess* (1973), *The Reckoning* (1978), *The Tide* (1980)**

Jellicoe is a former actress, teacher at the Central School of Dramatic Art and founder of the Cockpit Theatre club which was created to explore open-stage production. Her second play, *The Sport of My Mad Mother*, which won joint third prize in *The Ob-*

TRY THESE:
Royal Court Theatre which encouraged her earlier work; ▷Howard Barker, ▷David Edgar, ▷Charles Wood for dramatists commissioned by Jellicoe to write community plays; ▷John Osborne's *Look Back in Anger*,

server Play Competition in 1956, is a fantasy about a group of teddy-boys led by a sort of earth-mother. Based on action, not text, and exploiting the medium of theatre as her work has continued to do, it baffled audiences who had recently found *Look Back in Anger* revolutionary. Perhaps the most extreme example of this tendency is *The Rising Generation*, written in 1960 as a commission for the Girl Guides which, prefiguring her later work, needed a cast of thousands. In it a great mother-figure urges the girls to reject men, but the youngsters finally opt for co-operation and boys and girls set off together to colonise outer space. Unsurprisingly, the Girl Guides did not put it on, although a truncated version was eventually staged in 1967. *The Knack*, about the relationships and shifting power balances between a woman and three men sharing a house, could seem flat and confusing on the page but sparkles in performance and was a major success. *Shelley*, a documentary of the poet's life from university to his death, showed a more conventional approach.

From 1979, Jellicoe became involved in putting on plays with the people of Lyme Regis, Dorset, and channelled her energies into community theatre with casts of up to 150 in ▷ promenade performances and many more in support activities. Jellicoe has been the catalyst for their development, often as director and dramatist, through the Colway Theatre Trust which she helped found. Her style of working has been widely copied and she is now consulted internationally on such projects; her latest play has been written for the town of Holbaek in Denmark.

▷Arnold Wesker's *Trilogy*, ▷John Arden's *Serjeant Musgrave's Dance* for contrasting contemporary treatments of women with men by male writers; ▷Harold Pinter and ▷Samuel Beckett for break-up of form; the non-linear approach of many women's groups such as ▷Monstrous Regiment (which takes its name from one of the major concepts of *The Rising Generation*), the ▷Women's Theatre Group, Cunning Stunts, Scarlet Harlets; Welfare State, IOU for open-space spectacles; see also ▷community theatre, ▷promenade performances, ▷women-in-theatre.

JOHN, Errol [1924–88]
Trinidadian actor and dramatist

Plays include:
***Moon on a Rainbow Shawl* (1956)**

John's acting roles include Othello at the Old Vic in 1962, but he is best known for his play *Moon on a Rainbow Shawl*. Winner of 1956 *The Observer* Play Competition, this was produced at the Royal Court in 1958, directed by John as a revival at Stratford East in 1987 and has been seen most recently at the Almeida in 1988, directed by Maya Angelou. The play shows a trolley-bus driver abandoning the girl he has made pregnant in his determination to escape from the realistically presented back-yard life surrounded by prostitution, petty thieving and poverty. *The Dispossessed*, a published screenplay, presents the Caribbean predicament through a fisherman's son's rebellion against the life set out for him, though a robbery resulting in a killing leads to his death, not his escape. Other scripts and the television play *The Exiles* have shown black middle-class and intellectuals exiled in a white world, while *The Dawn* has a white protagonist and attempts to show the effect of his exposure to anti-black violence in Africa.

TRY THESE:
▷Shelagh Delaney's *A Taste of Honey* for a play of the same period dealing with similar issues to *Moon on a Rainbow Shawl*; ▷Willis Hall and ▷Keith Waterhouse's *Billy Liar* for contemporary escapism; for a 1980s view of the East End see ▷Karim Alrawi's *A Colder Climate*; for other treatments of strain put onto personal relationships through poverty and racism, see ▷Michael Abbensetts, ▷Caryl Phillips, ▷Mustapha Matura, ▷Tunde Ikoli, ▷Barry Reckord; see also ▷Black Theatre Forum, ▷Temba.

JOHNSON, Terry [1955–]
British dramatist and director

Plays include:
***Days Here So Dark* (1981), *Insignificance* (1982), *Unsuitable for Adults* (1984), *Cries from the Mammal House* (1984), *Tuesday's Child* (1986; with Kate Lock)**

TRY THESE:
▷Brecht's *Galileo* and ▷Howard Brenton's *The Genius* also deal with the responsibilities of scientists; ▷Dürrenmatt's *The*

Clare Benedict and Trevor Etienne in Errol John's ***Moon On A Rainbow Shawl***, directed by Maya Angelou (her directorial debut in Britain) at the Almeida, 1988.

Johnson, who has worked in ▷ community theatre and with the Science Fiction Theatre of Liverpool, is best known for *Insignificance* (which was filmed in 1985) and, increasingly for his work as a director (he directed the superb 1988 television adaptation of ▷ Ayckbourn's *Way Upstream*). His other work includes the somewhat portentous Viking/Scottish *Days Here So Dark*, and *Tuesday's Child* which deals with the complications that arise following the discovery of an Irish virgin's apparently immaculate pregnancy. *Cries from the Mammal House* is a dramatically powerful meditation on themes of conservation, religious and political enlightenment, family life and child abuse which deserves to be more widely staged. On the other hand, *Insignificance* is a heady mix of issues and characters as Marilyn Monroe and Einstein demonstrate the theory of relativity with interruptions from di Maggio and McCarthy. Witty, imaginatively concerned with important questions about natural and personal power and responsibility, the creation of myth and the gap between public and private personas, Johnson's plays are impressively willing to address the big themes, and even if he occasionally loses his way (as in *Tuesday's Child*), his readiness to tackle the wider canvas makes his a refreshing talent in a climate increasingly dominated by miniaturists.

Physicists takes a surreal look at scientists; ▷Caryl Churchill's *Top Girls* brings together a wide group of disparate characters out of historical time; ▷Tom Stoppard's *Hapgood* juggles with theories of physics, espionage and the nature of responsibility; ▷Arthur Miller's *After the Fall* recalls echoes of Marilyn Monroe.

JOINT STOCK THEATRE GROUP,
British touring theatre company

Plays include:

***The Speakers* (1974), *Shivvers* (1974), *The Doomdockers' Ball* (1975), *Fanshen* (1975), *Yesterday's News* (1976), *Light Shining in Buckinghamshire* (1976), *Devil's Island* (1977), *A Thought In Three Parts* (1977), *A Mad World My Masters* (1977), *Epsom Downs* (1977), *The Glad Hand* (1978), *The Ragged Trousered Philanthropists* (1978), *Cloud Nine* (1979), *The House* (1979), *Say Your Prayers* (1981), *Borderline* (1981), *Real Time* (1982), *Fen* (1983), *Victory* (1983), *Vautrin* (1983), *The Great Celestial Cow* (1984), *Deadlines* (1985), *Amid the Standing Corn* (1985), *Fire in the Lake* (1985), *A Child in the Heart* (1988)**

Founded in 1974 by directors William Gaskill and Max Stafford-Clark, Joint Stock quickly became the most influential touring fringe company in Britain, developing a unique method of co-operative collaboration between actors, writers, directors and designers, and combining it with an impressive record of acclaimed and adventurous productions.

Rejecting the common practice in British theatre of a three- or four-week rehearsal period, Joint Stock employed a combination of lengthy workshops, detailed research, free discussion, long rehearsal periods – and above all co-operative effort – to produce a high degree of skilled ensemble playing and innovative, challenging scripts from some of the best writing talents in the country.

Joint Stock rapidly achieved symbolic value for the British fringe: showing what could be achieved when the conditions for producing a play were analysed seriously, and acted upon. Some of the most conspicuous talent in British theatre involved itself with Joint Stock. The company also became, for some, a symbol of committed left-wing theatre in Britain, mainly because of the rigour of the company's developing democratic working processes, and the subject matter of *Fanshen* (1975) – the Communist revolution in China. Rob Ritchie, Joint Stock's historian, suggests that the company, although clearly influenced at an early stage by its work upon, and the subject of, *Fanshen*, takes on the complexion of whatever material it works upon, in its effort to produce the highest artistic standards.

TRY THESE:
▷Karim Alrawi, ▷Howard Barker, Tony Bicât, ▷Howard Brenton, ▷Caryl Churchill, ▷Nick Darke, ▷Barrie Keeffe, David Halliwell, ▷David Hare, ▷Hanif Kureishi, ▷Stephen Lowe, ▷Sue Townsend, ▷Snoo Wilson are all writers who have worked with Joint Stock; other touring companies who have used improvisation include Monstrous Regiment, ▷Gay Sweatshop and ▷Paines Plough.

The original pool of 'Joint Stock actors' proved impossible to sustain over a long period of financial problems, and in recent times the company has depended heavily on co-productions with other theatres, although the method of working remains roughly the same. However, for the same reasons, the company has now been forced to adopt a conventional management structure.

Fanshen
An account of the Communist revolution in China as experienced in a single village, from the arrival of the first Party workers, through the overturning of the old order to the problems, triumphs and trials of establishing a new one. The performance of the play properly requires a disciplined ensemble style, with a multitude of characters played by a company of nine. The principle focus is an exploration of politics rather than of psychology, but it is not conventional agit-prop in that it does not take an overt political stance.

JONSON, Ben [1572–1637]
English dramatist, poet and actor

Plays include:
***Every Man in His Humour* (1598), *Every Man Out of His Humour* (1599), *Poetaster* (1601), *Sejanus His Fall* (1601), *Eastward Ho* (1605; with ▷ George Chapman and ▷ John Marston), *Volpone* (1605), *Epicene* or *The Silent Woman* (1609), *The Alchemist* (1610), *Catiline* (1611), *Bartholomew Fair* (1614), *The Devil is an Ass* (1616), *The Staple of News* (1625), *The New Inn* (1629), *The Magnetic Lady* (1633)**

Jonson worked as a bricklayer, served as a soldier, became an actor, escaped hanging after killing another actor in a duel by virtue of his ability to read Latin which meant he could claim what was called benefit of clergy, and became a highly successful dramatist in his own day, although his subsequent reputation has been eclipsed by that of his contemporary and fellow actor ▷ William Shakespeare. As well as being a successful dramatist, Jonson also wrote many of the Court entertainments known as Masques, working with architect and stage designer Inigo Jones until they quarrelled over the respective importance of their own contributions to the shows. Jonson was an energetic and somewhat turbulent figure who engaged in the theatrical controversies of his time in *Poetaster*, which attacked ▷ Marston and ▷ Dekker. He then collaborated with ▷ Marston on *Eastward Ho* which landed them and their co-author ▷ Chapman in prison for offending powerful Scots at the Court. His tragedies, *Sejanus* and *Catiline*, both on Roman subjects, are very seldom performed and his current theatrical fortunes tend to depend on *Volpone* and *The Alchemist* with occasional forays into other comedies. The ▷ RSC's Swan theatre, designed for staging the works of ▷ Shakespeare's contempories, has so far seen revivals of *Every Man in His Humour* (an imbroglio of jealous husband, braggart soldier, knowing servants and would-be gallants) and *The New Inn* (a saturnalian feast of role reversals with a spice of clothes fetishism). *The Devil is an Ass* (in which a trainee devil coming to London is mercilessly outplayed by the human devils) and *Bartholomew Fair* (which takes place in and around the famous annual fair as a wide cross section of society join in its pleasures and pitfalls) were fairly widely seen in the 1970s, particularly in versions adapted and directed by ▷ Peter Barnes. Perhaps surprisingly, *Epicene*, with its man who marries a woman who is supposed to be completely silent only to discover that she is not silent and eventually that she is not a woman, has not attracted recent theatrical interest.

The Alchemist
Jonson's galaxy of would-be street-wise dupes, get-rich-quick speculators, religious hypocrites, sexual opportunists and over-reaching con men (and woman) remains a devastating and delightful critique of the unacceptable faces of capitalism. There is

TRY THESE:
▷Marlowe's *Tamburlaine* and *Doctor Faustus* and ▷Massinger's *A New Way to Pay Old Debts* for portrayals of characters overreaching themselves; for satirical comedies about the acquisitive society see also ▷Middleton, the Restoration dramatists ▷Aphra Behn, ▷Wycherley and ▷Congreve, ▷John Gay's *The Beggar's Opera* and ▷Brecht's *The Threepenny Opera*, ▷Caryl Churchill's *Serious Money*; for Venetian capitalism see also ▷Shakespeare's *Merchant of Venice* and John Clifford's *Losing Venice*; Shakespeare and Jonson are characters in Edward Bond's *Bingo*. Michael Coveney described *The New Inn* as '*The Winter's Tale* meets *Nicholas Nickleby*'.

a kind of manic farcical drudgery in running this London dream factory with the partners reacting increasingly frenetically as new markets open up for their corporate strategy of marketing and planning consultancy, brothel-keeping and speculation in human and other currencies of all kinds. The alchemical jargon can be a problem if you read the play, but treat it as the equivalent of someone trying to sell you insurance or convert you to the beauties of the latest model computer (or car) and you won't go far wrong.

Volpone
Another satire on the acquisitive society, set in a Venice that reflects contemporary London, *Volpone* uses the beast fable to characterise its stereotypes: Volpone (the fox) and Mosca (the fly) prey on the carrion birds (Voltore, Corbaccio and Corvino, the vulture, the crow and the raven) who come to prey on the apparently dying Volpone. There is the same delight in trickery as in *The Alchemist* and we tend to admire the comic verve of the protagonists as they outsmart those who are trying to outsmart them. The whole play ends more sourly than most comedies with Volpone and Mosca overreaching themselves and an outbreak of near poetic justice that leaves you questioning the right of the venal judges to administer justice.

KAUFMAN, George S. [1889–1961]

HART, Moss [1904–61]
American dramatic collaborators

Plays include:
***Once In A Lifetime* (1930), *Merrily We Roll Along* (1934), *You Can't Take It With You* (1936), *I'd Rather be Right* (book for the Richard Rodgers musical; 1937), *The Fabulous Invalid* (1938), *The Man Who Came To Dinner* (1939), *The American Way* (1939), *George Washington Slept Here* (1940)**

For period pieces of Americana in towns both small and large and told with affection and wit, few playwrights could match this duo who, although they had other collaborators throughout their careers (Kaufman worked with Edna Ferber and Marc Connelly, among many others; Hart with Irving Berlin and Cole Porter), had their finest moments together. While their terrain shifted from Hollywood during the talkies (*Once In A Lifetime,* memorably revived by the ▷ RSC in 1980) to a remote Ohio town (*The Man Who Came To Dinner*), the two took pleasure in parody but remained sentimentalists at heart, particularly – as in *The Fabulous Invalid* – when the subject involved was the stage. ('We mustn't let that die,' the idealistic young director remarks stirringly of the theatre at the close of the play.) Even the potentially astringent *Merrily We Roll Along*, a story of lost ideals told in flashbacks, has gone on to exert an emotive pull that can be seen not only in Stephen Sondheim's ill-fated musical version of it (premiered in Britain at the Guildhall) but in such similar-themed pieces as ▷ Simon Gray's *The Common Pursuit* and films like *The Big Chill.* In their plays, emotional decency wins out over rules and regulations; they are foes of the reactionary, friends of the eccentric.

You Can't Take It With You
Set in New York in 1936, this three-act Pulitzer Prize winner is one of the most cheerfully anarchic of American plays and, unsurprisingly, one of the most often revived works in regional theatres throughout the USA. (Frank Capra's 1938 film adaptation won Oscars for Best Picture and Best Director.) A celebration of innocence and relaxation as well as personal eccentricity, it pitches the idiosyncratically zany Vanderhof clan against the boring money-minded conformists in the world around them. The part of Grandpa Vanderhof, a man who opted not to become rich 'because it took too much time', is one of the most delightful on the American stage, and Jason Robards performed it memorably on Broadway in 1982. The play sets off small comic explosions of fireworks, much like those being lit on stage, and Kaufman and Hart aren't beyond bringing in a Russian countess, Olga, at the eleventh hour to raise spirits again.

TRY THESE:
▷Noël Coward's *Hay Fever* for a more lethal hymn to family eccentrics; ▷Eugene O'Neill's *Ah, Wilderness!* and William Saroyan's *The Time of Your Life* for complementary comic Americana; ▷Philip Barry for deflations of pomposity; ▷Beth Henley, Harry Kondoleon, A. R. Gurney for contemporary comic shenanigans; ▷Charles Wood's *Veterans* and ▷Christopher Hampton's *Tales from Hollywood* for film-making; ▷George Abbott and John Cecil Holm's *Three Men on a Horse* for more warm-hearted live-and-let-live moralities.

KAY, Jackie [1961–]
British dramatist and poet

Plays include:
***Chiaroscuro* (1986), *Twice Over* (1988)**

Poetry includes:
A Dangerous Knowing* (1984), *Beautiful Barbarians

TRY THESE:
▷Ntozake Shange's *for colored girls who have considered suicide when the rainbow is enuf* for influence and similar outlook to do with the

(1986), *Angels of Fire* (1986), *Dancing the Tightrope* (1987), *Black Woman Talk Poetry* (1987), *Original Prints Volume II* (1987)

Brought up in Scotland and a graduate of Stirling University, part-time lecturer, a former editor with the feminist publishers Sheba, play worker and poet, Jackie Kay's *Chiaroscuro* was originally commissioned by Theatre of Black Women as a short thirty-minute performance. After more changes, workshops and yet more changes it emerged as a full-length play. Written in a mixture of forms – dreams, songs, poetry, naturalism – it is a delicate but potentially powerful piece of transformatory theatre in which cultural histories, friendship, 'coming out' as a lesbian and the difficulties of communication in a largely white-dominated and heterosexual world are confronted and overcome. For each of the four women it is a journey, their reunion and acknowledgement at the end a measure of how far they have travelled and how far they still have to go. *Chiaroscuro*, as the word itself implies, is about light and shade, variation and change and requires a subtle balancing act in performance, like the plays of ▷ Ntozake Shange, to bring out its full potential. But there is little doubt that time will prove the play to be a turning point in black women's theatre in Britain.

Kay's second play, *Twice Over*, given a rehearsed reading at ▷ Gay Sweatshop's 1987 workshop festival GS × 12, confirms her promise as a developing playwright whose black and lesbian perspective is only a starting point to further explorations. *Twice Over*, with great good humour and not a little pathos, elaborates on some of the issues introduced in *Chiaroscuro* – 'coming out' (this time the revelations turn on a recently deceased grandmother: can grandmothers really be lesbians?), and race, but also class and an implied plea for honesty as the basis of all relations, whatever their inclination.

intermingling of poetry and drama; also Audre Lorde for influence; see also ▷Jacqueline Rudet's *Basin* for another treatment of black women's friendship, labelling and lesbianism; ▷Gay Sweatshop; ▷Lesbian Theatre; ▷Black Theatre; ▷Theatre of Black Women; Bonnie Greer's *Zebra Days*, presented by ReSisters is another contemporary look at black women's identity.

KEARSLEY, Julia [1947–]

British dramatist

Plays include:

Wednesday* (1979), *Baby* (1980), *Waiting* (1982), *Leaving Home* (1986), *Under the Web* (1987)

A Northern dramatist who lives in Blackpool, Kearsley is highly regarded as an observer in the naturalistic, 'slice of life' mould, who uses irony as a leavening counterweight to the darker schisms revealed in the modern nuclear family. *Wednesday*, first produced at the Bush Theatre and later on Broadway, earned her the Susan Smith Blackburn Prize runner-up award for Best New Female Playwright. Whilst some commentators have commented on her somewhat shaky plotting techniques, others find her work overly televisual (*Leaving Home* actually did transfer to the small screen). Nearly all, however, agree on the emotional authenticity of her characters and her capacity to reveal hidden tensions and truths beneath the surface of family life, in looking after a retarded son (*Wednesday*) or an aged mother *Under the Web*), or coping with the consequences of a father leaving home (*Leaving Home*). *Waiting*, written in response to the Yorkshire Ripper murders, divided critics, some of whom saw it as an outright feminist tract. Kearsley does not see herself as 'a feminist writer': 'I think there would be a danger of not being able to be honest if one thought about it too much'. Nonetheless, from a female point of view, you can be sure that a Kearsley play will reflect contemporary disharmonies – the self-delusional defences, the aggressions – of women in the home, with faithful accuracy and not a little affection.

TRY THESE:
▷Alan Ayckbourn and ▷Mike Leigh for other scenes from family life; ▷Stephen Bill's *Curtains*, ▷Ayshe Raif's *Fail/Safe* and ▷Sharman Macdonald's *When I Was a Girl I Used to Scream and Shout* for mother/daughter relationships under stress; ▷De Filippo's *Ducking Out* for another portrait of post-stroke gallows humour; ▷Peter Nichols' *A Day in The Death of Joe Egg* for a surreally bitter view of caring for a mentally handicapped child; newcomer Lucy Gannon's *Keeping Tom Nice* for the ▷RSC is on a similar theme; see also ▷Graeae for alternative views of disabilities.

KEEFFE, Barrie [1945–]

British dramatist

Plays include:

***Only A Game* (1973), *Scribes* (1975), *My Girl* (1975), *Nipper* (1978), *A Mad World My Masters* (1977), *Gimme Shelter* (1977), *Barbarians* (1977), *Frozen Assets* (1978), *Sus* (1979), *Bastard Angel* (1980), *Black Lear* (1981;**

TRY THESE:
▷Hanif Kureishi, ▷Karim Alrawi, ▷David Hare, ▷David Edgar, ▷Howard Brenton and ▷Howard Barker for committed topical

revised as *King of England*, 1987), *Chorus Girls* (1982), *Better Times* (1985)

Films include:

The Long Good Friday (1980), _The Killing of Joelito_ (1988)

Television includes:

Substitute (1972), _Not Quite Cricket_ (1977), _Gotcha_ (1977), _Nipper_ (1977), _Champions_ (1978), _No Excuses_ (1983), _King_ (1984), _Betty_ (1988)

An East Londoner who began his career as an actor and journalist, Keeffe has established a career as a gritty, hard-driving writer whose affiliation with the East End is maintained via his sustained relationship with the Theatre Royal, Stratford East, where his last three plays have premiered. Known for his topicality and the controversy it can cause, Keeffe paints an unromanticised portrait of contemporary England, occasionally using past events, as in *Better Times*, about the 1921 imprisonment of thirty East End labour councillors who refuse to levy an unfair government rate to illuminate today's headlines. His *A Mad World My Masters*, written in 1977 and revised in 1984, placed a Margaret Thatcher look-alike amidst an updated response to ▷ Thomas Middleton's similarly titled 1608 comedy. In *King of England*, a revision of his earlier *Black Lear* for ▷ Temba, a widower decides to return to the West Indies after thirty-five years in England, only to find that one of his daughters doesn't share his feelings of gratitude towards the UK. *Sus*, written in the year of Thatcher's election is a prophetic view of relations between young blacks and the police. A playwright with a vigorous sense both of comedy and of social responsibility, Keeffe is still best-known for his debut film script in 1980 for John MacKenzie's gangster drama *The Long Good Friday*.

writing (though, like Hare, Keeffe claims he does not 'set out to write political plays'); ▷Sam Shepard's *Tooth of Crime* for a *Bastard Angel*-like rock star on the skids; ▷Thomas Middleton's *A Mad World*, ▷Shakespeare's *King Lear*, ▷Edward Bond's *Lear* for another modern version of Shakespeare's play.

KEMP, Lindsay [1939–]

British mime artist, choreographer, director and painter

Key performances include:

Flowers (1974), _The Parade's Gone By_ (1975), _Salomé_ (1977), _Cruel Garden_ (1977)

Born in Scotland, Kemp studied painting at Bradford before attending the Rambert School of Ballet and went on to study mime with Marcel Marceau. He mounted events ranging from Soho strip shows to 1960s 'happenings', first forming a company in 1962. He attracted popular attention with the Ziggy Stardust concerts staged for David Bowie, a former company member, in 1974. *Flowers*, a fantasy based on ▷ Jean Genet's *Notre Dame des Fleurs*, brought cries of both outrage and acclaim. This was followed by a production of ▷ Oscar Wilde's *Salomé*, and two ballets for Ballet Rambert: *The Parade's Gone By* and *Cruel Garden*, with choreography by Christopher Bruce, before Kemp decided to base his company in Spain, returning for occasional seasons. His own version of *A Midsummer Night's Dream* and *Nijinsky* and *The Big Parade* (like the similar Rambert ballets exploring old Hollywood themes) have continued to divide critics. In *Cruel Garden*, based on the life of ▷ Federico Garciá Lorca and using many bullfight themes, Kemp and Bruce created a vital and magnificent ballet. Whether his other works have been flawed by crude excess or that excess is part of their beauty depends on individual reaction. Kemp is certainly an innovator with a touch of genius.

Kemp's own performances have been characterised by slow movement and flickering gesture. Their power is illustrated by the way in which his grotesque impersonation of Salomé, instead of a whirling sinuous dance of the seven veils, offered a slow motion mixture of the coy and the lascivious, his protruding tongue provocatively roaming, at first revolting and then hypnotically imposing its wayward sensuality. Even in a female role Kemp is in no way a drag artiste, he does not impersonate but seems to embody the femininity he seeks to present. He is not equipped to look like either a pretty boy or a pretty girl but can generate a feeling at odds to the physical appearance and, in *Flowers* for instance, has been able to show the beauty and

TRY THESE:
▷Performance Art; Neil Bartlett for another high-definition performer, particularly his *A Vision of Love Revealed in Sleep* about the gay poet, painter and friend of ▷Oscar Wilde, Simeon Solomon; ▷Steven Berkoff as another iconoclastic performer/writer/ director.

sensitivity that can grow from apparent brutality and pornography. Often Kemp seems to be trying to shock but then caps that with moments of great theatrical beauty that outweigh his lapses into the banal.

KESSELMAN, Wendy [1940–]
American dramatist, adaptor, translator

Plays include:

***Becca* (1977), *My Sister in This House* (1981), *The Juniper Tree: A Tragic Household Tale* (1982), *Maggie Magalita* (1985), *Merry-Go-Round* (1987), *I Love You, I Love You Not* (1987)**

Originally a songwriter and author of children's books, New Yorker Kesselman is known in Britain through Nancy Meckler's 1986 ▷ Monstrous Regiment Leicester Haymarket co-production of *My Sister in This House* which won the Susan Smith Blackburn Prize. This is a reworking of the same incident in Le Mans that inspired ▷ Genet's *The Maids*, namely two sisters who murdered their mistress, although ▷ Genet's play – which invariably has the roles played by men in drag – takes the murder as the starting point for an extravagant fantasy on such favourite Genet themes as domination, humiliation, and self-hatred. Kesselman's version places the sisters in a realistic social context, and is a much more recognisable and subtle indictment of French bourgeois values with its claustrophobic female household, petty obsessions, oppressions, and stifled emotions. Though Kesselman does not necessarily pin her colours to the feminist mast, *My Sister in This House*, by virtue of its reworking, places her in a feminist mould. Interestingly male critics have received the play perhaps better than their female counterparts for whom the horrific act of violence, juxtaposed as it is with such a strong image of love between women, remains problematical.

Quintessentially, a writer who works out of her own experiences, Kesselman became obsessed with the sisters after reading about the incident in Janet Flanner's *Paris Was Yesterday*; similarly the bi-lingual *Maggie Magalita*, about assimilation (the central character only feels she is accepted when she drops her Spanish name), came from Kesselman's experiences working with young Hispanics in a New York hospital. Other plays, yet to be seen in Britain, but which deserve a wider showing include *Becca*, a Coppelia-like children's musical with dark psychological undertones boasting some hauntingly lyrical songs, written and recorded by Kesselman (she is also a talented musician), and *I Love You, I Love You Not*, a delicate tracing of generational relationships between a Jewish grandmother and grand-daughter set against a background of German war-time memories.

TRY THESE:
▷Genet for a contrasting treatment of *The Maids*; ▷Blood Group's *Barricade of Flowers* takes *The Maids* as its starting point for a female imagistic treatment; Sartre for a different kind of claustrophobic household in *Huis Clos*; ▷Pam Gems' *Dusa, Fish, Stas and Vi* and *Piaf*, ▷Caryl Churchill's *Top Girls* and *Fen* for other treatments of women and class; ▷Catherine Hayes' *Skirmishes* for a contrasting treatment of sisters; ▷Jacqui Shapiro's *Winter in the Morning* for an extended image of the Holocaust in the Warsaw Ghetto.

KILROY, Thomas [1934–]
Irish dramatist

Plays include:

The Death and Resurrection of Mr Roche* (1968), *The O'Neill* (1969), *Tea and Sex and Shakespeare* (1976), *Talbot's Box* (1977), *Double Cross* (1985), and has also adapted ▷ Chekhov's *Three Sisters

Born in Callan, County Kilkenny, in southeast Ireland, Tom Kilroy is an academic dramatist; like ▷ Jack Gelber in America, he combines playwriting with teaching, and was a lecturer in the English department at University College, Dublin, before becoming Professor of English at University College, Galway. One of Ireland's leading playwrights, Kilroy draws on different theatrical genres and moments of history, and he unapologetically requires a commitment from his audience in an effort to elicit 'an intellectual response to what's happening on-stage'. Like many of his colleagues, Kilroy casts a sceptical glance at his country, and *The Death and Resurrection of Mr Roche* takes place at a celebratory party for an Ireland described, somewhat ironically, as 'on the move. . .up and up'. In *Talbot's Box*, Kilroy uses the story of a real-life Dublin labourer, Matt Talbot, to address the nature of modern-day sainthood. *Double Cross*, written for the Derry-based touring company Field Day, applies the psychology

TRY THESE:
▷Tom Stoppard for overtly intellectual theatre which often plays fictional games with fact (see *Travesties* and particularly *Hapgood* for dealing in, amongst other things, the philosophical similarities of 'double agents' and physics); ▷Hugh Leonard ▷Brian Friel for Irish contemporaries, both of whom write in more immediately recognisable modes; ▷Pirandello, ▷Brecht, ▷Ariane Mnouchkine's *Mephisto* for plays that link theatrics with power.

of dissimulation to two Irishmen who were roughly contemporary: Brendan Bracken, Churchill's Minister of Information, and William Joyce (Lord Haw-Haw), the Nazi sympathiser and fascist who was hanged in 1946, to explore, with unfashionable non-partisanship, the nature of 'treason', national identity and racism.

KLEIST, Heinrich von [1777–1811]

German dramatist

Plays include:

***Der zerbrochene Krug* (*The Broken Jug*; 1808), *Penthesilea* (1808; produced 1878), *Käthchen von Heilbronn* (1810), *Die Hermannschlacht* (*The Battle of Arminius*; 1810, produced 1860), *Prinz Friedrich von Homburg* (*The Prince of Homburg*; 1811, produced 1821)**

Kleist never really recovered from leaving the Prussian army and taking up the study of Kantian metaphysics; he was given to asking his friends of both sexes to join him in a suicide pact, and eventually a faithful female friend agreed. Most of his plays (except *The Broken Jug*, which is a good broad comedy using the structure of *Oedipus Rex*), display a neurotic emotional power, with verse to match; several were not performed until well after his death. A surprising number of versions of his plays have appeared in recent years; the most ambitious was a fine attempt to stage the epic mythological *Penthesilea* at the Gate at Latchmere in 1983 on a tiny stage, with the clash of Greek and Amazon armies indicated by sound and light alone, and Susannah York as the Amazon queen sinking her teeth into Achilles' bleeding heart and then killing herself in a frenzy of erotic violence. (Kleist changed the story from the usual versions in which Achilles kills Penthesilea.) *The Prince of Homburg*, a play that has been variously described as both fascist and subversive, in which the hero is sentenced to death for disobeying an order, even though his action won the battle, and comes to agree with the verdict (and be pardoned), was produced at the Cottesloe in 1982. Henry Livings' broad version of *Der zerbrochene Krug* as *Jug!* was put on at the Theatre Royal Stratford East in 1986; and James Saunders' dramatisation of a Kleist novella, *Michael Kohlhaas*, (which he called *Hans Kohlhaas*), about justice and class in Martin Luther's Germany, appeared at the Gate in 1983 and at the Orange Tree in 1986. One Kleist play that has yet to appear in English is *The Battle of Arminius*, a patriotic play (aimed at Napoleon) dealing with the German defeat of the Roman army; it includes a German maiden called Thusnelda who sets a bear on her faithless Roman lover (surely a natural for the ▷ Glasgow Citizens').

TRY THESE:
▷Schiller's *William Tell* for a historical play proclaiming national freedom; Grillparzer for plays in German dealing with mythology and with strong parts for women; ▷Sarah Daniels' *Byrthrite*, ▷Shakespeare's *The Winter's Tale* and ▷Jarry's *King Ubu* for plays in which bears appear on stage.

KOPIT, Arthur [1937–]

American dramatist

Plays include:

***The Questioning of Nick* (1957), *On the Runway of Life, You Never Know What's Coming Off Next* (1958), *Across the River and Into the Jungle* (1958), *Sing To Me Through Open Windows* (1959), *Aubade* (1959), *Oh Dad Poor Dad Mama's Hung You In the Closet And I'm Feelin' So Sad* (1960), *Asylum, or What the Gentlemen Are Up To, Not To Mention the Ladies* (1963), *The Conquest of Everest* (1964), *The Hero* (1964), *The Day the Whores Came Out To Play Tennis* (1965), *Indians* (1968), *Wings* (1978), *Nine* (book of the musical; 1980), *End of the World (with Symposium to Follow)* (1984)**

Born in New York the son of a jeweller, Arthur Kopit has been writing some of the most intriguing American drama for three decades, in a career that stretches from Ionesco-like comic absurdism (the celebrated *Oh Dad Poor Dad*) to the libretto for a Tony-winning musical inspired by Federico Fellini's *8½* (*Nine*). In between are some lengthily titled black comedies and two acclaimed dramas diametrically opposed in style and scope. *Indians*, which had its world premiere at the ▷ RSC, a Pirandelloian piece about cultural imperialism, with Buffalo Bill Cody as an early white liberal confronted by the ghosts of Indians who

TRY THESE:
▷Pirandello, ▷Tom Stoppard for theatrical self-consciousness; ▷Jack Gelber and ▷Murray Schisgal for similar 1960s iconoclasm, America-style; ▷Howard Sackler, ▷Bernard Pomerance for analogously liberal looks at American history; ▷Brian Clark's *The Petition*, ▷Lanford Wilson's *Angels Fall*, ▷Nick Darke's *The Body* ▷Sarah Daniels' *The Devil's Gateway*, ▷David Edgar's *Maydays* for other contemporary plays about the Bomb along the lines of *End of the World*; ▷Jean-

resented being put on display at his Wild West show; and *Wings*, an intimate, fragile play about an aviatrix, Emily Stilson, who suffers a stroke.

Claude Van Itallie's *The Traveller* for another recent play about a stroke victim; see also ▷De Filippo's *Ducking Out* for a play on a similar theme.

Oh Dad Poor Dad Mama's Hung You In the Closet and I'm Feelin' So Sad

The man-eating and violent matriarch Madame Rosepettle arrives in Cuba on holiday with a silver piranha and two belligerent flowers, as well as her stammering twenty-six-year-old son, in this crazed and noisy comedy, a deliberate pastiche of ▷ Ionesco and ▷ Tennessee Williams that made Kopit's international name. The son begins to discover women, but his efforts at seduction are continually thwarted – ▷ Joe Orton-style – by the tumbling corpse of his embalmed father. In between, his mother is pinioning him under blankets in order to keep him under control, and the domestic comedy spirals into a kind of chaotic disorder that suggests ▷ Kaufman and Hart on speed.

KOPS, Bernard [1926–]

British poet, novelist and dramatist

Plays include:

***The Hamlet of Stepney Green* (1957), *The Dream of Peter Mann* (1960), *Enter Solly Gold* (1962), *Ezra* (1981), *Simon at Midnight* (1985)**

First produced at about the same time as ▷ Arnold Wesker, and from the same East End Jewish background (the privations and vigour of which are both reflected in his work), Kops declared in 1962 that he and his contemporaries ▷ John Arden, Alun Owen, ▷ Robert Bolt, ▷ Willis Hall and ▷ Wesker would ensure that theatre would never again be a 'precious inner-sanctum for the precious few'. He believed then that by tackling issues of immediate social concern they could change the way the world works. However, his issues are the rather broad ones of the poor quality of working-class life, the futility of riches and the need for love and joy rather than hard political polemic. In *The Hamlet of Stepney Green* his Hamlet seeks revenge, but not against an actual murderer, and he ends the play optimistically, the ghost satisfied by the reconciled characters' promise to always carry a little revolution in their hearts. All his work is not so optimistic, though the con-man 'rabbi' in *Enter Solly Gold*, posing as the long awaited Messiah, brings a sense of real values and a new joy to the materialistic family he cons. The title character of *The Dream of Peter Mann*, like his namesake ▷ Ibsen's Gynt, sets out on a quest for riches, while in the dream which forms the second part of the play he finds himself in a world preparing for nuclear war, waking when the bomb explodes, and ending reconciled to home. Kops' plays are always lively, though sometimes dramatically overstated and given to over-sentimentality and naivety.

TRY THESE:
▷Arnold Wesker and ▷Harold Pinter write from the same background; ▷Tom Stoppard's *Rosencrantz and Guildenstern are Dead* for one of many dramatic responses to Shakespeare's plays; ▷De Filippo and ▷Alan Ayckbourn, ▷David Lan's *Flight* and ▷Neil Simon's *Brighton Beach Memoirs* for plays of family drama.

KRAMER, Larry [1936–]

American author and dramatist

Plays include:

***Sissies' Scrapbook* (1972), *The Normal Heart* (1985)**

Films include:

***Women In Love* (adapted from the D. H. Lawrence novel; 1970)**

A graduate of Yale, Larry Kramer began his career in London in the 1960s working as a story editor for Columbia Pictures. As a playwright, he is best known for *The Normal Heart*, a semi-autobiographical drama which made such an impact that its author merits an entry for sociological and historical reasons as much as anything else. Set in Manhattan over a three-year period from 1981 to 1984, the play is a howl of rage from a writer incensed at his city's sluggishness in responding to the alarms of AIDS. A founding member of the Gay Men's Health Crisis Centre, Kramer casts as his on-stage alter ego one Ned Weeks, a consciousness-raising writer who refuses to rest until such disparate institutions as *The New York Times*, the Mayor's office, and the national government have given the fatal disease the attention it

TRY THESE:
▷Ibsen's *An Enemy of the People* as a play of ideas centred on illness; ▷Clifford Odets for social arousal; playwrights listed above for AIDS-related literature; also ▷Sherman's *Passing By*, for a pre-AIDS treatment of illness; see also ▷Gay Sweatshop for other gay plays dealing with social issues.

Joint Stock's seminal 1975 production of David Hare's ***Fanshen***, directed by Bill Gaskill and Max Stafford-Clark.

Martin Sheen and Frances Tomelty in Larry Kramer's ***The Normal Heart***, Royal Court, 1986, which subsequently transferred to the West End.

deserves. Wildly polemical and issue-obsessed – Kramer claims he was emboldened to write the play after seeing ▷ David Hare's *A Map of the World* at the ▷ National Theatre – the play is basically a harangue written at white heat, and it ends with a deathbed scene that recapitulates dozens of 1930s movies, this time from a gay vantage-point. Other playwrights on both sides of the Atlantic – William M. Hoffman (*As Is*), ▷ Harvey Fierstein (*Safe Sex*), Paul Selig (*Terminal Bar*), Andy Kirby (*Compromised Immunity*) – have addressed the illness on-stage, but Kramer's play, if not the best, is certainly the most well-travelled. Productions have been seen in eighteen countries, including in Britain at the Royal Court and then at the Albery, and Barbra Streisand plans to produce and direct a film version, possibly starring her *Nuts* colleague, Richard Dreyfuss.

KROETZ, Franz Xaver [1946–]
West German dramatist

Plays include:

***Heimarbeit* (*Homeworker*; 1971), *Stallerhof* (*Staller Farm*; 1972), *Wunschkonzert* (*Request Programme*; 1972), *Agnes Bernauer* (1973; from Hebbel's play), *Das Nest* (*The Nest*; 1975), *Wer durch's Laub geht* (*Through the Leaves*; 1976)**

Kroetz is one of a number of contemporary German playwrights, both East and West (including Martin Walser, Jochen Ziem, and Martin Sperr), who have been influenced by the post-war rediscovery of ▷ Horváth and the 'Volksstück', a genre dealing with the lives of ordinary people in ways accessible to them, and which also uses the conventions of television drama. His first plays often had a *succès de scandale* – *Homeworker* includes, on stage, an unsuccessful abortion and the murder of a deformed child, and *Staller Farm* the seduction of a mentally defective girl and masturbation on a lavatory. But since then his scenes from the lives of inarticulate people trapped in their economic situation have become lower-keyed and more effective, and his political commitment more clear. Several of his plays have been successfully put on in Britain: *The Nest*, at the Orange Tree in 1981 and at the Bush in 1986, shows in short simple scenes the clichéed conversation and domestic detail of the lives of a lorry-driver and his wife, including a long silent sequence where he dumps barrels of industrial waste in a bathing-pool; theatricality takes over when their baby is burnt by the waste, and he is thus driven to join the union. *Through the Leaves*, a Traverse transfer to the Bush in 1985, almost eschews plot in showing the relationship between a lonely middle-aged pair, a female offal-seller and a construction worker, finally destroyed by the conditioned inadequacies of their language and their sexual assumptions. *Request Programme* also transferred from the Traverse to the Bush in 1986. This finely tuned Nancy Duguid production (with a harrowing performance from Eileen Nicholas) takes the portrayal of inarticulacy to extremes. After an hour's silence, except for the radio, we know a great deal about the lonely single woman who is the only character, as she goes about her evening's fussy, meticulous routines, and at the end quietly and inevitably commits suicide.

TRY THESE:
▷Michel Vinaver for the '*Théâtre du quotidien*', though Kroetz's political message is clearer; ▷Edward Bond's *Saved* was admired by many 1970s German playwrights for the way it shows the violence that goes with inarticulacy; there is a line of influence through ▷Horváth back to ▷Büchner's *Woyzeck*; see ▷Daniel Mornin's *The Murders* and ▷Hanif Kureishi's *Tomorrow-Today!* and *Outskirts* for contemporary inarticulacy and violence; Gerhart Hauptmann was a late nineteenth-century champion of naturalistic drama.

KUREISHI, Hanif [1954–]
British dramatist and screenwriter

Plays include:

***Soaking the Heat* (1976), *The King and Me* (1979), *The Mother Country* (1980), *Tomorrow-Today!* (1980), *Outskirts* (1981), *Borderline* (1981), *Cinders* (adaptation, from Christina Paul's translation, of a play by Janusz Glowacki; 1981), *Artists and Admirers* (with David Leveaux, from ▷ Ostrovsky; 1982), *Birds of Passage* (1983)**

Films include:

***My Beautiful Laundrette* (1986), *Sammy and Rosie Get Laid* (1988)**

TRY THESE:
▷Karim Alrawi's *A Colder Climate* charts racism in the East End; ▷Harwant Bains is a new British Asian writer; ▷Sue Townsend's *The Great Celestial Cow* was Joint Stock's second Asian venture; ▷Mustapha Matura's *Playboy of the West Indies* and *Trinidad Sisters* are reworkings

Rita Wolf and Vincent Ebrahim in Hanif Kureishi's ***Borderline***, directed by Max Stafford-Clark for Joint Stock, 1981.

Kureishi's theatre and film work shares the same preoccupation with the difficulties of making and establishing meaningful personal contacts in the face of major cultural obstacles, particularly those deriving from prejudice. Kureishi evokes brilliantly the wastelands of the inner cities and the casualties of endemic poverty of vision and racism, both white and non-white. *The King and Me* is a study of a young couple on a housing estate who are at once sustained and trapped by adherence to the Elvis Presley cult, but who eventually make a new start; *Cinders*, incidentally, shares the same concern with the role of media mythologies in shaping people's lives and responses. In *Tomorrow-Today!* urban blight is given added poignancy and urgency by the young characters' inability to believe in the future because of the nuclear threat. In *Outskirts* scenes from the past and present of two South London white men who once joined in a violent racial attack are intercut in a landscape of despair from which one has escaped to become a liberal teacher while the other has become involved with a fascist organisation. *Borderline*, which caused some controversy in the Asian community because white actors doubled both white and Asian parts in the ▷ Joint Stock production, is a fine evocation of the strains of living on the borderlines of different cultures and different conventions which shows a complex picture of class, racial and gender expectations across Asian and white communities, breaking through stereotypes to show the complexities, tensions and possibilities for good and bad in Britain now. *Birds of Passage*, a Sydenham *Cherry Orchard*, shows the erosion of old loyalties to neighbourhood, class and family in the face of socio-economic changes made concrete in the shape of the Pakistani former lodger who buys the house he lodged in.

of classics to West Indian settings; ▷Peter Flannery's *Savage Amusement*, ▷Trevor Griffiths' *Oi for England* and ▷Nigel Williams' *Class Enemy* tackle themes of urban deprivation as do the young stream of playwrights, Johnny Quarrel, Mick Mahoney, ▷Gregory Motton and ▷Jim Cartwright; ▷Alan Bleasdale's *Elvis* was a musical portrait of the 'King'.

KYD, Thomas [1558–94]

English Renaissance dramatist

Plays include:

The Spanish Tragedy (c 1589)

Kyd's *The Spanish Tragedy* is, for all practical purposes, the play that started the vogue for revenge tragedy in the Elizabethan theatre but unlike many trendsetters it still bears comparison with its successors. The details of Kyd's life and career are somewhat obscure: London born, he may well have followed his father's profession of scrivener and he was working in the theatre by 1585. The main biographical information we have about him comes from 1593 when he was arrested and charged with blasphemy. After ▷ Marlowe's suspicious death Kyd claimed that the 'blasphemous' material found in his home had belonged to Marlowe since they had shared a room at one point. Whatever the truth of the matter, Kyd's death just over a year after he was released may well have been related to his sufferings in prison. Kyd is thought to have been the author of an earlier version of *Hamlet* as well as other works, most of which have not survived. All the ingredients of the later revenge plays are to be found in *The Spanish Tragedy*, some derived from ▷ Seneca, some indebted to the Elizabethan picture of ▷ Machiavelli: the search for justice thwarted by corruption, ingenious murders, the masque that converts pretend deaths into real ones, the ghost, the play within the play, madness, the dumb show, and the Machiavellian villain. But there is more to it than sensationalism: the theme of revenge serves as a way of dramatising and heightening everyday conflict, thus opening up revenge tragedy as a medium for presenting major issues in a dramatically effective way.

TRY THESE:

Most Renaissance tragic dramatists used revenge plots and malcontent figures – ▷Shakespeare's *Hamlet* is the most famous example of both, and there are notable examples in ▷Tourneur, ▷Webster and ▷Middleton; see ▷Bernard Kops' *The Hamlet of Stepney Green* for a contemporary, Jewish variation.

LABICHE, Eugène [1815–88]
French dramatist

Plays include:

***Un Chapeau de paille d'Italie* (*An Italian Straw Hat*; 1851), *Le Voyage de M Perrichon* (*M Perrichon Takes a Trip*; 1860), *La Poudre aux Yeux* (*Dust in Your Eyes*; 1861), *Célimare le Bien-Aimé* (*Beloved Célimare*; 1863), *La Cagnotte* (*The Piggy-Bank*; 1864)**

The most successful writer of French farce, and certainly the most prolific, Labiche published fifty-seven plays, but had a hand in perhaps a hundred more. Given this vast output, it is not surprising that he is distinguished less for originality than for the professionalism with which he reworks all the oldest and most reliable jokes. His satire of the bourgeois is often sharp but his plays are more genial and less manic than ▷ Feydeau's. He had a sunny temperament, helped no doubt by the success that brought him the money for a chateau in Sologne and eventually a seat in the French Academy. Many of the plays would bear revival. *An Italian Straw Hat* has an unequalled chase theme, as a hapless bridegroom, followed by his entire wedding party, rushes around Paris in search of a replica straw hat for one that has been eaten by his horse in circumstances of maximum embarrassment to the owner. This play is usually reliable, and René Clair's 1927 film version still has great charm; but the 1986 Ray Cooney production fell flat on its face, as did one by Orson Welles in 1936, retitled *Horse Eats Hat.*

TRY THESE:
▷Feydeau for nineteenth-century French farce; ▷Pinero, ▷Ben Travers; ▷Joe Orton and ▷Alan Ayckbourn for English variations; ▷Michael Frayn's *Noises Off* for the best theatrical exposure of the mechanisms of farce.

LAN, David [1952–]
South African born dramatist

Plays include:

***Painting a Wall* (1974), *Bird Child* (1974), *Paradise* (1975), *Homage to Bean Soup* (1975), *Winter Dancers* (1977), *Red Earth* (1978), *Sergeant Ola and his Followers* (1979), *Flight* (1986), *A Mouthful of Birds* (with Caryl Churchill; 1986)**

Born in Cape Town, where he was a teenage magician and puppeteer, Lan went to Britain in 1972 to study social anthropology and lived in Zimbabwe from 1980 to 1982. Considerations of racism and anthropology are central to his plays which concern themselves with the search for both political and personal freedoms. *Paradise*, set during the Peninsular War, lacks the basis of personal experience or research which gives substance to his other work, whether the Canadian Indian culture of *The Winter Dancers*, the cargo cult of *Sergeant Ola and his Followers* or the African background of his other plays. *A Mouthful of Birds*, developed with ▷ Caryl Churchill for ▷ Joint Stock from the cast's improvisations, is a collage of variations growing from the Dionysus story. Exploring sexism, racism and other forms of exploitation through ritual, dance, and strong visual theatre rather than any verbal dialectic it is a totally different experience to its predecessor *Flight.*

TRY THESE:
South African born playwrights ▷Athol Fugard, ▷Ronald Harwood and ▷Nicholas Wright; ▷Stephen Poliakoff's *Breaking the Silence* for another family chronicle of Jewish origins.

Flight

Flight is a Jewish family chronicle demonstrating the compromising of political, personal and religious standards and the effects both of refusal to do so and of refusal to recognise one's tacit acceptance of such compromise. A long and demanding play which would benefit from cuts, it nevertheless totally held the attention in the 1986 ▷ RSC Other Place production.

LAVERY, Bryony [1947–]
British dramatist

Plays include:
***I Was Too Young at the Time to Understand why my Mother was Crying* (1976), *Sharing* (1976), *Grandmother's Footsteps* (1976), *The Catering Service* (1977), *Helen and her Friends* (1978), *Bag* (1979), *The Wild Bunch* (1979), *Gentlemen Prefer Blondes* (from the Anita Loos novel; 1979), *Family Album* (1980), *Missing* (1981), *Zulu* (1981), *The Black Hole of Calcutta* (1982), *Götterdämmerung* (1982), *For Maggie, Betty and Ida* (1982), *Hot Time* (community play; 1984), *Calamity* (1984), *Origin of the Species* (1984), *Witchcraze* (1985), *The Mummy* (1987), *The Headless Body* (1987)**

Television includes:
***Revolting Women* (co-written with ▷ Sue Townsend, Sue Frumin, Vicky Pile)**

Vet/nun/comedienne/detective/lifeguard/Scarborough trawler worker manqué, Lavery has in the end settled for being a feminist writer of prodigious output and variety: satire, sketches, plays for children (she is currently writer-in-residence for the Unicorn children's theatre, and previously the Theatre Centre), ▷ cabaret (she wrote the script for Pamela Stephenson's one woman show in 1981), television and radio. She is at one extreme scriptwriter for the highly original National Theatre of Brent (anarchic dismemberers of grand myths and legends usually played by two or at most three performers), at the other a frequent provider of what *The Guardian* called 'wistful satire, ingenious fantasy'. However, the critics do not all agree (*The Daily Telegraph* called the same show, *Female Trouble*, 'aggressive with a cruel edge to it'). Lavery's peculiarly wonderful send-up/celebration of female suburbia was encapsulated in the Wandsworth Warmers (to be a Warmer, you had to live in Wandsworth, have little sleeps in the afternoon and tie bits of wool round your wrists to keep your arms warm). But behind the satire Lavery has also sought to question and challenge a whole range of man-made assumptions. An open lesbian feminist writer, 'I am passionately dedicated to the rediscovery of women's strength through positive theatrical presentation', her problem has been in finding the right balance between content and style. *Calamity* is a spoof on the Wild West reflected through the eyes of Calamity Jane and other pioneering women. *Witchcraze* deals with connections between witches past (seventeenth century) and present (Greenham), while *Mummy* is about death, mothers and daughters. *Origin of the Species* shows Darwinism revisited or the re-writing of his/her-story. All these plays received criticism for being 'ill-organised' – a drawback that had been avoided in earlier, shorter plays, such as *Helen and her Friends*, *Bag* (about the various definitions of the word), *Family Album* (family pressures seen through a child's and then adult's eyes), *Catering Service* (an allegory on paramilitarism), and *For Maggie, Betty and Ida* (about the stories present inside every woman). Or is it that women writers, breaking new ground, simply have a hard time having their work accepted by a different set of criteria? In any event, *Floorshow*, written with ▷ Caryl Churchill, ▷ Michelene Wandor and David Bradford (see ▷ Monstrous Regiment) remains one of the most interesting subversions of traditional stand-up comedy. Much of her early work was produced through Lavery's own company, set up with friends, the anarchically titled Les Oeufs Malades which metamorphosed by stages into Female Trouble.

TRY THESE:
For a lesbian version of the Wild West, see ▷Tasha Fairbanks; for other zany women's groups, see Cunning Stunts; see also ▷Women's Theatre Group, ▷Monstrous Regiment, ▷Cabaret, ▷Women in Theatre.

LEIGH, Mike [1943–]
British dramatist, director

Plays include:
***The Box Play* (1966), *Bleak Moments* (1970),**

TRY THESE:
Mike Bradwell's early work with Hull Truck is similar in approach to Leigh's; ▷Alan

***Wholesome Glory* (1973), *The Jaws of Death* (1973), *Babies Grow Old* (1974), *Oh What!* (1975), *Abigail's Party* (1977), *Ecstasy* (1979), *Goose Pimples* (1981)**

Television includes:

***A Mug's Game* (1972), *Hard Labour* (1973), *The Permissive Society* (1975), *Nuts in May* (1975), *Knock for Knock* (1976), *The Kiss of Death* (1977), *Who's Who* (1979), *Grown-Ups* (1980), *Home Sweet Home* (1982)**

Films include:

***Bleak Moments* (1970)**

Salford born Leigh trained as an actor at the Royal Academy of Dramatic Art, moved to the Camberwell and Central Schools of Art and the London Film School, before becoming Associate Director of the Midlands Arts Centre, Birmingham. His first original play, *The Box Play* evolved from improvisation work in Birmingham. He has since directed for the Royal Court, and the Hampstead Theatre Club, and between 1967 and 1968 was an assistant director for the ▷ RSC.

Leigh has developed a form of theatre which can best be described as structured improvisation; as he has said: 'It's necessary that the improvisations serve a particular theme or idea. I discover the substance of the play during rehearsals. . .' Working closely with actors, his plays develop out of a long process of workshops and improvisation from which Leigh devises a final script. Actors work in great detail with their characterisation, often beginning by developing their character alone with Leigh, and then moving towards meeting other characters gradually over the rehearsal period. For example, Anthony Sher has described his experience of preparing for his role as an Arab in *Goose Pimples* by dressing the part, exploring the West End of London in character and taking great pride in being treated in character by a London taxi driver. The process has the effect of constructing a very intense and stylised form of naturalistic theatre. This works very well for television, for which he has devised over twenty plays: notably *Nuts in May*, in which a couple go on a camping trip, *Who's Who*, a study of class, in its intercut story of an upper-class dinner party and a cat breeder, and *Home Sweet Home*, the story of the marriages of a group of postmen. *Bleak Moments*, Leigh's tenth improvised play, which explores the relationship between two painfully lonely people, transferred beautifully into a feature film, which won prizes at the Chicago and Locarno Film Festivals.

Abigail's Party

Abigail's Party is structured around a group of neighbours who meet for drinks while one couple's teenage daughter is holding a party. The play is set in the living room of the fearsome hostess, Beverley. Alison Steadman, Leigh's wife, won the *Plays and Players* and *Evening Standard* best actress awards for her performance. The play charts the tensions of the relationships as they move over the course of the evening to a final dramatic conclusion. The experience of the play is something like spending an evening among a group who become increasingly embarrassing and painful to watch. A wickedly sharp satire on lower-middle-class social pretensions, if over-played, it comes close to the bitterest form of parody.

Ayckbourn and ▷Joe Orton for fierce demolition of middle-class pretensions; ▷Edward Albee's *Who's Afraid of Virginia Woolf* for an American equivalent of fierce satire; ▷de Filippo for domestic satires of a gentler nature; ▷Alan Bennett for another form of satire on a whole range of middle-class mores.

LEONARD, Hugh [1926–]

Irish dramatist

Plays include:

The Big Birthday* (1956), *A Leap In the Dark* (1957), *Madigan's Lock* (1958), *Walk On the Water* (1960), *The Poker Session* (1964), *The Family Way* (1964), *Mick and Mick* (1966), *The Au Pair Man* (1968), *The Patrick Pearse Motel* (1971), *Da* (1973), *Summer* (1974), *Irishmen* (1974), *Time Was* (1976), *A Life* (1978), *The Mask of Moriarty* (1986); adaptations include *The Passion of Peter Ginty* (1961; from ▷ Ibsen's *Peer Gynt*), *Stephen D.* (1962; from Joyce's *Portrait of the Artist. . .*), *When the Saints Go Cycling In* (1965; from Flann O'Brien's *The Dalkey

TRY THESE:

▷Brian Friel, ▷Thomas Kilroy and Tom Murphy for Leonard's pre-eminent contemporaries, who examine the Irishman's relationship to his country; ▷Eugene O'Neill, ▷John Mortimer's *A Voyage Round My Father* and ▷J. M.

***Archive*), *Some of My Best Friends Are Husbands* (1976; from ▷ Labiche's *Celimare*)**

Born John Keyes Byrne, Leonard is one of Ireland's most popular current playwrights, and his success has led to the same sorts of misconceptions that plague ▷ Alan Ayckbourn in England. Indeed, like Ayckbourn, Leonard frequently indicts the same moneyed bourgeois audience who flock to see his plays, and even his most crowd-pleasing works (such as *The Patrick Pearse Motel,* which uses the conventions of French farce to comment on the development of modern-day Ireland) have their moments of bile, as well. The link between the present and the past, and between people and their country, are twin themes Leonard explores repeatedly. In *A Walk On the Water*, the exiled protagonist comes home to Ireland for his father's funeral, only to encounter his erstwhile companions dating back to an era which now seems lost both to them – and to their city. *Mick and Mick* refracts the same sentiment through the eyes of an Irishwoman working in Britain, who returns to Ireland with the clarity of an outsider.

Leonard has written many adaptations (his *Stephen D.*, taken from James Joyce, remains a model of its kind) and pastiche (*The Mask of Moriarty*, about Sherlock Holmes' sidekick), but he's best known for *Da* and *A Life*, two plays opposed both in tone and subject matter – the first finds life in death, the other death in life.

Barrie's *Mary Rose* for familial ghosts, both literal and figurative; ▷Lanford Wilson's *Lemon Sky* and ▷Tina Howe's *Painting Churches* for analogous contemporary American plays about grown children and their parents.

Da

The middle-aged Charlie comes to terms with his dead foster-father, the 'da' of the title, in Leonard's quasi-autobiographical comedy/drama, which was a Tony-winning Broadway smash, abetted by superb leading performances from Brian Murray and Barnard Hughes as Charlie and his crusty old 'da'. A gardener who has made a lifetime career out of exasperating his son, 'da' is a ghost who just won't lie down, and the play is a comic exorcism with darker shades, as well. The man who gave Charlie his first job, the civil servant Desmond Drumm, takes centre-stage in *A Life*, in which he is diagnosed as having cancer.

LESBIAN THEATRE

TRY THESE:
▷Gay Sweatshop; ▷Women-in-Theatre; ▷Women's Theatre Group; ▷cabaret; ▷Performance art; ▷Theatre of Black Women; see also ▷Tasha Fairbanks, ▷Jacqueline Holborough, ▷Sarah Daniels, ▷Maureen Duffy, ▷Jackie Kay, ▷Jackie Rudet.

As one of society's taboos, lesbian theatre, it seems, has always had a hard struggle to exist. Plays showing women together seem fair game for main-stream runs (think of Nell Dunn's *Steaming* or Sharman Macdonald's *When I Was A Girl I Used to Scream and Shout*) with the proviso that female interaction stays this side of the sexual divide.

It may, therefore, seem as if lesbian theatre is invisible but there is plenty of life going on – albeit mostly away from the main stages. Like the history of gay (male) theatre in Britain, much of the creation of lesbian theatre goes back to ▷ Gay Sweatshop who presented Jill Posener's 'coming out' play *Any Woman Can* in their first season. ▷ Gay Sweatshop's women's company, including Kate Crutchley, Nancy Duguid, Kate Phelps and ▷ Tasha Fairbanks also created *Care and Control* about lesbian mothers and custody (scripted by ▷ Michelene Wandor). Duguid, Crutchley and ▷ Fairbanks have all gone on to be instrumental in the creation and support of feminist and lesbian feminist work, particularly Crutchley whose tenure at the Oval House in London has guaranteed a steady stream of gay, lesbian and feminist plays. It has been at the Oval for example that the American groups Spiderwoman, Hot Peaches and Split Britches made their British debuts. In 1987 Split Britches returned with the high energy/stream-of-consciousness and fairly controversial view of lesbian love and American landscapes *Dress Suits To Hire*, with Lois Weaver, and Peggy Shaw, written by Holly Hughes. The Oval has also hosted Hard Corps (Adele Saleem and Sarah McNair) in their 'whodunnit and who she did it with', *John* (about Radclyffe Hall and her life-long companion

Una Troubridge); the cabaret duos Parker & Klein and Donna & Kebab; Sue Frumin's comedies of life, love and women's friendship; Crutchley's production of Sandra Freeman's comic saga of lesbian loves *Supporting Roles* and the Sadista Sisters' sci-fi feminist fantasy *The Virgin's Revenge*.

▷ Tasha Fairbanks has been instrumental in setting up the lesbian group Siren, and Duguid's varied career includes directing *Patterns* by Barbara Burford, a multi-racial mythic treatment of women's history, at the Drill Hall. The Drill Hall, another haven for lesbian and women's work (under the encouragement of ex-Gay Sweatshopper, Julie Parker) has hosted, amongst many: ▷ Gay Sweatshop (*More*), ▷ Theatre of Black Women (*Chiaroscuro*), Siren (*PULP*), and singer Michelle Shocked as well as groups such as Burnt Bridges, Blood Group, ▷ Women's Theatre Group and ▷ Rose English.

Lesbian theatre nonetheless has yet to break into the mainstream with any force. There are no television soap lesbian characters (though they are gradually stealing into film, eg *Desert Hearts* and *I've Heard The Mermaids Singing*) and, since ▷ Frank Marcus's by now legendary *The Killing of Sister George* (which, unintentionally since it was intended as farce, set up irrevocable lesbian stereotypes), almost no West End productions. However, Win Wells's *Gertrude Stein and Companion* with Miriam Margoyles and Natasha Morgan did transfer respectably from the ▷ Edinburgh Festival fringe to the Bush for a sell-out run and Rainer Werner Fassbinder's *The Bitter Tears of Petra von Kant*, a typically melodramatic though theatrically gripping treatment of lesbian relationships, was given a particularly fine production in 1987 at the small Latchmere fringe theatre in London. Lesbian characters have also regularly appeared in the plays of ▷ Clean Break and with particular credibility in ▷ Jacqueline Holborough's first full length play *The Garden Girls*. ▷ Sarah Daniels' *Neaptide*, about lesbian mothers and child custody surfaced briefly at the National's Cottesloe in the 1980s as did ▷ Maureen Duffy's *Rites* in a short season of experimental plays in 1969.

Lesbian theatre, by its nature on the fringes of society is, like much other women's theatre, starved of resources, and, on the whole small-scale. For all that, it has flourished and fed into the repertoire of many women's companies such as Burnt Bridges, Scarlet Harlets, and ▷ Women's Theatre Group.

Lesbian theatre can be celebratory and autobiographical (as in Nicolle Freni's *Brooklyn E5* presented at the London Lesbian and Gay Centre, another venue which has regularly hosted lesbian work) or it can highlight women's friendship as in Sue Frumin's *Rabbit in a Trap* and *Home Sweet Home* or Isobel Miller's *Patience and Sarah*. It can explore racial and cultural roots and homophobia as in ▷ Jackie Kay's *Chiaroscuro* or ▷ Jackie Rudet's *Basin*, or it can be abstract, stylistic and almost epic (*Madonna in Slag City* by Sadista Sisters' founder Jude Alderson). It can also be experimental as in Maro Green and Caroline Griffin's *More*, about hidden disabilities, and *The Memorial Gardens*, about sexual abuse and self-insemination; or in the now defunct Hormone Imbalance's blank verse parody of Shakespeare, *Ophelia*. Lesbian plays can, as in the work of Siren, take the form of a re-examination of the value system within which we live – of patriarchy (with its overtones of militarism), masculinity, femininity, and the female images most popularly transmitted in society. Much of lesbian theatre has absorbed the tenets of feminism into its work – but not all lesbians are feminists or vice versa! It also does not necessarily follow that it must be, as male critics often accuse women's theatre of being, man-hating (though it may be), or shrill, or strident. It may be didactic, it may be subversive; it can also be an eye-opener as in Random Pact's *As My Eyes Close, So Yours Will Open*, the true story of Herculine Baroin, a French nineteenth-century hermaphrodite. The plays may be about abuse or a sense of grievance but lesbian theatre also shows a remarkable capacity for imaginative leaps (see the plays of ▷ Bryony Lavery and Berta Freistadt, and the Ortonesque farces of Jill Fleming). Lesbian theatre at its best is about rediscovery, re-examination, honesty, laughter, compassion, imagination, and a positive response to the mistrusts, mistakes and misunderstandings of society – a good place for any theatre to be, though in Britain in April 1988 overshadowed overwhelmingly by the advent of legislation banning the 'promotion' of homosexuality with local government funds, the effects of which, future theatre will undoubtedly chart.

LESSING, Gotthold Ephraim [1729–81]
German dramatist and critic

Plays include:

***Miss Sara Sampson* (1755), *Minna von Barnhelm* (1767), *Emilia Galotti* (1772), *Nathan the Wise* (1779)**

Lessing combined the theory and practice of drama in much the same way as ▷ Granville Barker and ▷ Shaw; his witty and influential theatre criticism, collected as the *Hamburgische Dramaturgie* (1769), includes both reviews of live performances at the National Theatre in Hamburg and general thoughts on the way German drama should develop. The direction he advocated was away from the previous influence of French Classical tragedy and towards ▷ Shakespeare and Diderot as models for the writing of plays about everyday bourgeois life (though not with everyday incidents). He wrote several plays following his own precepts: *Miss Sara Sampson* is a domestic tragedy owing much to Richardson's *Pamela*, but too sententious and violent in its end. *Emilia Galotti*, though equally emotional, works much better, as the story of the father killing his daughter (at her request) to save her from dishonour; the narrative line is strong, and the political protest at the princely abuse of power is striking, though it is carefully distanced by an Italian Renaissance setting. The young p.l.c. company revived it in 1987 at the Young Vic for the first time in Britain since the eighteenth century, in modern dress but in a somewhat flowery Victorian translation, and with considerable success. They also did well with *Minna von Barnhelm*, the enjoyable romantic comedy of a penniless officer discharged under a cloud at the end of the Seven Years' War, and scrupulously refusing to marry his betrothed because she is an heiress. She gets him in the end, of course. Someone should try an English version of *Nathan the Wise*, Lessing's great plea for religious tolerance.

TRY THESE:
▷Goethe and ▷Schiller for eighteenth-century German drama and the influence of ▷Shakespeare; *Minna von Barnhelm* is not dissimilar in tone to ▷Sheridan and ▷Goldsmith; ▷Corneille's *Le Cid* in ▷Cheek By Jowl's luminous production brought the issues of women's honour related to man-made social codes firmly to the fore.

LEVY, Deborah [1959–]
South African-born dramatist, poet

Plays include:

***On New Land* (1981), *Eva and Moses* (1983), *Pax* (1984), *Dream Mama* (1985), *Ophelia and the Great Idea* (1985), *The Naked Cake* (1986), *Our Lady* (1986), *Heresies* (1986)**

Levy is one of the most exciting new writers of the past five years. A self-confessed avant-gardist, with a prodigious intellectual and political curiosity, she made her mark quite suddenly in 1984 with *Pax*, written for the ▷ Women's Theatre Group, following it up with another five plays in the short space of two years (for a variety of women's groups, and culminating in *Heresies*, commissioned for the short-lived ▷ RSC women's group. Created through workshop improvisations, this distillation of contemporary modes around sexual and other politics, seen through the eyes of different archetypes (Cholla, the Displaced Person; Leah, the Composer etc) seemed unusually short on plausibility (Roger Allam's Lonely Businessman male character was a particular casualty). But even when not sparking on all plugs, the power and intelligence of Levy's writing (she has always been the mistress of aphorism triggering a thousand and one allusions) and the breadth of her vision about such recurrent themes as grief, displacement, the nuclear threat, resistance, the importance of female values, and survival make Levy a writer to watch, though she is not always easy to understand. She is also a poet/performance artist. Using the name Lotte Literati, she performs a poetry/performance act on the fringe circuit with Mine Kylan. Her

TRY THESE:
Hilary Westlake and Lumiere and Son's *Panic* for a sound/visual equivalent of women exploring external and inner realities; Burnt Bridges' *Deals* is a stylised feminist encounter with the Big Bang and 1986 City psyche, pre-dating ▷Caryl Churchill's *Serious Money* by several months; ▷Susan Yankowitz's *Alarms* for a heightened Cassandra treatment of the nuclear future; ▷Bryony Lavery's *Origin of the Species* for a feminist reassessment of history; ▷Berta Freistadt's *The Celebration of Kokura* and ▷Stephen Lowe's *Keeping Body*

Deborah Levy's ***Heresies***, directed by Sue Todd for the RSC in 1986. From left to right: Nimmy March, Tina Marian, Susan Tracy, Penelope Freeman.

love of words is matched by a desire to give visual images equal weight, a balance, which Levy herself agrees, makes considerable imaginative demands on a director.

Pax
As time goes on, this play has taken on something of the lustre of a legend. Complex, densely worded, and a play so rich in allusion and ideas as to feel like a hallucinatory journey into the contemporary female psyche, this rummage through female archetypes with its confrontations with past, present and warnings of a precarious future in a nuclear age remains a landmark in mid-1980s feminism with its exploration of mothers and daughters, philosophical meditations on death, patriarchy, the Holocaust and survival. It was directed by Sue Todd (who also directed *Heresies*) and Anna Furse, in a production that matched Levy's adventurousness with equal visual audacity.

and Soul Together for more plays on peace themes; newcomer ▷April de Angelis for a similarly allusive use of language; ▷Red Shift for a parallel aspiration to visual/ verbal theatre.

LIFT (London International Festival of Theatre)

This biennial festival was launched in 1981 by Lucy Neal and Rose de Wend Fenton, who on leaving Warwick University travelled the European festival circuit and returned with a determination to widen theatrical horizons at home. LIFT is not a replacement for the much-lamented Peter Daubeny's World Theatre Seasons which brought productions by major international companies to London which, like the visit of the Berliner Ensemble, left an indelible influence on future British theatre.

The organisers define their criteria for inclusion as that all productions should be easily understood by an English-speaking audience and claim that LIFT is not esoteric, elitist, or fringe but simply stages performances that can be enjoyed by anyone with a curiosity about the world. However, ever since its inception, responses have been divided between ardent supporters and furious hostility, and certainly the standard of shows has varied widely with some gems, some dross. For example, the 1987 festival provoked the *Daily Telegraph* to call the Catalonian La Cubana company's *La Tempstad* 'the worst theatrical experience of this reviewer's life. . .a juvenile farrago of audience debasement that defies comprehension'. Irving Wardle, however, in *The Times*, said of the Canadian Theatre Repere company's *The Dragon Trilogy* that 'this production alone is worth staging the festival for'. Such diversity is the staple of these festivals, and if some productions have been bafflingly hermetic, the overall vitality and innovation of each festival continues, on the whole, to win acclaim. Given the increasing problems of funding (Neal and Fenton spend at least half their time between festivals touting for sponsorship), the fact that the festival continues to happen at all says much for the organisers' persuasive powers.

For audiences willing to have their imaginative sinews stretched, LIFT can still offer a plethora of experiences. The emphasis is on the visual and from an increasingly feminist perspective although Neal and Fenton say they don't go out of their way to book women's work which would be ghettoising, but 'judge things on their artistic merit'. In 1987 the range spanned the four-hour *Cerceau* from the Taganka Theatre in Moscow, the explosive tele-musical from the US's poorest black ghetto – called the *Cabrini Green Project* (described by the *City Limits'* critic as 'the *West Side Story* for the 1980s'), Polish and Japanese mime, and the sonorous rituals of percussion on old machines from the British Bow Gamelan group played in an abandoned boat-yard. Previous years have featured the Catalan Els Comediants rampaging through Battersea Park with a riot of devils erupting with fireworks and flame, and the mesmeric wailing of the French Urban Sax (a platoon of saxophonists dressed in white boiler suits) descending from the roof of Covent Garden Market.

London listings magazine *City Limits* said, 'you never know what to expect with LIFT', and it's true – an Argentinian psychologist in a bravura anti-Junta tirade, a Mexican feminist version of *Don Giovanni*, an American drag artist in cabaret revamping *Phèdre* and *King Lear*, the visually and aurally

TRY THESE:
Glasgow Mayfest, ▷Edinburgh Festival, Dublin and York Festivals are all larger in scale; Cardiff's Chapter Arts Centre also now holds a theatre/ dance festival with emphasis on the 'new'; in Europe The Festival of Fools in Rotterdam offers a comparable performance-based showcase, elsewhere the Avignon Festival, and the Paris and Berlin Theatre Festivals are mixtures of the established and the eccentric.

Donna Giovanni by the Mexican Divas Compania – a feminist version of *Don Giovanni*, at the Shaw Theatre, part of LIFT 1987, showing the exciting visual theatre which is characteristic of the Festival.

stunning Red Pilot group from Yugoslavia, or a searing women's group from a South African black township, the Vusisizwe Players in *You Strike the Woman, You Strike the Rock*, the Australian Circus Oz. What all will have in common is a strong theatricality.

LIFT has also commissioned work especially for the festival, giving Londoners a rare chance to see some British groups such as Welfare State's *Raising of the Titanic* in Limehouse Basin, and Pip Simmons' *Gor Hoi*, an extraordinary outdoor multimedia 'happening' on the theme of the Vietnamese 'boat' people's experiences, or the Nigerian dance drama *New Earth*, created because the organisers found Nigeria's existing 'ethnic' performances were aimed at a tourist audience.

Accusations of elitism, theatrical rubbish, over-pricing, and incomprehensibility may well still be flung regularly at the festival, but Neal and Fenton's optimism and remarkable dedication to this cultural bonanza – even if their choices seem sometimes unnecessarily idiosyncratic – guarantee that this is a festival that will continue to be not quite like any other.

In the first four festivals over sixty companies have been presented – including seminars, workshops, cabaret in the festival club and special performances for children.

LINNEY, Romulus [1930–]

American dramatist

Plays include:

***Goodbye Howard* (1970), *Love Suicide At Schofield Barracks* (1972), *Holy Ghosts* (1974), *The Seasons, Man's Estate* (1974), *Democracy and Esther* (1975), *The Sorrows of Frederick* (1976), *Just Folks* (1978), *Tennessee* (1979), *El Hermano* (1981), *The Captivity of Pixie Shedman* (1981), *Childe Byron* (1981), *Why the Lord Came to Sand Mountain* (1986)**

Raised in Tennessee and North Carolina but educated in the Midwest at Oberlin and then at the Yale Drama School, Romulus Linney writes heady, if messy, dramas in an American Gothic mode – works that cannot be easily categorised but make for intriguing theatre nonetheless. Whether his topic is American eccentrics or real-life historical heavyweights, Linney never condescends to his material, and he seems likely to be one American playwright whose reputation will improve over the years. Already, he has had some success off-Broadway, and his *Childe Byron*, about the relationship between the poet and his daughter, was a notable early acting success for William Hurt. Linney's interest in biography continued in *The Sorrows of Frederick*, the story, via flash-backs, of the septuagenarian Frederick the Great of Prussia, who wants nothing more than to be rid of his army so he can go home to bury a dog. *Democracy and Esther* draws on two novels by Henry Adams set during the corrupt administration of America's eighteenth president, Ulysses S. Grant, and *Love Suicide At Schofield Barracks* used the double suicide of an army general and his wife at a 1970 Hallowe'en party in Hawaii to raise questions about the Vietnam War. His *Holy Ghosts*, about an unhappily married southern couple drawn into a snake-handling cult, was successfully revived by the San Diego Repertory Theatre in 1987 and presented off-Broadway for a season.

TRY THESE:
▷Christopher Hampton's *Total Eclipse*, ▷Howard Brenton's *Bloody Poetry* for plays about nineteenth-century poets; ▷Sam Shepard for an alternative mode of American Gothic; James Duff's *The War Back Home* as an anti-Vietnam play with a domestic setting.

LITTLEWOOD, Joan [1914–]

English actress and director

Writing in *Encore* in 1961 Littlewood declared 'I do not believe in the supremacy of the director, designer, actor or even of the writer. It is through collaboration that this knockabout art of theatre survives and kicks.'

Best known as founder-director of Theatre Workshop Littlewood was born in Stockwell, London, and went to RADA but left without completing the course, reacting against the teaching and against West End theatre in general. In Manchester she became involved with Ewan McColl's Theatre of Action, a left-wing group

TRY THESE:
For Littlewood's style of collective script techniques, see ▷Joint Stock, and much of the early work of companies such as ▷Monstrous Regiment, ▷Women's Theatre Group and socialist companies like ▷7:84, Belt and

inspired by the theories of Adolphe Appia and described by one critic as 'the nearest thing any British theatre has got to Meyerhold.' Reconstituted after a wartime gap as Theatre Workshop, the company toured throughout the country – often with one-night-stands, in new plays created by the company and occasional classics, until finding a permanent home at the Theatre Royal, Stratford, in East London. Largely unacknowledged by British critics, though invited to perform abroad with great success, Littlewood overcame conditions of continuous financial crisis to create productions of great energy and power from negligible resources. One of the first British directors to make extensive use of improvisation, she had remarkable skills in developing performances. She was sometimes accused of working best with second-rate material but a great many fine actors – not to mention designer John Bury – look back on their days with Theatre Workshop as a key period in their careers.

Littlewood was trusted by ▷ Brecht with the first British production of *Mother Courage* (Barnstaple 1955), which she directed as well as playing the title role, and should be remembered as much for the anti-nuclear war *Uranium 235*, a pro-peace *Lysistrata* and classic productions of *Volpone* and *Richard II* as for the plays by ▷ Behan, ▷ Delaney and Lionel Bart which gained wide audiences when Theatre Workshop productions transferred to the West End. These transfers meant that each time a new company had to be built at Stratford.

In 1961 Littlewood went to Nigeria and there were no new Workshop productions for two years. Then in 1963 came another smash hit *Oh What a Lovely War*, a World War I documentary built around popular songs and presented as a pierrot show. But the long-running transfer again removed the company.

Littlewood does not see theatre as existing only in theatres; with a group which included Buckminster Fuller, Lord Harewood and Yehudi Menuhin, she made plans in the late sixties for an ambitious 'Fun Palace' which she described as 'a place of toys for adults, a place to waste time without guilt or discomfort, to develop unused talents, to discover the fund of joy and sadness within us.' It was to have such features as warm air curtains, optical barriers and vapour zones, but potential sites fell through, funding did not materialise and her theatre colleagues did not share her enthusiasm for the idea.

In 1967 *Mrs Wilson's Diary*, a satire on life at 10 Downing Street developed in improvisations from material supplied by John Wells and Richard Ingrams, was Littlewood's last Workshop success to transfer to the West End but although she did four more productions in 1972–3. The demolition of the district around the theatre and failure of funding eventually led to the end of Theatre Workshop. Since the early death of Gerry Raffles, her partner in life and work, Littlewood has not worked in theatre.

Braces; for community oriented companies see ▷Ann Jellicoe and ▷Community Theatre; for companies committed to new writing see ▷Foco Novo, ▷Paines Plough, ▷Theatre of Black Women; for a vision, though unacceptably middle-class of Joan's 'fun palace', see, ironically, the National Theatre; for smaller theatres round the country see Peter Cheeseman at Stoke-on-Trent, Sheffield's Crucible, Leicester Haymarket, Solent People's Theatre, Theatre Foundry, and in London, The Albany in Deptford and Battersea Arts Centre.

LORCA, Federico Garciá [1898–1935]

Spanish dramatist, poet, artist

Plays include:

***The Butterfly's Evil Spell* (1920), *Mariana Pineda* (1927), *In Five Years' Time* (1930), *The Public* (1930), *Blood Wedding* (1932), *Yerma* (1934), *Dona Rosita la Soltera* (1935), *The House of Bernarda Alba* (1935)**

Lorca was brought up on the family farm near Grenada and always said that he was unable to speak and walk until the age of four because of illness as a baby. As a student he forged close friendships with Salvador Dali and Luis Buñuel. Surrealism was something that sat easily with Lorca – *The Public* and *In Five Years' Time* are Surrealistic fantasies – but he was mistrustful of intellectual and literary élites, and his plays are rooted in Spanish folk lore and traditions. His second play, *Mariana Pineda*, told the story of a heroine of the revolution of the 1830s. Lorca thought of himself as a playwright for the Spanish people; he became involved in 1931 with a travelling theatre group, La Baracca, which toured classic Spanish drama throughout the regions of Spain. Many of his texts employ farce, folk tale and poetry, popular and traditional forms, to make them accessible.

His most important works are those which bring together Lorca's passionate feeling for the history and traditions of Andalusia with his poetic power. The 'trilogy of the Spanish Earth';

TRY THESE:
▷Joe Orton and Lorca write with a bitter awareness of sexual hypocrisies; ▷Lindsay Kemp has mounted a dance version of *Blood Wedding* and with Christopher Bruce of Ballet Rambert a superb dance/drama portrait of Lorca, called *The Cruel Garden*; Lorca shared with ▷Brecht, ▷7:84, ▷Trevor Griffiths, ▷John McGrath and David Edgar a commitment to bringing the theatre to the people; ▷Wendy Kesselman's *My Sister in This House* is another claustrophobic

Blood Wedding, *Yerma* and *The House of Bernarda Alba*, are firmly rooted within Spanish communities, and are all concerned with marriage, sexuality and the constraints and commitments of the community. *Blood Wedding* is based on an actual story Lorca came across in a newspaper fragment which told of a family vendetta and a bride who ran away with the son of the enemy family. In his play the first act is relatively naturalistic, but in the second, the moon and death appear in an extraordinarily powerful image to oversee the fleeing lovers. *The House of Bernarda Alba* is a play exclusively of women, in which the destructive power of the matriarch Bernarda Alba becomes a metaphor for sexual repression and constraints on liberty.

On August 19, 1936 Lorca was shot by the fascist paramilitary Black Squad in the early days of the Spanish Civil War. His body lies in an unmarked grave, but he remains Spain's most celebrated playwright.

household of sexual repression.

Yerma

Yerma means 'the barren one'. The play is a powerful study of a peasant woman, obsessed with the desire for a child. But childlessness in Lorca's hands becomes a metaphor for other kinds of barrenness: Yerma's marriage is not only sterile because it has not produced children, her racking pain is quite clearly a desire for another way of being. Yerma and her marriage are firmly located in a community of traditional wisdoms and attitudes to marriage. She is offered the commandments of marriage: 'You must obey your husband who is your owner and master'; and while keeping to her own code of honour, recognises that she is alone in her integrity. In one scene a group of bawdy women offer her their own experiences of wifehood, in another an old woman advises her to he unfaithful. In a final act of revenge she strangles her husband, with the recognition that he can never satisfy her and that she has been denied the one positive outcome of her marriage, a child. The play is a powerful study of sexual hypocrisies, of the constraints on women of traditional 'femininity', and of the 'macho' on men. Yerma was given a magnificent and legendary production by Victor Garcia (later revived by Nuria Espert) in which the play was performed on a huge trampoline and billowing drapes.

LOWE, Stephen [1947–]

British dramatist

Plays include:

Cards (1971), *Stars* (1976), *Touched* (1977), *Shooting Fishing and Riding* (1977), *Sally Ann Hallelujah Band* (1977), *The Ragged Trousered Philanthropists* (1978; from the book by Robert Tressell, *Glasshouses* (1981; retitled as *Moving Pictures*), *Tibetan Inroads* (1981), *Strive* (1982), *Trial of Frankenstein* (1984), *Seachange* (1984), *Keeping Body and Soul Together* (1984), *Desire* (1986), *Demon Lovers* (1987), *The Storm* (1987; from Ostrovsky)

Nottingham-born Lowe worked as an actor at the Stephen Joseph Theatre at Scarborough under the artistic directorship of ▷ Alan Ayckbourn before becoming Resident Playwright at Dartington and at the Riverside Studios. His work has tended to centre on socialist and feminist themes which he has tackled from a wide variety of angles: in *Cards* the idea is that Donald McGill-style seaside postcards are actually photographs of real people who we see discussing their work as they wait for their photographs to be taken; *Stars* shows two couples acting out film fantasies during World War II; *Shooting Fishing and Riding* is a play about rape, based on Susan Brownmiller's *Act of Will.* Lowe has written about the Falklands in *Strive* and, allegorically, in *Seachange* and about the Chinese annexation of Tibet in *Tibetan Inroads.* He is always a challenging playwright with a strong concern for human dignity and a firm commitment to the idea of 'a decent, equal, peaceful future', which comes over strongly in his two best known works, *Touched* and *The Ragged Trousered Philanthropists. Touched*, set in Nottingham in the period between the end of Word War II in Europe and the surrender of Japan, explores the relationship between a group of working-class women as they hope and fear for the future, set against

TRY THESE:
▷David Hare's *Fanshen*, another ▷Joint Stock play, shows the Chinese working-classes reaching an understanding of the roots of their situation; ▷Howard Brenton and David Hare, separately and together, have written plays which, like *Touched*, take Angus Calder's *The People's War* as their inspiration; other writers who have taken the Falklands war as their theme are ▷Louise Page in *Falkland Sound/Voces de Malvinas*, ▷Tony Marchant in *Coming Home*, and Greg Cullen in *Taken Out*; ▷Noël Greig's *Poppies* takes a look at pacificism from a gay perspective.

the background of the discovery of Belsen, the election of the Labour government and the dropping of the first atomic bombs. Lowe's version of the socialist classic *The Ragged Trousered Philanthropists*, first developed in workshops with ▷ Joint Stock, is a moving account of the struggle of working men to come to an understanding of their oppression and carry the fight back to the capitalists.

LUCIE, Doug [1953–]

British dramatist

Plays include:

***John Clare's Mad Nuncle* (1975), *Rough Trade* (1977), *We Love You* (1978), *Oh Well* (1978), *The New Garbo* (1978), *Heroes* (1979), *Poison* (1980), *Strangers in the Night* (1981), *Hard Feelings* (1982), *Progress* (1984), *Key to the World* (1984), *Force and Hypocrisy* (1986), *Fashion* (1987)**

Lucie has made a reputation as the satirical chronicler of the underside of the bright new world of style, be it that of the liberated new man in *Progress* or the marketing of politicians in *Fashion*. Lucie reserves his attacks for those who use current trends for their own egocentric ends, but since that is almost everyone in his plays they achieve major heights of misanthropy in their depiction of a hard, uncaring, manipulative lifestyle. Lucie can be very funny in his presentation of the mannerisms and jargon of his characters but there is no compensating warmth and little hope in a world in which cynicism is the norm and where the plots ensure that what little progress is made is ignored by the other characters.

Progress

Progress is an uncomfortably accurate presentation of right-on people attempting to grapple with all the hazards and pitfalls of negotiating the contradictions of patriarchy and capitalism while using a working-class battered wife as a medium for their own antagonisms. Many of the characters are homo- or bi-sexual and there are important points about the manipulation of trendy ideas to give people sexual credibility, particularly the Men's Group's attempt to discuss pornography. Under the comedy of manners surface, there is a genuine sense of the waste of human potential as relationships collapse and sexual politics becomes sexual warfare. Lucie's vitriolic comedy worked brilliantly at the Bush in 1984 with Lindsay Duncan and Gregory Floy as the trendy middle-class couple whose marriage is foundering, but in the much larger space of the Lyric Hammersmith in 1986 and with a changed cast it seemed altogether more brittle and the sense of waste was lost in the glittering surface. It remains *the* sexual politics play (male variety) for the 1980s.

TRY THESE:
▷Noël Coward, ▷Wycherley, ▷Congreve, ▷Aphra Behn, ▷Joe Orton for manipulative societies where wit is at a premium; ▷Sarah Daniels' *Masterpieces* for a contemporary feminist approach to the question of pornography; ▷Caryl Churchill's *Cloud Nine* for polymorphous sexuality; ▷Deborah Levy's *Heresies* for another contemporary view of sexual politics; ▷Christopher Hampton's adaptation of Laclos' *Les Liaisons Dangereuses* as *the* portrait of cunning and viperish manipulation.

LUCKHAM, Claire [1944–]

British dramatist

Plays include:

***Scum* (with Chris Bond; 1976), *Yatsy and the Whale* (1977), *Tuebrook Tanzi the Venus Fly Trap* (1978, later known as *Tugby Tanzi* and then *Trafford Tanzi*; 1980), *Aladdin* (1978), *Fish Riding Bikes* (1979), *Finishing School* (1982), *The Girls in the Pool* (1982; later known as *Gwen*), *Walking on Water* (1983), *Moll Flanders* (1986 from Defoe's novel), *Imber* (1986), *Alice in Wartime* (1986), *Mary Stuart* (1988; adapted from ▷ Schiller)**

Nairobi-born Luckham stands somewhere between the 'older generation' of female playwrights who won commercial success in the 1970s such as ▷ Pam Gems, ▷ Caryl Churchill, ▷ Mary O'Malley, and ▷ Nell Dunn and the next generation of ▷ Sarah Daniels, ▷ Louise Page, and ▷ Sharman Macdonald in the mid-1980s. With her husband, director Chris Bond, she was initially associated with Liverpool's Everyman and is best known for *Trafford Tanzi* which has now been performed all round the world and translated into more than a dozen languages. Her other plays have also explored female issues, particularly relationships

TRY THESE:
For taking men on in their own sphere, see ▷Timberlake Wertenbaker's *The Grace of Mary Traverse*; for an earlier counterpart, ▷Middleton and ▷Dekker's *The Roaring Girl*; Robert David McDonald has also adaptated ▷Schiller's *Mary Stuart*; for early feminist work, see ▷Monstrous Regiment and ▷Women's Theatre Group; ▷Arnold Wesker's *The Kitchen* is another industrially based piece, also

between women, to each other and to work, with the series of monologues (*Fish Riding Bikes*, *Finishing School*) about women's friendship, a typists' strike at Liverpool Council (*The Girls in the Pool)*, and the adaptations of Defoe's *Moll Flanders* and ▷ Schiller's *Mary Stuart*. But there have also been a couple of ▷ community plays including one about the whaling industry and the army occupation of Salisbury Plain (*Imber*). *Scum*, commissioned by Monstrous Regiment and directed by Sue Todd, set in a laundry during the Paris Commune of 1871, an early exploration of sexual and socialist politics entwined in women's relationships to work and society, was co-written by Luckham and Bond. (Recently, there seems to have been a sudden resurgence in laundry-set pieces with the French women's company from Amiens, Théâtre Basouche performing their much acclaimed *Le Lavoir* at the 1987 Edinburgh Festival, and the excellent Scottish company Wildcat reviving *The Steamie* by David McNiven.) Whilst *Mary Stuart* is Luckham's most recently produced play, *No Fury* is another commission awaiting production with the Women's Playhouse Trust.

Trafford Tanzi
Trafford Tanzi, a storming visual and physical metaphor of female liberation (as it was then seen) enacted through an actual wrestling match between Tanzi and the various characters in her life, first started out doing the rounds of the pubs of Liverpool. Taken up and toured by various companies, including the Contact Theatre in Manchester, the Traverse in Edinburgh, ▷ 7:84, and the Half Moon, it finally settled into a long and successful run at the Mermaid. No doubt about it, *Trafford Tanzi*, with its direct appeal to audience participation, gives value for money as a theatrical experience as Tanzi changes from socially conditioned, feminine little girl to renegade and ultimate wrestler, meeting her husband on equal terms and literally throwing him. However, from a current point of view, some of its sexual politics leave a good deal to be desired, particularly if you are no great lover of the right-by-might or blood sports lobby.

▷John Byrne's *The Slab Boys Trilogy*, Robert Tressell's *The Ragged Trousered Philanthropists*, adapted both by ▷Stephen Lowe and ▷7:84 (re-titled *The Reign of Terror and the Great Money Trick*); for other realistic sporting images, Johnnie Quarrell's *The Wednesday Night Action*, ▷Howard Sackler's *The Great White Hope*, ▷John Godber's *Up 'n' Under*, ▷Louise Page's *Golden Girls*; many agit-prop companies in the 1970s set their plays in places of work to highlight the inter-relationships between individuals, capital, class and gender – see ▷7:84, Red Ladder, Belt and Braces; ▷Caryl Churchill's *Top Girls* and *Serious Money* are perhaps two of the most commercially successful variants of women making it on male terms.

LUKE, Peter [1919–]
British dramatist

Plays include:
Hadrian the Seventh **(1967),** ***Bloomsbury*** **(1974),** ***Married Love*** **(1985)**

Peter Luke has written relatively few plays in the course of a variegated career (wine trade, Head of Scripts for ABC Television, farming in Andalucia, director of the Abbey Theatre, etc), but his version of Frederick Rolfe/Baron Corvo's novel *Hadrian VII* reproduced much of the neurotic fascination of that amazing piece of wish-fulfilment, gave a superb part to Alec McCowen at the Mermaid theatre, and became an international hit. Later plays, such as *Bloomsbury*, about Virginia Woolf, and *Married Love*, about Marie Stopes, have had only moderate success.

Hadrian the Seventh
Hadrian VII, like Rolfe, was a failed priest but, unlike Rolfe, he was made Pope, forgave all his enemies at great and self-righteous length, and revolutionised the Church and the world before being assassinated by a crazed Irishman. Luke's play uses details from Rolfe's life and his other books as an effective frame for the story – at the end we see Rolfe standing on stage, clutching his manuscript, as he watches Hadrian's funeral.

TRY THESE:
▷Mike Alfreds and ▷Shared Experience for other successful adaptations of novels, ▷Shared Experience's latest is Olwen Wymark's adaptation of Zola's *Nana*, ▷David Edgar's adaptation of *Nicholas Nickelby*; actress Pauline Devancy's *To Marie with Love* is another, one-woman version of the contradictory personality of Marie Stopes; see also ▷adaptations.

MacARTHUR, Charles

see HECHT, Ben

MacDONALD, Robert David

see GLASGOW CITIZENS' THEATRE

MacDONALD, Sharman [1951–]

British actress and dramatist

Plays include:

***When I Was a Girl I Used to Scream and Shout* (1984), *The Brave* (1988)**

It's the kind of story that all playwrights must dream about – a first play, taken up by a good fringe venue, hailed by the press, jumps sprightly into the West End. So it was for Glasgow-born actress Sharman MacDonald. First performed at the Bush Theatre, MacDonald's painful, bitterly funny study of a Scottish childhood and adolescence went, as it were, straight to No. 1, winning the *The Evening Standard*'s Most Promising Playwright award for 1984. Was it just another case of sophisticated theatrical voyeurism, titillating tales from a girl's locker room that seldom get aired in public? In fact, though much of its popularity came from the caustic humour of adolescent sexual curiosity, the play's core is an impressively honest study in stunted womanhood – of compromised choices, emotional warfare between mother and daughter, the dead hand of Presbyterianism and the pull of the past in the present (the girl is midwife to the woman theme). Structurally, *When I Was a Girl*'s strain for cause and effect has its problems, but as a first play, its wit and stinging observations mark it out as a worthy successor to ▷ Shelagh Delaney's *A Taste of Honey*. Like ▷ Nell Dunn's *Steaming*, its success begs the question that whilst plays by women still have a hard time making it into the Big Time, you are likely to capture more of the headlines if the play just happens also to have a strong sexual element. Its success also reaffirmed the Bush Theatre's indispensable talent for seeking out and supporting unknown talents: MacDonald's was just one of over a 1000 scripts that turned up unsolicited at the Bush that year.

TRY THESE:
Nell Dunn's *Steaming*; for a Catholic variation on sexual repression, see ▷Mary O'Malley and ▷Christina Reid; for mother and daughter relationships, see ▷Julia Kearsley, ▷Louise Page, ▷Shelagh Delaney; for comparisons with male adolescence, see ▷Neil Simon's *Brighton Beach Memoirs*, or even the film *Gregory's Girl*; for Scottish adolescence see Muriel Spark's *The Prime of Miss Jean Brodie* and ▷John Byrne's *The Slab Boys Trilogy*.

MACHIAVELLI, Niccolo di Bernardo dei [1469–1527]

Italian political theorist and occasional dramatist

Plays include:

***La Mandragola* (1518), *Clizia* (1525)**

Machiavelli was a civil servant in Florence under the republican government that succeeded the rule of Savonarola. He wrote his plays, and also *The Prince* (1513), in compulsory retirement in the country after the restoration of the Medici. *The Prince* was inspired by the expedient political methods of Cesare Borgia, rather than vice versa, but it led to his black reputation in England and elsewhere for advocating the ruthless and amoral pursuit of power. Although *La Mandragola* is one of the best of

TRY THESE:
▷Marlowe for using 'Machiavel' as a prologue; ▷Shared Experience for adapting Ruzzante as *Comedy Without a Title*; Giordano Bruno's *Il Candelaio* is another Italian Renaissance comedy that surfaces in the modern repertory.

Italian Renaissance comedies, it is probably Machiavelli's reputation as the Demon King (see for example ▷ Marlowe's prologue to *The Jew of Malta*) which leads to its occasional appearance on the modern stage (as against plays by, say, Bembo or Ruzzante). It is a classical example of academic wish-fulfilment; the rich old lawyer Nicia is cuckolded by the dashing young scholar Callimaco, with the assistance of the parasite Ligurio and a pretended potion made from the mandrake root. Surprisingly, all live happily ever after. The ▷ National Theatre attempted an updated musical version in 1984, but might have done better to have left it in period.

MAMET, David [1947–]

American dramatist

Plays include:

***American Buffalo* (1975), *Sexual Perversity in Chicago* (1976), *Duck Variations* (1976), *Reunion* (1977), *The Woods* (1977), *The Water Engine* (1977), *A Life In the Theatre* (1978), *Lakeboat* (1981), *Edmond* (1982), *Glengarry Glen Ross* (1983), *Vermont Sketches* (1984), *Prairie du Chien* (1985), *The Shawl* (1985), *The Frog Prince* (1985), *Speed-the-Plow* (1988)**

Films include:

David Mamet's original scripts include *The Verdict* (1982) and *The Untouchables* (1987), as well as an adaptation of *The Postman Always Rings Twice* (1981); in 1987, he wrote and directed *House of Games*, starring his wife, Lindsay Crouse

The Chicago-born playwright David Mamet is that unique American dramatist whose work seems simultaneously absolutely indigenous to the USA and peculiarly European. While his expletive-laden language and volatile situations seem part of an innately American idiom, his understanding of linguistic wordplay and of silence recalls such English and European forbears as ▷ Beckett and ▷ Pinter, and Mamet's British acclaim both at the ▷ National Theatre (where *Glengarry Glen Ross* had its world premiere) and the Royal Court is not surprising. Still, as the co-founder of Chicago's St Nicholas Theatre Company, where he functioned as both playwright-in-residence and artistic director, he writes with that city's street-wise, colloquial rhythm, whether on subjects as dense as the underside of American capitalism (*American Buffalo*, *Glengarry Glen Ross*) or as relatively benign as the intertwined lives and careers of two actors (*A Life In the Theatre*). His plays rarely have more than two or three characters (*Speed-the-Plow*, his three-character Broadway hit of 1988, marked the Broadway debut of Madonna), and works like *Edmond* – an impressionistic tableau about one man's descent into Sodom and Gomorrah in New York – are unusual. More typical is a piece like *The Shawl*, a three-character play about a charlatan seer, which further dissects a topic – the psychology of the con game – that Mamet returns to time and again (it's the raison d'être of *House of Games*, the 1987 film on which he made his directorial debut). His plays, of course, speak of another kind of shawl: the cloak of language beneath which lies a multiplicity of human instincts too few playwrights address with Mamet's courage.

TRY THESE:
▷Arthur Miller (especially *Death of A Salesman*) and ▷Clifford Odets for socially conscious writing, often about the limits of American capitalism; ▷Georg Büchner's *Woyzeck* for *Edmond*-like descents into a psychological hell; ▷Kaufman and Hart, and Terrence McNally's *It's Only A Play* for works about the theatre; ▷Sam Shepard, ▷Harold Pinter, ▷Samuel Beckett for charting that elusive terrain midway between speech and silence.

American Buffalo

Three small-time crooks bungle a coin robbery, and out of their comedy of frustration Mamet weaves an exhilaratingly telling and poignant account of avarice and ambition in which the promise of monetary gain makes everyone both victor and victim. (The title refers to an American coin, an old nickle that Bobby, the young addict, finds in Act Two.) At once edgy and elegiac in tone, the play is also a rending treatment of friendship under stress, and its three roles – the mastermind Teach; the older shop-owner Donny; and his side-kick, Bobby – are so superbly written that it's small wonder the play pops up on the London fringe and in regional theatre, perhaps more than any other American drama. 'Fuckin' business' reads the last line of Act

One, and a few plays have summed up the price of the capitalist ethic with such terse and moving irony.

MANCHESTER SCHOOL

This is the name commonly given to a small school of regional playwrights who flourished at the Gaiety Theatre in Manchester from 1908. This theatre was bought and equipped by Miss Annie Horniman (1860–1937), who had first provided the money to build the Abbey Theatre in Dublin (in 1904), but moved to Manchester after being ousted by ▷ Lady Gregory and others, taking with her Ben Iden Payne as her artistic director. She managed the Gaiety as a repertory theatre until 1917, specialising in naturalistic productions of local plays, many of them with 'strong' parts for women (often played by Sybil Thorndike); the Gaiety put on some two hundred plays in ten years or so, more than half of which were new work. The two playwrights whose work still appears most often, ▷ Harold Brighouse and ▷ Stanley Houghton, were both from Manchester (and indeed from Manchester Grammar School, as was Ben Iden Payne).

The 'Manchester School' did not survive World War I, but other plays produced at the Gaiety would be worth reviving, eg Allan Monkhouse's *Mary Broome* (1911), not a Lancashire play, but in the same vein of careful naturalism and social questioning (a middle-class man makes an unsatisfactory marriage to a parlourmaid when the girl becomes pregnant; again the girl has the strongest part, showing qualities of survival); or Elizabeth Baker's *Chains* (1911), a fresh, understated, non-didactic play whose characters come to question their reasons for either staying in boring jobs or marrying to get free of them.

TRY THESE:
Other repertory theatres past and present – the Court Theatre under Granville Barker, which provided the pattern for the Gaiety's seasons; the Abbey Theatre, Dublin; the ▷Glasgow Citizens' Theatre; and Lilian Baylis whose efforts at the Old Vic, to turn it into a popular cheap theatre, predated the ▷National Theatre by a good half century, and was a precursor to ▷Joan Littlewood's still unfulfilled dream of a 'fun palace' for the people; see also ▷Harold Brighouse and ▷Stanley Houghton.

MARCHANT, Tony [1960–]
British dramatist

Plays include:
***Remember Me?* (1980), *London Calling* (1981), *Thick as Thieves* (comprising *London Calling* and *Dealt;* 1981), *Stiff* (1982), *Raspberry* (1982), *The Lucky Ones* (1982), *Welcome Home* (1983), *Lazy Days Ltd* (1984), *The Attractions* (1987), *The Speculators* (1987)**

Television includes:
***Reservations* (1985), *This Year's Model* (1987), *Home and Away* (1988)**

One of the most likeable of today's young playwrights, Marchant may well be also one of the most talented. A grammar school-educated, working-class native of Wapping, with Catholic parents, Marchant has been consistently praised since the age of nineteen and shows every sign of maturing into the front rank of contemporary British playwrights. He has a remarkable feel for character, for the underdog (in the early plays invariably the young unemployed) and, more than any other of his contemporaries, a finely tuned sense of what is topical and important, to which he responds with flair. His plays (frequently based on months of well-informed research) are distinguished by naturalistic dialogue, a sensitivity and subtlety towards his characters, and enormous compassion. Frequently they are set in the East End, a world he knows well (several of his plays have first seen the light, appropriately, at Stratford East's Theatre Royal). A Marchant world, too, is a jungle where the scavenging law of economics is never very far away: *Remember Me?* is a young, unemployed school-leaver's cry of outrage against an educational system he feels failed him; *The Lucky Ones* (who have jobs), an equally passionate, if witty, riposte to the argument for a job at any price has an emblematic working-class rebel/anti-hero who refuses to bend the knee to the system (winningly played by Phil Daniels in the Theatre Royal's production, which also boasted a set of superb scale by Jenny Tiramani). In contrast, *Raspberry* is a short study of the social stigmas around abortion and infertility, treated with great skill, and shown

TRY THESE:
▷R.C. Sherriff's *Journey's End* makes similar points about the psychological traumas of war, albeit related to World War I; ▷Noël Greig's *Poppies* for ▷Gay Sweatshop explored a pacifist ethic; ▷Robert Holman, ▷Louise Page, and Greg Cullen are other writers who have dealt with aspects of the Falklands; ▷Doug Lucie's *Fashion* is a similarly jaundiced study of contemporary go-getting as *Speculators*; Burnt Bridges' *Deals* pre-dated ▷Caryl Churchill's *Serious Money* by several months; ▷Michael Ellis' *Chameleon* looks at being on the make from a black perspective; ▷Tony Craze's *Angelus* and Billy Roche's *A Handful of Stars* are examples of contemporary protest expressed through anti-heroes, (Roche's is an Irish counterpart

through the growing friendship between two women who find themselves in adjoining hospital beds.

Marchant's two most recent plays are perhaps different sides of the Thatcher coin. *The Attractions* is a compulsively fascinating study of violence triggered, once again, by one of those not enjoying the fruits of Thatcherism, and uncomfortably juxtaposing violence in the past (it is set in a museum of horrors on the south coast) with its present day manifestations. *The Speculators*, on the other hand, digs into the equally gory and compulsive arena of Big Bang City and financial greed, and is inevitably compared with ▷ Caryl Churchill's *Serious Money*, though they deal with quite different markets – Marchant's is the foreign exchange where, he says, the jumping pound is more synonymous with national identity. Truly, a playwright for all seasons and our times, and, not surprisingly, much sought after in the past three years by television and film producers.

of the young James Dean's *Rebel Without a Cause*); ▷Jim Cartwright's *Road* is an outcry against unemployment.

Welcome Home

Commissioned by ▷ Paines Plough, this was one of the first plays to take a look at the Falklands. Characteristically, Marchant spent time with an army unit before sitting down to write and his beautifully constructed play, centred round a group of paras assembled to bury one of their number with full military honours, constantly mirrors that authenticity: in its refusal to present its soldiers as ciphers, and in its understanding of the army mentality and its disadvantages (in the shape of an over-zealous corporal whose belligerence and neo-fascism are barely under control). In its obvious awareness of the emotional and psychological price paid in that South Atlantic exercise, Marchant's play makes a tangible plea for a new kind of masculinity, based on an acknowledgement of weakness as much as forced machismo.

MARCUS, Frank [1928–]

British dramatist and critic

Plays include:

***The Formation Dancers* (1964), *The Killing of Sister George* (1966), *Notes on a Love Affair* (1972)**

Born in Germany, but coming to Britain in 1939, Marcus acted, directed and ran an antiques business as well as writing. With well over a score of plays produced, he is best known for *The Killing of Sister George*, a study of a disintegrating lesbian partnership in which the butch half is a radio soap lead about to be killed off in the programme. A serious study of caring, need and dominance, its sadness is heightened by its hilarity. Unfortunately, due to the paucity of mainstream plays with lesbian characters, *The Killing of Sister George* has become to the general public the stereotypical image of lesbians and their relationships – an image which to some extent is counteracted by plays on the fringe which, however, seldom percolate through. Marcus' earlier success, *The Formation Dancers*, a much lighter four-hander, presents feigned infidelity as a method of regaining an unfaithful husband, but the treatment of women and love is a recurrent theme in much of his later work.

Marcus' work has some echoes of ▷ Molnar and ▷ Schnitzler whose work he has adapted. He has also adapted Kaiser and Hauptmann.

TRY THESE:
▷Charles Dyer's *Staircase* for a comparable treatment of male homosexuality; see also ▷Lesbian Theatre and ▷Sarah Daniels.

MARIVAUX, Pierre Carlet de Chamblain de

[1688–1763]

French dramatist and novelist

Plays include:

***Arlequin Poli par L'Amour* (*Harlequin Polished by Love*; 1720), *La Double Inconstance* (*The Double Inconstancy*; 1723), *Le Jeu de L'Amour et du Hasard* (*The Game of Love and Chance*; 1723), *Le Triomphe de l'Amour* (*The Triumph of Love*; 1732), *L'Heureux Stratagème* (*Successful Strategies*; 1733), *Les Fausses Confidences* (*False Admissions*; 1737), *L'Epreuve* (*The Test*; 1740), *La Dispute* (*The Dispute*; 1744)**

TRY THESE:
▷Beaumarchais for eighteenth-century French comedy, though with much broader brushstrokes and a larger canvas; ▷Turgenev's *A Month in the Country* for a comparable game of love and chance, but without a happy ending; ▷Noël

MARIVAUX, PIERRE CARLET DE CHAMBLAIN DE

Marivaux was born of a nouveau riche family (his father started as Carlet and added the 'de Chamblain' and 'de Marivaux' as he moved up the pecking order), but lost his money in the Mississippi scheme (the French equivalent of the South Sea Bubble), and so was forced to make his living by writing plays, novels and journalism, and by relying on the generosity of various noble ladies who welcomed his wit in their salons; he made it to the Academy in 1742. His long association with the Comédie-Italienne and their lively acting helped to make his plays successful; indeed it was noticeable that those of his plays put on by the Comédie Française worked much less well. His best known plays deal with the beginnings of love, often unrecognised and sometimes unwelcome, through subtle dialogue rather than complicated plots. This delicate dialogue was found affected by some of his contemporaries, who called it 'marivaudage', but in fact it wears (and acts) very well. He has been out of fashion in Britain for most of the twentieth century, though Parisian productions have been fairly common and have ranged from the stylish (Jean-Louis Barrault and Madeleine Renaud in the 1950s to the perverse (Patrice Chéreau's *La Dispute*, with its smoking moat and vast moving white walls, seen at the ▷ National Theatre in 1976) and the bizarre (Alfredo Arias' 1987 version of *The Game of Love and Chance*, with all the characters played as monkeys). However, he now seems to be doing rather better in Britain, especially through ▷ Shared Experience's 1983 productions of *False Admissions* and *Successful Strategies*, translated by ▷ Timberlake Wertenbaker. These avoided directorial gimmicks and successfully brought out the complexity and ambiguity of these delightful plays. *The Triumph of Love* was also put on at the Gate in 1987, in another smooth translation, this time by Guy Callan. Clearly Marivaux is not as difficult to translate as people have long said. There are at least thirty other plays that have never been produced in Britain.

Coward's *Private Lives* for a set of mixed doubles like *The Double Inconstancy*.

MARLOWE, Christopher [1564–1593]
English Renaissance dramatist

Plays include:

***Tamburlaine the Great, I and II* (1587), *Doctor Faustus* (c 1588), *The Jew of Malta* (c 1589), *Edward II* (c 1592), *The Massacre at Paris* (c 1592), *Dido, Queen of Carthage* (c 1593)**

Marlowe led a brief and turbulent life in which he was involved in espionage, accused of heretical opinions and killed in a pub brawl before the case was tried in circumstances which suggest that he may have been eliminated to avoid political embarassment. He also managed to write plays which gave a new impetus to Renaissance theatre writing. Unfortunately, some of them have only been preserved in mangled form but, with the exception of the two last plays, they are still staged fairly regularly and even *The Massacre at Paris* has been staged by the ▷ Glasgow Citizens' Theatre. *Tamburlaine* is interesting because of Marlowe's use of what ▷ Ben Jonson called the 'mighty line' to display the superhuman characteristics of its hero, who starts off a shepherd in Part I, conquers the world, and then dies in Part II. The play presents a full circle of Fortune's Wheel but there is little dramatic conflict and no particular tension within the presentation of Tamburlaine himself – his tragedy arises simply from the fact that, in the end, he is not superhuman. *The Jew of Malta* also has a larger than life protagonist, the comic villain Barabbas, who indulges in wholesale Machiavellian slaughter until he, literally, falls into one of his own traps. The 1988 ▷ RSC production rightly treated it as a savage farce. *Edward II* has a more developed set of conflicts between characters and, although the verse is less obviously memorable than in some of Marlowe's other plays, there is a satisfying movement in the play as Edward's fortunes decline and Mortimer's rise only to fall again.

TRY THESE:
Other plays which use the Faust legend are ▷Goethe's *Faust*, ▷Howard Brenton and ▷David Hare's *Pravda*, and Czech dramatist ▷Vaclav Havel's *Temptation*; ▷Shakespeare's *Merchant of Venice* offers an interesting comparison with Marlowe's treatment of the Jews; ▷Brecht adapted *Edward II* and the English version of his play is sometimes staged.

Doctor Faustus

Faustus sells his soul to Mephostophiles in return for twenty-four years of magic power but those years are spent mainly in comic conjuring exercises and slapstick. So, although there is powerful verse and a real tragic situation at the beginning and at the end, the play can tend to sag in the middle since many directors find it hard to reconcile the clowning with the sense of Faustus' tragic situation. The best productions are those which try to bring out the way in which these scenes show Faustus frittering away the possibilities open to him, thus emphasising the tragedy of his bargain. ATC (Actors Touring Company) pared the play down to three actors, successfully transposing Faustus into a latter-day hedonistic trendy, complete with Crippen specs and short haircut.

MAROWITZ, Charles [1934–]

American-born director and dramatist

Marowitz, born in New York, came to Britain in the 1950s to act and direct; he worked with ▷ Peter Brook on *King Lear* in 1962, and on the experimental Theatre of Cruelty season at LAMDA in 1963. ▷ Brook and ▷ Artaud have been continuing influences on his work. He was Artistic Director of the Open Space Theatre from 1968 to 1979, with his indispensable colleague Thelma Holt as administrator and actress. They put on a wide range of plays, including new or previously unproduced work by ▷ Howard Brenton, ▷ Peter Barnes, ▷ David Edgar, ▷ Howard Barker, ▷ Trevor Griffiths, and ▷ Sam Shepard; they also staged a number of Marowitz's own 'collage' or cut-up versions of ▷ Shakespeare (*Hamlet*, *Macbeth*, *An Othello*, *The Shrew*, *Measure for Measure*, and *Variations on the Merchant of Venice*). *Hamlet* is probably the most successful of these, perhaps because the play is so familiar to most audiences, but the Black Power *Othello* and the feminist *Shrew* are also effective, and are still put on reasonably often by student and experimental groups. All his work, both as author and director, displays and enjoys great power to shock. In his collage works he used film-like techniques to switch rapidly from one image to another, dream or nightmare sequences, verbal and visual shock tactics, simple sets, and aggressive lighting. In other productions he used 'environmental' staging –for example in the opening production, John Herbert's *Fortune and Men's Eyes* (1968), he transformed the theatre into a prison; in *Palach* he used multiple stages; and in his production of Picasso's *Four Little Girls* the audience entered through a tiny door into a colourful Alice in Wonderland fantasy world, which cost more than the Open Space's total grant for a year.

Marowitz has written lively accounts of his work with Brook and his ideas on acting, and he is a fine bruising critic of other people's theatre – see for instance *Confessions of a Counterfeit Critic* (1973) and *The Method as Means* (1981); and some of his Open Space productions would be interesting to revive. Though few of the Open Space productions reached the West End, one of his 'potboilers' (*Sherlock's Last Case*) did quite well on Broadway in 1987–8.

TRY THESE:
▷Peter Brook, for collaboration on Artaud-influenced work; ▷Genet's *Deathwatch* for prison and homosexual themes; see also the ▷Wooster Group for a company of collage makers; ▷Tom Stoppard's *Rosencrantz and Guildenstern are Dead* draws on *Hamlet*, as does W.S. Gilbert's *Rosencrantz and Guildenstern*; the Yugoslav radical theatre group Red Pilot, and Germany's Peter Stein also transform their spaces into part of the theatrical experience.

MARSTON, John [1576–1634]

English Renaissance dramatist

Plays include:

***Antonio and Mellida* (1599), *Antonio's Revenge* (1600), *The Dutch Courtesan* (1604), *The Malcontent* (1604), *The Fawn* (1605; also known as *Parasitaster*)**

Marston, like John Donne, eventually became an Anglican clergyman but before that he had a fairly successful career as a satirical poet and dramatist, being heavily involved in the so-called 'War of the Theatres' in which a number of dramatists, including ▷ Jonson, attacked one another in a succession of plays. He often wrote within the popular revenge conventions of his day but both *Antonio and Mellida* and *The Malcontent*, despite the sordidness and corruption of their court worlds and their apparently tragic dynamic, have 'happy' endings. *The Dutch Courtesan* also operates on the fringes of tragi-comedy. *Antonio's Revenge*, the second part of *Antonio and Mellida*, is, however, a fully fledged revenge tragedy in the traditional Elizabethan mode. Although his tendency to dwell on excretion and sexuality is probably more acceptable than it might once have been, Marston tends to be an occasional rather than a regular feature of the contemporary repertory, perhaps because so many of his

TRY THESE:
Most Renaissance dramatists used revenge plots and malcontent figures – ▷Shakespeare's *Hamlet* is the most famous example of both, but ▷Kyd's *The Spanish Tragedy* started the vogue for revenge and there are notable examples in ▷Tourneur, ▷Webster and ▷Middleton; there are disguised Dukes (like Malevole in *The Malcontent*) in many Renaissance plays, notably *Measure for Measure* and *The Tempest*; Malevole has also been

characters, situations and plots are to be found elsewhere in Renaissance drama, handled in ways that have proved more acceptable to modern audiences. A recent ▷ National Theatre production of *The Fawn* did little to suggest it would replace *The Malcontent* as the Marston play most likely to be staged.

compared to the protagonist of ▷Brecht's *The Good Person of Sezchuan.*

MASSINGER, Philip [1583–1640]

English Renaissance dramatist

Plays include:

***A New Way to Pay Old Debts* (1625), *The Roman Actor* (1626), *The City Madam* (1632)**

Massinger eventually succeeded ▷ Fletcher as resident dramatist with the King's Men, writing jointly or singly some fifty-five plays. The manuscripts of eight of them were used to line pie dishes in the eighteenth century and others have also failed to survive. Only *A New Way to Pay Old Debts*, a satirical comedy of contemporary manners, which uses stock elements such as young lovers outwitting parental marriage plans, a young man reduced to poverty who is still a gentleman at heart, and a wily servant outwitting his master, survives in the contemporary repertory. Much of its success has been due to the popularity of its apparently larger than life protagonist Sir Giles Overreach, whose extravagant extortions and ultimate madness have long been a favourite with actors and audiences. In fact, Overreach is based on the historical Sir Giles Mompesson, a particularly outrageous figure of the period who was eventually tried and convicted for his corrupt practices. *The City Madam* (also a citizen comedy but its prodigal turns out to be corrupt when given a second chance) was revived in the 1960s and is probably due for another production but *The Roman Actor*, despite its use of three plays within plays and a speech defending the profession of actor which should make it appeal to the post-modernist sensibility, has not yet had a contemporary revival.

TRY THESE:
▷Marlowe's characters Tamburlaine and Faustus are probably the most famous Renaissance over-reachers, though ▷Shakespeare's *Twelfth Night* contains another fine comic example in Malvolio; ▷Dekker, ▷Heywood, ▷Middleton and ▷Jonson wrote comedies of contemporary London life; many Restoration comedies tackle similar themes, as does ▷Caryl Churchill's *Serious Money*; ▷Howard Brenton and ▷David Hare's *Pravda* offers a contemporary portrait of the megalomaniac businessman; for plays about the theatre see ▷Michael Frayn's *Noises Off*, ▷Pirandello's *Six Characters in Search of an Author*, ▷Bulgakov's *Molière*.

MATURA, Mustapha [1939–]

Trinidadian dramatist

Plays include:

***Black Pieces* (1970), *As Time Goes By* (1971), *Bakerloo Line* (1972), *Nice* (1973), *Play Mas* (1974), *Black Slaves, White Chains* (1975), *Rum an' Coca Cola* (1976), *Bread* (1976), *Another Tuesday* (1978), *More More* (1978), *Independence* (1979), *Welcome Home Jacko* (1979), *A Dying Business* (1980), *One Rule* (1981), *Meetings* (1981), *The Playboy of the West Indies* (1984), *Trinidad Sisters* (1988)**

Trinidad-born Matura, one of the major British black dramatists, co-founder of ▷ Black Theatre Co-op, has also written extensively for television, particularly the series *No Problem* and *Black Silk*. His work has concentrated both on the black experience in Britain and on Trinidadian issues, with a recent development into versions of classics adapted to his own interests. The common thread that links both the Trinidadian and the British-set plays is Matura's interest in the contradictions that arise when people drawn from different social and racial groups interact. This stems partly from Trinidad's rich mixture of people of African, East Indian, Chinese, Spanish, British, Portuguese and French descent, as a result of its colonial past. Like many contemporary writers Matura is particularly interested in colonialism as a state of mind as well as a physical institution. Thus in *Play Mas* people of Indian and African descent work out power relations against the background of Carnival and of independence; in *Independence* different versions of independence are mobilised in contradiction; and in *Meetings* we see the tensions between old and new

TRY THESE:
▷Tunde Ikoli, another black dramatist whose early career was also fostered by the director Roland Rees, successfully adapted ▷Gorki's *The Lower Depths* for a mainly black cast; ▷Caryl Churchill's *Cloud Nine* looks at the relationship between the patriarchal and the colonial impulses; ▷Brian Friel's *Translations* offers an Irish dimension; ▷Barrie Keeffe is a white writer who has used a theme drawn from the classics to underpin his portrayal of black British experience, in *Black Lear (revised as King of England)*; ▷Derek Walcott, ▷Trevor Rhone, ▷Barry Reckord, ▷Errol Hill,

(foreground): Joan-Ann Maynard (Olga), Joanne Campbell (Irene), Pauline Black (Marsha); (background): Ram John Holder (Dr Charles) in the Tricycle Theatre's production of Mustapha Matura's ***Trinidad Sisters***, (adapted from Chekhov's *Three Sisters*), directed by Nicolas Kent. The Tricycle Theatre was burnt down in May 1987; this production was therefore presented in February 1988 at the Donmar Warehouse.

focused in a wealthy couple, one nostalgic for traditional cooking (and, by extension, a life rooted in the old values), the other enslaved to the values of American economic colonialism. Matura has a great gift for witty and revealing dialogue which he puts to particularly good use in his adaptations of the classics; *The Playboy of the West Indies* is an adaptation of ▷ J.M. Synge's *Playboy of the Western World*. *Trinidad Sisters* is a particularly poignant re-location of ▷ Chekhov's *Three Sisters*, as a statement of 'mother country' and its mental stranglehold.

▷Errol John, ▷Edgar White, ▷Caryl Phillips are other Afro-Caribbean writers; see also ▷Jacqueline Rudet and ▷Theatre of Black Women.

MAUGHAM, William Somerset [1874–1965]

English novelist and dramatist

Plays include:

***A Man of Honour* (1903), *Penelope* (1909), *Our Betters* (1917), *Caesar's Wife* (1919), *Home and Beauty* (1919), *The Circle* (1921), *East of Suez* (1922), *The Constant Wife* (1926), *The Letter* (1927), *The Sacred Flame* (1928), *The Bread Winner* (1930), *For Services Rendered* (1932), *Sheppey* (1933)**

His twenty-two plays, mainly neatly constructed comedies, are entertaining and witty. They often tend to moralise, but though set in the fashionable middle class to whom he was seeking to appeal he by no means toes the establishment line. Although his closet homosexuality does not figure in his plays, his unsatisfactory marriage may have influenced the criticism of the divorce laws found in *Home and Beauty* and the debate on economic and social sexism in *The Constant Wife*.

In *For Services Rendered* his cynical wit is put aside to show the caustic effect of war on family life and in *Sheppey* he shows hostile public reaction to a barber who, on winning a lottery, attempts to use his winnings according to Christ's teaching. *The Sacred Flame*, probably the best of his serious dramas, shows his greatest depth of feeling in a study of unrequited love, part of a murder story that offers a defence of euthanasia.

The Circle

Maugham's finest comedy, *The Circle* was booed at its premiere. An MP and his wife await the arrival of his mother, whom he has not seen since childhood, when she ran away with a married man. When she and her lover arrive, no longer a romantic couple but she a middle-aged, over made-up, scatterbrain and he an elderly balding man, who was forced out of a brilliant political career, they bicker over the 'sacrifices' each made to be with the other. When the young wife then falls for a house guest the parallels between wife and mother become clear. Though others try to dissuade her from throwing away her marriage, she is eventually won by her lover's realistic, if romantic, declaration, 'I don't offer you peace and quietness. I offer you unrest and anxiety. I don't offer you happiness. I'm offering you love.'

TRY THESE:
▷Noël Coward for similar cynical wit with flashes of social comment; ▷Terence Rattigan for comparable neat construction and subversive tackling of socially unacceptable themes.

MAYAKOVSKY, Vladimir Vladimirovich [1893–1930]

Russian poet and dramatist

Plays include:

***Vladimir Mayakovsky* (1913), *Mystery-Bouffe* (1918), *A Comedy Of Murder* (1927), *The Bedbug* (1929), *The Bathhouse* (1930)**

Born in Georgia, Mayakovsky espoused the Bolshevik cause at an early stage, and became a champion of Futurism. After the 1917 Revolution he was a leading activist in the new art forms, but after initial success and acclaim he gradually fell from official favour until with the rise of Stalinism he was subjected to increasingly severe criticism from the Communist Party bureaucracy for individualism and Formalism. The fact that he never joined the Party was also offered as evidence of his weakness. In the early 1920s he was a great experimenter with form, writing many fragments and one-act pieces, drawing on a great variety of sources, but he is best known for his two last plays –brilliantly inventive satires on the Soviet Bureaucracy of the late 1920s. These attacks hardly endeared him to his opponents, and in

TRY THESE:
Dusty Hughes' *The Futurists* is in itself a political satire featuring Mayakovsky as a character; Meyerhold directed the plays of Mayakovsky; ▷David Pownall's *Master Class* is a vivid evocation of Stalinist pressure on artists; ▷Mrozek, and ▷Havel are modern East European dramatists who have clashed with their states; ▷Gogol's *The Government Inspector* is the classic Russian

1930 he committed suicide in a fit of depression, convinced that the Revolution had been subverted.

bureaucracy play.

The Bathhouse
A deeply corrupt official, Pobedonosikov, is informed that a man called Kranov has invented a time-machine, with the intention of employing it in the service of the Peoples' Revolution. Pobedonosikov refuses to listen to the inventor, finding the present power he wields entirely satisfactory and unwilling to risk any change, initiative or responsibility. However, when a miraculous Woman from the Future appears from 2030 AD to assist the Soviet people, Pobedonosikov claims the time-machine as his own. He is left behind when the Woman transports the ordinary people off to the glorious future, leaving only his fellow bureaucrats to console him.

McGRATH, John [1935–]
British dramatist and director

Plays include:
***A Man Has Two Fathers* (1958), *Events While Guarding the Bofors Gun* (1966), *Random Happenings in the Hebrides* (1970), *Sharpeville Crackers* (1970), *Trees in the Wind* (1971), *Soft or a Girl* (1971; revised as *My Pal and Me*), *Fish in the Sea* (1972), *The Cheviot, the Stag and the Black, Black Oil* (1973), *The Game's a Bogey* (1974), *Boom* (1974), *Lay Off* (1975), *Little Red Hen* (1975), *Yobbo Nowt (1975; also known as Mum's the* Word and *Left Out Lady*), *Oranges and Lemons* (1975), *The Rat Trap* (1976), *Out of Our Heads* (1977), *Trembling Giant* (1977), *The Life and Times of Joe of England* (1977), *If You Want to Know the Time* (1979), *Big Square Fields* (1979), *Joe's Drum* (1979), *Bitter Apples* (1979), *Swings and Roundabouts* (1980), *Blood Red Roses* (1980), *The Catch* (1981), *Nightclass* (1981), *Rejoice!* (1982), *On the Pig's Back* (with David MacLennan; 1983), *The Women of the Dunes* (1983), *The Baby and the Bathwater* (1984), *Behold the Sun* (1985; opera libretto with Alexander Goewr), *Mhàri Mhór* (1987)**

Television includes:
***The Day of Ragnarok* (1965), *Shotgun* (with Christopher Williams; 1966), *Diary of a Nobody* (with Ken Russell, from George and Weedon Grossmith; 1966), *Orkney* (1971; from George Mackay Brown), *Bouncing Boy* (1972), *Once Upon a Union* (1977), *The Cheviot the Stag and the Black, Black Oil* (1974), *The Adventures of Frank* (1979), *There is a Happy Land* (1986)**

Films include:
***Billion Dollar Brain* (from Len Deighton; 1967), *The Bofors Gun* (1968), *The Virgin Soldiers* (from Leslie Thomas; 1969), *The Reckoning* (from Patrick Hall; 1970)**

McGrath is among the most inventive and prolific of contemporary socialist dramatists; an Artistic Director of 7:84, he developed much of his work with them and has in turn brought their work to wide public attention through his experience in television. He became actively involved in theatre on leaving Oxford University, joining the Royal Court as a playreader, and directing for the Questors Theatre (an amateur group in Ealing), and for Live New Departures, a literary road-show. From the Royal Court he joined the BBC script department, went on to do a Directors' course there, and began directing television plays. He was a co-founder of *Z Cars* (an innovation in television police series), and directed arts shows, documentaries, and new plays until 1965 when he left full-time television work to concentrate on writing his own plays. In 1971 he founded 7:84 and became its Artistic Director; much of his theatre work as a writer and director since then has been based with them, but he has continued to write and direct for television and film. In 1983 he founded Freeway films, an independent company to make films for the new Channel Four. McGrath has consistently contributed reviews and articles on drama to a range of newspapers and journals and is an insistent

TRY THESE:
▷7:84, which McGrath founded, and with whom he has developed his work; ▷Brecht (*Caucasian Chalk Circle*; 1972), ▷Peter Terson (*Prisoners of the War*, 1972), ▷John Arden (*Serjeant Musgrave Dances On*; 1972), and ▷Aristophanes (*Women in Power; or Up the Acropolis*; 1983) are among the dramatists McGrath has reworked; ▷Brecht is a central influence for McGrath; ▷John Arden and ▷Margaretta D'Arcy, ▷David Edgar, ▷Trevor Griffiths and ▷Howard Brenton are contemporary 'political' dramatists who have differing views of the most effective ways of reaching audiences; *Swings and Roundabouts* is a reworking of ▷Noël Coward's *Private Lives*.

and important voice in socialist debates around drama, theatre and cultural forms, both in his theory and his practice.

Besides his own plays, much of McGrath's writing has been a reinterpretation of classic theatre texts. His version of *The Seagull* sets ▷ Chekhov's play in the contemporary Scottish Highlands; *The Caucasian Chalk Circle* is set in a building site and McGrath has added a prologue spoken by Liverpool workers (a reworking which ▷ Brecht would surely have approved).

The Cheviot, the Stag and the Black, Black Oil

The Cheviot, the Stag and the Black, Black Oil is a musical, which takes the form of a traditional Highland ceilidh, exemplifying the 7:84 principle of political theatre which is also a 'good night out'. It was developed with the 7:84 Scotland Company, who researched the text, and devised the music and performance in rehearsal with McGrath. The play is a history of the economic exploitation of the Highlands, from the nineteenth-century 'clearances', which cleared land for profits from the Cheviot sheep, through the migration of Highlanders to Canada, to the appropriation of land for grouse-shooting, the development of North Sea Oil and tourism. The play also celebrates working-class struggle, from the refusal to enlist for the Crimean War to organised resistance against landlords. *The Cheviot, The Stag and the Black, Black Oil* was performed as the first production of 7:84 Scotland at the 'What Kind of Scotland?' conference in Edinburgh in 1973, toured throughout Scotland and was televised, in performance to a Highlands audience, in 1977, using Brechtian alienation effects to demonstrate the mythologising of Scottish history.

McGRATH, Tom [1940–]
British dramatist

Plays include:

***The Great Northern Welly Boot Show* (1972), *Laurel and Hardy* (1976), *The Hard Man* (1977), *The Android Circuit* (1978), *Sisters* (1978), *The Innocent* (1979), *Animal* (1979), *123* (1981), *The Nuclear Family* (1982), *The Gambler* (1984), *End of the Line* (1984), *Pals* (1984), *Kora* (1986), *Thanksgiving* (1986), *Trivial Pursuits* (1988)**

Already known as a musician and the creator of *International Times*, McGrath joined with Billy Connolly to celebrate the UCS work-in with *The Great Northern Welly Boot Show*, and since then has built a solid reputation as a playwright. To date his work has taken most of its impetus from autobiographical incident or from real events: *The Hard Man* is closely based on the life of Jimmy Boyle, Scotland's best-known ex-convict; *The Innocent* stems from his own involvement with drugs and the 'alternative society' of the 1960s; *123* clearly drew on personal experience of attempts to shake off society's demands with the aid of Buddhism and mythology. *Animal* is probably his most exotic piece, presenting a colony of apes under scrutiny from zoologists, with delightful and frequently comically surreal visions of ape movement and relationships before tragedy results from contact with the humans.

The Hard Man

A startling impressionistic account of a life of violence, based on the life of Jimmy Boyle. A clever use of non-naturalistic devices and direct address to the audience establishes a terrifying underworld of unthinking brutality and exposes the conditions which breed it, only to uncover an equally appalling world in the violence of prison life as authority tries to contain and break the spirit of dangerous inmates. It is a measure of McGrath's honesty that he does not turn his central figure into a stereotyped 'victim of society', but that having established him as a truly terrifying figure wedded to uncontrollable violence – telling his own version of the events depicted – he then finds in him a symbol for the enduring human spirit, at a point when he crouches naked in a cage smeared with excrement to protect himself from the attacks of prison officers. The play is a stimulating exercise in sustained anti-naturalism and theatricality in the service of serious thought.

TRY THESE:
▷Eugene O'Neill's *The Hairy Ape*, Terry Johnsons' *Cries from the Mammal House* are zoological allegories; for more prisoner portraits see also ▷Genet's *Deathwatch*; and John Herbert's *Fortune and Men's Eyes*.

McINTYRE, Clare [1953–]

British dramatist

Plays include:

***I've Been Running* (1986), *Low Level Panic* (*Don't Worry, It Might Not Happen*; 1988)**

McIntyre has turned to writing plays after spending some years acting in them, on stage and in television and films. Of her plays *Low Level Panic* has made the biggest splash. Opening with a bathroom scene, it is about three young women sharing a flat together, with some sharp and revealing writing (naturalistic dialogue and monologues of internalised thoughts) on images, commercialisation, female sexual fantasies, and the more frightening realities as women experience them on the street. The action seldom extends beyond the bathroom (except for a monologue scene recounting a street attack on one of the women and a fantasised revenge sequence to do with an advertising hoarding), and lacks overall development. Nonetheless, *Low Level Panic* accurately articulates the current thoughts, fears and feelings of many young women – also achieved in *I've Been Running*. A sharp two-hander, McIntyre's first play delved into the murky waters of contemporary sexual politics to take a look at the division between the young modern woman (a bit of a health freak, but questioning and curious about life) and her sluggish, complacent boyfriend who can't understand what she is on about at all. (*I've Been Running* was directed at the Old Red Lion, London by Terry Johnson, whose pessimism about the male of the species and trust in the female has become more pronounced as time has gone on). The outlook does not look good for the sexes but brighter for McIntyre who has just finished a commission for the Royal Court.

TRY THESE:
▷Winsome Pinnock draws attention to similar issues in *Picture Palace*; ▷Jacqui Shapiro's *Dead Romantic* is another contemporary look into the sexual politics scrum; ▷Ted Whitehead's *Alpha Beta* is an older, male though equally pessimistic view of coupledom; Lumiere and Son have dealt with street and other female anxieties in *Panic*; ▷Nell Dunn's *Steaming* is set in a larger, public, bath; ▷Michel Tremblay's *Albertine in Five Times* for an even more extended application of the monologue technique to express internal thoughts and feelings; ▷Kay Adshead; ▷Sharman Macdonald and ▷Julia Schofield are other actress/writers.

MEDIEVAL DRAMA

The most commonly produced medieval plays are the so-called mystery plays drawn from the cycles staged in the open air once a year by the craft guilds (also called mysteries, hence the name) in many English towns. They take biblical stories as their subject matter and a complete cycle could run from the Creation to the Last Judgement, with each individual play staged by an appropriate guild – at York the plasterers were responsible for the Creation, the shipwrights, fishmongers and sailors took charge of the Noah story and the Crucifixion was done by the nail makers! This division of responsibility was related to the enormous community effort that went into the stagings and to the didactic purpose of the plays, which was to give readily understandable religious instruction to a largely illiterate population. This does not mean that the plays are solemn: they include such figures as the hen-pecking Mrs Noah, and the sheep-stealing Mak in the Wakefield Master's *Second Shepherd's Play*. The cycles continued to be staged, despite official disapproval after the Reformation, until late in the sixteenth century, even after the erection of the first purpose-built professional theatre in London in 1576. They had a considerable influence on Renaissance playwriting and theatrical practice, and they have found a new popularity both in Bill Bryden's highly successful promenade staging for the ▷ National Theatre and in the regular stagings now offered at Chester, Coventry and York.

Also from the late medieval period are the Moralities which use personification and allegory to make their didactic points. The most famous are probably *The Castle of Perseverance* (from the early fifteenth century), *Mankind* (from the 1460s) and *Everyman* (from the 1490s). They make effective theatre, particularly in such scenes as Everyman's descent into the grave deserted by all his companions (Beauty, Strength, Goods and so on) except Good Deeds. *A Satire of the Three Estates* (1540) by Sir David Lindsay (1468–1555), a Scottish Morality, is noteworthy as the surprise hit of the 1948 ▷ Edinburgh Festival in Tyrone

TRY THESE:
▷John Arden and ▷Margaretta D'Arcy's *The Business of Good Government*, and *The Non-Stop Connolly Show*, ▷Ann Jellicoe, ▷Promenade Performances and ▷Community Theatre for modern approximations to the dynamic behind the Mysteries; ▷Brecht for didactic theatre; ▷Women Dramatists for other neglected female playwrights; ▷Marlowe's *Doctor Faustus* for the influence of the medieval tradition on Renaissance dramatists; ▷T. S. Eliot's *Murder in the Cathedral* for medieval influence (and, interestingly, toured by the ▷RSC in a promenade production); The Medieval Players is a professional touring company that produces medieval and pre-

Brian Glover as God on a fork lift truck in Bill Bryden's invigorating National Theatre promenade production of ***The Mysteries***, staged in various versions from 1977 to 1985.

Guthrie's inspired staging which rescued it from four hundred years of oblivion, and was recently revived, again with great success, by Tom Fleming.

The earliest medieval writer who is likely to be produced is the tenth-century nun Hroswitha (also known as Roswitha) who wrote six Latin plays dealing with Christian subjects, modelled on the Roman comic dramatist Terence. Apart from their historical significance as the first known plays by a woman and as an outcrop of literary dramatic activity in an otherwise barren period, they deserve professional revival.

Shakespearian drama.

MEDOFF, Mark [1940–]

American dramatist

Plays include:

***The Kramer* (1973), *The Wager* (1973), *When You Comin' Back Red Ryder?* (1974), *The Conversion of Aaron Weiss* (1977), *Children of A Lesser God* (1979), *The Hands of An Enemy* (1986), *The Heart Outright* (1986), *The Homage That Follows* (1987)**

The Illinois-born son of a doctor and a psychologist, Medoff teaches English at New Mexico State University where he premieres many of his plays. His reputation has been built on three works: *The Wager*, a study of honour between two university graduate students who make a bet about seducing a woman called Honor; *When You Comin' Back, Red Ryder?*, a play about blighted lives set in a third-rate Southwest diner at the end of the 1960s; and *Children of A Lesser God*, a love story between a hearing therapist for the deaf, James Leeds, and his stubborn and proud non-hearing student, Sarah Norman. A substantial success on Broadway, in London, and as a film, the play prompted the predictable backlash that Medoff was simply milking the tear-jerking potential inherent in any disability drama; still, the play is more worthy than that, and the role of Sarah has given long-overdue exposure to several deaf actresses including Phyllis Frelich, Jean St Clair, Marlee Matlin, and Elizabeth Quinn who scored a great personal triumph in the play's long-running success at London's Albery Theatre. Ms Frelich starred in Medoff's follow-up play *The Hands of An Enemy*, which failed to repeat the earlier success.

TRY THESE:
▷William Inge (especially *Bus Stop*), Robert Sherwood's *The Petrified Forest* and Ed Graczyk's *Come Back to the Five and Dime, Jimmy Dean, Jimmy Dean* for plays about small-town America roadside gatherings: ▷Phil Young's *Crystal Clear* and ▷Bernard Pomerance's *The Elephant Man* for comparative treatments of disability; see also ▷Graeae.

MERCER, David [1928–80]

British dramatist

Plays include:

***The Buried Man* (1962), *The Governor's Lady* (1965), *Ride a Cock Horse* (1965), *Belcher's Luck* (1966), *After Haggerty* (1970), *Flint* (1970), *White Poem* (1970), *Duck Song* (1974), *Cousin Vladimir* (1978), *Then and Now* (1979), *No Limits to Love* (1980)**

Television includes:

***The Generations* (1961–63), *In Two Minds* (1967), *The Parachute* (1968), *Find Me* (1974), *Huggy Bear* (1976)**

Films include:

***Morgan! – A Suitable Case For Treatment* (1965), *Providence* (1977)**

The son of an engine driver in a working-class Northern family, David Mercer trained at art school. Heavily influenced at certain periods in his life by, on the one hand, R.D. Laing (he himself had a mental breakdown in 1957) and marxism on the other, his work reflects a disturbingly penetrating analysis of the individual in relation to society, with a critical judgement that left him politically unaligned – and subject increasingly to attacks by left-wing critics. As such he has brought a variety of perspectives to bear on situations ranging from the Orton-esque black comedy of *Flint* (about an agnostic vicar and a suicidal young girl) to the examination of infantilism in *Ride a Cock Horse* (in which a writer finds himself regressing emotionally following three unfortunate encounters with women). In *After Haggerty*, the title character –

TRY THESE:
▷Peter Shaffer (especially *Equus*) for exaltations of passion over reason; ▷David Hare (especially *Plenty*) and ▷Howard Brenton (especially *The Weapons of Happiness*) ▷Michael Frayn's *Benefactors* for left-wing disillusionment and lapsed idealism; ▷David Edgar's *Maydays* for another encounter between a dissident and the English; also ▷David Pownall's *Master Class* for another treatment using artistic freedom of the individual against political dogma; also some ▷Stoppard for a more right-wing view.

Helen Mirren as Moll Cutpurse, the heroine, in Barry Kyle's 1983 RSC production of Thomas Middleton and Thomas Dekker's ***The Roaring Girl***.

Godot-like – never arrives; instead the stage is occupied by a drama critic and, at times, an American woman. His fondness for disorienting monologues is echoed in *Duck Song*, a philosophical pastiche set in the home of a wealthy artist. *Cousin Vladimir* is a 'whither England?' piece, pitting a morally neutral Russian dissident against an acute and incisive Englishman; whereas *Then and Now* examines the mounting despair felt by two people seen at two points in their lives – aged twenty and fifty. Mercer's stage success was surpassed by his acclaim on television and film, and his screenplay for Karel Reisz's film *Morgan!*, about an eccentric artist hovering on the brink of insanity, is a classic of the 1960s.

MIDDLETON, Thomas [1580–1627]

English Renaissance dramatist

Plays include:

> ***A Mad World, My Masters* (1606), *A Chaste Maid in Cheapside* (1611), *The Roaring Girl* (with ▷ Thomas Dekker; 1611), *A Fair Quarrel* (with ▷ William Rowley; 1617), *Women Beware Women* (1621), *The Changeling* (with Rowley; 1622). [Middleton is now often credited with writing *The Revenger's Tragedy* (1607), previously ascribed to ▷ Cyril Tourneur, under whose name it is discussed in this book.]**

The current interest in themes of gender, class and power has made Middleton a more widely staged dramatist than ever before, since his plays are particularly concerned with female psychology and preoccupied with the relationship between love, duty and money. His Citizen Comedy, *A Chaste Maid in Cheapside* has been seen as one of the theatre's richest investigations of the topics of money, sex and society but his best known works are the two tragedies *Women Beware Women* and *The Changeling* in which he again treats the relationship between money, sex and power. A recent RSC production of *The Roaring Girl* has shown the continued relevance of this fictionalised account of the life of Moll Cutpurse, based on a real woman who scandalised early seventeenth-century society by her non-conformist ways (see ▷ Dekker for more on *The Roaring Girl*)

The Changeling

There are no great affairs of state at stake in *The Changeling*, no kingdoms fall, no royal houses die out. It is far more of a domestic tragedy than many of the great Renaissance tragedies and it is very much a play about lack of perception and failure, sometimes deliberate, to understand the probable results of actions. In particular, the heroine, Beatrice-Joanna, fails to see that playing on the malcontent De Flores' passion for her in order to get him to rid her of her unwanted betrothed in favour of another man is unlikely to be without consequences for her own future freedom of action and she becomes sucked into the vortex of passion which brings them both to their deaths. There is the usual Renaissance pattern of dumb shows, dropped handkerchiefs, severed fingers, dances of madmen and so on, but it is almost all still credible in modern terms (with the exception of the virginity test potions) and the result is a powerful unmasking of not only individual psychology but also, particularly in the subplot, of the constraints which determine the subordinate status of women within society.

TRY THESE:
The modernity of Middleton's interests has encouraged contemporary dramatists to adapt his work, notably ▷Barrie Keeffe with his modern version of the comedy *A Mad World, My Masters* and ▷Howard Barker with his rewriting of the later parts of *Women Beware Women*; most Renaissance dramatists used revenge plots and malcontent figures – ▷Shakespeare's *Hamlet* is the most famous example of both, and there are notably examples in ▷Tourneur and ▷Webster; for modern equivalents of *The Roaring Girl*, see ▷Timberlake Wertenbaker's *New Anatomies* and *The Grace of Mary Traverse*; see also ▷Aphra Behn for a late-seventeenth-century female view of similar themes.

MIKRON,

British narrowboat-based touring theatre company

Since 1972 Mikron, founded by Mike Lucas, Sarah Lucas and Danny Schiller, have toured Britain's inland waterways by boat performing their shows mainly at waterside pubs, and almost exclusively in non-theatrical venues. Their policy is to promote recreational and commercial use of the waterways and improve awareness of the environment. Their work is specially written, features music and tends to be concerned with social, historical and environmental interpretation. In 1988 *Flight of Fancy* recreates life on the Worcester and Birmingham Canal in the

TRY THESE:
for other companies with a long-term touring record see ▷Foco Novo, ▷Joint Stock, Red Ladder, ▷7:84; see also ▷Ann Jellicoe and ▷Community Theatre for other works based on particular communities.

1930s and *Rise and Fall* deals with the building of the first boat lifts. Theirs is a unique contribution to the contemporary theatrical scene.

MILLER, Arthur [1915–]
American dramatist

Plays include:
***The Man Who Had All the Luck* (1944), *All My Sons* (1947), *Death of a Salesman* (1949), *The Crucible* (1953), *A View From the Bridge* (1955), *Memory of Two Mondays* (1955), *After the Fall* (1964), *Incident at Vichy* (1964), *The Prince* (1968), *Fame* (1970), *The Creation of the World and Other Business* (1972), *Up From Paradise* (1974), *The Archbishop's Ceiling* (New York 1978; London 1986), *The American Clock* (New York 1980; London 1986), *Danger: Memory!* (1987); and adaptations include *An Enemy of the People* (1950; from Ibsen)**

Films include:
***The Misfits* (1960)**

Television includes:
***Playing for Time* (1980)**

TRY THESE:
▷Ibsen, ▷G.B. Shaw ▷Clifford Odets and ▷Lillian Hellman for a variety of dramatic moralists; ▷David Mamet (especially *Glengarry Glen Ross*) for similarly soured visions of the American dream.

The son of a clothing manufacturer hard hit by the Depression, Miller, a native New Yorker, is nowadays better-regarded in Britain than in America, as the result of a series of superior stagings of his plays – from Michael Blakemore's 1982 version of *All My Sons* through to ▷ Alan Ayckbourn's 1987 production of *A View From the Bridge* with Michael Gambon. Along the way, two fast flops in America – *The American Clock*, inspired by Studs Terkel's *Hard Times*, and *The Archbishop's Ceiling* – were reclaimed as well, as Britain took to heart a writer whose intentions are always superb, even when his dramas themselves disappoint.

Miller's reputation began with *All My Sons*, a deceptively timely tale of World War II venality that up-ends the cosy world of small-town America in which it is set. *Death of a Salesman*, his Pulitzer Prize-winning parable about the failure of the American dream, remains potentially his most powerful play, although *The Crucible* – an exposure of McCarthyism in 1950s America filtered through the Salem, Massachusetts, witch trials of the seventeenth century – remains his most politically charged. *A View From the Bridge* is a story of private morality and public pressure, involving a Brooklyn longshoreman, Eddie Carbone, in love with his young niece, Catherine. *After the Fall* attracted attention for reasons primarily of gossip: to what extent could the suicidal Maggie in Miller's play be read as the writer's portrait of his late wife, Marilyn Monroe? The prices people pay for choices they have made is an obsessive Miller theme, made explicit in *The Price* and also in his recent *Danger: Memory!*, in which efforts to forget pain cost people their memories.

While inevitably included in any list of the top five or so American playwrights, Miller falls short of his peers in various areas, lacking ▷ Tennessee Williams' sheer lyricism and ▷ Eugene O'Neill's headlong plunge into the psychological heart of darkness. His pontifical tendencies can also drag him down, and fans of *A View From the Bridge* have difficulty defending the character of the lawyer Alfieri, whose function is to explicate for us a play which is immediately comprehensible without him. Still, at his best Miller is the kind of fervid authorial stimulus the American theatre nowadays needs and lacks – a man emboldened by his own vision both to demand and to produce the acute perception and moral clarity that the best art offers. As he has said: 'I am simply asking for a theatre in which an adult who wants to live can find plays that will heighten his awareness of what living in our time involves.' And how many playwrights ask for that?

Death of a Salesman
Despite its portentous subtitle, 'Certain Private Conversations In Two Acts and A Requiem', Miller's play is still capable of packing a wallop, and its frequent programming on the British regional circuit no doubt attests in part to its harsh look at the

Michael Gambon (Eddie Carbone) and Suzan Sylvester (Catherine, his niece) in the National Theatre's production of Arthur Miller's ***A View From The Bridge***, directed by Alan Ayckbourn, Cottesloe, February 1987. It subsequently transferred to the Aldwych Theatre.

psychological costs paid by devotees of American capitalism. Willy Loman, the pathetic American Everyman, loses his job at age sixty-three and kills himself in a car accident in a last-ditch effort to raise the money his family needs. At once particular and general, lean and overripe, linear and abstract in its cross-cuttings in time, Miller's play is one of the profoundest examinations yet of the American dream, and it's a pity that he doesn't trust his own technique enough to do without Willy's wife Linda's sententious (if famous) exhortation: 'Attention, attention must be finally paid to such a person.' That we pay attention nonetheless is due to the level of characterisation – not just the eternal scrapper Willy, who has provided a landmark role for actors as varied as Lee J. Cobb, George C. Scott, and Dustin Hoffman on Broadway, and Paul Muni and Warren Mitchell in London, but also Willy's long-suffering wife Linda and their two sons, Biff and Happy. A production of it in China prompted Miller's 1984 memoir, *Salesman In Beijing*.

MINGHELLA, Anthony [1954–]

British dramatist

Plays include:

***Child's Play* (1978), *Whale Music* (1981), *A Little Like Drowning* (1984), *Two Planks and a Passion* (1984), *Love Bites* (1984), *Made In Bangkok* (1986)**

Television includes:

***Whale Music* (1983); *What If It's Raining* (1986), *The Dead of Jericho* (1987), *The Storyteller* (1987)**

Of Italian parentage, brought up on the Isle of Wight, Minghella, a former lecturer at Hull University, has established himself as a leading young dramatist capable of an impressive breadth of themes and periods, even if he has yet to come up with one play that would cement his reputation. *Made In Bangkok*, his most recent, is the best-known, in light of its 1986 West End run and its 1988 American premiere in Los Angeles. In *A Little Like Drowning*, an episodic flashback drama about an Italian family uprooted to England, a conversation between the elderly Nonna and her granddaughter Anastasia gives way to a series of pained recollections about her now-dead husband, Alfredo, who left her for an English mistress. Domestic discord continues in *Love Bites*, about a family reunion that disintegrates into recriminations. *Two Planks and a Passion* shifts the scene to 1392 and to preparations in York for a Passion play at the Feast of Corpus Christi, a religious event turned all too secular by the greed and avarice of a community suddenly visited by Richard II. *Made In Bangkok* continues Minghella's interest in issues of ethical and moral compromise, but he remains, as of now, a writer whose intentions outstrip his achievements.

Made In Bangkok

Commissioned by Michael Codron for a commerical engagement at the Aldwych in 1986, *Made In Bangkok* was a risky venture about sexual exploitation that must have surprised tourists who thought it would be a spicy follow-up to *No Sex Please, We're British.* Five Britons arrive on an 'Eastern Promise' holiday in Asia – one woman, Frances, and four sex-starved men – only to find that geographical displacement leads to its own emotional truth-telling as the men are revealed to be rapacious wolves and Frances becomes an all-too-obvious authorial stand-in. An extended essay about exploitation, the play is too smart to be prurient itself, but it never quite packs the punch Minghella seems to assume it will, and Frances' moralistic editorialising ('It's got nothing to do with Bangkok; it's to do with us,' she decides, sensibly) is a bit wearisome.

TRY THESE:
▷Stephen Lowe, ▷Caryl Churchill and ▷Dusty Hughes for a similar kind of peculiarly English staccato rhythm; Mark Brennan's *China* for sexual exploitation closer-to-home in a Soho hostess bar; ▷Robert Bolt's *A Man For All Seasons* for the sort of conventional history play *Two Planks and a Passion* reacts against; Julia Schofield's *Love On the Plastic,* ▷Kay Adshead's *Thatcher's Women* and ▷Peter Terson's *Strippers* as plays about the sexual exploitation of women.

MITCHELL, Julian [1935–]

British novelist, dramatist and historian

Plays include:

***Half-Life* (1977), *The Enemy Within* (1980), *Another Country* (1981), *Francis* (1983), *After Aïda* (originally *Verdi's Messiah*; 1986)**

TRY THESE:
▷Alan Bennett's *The Old Country* and television play *An Englishman Abroad* for secret agents; Saint Joan is the

Mitchell is best known for *Another Country* (filmed with Rupert Everett as the iconic gay/rebel) which explored the link between sexual identity and political awareness in a public school setting, echoing the background of the MI5 spy Guy Burgess. Critics were less kind to his bio-piece on St Francis of Asissi, Francis, which smacked somewhat of unimaginative school's radio unable to match his sharp political edge in religious ideology.

Mitchell's earlier stage success was in adapting two Ivy Compton-Burnett novels, *A Heritage and its History* (1965) and *A Family and a Fortune* (1966) and he has also translated ▷ Pirandello's *Henry IV* (1983). *After Aïda*, in response to a commission from the Welsh National Opera, uses opera singers performing extracts from Verdi's music as an integral part of the story of the composer's return from musical retirement to answer the challenge of Wagner's music dramas in the final flowering of his later work. *Adelina Patti, the Queen of Song* is another piece devised for the Welsh National Opera.

most popular theatrical saint; see ▷Shakespeare's *Henry VI*, ▷Shaw, ▷Brecht, ▷Terson, and ▷Anouilh for good examples.

MNOUCHKINE, Ariane [1938–]

French director and dramatist, founder-member and manager of the Théâtre du Soleil

Key productions include:

***Les Clowns* (1969), *1789* (1970), *1793* (1972), *L'Age d'Or* (1975), *Méphisto* (1979), ▷ Shakespeare's *Richard II* (1981), and *Henry IV* (1984), *L'histoire terrible mais inachevée de Norodom Sihanouk, roi du Cambodge* (1985), *L'Indiade* (1987)**

Mnouchkine is one of the most important French directors, and demonstrates what can be done with a devoted company, one production every two years, a substantial subsidy, and very considerable talent. The Théâtre du Soleil was founded in 1964 as a theatre co-operative, and the early successes included ▷ Gorki's *Philistines* and ▷ Arnold Wesker's *The Kitchen*, but they are best known for four *créations collectives* – improvised and devised plays – *Les Clowns*, *1789*, *1793*, and *L'Age d'Or*. *1789* used all the devices of popular theatre to look at the people's view of the French Revolution: clown techniques, puppets of all sizes, fairground turns, a narrator like a fairground barker, and a set with a ring of five small stages and the audience standing in the middle. The production came to London's Round House in 1971, and proved an enormously exciting use of stage space. For *L'Age d'Or*, the story of a Moroccan immigrant worker in contemporary France, the whole theatre was filled with sand shaped into four large hollows, in which the audience sat in close proximity to the actors.

Since 1975 they have made a film on the life of ▷ Molière, put on Mnouchkine's adaptation of *Méphisto* (Klaus Mann's novel about his brother-in-law Gustav Gründgens), and worked on some colourful Shakespearean productions in a style based on Kabuki. The two most recent productions have applied these new techniques to texts written for and with the company by the radical feminist writer ▷ Hélène Cixous; these are substantial historical plays on the terrible story of Sihanouk and Cambodia, and on the partition of British India.

The company is based in a disused munitions factory beyond the end of the métro at Vincennes, to which they have attracted consistently large audiences, though perhaps not the popular audience which their techniques seem to invite. There has also been a hilarious one-man parody of Mnouchkine's directing style running in Paris, *Ariane ou l'Ange d'Or*, by Philippe Caubère, not something that commonly happens to directors.

TRY THESE:

▷Peter Brook, for inventive direction and use of space, though Mnouchkine is more politically committed; ▷Goethe's *Faust*, for Mephistopheles; Jerome Savary's *Le Grand Magic Circus* also use theatre space in its totality; Peter Stein in Germany and the radical Yugoslav Group, Red Pilot, are two of the many Europeans who use space imaginatively (see ▷LIFT for others); also Jan Fabre and Pina Bausch who are more performance art oriented; in Britain the equivalents, though different in scope, could range from Lumiere and Son, to Welfare State to the ▷National Theatre's ▷promenade performances, or ▷Ann Jellicoe's community theatre; see also ▷performance art.

Méphisto

The play is built around a series of oppositions (Nazi/Communist, mainstream theatre/satirical cabaret, and above all theatre/life). In a series of short scenes, it puts questions (as did the ▷ Molière film) about the actor's responsibilities to society. It is a pity that this is the only example of Mnouchkine's work that has been seen in Britain since the visit of *1789* in 1971. It worked very well in the Oxford Playhouse's shortened version at the Round House in 1981, with Ian McDiarmid as the diabolic Höfgen but by the time it reached the Barbican in 1986, in Timberlake

Wertenbaker's version, either the time was no longer right, or the production was too heavy-handed.

MOFFATT, Nigel [1954–]
Jamaican dramatist

Plays include:
***Mamma Decemba* (1985), *Celebration* (1986), *Walsall Boxed In* (1987)**

Poet, musician, songwriter (in 1983, he recorded with ex Jam and Style Counsel lead singer Paul Weller, and has played the folk club circuit), now living in the West Midlands. Moffatt's *Mamma Decemba*, written for ▷ Temba, won the ▷ Samuel Beckett award for 1986. Like so many before him, Moffatt's play centres on the disillusionment of Caribbean immigrants with 'the home country', seen through the eyes of two older women, Mamma Decemba and her friend. But in Mamma Decemba, written in patois though set in 'inner-city England', Moffatt has created a unique character whose shifts of mood and impenetrable grief as she mourns her recently deceased husband are handled with a sensitivity that goes beyond the individual and gives the play a universal appeal.

Moffatt has also been part of the National Theatre's studio workshops out of which came two plays *Tony* and *Rhapsody 'N Black 'N' White* performed to invited audiences. *Tony* subsequently appeared at the Oval under the title of *Thriller* in a version not approved of by the author.

TRY THESE:
▷Caryl Phillips, ▷Mustapha Matura, ▷Edgar White for other plays on the theme of disillusionment with the mother country.

MOLIÈRE (Jean-Baptiste Poquelin) [1622–73]
French dramatist and actor-manager

Plays include:
***Les Précieuses Ridicules* (*The Affected Ladies*; 1658), *L'École des Femmes* (*The School for Wives*; 1662), *Don Juan* (1665), *Le Misanthrope* (*The Misanthrope*; 1666), *Le Tartuffe* (*Tartuffe*; written 1664, produced 1667), *Georges Dandin* (1668), *Le Bourgeois Gentilhomme* (*The Would-be Gentleman* or *The Bourgeois Gentleman*; 1671), *Les Fourberies de Scapin* (*The Tricks of Scapin* or *Scapino*; 1671), *Les Femmes Savantes* (*The Learned Ladies*; 1672), *Le Malade Imaginaire* (*The Hypochondriac* or *The Imaginary Invalid*; 1673)**

Molière was the eldest son of a wealthy Paris tapestry merchant in the King's service, and was well educated with a view to following his father. However, Molière went off with a troupe of actors and toured in the provinces for fifteen years before making any success in Paris; this apprenticeship, and having to share the Palais-Royal theatre for half the week with an Italian *commedia dell'arte* troupe, gave him a very thorough theatrical grounding. He became France's most complete man of the theatre; he was as good a comic actor as he was a comic dramatist. He produced his own plays and managed his company against strong attacks from the respectable (though with the firm support of King Louis XIV) and he died with his make-up on. His output ranges from knockabout farce to conversation pieces, to political satire, to Court spectacles with elaborate machinery, and to subtle comedies of character, all happily still holding the stage. His only failure was a heroic drama, *Don Garcie de Navarre*; being disinclined to waste, he salvaged some of the text and used it for Alceste's more lofty sentiments in *The Misanthrope*.

Molière's plays (like ▷ Shakespeare's) can survive almost anything a director feels like doing to them. British directors tend to be more respectful of the text than Planchon or Vitez, but in recent years the ▷ National Theatre has moved *Scapino* (1970) to modern Italy, with motor-bikes, and *The Misanthrope* (1973), in Tony Harrison's elegant rhymed couplets, to de Gaulle's France. The productions of *Don Juan* (1981) and *The School for Wives* (1987) were comparatively straight, but Bogdanov (1981) added a speeded-up version of an earlier Molière doctor farce (*Le Médicin Volant*) as a carnival extra to *The Hypochondriac* and killed off his main actor at the end, in reference to Molière's own

TRY THESE:
▷Racine for seventeenth-century French theatre, though they were on bad terms, and there is very little to compare; English Restoration comedy (eg ▷Etherege, ▷Wycherley) has much in common with Molière; ▷Christopher Hampton's *The Philanthropist* is an 'answer' to *The Misanthrope*; see also ▷Bulgakov's *Molière*.

death. The 1983 ▷ RSC *Tartuffe* (▷ Christopher Hampton's version) was successful in spite of having a striking main actor (Anthony Sher) who was clearly in a different play from everyone else. A certain amount of Molière's effect is lost in English translation (except when it is by Tony Harrison), but British directors sensibly keep on trying, and the plays take surprisingly well to Scottish dialect (*Le Bourgeois Gentilhomme* as *A Wee Touch o' Class*, Edinburgh, 1985; *The Hypochondriak*, Edinburgh 1987).

The Misanthrope
Q. Will the noble, uncompromising, universally admired Alceste win his lawsuit despite his refusal to butter up the judges and his inability not to tell the truth about the awful verses of the powerful Oronte? A. No. Q. Will he marry the brilliant, beautiful, bitchy Célimène or the quiet, devoted Eliante? A. Neither: Célimène cannot face the thought of all that rustic high thinking, and Eliante very sensibly decides that she will be happier with Alceste's more worldly and less demanding friend, Philinte. The rest is just brilliant conversation. The world divides into those who think Alceste is Molière's funniest creation, and those (like Rousseau) who are shocked that Molière should have held up to ridicule this virtuous and Rousseau-like man.

MOLNAR, Ferenc [1878–1952]
Hungarian dramatist

Plays include:
Liliom (1909), _The Guardsman_ (1910), _The Swan_ (1914), _The Play in the Castle_ (as _The Play's the Thing_ in the USA; 1924), _Olimpia_ (1927), _The Good Fairy_ (1931)

Beginning as a writer of farces and light-hearted satirical comedies of Hungarian city life but later gaining international success, Molnar's work is probably better known than his name. *The Devil* (1907), a reworking of the Faust theme, was an early success; *The Wolf* surfaced in the West End in 1973 with Judi Dench; *The Swan* is best known through a Grace Kelly/Alec Guiness film version and *Liliom* in its musical adaptation *Carousel*. ▷ Tom Stoppard reworked *The Play in the Castle* as *Rough Crossing* (▷ National Theatre 1984) with disastrous results – changing the setting to a transatlantic liner, adding a parody musical, complicating the plot and turning an elegant trifle into a heavy-handed wreck. The P. G. Wodehouse version for Broadway is much closer to the spirit of the original. In the original version a young composer overhears his fiancée in a passionate exchange with another man; to save the situation a playwright dashes off a short play (a pastiche of one by Sardou) to convince the composer that all he heard was a snatch of a rehearsal. Molnar's touch is almost always light and his work often has elements of fantasy as in the father's return to earth in *Liliom* and the usherette's dream adventures in *The Good Fairy*.

TRY THESE:
His work has been adapted by ▷Frank Marcus and ▷Tom Stoppard; Nicolle Freni's *Brooklyn E5* for a lesbian variation involving the return of a ghostly (and benevolent) father; ▷J. M. Barrie's *Mary Rose* for returning ghosts; ▷Anouilh, ▷Giraudoux for elements of fantasy.

MONSTROUS REGIMENT
British women's theatre company

Plays include:
Scum (by ▷ Claire Luckham and C.G. Bond; 1976), _Vinegar Tom_ (by ▷ Caryl Churchill; 1976–77), _Kiss and Kill_ (by Ann Mitchell and Susan Todd; 1977–78), _Floorshow_ (by ▷ Caryl Churchill, ▷ Bryony Lavery, ▷ Michelene Wandor and David Bradford; 1977–78), _Time Gentlemen Please_ (by ▷ Bryony Lavery; 1978), _Teendreams_ (by ▷ David Edgar with Susan Todd; 1979), _Gentlemen Prefer Blondes_ (by ▷ Bryony Lavery; 1979–80), _Dialogue Between a Prostitute and one of Her Clients_ (by Dacia Maraini; 1980), _Mourning Pictures_ (by Honor Moore; 1981), _Yoga Class_ (by Rose Tremain; 1981), _Shakespeare's Sister_ (presented by Théâtre de l'Aquarium; 1982), _The Execution_ (by ▷ Melissa Murray; 1982), _Fourth Wall_ (by ▷ Franca Rame and ▷ Dario Fo; 1983), _Calamity_ (by ▷ Bryony Lavery; 1983–84), _Enslaved by Dreams_ (devised by

TRY THESE:
▷Women's Theatre Group, ▷Foco Novo, ▷Paines Plough, ▷Black Theatre Company, ▷Temba, ▷Theatre of Black Women, ▷Joint Stock for other touring companies devoted to new writing; also ▷Cheek by Jowl and ATC for ensemble companies who are also extremely innovative in their style of presentation of classic texts; Blood Group, Burnt Bridges

Chris Bowler; 1984), *Origin of the Species* (by ▷ Bryony Lavery; 1984–85), *Point of Convergence* (by Chris Bowler and Cockpit Youth Theatre; 1985), *My Song is Free* (by ▷ Susan Yankowitz; 1986), *Alarms* (by ▷ Susan Yankowitz; 1987), *My Sister in This House* (by ▷ Wendy Kesselman; 1987), *Waving* (by Carol Bunyan; 1988)

A long-standing and influential feminist theatre company, founded in 1975 by ex-Belt and Braces performer Gillian Hanna with Mary McCusker, Chris Bowler, Linda Broughton, and Helen Glavin, Monstrous Regiment take their name from John Knox's misogynistic pamphlet of the sixteenth century (a half-ironic self-consciousness reflected in other company titles of the 1970s such as ▷ Gay Sweatshop, Welfare State, Belt and Braces).

Originally conceived by its founders as a way of breaking out of the poverty of roles for women – 'If I have to play another tart in a pvc skirt, usually with a heart of gold, I'll puke,' (McCusker); 'If I have to play another earth-mother/shop steward in orange dungarees, I'll go mad,' (Hanna) – the collective was a way for performers, particularly women performers, to gain more control of their working lives. Although they have consistently employed male actors in productions, since the early 1980s the company has been run by women only, and retains its identity as a collective more in administrative terms than actual performance – a change which in large part has been the consequence of diminishing subsidy. As such, sexual politics have always been a cornerstone of the company's work as well as the manner and form of its presentation which, in the past, often contained strong visual and musical elements in a variety of styles, from epics to collages, monologues to political sagas, ▷ musicals to ▷ cabaret (music was an important element of all their early shows).

The primary focus has been to challenge stereotypes of women in a dozen different ways, whether at work, in the home, as performers, or as victims of history (witches) or the present day (prostitutes on the one hand, older women on the other). Some of the issues covered include: violence (*Kiss and Kill*); women and work (*Scum* and *Floorshow*). These issues are probably familiar to any feminist-oriented company and have become part of the theatrical furniture. The company themselves recognise they are perhaps at a crossroads in their fortunes but have an impressive track record of past work to look back on which has laid the foundations for future companies to build on. They have re-assessed women's role in history in a number of different ways: through epic; ▷ Melissa Murray's *The Execution* and Chris Bowler's *Enslaved by Dreams* which looks at Florence Nightingale through her own writings; ▷ Caryl Churchill's *Vinegar Tom* dealing with the seventeenth-century witch craze through its social ambience and in particular the fear of women's sexuality; ▷ Bryony Lavery's *Origin of the Species* looking at the man-made nature of history. Some of their most controversial work in the early period explored women as performers in popular entertainment, as stand-up comics, or looked at women and work (*Floorshow*) and women and glamour (*Time Gentlemen Please*). Other shows have looked at prostitution (*Dialogue Between a Prostitute*), whilst *Shakespeare's Sister*, using striking visual images, dismantled a few ideas to do with marriage as well as imagining the possibilities of a writing career for Shakespeare's (imagined) sister. More recently, *My Song is Free* was an account by four women imprisoned in Chile; *Point of Convergence*, a physical piece of theatre about survival skills and collective strength; while Carol Bunyan's *Waving* tackled the rare subject of older women, scoring neat comic points about independence, in relation to marriage and disability.

The company has also consistently been committed to new writing, commissioned often from outside writers and developed with the company in workshops. Writers like ▷ Caryl Churchill (*Top Girls* in fact resulted from a period of workshops with Monstrous Regiment), ▷ David Edgar, ▷ Michelene Wandor, ▷ Melissa Murray, ▷ Bryony Lavery, ▷ Claire

and the American group Split Britches for innovative women's groups; also The People Show, one of the longest running and still most consistently inventive cabaret/ performance groups around; see also ▷Women in Theatre, ▷New Writing, ▷Graeae.

Luckham, Susan Todd, have all been associated with the group at one time or another.

MORNIN, Daniel [1956–]

Northern Irish dramatist

Plays include:

***Mum and Son* (1981), *The Resting Time* (1981), *Kate* (1983), *Short of Mutiny* (1983), *Comrade Ogilvy* (1985), *Built on Sand* (1987), *Weights and Measures* (1988)**

Belfast-born Mornin spent three years in the navy, travelled extensively in Asia and North Africa before coming to rest in London and deciding to become a writer. *Short of Mutiny* was in fact his first play. A sort of 'navy lark' below stairs with, for these days, a large cast (over twenty), it suffered from being produced in a post-Falklands context but was admired for its authenticity of crew life, social dynamics and observation about the wretchedness of life aboard for those at the wrong end of command. Mornin has really come to prominence however with his trio of plays about Belfast. As though trying to find answers to his own inner questions, the three plays have tried to explore the complex strands of the conflict, its effects on Irish people and how those strands go on being perpetrated. *Built on Sand*, a non-naturalistic piece that uses flashbacks, is as much a study in political cynicism as it is about young Belfast journalist Andrew's obsession with finding answers to the murder of his girlfriend; and *Kate* which tries to show the daily pressures of living in Belfast, is as harrowing in its depiction of the young, sullen son, already 'lost' and committed to violence and the loyalist paras, as it tries to be optimistic in its portrait of Kate, determined to get a typing qualification despite life falling apart all around her. *The Murderers* is the inevitable end of the conundrum, going behind the scenes of a bloody sectarian killing, to reveal the same inevitable bigotry that both IRA and Loyalist leaders in *Built on Sand* feed into and off. There is also concern about the nature of 'maleness' and 'femaleness' in which the killing is seen as part of some atavistic male initiation rite, whilst the only female character, the sister of the Protestant and sullenly avenging brother, is free of such constraints and so sleeps with a Catholic. However you take these theses there is no doubt that Mornin remains a playwright of unquestionable dramatic grip. Though *The Murderers* won the 1985 George Devine award, *Kate* is the one that lingers in the mind and may prove more durable.

TRY THESE:
▷Christina Reid, ▷Ann Devlin, ▷Charabanc for more plays on Belfast and its effect on women; also Seamus Finnegan for historical and social explorations of Northern Ireland conflicts; Stephen Lowe's *Seachange* has particular affinities in its flashback style though Lowe's was to do with the Falklands; ▷Louise Page; Robert Holman's *Lost in Making Noise Quietly* for more post-Falklands reprises, both army and navy; ▷Willis Hall's *The Long and the Short and the Tall* for more portraits of inter-ranks service strife.

MORRISON, Bill [1940–]

Northern Irish dramatist, actor and director

Plays include:

***Please Don't Shoot Me When I'm Down* (1969), *Patrick's Day* (1972), *Tess of the D'Urbervilles* (1971; from Thomas Hardy), *Conn and the Conquerors of Space* (1972), *Sam Slade is Missing* (1972), *The Love of Lady Margaret* (1973), *The Irish Immigrant's Tale* (1976), *The Emperor of Ice Cream* (from Brian Moore; 1977), *Flying Blind* (1977), *Ellen Cassidy* (1978), *Dr Jekyll of Rodney Street* (1979), *Scrap!* (1982), *Cavern of Dreams* (musical with Carol Ann Duffy; 1984)**

Morrison's greatest success is *Flying Blind*, one of a number of plays produced during a fruitful association with the Liverpool Everyman. Set in contemporary Belfast it uses broadly farcical mechanisms and devices – overheard conversations, inopportune exits and entrances, frustrated seductions, robings and disrobings – to present a portrait of a society impotent to solve its problems (the fact that none of the men can achieve an erection is metaphorically as well as farcically appropriate). The old certainties and convictions have given way to male withdrawal into the safer world represented by the music of Charlie Parker or to the fanaticism of the paramilitaries. Everyone is 'flying blind' without navigational aids, including the Protestant paramilitary who has to keep taking off his hood because he can't see without his

TRY THESE:
The issues raised have counterparts in plays by ▷Sean O'Casey and ▷Brian Friel; ▷Joe Orton provides an example of the extension and subversion of the boundaries of farce in *Loot* and *What the Butler Saw*; Hector MacMillan's *The Sash* offers a Scottish angle on the Irish situation; ▷Charabanc's *Somewhere Over the Balcony* also takes a farcical, surreal approach to present day Belfast; for other Belfast-touched subjects see ▷Ann Devlin, Seamus Finnegan, ▷Christina Reid,

glasses and the female babysitter who wants to borrow *Fear of Flying*. This powerful, disturbing and funny play ends in a welter of gunfire, urine, death and reconciliation which defies conventional theatrical expectations, just as the characters' lives have been forced out of conventional moulds by the political situation.

▷Daniel Mornin, Allan Cubitt.

MORTIMER, John [1923–]

British dramatist, journalist, novelist, barrister

Plays include:

***The Dock Brief* (1957), *What Shall We Tell Caroline* (1958), *Lunch Hour* (1960), *The Wrong Side of the Park* (1960), *Two Stars for Comfort* (1962), *A Flea in Her Ear* (1966; from ▷ Feydeay), *The Judge* (1967), *Come as You Are* (1970; comprising: *Mill Hill, Bermondsey, Gloucester Road, Marble Arch*), *A Voyage Round My Father* (1970), *Collaborators* (1973), *Heaven and Hell* (1976; comprising *The Fear of Heaven, The Prince of Darkness*, later retitled *The Bells of Hell*), *The Lady From Maxim's* (1977; from ▷ Feydeau), *A Little Hotel on the Side* (1984; from ▷ Feydeau)**

Television includes:

***I, Claudius* (1972; adapted from Robert Graves' novels), *Brideshead Revisited* (1981; adapted from Evelyn Waugh), *Rumpole of the Bailey* (series; 1975–87), *Will Shakespeare* (1978), *Paradise Postponed* (1986)**

Films include:

***Ferry to Hong Kong* (with Lewis Gilbert and Vernon Harris; 1959), *The Innocents* (with Truman Capote and William Archibald; 1961), *Guns of Darkness* (1962), *I Thank a Fool* (1962), *Lunch Hour* (1962), *The Running Man* (1963), *Bunny Lake is Missing* (with Penelope Mortimer; 1964), *A Flea in Her Ear* (1967), *John and Mary* (from the novel by Mervyn Jones; 1969)**

Mortimer has been enormously prolific; he regularly contributes to newspapers and to television, has kept up a regular flow of plays and novels, and has remained a working barrister. Despite a very Establishment and traditional background, he has consistently espoused liberal positions in his writing and involvement in theatre. He has been a key figure in anti-censorship debates, acting for the defence in the prosecution of the magazine *Oz* for obscenity, giving testimony which was active in abolishing the power of the Lord Chamberlain and speaking out against the attacks on ▷ Howard Brenton's *The Romans in Britain*. There is very little danger of his own plays suffering censorship, however; his own writing is, for the most part, very gentle and often nostalgic.

Born in Hampstead, Mortimer was educated at Harrow School and Oxford University, and qualified as a barrister in 1948. He began writing professionally during World War II, when he was posted as an assistant director and later a scriptwriter with the Crown Film Unit. His first plays were written as radio plays, and were later produced in the theatre as one-act plays. *The Dock Brief* was the first play which really made his name; it went through the process that has been true of many of Mortimer's plays, first written for radio, it was then staged, and finally televised.

Voyage Round My Father

Voyage Round My Father is an autobiographical account of Mortimer's father, a lawyer who resolutely denied his own blindness. It is a powerful and moving study of a man who is clearly monstrous in some aspects but who is, nonetheless, drawn with enormous affection. The play is almost an elegy for him, and for Mortimer's stalwart mother who forebore his father's eccentricities with enormous patience. First produced as a radio play, it was then staged in a final version at the Haymarket theatre, and later televised with Laurence Olivier as the father.

TRY THESE:
▷Feydeau, whom Mortimer has translated with enormous success; ▷John Osborne whom Mortimer acknowledges as an influence; ▷De Filippo's *Ducking Out* and ▷Edgar White's *The Nine Night* both have central, *monstres sacrés* father figures, as does ▷Eugene O'Neill's *Long Day's Journey into Night*.

MOTTON, Gregory [1962–]

British dramatist

TRY THESE:
▷Gorki, ▷Beckett for

Plays include:

***Rain* (1984), *Chicken* (1987), *Ambulance* (1987), *Downfall* (Royal Court commission; 1988)**

A quirky young dramatist, London born Motton is yet the latest in the Royal Court's seemingly inexhaustible stream of young writers who see contemporary society with a jaundiced but compassionate heart. Motton's plays recall all too quickly those urban wastelands of confusion and deprivation made famous from ▷ Gorki to ▷ Pinter – his characters, like theirs, are misfits and social outcasts who have fallen through the system but whom the system still menaces. *Chicken* is set in a café which turns customers away and a rubbish strewn Islington street; *Ambulance*, somewhere between the cosmos and the stinking gutter. One of Motton's characters in *Chicken* has a memory problem and forgets who he is because no one ever asks him. Like ▷ Beckett, without the jokes, these young losers and down-and-outs of Thatcher's Britain – the alcoholic, the mentally and physically scarred – have dreams and aspirations that are already a thing of the past. A brutal surrealism is Motton's stock in trade, and a style which has yet to find its own full voice, but it is one to be watched.

similar visions of social outcasts and yearning; ▷Tunde Ikoli's *The Lower Depths* for a multi-racial East End version; ▷Jim Cartwright for another version of contemporary disenchantment; ▷Harold Pinter for characters as menacing symbols of external reality; ▷Tennessee Williams for a contrasting American treatment of the loss of dreams.

MROZEK, Slawomir [1930–]

Polish dramatist and cartoonist

Plays include:

***Police* (1958), *Charlie* (1961), *Out at Sea* (also known as *The Ship-Wrecked Ones*; 1961), *The Party* (1962), *The Enchanted Night* (also known as *What a Lovely Dream*; 1963), *Tango* (1964), *Emigrés* (1975), *The Hunchback* (1976), *A Summer's Day* (1983)**

Mrozek is probably the Polish playwright best known in the West, if only because he found himself there after protesting about Poland's role in the occupation of Czechoslovakia; his passport was withdrawn, but he managed to escape to Paris. His plays are often absurdist in style, but the background is not so much a meaningless universe as an irrational and arbitrary totalitarian state, and his tone is satirical and sardonic rather than despairing. His plays have been put on in Britain with reasonable frequency since Martin Esslin adapted a short story, *Siesta*, for radio in 1963; three short plays were put on at the Traverse in 1964 (*The Enchanted Night, The Party,* and *Charlie*) and two at the Edinburgh Lyceum in 1965, *Out at Sea* and *Police* and *Tango*, adapted by ▷ Tom Stoppard, was produced by the ▷ RSC in 1966. Two other Mrozek plays have appeared in recent years: *Emigrés* at the Young Vic in 1975 and at New End in 1981, a two-hander between AA the Intellectual and XX the Worker, both exiles in a sordid basement somewhere in the free world, fantasising and bickering on New Year's Eve; and *A Summer's Day* at London's Polish Theatre in 1985, another two-handed philosophical tug-of-war between Sux, an over-achiever, and Unsux, an under-achiever, both of whom wish to commit suicide; there is an intervening lady (who goes off with Sux, of course). There are plenty more of his plays for enterprising directors to try.

Tango

In this play, questions of freedom and authority in the modern state are raised through the metaphor of an anarchic family with an intellectual but authoritarian son who is trying to reform it; he fails to maintain control, and brute force takes over in the form of Eddie the butler. The play, besides being full of logical paradoxes and knotty arguments of the ▷ Stoppard kind, is also very funny, and Lou Stein's revival at the Gate in 1981 will probably not be the last.

TRY THESE:
▷Vaclàv Havel for another Eastern European playwright writing under political difficulties, and using the devices of absurdist theatre to comment on the state of his country; ▷Tom Stoppard for *Professional Foul*, *Every Good Boy Deserves Favour*, and *Squaring the Circle*, which treat similar themes; ▷Brecht's *Conversations in Exile* has similarities to *Emigrés*, Witold Gombrowicz is the other Polish dramatist well known in the West; Janusz Glowacki's *Cinders* was co-adapted by ▷Hanif Kureishi, ▷Pam Gems adapted Stanislawa Przybyszewska's *The Danton Affair*.

MURRAY, Melissa [1954–]

British dramatist, poet

Plays include:

***Bouncing Back with Benyon* (with Eileen Fairweather; 1977), *Hot Spot* (1978), *Belisha Beacon* (with Eileen Fairweather; 1978), *Hormone Imbalance* (revue; 1979),**

TRY THESE:
For states of isolation see ▷Ayshe Raif's *Another Woman*, ▷Botho Strauss' *Great and Small*, and ▷Barry Collins'

MURRAY, MELISSA

***Ophelia* (1979), *The Admission* (1980), *The Execution* (1982), *The Crooked Scythe* (1982–83), *Coming Apart* (1985), *Body-cell* (1986)**

Radio includes:
***A Grain of Salt* (1985), *Body-cell* (1988)**

A feminist, Murray's output, coincidentally, reflects the diversity of styles women playwrights have adopted in the search for ways of expressing the female experience: revue (*Hormone Imbalance*, a surreal gay cabaret), agit-prop (*Bouncing Back with Benyon*, a pro-abortion piece), blank verse (*Ophelia*, a parody of Shakespeare seen from a lesbian feminist perspective), rhyming verse (*The Crooked Scythe*) and historical epic (*The Execution*). They have had their share of brickbats (women's writing is either criticised for being too aggressive or too humourless, too unfocused, or too benign). However, *Coming Apart*, which won the Verity Bargate award, showed the best and the worst of Murray's style: a certain lack of conviction in the overall plot – the interaction of four characters upon each other, trapped in memories of the past in a Berlin boarding house – but a haunting, elusive quality capable of evoking a disturbing sense of paranoia, fear and disorientation, and a considerable sympathy for the vulnerable and isolated. Murray touched on this theme in a different way in the earlier *The Admission*, an angry forty-minute piece about society's approach to treating women and mental illness. *Body-cell* (produced whilst she was writer-in-residence at the Soho Poly in 1986) combines these themes of isolation and society's controlling techniques, in the portrait of a female political prisoner in Durham prison, confined to solitary for disruptive behaviour, and her increasing withdrawal from human contact as a result of it.

Judgement; for women and mental illness, see ▷Tony Craze's *Shona*, ▷David Mercer's *In Two Minds*, ▷Alan Ayckbourn's perhaps overpraised but nonetheless moving *A Woman in Mind*, Charlotte Perkins Gilman's Edwardian account of a wife's deterioration in her novel *The Yellow Wallpaper*, and ▷David Edgar's *Mary Barnes*; for images of women in prison, see ▷Clean Break and ▷Jacqueline Holborough; for other images of the brutalising effect of prison on the human spirit, see ▷Wisdom Bridge Theatre Company's *In the Belly of the Beast*.

MUSICALS

Are musicals the great Broadway art form, America's one truly indigenous contribution to the theatrical spectrum? Or are they mere song-and-dance palliatives that assuage tired egos even as they drain our pockets? People will no doubt espouse both points of view, but one truth remains: at its best, the Broadway musical produces a sense of exhilaration and speed that few creations can match; at its worst, particularly when bloated into technologically top-heavy, impersonal leviathans, few theatrical genres seem more cynical or more calculated.

The history of the musical is really that of musical *comedy*, as distinct from plays with music (much of ▷ Shakespeare, for example, or modern works like ▷ Caryl Churchill's *Serious Money*) or fully fledged opera, although nowadays the distinction is beginning to blur. The origin of the musical lies in turn-of-the-century operetta, in such European – or, at least, European-influenced – works as *Naughty Marietta*, *The Merry Widow*, and the rippingly sung pastiche of Gilbert and Sullivan. Prior to World War II, George and Ira Gershwin, Cole Porter, and Jerome Kern were the musical names to reckon with, but the genre really took off after World War II in the golden-toned decades of the 1940s and 1950s, in musicals by Leonard Bernstein (*Wonderful Town*, *Candide*), Richard Rodgers and Oscar Hammerstein II (*The King and I*), Alan Jay Lerner and Frederick Loewe (*Brigadoon*, *My Fair Lady*), and Frank Loesser (*Guys and Dolls*, *The Most Happy Fella*), to name just a few.

From the late 1960s and early 1970s onward, the director became king, men – like Hal Prince, Bob Fosse, and Michael Bennett – who placed their unmistakable touch on shows that might not otherwise have found a public (*Sweet Charity*, *Cabaret*, *Dreamgirls*). The British, too, entered the fray, once Trevor Nunn found that after decades working in the classics, he could become a millionaire by staging the most financially lucrative musical of all time – Andrew Lloyd Webber's *Cats*. Since *Cats*, discussion of the British musical invasion has produced endless amounts of journalistic copy, but it is really a tribute to two men alone: Lloyd Webber and Nunn, either one of whom has been responsible for all the international British

TRY THESE:
▷G.B. Shaw's Pygmalion is the basis of *My Fair Lady*; ▷T. S. Eliot's *Old Possum's Book of Practical Cats* is the source of *Cats*; ▷Brecht's *Threepenny Opera* and John Gay's *The Beggar's Opera* are satirical musicals; among contemporary British small-scale musicals are Felix Cross' *Blues for Railton* and *Mass Carib and Colin Sell's Black Night Owls* and *Iron Harvest;* many of ▷Paines Plough's productions have a strong musical base; *Ain't Misbehavin'*, *Bubbling Brown Sugar*, *One Mo' Time* and Sheldon Epp's *Blues in the Night* are a few of the successful black American musicals to have been seen in Britain in recent years. ▷Robyn Archer offers an alternative perspective on 'the musical'.

Everybody's favourite, ***42nd Street***, the musical that sums it all up: from the book by Michael Stewart and Mark Bramble, music by Harry Warren, lyrics by Al Dubin, directed by Lucia Victor (from orginal direction by dances by Gower Champion); opened Theatre Royal, Drury Lane, August 1984.

Jack Lemmon in Eugene O'Neill's ***Long Day's Journey Into Night***, directed by Jonathan Miller, Theatre Royal, Haymarket, August 1986.

musical smash hits from *Cats* and *The Phantom of the Opera* to *Evita*, *Chess*, and *Les Miserables*. (*Me and My Girl*, the hit revival of Noël Gay's 1937 warhorse, is a decided exception; Howard Goodall's *The Hired Man*, also showed a rising new star on the way.)

On Broadway, musical output has lessened due to greater critical severity (many a London hit dies a quick death there) and much greater production costs ($4 million per musical, on average, and mounting). New York's shining musical light remains Stephen Sondheim, who began his career as the lyricist for *Gypsy* and *West Side Story*, and has gone on to write and compose a string of landmark shows, from *Follies* and *Company* through to *A Little Night Music* and *Sunday in the Park With George*. With the exception of his early collaborations, Sondheim's shows have never been long-running hits, and one wonders how long he can keep producing top-quality work for an ever-dwindling, minority-interest public.

MUSIC HALL/VARIETY

TRY THESE:
▷Trevor Griffiths' *Comedians* for would-be stand up comics and the aggressive use of comedy as a tool of social criticism; ▷Peter Nichols' *Privates on Parade* for a concert party; see also ▷cabaret.

Music hall and variety flourished in Britain for almost a hundred years, starting in the early to mid-nineteenth century in pubs and song and supper rooms, and gradually developing into vast Empires and Alhambras with twice-nightly programmes. The spectacular shows at the Coliseum in the early years of the century, with ballet, operatic numbers, horses, and many changes of scene are about as far from music hall's origins as one can get. The large halls gradually closed after World War I and the coming of cinema, but music halls and variety acts on radio, lingered on after World War II. Nostalgia lingers still, mostly because of the marvellous songs that were generated and the associated myth of a lively, subversive and essentially working-class culture. Some London pubs, such as The Pindar of Wakefield, still put on music hall evenings, most people can still sing many of the choruses and the Good Old Days continues relentlessly on television. The interesting and invigorating thing about current variety entertainment is that it is often alternative cabaret, with individual stand-up acts, comic or musical or both, which has the closest affinity to music hall. Variety still also flourishes in larger pubs and clubs throughout Britain.

London's Players' Theatre Club, under the Arches at Charing Cross (currently being rebuilt) still does something akin to the original music hall, though for a predominantly middle-class audience, and has been running since the 1930s. A normal evening at the Players' consists of a highly ritualised introductory dialogue between the audience and the chairman, about fifteen authentic music hall songs, delivered in costume by performers rather than singers, with the audience joining vigorously in the choruses, and another ritual chorus to close the proceedings. It is not a very accurate reproduction of a music hall at any period – it has the beer, but lacks the speciality acts and the sketches and (happily) the more awful songs. Its merits are that the singers always know their business, sometimes very well (for example, in the early days there was Robert Eddison's alter ego, the Honourable Maud Eddison and more recently Hattie Jacques singing 'She was Only a Bird in a Gilded Cage'), a receptive and vociferous audience, and above all the magnificent quality of the songs. It is somehow typical that the annual 'Players' Panto', although one of London's most enjoyable Christmas entertainments, is not in fact what the Victorians would have called a ▷ pantomime, but a Burlesque Extravaganza.

There are two other legacies from the music hall: one is its direct influence on plays, as in the use of authentic songs in *Oh What a Lovely War* to counterpoint the facts about the war, and the extended use of a second-rate music hall act in ▷ John Osborne's *The Entertainer* to make points about the state of Britain; and the use of techniques of cross-talk dialogue and comic monologue by playwrights such as ▷ Beckett and ▷ Pinter, with the accompanying bonus of Max Wall's great success in *Waiting for Godot* and *Krapp's Last Tape*. The other legacy stems from nostalgia and the glamour that has always been attached to the 'Idols of the Halls': various one-person shows and plays based on the acts and the lives of real music hall figures, such as Max Miller, Flanagan and Allen, and above all Marie Lloyd (the most recent being Steve Trafford's *Marie* at the Drill Hall in 1988, with Elizabeth Mansfield alternating the songs with narrative about her somewhat depressing life, and presenting her as a feminist and a union activist). The best of the plays so far is probably Alan Plater's *On Your Way, Riley!* (Theatre Royal, Stratford East, 1982), which neatly counterpoints the stage personae of Arthur Lucan and Kitty McShane with their Strindbergian marital battles, and includes the whole of their popular sketch *Bridget's Night Out*, in which Old Mother Riley smashes 250 plates. There will no doubt be more such plays – there were plenty of remarkable people on the halls.

NATIONAL THEATRE, THE

The idea of a national, state-supported theatre in Britain was floated for decades before it was actualised in the cement and concrete of its present form on the South Bank in London. It was David Garrick who first, in the eigthteenth century, publicly suggested a permanent state-supported theatre in London on the lines of the Comédie Française, and Bulwer-Lytton and Henry Irving were among the nineteenth-century champions of the cause. Harley ▷ Granville Barker and William Archer formulated definite plans for such a theatre in *The National Theatre: A Scheme and Estimates*, published in 1903, and a committee was set up to investigate the practical foundation of a national and subsidised theatre in 1908, with plans to celebrate the tercentenary of Shakespeare's birth in 1916 with the opening of a National Theatre building. Sixty years after that projected date the first theatre in the National's own building opened.

Sir Peter Hall, the artistic director who took the company into the South Bank, said: 'for 150 years, the radicals of the theatre have been fighting for a National Theatre: they have collected money for it, given up their careers for it, and spent their energies in a most prodigal and altruistic way for it'. In 1949, that fight came to some sort of fruition with the passing of a National Theatre Bill. The then Queen optimistically laid a foundation stone on the South Bank site in 1951. It was the third such ceremony; the second had been undertaken by ▷ Shaw, at a South Kensington site for a projected building designed by Lutyens, but which was never built. The final site for the theatre (although not the one where the Queen laid her foundation stone) was provided by the London County Council, forerunner to the late lamented GLC which contributed substantially to the theatre's subsidy until its demise. Work on a National Theatre building designed by Denys Lasdun and comprising three theatres, finally began under the Labour Minister for the Arts, Jennie Lee, in 1969, and the first theatre opened to the public in 1976.

Although the building and siting of a National Theatre took so long, a National Theatre Company had been in existence since 1963, transformed from the Old Vic company, under the auspices of Laurence Olivier and the Old Vic theatre was for many years the base for the National Theatre. The Old Vic company had been founded by Lilian Baylis, an enormously influential theatrical manager whose aim was to bring art and culture to the people, and who was instrumental in establishing national opera and ballet companies in Britain; without her there would have been no National Theatre. Her efforts are recorded at the National, in somewhat curmudgeonly fashion with a terrace being dubbed 'The Baylis terrace' in her honour.

The National Theatre is now made up of three theatres, a proscenium theatre, the Lyttleton (named after Lord Chandos, the National Theatre Board's first chair), the largest, the open stage Olivier (after Laurence Olivier), and the versatile workshop space, the Cottesloe (after the first Chair of the South Bank Theatre Board). The original plan was that the Lyttleton should concentrate on new writing, touring and retrospective seasons, the Olivier should continue the work of the Old Vic company and that the Cottesloe should be a space for new and experimental drama. In fact, the National is not at the moment the place to go for experimental work; government cutbacks and underfunding over the past ten years or so have meant that the National is no longer in a position to take many risks. There have been exceptions; Bill Bryden's tenure developed a 'promenading' style in the Cottesloe which produced several outstanding productions culminating in ▷ Tony Harrison's adaptations of the *The Mysteries*, a truly outstanding cycle of mystery plays that showed just what a national subsidised theatre could do. It has been followed up, to a lesser extent, by ▷ David Edgar's community-adapted play *Entertaining Strangers*. On the whole the National has, in these straitened years, tended to work with tried and tested actors, directors and texts, often picking up on the proven successes of fringe theatre.

Where they have scored is in the revival of neglected European classics by writers such as ▷ Schnitzler and ▷ von Horváth; and first-rate productions of some British and American classics: ▷ Thomas Otway's *Venice Preserv'd*, ▷ Kyd's *The Spanish Tragedy*, a glittering Philip Prowse production of ▷ Webster's *The Duchess of Malfi*, Harley Granville Barker's *Waste*. In the American sector ▷ Arthur Miller's *A View from the Bridge* had a towering performance from Michael Gambon and the Cottesloe was the scene of Bryden's very fine productions of ▷ David Mamet's (*Glengarry Glen Ross*), ▷ Mike Alfreds' adaptation of *The Cherry Orchard*, Hall's production of George Orwell's *Animal Farm*, ▷ Athol Fugard's *The Road to Mecca*, The Olivier, though proving a more challenging space than perhaps envisaged, has nonetheless produced its own share of memorable productions including the ▷ David Hare and ▷ Howard Brenton's *Pravda*, ▷ Ayckbourn's *Chorus of Disapproval*, ▷ Christopher Hampton's *Tales from Hollywood*, the Tony Harrison/Peter Hall *Oresteia*, ▷ Peter Shaffer's *Amadeus*, and Hall's *Antony and Cleopatra*. The Lyttleton too has had its share of thrills (though again, the auditorium is less hospitable than one might have hoped), a glorious revival of ▷ Kaufman and Hart's *You Can't Take It With You* and ▷ Michael Frayn's adaptation of ▷ Chekhov's *Wild Honey*.

The National, despite its financial strictures, also, under Thelma Holt's supervision, staged an international season in 1987 which brought a welcome whiff of adventure with visits from Peter Stein's Schaubühne company in a visually stunning version of ▷ O'Neill's *The Hairy Ape* (the scene changes took half an hour in themselves), Tokyo's Ninagawa Company with equally outstanding productions of *Medea* and *Macbeth* and the Russian Mayakovsky Theatre in the distinctly pro-individual *Tomorrow Was War*.

Peter Gill's studio wing in the annexe of the Old Vic also attempts to meet its experimental obligations with continuing workshops, encouragement of young writers and studio performances. Its last short season of new plays included plays from ▷ Daniel Mornin (*The Murderers*), ▷ Debbie Horsfield's final two plays of her football trilogy (*True Dare Kiss* and *Command or Promise*), Peter Cox's *The Garden of England*, Mick Mahoney's *Up For None*, plus first-timers Rod Smith, Rosemary Wilton and Alex Renton. Somewhat oddly, for a season of new writers, it also included Gill's adaptation of William Faulkner's *As I Lay Dying* and Gill's own *In The Blue*.

The National also present early evening Platform performances which enable a wide variety of events to be showcased – short plays, poetry readings etc – and one of the successes of Sir Peter Hall's regime has been to give the ungainly concrete building a sense of popular hubbub with pre-theatre music in the foyer, outdoor summer activities on the terraces, to add to a well-stocked bookshop, continual theatre exhibitions and all-day restaurant facilities. There is too an educational programme; study packs and workshops are available to go with some of the productions, and local schoolchildren were involved in the production of Adrian Mitchell's splendid adaptation of *The Pied Piper* in 1987.

Peter Hall, one of the founders of the Royal Shakespeare Company has been director of the National since he succeeded Olivier in 1972 (Hall's account of the trials and tribulations of the early years on the South Bank is to be found in his published diaries, edited by his Head of Publicity, John Goodwin). Under his policies, the National resolved themselves into several companies under different directorships eg the

McKellen/Petherbridge group, the ▷ Mike Alfreds group, the Michael Rudman group, etc. With his retirement as Artistic Director and the appointment of Richard Eyre (film and theatre director) along with that of producer David Aukin as Executive Director, the National is poised for yet further changes in its volatile history.

NEGRO ENSEMBLE COMPANY, THE

New York non-profit theatre

Started in April, 1967, by a trio comprising actor Robert Hooks, author/director Douglas Turner Ward and producer Gerald Krone, the Negro Ensemble Company (NEC) is America's premier non-profit theatre devoted to black drama. Ever since Ward's celebrated *New York Times* article in 1966 demanding the establishment of such a venue, the NEC has been responsible for developing an awareness of – and audience for – black drama without which such vast commercial successes as ▷ August Wilson's *Fences* might not have happened. Wilson has never been seen at the NEC, but most other leading black playwrights – whether American or otherwise – have, including ▷ Wole Soyinka (*Kongi's Harvest*), Lonne Elder III (*Ceremonies In Dark Old Men*), Leslie Lee (*The First Breeze of Summer*), Steve Carter (*Eden*, *Nevis Mountain Dew*) ▷ Trevor Rhone (*Two Can Play*), and ▷ Derek Walcott (*The Dream On Monkey Mountain*).

The NEC first visited London as part of the 1969 world theatre season at the Aldwych. In 1985, they took part in the American Festival with Samm-Art Williams' poetic *Home*, a gentle picaresque tale about a young black man's journey from his bucolic Southern 'home' to a grim Northern city. In 1984, their production of *A Soldier's Play* came to the ▷ Edinburgh Festival, broadening exposure for Charles Fuller's Pulitzer Prize-winning drama which became an Oscar-nominated film (*A Soldier's Story*). Operating out of the 299-seat Theatre Four off-Broadway, the NEC has faced the struggle for financial survival that all non-profit theatres confront, and the two-year run of *A Soldier's Play* offered a needed financial boon to a venue that is an integral part of the New York theatre.

TRY THESE:
▷August Wilson and ▷James Baldwin as American black dramatists who found success outside of the NEC; see also ▷American Theatres for general discussion of the non-profit scene; ▷Steppenwolf and ▷Wisdom Bridge for other important venues, both in Chicago; see also ▷Black Theatre for British counterparts.

NELSON, Richard [1950–]

American dramatist

Plays include:

***The Killing of Yablonski* (1975), *Conjuring An Event* (1976), *Jungle Coup* (1978), *The Vinna Notes* (1978), *Bal* (1979), *Rip Van Winkle or The Works* (1981), *The Return of Pinocchio* (1983), *An American Comedy* (1983), *Between East and West* (1984), *Principia Scriptoriae* (1986); commissioned to write the book for the musical *Chess* (1988)**

Chicago-born Nelson is one of the few American playwrights to address political issues in a manner taken for granted in Britain; indeed, he says his interest in 'primarily social' themes 'can be lonely' for an American writer. His additional experience as a translator and adapter allies him more to men like ▷ Michael Frayn and ▷ Trevor Griffiths than to such American peers as ▷ Albert Innaurato, ▷ Christopher Durang, and the rest of the Playwrights' Horizons New York school of intensely domestic drama. The frequent recipient of foundation awards and grants, Nelson writes both large, sweeping works (his near four-hour *Rip*

TRY THESE:
▷Clifford Odets and ▷Arthur Miller are earlier writers with an overt social conscience; ▷David Hare's *A Map of the World*, Donald Freed's *The Quartered Man*, and ▷Dusty Hughes' *Jenkins' Ear* for contrasting treatments of contemporary *realpolitik;* ▷Manuel Puig's *Kiss of the Spider Woman*, ▷Trevor Griffiths' *The Party*, ▷David Hare's *Fanshen*, ▷Harold Pinter's *One for the Road* and ▷Samuel Beckett's *Catastrophe*

Van Winkle plays like a parody of *Faust* crossed with *Peer Gynt*) and more focused two-character dramas such as *Between East and West*, (a two-hander about a Czech director and his wife experiencing culture shock in New York), and he frequently makes use of titles above his scenes for ironic or distancing effect. His embrace of private and public concerns no doubt prompted the producers of *Chess* to call on him when they needed someone to revise their troubled musical's book, but how Nelson will fare amidst the shark-like climate of Broadway – an environment he has so far eschewed – remains to be seen.

are just some of the contemporary treatments of similar themes.

Principia Scriptoriae
An ambitious if flawed work set in an unnamed Latin American country, the play starts in 1970 under a right-wing government, moving to 1985 under a new leftist regime. Enmeshed in the political shift are two writers who find themselves on opposite sides of the ideological fence: the Cambridge-educated Ernesto, a Latin American dissenter who returns in the second act as the secretary to the Minister of Culture, and Bill, a middle-class American midwesterner who believes that 'you can't ever stop asking yourself questions'. Nelson's play ultimately poses more questions than it answers, but it's refreshing to see a writer reaching beyond his nation's boundaries in an attempt to consider how other nations breathe, speak, and think.

NESTROY, Johann Nepomuk [1801–62]
Austrian actor, singer and dramatist

Plays include:
 ***Einen Jux will er sich machen* (*He's Out for a Fling*; 1842)**

Nestroy's range of talents was even wider than ▷ Molière's (his first professional appearance was as Sarastro in *The Magic Flute*) and his seventy-seven surviving plays (most of them satirical comedies) still hold the stage in Vienna, but little of his work has so far been translated into English. However, *Einen Jux will er sich machen* (itself based on two English farces) forms the basis both of ▷ Thornton Wilder's successive versions, *The Merchant of Yonkers* (1938) and *The Matchmaker* (1954) (musicalised as *Hello, Dolly!*, 1963), and of ▷ Stoppard's *On the Razzle* (▷ National Theatre, 1981). Stoppard dealt with the problem of translating the rich Viennese dialect by ignoring it altogether, omitting sub-plot, comic songs, and local references, and letting his own line in outrageous wordplay enliven a good basic farce plot about two shop assistants having a stolen day out on the town (Vienna, of course).

TRY THESE:
▷Horvath, for adding a political element to Nestroy's folk play tradition; ▷Labiche's *La Cagnotte* for the theme of country folk having a day out on the town (Paris, of course).

NEW PLAYWRITING

A constant turn-over of new playwrights is the life-blood of good theatre. Playwrights who end up as household names on television frequently start off plugging their wares round the fringe, pub and small touring companies.

New plays are always a financial risk; larger companies like the ▷ RSC and the ▷ National Theatre perhaps have more to lose in their large auditoria than a small venue on the fringe circuit with a new writer. On the other hand, they also have more funds at their disposal. It's a constant juggling act. On the whole, however, new writing still tends to test its muscles and make its mistakes on the fringe or occasionally on the regional circuit (Sheffield Crucible, Leicester Haymarket, Nottingham Playhouse, Bristol Old Vic, Edinburgh Traverse). Small-scale touring companies such as ▷ Paines Plough, ▷ Joint Stock, ▷ Red Shift, Bristol Express, ▷ Foco Novo, ▷ Women's Theatre Group, ▷ Monstrous Regiment, Siren, ▷ Theatre of Black Women have also shouldered much of the responsibility for new writing, (in the past, companies like ▷ 7:84, Red Ladder also consistently aired new work). Certain London fringe theatres too have fine records for seeking out and championing new writing, such as the Soho Poly, the Bush, the Half Moon, Old Red Lion, the Tricycle, Hampstead Theatre, Oval House, Drill Hall, Riverside, the Orange Tree at Richmond. But pre-eminently, the Royal Court has been at the forefront of new writing for well over thirty years (see ▷ English Stage Company). Some of the most innovative use of texts have also emerged through the multi-media performance art companies such as Hilary Westlake and Lumiere and Son, Blood Group, Burnt Bridges, Impact Theatre Co-operative, Intimate Strangers, and one of the newest groups, the Nottingham-based Dogs in Honey. Individual companies spring up constantly to produce individual plays but as project funding becomes the norm, disappear as quickly, returning us to the situation in the 1960s and 1970s where new writing was reliant on individual entrepreneurial producers such as Michael White and Michael Codron (who introduced ▷ Pinter, ▷ Beckett and ▷ Stoppard to West End audiences), and Oscar Lewenstein at the Royal Court (taking up the mantle left by George Devine). In the 1970s, Ian Albery was one of the few theatre managers to inject a little experimentation into the West End with transfers of ▷ Dario Fo's *Accidental Death of an Anarchist* and *Can't Pay Won't Pay* by the fringe company, Belt and Braces.

These days, at one end of the spectrum, new writers may emerge through ▷ RSC commissions (like ▷ Nick Darke, ▷ Nick Dear, and Nick Ward). ▷ Pam Gems, ▷ Caryl Churchill, ▷ Louise Page, ▷ Timberlake Wertenbaker and newcomer Heidi Thomas are also amongst the few women who have been sought out. On the whole, the major companies do not have as good a record as they might in encouraging new writing across the social spectrum, though there have been a number of new plays commissioned at the ▷ National Theatre from such established names as ▷ Tom Stoppard, ▷ Christopher Hampton, ▷ Alan Ayckbourn, ▷ David Hare and ▷ Howard Brenton. However, new young writers from the Asian and West Indian communities (or the Irish or gay community for that matter – ▷ Sarah Daniels' *Neaptide* being a notable exception) have not generally found their way onto the ▷ National's stages, leading, not surprisingly, to cries of cultural apartheid. For the past few years, the ▷ National has run a studio wing under director Peter Gill which serves as a forum for new writing. In addition, there are several playwriting schemes that have sprung up since 1982 to encourage new writing, particularly amongst young women and young black writers.

At the other end of the spectrum many more new writers come up through such schemes as the Soho Poly's Verity Bargate award, the Royal Court's Young Playwright Scheme (▷ Andrea Dunbar, ▷ Ayshe Raif and the founders of the ▷ Theatre of Black Women, Bernadine Evaristo and Patricia Hilaire are just a few to have started their careers through this scheme), the Albany's Second Wave festival of new writing for young women (which has already produced a writer of promise in ▷ April de Angelis) or the Manchester Royal Exchange's Mobil Playwriting competition.

In 1987, the Bristol Express touring company were responsible for an impressively inaugurative development and research scheme, 'The Play's the Thing', which organised staged workshops and readings over a period of several weeks; the ▷ Red Shift theatre company, in conjunction with *City Limits* magazine ran a New Expressionism season in which plays encouraging a strong visual element were sought. The Playwright's Co-operative and New Playwrights Trust have also held enterprisingly ambitious staged readings and workshops specifically to encourage new writing.

Such initiatives could well be the trend for the future. Declining support for subsidy means new writing faces a precarious future. Untried new writing is less attractive to sponsors than tried and tested classics. In 1988, some of the smaller touring companies such as those mentioned who specialise in new writing have received sizeable cuts in their grants for 1988–89. The result may well mean not only fewer new playwrights emerging but also a qualitative change in the kind of plays produced with more encouragement of the status quo and less anti-establishment criticism.

NICHOLS, Peter [1927–]
British dramatist

Plays include:
***A Day in the Death of Joe Egg* (1967), *The National Health* (1969), *Forget-Me-Not-Lane* (1971), *Chez Nous* (1974), *The Freeway* (1974), *Harding's Luck* (1974), *Privates on Parade* (1977), *Born in the Gardens* (1979), *Passion Play* (1981), *Poppy* (1982), *A Piece of My Mind* (1986)**

Television includes:
***Ben Spray* (1961), *The Reception* (1961), *Continuity Man* (1963), *The Heart of the Country* (1963), *When the Wind Blows* (1964), *Daddy Kiss it Better* (1968), *Hearts and Flowers* (1971), *The Common* (1973), *The Atkinsons* (serial; 1978), *Funny Ideals* (1983)**

Nichols was born in Bristol, trained as an actor with the Bristol Old Vic and worked there until he was called up to National Service in the RAF and went to India and Malaya, a crucial experience for *Privates on Parade* which is set in a song and dance unit in Malaya. During National Service Nichols became involved in camp concert parties, which included Kenneth Williams and Stanley Baxter. His first stage play was the autobiographically based *A Day in the Death of Joe Egg*, which was produced by the Glasgow Citizens' Theatre, directed by Michael Blakemore. Nichols writes very unsettling comedies, even the tragic subject of *A Day in the Death of Joe Egg* is handled with a bitter wit and he has taken a delight in experimenting with popular forms, often using an improbable form to make a satirical point. *The National Health* deals with a hospital ward full of patients who are in pain or dying, and puts them together with a hospital romance *Privates on Parade* uses the form of the revue show to explore army life and the British presence in Malaya. *Poppy* uses ▷ pantomime and ▷ music hall to chart the British involvement in the Chinese Opium Wars, and has a wonderful alienation effect, the pantomime horse gets shot. *Poppy* also employs a pantomime sing song, in which a character uses all the pantomime devices to encourage the audience to sing along, only to confront them with the awareness of the racist and imperialistic implications of what they are singing.

His most recent play *A Piece of My Mind* was a bitter comedy about his own difficulties with writing, and his resentment that his challenging and uncomfortable comedy was not more successful. Unsurprisingly it was badly reviewed, but contains some bravura writing and effects. According to Nichols: 'To make an audience cry or laugh is easy –they want to. . .this is only worth doing if one thereby catches a whiff of life, a true tang of the bitter mixture we all have to drink.'

A Day in the Death of Joe Egg
A Day in the Death of Joe Egg was Nichols' first stage play, and still the play with which he is most associated. It is openly autobiographical, drawn from the experience of his own disabled daughter. The play employs bitterly funny backchat between the father and mother, and brings in jazz and tap dance, in its exploration of the strains on a relationship of living with what the father, Bri, calls a 'human parsnip'. The name Joe Egg comes from a children's rhyme 'Joe Egg's a fool, he tied his stocking to a stool. . .' Most theatrical managements shied off producing such a subject, but one critic has said: 'there was a sudden rush of approval as a new barrier of inhibition was swept away'.

TRY THESE:
▷Harold Pinter and ▷John Osborne also trained and worked as actors before becoming playwrights; ▷Alan Bennett, ▷Arnold Wesker and ▷John McGrath are among the (male) playwrights for whom National Service was a significant experience; ▷Tom Stoppard appears thinly disguised as Miles Whittier (a pun!) in *A Piece of My Mind*; ▷Graeae has affinities with Nichols in their ability to laugh at their own disabilities ▷Joe Orton shares Nichols' sense of the macabre in humour.

NORMAN, Marsha [1947–]
American dramatist

TRY THESE:
▷Tennessee Williams'

NORMAN, MARSHA

Plays include:

***Getting Out* (1977), *Third and Oak* (also known as *Circus Valentine*; 1978), *Laundromat* (1979), *'Night Mother* (1982), *The Holdup* (1983), *Traveller In the Dark* (1984), *The Shakers* (1988)**

The Kentucky-born daughter of an estate agent, Marsha Norman has made a deservedly strong reputation on the basis of two widely-acclaimed plays – *Getting Out*, her debut play commissioned for the Actor's Theatre of Louisville, and *'Night Mother*, which became a film co-starring Sissy Spacek and Anne Bancroft. The former is a terse and aggressive account of a woman's re-assimilation into society after an eight-year prison term, with two women representing the central character at different phases of her life; the incarcerated, wilder Arlie and her liberated, yet domesticated, Arlene. *'Night Mother*, which won the 1983 Pulitzer Prize and was seen at Hampstead in 1985, ruthlessly up-ends the American family-in-crisis play in its spare, merciless portrait of the suicidal Jessie Cates and her panic-stricken mother, Thelma. In telling its story to the on-stage ticking of six clocks, *'Night Mother* is also that unusual play where stage time equals real time.

The Glass Menagerie, Paul Zindel's *The Effect of Gamma Rays. . .*, ▷Louise Page's *Real Estate* as some of the many plays showing mothers and daughters locked in terminal combat; Greek tragedy (particularly *Medea*) and ▷Ibsen's *Hedda Gabler* for dramas with an inexorable pull towards an event we cannot imagine happening that nonetheless shatters us when it does; ▷Thomas Babe, ▷Wallace Shawn for the willed aggression of the writing; ▷David Mamet for a comparable sense of the weight of silence, and the use of real time, also in ▷Lanford Wilson's *Talley's Folly*; see ▷*Clean Break* for treatments of women in prison.

O'BRIEN, Richard

Australian actor, composer, lyricist, director and dramatist

Plays include:

***The Rocky Horror Show* (1973), *Top People* (1984)**

Richard O'Brien was responsible for one of the great cult successes of the 1970s and one of the great cult failures of the 1980s. *The Rocky Horror Show*, a camp combination of transvestism, the Frankenstein story and music, began at the Royal Court Theatre Upstairs and has now achieved a kind of independent existence of its own, virtually impervious to criticism, as much a cultural monument in its own way as ▷ Agatha Christie's *The Mousetrap*. Its initial success owed much to the energy and commitment of its first cast who included Tim Curry, Julie Covington and O'Brien himself but it has now become equally its audience's property with people regularly dressing up as their favourite characters, joining in the songs and dialogue, throwing confetti at the wedding and so on. There are, particularly in the USA, conventions and fan clubs and the whole camp cult has become a phenomenon that transcends the bounds of theatre or of cinema (the film version, made in 1975 with many of the original cast, has much the same effect as the stage version). *Top People* was an unmitigated disaster that deservedly lasted less than a week in London.

TRY THESE:

For aspects of camp see ▷Joe Orton the deliciously outrageous Bloolips and the superb American drag/performance artist, Ethyl Eichelberger; for contrast see Tilda Swinton's trans-sexual male in the socialist-surreal *Man to Man* by East German Manfred Karge; for Frankenstein variations, see ▷April De Angelis' *Breathless*, ▷Graeae; the physicality and energy of *The Rocky Horror Show* can also be found in the work of ▷Steven Berkoff, ▷performance art and some ▷cabaret artists.

O'CASEY, Sean [1880–1964]

Irish dramatist

Plays include:

***The Shadow of a Gunman* (1923), *Juno and the Paycock* (1924), *The Plough and the Stars* (1926), *The Silver Tassie* (1928), *Within the Gates* (1933), *The Star Turns Red* (1940), *Purple Dust* (1940), *Red Roses for Me* (1942), *Cock-a-Doodle Dandy* (1949), *The Bishop's Bonfire* (1955), *The Drums of Father Ned* (1960)**

One of the great dramatists of the twentieth century, O'Casey is best remembered in Britain for the early Dublin plays but his later exuberant, equally politically conscious, tragi-comic epics deserve as wide an audience as the so-called Dublin Trilogy (*The Shadow of a Gunman*, *Juno and the Paycock*, *The Plough and the Stars*). O'Casey, largely self taught, and politically active, was initially fostered by the Abbey Theatre but ▷ Yeats' rejection of *The Silver Tassie*, which now seems astonishingly misguided, led to O'Casey's departure from Ireland and a career marked by further controversy and misunderstanding. *The Silver Tassie* is an anti-war play which extends O'Casey's dramaturgy into a highly stylized quasi-liturgical second act; the mixture of styles suggests the difference between the normal world and the world of the war. O'Casey's socialism, his hatred of priestly influence in

TRY THESE:

O'Casey declared that he was influenced by ▷Shakespeare and ▷Boucicault; ▷Joe Corrie and ▷Brecht's theatre have much in common with O'Casey's; Frank McGuinness' *Observe the Sons of Ulster Marching Towards the Somme* is another play that deals with the Irish and World War I; ▷Brendan Behan had much of the energy, if less of the discipline, of O'Casey; ▷Sherriff's *Journey's End*, ▷Willis Hall's *The Long and the Short and the Tall* and Theatre Workshop's *Oh What*

Ireland and his ceaseless experimentation with form all contributed to his relative eclipse in the professional theatre and it is surprising that, in an era more receptive to large-scale non-linear political work, some of the later plays have yet to be given productions by the ▷ RSC or the ▷ National Theatre. *Cock-a-Doodle Dandy* in particular deserves a wider audience, with its life-size dionysiac Cock struggling against the forces of repression in the form of capitalism and the church which attempt to quell the human spirit. Not that the earlier plays have outlived their welcome: O'Casey's presentation of the heady contradictions of the struggle for Irish independence is still horribly relevant to the present, not only in terms of an understanding of the intractability of that situation, but also in more general terms of an analysis of the sheer messiness and mixture of impulses and dynamics in any political situation.

Juno and the Paycock
A brilliant mixture of the comic and tragic which takes in the abduction and murder of Juno's son (Johnny) who has informed on a Diehard colleague, her unmarried daughter Mary's pregnancy and attitudes to it, the posturings of her feckless husband (the Paycock of the title), the apparent rise in the social status of the family as the result of a supposed inheritance, and its collapse when the will turns out to have been badly drafted. There are major issues here about the poisoned inheritance of Ireland, the importance of received attitudes in determining people's responses to both political and personal issues, the role of women in both sustaining and fracturing male vanities; but they emerge for use in truly epic style as we are faced with a necessity for practising complex seeing and thinking above the flow of the action as well as with it. The final scene, with the room stripped of furniture, Juno and Mary departed to Juno's sister's, Johnny dead, and the drunk and oblivious Paycock telling his pal Joxer that the whole world is 'in a terr. . .ible state o'. . .chassis', is a fine example of O'Casey's ability to present contradictions simultaneously and in memorable theatrical form.

The Plough and the Stars
Set during the Easter Rising of 1916, *The Plough and the Stars* is more directly concerned with great political events than *Juno and the Paycock*, but the focus is still largely on ordinary people and their reactions to events; although some of Padraic Pearse's speeches are spoken by the Voice in Act Two, he is not identified by name. Again we have a tenement setting, an assortment of representative characters and the mixture of the comic and the tragic, but here the mood is darker and the dispossession of the Irish is clearer. The play ends in another fine dramatisation of contradiction, with Dublin burning as two English soldiers sit drinking tea and singing 'Keep the Home Fires Burning' in the room from which the Irish inhabitants have been expelled; the hope embodied in the women and the pregnancy in *Juno* has been snuffed out in this play by death and by madness, and the men are generally as ineffectual as before.

a Lovely War offer different accounts of war; ▷Howard Brenton and ▷David Edgar have something of the same energy and willingness to experiment in order to make political points; of the many writers now writing about Northern Ireland, ▷Ann Devlin's *Ourselves Alone*, ▷Seamus Finnegan's *North*, and ▷Charabanc's *Gold in the Streets* attempt to show the intractable contradictions of the situation in all their socio-politico-religious complexity.

ODETS, Clifford [1906–63]
American dramatist

Plays include:
Awake and Sing (1935), _Waiting For Lefty_ (1935), _Till the Day I Die_ (1935), _Paradise Lost_ (1935), _Golden Boy_ (1937), _Rocket to the Moon_ (1938), _Night Music_ (1940), _Clash By Night_ (1941), _The Big Knife_ (1949), _The Country Girl_ (1950), _The Flowering Peach_ (1954), _The Silent Partner_ (written in 1937; produced posthumously in 1972)

Films include:
adaptations of _Golden Boy_ (1939), _The Country Girl_ (1954; for which Grace Kelly won an Oscar, and _The Big Knife_ (1955); other scripts include _None But the Lonely Heart_ (1944) and _Deadline At Dawn_ (1946)

'I would say that I have shown as much of the seamy side of life as any other playwright of the twentieth century, if not more', the Philadelphia-born Odets once commented. And as a chronicler

TRY THESE:
The early plays of ▷Eugene O'Neill (especially *The Hairy Ape*) and Marc Blitzstein's folk opera *The Cradle Will Rock* for both subject matter and experimental form; ▷Beckett's *Waiting for Godot*, ▷David Mercer's *After Haggerty* for other plays where the title character never appears ▷David Rabe's *Hurlyburly* for later, equally bitter writing about Hollywood; ▷Arthur

of moral malaise, Odets is hard to beat, even when his chosen milieus (as in the Beverley Hills playroom of *The Big Knife*) deceptively evoke a ▷ Noël Coward comedy, not a scabrous indictment of the 'noisy, grabbing world' of Hollywood. Odets was the star dramatist of the Group Theatre – Harold Clurman, Cheryl Crawford and Lee Strasberg's 1931–41 New York enterprise that grew out of the Theatre Guild – and his keystone early plays *Waiting For Lefty* and *Awake and Sing* were both premiered there. Although his plays can seem melodramaic and ponderous, at their best, their moral vigour is stirring, and they provide notable acting opportunities, particularly of a dry, hard-boiled sort. *Golden Boy*, a play about a violinist-turned-boxer that makes genuine individuals out of archetypes was memorably revived at the ▷ National Theatre in 1984 by director Bill Bryden, with American actress Lisa Eichhorn as Lorna and Jack Shepherd in top form as the manager, Fuseli. Generally British interest in Odets is due to Robin LeFevre, who staged variable revivals of *Rocket to the Moon*, *The Country Girl*, and *The Big Knife* in 1982, 1983, and 1987, respectively.

Waiting For Lefty

A taxi union votes to go on strike in Odet's landmark 1935 drama, as important for its radical Socialist form as for its message. Produced by the Group Theatre and directed by its co-founder, Harold Clurman, the staging planted actual cabbies in the audience, which gave a charge to the final rallying cry, 'Strike!' The Lefty of the title, one of the union leaders, never arrives, but Odets uses the drivers and their families to launch an assault on capitalism in the kind of denunciation of avarice that few American playwrights have fielded since. The play is didactic agit-prop, to be sure, but also testimony to an era in American playwriting when plays were seen to make a difference – not marginalised, escapist 'entertainments' as they are all too often viewed now, despite genuine inheritors of Odets' vision like Arthur Miller and ▷ David Mamet.

Miller and ▷David Mamet for comparable emphases on the playwright as conscience.

O'MALLEY, Mary [1941–]

British dramatist

Plays include:

***Superscum* (1972), *A 'Nevolent Society* (1974), *Oh If Ever a Man Suffered* (1975), *Once a Catholic* (1977), *Look Out. . .Here Comes Trouble* (1978), *Talk of the Devil* (1986)**

Television includes:

***Percy & Kenneth* (1973), *Shall I See You Now* (1974), *Oy Vey Maria* (1976), *On the Shelf* (1984)**

London born chronicler of north London and the London Irish, O'Malley's satire on convent eduction, *Once a Catholic*, was the play that took 1977 by storm. It had, in fact, taken five years since she first saw an article in *The Stage* about a school-chum who was writing plays for the ▷ RSC and she felt she could do as well. *Superscum*, about a man living well on social security, *A 'Nevolent Society*, about three Jewish boys in Stoke Newington and *If Ever a Man Suffered*, about incest in an Irish family in Cricklewood all followed quickly. But the big break came with *Once a Catholic*, originally sponsored by the Royal Court for the Thames Television Playwright Scheme which O'Malley won – the first woman to do so – and which brought her a year's writer-in-residency at the Court. Semi-autobiographical and set in a north London convent school, our Lady of Fatima, her hysterically funny dig at Catholicism, damnation and the sexual stirrings of adolescent girls won her both the *Evening Standard* and *Plays & Players* awards as 'most promising playwright'. Cathartically, *Once a Catholic* seems to have been one way of O'Malley releasing herself from the oppression of school life which felt 'like a big black cloud hanging overhead' and where she was told, 'Mary O'Malley, you'll never be any good' (she was told to leave school at sixteen because she was always playing truant). 'Really it was an epitaph to the Irish living in England as I remember them in my youth and Catholicism as taught before the 2nd Vatican Council.' She continued in the same vein, to some extent in *Talk of the Devil*, a family saga with Ortonesque echoes with its

TRY THESE:
For scenes from school life, see Denise Deegan's Angela Brazil spoof *Daisy Pulls It Off*, Muriel Spark's classic Presbyterian variation *The Prime of Miss Jean Brodie*; for adolescent female yearnings, see ▷Sharman Macdonald and ▷Wedekind's *Spring Awakening*; for a male Irish view, see ▷Hugh Leonard's adaptation of James Joyce's *Portrait of the Artist as a Young Man* or *Stephen Dedalus*; for an English view, see ▷Alan Bennett's *Forty Years On* and John Dighton's *The Happiest Days of Our Lives*; for a complete contrast, black American Adrienne Kennedy's *A Lesson in Dead Language* which uses visual imagery bordering on the grotesque to make its point about the education of young women;

mixture of sex, religion and death (including visitations from an imaginary Devil got up in black leather). Her early experiences too as a young wife and mother, married to a Jew, and contemplating Judaic conversion also ended up as a comedy *Oy Vey Maria* in the BBC's Play for Today slot. *Once a Catholic*, with its emblematic Marys (all the girls are called Mary) however remains her pièce de résistance – a rare and hilarious female expression of adolescent retaliation against Catholic dogma and the authoritarianism and hypocrisy of school which should be compulsory viewing for every generation.

▷Nigel Williams' *Class Enemy* is a contemporary version of waste of potential in schools.

O'NEILL, Eugene [1888–1953]

American dramatist

Plays include:

***Beyond the Horizon* (1920), *The Emperor Jones* (1920), *Anna Christie* (1921), *The Hairy Ape* (1922), *Welded* (1924), *All God's Chillun Got Wings* (1924), *Desire Under the Elms* (1924), *The Great God Brown* (1926), *Marco Millions* (1928), *Strange Interlude* (1928), *Lazarus Laughed* (1928), *Mourning Becomes Electra* (1931), *Ah Wilderness* (1933), *More Stately Mansions* (1938), *The Iceman Cometh* (1939; performed 1946), *Long Day's Journey Into Night* (1940; performed 1956), *A Touch of the Poet* (1940), *A Moon For the Misbegotten* (1943)**

One of the two or three premiere American playwrights of this century, Eugene O'Neill was born in New York the son of the actor, James O'Neill. His own tortured and often sorrowful upbringing prompted several of the greatest family dramas ever written – works that take a scalpel to the blood ties that bind, finding the inextricable link between pain and passion whereby affections hover forever precariously over the abyss. Greatly influenced by the Greeks (his *Mourning Becomes Electra* is a New England reworking of *The Oresteia*), his plays can seem cumbersome and pedantic, and his aspirations occasionally exceed his achievement. Recently, however, European and British directors have taken a stylised approach to the works – Keith Hack with his staging of *Strange Interlude*, David Leveaux with *A Moon For the Misbegotten*, Germany's Peter Stein with *The Hairy Ape*, Patrick Mason with *Desire Under the Elms* – finding the poetry in what might have been pompous. The plays themselves avoid easy classification, whether tending towards the modernist (*Strange Interlude*, with its Faulknerian stream-of-consciousness) or the opaque (*The Great God Brown*), the surprisingly comic (*Ah Wilderness*) or the ineffably sad (*Long Day's Journey. . .*). A four-time recipient of the Pulitzer Prize, O'Neill also became, in 1936, the first American to win the Nobel Prize.

TRY THESE:
▷Shakespeare (especially *King Lear*), ▷Ibsen (especially *Ghosts*) for distilled family tragedies; E.A. Whitehead's *Alpha Beta*, ▷Edward Albee's *Who's Afraid of Virginia Woolf?* for more recent domestic plays which have a cathartic effect; ▷Athol Fugard for a portrait of the artist-as-a-young-man (*'Master Harold'. . .and the Boys*); ▷Tennessee Williams' *Cat on a Hot Tin Roof*, and ▷Lillian Hellman's *Little Foxes* for probing treatments of 'mendacity'; ▷Gorki's *The Lower Depths* for earlier images of barflies; ▷Ibsen's *The Wild Duck* for another treatment of the saving lie.

The Iceman Cometh

Written in 1939 but not performed until seven years later, the play remains associated with its 1956 off-Broadway revival, which made the reputations of star Jason Robards and director Jose Quintero. (The two re-teamed in 1985 for a commercially unsuccessful Broadway staging.) *The Iceman Cometh* shows O'Neill at both his most ponderous and his most profound, as his lumbering symbolism and sometimes archaic language (the Biblical 'cometh' of the title) yield before the cumulative majesty of a text which does not let the audience out of its grip until both they and the characters have been brought up short by the death of their collective illusions. Set in Harry Hope's saloon in 1912, the play is a devastating evening of pipe dreams gone sour, with Hickey as the Virgil of the occasion leading us through this barroom Inferno. With a large cast (nineteen) and a long running-time (about five hours), the play has both marvellous vignettes and rending monologues, and it highlights the emphasis on personal truth-telling that would obsess O'Neill through all his late plays.

Long Day's Journey Into Night

O'Neill's patterning of family pathology – a lifelong interest spanning the Oedipal tensions of *Desire Under the Elms* and the father/daughter relationship of *A Touch of the Poet* – reaches its most lacerating pitch in this play written 'in blood and tears', but not performed until 1956, three years after the author's death.

Tilda Swinton as Max Gericke in the Traverse Theatre's production of Manfred Karge's ***Man To Man***, translated by Anthony Vivis, directed by Stephen Unwin: Traverse Theatre, July 1987; Royal Court, January 1988.

The most directly autobiographical of O'Neill's plays, it plunges directly to the heart of familial darkness in its account of a single day amongst the tormented Tyrone clan: the Irish-born father James, the miserly paterfamilias feeding on his memories as a stereotyped matinee idol; his morphine-addicted wife Mary; and their two sons, the ruthlessly honest drinker Jamie and his younger brother Edmund, O'Neill's unsparing vision of himself as a young, tubercular artist. The roles are as challenging as any in the English-language theatre, and actors as diverse as Laurence Olivier, Robert Ryan, and Jack Lemmon have taken on the part of the father, while Florence Eldridge and Constance Cummings were two notable Marys.

ONE PERSON SHOWS

It may be no coincidence that the period of cuts in arts funding has also seen a proliferation of one person shows: the cheapest possible form of a company. The Perrier fringe awards of the last few years at the ▷ Edinburgh Festival have been dominated by one person shows (stand-up comics like Arnold Brown, Hattie Hayridge, Jeremy Hardy and John Hegley).

The only definition of a one person show is that it should, indeed contain only one person; within that format there is a huge range of possibilities. One person shows have been used to present a biographical study of a single individual: Alexandra Kollontai (devised and performed by Barbara Ewing), Queen Victoria, Kafka and Frances de la Tour's memorable evocation of Lillian Hellman in *Lillian* written by American William Luce. Emlyn Williams performed readings of Dickens, and also devised a biographical show about him, Michael Pennington has done the same for ▷ Chekhov and Eileen Pollock has toured *Fight Like Tigers*, an energetic rip-roaring portrait of the American trade unionist, Mother Jones.

Jack Klaff has employed the one man show to present an indictment of South Africa in *Nagging Doubt* in which he played a range of characters, as did Cordelia Ditton whose thirty-five-character tour de force in *About Face* (compiled with Maggie Ford) about the 1984 Miners' Strike included playing a police horse, a jazz band and a super pit as well as housewives and Ian McGregor.

The one person show can also be a form in which to present a particular text; Alec McCowen has performed *St Mark's Gospel*, Kerry Shale acted the entire novel of John Kennedy Toole's *A Confederacy of Dunces* in which he played all fifteen characters; and John Sessions offered *Napoleon* in voices which ranged from Angie and Den of *East Enders* to Sir Laurence Olivier.

Simon Callow has devised a performance of ▷ Shakespeare's sonnets as a ▷ National Theatre Platform Performance; and in a tightly structured performance which appeared to be an informal conversation with the audience, Ian McKellen's *Acting Shakespeare* toured with the British Council and across the USA offering an insight into the making of the actor and his own approach to Shakespearean verse.

Many women performers have recently used the monologue which has ranged from play form, such as Frances McNeil's effective and poignant study of a young northern woman's emancipation through becoming a Muslim, *Jehad*, unspecifiable categories, such as ▷ Rose English's amalgam of ▷ music hall patter and philosophical exploration, and Janice Perry's musical mimicry and dramatic sketches.

▷ Samuel Beckett and ▷ Alan Bennett, in very different ways, are also master exponents of the monologue (funnily enough, many of them for women, and Bennett's owing a good deal to Joyce Grenfell). Dramatic monologues have also been used very successfully by such writers as ▷ Barry Collins whose *Judgement* remains a harrowing tour de force by any standards; ▷ Alan Drury (*The Man Himself*), ▷ Franca Rame (*The Mother, Female Parts*), ▷ Berta Freistadt (*Woman with a*

TRY THESE:
▷Beckett for more on monologues; ▷cabaret for more on one-person performers; ▷Robyn Archer for one-woman shows; see Theatre of Black Women for more on *The Cripple*.

Shovel), Ruth Harris (*The Cripple*) are others who have all used the monologue to great effect.

Maurice Chevalier was a huge hit in London with his one man shows, and Ruth Draper became an important name in the 1930s and 1940s with her one woman shows. So too the irreplaceable Joyce Grenfell whose comic sketches, like Ruth Draper's, tread a fine line between comedy/mimicry/impersonation and the stand-up comic routine. Victoria Wood is the contemporary equivalent. Harry Enfield's Stavros and Loadsamoney have become one person performances from their origins as sketches and, of course, much of the 'alternative comedy' circuit rests on the single stand-up comic phenomenon.

Which leads up finally to housewife superstar, Dame Edna Everage, the ultimate one person show holding court at Drury Lane, London's largest theatre, cajoling an entire audience to wave their 'gladdies' and rising to the ceiling on a fork lift truck in the ultimate apotheosis of self-aggrandisement.

ORTON, Joe [1933–67]

British dramatist

Plays include:

***The Ruffian on the Stair* (broadcast 1964; staged 1966), *Entertaining Mr Sloane* (1964), *Loot* (1965), *The Erpingham Camp* (televised 1966; staged 1967), *The Good and Faithful Servant* (televised 1967; staged 1971), *Funeral Games* (televised 1968; staged 1970), *What the Butler Saw* (1969)**

Orton shocked delighted audiences by offering taboo subjects discussed in dialogue of the greatest propriety by characters moving through plots of sometimes Byzantine contrivance. He claimed to draw incident and dialogue straight from life, making full use of the phraseology and platitudes of official jargon, the contrived headlines of the tabloid press and the euphemisms of pretentious respectability. His characters adopt the moral values of the world as he observed it –a police inspector is by nature corrupt, a man is expected to have an affair with his secretary, a psychiatrist is himself habitually deranged, exceptional genital endowment is a natural feature of a heroic statue (even of Winston Churchill). Though the audiences that gave Orton West End success probably dismissed this as a world of high camp fantasy, its parallels can be found in the pages of the daily and Sunday papers. Orton is not setting out a critique of society he is simply holding a mirror up to it – and not even a distorting mirror! Nevertheless, the humour of his plays does come largely from this apparent dislocation, in which the socially unacceptable is treated as the commonplace, authority figures are stripped of their disguises and all is orchestrated with the physical and coincidental mechanisms of black farce. Orton is unlikely to really shock you, most audiences will lap up his apparently outrageous naughtiness – but take him seriously and you will find that today's world is even nearer to the world he created.

It is now almost impossible to view Orton's work without remembering his own life, so graphically described in John Lahr's *Prick Up Your Ears* and the film based on it, and recorded in Orton's own diaries, but his promiscuous cottaging and murder by his male lover affected his work only in bringing it so suddenly to an end. *Entertaining Mr Sloane*, in which an attractive young murderer thinks he has captivated a woman and her brother into giving him a cushy life but finds the tables turned and himself trapped as their sexual toy, is perhaps his most accomplished play. *The Good and Faithful Servant* shows a compassion not evident in his other work and a more conscious criticism of the way in which society treats its nonachievers.

TRY THESE:
Ray Cooney farces for simple laughter; ▷Alan Ayckbourn's *Absurd Person Singular* and *Bedroom Farce* for more abrasive comedies of suburbia; ▷Alan Bennett's *Habeas Corpus* and *Enjoy* for darker shades of grey along Orton lines.

Loot

Basically a parody of a stock detective play, *Loot* presents a pair of young male lovers who have robbed a bank and hide the loot in the coffin of one boy's mother – who had been murdered by her nurse who plans to marry the father before disposing of him in turn. A bent detective, posing as a Water Board official, completes the main cast. Contrasts between the manner of the dialogue (often quite formally stylised) with situation and substance, opportunities for hilarious business with the body to prevent discovery, and other farce devices keep the laughs coming. In the end everyone gets a piece of the share-out except the murdered woman's husband, the only truly innocent, who is hauled off to jail to take the rap. Or is he actually the most culpable for his blindness to the corruption of the world around him and complicity in preserving the facades of respectability?

OSBORNE, John [1929–]
British dramatist

Plays include:
***The Devil Inside Him* (with Sheila Linden; 1950), *Personal Enemy* (with Anthony Creighton; 1955), *Look Back in Anger* (1956), *The Entertainer* (1957), *Epitaph for George Dillon* (with Anthony Creighton; 1958), *The World of Paul Slicky* (1959), *A Subject of Scandal and Concern* (1961), *Luther* (1961), *Plays for England*: *The Blood of the Bambergs, Under Plain Cover* (1963), *Inadmissible Evidence* (1964), *A Patriot for Me* (1966), *The Hotel in Amsterdam* (1968), *Time Present* (1968), *West of Suez* (1971), *A Sense of Detachment* (1972), *The End of Me Old Cigar* (1975), *Watch it Come Down* (1975)**

Adaptations include:
***A Bond Honoured* (from ▷ Lope de Vega; 1966), *Hedda Gabler* (from ▷ Ibsen; 1972)**

Screenplays include:
***Look Back in Anger* (with Nigel Kneale; 1959), *The Entertainer* (with Nigel Kneale; 1960), *Tom Jones* (1963), *Inadmissible Evidence* (1968), *The Charge of the Light Brigade* (with Charles Wood; 1968)**

Born in London of what he describes as 'impoverished middle-class' parents, John Osborne worked as journalist for a number of trade magazines before he became an Assistant Stage Manager and acted in repertory companies (an experience he draws on in *The Entertainer*).

Osborne's *Look Back in Anger* seemed to mark a watershed between the theatre of the 1930s and 1940s, and the new 'contemporary style' of the 1950s and 1960s which developed at the Royal Court and at the Theatre Royal, Stratford East. In a contemporary review Kenneth Tynan described it as 'the best young play of its decade' and journalists christened a whole group of new writers as the 'Angry Young Men'; they included ▷ Arnold Wesker and ▷ John Arden among the dramatists.

Osborne's first stage plays were collaborations; *Personal Enemy* was banned by the Lord Chamberlain because of its homosexual elements. *Look Back in Anger*, sent to George Devine in response to an advertisement in *The Stage* for new plays for the English Stage Company was Osborne's first produced play. Previously turned down, according to Osborne, by twenty-five managers and agents, it was the only play elicited from the advertisement which was considered worth a production. Directed by Tony Richardson it was the second English Stage Company production. Osborne, previously unknown, was hailed by one critic as 'the voice of our generation', and became the first of the many 'discoveries' of the Royal Court's policy of a Writer's Theatre. It was the first of the Royal Court plays to be recognised internationally, and toured to the USSR in 1957 as part of the World Youth Festival. Osborne thus became a significant figure in turning international attention to the developments in new British drama.

His next play *The Entertainer* explored the 'state of England' through the music hall act of a shabby song and dance man. Laurence Olivier had expressed interest in performing in an Osborne play, after *Look Back in Anger*, and although the ESC committee were uncertain about staging it, Olivier's participation clinched the production. It was a smash hit, transferred to the West End, and was turned into a film directed by Tony Richardson. The Court also produced *Epitaph for George Dillon*, which Osborne had written with Anthony Creighton four years prior to

TRY THESE:
Osborne says he 'couldn't abide' ▷Ionesco's plays and used to quarrel with George Devine about the Court's productions of them; ▷John Arden, ▷Arnold Wesker and ▷Willis Hall were categorised with Osborne as 'Angry Young Men'; ▷Shelagh Delaney, ▷David Storey, ▷Arnold Wesker, Alan Sillitoe, ▷N.F. Simpson and ▷Ann Jellicoe were among the writers whose plays were filmed for Woodfall; ▷Arthur Miller saw *Look Back in Anger* as the play which launched a new realism in a theatre that had been 'hermetically sealed from reality'; ▷Tony Craze's male protagonist in *Angelus* is a Jimmy Porter for the 1980s; Osborne's misogyny has Strindbergian elements; ▷Trevor Griffiths' *Comedians* is a very different treatment of stand-up comedy from *The Entertainer*.

Look Back in Anger. Osborne wrote the part of Baron von Epp in *A Patriot for Me* for George Devine, but the play was censored by the Lord Chamberlain, and could only be staged as a club production. This led to the Court's decision to become a club theatre until the Theatres Act of 1968 made it no longer necessary.

Osborne became a director of Woodfall films with Tony Richardson, a company which filmed *A Taste of Honey*, *Look Back in Anger*, *This Sporting Life* and many other classic texts of the 1950s and 1960s and which Lindsay Anderson credited with 'changing the face of British Cinema'. Osborne has also written extensively for television, but has been scathing about the more radical developments of the Royal Court, particularly loathing the Young People's Theatre Scheme.

Tony Richardson, the first director of *Look Back in Anger*, said of Osborne: 'He is unique and alone in his ability to put on the stage the quick of himself, his pain, his squalor, his nobility – terrifyingly alone'. Unfortunately the 'Angry Young Man' of the 1950s has soured in middle age (as the title of his 1981 autobiography *A Better Class of Person* suggests).

Look Back in Anger

Although it may not be the best of Osborne's plays, nor the best play of his generation of writers, it has come to stand as a key text for modern British drama. It came to express the disillusion with post-war England that was felt by many, and contains a central statement of frustration from its anti-hero Jimmy Porter, which became a cry for a whole generation: 'there aren't any good brave causes left'. Jimmy Porter became the epitome of the Angry Young Man in his harangue of contemporary values. Jimmy is the single figure who dominates the stage, his bitterness the point of identification for the audience. His wife, the middle-class Alison, takes the brunt of his onslaughts, and leaves him. She spends much of the play ironing, and taking abuse from Jimmy. The play ends with Alison's return, and the two cling together, addressing each other in child's language in an attempt to forge some kind of intimacy. Jimmy's treatment of Alison is now far harder to endorse than it was in the 1950s, and the play has therefore now lost some of its power. The play's setting and form is very social realist, the dingy bedsit where Jimmy and Alison live gave rise to the term 'kitchen sink' drama. Osborne himself has described *Look Back in Anger* as 'a formal, rather old fashioned play', and in retrospect, it is.

OSTROVSKY, Alexander Nikolayevich [1823–86]

Russian dramatist

Plays include:

***The Bankrupt* (later *It's All in the Family*, or *A Family Affair*; 1848), *Stick to Your Own Sleigh* (1853), *The Storm* (1859), *The Scoundrel* (or *Diary of a Scoundrel*; 1868), *The Forest* (1871), *Artists and Admirers* (1881)**

Ostrovsky was the virtual founder of the Russian theatre. He wrote forty-seven plays, many more than ▷ Gogol or ▷ Turgenev, and unlike them was a professional man of the theatre, ending as Supervisor of Repertoire of Moscow's Imperial Theatres and Head of the Dramatic School. He studied at Moscow University but failed Roman Law, and then worked as a clerk in the commercial courts until he was forced to resign in 1851 after the publication of his second play, *A Family Affair*. Although the play was banned, Ostrovsky's readings of it were a wild success in intellectual high society in Moscow, and this made his name. It, and his liaison with a charming but plebeian actress, also got him cut off without a shilling, and he spent the next few years as a well-respected but very poor literary hack in Moscow. The first of his plays to be performed was *Stick to Your Own Sleigh* (ie 'know your place') in 1853, and from then until his death in 1868 he was Russia's most important playwright. His plays range from broad comedies to the nightmare tragedy *The Storm* (which is the source for Janacek's *Katya Kabanova*). They are all set in more-or-less contemporary Russia, sometimes back-dated to appease the censor, and are all vigorously critical

TRY THESE:
▷Gogol's *The Government Inspector*, for an earlier satire on corruption in provincial Russian society; ▷Jonson's *Volpone* for satire on greed and over-reaching plotters; ▷Ayckbourn and ▷de Filippo for modern critical social comedies.

of the society they depict, actors being the only group shown in a consistently favourable light.

A Family Affair
The censor said it all: 'A rich Moscow merchant deliberately declares himself bankrupt. He transfers all his property to his clerk, whose interests he hopes to identify with his own by marrying him to his daughter. Being as great a rogue as himself, the clerk accepts daughter, property and money and then allows his father-in-law to be thrown into a debtors' prison. All the characters in the play – the merchant, his daughter, the lawyer, the clerk and the matchmaker – are first-rate villains. The dialogue is filthy. The entire play is an insult to the Russian merchant class.'
As played by ▷ Cheek by Jowl in 1988, it is also very funny indeed.

OTWAY, Thomas [1652–85]
English dramatist

Plays include:
***Alcibiades* (1675), *Don Carlos* (1676), *Titus and Berenice* (after Racine; 1676), *The Cheats of Scapin* (based on Molière; 1676), *Friendship in Fashion* (1678), *The History and Fall of Caius Marius* (1679), *The Orphan; or, The Unhappy Marriage* (1680), *The Soldier's Fortune* (1680), *Venice Preserv'd; or, A Plot Discovered* (1682), *The Atheist; or, The Second Part of the Soldier's Fortune* (1683)**

Otway began his theatrical career as an actor but suffered from such stage fright at his undistinguished debut that he switched to play writing. *Don Carlos* is written in rhyming couplets, other plays in blank verse. Otway became known as 'the tragedian of love' but although his work was popular he died in penury. From its premiere until the mid-nineteenth century his most successful play, *Venice Preserv'd*, was probably revived more frequently than any other play not by Shakespeare and is still occasionally revived. Tim Albery's production at the Almeida, rather than the ▷ National Theatre's starry revival, demonstrated that it still has considerable theatrical power. A bleak blank verse tragedy about the family and the state, loyalty and personal honour, and sexual politics, it includes a scene of grotesque comic sexuality and self abasement by a masochistic nobleman, echoing the corruption of the Venetian state against which the protagonists Pierre and Jaffeir plan revolt. *The Orphan*, once almost as popular as *Venice Preserv'd*, is seldom revived today but *The Soldier's Fortune*, a typical example of Restoration comedy, is occasionally staged.

TRY THESE:
For other post-Restoration writers of verse tragedy whose work is still staged, ▷Dryden and ▷Shelley; other Restoration comic dramatists are ▷Aphra Behn, ▷Congreve, ▷Etherege and ▷Wycherley; for more satire on sexual abasement, see particularly *Nana*, in Olwen Wymark's *Zola* adaptation for Shared Experience, and, for a high camp lesbian variety, Split Britches' stylish *Dress Suits to Hire*; see also ▷Shakespeare (*Caius Marius* is an adaptation of *Romeo and Juliet*).

OWENS, Rochelle [1936–]
American dramatist

Plays include:
***The String Game* (1965), *Istanboul* (1965), *Futz* (1968), *Homo* (1966), *Beclch* (1966), *Kontraption* (1971), *He Wants Shih* (1971), *The Karl Marx Play* (1973), *K.O. Certaldo* (1975), *Emma Instigated Me* (1976), *The Widow and the Colonel* (1977), *Mountain Rites* (1978), *The Writer's Opera* (1979), *Chucky's Hunch* (1981), *Who Do You Want Peire Vidal* (1982), *The Mandrake* (1983)**

Brooklyn-born Owens belongs to the school of formally innovative and iconoclastic playwrights associated with the rise of off-Broadway in the 1960s – people who had a highly emotive, deeply contradictory attitude to the theatre, a medium whose form they tended to admire even as they distrusted or alienated the audience. (Owens has said that she sees theatre as a 'life-sustaining force' for a public that 'wishes to be summoned from its sleep'.) Her best-known work, *Futz*, made into a controversial 1969 film directed by the original director of *Hair* (Tom O'Horgan), is – in the words of New York critic Michael Feingold – 'the keystone play of the decade'; it's a violent piece about a man, Cyrus Futz, in love with a pig, Amanda, and the menage à trois between the two of them and a woman, Marjorie Satz. Images of excess and shock often figure in her work: *Beclch*, a play

TRY THESE:
▷Amiri Baraka, ▷Lorca for theatre as ritual; ▷Jean-Claude Van Itallie's *America Hurrah* for benchmark avant-garde American plays of the 1960s, *Futz*-style; early ▷Arthur Kopit and ▷Jack Gelber for hallucinogenic, surreal drama; ▷Caryl Churchill and ▷David Lan's *A Mouthful of Birds* for another disturbing pig image; adaptations of Orwell's *Animal Farm* for a political parable of porcine dimensions; ▷Nick Darke's *The Monkey* for a less successful handling of the animalistic menage à

about four white adventurers in Africa, includes a lethal cock-fight; in *String Game*, a priest chokes to death on spaghetti among a community of Eskimos whom he has just chided for thinking erotic thoughts. *The Karl Marx Play* is, in many ways, her freest and funniest work – a surrealist pastiche in which the black jazz musician, Leadbelly, Friedrich Engels and his wife wait for Marx to write *Das Kapital.*

trois; ▷Susan Yankowitz's *Slaughterhouse* and Adrienne Kennedy's *A Rat's Mass* offer further theatrical images of the grotesque; for British equivalents, see ▷Women in Theatre and ▷Bryony Lavery who has tried to come close.

PAGE, Louise [1955–]

British dramatist

Plays include:

***Want-Ad* (1976), *Lucy* (1977), *Tissue* (1978), *Hearing* (1979), *Housewives* (1981), *Salonika* (1982), *Falkland Sound/Voces de Malvinas*; (1983), *Real Estate* (1984), *Golden Girls* (1984), *Beauty and the Beast* (1985), *Goat* (1986)**

Television includes:

***D.I.Y. in Venice* (1982), *Legs Eleven* (1984), *Birds Heads and Fishes Tails* (1986)**

Radio includes:

Adaptations of *Tissue* (1979), *House Wives* (1981), *Real Estate* (1984), *Golden Girls* (1986), *Armistice* (1983–84)

A London-born writer now living in Sheffield, Page is leading light of what for a short time in the early 1980s was known as the 'second wave' of young women playwrights. A graduate of Birmingham University's drama course (where she was taught by ▷ David Edgar), she has been writer-in-residence at the Royal Court, a Fellow in Drama and TV at Yorkshire Television, and Associate Director at Theatre Calgary in Alberta, Canada.

Something of a minimalist and writer of spare dialogue, her plays reflect a generation of women where feminism is assumed, if not overt. An early play, *Tissue*, touches sensitively on the trauma of a young woman facing breast cancer whilst the later *Golden Girls*, about women and sport, takes a leaf out of ▷ Caryl Churchill's book in tackling women and ambition. This issue is also touched on in the earlier *Real Estate*, an unflattering picture of post-feminist woman and the selfishness of daughters, in which the mother definitely has the last and better word – mother/daughter relationships are a recurring theme in Page's work. Much of her reputation, however, rests on *Salonika*, with which she won the 1982 George Devine award at the age of twenty-four.

By thirty, she was reputedly one of the few younger playwrights earning her living from writing, (all her subsequent plays from *Salonika* have been commissions). Her plays have ranged from the unpredictable and surreal time-warp of *Salonika* to the hermetic domesticity of *Real Estate*, and the large-scale and ambitious re-working of the old fairy tale *Beauty and the Beast*. Her plays have been produced all over the world, in New Zealand, the USA, Denmark, Greece, Australia, Norway.

Salonika

A surrealistic account of the effect of World War I on a widow returning to the Grecian beach where her husband had died sixty-five years earlier (he re-appears during the course of the play), and on her elderly spinster daughter. Critics hailed it as 'haunting' and a remarkably mature piece of work on the themes of futility and the frictions of mother/daughter relationships.

TRY THESE:
For ghosts of other generations brought on stage, see Greg Cullen's *Taken Out*, ▷Stephen Lowe's *Seachange*, ▷T.S. Eliot's *The Family Reunion*, ▷J.M. Barrie's *Mary Rose*, ▷Ibsen's *Ghosts*, ▷Edward Bond's *Summer*; for other plays on the friction of mother/daughter relationships, see ▷Ayshe Raif, ▷Julia Kearsley, ▷Sharman Macdonald; for images of the post-feminist woman see ▷Caryl Churchill's *Top Girls*, ▷Jacqueline Holborough's *Dreams of San Francisco*, ▷Deborah Levy's *Heresies*.

PAINES PLOUGH

British touring theatre company

Started in 1975 by the dramatist ▷ David Pownall and the

TRY THESE:
For new writing see the ▷English Stage Company at the

director John Adams, Paines Plough has established a reputation as one of the leading producers of new plays, both under its founders and under the current artistic direction of Pip Broughton. Pownall himself has written eight plays for the company and there have been two each by Stephen Jeffreys and Elisabeth Bond. Where ▷ Joint Stock's work has been characterised by its workshop method and ▷ Foco Novo has championed black writers, Paines Plough has been more eclectic, though there is a strong thread of interest in the other arts, particularly music, in many of ▷ Pownall's plays, ▷ Donna Franceschild's *Songs for Stray Cats* and Nigel Gearing's *Berlin Days, Hollywood Nights,* and literary figures such as John Evelyn (Elisabeth Bond's *The Messiah of Ismir*), George Orwell (Pownall's *Richard III, Part Two*). Many of their writers like ▷ Terry Johnson (though his Paines Plough play, *Days Here So Dark*, was not one of his best), ▷ Tony Marchant, ▷ Louise Page, ▷ Doug Lucie and ▷ Christina Reid have already made or gone on to make a significant impact in the contemporary repertory. The value of their workshop and play reading work with new writers is shown in the testimony of, for example, ▷ Jacqueline Rudet, Charlotte Keatley and Rona Munro all of whom have had rehearsed readings of their plays. New writing is the lifeblood of theatre; companies like Paines Plough and their peers perform one of the most essential tasks in theatre as, in effect, the research and development wing of the theatre.

Royal Court, ▷New Writing, the Bush Theatre; see also ▷Women's Theatre Group for Elisabeth Bond's *Love and Dissent*; ▷Gay Sweatshop, ▷Black Theatre Company and ▷Temba for more companies committed to new, especially black, writers.

PANTOMIME
(Greek: 'all-mime')

Pantomime can mean any kind of dumb-show in which words are replaced by gesture and body signals, whether entertainment or communication. The Romans also used it to describe a dumb-show performer. In Britain it is now specifically used to describe a traditional Christmas entertainment, usually loosely based on a fairy-tale or well-known children's story, featuring lavish sets, songs, dances, humour and farcical episodes. There will usually be an element of cross-dressing, with the romantic male lead – the 'Principal Boy' – played by an attractive woman and a comic female role – the 'Dame' – by a male comedian. The Principal Boy is not a male impersonator, but the sex reversals are usually deemed to allow greater liberties to be taken in humour without causing offence.

With the nineteenth-century rise of the music hall, variety artists, acrobats and speciality acts began to appear in pantomime and characters and plots were shaped to allow them to display their particular skills. The pattern continues today, with pop stars in leading roles, television comic double-acts as the broker's men in *Cinderella* or a conjurer playing a magician. To enable the casting of male pop singers some 'breeches' roles have recently been played by men but spectacle, romance, popular cultural references and songs – including a segment for the audience to sing along with – are still the hallmark of the popular pantomime. Complaints that comedians use too much blue material for a family audience have led to calls for a return to old standards, but pantomime humour has always included a certain amount of bawdy.

Pantomimes are still great money spinners, running anything from a week at Christmas right through to Easter, and often supporting the losses of the rest of the year. Many theatres now offer a 'children's play' as well, but it is inconceivable that panto will not survive even in its current 'watered down' version. Ironically, one of the best traditional pantomimes is staged annually by the innovative ▷ Glasgow Citizens' Theatre. Cheryl Moch's *Cinderella, The Real True Story* (1987) and ▷ Gay Sweatshop's *Jingle Ball* (1976) have both subverted the tradition by having Cinderella fall in love with a woman, no great elaboration when you consider the 'Principal Boy' is usually played

TRY THESE:
Contemporary plays that owe something to the pantomime tradition are ▷Nichols' *Poppy*, ▷Caryl Churchill's *Cloud Nine*, ▷Louise Page's *Beauty and the Beast*; Theatre Workshop's *Oh What a Lovely War* uses the pierrot show, ▷Trevor Griffiths' *Comedians*, the stand up comic, and ▷John Osborne's *The Entertainer*, the music hall; Dame Edna Everage as a grotesque, wildly popular manifestation of cross-dressing satire.

by a woman anyway – but enough to set certain newspapers baying for blood!'

PARKER, Stewart [1941–]

Northern Irish dramatist

Plays include:

***Spokesong* (1975), *Catchpenny Twist* (1977), *Kingdom Come* (1977), *I'm A Dreamer, Montreal* (1979), *The Kamikaze Ground Staff Reunion Dinner* (1979), *Nightshade* (1980), *Iris in the Traffic Ruby in the Rain* (1981), *Blue Money* (1984), *Heavenly Bodies* (1984), *Northern Star* (1984), *Pentecost* (1987), *Lost Belongings* (1987)**

Born in Belfast, educated at Queen's University, Parker has received a number of awards including the Evening Standard Award in 1977, a Thames Television Bursary in 1977, and the Banff International TV Festival Prize in 1985. With a skilful grasp of the surreal effects of everyday speech, and an obvious delight in word-play, Parker's plays are fast-moving, openly surreal, and very entertaining, although they frequently deal with the serious issues of the Troubles and their consequences for the lives of individuals. He repeatedly asserts that there is a force for life and independence which transcends political slogans and allegiances. In *Catchpenny Twist* the main characters are forced out of Ireland by violence and killed by a terrorist bomb in a foreign airport, but in the end their dreams of songwriting fame seem vastly superior to those of the politically 'enlightened' who condemn them for the irrelevance of their lives to the historic cause. In *Northern Star* Parker attempts a theatrical tour de force in a study of Irish history through the lives of its greatest playwrights from ▷ Sheridan to ▷ Beckett, a breathtaking exercise in skill and imagination with an operatic use of theatrical styles to present the response of each dramatist to his particular period.

Spokesong

Spokesong charts a family history through twentieth-century Ulster, in which a tenuous survival of individual eccentricity over political violence and faceless bureaucracy finally blossoms, despite the dehumanising forces ranged against it. Frank struggles to maintain the family bicycle-shop against threats of redevelopment, the car-culture, and the bombs of terrorists, and battles with his hostile brother Julian for the hand of the beautiful Daisy. Interwoven with Frank's story is that of his grandparents. The bicycle and its adherents take on symbolic value as the preservers of humanity, hope and simplicity, and Daisy finally rescues Frank from defeat and despair. The play is effectively allied to music hall and the 'good night out' philosophy, with songs, illustrative episodes and emphatic good nature underlining its central theme.

TRY THESE:
▷Sean O'Casey for his sagas of Irish family life; Seamus Finnegan, ▷Daniel Mornin and ▷Christina Reid for varying views of the Troubles; see also ▷Charabanc who share a similar ebullience of spirit in the face of dehumanising forces.

PERFORMANCE ART

Performance art is almost as much of a catch-all term as 'Theatre of the Absurd'; RoseLee Goldberg defines it as 'live art by artists', which is far too wide. It could be defined as something that happens before an audience and does not fit under the labels of theatre, ballet, opera, music, or strip-tease, though it may contain elements of all these. It is more a matter of visual artists turning to performance as a means of expressing their ideas than of anything to do with conventional theatre. The visual image is almost always central, though often accompanied or contradicted by complicated soundtracks using the latest technology. It often uses a variety of media, including music and dance, video, film and slides. The term has become current only since the 1970s, when the form began to be institutionalised, especially in the USA, in festivals, performance courses in art colleges, and specialist magazines.

It is difficult to write about performance art productions in standard critical terms, because they tend to be experimental

TRY THESE:
▷Rose English, ▷Deborah Levy for writers with performance art antecedents; ▷LIFT for more on their biannual festival; ▷Ken Campbell for other streams of anarchy; ▷Spalding Gray, ex-Wooster Group member for more on the ▷Wooster Group.

and open-ended, and groups by definition wish to subvert standard art forms. Their ancestry can be traced to Italian Futurism, the Dada movement, Surrealism, and the Jarry-Apollinaire-Artaud line, but this does not add much precision to the discussion. The 'Happening' made popular in the late 1950s and early 1960s in the USA by artists such as Allan Kaprow (who coined the term) and Claes Oldenburg, is clearly related, but was on the whole more anarchic and spontaneous; performance art productions tend to be carefully planned, even in the variable bits (witness The People Show). The line is often hard to draw – the term performance art has been used to encompass a range of projects from Welfare State's vast outdoor shows, through the ambitious large-scale works of ▷ Robert Wilson and of Richard Foreman's Ontological-Hysteric Theatre, Pina Bausch's ritualistic and imaginative dance theatre, to Miranda Payne hanging alone from a wall in the Riverside Studios in her *Saint Gargoyle*. The only constants seem to be that the event is probably non-linear, that unexpected juxtapositions will occur, and that any number of media may be brought into play.

Performance art has had something of a vogue in Britain over the past decade, with the Chapter Arts Centre in Cardiff, where one of the seminal groups, Geoff Moore's Moving Being, were based, as one of its key springboards. Rational Theatre and Impact are two other influential groups whose members have subsequently gone on to form other conglomerations of like-minded artists. Constant re-arranging of personnel is a typical feature of performance art. Some Rational Theatre members split off from the company to become The Hidden Grin, whilst ex-Impact members such as Steven Shill are now pursuing their own lines of enquiry. There is too an emphasis on working through complementary disciplines – musicians with actors, with dancers, with video and film-makers. Another has been a concern with deconstruction as a process and as a means to creating a different kind of theatrical language, overlapping musical and textual sound, visual images and movement, often in repetitious but rigorously disciplined physical sequences. Describing the evolution of his 1987 piece, *Dungeness – The Desert in the Garden*, Graeme Miller, a co-founder of Impact put it: 'Essentially *Dungeness* is an arbitrary landscape. . .and over the years I've collected from it in a random way. Now I'm treating real material as if it were false and throwing together fragments of theatre, film, tape and music into a continuous choreographic process that begins to make sense and then doesn't. . .*Dungeness* is an anti-Down Your Way. It's different from the original, but also closer to it'. Another group with a long-standing reputation is Lumiere & Son founded in 1973 by Hilary Westlake and David Gale whose *Circus Lumiere* (1980–81) presented in a tent showed how popular performance art can be and that electronic musical scores (in *Brightside* and *Panic*) can be positively haunting. Their outdoor event *Deadwood* in Kew Gardens (1986) also showed the company's versatility, and the audience interest in performance art as a large-scale project, as pioneered by Welfare State and now practised as well by IOU (an off-shoot of Welfare State), and events in the 1987 ▷ LIFT by Pip Simmons (*Gor Hoi*) and the Bow Gamelan Ensemble (*Offshore Rig*).

Apart from the Chapter Arts in Cardiff performance art in Britain has evolved largely outside London; with American Jim Haynes at the Traverse in the early 1960s (later at the Arts Lab in London), at the Birmingham Arts Lab, and currently in and around the Midland Group based in Nottingham. However, much of the existence of performance art in this country is due to the steady support of Ritsaert ten Carte of the Mickery Theatre in Amsterdam, who has been the commissioning agent behind many of the groups who have eventually been seen in London at the ICA. There is too, now, a growing feminist movement, the Magdalena Project centred on Chapter Arts, which is bringing women artists together from many countries to explore the role of women and language.

During John Ashford's tenure as the ICA's theatre director this venue was the main London showcase for performance art and played host to a range of European artists including one of Europe's current major exponents, Jan Fabre from Holland (whose 5–8 hour productions are as much tests of stamina for his audience as they are lessons in iconoclasm). The French Canadian company Theatre Repere's *The Dragon Trilogy* directed by Robert Lepage also made a considerable impact when seen at the ICA in ▷ LIFT 1987.

Of other recent visits, the New York ▷ Wooster Group also (almost) gained critical acceptance with *The Road to Immortality Part Two* at the ▷ Edinburgh Festival and Riverside Studios in 1986. Produced by Elizabeth LeCompte, it presented a collage of readings from American beat writers, musical, film and television interludes, and a cut-down version of *The Crucible*, done twice, once supposedly under the influence of LSD. This was well received, partly because it had more plot than most; no such tolerance was extended to the French Théâtre du Radeau, who brought an interesting two-hour piece of almost pure imagistic theatre, *Mystère Bouffe*, to the Almeida in 1987; and ▷ Robert Wilson's direction of Heiner Müller's *Hamletmachine* at the Almeida in 1987, showing five variations on the text in slow, precisely choreographed movement and sound, produced very mixed reviews, but at least was sold out during its run. At the other end of the spectrum is the carefully constructed anarchy of The People Show, where the only constant seems to be Mark Long, despite a move over the years towards plot and away from nudity and paint-splashing.

PHILLIPS, Caryl [1958–]
Caribbean dramatist

Plays include:
***Strange Fruit* (1979), *Where There is Darkness* (1982), *The Shelter* (1983)**

Films include:
***Playing Away* (1986)**

Television includes:
***The Record* (1984), *The Hope and The Glory* (1984)**

Radio includes:
***The Wasted Years* (1984; Giles Cooper award for best radio play), *Crossing the River* (1985), *Prince of Africa* (1987)**

'Cass' Phillips was born in St Kitts but came to Britain in 1958 and was brought up in Leeds and Birmingham, before going to Oxford University to study English Literature. His plays express the generational conflicts and bitter reproaches of that generation of young blacks brought up in Britain but with deep roots in the Caribbean culture, the most powerful statement of which is *Strange Fruit*, a tragic tale of disillusionment and lives blighted by race. *Where There is Darkness* is another passionate treatment of a similar theme: a West Indian father, successfully settled in this country as a social worker, is on the point of returning to the Caribbean. The conflict between him – chauvinistic, aggressive and clearly intended by Phillips as symbolic of racism's brutalising effect – and his quieter son who is about to thwart his father's ambitions, reflects wider social ills and is drawn with great persuasion and subtlety. *Shelter*, on the other hand, a more schematic treatment of colonialism and its repercussions contrasts eighteenth and twentieth-century relations between the sexes (the first half has a white woman-black man/master-slave *Robinson Crusoe* type twist to it) but is less successful in creating credible human beings.

Apart from his stage output, Phillips has been prolific in every other writing medium with films, novels, television documentaries, radio (plays, and interviews including an extended one with ▷ James Baldwin) and extensive lecturing.

Strange Fruit
Premiered at the Sheffield Crucible in 1980 and revived fre-

TRY THESE:
Many of the major black Caribbean writers have dealt with the theme of disillusionment with the old country but particularly ▷Mustapha Matura, ▷Edgar White, Felix Cross, ▷Barry Reckord; ▷Tunde Ikoli's *Scrape Off the Black* focuses on two brothers; ▷Derek Walcott's *Pantomime* is another twist on the Robinson Crusoe theme; ▷Arthur Miller's *A View From The Bridge* has the father protagonist as a complex victim/aggressor; Nigel Moffatt's *Mamma Decemba* is a new generation's recent treatment of disillusionment; ▷Hanif Kureishi's *Borderline* examines living on the borderlines of cultures from an Asian perspective; ▷Karim Alrawi's *A Child in the Heart* is equally concerned abour mixing cultures; see also ▷Ntozake Shange, George Wolfe's *The Colored Museum* and Kalamu Ya Salaam's *Black Love Song No 1* for satirical accounts of

quently since, *Strange Fruit* is one of those plays that, as time goes on, may emerge more and more as one of the landmarks of British black theatre. Centred around a schoolteacher, Vivien Marshall, and her two sons, it is a graphic, painful account of a family caught between two cultures, tearing each other apart as they fight out their destinies; the mother still upholding white values, one son opting for Rastafarianism, the other ultimately rejecting everything the mother (ie 'mother country') has stood for. *Strange Fruit* offers no optimistic ending; its naturalism is raw, and angry (its two sons are uncomfortably harsh on the single parent, upright mother). Far from unique in its theme of disillusionment with the old country, it remains one of the most potent expressions of it.

how white society has created 'the black image'.

PINERO, (Sir) Arthur Wing [1855–1934]

British dramatist

Plays include:

***The Magistrate* (1885), *The Schoolmistress* (1886), *Dandy Dick* (1887), *The Second Mrs Tanqueray* (1893), *The Benefit of the Doubt* (1895), *Trelawney of the 'Wells'* (1898), *The Gay Lord Quex* (1899), *His House in Order* (1906)**

During his lifetime, Pinero was most renowned for his 'problem plays', above all *The Second Mrs Tanqueray* which starred Mrs Patrick Campbell. (Students of Belloc will recall that it was while her aunt was Off to the Theatre To see that Interesting Play *The Second Mrs Tanqueray* that Matilda, and the House, were Burned.) These, despite the skill of their construction, have virtually died with the problems they dealt with. However, *Trelawney of the 'Wells'* remains a charming if sentimental picture of the mid-Victorian theatre, in which the passage of time has made the realistic characters seem stagey and the theatrical characters seem drawn from life; and his excellent farces are still regularly revived (*The Magistrate* most recently at the ▷ National Theatre in 1986).

The Magistrate

The plot has elements in common with ▷ Feydeau's *A Little Hotel on the Side* – the visit to the dubious hotel in Act II by most of the characters, unknown to each other, the police raid, the desperate attempts to avoid discovery – but the taboos that are transgressed, this being nineteenth-century England, are not sexually oriented; Mr Poskett, a metropolitan magistrate, is merely trying to conceal the fact that he has been taken for a night out by his stepson, and Mrs Poskett is trying to hide the fact that this stepson, who is thought to be a precocious fourteen, is actually nineteen, she having lied about her age. Similarly, in *Dandy Dick*, the dreadful secret that involves the Dean of St Marvells in a night in prison is merely that he has placed a bet on a horse to save his tottering spire (and he doesn't even win the bet); but the nimble plotting and the lively dialogue can still effortlessly keep our attention.

TRY THESE:
▷Feydeau for well-crafted farces; ▷Dumas fils and ▷G. B. Shaw for plays about the 'woman with a past' – *Mrs Warren's Profession* is partly an attack on the glamorising of that attractive figure; ▷Goldsmith's *She Stoops to Conquer* for another comedy that partly hinges on the age of a stepson.

PINNOCK, Winsome [1961–]

British dramatist

Plays include:

***A Hero's Welcome* (rehearsed reading; 1986), *The Wind of Change* (1987), *Leave Taking* (1987), *Picture Palace* (1988)**

London-born Pinnock is a young, black woman playwright, much in demand, whose hardest job may well be keeping up with others' expectations of her. *Picture Palace*, commissioned by the ▷ Women's Theatre Group, is an entertaining though ultimately somewhat depressing piece about escapism, media sexism and male violence. Four usherettes, indulging in celluloid dreams and fantasies about themselves and men, are confronted with the reality of their lives and real-life male violence. Pinnock shows a nice line in light humour and characterisation though as yet it does not go very deep and it is not a particularly new theme (though one which seems a particular preoccupation with

TRY THESE:
▷Clare McIntyre's *Low Level Panic* for a more single-minded and intense exploration of the themes of male violence and the female image; Lumiere and Son's *Panic*, for a superbly rendered piece of multi-media, physical theatre expanding the theme to panic attacks of all kinds; see Siren Theatre's *PULP* for a (Philip) Marlowesque, lesbian

younger women playwrights in 1988). One outstanding sequence – in which the described movements of a camera over a woman's body become the embodiment of erotic voyeurism/ male domination and control –indicates that her forte may well lie far from naturalism. Commissions in the pipeline include one for the Royal Court, another for their Young People's Theatre (entitled *Claudia Jones*), the Women's Playhouse Trust, the ▷ National Theatre Studio and the BBC.

thriller treatment of images, choices, compromises and survival; ▷Gregory Motton, a contemporary male voice, treats dreams and fantasies very differently.

PINTER, Harold [1930–]
British dramatist, actor, director

Plays include:
***The Room* (1957), *The Birthday Party* (1958), *The Hothouse* (written 1958; staged 1980), *A Slight Ache* (1959), *The Dwarfs* (1960), *The Dumb Waiter* (1960), *The Caretaker* (1960), *A Night Out* (1960), *The Collection* (1961), *The Lover* (1963), *Tea Party* (1965), *The Homecoming* (1965), *The Examination* (1966), *The Basement* (1967), *Landscape* (1968), *Silence* (1969), *Night* (1969), *Old Times* (1971), *Monologue* (1973), *No Man's Land* (1975), *Betrayal* (1978), *Family Voices* (1981), *Other Places* (1982, made up of *Family Voices*, *Victoria Station*, *A Kind of Alaska*), *One for the Road* (1984)**

Films include:
***The Caretaker* (1964), *The Servant* (1963), *The Pumpkin Eater* (1964), *Accident* (1967), *The Quiller Memorandum* (1966), *The Birthday Party* (1968), *The Homecoming* (1971), *The Go Between* (1971), *The French Lieutenant's Woman* (1981), *A La Recherche du Temps Perdu* (published 1977, unfilmed)**

Pinter has become notorious as the writer of dialogue with lengthy pauses; 'Pinteresque' has come to mean the dialogue of evasion. He has been claimed as a British exponent of the Theatre of the Absurd, although his plays often begin from an ostensibly naturalistic context, which breaks down into a threatening, and sometimes surreal world. The plays are often structured around the instrusion of a menacing stranger into an apparently safe world, who then becomes a catalyst for the return of the repressed. The theatre critic Irving Wardle has termed Pinter's work the 'Comedy of Menace'. Pinter has said that his fascination with oblique communication was something that he learned as a Jew bought up in an anti-semitic area of London, where evasion was a means of survival.

Born in the East End, the son of a Jewish tailor, Pinter worked as an actor before turning to writing. He was called up for compulsory National Service, but refused as a conscientious objector, risking imprisonment. He began writing poetry for small magazines, then short stories; his first play, *The Room*, was peformed by students at Bristol University.

The first London production of a Pinter play was received with criticial incomprehension and was a commercial disaster. *The Birthday Party*, in which two menacing figures threaten the banality of a seaside boarding house, was variously described in the national papers as: 'half-gibberish', 'puzzling' a 'baffling mixture'. Consequently, *The Dumb Waiter* had its first performance in Hamburg, and it was not until *The Caretaker* in 1960 that Pinter was recognised as a major writer.

All the plays sound an enigma, the threat in them is all the more frightening for never being directly explained. Pinter's work has been interpreted in a host of different ways; among other theories, Freud and the Bible have been hauled in to account for their obscurity, but Pinter resolutely insists that the plays mean no more than they say: 'I can sum up none of my plays. I can describe none of them, except to say: That is what happened. That is what they said. That is what they did.'

Old Times
With many of the characteristic Pinteresque themes, this play is concerned with power within relationships, with possessiveness over people and territory, with the fraudulence of memory, and

TRY THESE:
▷Terence Rattigan, who interpreted *The Caretaker* as an Old Testament allegory; ▷Ionesco for similarities in *The Birthday Party*; ▷Beckett with whom Pinter shares a refusal to analyse his plays and his paradoxical precision of language but ambiguity of meaning; ▷Joe Orton for an extension of the mundane into Surrealism, ▷Tom Stoppard for his interest in the fraudulence of memory; ▷Manuel Puig's *Mystery of the Rose Bouquet* as a multi-faceted exercise in memory; also ▷Michel Tremblay's *Albertine in Five Times* for a Proustian play; Elizabeth Bowen's *The Heat of the Day* (adapted for Shared Experience) also explores the slipperiness of language and betrayal; ▷N. F. Simpson as a Pinter contemporary and exponent of the British vein of Absurdism.

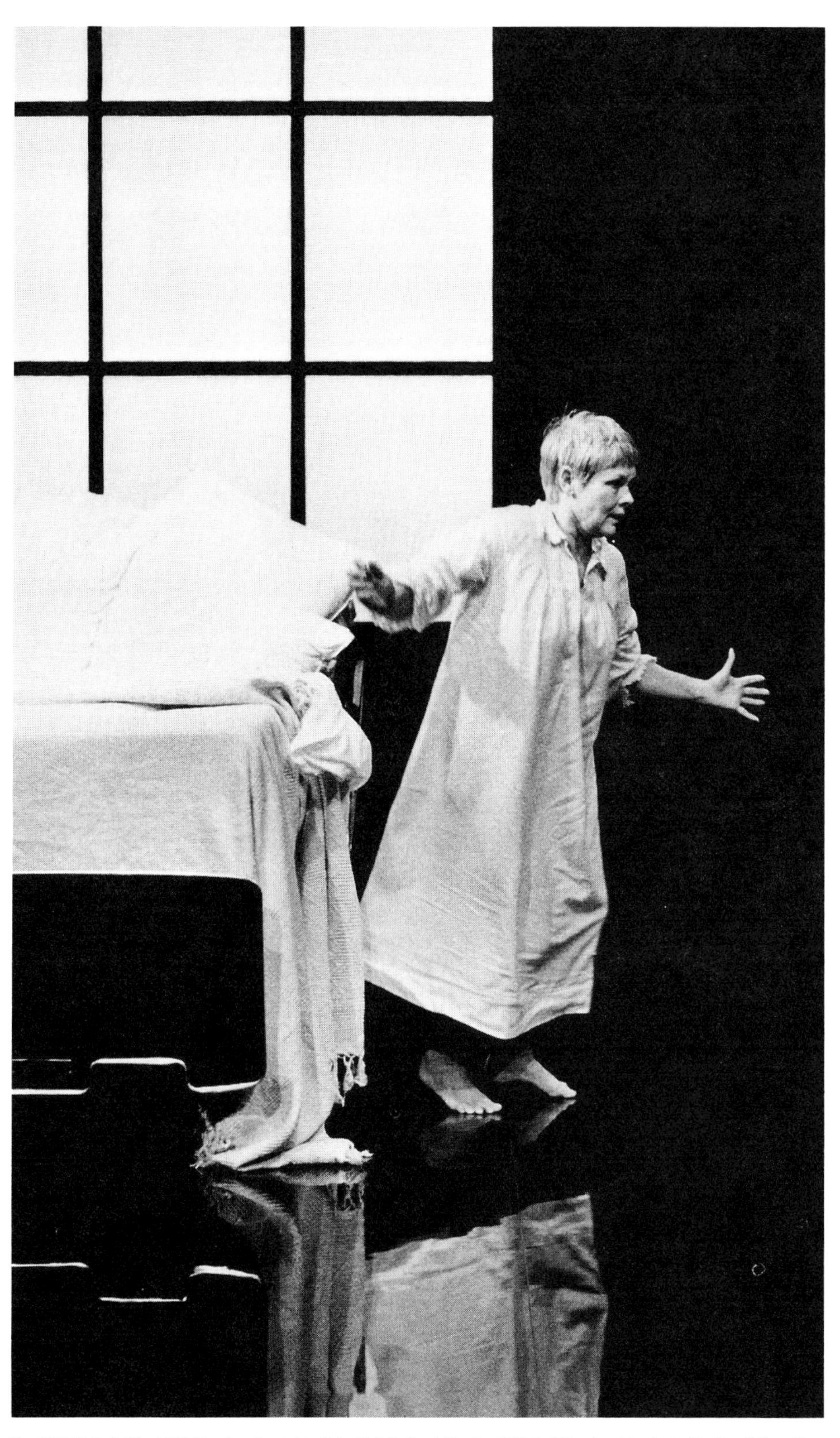

Harold Pinter's ***A Kind Of Alaska***, directed by Peter Hall, National Theatre, 1982. Judi Dench waking from virtually a lifetime of catatonia.

the subtexts of social dialogue. The play is organised around an intrusion into an established relationship, an intrusion which invokes the tensions, contradictions and power relations between a married couple, which had remained unspoken. The environment of the play initially appears to be a safe haven from the world, an attractive middle-class home, inhabited by an attractive, articulate couple, until Anna arrives to stay with her old friend Kate and her husband, Deeley. Over the course of the play, a power struggle between Anna and Deeley emerges, and it becomes clear that both are battling for Kate. Their conflict is fought over the memory of the past; each character reminisces about their shared experiences, but each has a very different version of events. The play does not have the menacing violence of *The Birthday Party* or *The Caretaker*, but is nonetheless very unsettling; it offers no help in untangling the 'truth' of the past, but suggests, like *Betrayal*, the slipperiness of truth, of memory and of language.

PIRANDELLO, Luigi [1867–1936]

Italian dramatist

Plays include:

***The Vise* (1898), *Scamander* (1909), *Sicilian Limes* (1910), *Liola* (1916), *Right You Are – If You Think So* (1917), *Cap and Bells* (1917), *The Pleasure of Honesty* (1917), *Man, Beast, and Virtue* (1919), *Mrs Morli, One and Two* (1920), *Six Characters in Search of an Author* (1921), *Henry IV* (1922), *Each In His Own Way* (1924), *Diana and Tuda* (1926), *The New Colony* (1928), *Lazarus* (1929), *Tonight We Improvise* (1930), *To Find Oneself* (1932), *When Someone is Somebody* (1933), *No One Knows How* (1934), *The Mountain Giants* (1937)**

Born into a wealthy Sicilian family with a history of liberal and revolutionary beliefs, Pirandello attended the Universities of Rome and Bonn. In 1894 the family business began to slide towards financial collapse and in 1897 he was forced to seek employment at a Women's College in Rome, where he remained until 1923. His father was bankrupt by 1904, and his wife suffering from mental disorder, obsessed with the notion that Pirandello was unfaithful. He continued to live a miserable and withdrawn life until his wife was consigned to a mental institution in 1919. During this period of withdrawal he began writing plays, and in the early 1920s he achieved considerable fame, winning the support of Mussolini and world-wide acclaim. He won the Nobel Prize in 1934. Pirandello's influence is particularly powerful on the Theatre of the Absurd. His plays are about a deeply perplexing, frequently hostile universe populated by characters who are themselves inconstant; he is fascinated by the masks people adopt in altering social circumstances, by the possibilities of multiple personality and the relativity of truth. Again and again his plays return to themes of deception and self-deception, entangling the audience in nets of paradox. The surface naturalism of his style of writing serves to heighten the contradictions which beset his characters, who are generally speaking unspectacular minor bourgeois figures rather than Promethean heroes. The plays have an obvious intellectual appeal; Pirandello's great achievement is to make them also highly theatrical.

TRY THESE:
▷Tom Stoppard, and ▷Thomas Kilroy for similar interest in role-playing, also ▷Anouilh's *The Rehearsal* has Pirandellian influences; ▷Noël Greig's *Angels Descend on Paris* and Siren's *PULP* are two gay plays that deal in sexual role-playing; Don Hale's *Every Black Day* mixes fiction and real-life episodes; ▷Günter Grass' *The Plebians Rehearse The Uprising* plays with the notion of the play-within-the-play from a political perspective; for plays about theatrical illusion, and identity see ▷Shakespeare's *Hamlet* (the most recent ▷National Theatre production in 1987 of *Six Characters* made *Hamlet* the play the actors were rehearsing) and *A Midsummer Night's Dream*; for other dramatists of the Absurd, see particularly ▷Genet and ▷Ionesco.

Six Characters in Search of an Author

A rehearsal in the theatre is disrupted by the unexpected intrusion of a strange family group, who claim to be characters from an incomplete play. In the hope that the actors can finish the work, the family act out scenes from their life, but these prove full of contradiction and contention. The Father has become estranged from his wife early in their marriage, he has brought up their son in isolation, while she has lived with the man she loved and had three children by him. The Father interprets this as proof of his benevolence; the Wife accuses him of ruthless self-interest, cruelty and lechery. The Father confesses that he encountered the Daughter in a brothel. The Stepdaughter blames the Father for her life of shame. The Son turns his back both on the Father and the rest of the family. Then the Little Girl is discovered drowned, and the Younger Boy kills himself. In the horrified confusion which follows in the theatre, the family insist that the events witnessed have been real, while the actors insist that they must be illusion.

POLIAKOFF, Stephen [1952–]
British dramatist

Plays include:
***Granny* (1969), *A Day With My Sister* (1971), *Lay-By* (1971; with ▷ Howard Brenton, ▷ Brian Clark, ▷ Trevor Griffiths, ▷ David Hare, Hugh Stoddart and ▷ Snoo Wilson), *Berlin Days* (1973), *Hitting-Town* (1975), *City Sugar* (1975), *Strawberry Fields* (1977), *Stronger Than The Sun* (1977), *Shout Across The River* (1978), *American Days* (1979), *Caught On A Train* (1980, television), *Soft Targets* (1982, television), *Breaking The Silence* (1984), *Coming In To Land* (1987)**

Although he began writing plays in 1969 Poliakoff first came to prominence with *Hitting Town* and *City Sugar*, by the understated precision with which he evoked the sham comforts of anonymous shopping malls, fast-food outlets and motorway service areas, while exploring readily identifiable, unlikeable and deeply alienated characters. He is particularly effective in capturing the curious absence of real passion in people smothering in webs of superficiality, and the sense of conscious distress behind even the most glibly desperate – exemplified by the radio DJ in *City Sugar*. The plays are notable for a strong sense of isolation and of communication replaced by half-hearted buzzwords and slogans. He conveys – rather suprisingly given his settings –an accurate sense of particular physical spaces, underlined by their actual emptiness: public spaces deserted at night; the enclosed but lonely world of the late-night radio phone-in; surveillance cameras and unseen observers render even his most aggressive characters exposed and vulnerable. His most recent plays however have seen an expansion away from urban blight. In *Breaking the Silence* a scientist-inventor (Poliakoff's own grand-father) on the run from the Russian Revolution is holed up with his family in a railway carriage. In *Coming in to Land* another political refugee, a Polish woman seeking asylum in Britain, is the focus for a study on the nature of oppositional attraction, bureaucracy, immigration and East and West. Poliakoff's concerns have also transferred very effectively to television, particularly in *Caught on a Train* which starred Peggy Ashcroft.

TRY THESE:
▷Jonathan Gems and ▷Gregory Motton are contemporary newcomers whose characters are equally in flight; ▷Tom Stoppard for political dissidents; ▷Robert Bolt's *Flowering Cherry* for portraits of grandiose dreamers sacrificing their families as in *Breaking the Silence.*

Strawberry Fields
The play charts a journey through service stations and lay-bys almost devoid of people as Kevin and his sister Charlotte travel to meet other members of their neo-Nazi sect. At the end of the first act, they shoot a hitch-hiker; at the end of act two they kill a policeman. Although they romanticise themselves as renegades and guerrillas, they seem to be in flight from nothing more tangible than their own imagined fears of pursuit. Non-communication is a strong element in the play.

POLLOCK, Sharon
Canadian dramatist

Plays include:
***Compulsory Option* (1971), *Walsh* (1973), *And Out Goes You* (1975), *The Komogata Maru Incident* (1976), *Blood Relations* (1980)**

Pollock, who also works as a director and actress and writes plays for children, is known in Britain for *Blood Relations*, inspired by the true story of Lizzie Borden who, according to popular rhyme 'took an axe/ And gave her mother forty whacks' and then gave her father forty-one (she was actually acquitted of murdering them but it makes for a less interesting rhyme!). In Pollock's version whodunnit is less important than why it was done: the claustrophobic tensions, repressions, and slow violences of family life, are refracted through the device of having her story acted out ten years after the historical events

TRY THESE:
▷Michel Tremblay for another Canadian dramatist; ▷Genet's *The Maids* and ▷Wendy Kesselman's *My Sister in This House* both based on an actual case, are also concerned with role playing and family tensions leading to murder; parent killing is a staple of drama from Orestes in ▷Aeschylus's *Oresteia*, Oedipus in

by her actress friend while the 'real' Lizzie plays the role of the family maid. Women have come to the fore in Pollock's later plays but she has always been interested in the borderlines between normal and abnormal behaviour, the central and the marginal in a culture, as in the historically based *Walsh*, in which the Mountie Major of the title is torn between the values of his government and those of Sitting Bull, and *The Komagata Maru Incident*, in which a government agent who is himself of mixed race is sent aboard a ship full of Asian refugees who are being refused entry into Canada. Her work deserves to be more widely seen outside Canada.

▷Sophocles' *Oedipus Rex*, Hamlet in Shakespeare's *Hamlet* to ▷Stephen Bill's *Curtains*; ▷Arthur Kopit's *Buffalo Bill and the Indians* is another meditation on the Red Indian/white culture clash.

POMERANCE, Bernard [1940–]

American dramatist

Plays include:

***Foco Novo* (1972), *Someone Else Is Still Someone* (1974), *The Elephant Man* (1977), *Melons* (1985), he has adapted ▷ Brecht's *A Man's A Man* and *The Elephant Calf* (1975)**

A Brooklyn-born American expatriated to London, Pomerance seems – on the basis of his few widely seen plays – to be drawn to dialectics often at the expense of powerful writing. In *Foco Novo*, which gave its name to the theatre troupe Pomerance helped to found, an unnamed Latin American military dictatorship (Brazil?) pits its citizens against the state, the guerilla outsiders against the technologically obsessed Americans. *The Elephant Man*, his best-known play, is based on a true life story in which a Victorian doctor, an anatomist named Treves, finds his definition of normality challenged by the Elephant Man of the title, a physically deformed, dream-obsessed visionary. *Melons*, set in a New Mexico melon patch in 1906, has its own would-be Treves: Carlos Montezuma, an Indian rights activist torn between the new world of the American colonialist and the ageless rituals of the native Indians. Pomerance's moral and ethical concerns are laudable, but he remains a playwright who may, perhaps, be creatively hamstrung by the burden of a monster hit.

TRY THESE:
▷Peter Shaffer's *Equus* for doctor-patient conflict as metaphor; ▷Arthur Kopit's *Indians* for stage treatment of an often-ignored area; ▷Richard Nelson for his spare, enunciatory style and a shared interest in history and politics.

The Elephant Man

In twenty-two short scenes with titles, Pomerance has written a major play that goes beyond prurient interest in its hunched, malformed central figure to touch on matters of faith, romance, and theatricality itself. To the left of the stage stands a strapping, well-built actor, who, as the description of his character is heard, assumes the stooped posture and slurred diction of the grotesquely misshapen John Merrick, labelled 'the elephant man' by nineteenth-century circus owners who used him as a freak attraction. A compassionate but career-minded physician, Treves, takes Merrick under his wing, undergoing a painful self-analysis that strips bare Victorian preconceptions about normality and the parameters of faith. The play features a superb part for a woman – the actress Mrs Kendal, who offers Merrick his one brief moment of eros. A raging success both in Britain and on Broadway, the play sparked interest in its subject, and a 1980 film was made with the same title, bypassing Pomerance's text.

POWNALL, David [1938–]

British dramatist and novelist

Plays include:

***Crates on Barrels* (1975), *Ladybird, Ladybird . . .* (1975), *Music to Murder By* (1976), *Richard III Part Two* (1977), *Barricade* (1977), *Motocar* (1977), *An Audience Called Edouard* (1978), *Livingstone and Sechele* (1978), *Beef* (1981), *Master Class* (1983), *The Viewing* (1987), *King John's Jewel* (1987), *Dark Star* (1987)**

Pownall spent some years as a personnel officer at Ford in Britain and working in the Zambian Copperbelt where he began writing plays for the local theatres. On his return to England he worked with the Century Theatre and the Duke's Playhouse in

TRY THESE:
▷Snoo Wilson is like Pownall with the brakes off; ▷Terry Johnson's *Insignificance* brings together mythic figures in a similar way to much of Pownall's work, but without the time shifts; ▷Tom Stoppard's *Every Good Boy Deserves Favour* also tackles

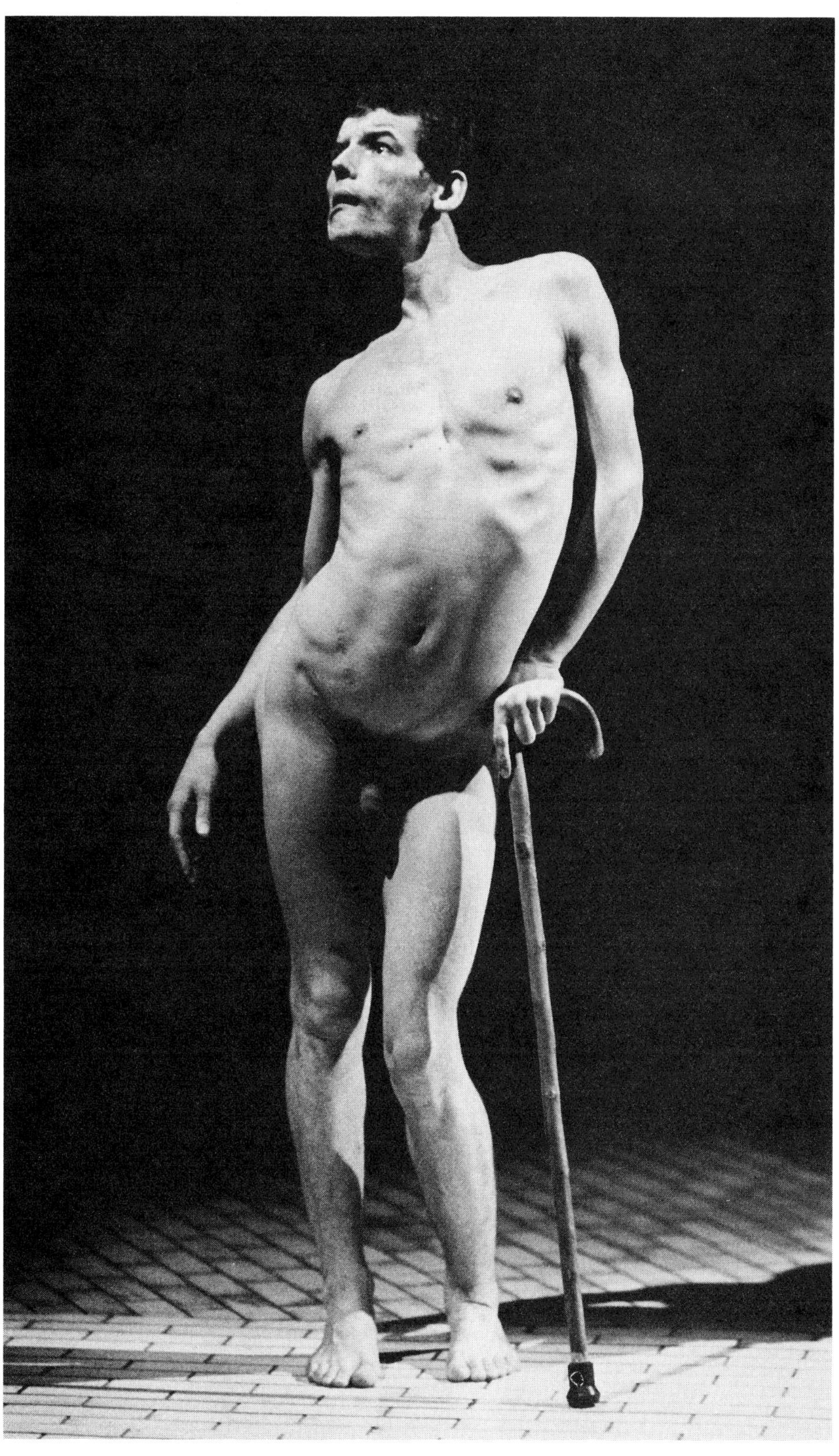

David Schofield repeating his original stunning Foco Novo portrayal of John Merrick, the Elephant Man, in Roland Rees' National Theatre production of Bernard Pomerance's ***The Elephant Man***, 1980.

Lancaster before co-founding the touring company ▷ Paines Plough with John Adams. He is an inventive dramatist who characteristically yokes together apparently disparate material to create plays in which the audience is invited to enjoy itself by engaging with complex issues and the deconstruction of received patterns of thinking. His main interests so far have been in politics, history, the arts, music, and Africa. *Music to Murder By* combines both music and history in its study of the composer Peter Warlock reincarnating himself as the sixteenth-century composer Gesualdo in order to, literally, kill his writing block; *Motocar*, set in a mental hospital in Zimbabwe just before independence, is a powerful evocation of history and the relationship between personal and public madness; *Richard III Part Two*, a meditation on the construction and uses of history, begins with George Orwell telling us about *1984* and switches to an Orwellian present in which the Ministry of Sport is about to market its new game 'Betrayal' about Richard III and the Princes in the Tower. *An Audience Called Edouard* starts with the actors on stage in the attitudes of Manet's painting *Déjeuner sur l'herbe* with Manet supposed to be out front in the audience painting the scene; add to this the arrival of an incognito Karl Marx and we have a potent brew. After the success of *Master Class*, Pownall's touch seems to have deserted him, at least as far as the critics were concerned. *The Viewing*, in which a mysterious potential house buyer turns out to be God come to stop a blind scientist from destroying the world, was generally thought to be emptily portentous, and *King John's Jewel*, in which we see a different John to the normal version, seemed to be too static for many tastes. With Pownall there is always the chance that the material brings together will fail to gel, but when it does he can be one of the most exciting and entertaining dramatists around.

the theme of music in Russia, as does ▷Michael Wilcox's *78 Revolutions*, whilst ▷C.P. Taylor's *Good* does the same for Nazi Germany; ▷Shakespeare's *Richard III* is the effective starting point for modern popular attitudes to Richard; ▷J.B. Priestley's *An Inspector Calls* is the best modern God-in-disguise play.

Master Class

In an imagined encounter in 1948 Stalin, Prokofiev, Shostakovich and Zhdanov engage in debate about the right formula for socialist music, but the terms of the debate are skewed by the composer's knowledge that Stalin can simply have them killed if they don't fall into line. Stalin equates artistic freedom, atonality and lack of melody with political irresponsibility: the people need uplifting with simple music they can understand to get them through the aftermath of war and the composers have a duty to provide it. The whole relationship between the state and the individual is brought into play in a way that is both entertaining and chilling, particularly at the end of the first act when Prokofiev is asked to choose his favourite record and Stalin proceeds systematically to destroy the record collection so that the second act is played on a visual and aural carpet of broken music.

PRIESTLEY, J.B. (John Boynton) [1894–]

British dramatist, novelist, commentator and essayist

Plays include:

***The Good Companions* (with Edward Knoblock, from his own novel; 1931), *Dangerous Corner* (1932), *Eden End* (1934), *Time and the Conways* (1937), *I Have Been Here Before* (1937), *When We Are Married* (1938), *Music at Night* (1938), *Johnson Over Jordan* (1939), *Desert Highway* (1943), *They Came to a City* (1943), *An Inspector Calls* (1945), *The Linden Tree* (1947), *Summer Day's Dream* (1950), *The Scandalous Affair of Mr Kettle and Mrs Moon* (1955)**

Priestley wrote forty-seven plays (including one for Pollock's toy theatres, an opera libretto, films, television and radio plays and twenty-eight novels – quite apart from a much greater number of books of travel, political comment, literary biography etc. Most of his plays are carefully plotted and mainly conventional in form, even allowing for the split, serial and circular theories of time which shape the three 'time plays': *Dangerous Corner*, *Time and the Conways* and *I Have Been Here Before*. More unconventional in breaking out of the domestic box set are: *Johnson Over Jordan*, which follows its protagonist through the fourth dimension of immediate after-death; *Music at Night*, which explores the thoughts and lives of the audience at a concert; *They Came to a City*, which pictures a socialist utopia; and *Desert Highway*,

TRY THESE:
Harold Brighouse, ▷Keith Waterhouse and ▷Willis Hall, ▷Willy Russell for other plays rooted in the North of England; ▷Somerset Maugham's *For Services Rendered* for a critique of conventional values within a traditional form; ▷Trevor Griffiths and ▷Arnold Wesker as socialist dramatists who tend to work with available forms; ▷Edward Bond and ▷Howard Brenton as socialist dramatists who use more radical approaches; ▷Brecht for communal responsibility; ▷Enid Bagnold for domestic

written for army actors, which shows a tank crew marooned in the desert with a flash-back to their prototypes in ancient times. Priestley was much more adventurous than most dramatists being performed on Shaftesbury Avenue at the time, but he quite consciously sought to work within the limits acceptable to contemporary audiences; while experimenting in one direction he felt, 'it is dangerous to try and advance on all fronts at once'. Nevertheless, although the demands he makes may be slight compared with those some dramatists make of audiences, even his lightest comedies embody a critique of society and behaviour and a presentation of ideas beyond the humour and narration of their surface. Their optimism now dates his more overtly political pieces, but *When We Are Married* and *An Inspector Calls* are frequently revived and may outlive much contemporary writing.

revelations; ▷Ronald Harwood's *The Dresser* for other views of theatre life.

An Inspector Calls
A totally believable middle-class Yorkshire household is visited by a detective – originally created rather enigmatically by Ralph Richardson, though there is no reason why he should not be much more mundane in manner – who is investigating the death of a young woman. As the background to the tragedy is revealed, the circles of responsibility and guilt spread to affect almost everyone. At the end of the play, the announcement of the visit of a detective inspector questions the detective's real identity and reveals the play as a metaphor for our own failure to accept our responsibility to others.

PROMENADE PERFORMANCES

This is an expression originally used to describe concerts, like the annual London series begun by Henry Wood in 1895, at which the audience is free to walk about. It is today sometimes used of special low-price performances which aim to attract new audiences and for which they must queue on the day. Since 1977, when the term was borrowed by the ▷ National Theatre as less off-putting than saying that audiences had to stand, it has been used to describe performances such as the Bill Bryden productions of *The Mysteries* which played to popular and critical success (1977–85), and Keith Dewhurst's adaptation of *Larkrise to Candleford*. The promenade style has been used for such widely acclaimed productions as Le Théâtre du Soleil's *1789* (1970), an ▷ RSC production of ▷ Arthur Miller's *The Crucible*, ▷ Ann Jellicoe's community plays and numerous ▷ Shakespeare productions including Peter Stein's Berlin *As You Like It*. It can take two quite different forms: in one the audience and actors share a performance area, with the action flowing through the space; in the other the action moves on from place to place, the audience following from one location to another. In both cases some seating is usually provided for those not wishing to stand for the whole performance.

TRY THESE:
▷Nick Darke's *Ting Tang Mine*, ▷David Edgar's *Entertaining Strangers* and ▷Jim Cartwright's *Road* are recent promenade productions; see also ▷Ann Jellicoe, ▷Community Theatre, ▷Adaptations and Adapters.

The processional form may exploit actual locations, indoor or outdoor, through which it passes or it may move through specially created environments. The ▷ RSC's *The Dillon* (1983 and 1985), based on the life of a Stratford man, actually wound its way through the town. Bread and Puppet Theatre have frequently used processional forms to draw audiences into participation, and Welfare State is one of the British groups that have used a trail both to provide a series of dramatic and visual experiences and to increase awareness of the environment itself. Audiences can be offered a multitude of animate and inanimate images, in addition to human performers, and the extent of communication will depend upon the keenness of their observation. Interaction in this form may be more with the environment than with performers. Even when outdoor promenades encompass large territories, performance elements and any simultaneous, as opposed to sequential, experience will limit the number of participants. Many were turned away from events such as Lumière and Son's *Deadwood* at Kew Gardens.

Plays presented in promenade style within a limited theatrical space force audience and actors to share that space. As the action moves from one area to another the audience change their perspective and probably their position. The spectator

A promenade performance: Jim Cartwright's ***Road*** at the Royal Court, 1986, in Simon Curtis' production with Edward Tudor-Pole in the shopping trolley, Lesley Sharp (left), Mossie Smith (right) and members of the audience.

chooses his or her constantly changing relationship with the action, as opposed to the passivity of a fixed seat. Offering a literal contact with the actors that is the extreme opposite of fourth-wall theatre, promenade performance paradoxically both emphasises the theatrical nature of the event and reinforces empathic involvement.

PROWSE, Philip

see GLASGOW CITIZENS' THEATRE

PUB/CAFÉ THEATRE

TRY THESE:
▷Cabaret.

Café theatre in Britain is almost non-existent, with the honourable exceptions of London's Canal Café Theatre in Little Venice and La Bonne Crêpe in Battersea, but pub entertainment is more common. Entertainment in pubs comes in three kinds: the most basic is the band at one end of the bar, which is primarily there to encourage the clientèle to do their drinking in this pub rather than any other. The second type is the large room with a stage at one end, and often a bar down one side, where a charge is made for admission but drinking is an expected part of the evening; this is very much the way the music hall started, but it is now the homeland of the 'alternative ▷ cabaret' circuit, above all stand-up comedians of both sexes, but also including singers, comic groups, and the odd poet, which can be very good indeed, and at any rate is rarely dull. The third type, pub theatre proper, which is mainly a London phenomenon except during festivals in other towns, is one end of a continuum at the other end of which is the Donmar Warehouse or the Cottesloe and which makes up a large proportion of the London fringe – analagous to the kind of performance spaces which house the fringe activity of New York's off-off Broadway, or the ▷ Edinburgh Festival fringe. The very high costs involved in keeping a play on in the West End leave an unsatisfied supply and demand. On the supply side, there is not only the steady flow of young people who would rather act or direct for peanuts than not at all, but also the relatively substantial touring companies who like occasionally to display their talents within reach of the metropolitan critics and the Arts Council. On the demand side, London contains many theatre enthusiasts who actively wish to see plays by ▷ Kleist or ▷ Marivaux or new authors, even if this means tolerating a low standard of comfort and the sort of staging which uses brains instead of money. What both sides therefore need are simple, cheap places where plays can be put on, and one source of these places is upper rooms in Victorian pubs, originally intended for the sort of 'function' which no longer happens or happens somewhere else – Oddfellows' banquets or wedding receptions. There are other sources for such rooms – 'studios' in modern theatre or arts complexes, made-over church or drill halls, even the basement of a bookshop for the Theatre Downstairs – but pubs tend to have the cheapest ones. They also have the advantage that you can take your beer with you, as in the music halls, which makes for a pleasant informality. The type of performance seen in these London pub theatres varies with the management. Some of them – the Orange Tree at Richmond, the Old Red Lion in Islington, the Bush, the Gate and the Latchmere under Lou Stein (now at Watford) – have strong managements and highly individual repertoires. Others are just 'venues', open to anybody who can put down the money, and liable to close as quickly as they opened. Other pub theatres that currently put on plays regularly if not all the year round include the Man in the Moon, the Sir Richard Steel, the Corner Theatre, the Etcetera, the Duke of Cambridge, Pentameters and the Tabard at Acton, a comparative newcomer that encourages new authors. London's only punk theatre company, Chris Ward's Wet Paint, also turn up from time to time in various pub venues.

Of those with a more or less continuous programme, the Bush is the most successful example of pub theatre – its record of discovering new writers and consistently high production standards place it on a par with larger theatres such as the Royal Court. In the past few years, it has put on plays by ▷ Snoo Wilson, ▷ Sam Shepard, and 'discovered' many more including ▷ Nick Darke, ▷ Terry Johnson, ▷ Beth Henley, ▷ Jacki Holborough ▷ Sharman Macdonald, ▷ Daniel Mornin, and ▷ Julia Kearsley; their two recent authors, Lucy Gannon (*Raping the Gold*) and Billy Roche (*A Handful of Stars*) look set to continue the Bush's sure touch. It has also presented a fine adaptation of ▷ Manuel Puig's *Kiss of the Spider Woman* as well as Nancy Duguid's much-praised revival of ▷ Franz Xaver Kroetz's *Request Programme*. The Gate, Notting Hill, and the Latchmere in Battersea both have similarly adventurous repertoires and imaginative staging, and will tackle rare foreign classics such as ▷ Kleist's *Penthesilea*, Lesage's *Turcaret*, and Fassbinder's *The Bitter Tears of Petra von Kant* (John Clive's 1988 revival was a particularly stylish rendering of this distinctly over-heated play). The Latchmere has a bigger room and a decent restaurant, but the Gate is essentially a pub. The King's Head has offered a varied and sometimes distinguished programme of work for many years (Robert Patrick's *Kennedy's Children* and Vivien Ellis's *Mr Cinders* both started at the King's Head before transferring to the West End) and is now trying to survive without its Arts Council grant. The Orange Tree, Richmond, under Sam Walters' direction, has a well-established high reputation for its acting and for the staging of lost classics, such as Tolstoy's *Power of Darkness* and foreign revivals such as ▷ Havel's *Largo Desolato*; it sometimes fits astonishingly large casts into the small acting space in the round. The seats are pews and not very comfortable, but the pub and basement restaurant are excellent, and the theatre has good local support.

On the whole, and within the limits of the form, the quality of the work put on in pub theatre is fairly high, because it is done by enthusiasts for a discriminating and demanding audience. However, it is intended for people who know what to expect, and it seldom really attempts either the avant garde or experimental (unlike off-off Broadway, or the London fringe in the 1970s). Pub theatre will generally be interesting – it may or may not be entertaining – but it still provides a seed-bed of activity out of which emerge eventually the actors, writers and directors who become household names, nationally, internationally and on television.

PUIG, Manuel [1932–]

Argentine novelist, dramatist and film director

Plays include:

> ***Kiss of the Spider Woman* (1981), *Mystery of the Rose Bouquet* (1981), *Under the Mantle of Stars* (1982)**

Puig studied at film school in Rome and became a successful novelist before having his first play produced. *Kiss of the Spider Woman*, based on his own novel, is widely known from the film version which he also directed. Both this and *Mystery of the Rose Bouquet* are two-handers for contrasting characters, offering marvellous opportunities for actors, and exploring stormy and intricate relationships. Puig uses these small-scale pieces to reflect the culture in which they are set and perhaps suggests – in the transformation which the interaction works on each character – a possibility of social change. Both are set in enclosed worlds, *Mystery of the Rose Bouquet* in an expensive health clinic where a rich and mischievous old woman who has already sacked four nurses, and the poor, apparently unqualified nurse who is now looking after her, begin to find a pattern of similarity in their lives.

TRY THESE:
For other homosexuals in prison John Herbert's *Fortune and Men's Eyes*, ▷Genet's *Deathwatch*, ▷Martin Sherman's *Bent*; for studies of power relationships ▷Harold Pinter's *One for the Road* and *No Man's Land*, ▷Beckett's *Endgame* and *Catastrophe*; for contrasting two-handed female relationships, see ▷Catherine Hayes' *Skirmishes*, Holly Hughes' *Dress Suits*

As they relive their memories of sadness, failure and sometimes of roses, they both torment and rehabilitate each other. As in his novels, such as *Betrayed by Rita Hayworth*, the character's imagination and fantasies are explored, thus lifting his plays out of strictly naturalistic forms.

Kiss of the Spider Woman

Kiss of the Spider Woman is set in an Argentinian prison cell where a camp window-dresser, found guilty of fooling around with a fifteen-year old, is shut up with a macho, Marxist revolutionary and promised release if he can pry secrets from him. As affection and dependence develop between the man, climaxing in physical consummation, the fey-gay who escapes from reality in reliving B-picture romances (oblivious to their fascist background and ideology) learns that caring for individuals is not enough, accepts social responsibility and recognises his own integrity, while the revolutionary learns reciprocal respect and the value of the individual. This is a homosexual love story, a study of power – not only of authority over the individual but between the prisoners themselves – and an argument for the innocence of love. It demolishes conventional bourgeois values while skilfully embroiling the audience in the conflicts of loyalty and betrayal.

to Hire (Split Britches); Win Wells' *Gertrude Stein and Companion.*

RABE, David [1940–]
American dramatist

Plays include:

***The Basic Training of Pavlo Hummel* (1971), *Sticks and Bones* (1971), *The Orphan* (1973), *In the Boom Boom Room* (1973), *Streamers* (1976), *Goose and Tom-Tom* (1980), *Hurlyburly* (1984)**

Films include:

***I'm Dancing As Fast As I Can* (1982), *Streamers* (1983), *Casualties of War* (1988)**

A tough, gritty, often abrasive writer who bides his time between plays, Rabe is distinguished by his trilogy about the Vietnam War. This begins with the untidy *The Basic Training of Pavlo Hummel*, continues on to the stark, ironic *Sticks and Bones* and climaxes with the altogether startling *Streamers*, one of the great American plays of the 1970s. Set in 1965 in a Virginia army barracks, the play makes the scabrous point that we carry war with us, that war is an internal condition which occasionally finds an external release. It takes its title from the word for a parachute which fails to open, but the play itself floats on a bloody and pained compassion for all of society's victims. This natural state of aggression finds its peace-time equivalent amongst the Hollywood sharks who populate *Hurlyburly*, a sour and rancid end-of-the-world play which is as flowery and overwritten as *Streamers* is swift and sharp.

TRY THESE:
▷Genet's *Deathwatch*, Miguel Pinero's *Short Eyes* for similar dramas of enclosure; ▷Thomas Babe for often jagged, sometimes over-literary language; for Vietnam plays, James Duff's *The War at Home* traces the experience without illuminating it, ▷C.P. Taylor's *Lies About Vietnam* links the public problem with the personal, the Vietnam Veterans Ensemble's *Tracers* and Emily Mann's *Still Life* providing haunting documentary-like responses; plays about the LA malaise are also often second-rate (Nick Darke's *The Dead Monkey* for example).

RACINE, Jean [1639–99]
French dramatist and historiographer-royal

Plays include:

***Le Thébaïde* (*The Theban*; 1664), *Alexandre le Grand* (*Alexander the Great*; 1665), *Andromaque* (*Andromache*; 1667), *Les Plaideurs* (*The Litigants*; his only comedy; 1668), *Britannicus* (1669), *Bérénice* (1670), *Bajazet* (1672), *Mithridate* (*Mithridates*; 1673), *Iphigénie* (*Iphigenia*; 1674), *Phèdre* (*Phaedra*; 1677), *Esther* (1689), *Athalie* (*Athalia*; 1691)**

Racine was orphaned at the age of four, and brought up at Port-Royal by the Jansenists; he escaped them for most of his adult life, but they got him in the end. A good scholar and an admirer of the Greek dramatists, he took naturally to the neo-Aristotelian rules that ▷ Corneille found so constricting; his relentless dramas run their course in twenty-four hours or less, in one location, with no sub-plots to lessen the intensity. His characters manage to combine uncontrollable passion, self-interest, and a merciless lucidity; the restrictions of the rhymed Alexandrine couplets and the limited vocabulary help to channel the force of the events. After the comparative failure of *Phèdre*, Racine was reconciled with Port-Royal, and wrote no more secular plays; the last two, on Biblical subjects, were written for Madame de Maintenon's school for young ladies at St Cyr, but the subjects are from the Old Testament, and the doom is just as inevitable. It is used to

TRY THESE:
▷Corneille for seventeenth-century French tragedy and for the neo-Aristotelian rules, also for influence of the Greek dramatists (though ▷Corneille preferred subjects from Roman history); ▷Euripides, from whom he borrowed the plots of *Phèdre* and *Iphigénie*; ▷Molière for a seventeenth-century comic French dramatist.

be the received wisdom that Racine's plays were not successful in England because they were impossible to translate, but recent productions have disproved this; for instance Christopher Fettes' intense and well-acted productions of Britannicus and Bérénice in the Lyric Hammersmith Studio in 1981 and 1982 worked well in spite of the stilted Penguin translation. Tony Harrison's *Phaedra Britannica* (Old Vic 1975) moved the scene to British India; the Prowse/McDonald *Phaedra* (Old Vic 1984) had both Glenda Jackson and a palpable horse; both ▷ Cheek by Jowl (1985) and Jonathan Miller (1988) have recently made a fair success of *Andromaque*; indeed there seems to be a mini-boom in Racine productions. Someone ought to try putting on *Mithridate* –it has a solid main part for someone like Anthony Hopkins, a fine part for an actress (as in most of Racine's plays), and even (arguably) a happy ending.

Phèdre
This is based on ▷ Euripides' *Hippolytus*, but with concessions to the seventeenth-century French taste for *vraisemblance*; Hippolyte spurns his stepmother's forbidden love because he is in love with Aricie rather than because he is vowed to Diana, and the gods are obsessionally present in the characters' minds rather than appearing on the stage. The tension rises inexorably and logically from scene to scene; as often in Racine, if you pray to the gods your prayer is always answered (such as Thésée's prayer to Neptune to kill his son), but by then it is not what you want at all.

RAIF, Ayshe [1952–]
British dramatist

Plays include:
***Cafe Society* (1981), *Another Woman* (1983), *A Party for Bonzo* (1985), *Fail/Safe* (1986)**

Of Turkish-Cypriot parentage, Raif is a superb observer of emotional currents, with an ear for dialogue that is angry, and painful in its accuracy. Her plays thus far have been firmly embedded in the school of naturalistic drama – domestic, two- and three-handers showing life at the sharp end of urban existence: single women in lonely bed-sits (*Another Woman*), marriage torn apart by the effects of unemployment (*A Party for Bonzo*), and the repressive bonds that can tie mother/daughter relationships in knots (*Fail/Safe*). Though the plays are bleak, there is often a mordant humour at work which has yet to be fully unleashed. Some critics have found her work to be closer to television drama and Raif would herself admit the medium has its attractions. Her plays, thus far, have all been presented at the pint-sized Soho Poly (in keeping with its traditions of nurturing young writers). However, two commissions during a residency as writer at the Theatre Royal, Stratford East (a play with fourteen women and a male stripper and a second one, an East End version of Phèdre), may well herald a new, more expansive direction. In any event, she is a writer to look out for in the future.

TRY THESE:
For female monologue about isolation/alienation, see Jacqui Shapiro and Feroza Syal's *One of Us*; for relationships between mothers and daughters, see ▷Julia Kearsley; for marriage under stress, see ▷Strindberg, ▷Albee's *Who's Afraid of Viginia Woolf?*, ▷Ted Whitehead's *Alpha Beta*; for frustrated daughters, see ▷Catherine Hayes' *Skirmishes*.

RAME, Franca [c 1930–]
Italian actress, dramatist.

Plays include:
***The Mother*, and in collaboration with ▷ Dario Fo *It's All Bed, Board & Church* (1977, also known as *All House, Bed and Church* or *Female Parts* or *One Woman Plays* and comprising *Waking Up*, *Same Old Story*, *A Woman alone*, and *Medea*), *Tomorrow's News*; *Ulrike Meinhof; I Don't Move, I Don't Scream, My Voice is Gone* (1983; also known as *The Rape*), *The Open Couple* (1986–87)**

The fame of this remarkable actress-cum-playwright, daughter of one of the last of Italy's companies of strolling players, has been inextricably linked with that of Italy's premier political free-thinking socialist and satirist ▷ Dario Fo, with whom she has collaborated on several plays, and who together ran their own company/collective, La Commune.

A physical performer of enormous energy and dynamism,

TRY THESE:
▷Ayshe Raif's *Another Woman*, for its British equivalent of the solo woman; Dacia Maraini's *Dialogue Between a Prostitute and one of her Clients* for ▷Monstrous Regiment as an exercise in engaging audiences directly in the subject of prostitution; for a surreal account of rape, see Eve Lewis' *Ficky Stingers* (which with ▷Louise Page's

Rame's monologues reflect equally that emotional intensity and her political commitments, though she declines to label herself a feminist. Her plays, nonetheless, have focussed on a variety of women's issues, often as a result of her own experiences, and are testaments to the various forms of women's oppression in Italian society – from the state, the church and men. *The Mother* and the co-written *Ulrike Meinhof and Tomorrow's News* arose directly out of her activism on behalf of political prisoners; *The Rape* is an account, all the more chilling for its economy and understatement, of an attack on Rame herself motivated, she believes, by political opponents. Likewise, *Female Parts*, a series of monologues (co-written with Fo) performed in 1981 at the ▷ National Theatre by Yvonne Bryceland, a subversive mix of styles from the bitterly ironic and farcically anarchic to feminist reappropiation of fairy-tales and the Medea myth, reflects the problems of a range of Italian women (it was based on conversations with them), but has struck a common chord with female audiences from Japan to Brazil. *The Open Couple*, again co-written with ▷ Fo, from whom she has now split, is yet a further example of the comic and grotesque as a couple come to grips with the painful truths and double standards of extra-marital relationships.

The Mother and The Rape
These are classic Rame monologues. Both are blatant but bravura pieces of feminist agit-prop,, descriptive reconstructions in which simplicity is the key-note. A minimum of props is used – just a chair – but the emotional contents speak for themselves and the cumulative emotional effect can be shattering. In *The Mother*, the account by the mother of a young terrorist's trial and sentence, recreates not only the intensity of maternal feelings and their chilling climax, but instills a growing sense of society's collective responsibility towards the young man and his fate. Similarly, *The Rape* (which is often performed as part of a double-bill with *The Mother*) is a simple step-by-horrific-step description of a young woman being gang raped and tortured (with a cigarette) which is as powerful a statement about male violence – ▷ Sarah Daniels notwithstanding – as you are likely to see.

Tissue is an equivalent double bill of fear, anger and pain; ▷Sarah Daniels' *Masterpieces* for a contrasting treatment of male violence; see also ▷Dario Fo.

RATTIGAN, Terence (Mervyn) [1911–77]
British dramatist

Plays include:
***French Without Tears* (1936), *After the Dance* (1939), *While the Sun Shines* (1943), *Flarepath* (1942), *Love in Idleness* (1944), *The Winslow Boy* (1946, *Playbill* (*The Browning Version* and *Harlequinade*; 1948), *Adventure Story* (1949), *Who is Sylvia* (1951), *The Deep Blue Sea* (1952), *The Sleeping Prince* (1953), *Separate Tables* (1954), *Variation on a Theme* (1958), *Ross: a Dramatic Portrait* (1960), *In Praise of Love* (*Before Dawn* and *After Lydia*; 1974), *Cause Célèbre* (1977)**

A master craftsman in plot construction and writing telling dialogue, Rattigan first gained fame with *French Without Tears*, a bright comedy about would-be candidates for the Civil Service learning French in a crammer at a French resort. He maintained his light touch through plays such as *The Sleeping Prince*, an Olivier/Vivien Leigh vehicle about a middle-aged prince falling in love with a chorus girl, which Olivier filmed with Marilyn Monroe as *The Prince and the Showgirl*. In the late 1950s Rattigan's obvious commercial appeal led enthusiasts of the work of ▷ John Osborne and the new generation of more politically motivated dramatists to dismiss his work as irrelevant. Nevertheless, Rattigan, working within the format of the well-made play, tackled issues far deeper than those of conventional Shaftesbury Avenue entertainment, though he presented them with a skill that avoided alienating the respectable, middle-class, middle-aged theatre-goer whom he personified as 'Aunt Edna'.

In *Flarepath* he explored the strains on Battle of Britain flyers and their civilian friends and families; in the factually based *The Winslow Boy* his subject was the wrongful dismissal from a military academy of a boy accused of stealing a postal order; and in *The Browning Version* he examined the pressure on a teacher

TRY THESE:
▷Somerset Maugham and ▷Tennessee Williams for similar treatments of homosexual themes; ▷Brian Clark's, *Whose Life Is It Anyway?* for a play about incurable illness; many British comedies for jokes at the expense of funny foreigners, from ▷Shakespeare's *The Merry Wives of Windsor* onwards.

being forced into retirement with his wife unfaithful and even the pupil who seems to share his ideals abandoning him. *In Praise of Love* tackled incurable illness and *Cause Célèbre* was based on a famous case of a woman and her lover, who murdered her husband. *The Deep Blue Sea*, originally written as a story of male homosexuals following a tragedy concerning an actor with whom Rattigan was in love, touches tragic heights in its presentation of a woman leaving her husband for a man who does not return her love. Rattigan's understanding of the pain of relationships transcends sexual orientation, although *Adventure Story*, a psychological study of Alexander the Great, makes no attempt to explore the Alexander-Hephaiston relationship. Presumed homosexual rape is a central element in *Ross*, a presentation of T. E. Lawrence after Arabia, but the removal of censorship did not bring any overt exploration of his own sexuality to Rattigan's work.

Rattigan also wrote for television and, as well as adapting his own plays, was responsible for the screenplays for *Quiet Wedding*, *The Sound Barrier*, *The VIPs*, *The Yellow Rolls Royce*, and other major films.

Separate Tables

This is a double-bill (*Table by the Window* and *Table Number Seven*, both set in the same Bournemouth private hotel and with the same subsidiary characters), with each play offering a contrasting role for the leading lady and leading man. The first presents a drunken Labour ex-junior minister unexpectedly confronted with the ex-wife who divorced him for cruelty but for whom he still feels passionately. The second has a bogus major, bound-over on a charge of insulting behaviour in a cinema and shows reactions to his exposure, especially that of a repressed spinster with a bullying mother whom he has befriended. As in much of Rattigan's work, a comparatively slight idea is enriched by a deep understanding of the needs and inadequacies of human relationships. In his original review Ken Tynan regretted 'that the major's crime was not something more cathartic than mere cinema flirtation', but supposed 'the play is as good a handling of sexual abnormality as English playgoers will tolerate'. This was in the days of the Lord Chamberlain's control, and in fact Rattigan is said to have originally intended the charge to be a homosexual one.

RECKORD, Barry

Jamaican dramatist

Plays include:

***Adella* (1954; revised version, *Flesh to a Tiger*; 1958), *You in Your Small Corner* (1960), *Skyvers* (1963), *Don't Gas the Blacks* (1969), *A Liberated Woman* (1970), *Give the Gaffers Time to Love You* (1971), *X* (1972), *Streetwise* (1984)**

Television includes:

***In the Beautiful Caribbean* (1972)**

A black Jamaican, educated at Oxford, which he left in 1952, Reckord's first play centres on a woman in a Jamaican slum trying to choose between white medicine and local magic to save her dying baby. Insulted by the white doctor with whom she has begun to fall in love it ends melodramatically with her killing both her baby and the black 'shepherd' doctor in a parallel of her people's struggle to throw off both superstition and white domination. A later television play, *In the Beautiful Caribbean*, widens the picture of exploitation to include industry, drug traffic, and the exploitation of blacks by their own middle class, and shows the emergence of a black power agitator. Reckord's other work for the stage, however, has been more concerned with class than colour. *You in Your Small Corner* shows a black bourgeois Brixton family in which the successful mother looks down on the local poor whites; and in his best-known play, *Skyvers*, set in a London comprehensive school, the pupils react violently against the social inadequacy of their parents and teachers and the suppression of talent and lack of

TRY THESE:

▷Errol John, ▷Derek Walcott, ▷Edgar White, ▷Trevor Rhone for Caribbean-located plays; ▷Michael Abbensetts, ▷Mustapha Matura, ▷Caryl Phillips for plays about British blacks with roots in the Caribbean; ▷Barrie Keeffe and ▷Peter Terson for failures in the educational/social system; ▷Mary O'Malley for a contrasting comic swipe at the Catholic educational system, and ▷Wedekind's *Spring Awakening* for a study of school children; ▷Trevor Griffiths for a writer influenced by Wilhelm Reich; ▷Sophocles' *Oedipus*, ▷John

opportunity. Although his next two plays present, in *Don't Gas the Blacks*, a black couple in which the wife has a black lover, and, in *A Liberated Woman*, a black couple in which the wife has a white lover, he is concerned no less with racism as such than with personal freedom and the sexual politics which have obsessed him in recent years.

He claims now to be 'not really happy about any of my work, except perhaps *X*'. He is still 'attempting to write about sexual politics – and so far failing'. Refusal to compromise on the forthright content of his work has aborted several proposed productions of new plays in recent years, both on stage and on television.

X

Produced by ▷ Joint Stock at the Royal Court, *X* is a two-hander in which an Oxford don is visited in his college rooms by his daughter, a believer in the ideas of Wilhelm Reich. She strips preparatory to taking a shower and then settles down to an increasingly outspoken conversation with her father, in which they both describe their sexual disappointments and she reveals the 'X' of the title: a suppressed sexual longing for her father. In the premiere production some lines were played for laughs which made for an uneasy shift to the strong meat of the argument.

Ford's *'Tis Pity She's a Whore*, ▷Shelley's *The Cenci* for treatments of incest; Michel Tremblay's *Bonjour, Bonjour* for a quite different treatment of incest.

RED SHIFT,

British touring theatre company

Founded in 1982 by artistic director Jonathan Holloway and designer Charlotte Humpston, Red Shift has established a reputation for imaginative productions committed to bridging the gap between the naturalistic tradition of narrative theatre and more visually oriented and self-consciously experimental work. Working on the proverbial shoestring, and sometimes less than that, the company has toured extensively with imaginatively conceived shows derived from sources such as the Gothic horror story, the Wild West, the murder mystery, ▷ Shakespeare, ▷ Webster, revenge tragedy, ▷ Dostoyevski and George Eliot. The company won a Fringe First Award at the ▷ Edinburgh Festival in 1987 for Holloway's own production of his *In the Image of the Beast*, (loosely based on Chapman's *Bussy D'Ambois*) described as a science fiction revenge tragedy, which created a highly effective expressionistic vision of a future only too clearly extrapolated from our present. Funding permitted, future projects will no doubt reflect the company's adventurous eclecticism. They have also, like another small touring company, Bristol Express, initiated a scheme to encourage new-writing.

TRY THESE:
▷Expressionism and ▷Performance Art for other strongly visual forms of theatre; ▷New Writing, for other examples of recent innovation in the theatre; ▷Snoo Wilson, ▷Caryl Churchill for mixtures of naturalistically improbable material within the same play.

REID, Christina [1942–]

Northern Irish dramatist

Plays include:

***Tea in a China Cup* (1982), *Did You Hear the One About The Irishman. . .?* (1984), *Dissenting Adults* (rehearsed reading; 1985), *Joyriders* (1986), *The Bells of the Belfast City* (1987)**

Reid, currently writer-in-residence at the Young Vic, is an example of the Irish theatrical renaissance of the past ten years. Reid's way is not to use the Belfast troubles as the centrepiece of her plays, but their existence is never very far away, controlling and determining destinies. *Tea in a China Cup*'s irreverent humour is used to chart the domestic minutiae through which attitudes and communities reproduce themselves and their restrictive rituals through the female line in one working-class Protestant family over almost fifty years. *Joyriders*, on the other hand, takes a tougher, almost surreal tone to show the effect of the present troubles on four young no-hopers from Belfast's notorious Divis Flats, parallelling their lives with those in ▷ Sean O'Casey's *The Shadow of a Gunman*. *The Belle of the Belfast City* which won the 1987 George Devine award was

TRY THESE:
For other images of Belfast See ▷Ann Devlin's *Ourselves Alone* which, like *Tea in a China Cup*, focuses on women-centred responses to their environment; also Allan Cubitt, Daniel Mornin and ▷Seamus Finnegan and particularly ▷Charabanc's *From the Balcony* for another, even wackier, view of meeting every-day madness with madness.

commissioned by the Tricycle Theatre, but postponed when the theatre was burnt down in 1987.

RHONE, Trevor [1940–]
Jamaican dramatist

Plays include:
***Not My Fault, Baby* (1965), *The Gadget* (1969), *Smile Orange* (1970), *Comic Strip* (1973), *Sleeper* (1974), *School's Out* (1975), *Old Story Time* (1979), *Two Can Play* (1980), *Everyman* (1981), *The Game* (1982)**

Born in Kingston, Jamaica, Rhone came to Britain in the 1960s (where he studied at the Rose Bruford College) but returned to Jamaica disappointed with the roles offered to him as a black actor, which he later said didn't begin to express black lives. Out of this frustration eventually came the impetus to write plays that did, and a desire to set up a theatre in Jamaica. In 1965, with some colleagues, (including director Yvonne Brewster), he set up the Barn Theatre (in the beginning the garage of a friend's home) with a mix of both Caribbean and non-Caribbean plays.

Now one of Jamaica's leading playwrights, he is best known outside his own country for comedies like *Smile Orange*, *Two Can Play* and *School's Out*. Rhone specialises in broad situation comedy (one of his role models is ▷ Alan Ayckbourn) written with great verve and energy, inside which often lurk shrewd observations about Jamaican life. At his best, Rhone's language and comic timing are hugely enjoyable, but all too often his comic touch (or the way the productions are played) is allowed to swamp his sharper insights, leaving an impression simply of comic stereotypes. *Old Story Time*, considered to be Rhone's best play, proves he can be something considerably more; *Smile Orange*, a farcical treatment of tourists getting taken for a ride, also has something serious to say about Third World economics and methods of survival; *School's Out*, for all its playful characterisation is also a fairly pessimistic, highly critical portrait of the inadequacies of the Jamaican educational system, and reactionary attitudes that inhibit its change. *Two Can Play* is by far his most popular play and has been performed all over the world.

Two Can Play
Unlike *School's Out* this play shows the possibilities for human growth and is an enjoyable if sentimental two-hander on the old theme of marriage given a new twist to do with female enlightenment (although Rhone has commented that the imbalance in the marriage was partly the wife's fault for not confronting her husband sooner with her dissatisfactions!). Gloria and Jim are undergoing a crisis in their marriage; Gloria is the down-trodden, family organiser, Jim the usual male chauvinist. Gloria goes north to the USA to make a marriage of convenience (the two are planning on emigration to escape the Jamaican political unrest of the 1970s) and her return triggers a re-assessment and process of re-discovery for them both. Heart-warming and funny, the comedy can be overplayed (and its ending defies belief after what has gone before) but it clearly has appeal and should be around for some time to come.

TRY THESE:
For more sparring couples, and resurgent wives, see ▷Sarah Daniels' *Ripen Our Darkness* and *The Devil's Gateway*; for more acid marital conflicts, see ▷Ted Whitehead's *Alpha Beta*; ▷James Saunders' marital two-hander *Alas Poor Fred* performed by Unoja gave the play a whole new perspective; for other Caribbean writers, see ▷Derek Walcott, ▷Edgar White, ▷Errol Hill.

ROWLEY, William [c 1585–1626]
English Renaissance dramatist

Plays include:
***A Fair Quarrel* (c 1615), *The Witch of Edmonton* (1621), *The Changeling* (1622)**

Rowley, who was a comic actor, is noted for his collaborative works with others and probably had a hand in the writing of some fifty plays. His own works are not revived, but *The Changeling* and *A Fair Quarrel* (both with ▷ Middleton) and *The Witch of Edmonton* (with ▷ Ford and ▷ Dekker) are still performed.

The Royal Shakespeare Company's phenomenally successful production of Dickens' ***Nicholas Nickelby*** in David Edgar's adaptation, directed by Trevor Nunn and John Caird, which originally opened in London in 1980.

RSC (Royal Shakespeare Company)

The Royal Shakespeare Company is now to be found on two main sites, one the Shakespeare Memorial Theatre at Stratford-upon-Avon, and the other the Barbican Theatre in London. The Barbican has two stages, one main stage and one smaller space, the Pit; while Stratford has three; the main auditorium, the more intimate The Other Place, and The Swan Theatre, for the staging of Jacobean and later drama. RSC sponsored productions are however to be found outside their own bases: for example in early 1988, besides their many touring productions, *Kiss Me Kate*, the phenomenally successful musical *Les Miserables*, ▷ Christopher Hampton's *Les Liaisons Dangereuses* were all long running West End productions initiated at the RSC.

The idea that there should be a memorial theatre for ▷ Shakespeare based at the Bard's birthplace at Stratford-upon-Avon predated the theatre and the company by several centuries. David Garrick staged a jubilee celebration in 1769; in 1869 a festival was inaugurated with productions of six ▷ Shakespeare plays at Stratford, and in 1875 Charles Flower, a local brewer, launched a national campaign to build a permanent theatre, and donated a two-acre site himself. The Shakespeare Memorial Theatre was finally built there in 1879, and staged an annual festival of ▷ Shakespeare's work. The Gothic splendours of that building fell victim to a fire in 1926 (the remains now house the Swan). The new, and currently used, building at Stratford was opened in 1932.

In 1909 F. R. Benson, the then Director of the Stratford Theatre, stated the aim of the company: 'to train a company, every member of which would be an essential part of a homogenous whole, consecrated to the practice of the dramatic arts and especially to the representation of the plays of Shakespeare'. The RSC still claim this as their principle; the company is structured around a group of 'associates', including performers, directors, designers who work together throughout the season.

In 1960 the company (under the directorship of Peter Hall) acquired its first London base at the Aldwych Theatre, and transferred its productions for seasons in London. The company had toured productions to the USA and Australia since 1939, and had performed in Leningrad and Moscow in the 1950s, but after 1960, it began regularly to tour internationally, and in 1970 became the first British company to visit Japan. It took the name The Royal Shakespeare Company in 1961, although it had had a Royal Charter since 1925. Peter Hall expanded the repertoire from ▷ Shakespeare to include contemporary plays. He aimed for a company in which the techniques and discipline of classical drama would inform the performance of modern work, while modern work would inject a contemporaneity to the productions of classical plays. The importance of verse speaking has been central to his policy as a director, and continues to inform ▷ Shakespeare performances at the RSC.

The 1960s were a period which allowed the RSC to experiment with new forms of theatre, and to develop an awareness of world drama. ▷ Peter Brook established a Theatre of Cruelty company at the RSC which, influenced by ▷ Artaud and Grotowski, explored European dramatists and new techniques in theatre, the company led to the development of the play Marat/Sade, and to a film (*Tell Me Lies*) based on the RSC production *US*. In 1964 Peter Daubeney instituted the World Theatre Season at the RSC's home at the Aldwych, which was an unprecedented opportunity to see international theatre companies. Trevor Nunn joined as Joint Aristic Director in 1968. In 1974, a smaller auditorium known as The Other Place, was opened at the Stratford site, and in London, The Warehouse opened in 1977 – both theatres committed to the production of new British writing.

In 1982 the company moved from the Aldwych to the theatre in the Barbican Centre, a complex built by the Corporation of the City of London, which funds and manages the Centre. The Barbican Theatre was designed in collaboration with Peter Hall and John Bury, then Head of Design at the RSC. It has a versatile main stage (with lots of stage effects), and a smaller theatre space, The Pit.

The RSC is now severely underfunded, and the lack of government support for the arts does not allow for the experimentation which was so influential in the 1960s. Nonetheless it has continued to expand – some might say too much so, to the

TRY THESE:
▷John Mortimer is one of the Governors of the RSC, ▷David Edgar is a member of the New Play Committee; Heidi Thomas, ▷Timberlake Wertenbaker, ▷Louise Page, ▷Nick Darke ▷Doug Lucie are among the new writers who have been commissioned for work by the RSC recently. The ▷National Theatre, Royal Court and ▷Glasgow Citizens' Theatre for other British large-scale operations; ▷Peter Brook's *The Mahabharata* as a contrasting style of large-scale production; see also ▷Mnouchkine for contrast; Stratford Ontario in Canada is another ▷Shakespeare-based repertory.

detriment of its overall quality – with a large repertoire of plays each year as well as making regular tours in Britain, visits elsewhere, and small-scale tours. Some of their most exciting work has in fact come from the smaller theatres with The Other Place (TOP) consistently serving up the most varied and challenging productions of the season. Pam Gems' *Piaf* and *Camille* started off there; so too the premieres of David Lan's *Flight*, Doug Lucie's *Fashion*, Louise Page's *Golden Girls*, Stephen Poliakoff's *Breaking the Silence*, Nick Dear's *The Art of Success*, José Triana's *Worlds Apart* and Vaclav Havel's *Temptation*. Howard Davies made a delightful job of reviving William Saroyan's *The Time of Your Life*, likewise John Barton with Calderon's *Life's A Dream*, and John Caird with Gorki's *Philistines*. The Swan too has also seen some lively and much welcomed revivals of Ben Jonson (*Every Man In His Humour*), Aphra Behn (*The Rover*), Thomas Heywood (*The Fair Maid of the West*), Shakespeare and Fletcher (*The Two Noble Kinsmen*), and James Shirley (*Hyde Park*). Most of TOP's productions, and now the Swan's, transfer on to the Barbican. The RSC also had a summer season of Swan transfers and two American plays in 1987 at London's Mermaid Theatre.

But the cornerstone of the RSC's work remains Shakespeare. Their productions can sometimes suffer from the demands of having to produce the plays year in, year out, but many exciting and innovative productions still exhilarate audiences. These include Trevor Nunn's chamber version of *Macbeth*; Bill Alexander's 1950s set *Merry Wives of Windsor*; Howard Davies' world-weary *Troilus and Cressida*; Adrian Noble's *As You Like It* with Juliet Stevenson and Fiona Shaw as Rosalind and Celia and Alan Rickman as Jacques; Terry Hands' celebrated *Much Ado About Nothing* with Derek Jacobi; and recently, Deborah Warner's *Titus Andronicus* and Nicholas Hytner's *Measure for Measure* with Josette Simon as Isabella.

Nunn and Caird's 1981 production of *Nicholas Nickleby* in which David Edgar adapted Dickens' novel in collaboration with the company was a stunning two-part work which despite initially cool critical reception became a major success and toured Britain to packed houses.

It also marked a shift in RSC direction in encouraging large-scale, musically based productions: *Kiss Me Kate* and *Les Misérables* have followed. After Nunn's resignation as Artistic Director, Terry Hands has tended to go for the broadly popular because of considerable financial pressure and pushed increasingly into commercial sponsorship. There is some argument as to whether one of Britain's two major national subsidised companies *should* be putting on blockbuster musicals; *Carrie*, based on a Stephen King novel, was booked to go straight from Stratford to Broadway and on to London if a proven success. Its closure after five performances calls this policy seriously into question.

RUDET, Jacqueline [1962–]
British dramatist

Plays include:
Money to Live (1984), _God's Second in Command_ (1985), _Basin_ (1985)

Born in London's East End but brought up in Dominica, Rudet started out as an actress (appearing with Roland Muldoon's CAST company and Belt and Braces) before forming her own group, Imani-Faith, like ▷ Theatre of Black Women, to provide theatre for and about black women. However, her first play, *Money to Live* was actually presented by the ▷ Black Theatre Co-op and proved a success, with public and critics alike despite Rudet's own reservations about the way the production had been directed. A naturalistic writer with a television sense and lively line in dialogues she made a dazzling debut with the hard-hitting *Money to Live*, a domestic drama about stripping that tackled its subject with a rare lack of cant and undisguised anger at men who see women only as sexual objects. The play is centred on Charleen who is persuaded by a friend to become a stripper to escape from the poverty trap. Rudet also makes some trenchant observations about the relationship between

TRY THESE:
▷Peter Terson's *Strippers* for a rather more complex, and debatable treatment of the subject; ▷Pam Gems' *Treats* is set in a strip-club; ▷Kay Adshead's *Thatcher's Women* and ▷Julia Schofield's *Love on the Plastic* also look at the economic pressures and moral hypocrisies around prostitution; ▷Jackie Kay's *Chiaroscuro* for another play about black women exploring friendship, lesbianism and labels; ▷Winsome Pinnock is another contemporary

love, sex and money that leaves little room for sentimentality. If not necessarily a new subject, Rudet's treatment of it, in the context of a young, black female, and the timelessness of its theme probably ensures it will turn up regularly in future repertoires. And, as Rudet herself points out, the play is as much about getting through in hard times as about 'being a black play'. *Basin* however, has no such equivocation; a conversation piece, it is openly about the love and communality between black women with Rudet's sparky dialogue providing some easy humour amongst the sometimes tense encounters as three friends work out the meaning of friendship.

black playwright; see also ▷Theatre of Black Women.

RUDKIN, (James) David [1936–]
British dramatist

Plays include:

***Afore Night Come* (1960), *Burglars* (1970), *The Filth Hut* (1972), *Cries from Casement as His Bones Are Brought to Dublin* (1973), *Ashes* (1973), *No Title* (1974), *The Sons of Light* (1976), *Sovereignty Under Elizabeth* (1977), *Hansel and Gretel* (1980), *The Triumph of Death* (1981), *The Saxon Shore* (1986)**

Rudkin was hailed as a major playwright when *Afore Night Come*, already produced while he was an Oxford student, was taken up for production by the ▷ RSC in 1962. The play touches on themes which are developed in his later work such as concern for the countryside, abhorrence of atomic weapons, chemical and other pollution, the idea of homosexuality as a natural and innocent manifestation of love and an awareness of English-Irish confrontation; while the dialogue shows his accurate ear for the speech of the Black Country and the Worcestershire countryside. In *Afore Night Come* the continuity with the past seems ominous and evil but in other work, such as the television play *Penda's Fen* the past (in the persons of King Penda and Sir Edward Elgar) seems to be in guardianship, though the more recent *White Lady* showed nature overwhelmed by deadly petrochemicals.

Rudkin comes from a revivalist background but his plays question the idiology of sectarian religion and seek a closer communion with the natural world, sometimes using Christian symbolism. He affirms the continuity of the atavistic forces and beliefs which power systems – including the Church – suppress or twist to enable them to condition people to accept their own repression.

Afore Night Come remains the most accessible of Rudkin's major stage works. More complicated structures appear in *Ashes*, about an infertile couple (a fairly blatant metaphor for the sterility of the Northern Ireland situation) and self determinism, also which offers political, anthropological and psychological viewpoints, and *The Triumph of Death*, partly about Martin Luther, which is concerned with the way that organised Christianity seeks power through association with established forces.

Rudkin's adaptations and translations include ▷ Euripides' *Hippolytus* (1978), ▷ Genet's *Deathwatch* and *The Maids* (1987), and ▷ Ibsen's *Peer Gynt* (1983). Librettos include Schoenberg's *Moses and Aaron* (1965) and Gordon Crosse's *The Grace of Todd* (1969). The most characteristic of numerous television plays are perhaps *Penda's Fen* and *White Lady* and he has written screenplays for *Mademoiselle*, *Farenheit 451* and *Testimony*.

TRY THESE:
▷Trevor Griffiths and ▷Barry Reckord for Reichian influences; ▷David Edgar's *Mary Barnes* for contemporary treatment of schizophrenia; ▷Tony Craze's *Shona*, for Caribbean exploration of pre-Christianity; see also Felix Cross's *Mass Carib* and *Blues For Railton*.

The Sons of Light

The Sons of Light was worked on over eleven years (1965–76) resulting in an 8–9 hour play which was reshaped to about three hours playing time and then further cut for the published text as performed by the RSC in 1977. Dedicated to the late Dr Robert Ollendorf, a Reichian therapist, of whom the character Nebewohl is a portrait in reverse, it is divided into three main sections linked to the stages of the Christian mythology of the 'Harrowing of Hell'. A complex science-fantasy fable which operates on many levels it is set on a Scottish island ruled by a 'Benefactor' operating a religion of vengeance. Beneath the earth is a factory colony of workers kept from rebellion by a promise of heaven. Here a new pastor and his sons arrive, one of whom eventually descends among the workers, reawakens their self-awareness and destroys the subterranean complex to reclaim the island for its inhabitants. This is parallelled by the reclamation of a young girl from schizophrenia – a resurrection of both the individual and the culture.

RUSSELL, Willy [1947–]

British dramatist, song-writer and singer

Plays include:

***Keep Your Eyes Down* (1971), *Sam O'Shanker* (1972; musical version 1973), *When the Reds* (1972), *Tam Lin* (1972), *John, Paul, George, Ringo and. . .Bert* (1974), *Breezeblock Park* (1975), *One for the Road* (originally *Painted Veg and Parkinson*; 1976), *Stags and Hens* (1978), *Educating Rita* (1979), *Blood Brothers* (1981; musical version 1983), *Our Day Out* (1983, from 1977 TV play), *Shirley Valentine* (1986)**

Television includes:

***King of the Castle* (1973), *Death of a Young Young Man* (1975), *Break In* (1975), Our Day Out (1977), *Lies* (1977), *Daughters of Albion* (1979), *Boy with the Transistor Radio* (1979), *One Summer* (serial, 1980)**

One of the most often produced contemporary dramatists, Russell's work is closely linked with Liverpool (he was born in nearby Whiston) and the Everyman Theatre which mounted his first professional production and has commissioned other plays from him, including *John, Paul, George, Ringo and. . .Bert*. This musical about the Beatles brought him national success and was called 'a powerful statement about innocence and corruption that is also an hilariously funny evening out'. Such a balance between comment and exhilarating entertainment can be found right through Russell's work. *Educating Rita*, two-hander about a middle-aged lecturer and a 'raw-diamond' working-class woman student – especially in its film version – put Russell on the international map. Russell himself left school at fifteen, returning to college to study for 'O' and 'A' levels five years later because he had decided to become a teacher and a playwright, although the play probably owes as much to his regional background and time spent as a ladies' hairdresser. He is totally unpatronising about the working-class, and his female characters are particularly vivid. In both *Educating Rita* and *Shirley Valentine* - a scouse monologue with marvellous jokes (but little feminist consciousness) – he makes use of minimal resources, but he is equally adept at handling large groups of characters. A good example is *Stags and Hens*, in which a stag night and a hen night outing both chose the same club for their celebration. In this shrieking, puking world, with major sections set in the lavatories, Russell is no outsider and audiences can share both the fun and pain of his characters at grass-roots level.

Russell is an excellent introduction to theatre for anyone – and especially youngsters – who thinks that theatre is for the nobs and not for them. He can be commercial and popular without any compromise. He also writes smashing tunes!

Blood Brothers

Loosely based on the old 'Corsican Brothers' story of twins brought up in different classes, *Blood Brothers* has a superb creation in the character of the working-class mother (played and sung in the musical premiere by Barbara Dickson). It is a deeply felt picture of different social backgrounds, although its middle-class characters are perhaps less convincing than the working-class, and despite the parable-like nature of its overall construction. The songs are able to succeed outside the show, but they are an integral and necessary part adding to our understanding of the characters. A smash hit that offered a social document disguised as melodrama.

TRY THESE:
For Manchester, ▷Waterhouse and Hall's *Billy Liar*, Hobhouse, ▷Delaney, ▷Alan Bleasdale; ▷John Godber's *Bouncers* for a graphic, funny, but essentially damning portrait of British yobbism at play.

SACKLER, Howard [1929–1982]

American dramatist

Plays include:

***Uriel Acosta* (1954), *The Yellow Loves* (1959), *A Few Inquiries* (1964), *The Pastime of Monsieur Robert* (1966), *The Great White Hope* (1967), *Goodbye, Fidel* (1980), *Semmelweiss* (1981)**

Born in New York, Sackler started out as a poet and worked on films throughout his life, but he remains best known for his 1967 play *The Great White Hope*, a thinly fictionalised account of the celebrated black boxer Jack Johnson, who became the world heavyweight champion in 1908. Acclaimed on Broadway, on film, and in two separate London productions in 1985 (Tricycle) and 1987 (▷ RSC) (both directed by Tricycle director Nicholas Kent), the play is socially and ethically exemplary; as drama, however, it must be said it falls short. Sackler was writing from the viewpoint of undigested late-1960s white liberal guilt, and too many of the play's would-be challenges to the audience have more to do with assuaging Sackler's own uneasy conscience than with any genuine assault on the fourth wall. His follow-up plays were equally episodic, but nowhere near as successful, particularly *Goodbye, Fidel*, a sprawling saga about a patrician Cuban widow about to be exiled from a country in tumult.

TRY THESE:
▷Arthur Miller for social conscience; ▷James Baldwin and ▷Lorraine Hansberry for the kind of authentic black experience Sackler, as a white, wanted to reproduce on stage; ▷August Wilson, Charles Fuller, George C. Wolfe for contemporary black treatments of racism; ▷Louise Page's *Golden Girls* for a rare account of women and sport and racism; ▷Jack Gelber's *The Cuban Thing* and the works of ▷José Triana for plays set in and about Cuba.

SARTRE, Jean-Paul [1905–80]

French philosopher, novelist and dramatist

Plays include:

***Les Mouches* (*The Flies;* 1943), Huis Clos (*In Camera*; 1944), *Vicious Circle* or *No Exit*, *Les Mains Sales Crime Passionnel*, (*The Assassin*, or *Dirty Hands*; 1948), *Le Diable et le Bon Dieu* (*The Devil and the Good Lord*, or *Lucifer and the Lord*; 1951), *Kean* (from Dumas père; 1953), *Les Séquestrés d'Altona* (*Altona*; 1959)**

Play-writing was never Sartre's main occupation, but he had a high degree of success with it, and his plays and his philosophy interact in an interesting manner. His first known play is *Bariona*, a nativity play which he wrote while in a prisoner-of-war camp in 1940, and staged there with the help of priests; it was a semi-disguised anti-colonialist play about the occupation of Judaea. He subsequently favoured a 'theatre of situations' rather than a psychological theatre, with characters defined by their actions rather than their intentions, the better to explore his ideas about existentialism and the possibility of individual freedom. *The Flies* shows Orestes accepting full responsibility for the killing of Aegisthus, rather than being a prey to fate, as in the Greek versions; it also has overtones of French attitudes, including Sartre's own, to the Nazi occupation. *In Camera*, with its gradual revelation that the scene is hell, and its three characters who have lived in 'bad faith' must stay there for eternity, is perhaps his best bit of construction. In *The Devil and the Good Lord* the hero manages to achieve 'authenticity' in his actions (of which Sartre approved) by rejecting in turn attempts to be thoroughly evil or thoroughly good. By the time he reached *Altona*, however, Sartre had

TRY THESE:
Camus for French plays with philosophical content; ▷John Arden and ▷Margaretta D'Arcy for *The Business of Good Government*, another Nativity play with a political message; ▷Pirandello, for the questioning of the distinction between acting and life; ▷Brecht for anti-capitalist plays with non-Aristotelian forms.

given up hope about man's ability to choose how to act, and adopted a Marxist perspective towards what seems to be the development of post-war Germany but is in fact a metaphor for the French war in Algeria.

Sartre's plays were important in opening the post-war French drama to serious subjects, and in persuading playwrights to engage with politics and philosophy, but they were not experimental in form. For Sartre, anti-capitalism implied no break with Aristotelian models of theatre; unlike ▷ Brecht, he used fairly conventional and illusionistic forms of playmaking, though his characters do now seem to talk a lot. ▷ Ionesco called his plays political melodramas, but this underestimates their complexity and ambiguity.

Sartre's shorter plays were frequently performed in London in the 1940s and 1950s (▷ Peter Brook directed *Vicious Circle* in 1946, and *Men Without Shadows* and *The Respectable Prostitute* in 1947), but they have since had a period of eclipse; however, *The Assassin* was respectfully received at the Greenwich Theatre in 1982, and the first English production of *The Devil and the Good Lord* at the Lyric, Hammersmith in 1984 was a triumph for Gerard Murphy, in spite of four and a half hours of relentless metaphysical argument.

Kean

Kean is a reworking of Dumas père's Romantic drama, with substantial additions, and it is the play that displays most clearly Sartre's idea of theatre. Kean's ontological insecurities impel him to assume identities not his own (for he has none); at the same time, his free access to both princes and people gives him and others the illusion that it is easy for genius to move up in a class-ridden world. His constant awareness of his own psychological and social paradoxes allowed Sartre to turn theatre against itself without using Brechtian techniques of disjunction. Kean is also a marvellous part for a bravura actor, such as Alan Badel in 1971, and Jean-Paul Belmondo at the Théâtre Marigny in 1987.

SAUNDERS, James [1925–]

British dramatist

Plays include:

Alas Poor Fred (1959), _Next Time I'll Sing to You_ (1962), _A Scent of Flowers_ (1964), _The Italian Girl_ (1967; with Irish Murdoch, from her novel), _The Travails of Sancho Panza_ (1969; from Cervantes' _Don Quixote_, _The Borage Pigeon Affair_ (1969), _Bodies_ (1977), _The Girl in Melanie Klein_ (1980; from ▷ Ronald Harwood, radio version 1973), _Fall_ (1984)

For a while after *Next Time I'll Sing to You* Saunders was regarded as one of Britain's best dramatists but his subsequent career has not matched that early promise. *Next Time I'll Sing to You*, based on the true story of the hermit Jimmy Mason which also inspired ▷ Edward Bond's *The Pope's Wedding*, impressed many critics with its self-conscious theatricality and meditation on free will and determinism. Saunders, a prolific dramatist, has continued writing decent, questioning plays about liberal values but his work appears to have been overtaken by changing socio-political trends to the point where it seems to have little to offer to contemporary audiences. He often uses narrators, time shifts or monologues and displays an interest in the nature of theatricality but the whole enterprise currently seems curiously genteel and passé, though the black company Umoja's successful staging of his early *Alas Poor Fred* in 1986 suggests that there may be a renewed interest in his work from an unexpected direction.

TRY THESE:
The treatments of the aftermath of death in ▷Edward Bond's *The Sea* and ▷Alan Ayckbourn's *Absent Friends* offer interesting parallels to *A Scent of Flowers*; ▷Ayckbourn, as well as his other qualities, generally seems to offer a more robust version of Saunders; the atmosphere of *Fall* is distinctly Chekhovian, to the point of actually having three sisters; ▷Ted Whitehead's studies of modern marriage offer an interesting contrast to Saunders' *Bodies*; Saunders used to be classed as a dramatist of the Absurd, primarily on the strength of the subtitle to *Alas Poor Fred*, which is *A Duologue in the Style of Ionesco*.

SCHILLER, Johann Christoph Friedrich von

[1759–1805]
German dramatist and poet

TRY THESE:
▷Goethe for eighteenth-century

Plays include:

Die Räuber (_The Robbers_ or _The Highwaymen_; 1782), _Fiesco_ (1782), _Kabale und Liebe_ (_Intrigue and Love_; 1784), _Don Carlos_ (1787), the _Wallenstein_ trilogy (1798–9), _Maria Stuart_ (_Mary Stuart_; 1800), _Wilhelm Tell_ (_William Tell_; 1804)

Schiller was the son of an army surgeon, and was a young military doctor himself when his first play *Die Räuber* appeared – though safely set in the sixteenth century, it was an instant success for its contemporary revolutionary appeal, its *Sturm und Drang* claims for the rights of the individual, and its doubling of the parts of the good and bad brothers. He went on to become one of the major German verse playwrights, a professor of History at the University of Jena, and a close friend of ▷ Goethe; but he never had quite enough money to live on, and never quite achieved respectability.

Schiller's plays have been performed in Britain in recent years more often than ever before (not counting the various operatic versions); there was a tame version of *Die Räuber* (as *The Highwaymen*) at the Round House in 1974, of which the less said the better; and the p.l.c. company at Bridge Lane have made gallant attempts at both *Mary Stuart* (1985) and *Don Carlos* (1986). The Royal Exchange, Manchester, had some success with *Don Carlos* in 1987, in a new prose translation by James Maxwell with Ian McDiarmid as Philip II of Spain; but Frank Dunlop was probably right to use Joseph Mellish's 1801 verse translation of *Mary Stuart* for his 1987 production at the Assembly Rooms in Edinburgh. It came over as a powerful piece of rhetoric, with a fine confrontation between Hannah Gordon and Jill Bennett as the rival queens (though John Knox must have been spinning in his grave at the whole proceedings).

Maria Stuart

Maria Stuart has the characteristics of all Schiller's 'historical' plays – powerful language, long aria-like speeches, dramatic confrontations, and a somewhat cavalier attitude to historical fact. The 'big scene' is a meeting between Mary Stuart and Elizabeth Tudor which never happened, and both queens are courted by a vacillating Lord Leicester. It makes a splendid, somewhat operatic play (and indeed a fine opera by Donizetti); but its success in southern Britain is perhaps inhibited by the national difficulty in taking seriously a play which casts Elizabeth I as villainness. However it has done well at the ▷ Edinburgh Festival (1958 and 1987) and at the Glasgow Citizens' (1985, in Macdonald's translation).

German verse tragedy; ▷Dario Fo for a similar failure to understand Elizabeth I, ▷Corneille and ▷Racine for French classical tragedy; Shakespeare's history plays also take liberties with historical fact for dramatic effect, Liz Lochhead's *Mary Queen of Scots Got Her Head Chopped Off* for a contemporary Scottish perspective.

SCHISGAL, Murray [1926–]

American dramatist

Plays include:

The Typists (1960), _The Tiger_ (1960), _Luv_ (1964), _Fragments_ (1967), _The Basement_ (1967), _Jimmy Shine_ (1968), _A Way of Life_ (1969), _An American Millionaire_ (1974), _All Over Town_ (1974), _Twice Around the Park_ (1982), _Road Show_ (1987)

Films include:

The Tiger Makes Out (1967), _Tootsie_ (with Larry Gelbart; 1982)

Since he launched his playwriting career in London in 1960 with a series of one-act plays at the British Drama League, New York-born Schisgal has written fifty plays – many of them little-known one-acts – and a variety of television shows and films, pre-eminently the Oscar-winning smash *Tootsie*. His first New York success, *Luv*, is a three-character absurdist farce in which the suicidal Harry Berlin meets former schoolmate Milt Manville, who decides to unload his wife Ellen on the hapless Harry. The play once thought to make Schisgal 'a household word', it prompted critic Walter Kerr's dubious encomium that *Luv* was better than *Waiting For Godot*. In his 1968 *Jimmy Shine*, a comic vaudeville about despair, a failed abstract painter looks back on a life of frustration and fantasy. *All Over Town*, a Feydeau-esque farce set amidst Manhattan neurotics, is a mixed-identity comedy in

TRY THESE:
▷Neil Simon (especially *The Prisoner of Second Avenue*) ▷Jules Feiffer, Herb Gardner (*I'm Not Rappaport*) for New York neuroticism and urban misadventures; ▷Arthur Kopit's *Oh Dad, Poor Dad. . .* for ▷Ionesco-influenced hi-jinks comparable to *Luv*.

which a canny black delivery boy called Lewis is mistaken for an unemployed, lusty white youth called Louie Lucas. *Road Show* is a comedy about midlife crisis, centring on two high school lovers who meet twenty years on.

Schisgal's career is associated with certain performers who have repeatedly appeared in and/or directed his plays, including the husband/wife team of Eli Wallach and Anne Jackson, who brought his two one-act plays, *Twice Around the Park*, to the ▷ Edinburgh Festival, in 1984, and Dustin Hoffman, who played Jimmy Shine and directed *All Over Town.*

SCHNITZLER, Arthur [1862–1931]

Austrian dramatist

Plays include:

***Anatol* (1893), *Liebelei* (*Dalliance*; 1895), *Das Weite Land* (*Undiscovered Country*; 1911), *Reigen* (*La Ronde*; 1902), *Der Einsame Weg* (*The Lonely Road*; 1904)**

Schnitzler, the son of a rich Jewish doctor, studied medicine and psychoanalysis in late-nineteenth century Vienna, and his plays about the Viennese permissive society combine light comedy, satire, voyeurism, and apparent disapproval in an uneasy but appealing mixture. The plays are predictably popular today: ▷ Tom Stoppard's free translations *Undiscovered Country* and *Dalliance*, appeared at the ▷ National Theatre in 1979 and 1985 respectively; in 1985 Christopher Fettes directed both *The Lonely Road* at the Old Vic and *Intermezzo* at the Greenwich theatre; and the series of linked playlets, *Anatol* appeared at the Gate in 1987, with Jane Bertish putting in a bravura performance as seven contrasted women pursued by Anatol, the man-about-town. And in 1982, as soon as *La Ronde* came out of copyright, there were three stage and one televised version of it within three months (though, interestingly enough, nothing since).

La Ronde

The play is a series of ten episodes (the Prostitute picks up the Soldier; the Soldier seduces the Chambermaid; the Chambermaid seduces the Young Gentleman. . .the Count picks up the Prostitute). Its first performance in Berlin in 1920 was greeted with shock-horror and prosecutions of all concerned; it had a similar reception in Vienna in 1921, as did Max Ophüls' film version in 1950, though the film is far less sour and realistic than Schnitzler's original. Of the flurry of British productions in 1982 (Royal Exchange Manchester, as *The Round Dance*, ▷ RSC at the Aldwych, and ▷ Shared Experience at the Drill Hall), ▷ Mike Alfreds' new version for ▷ Shared Experience was the fastest and least heavy-handed. This was partly because of the quick changes of costume in full view to emphasise the degree of role-playing, and partly because two actors played all the roles; but the play was carrying more expectations that it can live up to, and Schnitzler's other plays seem more likely to hold the stage in future.

TRY THESE:
▷Wedekind's *Lulu* for the erotic cynicism, perhaps, though it is much less cool; ▷Molnár for Austro-Hungarian comedy, but with quite a different tone; ▷Nestroy for other Viennese dramatists translated by ▷Tom Stoppard; ▷Noël Greig's *Angels Descend On Paris* for more sexual role-playing; ▷Genet's *The Maids* and *The Balcony* for role-playing taken to a high art; and for the High Priest of them all, ▷Lindsay Kemp.

SCHOFIELD, Julia

British actress, director and writer

Plays include:

***Love on the Plastic* (1987)**

After ten years as an actress, some directing, a summer spent building a narrow boat and some scripts for television and radio Julia Schofield established herself as a stage dramatist with the success of *Love on the Plastic* at the Half Moon in 1987. The play is a witty, compassionate but coldly angry look at the almost respectable end of the sex industry in the form of the hostess clubs where business men buy female company, and more, on expenses. Its presentation of the underlying reasons for the women's presence in the clubs and their use of the only saleable commodity they have in a world dominated by the

TRY THESE:
▷Kay Adshead's *Thatcher's Women* and ▷Peter Terson's *Strippers* are contemporary accounts of the economics of the sex industry; much Restoration comedy (eg ▷Aphra Behn, ▷Congreve, ▷Wycherley) and Renaissance drama (eg ▷Middleton, ▷Webster) deals in

values of the marketplace is instructive, comic, moving and entertaining.

the relationship between sex and economic/political power.

SENECA, Lucius Annaeus [c 4 BC – 65 AD]
Roman philosopher and dramatist

Plays include:
Medea, Phaedra, Agamemnon, Oedipus, Thyestes **(nine plays in all are attributed to him)**

Seneca's verse plays were almost certainly not intended for the public stage but scholars disagree as to how (if at all) they were performed at Nero's court – the view that they were intended for dramatic recitation seems to owe something to their long rhetorical speeches, and something to so-called 'unstageable' scenes such as the reassembling of Hippolytus' dismembered body by his father. However, their static action and bloodthirsty plots were a major influence on the Elizabethan playwrights (eg Shakespeare's *Titus Andronicus* and ▷ Kyd's *The Spanish Tragedy*). Artaud, who regarded Seneca as the greatest Classical dramatist and the nearest in approach to his projected Theatre of Cruelty, planned to stage his own adaptation of *Thyestes* in 1934. Jean-Louis Barrault tried a production of the *Medea* at the Odéon in the 1960s and the Glasgow Citizens' had a go at *Thyestes* in the 1970s but the most recent major production of a play by Seneca was ▷ Peter Brook's *Oedipus*, in a version by Ted Hughes, at the Old Vic in 1968. The production combined a powerful and direct text, filled with violent images of bloodshed and horror, delivered in a distanced monotone by largely static actors; complex choral work broken up into separate sounds and rhythms, wails and hums and hisses, accompanied by electronic music; and a light political dusting of possible references to Vietnam. It was an interesting mixture of the Artaudian and the Brechtian, and was received with respect (though it was said of ▷ Brook that he had 'gradually become the purveyor of avant-garde clichés to the mass audience'). Its revival by the RSC in August 1988 should make a fascinating contrast.

TRY THESE:
▷Shakespeare for *Titus Andronicus*; ▷Euripides, ▷Racine for versions of the Hippolytus/Phaedra story; ▷Artaud for the Theatre of Cruelty.

7:84
British touring theatre company

7:84's name derives from a 1966 statistic in *The Economist*, which asserted that 7 percent of the population owned 84 percent of the capital wealth; although the figures may have fluctuated since then (the disproportion is probably now even greater), the principle of demonstrating the social and economic inequalities of life under capitalism still holds for the company. 7:84 began to work in 1971, and their first production, *Trees in the Wind*, by ▷ John McGrath (the Artistic Director), was performed at the Edinburgh Festival. In 1973 the company was organised as two companies, 7:84 England and 7:84 Scotland, but in 1985 the Arts Council withdrew its subsidy from 7:84 England, despite enormous support from audiences and the company has had to struggle to survive.

7:84 has strong links with the Trade Union and labour movements, Neil Kinnock is a director of 7:84 England, and the company receives financial support from Labour Councils the TUC and from individual unions. The first show from the Scottish company was *The Cheviot, the Stag and the Black, Black Oil* (by McGrath, developed with the company) which played to audiences in theatres, community halls and schools throughout Scotland; and became a text on Scottish history curricula in schools and colleges. The principle of touring has remained central to 7:84's policy; they have toured productions throughout Britain, often bypassing theatres in favour of community centres and colleges.

In 1983 the company toured a show about the effects of privatisation as part of NALGO's 'Put People First Campaign'.

TRY THESE:
▷John McGrath was Artistic Director, and developed much of his work with 7:84; ▷Trevor Griffiths, ▷John Arden and ▷Margaretta D'Arcy, David MacLennan, ▷Aristophanes and ▷Brecht have been performed by 7:84; for other contemporary touring theatre companies see ▷Foco Novo, ▷Paines Plough, ▷Joint Stock, ▷Temba, ▷Monstrous Regiment, Wildcat (which grew out of 7:84 Scotland), Red Ladder, ▷Women's Theatre Group, ▷Gay Sweatshop, ▷Cheek by Jowl, ▷Theatre of Black Women; Roland Muldoon's CAST company

7:84 are frequently to be found performing for benefits, for Socialist conferences and for particular political campaigns.

The theatres they have played in London have tended to be those with a radical history and a commitment to local audiences; the Royal Court, Unity Theatre, the Half Moon and The Theatre Royal Stratford East. They have toured Ireland, the Western Isles of Scotland, and internationally. In 1982 (before Glasnost), they toured Moscow, Leningrad and Tbilisi, have performed at the International Brecht Festival in Toronto, in Holland and Brussels, at the ▷ Berliner Ensemble.

Besides a commitment to bringing new work to working-class audiences, the company also has a policy of reviving Socialist texts, both novels and plays, and bringing them to a wider audience; their plays are, as McGrath puts it: 'based on the lives, the struggles past and present of our audiences, and on the aspirations of those audiences for a better future'. Among their productions are new versions of ▷ Brecht's *The Mother*, of ▷ Aristophanes and an adaptation of Miles Malleson's 1930s *Six Men of Dorset*, about the Tolpuddle martyrs. *Blood Red Roses* and *The Cheviot, the Stag and the Black, Black Oil* are among the 7:84 productions which have been televised.

7:84 says about themselves: 'of course we talk politics: because it is a reality of life today. And because theatre is about the way people relate to each other, and that is conditioned by economic structures from which spring social structures, like classes and cultural patterns.'

touring pubs and community venues in London kept political/socialist ▷cabaret alive for many years.

SHAFFER, Anthony (Joshua) [1926–]

British dramatist and novelist

Plays include:

***The Savage Parade* (1963), *Sleuth* (1970), *Murderer* (1975), *Widow's Weeds* (1977), *The Case of the Oily Levantine* (also known as *Who Done It*; 1979)**

Only *Sleuth* has gained both critical and popular acclaim. *The Savage Parade*, originally given only a Sunday night peformance but more recently revived, offers a very different topic: the secret trial of a Nazi war criminal in Israel. *Sleuth* is both a clever and intricate thriller and a parody of the genre. The protagonist is even a thriller writer, who plans to avenge himself on his wife's lover. With a construction like a series of chinese boxes it demonstrates great technical skill. Though the characterisations never attempt to rise above those of the conventional thriller, they offer the opportunity for bravura performances.

Shaffer wrote the screenplay for *Sleuth* and several other films, including *Frenzy*, *The Wicker Man*, *Masada* and *Death on the Nile*, and he has also written for television and collaborated on a number of novels with his twin brother, ▷ Peter Shaffer.

TRY THESE:
Robert Shaw's *The Man in the Glass Booth* for another play about the trial of a war criminal; ▷Tom Stoppard's *The Real Inspector Hound* for a rather less successful thriller parody; Ira Levins *Deathtrap* for a similar kind of plot; ▷Christopher Hampton's *The Portage to San Cristobal of A.H.* for a play about the Israelis and war criminals; see also ▷Thrillers.

SHAFFER, Peter [1926–]

British dramatist

Plays include:

***Five Finger Exercise* (1958), *The Private Ear* (1962), *The Public Eye* (1962), *The Royal Hunt of the Sun* (1964), *Black Comedy* (1965), *White Lies* (1967), *The Battle of Shrivings* (1970), *Equus* (1973), *Amadeus* (1979), *Yonadab* (1985), *Lettice and Lovage* (1987)**

Born in Liverpool and educated at Cambridge, Peter Shaffer is most interesting for what he is *not* – he is not a British resident, he is not politically motivated, and he is not interested in screenwriting, at a time when most playwrights are at least two out of the three. Instead, the New York-based Shaffer perpetuates infinite variations on a theme: the conflicts between reason and faith/mediocrity and genius/man and God, as examined from a variety of historical viewpoints. In *The Royal Hunt of the Sun*, the debate occurs between Atahualpa and Pizarro, the Inca and the atheistic Spanish conqueror of Peru. In *Equus*, it is a clash between a psychoanalyst and his charge – a self-tormenting

TRY THESE:
▷David Mercer for celebrations of the rebel; John Peielmeier's *Agnes of God*, ▷Bernard Pomerance's *The Elephant Man* for plays that pit doctors against patients, definitions of normality against an unhingement that may be preferable; for a historical sweep, see ▷Robert Bolt's *A Man for All Seasons*, ▷John Whiting's *The Devils* and by contrast, ▷Nick Dear's debunking *The*

doctor devoid of passion and the patient who has committed an extraordinary act of passion and violence. *Amadeus*, which became an acclaimed Oscar-winning film in 1984, shifts the argument to the creative arena, as it pits the aberrant genius Wolfgang Amadeus Mozart against the decent but uninspired court composer Antonio Salieri, who may or may not have poisoned him. In all three plays, Shaffer weds his argument to a strong sense of the theatrical, not to mention an underlying repressed homo-eroticism. The former, if not the latter, forsook him in the Biblical *Yonadab*, an *Amadeus*-like tale of envy drawn from the Old Testament's Second Book of Samuel.

Shaffer has written comedy, as well, including four plays for Maggie Smith: *The Private Ear, The Public Eye*, *Black Comedy*, and his most recent, *Lettice and Lovage*, in which the two heroines – Lettice Douffet and Lotte Schoen – enact their own variant on Shaffer's obsessive opposition of the eccentric outsider (Lettice) and the social conformist (Lotte). Is Shaffer a great playwright or merely a clever manipulator of the middlebrow? The verdict is out on that, but one thing is clear: Shaffer has a highly developed sense of the market second to none.

Art of Success for a similar and shocking reassessment of an artist.

Equus

A stable boy blinds six horses after a frustrated sexual liaison in Shaffer's award-winning play, which was a huge hit both in London (with Alec McCowen) and on Broadway (with Anthony Hopkins and – among others – Richard Burton, later in the run) in John Dexter's mightily theatrical, swift production. Burton starred in Sidney Lumet's ill-fated 1977 film, where the realism of the genre mitigated the thesis of the play. How could one put any stock in Dr Dysart's envy for the tormented Alan, when we had just seen, in full blood-drenched realism, the climactic episode which was supposed to have triggered such thoughts? The film has the odd effect of rendering hollow and emptily rhetorical what on stage is a verbal thrill: the agony between the self-laceratingly literate Dysart and his semi-articulate, disturbed young patient – a tension between the realms of intellect and passion that is a thematic constant for this playwright.

SHAKESPEARE, William [1564–1616]

English Renaissance dramatist

Plays:

***Henry VI, Parts II and III* (1591), *The Comedy of Errors* (1592), *Henry VI, Part I* (1592), *Richard III* (1593), *The Two Gentlemen of Verona* (1593), *The Taming of the Shrew* (1594), *Titus Andronicus* (1594), *Love's Labour's Lost* (1595), *A Midsummer Night's Dream* (1595), *Richard II* (1595), *Romeo and Juliet* (1595), *King John* (1596), *The Merchant of Venice* (1596), *Henry IV, Parts I and II* (1597), *Much Ado About Nothing* (1598), *As You Like It* (1599), *Henry V* (1599), *Julius Caesar* (1599), *The Merry Wives of Windsor* (1600), *Twelfth Night* (1600), *Hamlet* (1601), *All's Well That Ends Well* (1602), *Troilus and Cressida* (1602), *Measure for Measure* (1604), *Othello* (1604), *King Lear* (1605), *Macbeth* (1606), *Antony and Cleopatra* (1607), *Timon of Athens* (1607), *Coriolanus* (1608), *Pericles* (1608), *Cymbeline* (1609), *The Winter's Tale* (1610), *The Tempest* (1611), *Henry VIII* (1613; with ▷ Fletcher) *The Two Noble Kinsmen* (1613; with ▷ Fletcher)**

Shakespeare was a dramatist, actor, poet, theatre owner and landowner, who wrote most of his plays for the company of which he was part owner and worked in all the popular genres of his time. He also wrote the lost *Cardenio* with ▷ Fletcher and, most probably, part of *Sir Thomas More*. Many other Renaissance plays have been attributed to him, often on scanty or non-existent evidence; the strongest recent claims have been made for *Edmund Ironside* and *Edward III*.

Shakespeare's plays based on English history cover the period from King John to Henry VIII and include two tetralogies (*Richard II, Henry IV* Parts I and II, and *Henry V* form one and *Henry VI* Parts I, II and III, and *Richard III* the other), which are extremely effective when performed as a group (as done by the ▷ RSC in

TRY THESE:
For other Renaissance dramatists see ▷Beaumont, ▷Chapman, ▷Fletcher, ▷Ford, ▷Thomas Heywood, ▷Jonson, ▷Kyd, ▷Marlowe, ▷Marston, ▷Massinger, ▷Middleton, ▷Tourneur, ▷Webster; for adaptations/reworkings of Shakespeare see ▷Dryden and Davenant's *The Tempest*; Charles Marowitz's collage versions of several plays; Peter Ustinov's *Romanoff and Juliet*; the musical *West Side Story* is an updating of *Romeo and Juliet* to New York, and *Kiss Me Kate* is a reworking of *The Taming of the Shrew* into a clever showbiz musical in which the offstage lives of the stars parallel the story of

Antony Sher's extraordinary performance as Richard III in Shakespeare's play was the centrepiece of the RSC's 1984 Stratford and 1985 Barbican seasons. ***Richard III*** was directed by Bill Alexander.

Stephen Simms (Feste), Melinda McGraw (Maria). Cheek by Jowl's production of Shakespeare's ***Twelfth Night***, directed by Declan Donnellan at the Donmar, London, January 1987, is an example of an alternative approach to Shakespeare.

John Barton's adaptations under the title of *The Wars of the Roses* in the 1960s and re-adapted in 1988 by ▷ Charles Wood as *The Plantagenets*), even though they are perfectly viable as individual plays. The English Shakespeare Company has gone one further than the ▷ RSC in staging both tetralogies in tandem with considerable success. Richard III and Henry V have always attracted bravura interpretations, as has Falstaff in *Henry IV*. Shakespeare also wrote four plays drawn from Roman history (*Titus Andronicus*, *Julius Caesar*, *Antony and Cleopatra*, *Coriolanus*) of which *Julius Caesar* and *Antony and Cleopatra* form a linked pair, although the politics of *Julius Caesar* is geopolitical where that of *Antony and Cleopatra* is also sexual. *Titus Andronicus* is a fine example of revenge tragedy, considered unstageable until ▷ Peter Brook showed the way with Laurence Olivier in 1955, but now a fairly regular sighting (Deborah Warner's production in the 1987 Stratford season at The Swan was a particular triumph), as is *Coriolanus* (Peter Hall's 1986 production with Ian McKellen's Coriolanus was the most recent). *Coriolanus* is sometimes seen as a political vehicle, though there is dispute about whether its sympathies lean right or left, sometimes as a psychological study of mother-son relations and of repressed homosexual attraction between Aufidius and Coriolanus.

Shakespeare's comedies are almost exclusively of the romantic kind with 'boy meets girl/loses girl/finds girl' plots in which the young women, who are generally presented as intelligent, witty, down to earth, practical, resourceful and highly desirable, navigate their way through many complications (often associated with the fact that they are disguised as men) in order to arrive at marriages to men whose claim to our approval is that the women love them. Even in the most romantic plays there is a subplot to distance us from the romantic goings on. Bottom and his fellow amateur actors in *A Midsummer Night's Dream* provide incidental satire on the whole business of putting on a play and on the idea of romantic tragedy. In *Twelfth Night*, Malvolio's comic humiliation can easily turn into something that sours the whole romantic impulse of the play. Jacques compares the stream of couples about to get married at the end of *As You Like It* to the animals entering the Ark and, of course, Shylock in *The Merchant of Venice*, sometimes seen as a tragic hero, is always likely to cast a destabilising shadow over the romantic comedy mood of its final act. In *All's Well That Ends Well* and *Measure for Measure* there are similar tensions between the dynamics and conventions of comedy, the events portrayed and the means of characterisation which lead to them being dubbed 'problem plays'. Similarly *Troilus and Cressida* is a resolutely unheroic look at the Trojan war, which plays off its presentation of the sordid against an implied heroic image of a mythical period.

The tragedies *Othello, Hamlet, Macbeth* and *King Lear* have traditionally been regarded as the peak of Shakespeare's achievement and their heroes as amongst the greatest challenges for actors. Interpretations of the plays, and the parts, have differed greatly but there has generally been more interest recently in giving full weight to other characters, rather than concentrating simply on the hero. The group of tragi-comedies or romances Shakespeare wrote at the end of his career (*Pericles*, *Cymbeline*, *The Winter's Tale* and *The Tempest*), are noteworthy for their epic dramaturgy and refusal to be bound by naturalistic probability.

Shakespeare is one of the greatest challenges for directors, designers and actors and they adopt a wide variety of approaches, from the reverent to the iconoclastic. There is one tradition which attempts to give the full texts in an approximation of Renaissance stage conditions, and this tends to mean elaborate costumes, few lighting changes and an emphasis on verse speaking, all of which can quite easily become funereal; at the other extreme there is the jazzy update in which the text is heavily cut and altered, the period and setting are anywhere and nowhere and the whole thing becomes a vehicle for an imposed directorial concept. Most modern productions avoid the worst excesses of either approach but use the full resources of the modern theatre and attempt to bring out themes and issues which are at least latently present in the plays. Certain plays are particularly open to interpretation, such as *The Taming of the Shrew* which is a battleground between, crudely, those who believe that Shakespeare supported Petruchio in violence against

their musical adaptation of *The Shrew*; ▷Arnold Wesker's *The Merchant* is a counterargument to *The Merchant of Venice*; ▷C.P. Taylor's *Ophelia*, ▷Melissa Murray's *Ophelia* and ▷Tom Stoppard's *Rosencrantz and Guildenstern are Dead* are each rather more than *Hamlet* though the eyes of the supporting cast, as, in its way, is ▷W. S. Gilbert's *Rosencrantz and Guildenstern*; ▷Howard Brenton's *Thirteenth Night* reworks *Macbeth* and his *Pravda* (with ▷David Hare) draws on *Richard III*; ▷Edward Bond's *Lear* reassesses Shakespeare's, and his *Bingo* reassesses Shakespeare himself; ▷Barrie Keeffe's *King of England* is an Afro-Caribbean/East End transposition; ▷Terence Rattigan's *Harlequinade* is set during a rehearsal of *Romeo and Juliet*; ▷Shaw disliked *Cymbeline* so much he produced an 'improved' final act in *Cymbeline Refinished*; see also ▷Brecht (Shakespeare's world had a major influence on his dramaturgy); ▷Alan Ayckbourn for theatrical inventiveness and risk taking; ▷Beckett for striking theatrical images; composers from Berlioz to Prokofiev, Tchaikovsky to Cleo Laine have drawn on Shakespeare; see also ▷Cheek by Jowl as an example of a modern ensemble touring company successfully reinterpreting the classics, including Shakespeare.

women and those who see it as a play in which the only two lively characters deserve one another. A thorough-going feminist interpretation still has problems with this play, as evinced by the all-female production at the Theatre Royal, Stratford East in 1985, though it was in fact directed by a male director. Two significant tendencies in modern British productions are the ▷ RSC's move back into elaborate sets and a heavy burden of incidental music in mainhouse productions, and a vogue for a kind of vulgar deconstruction, in which a director elicits brilliant line by line performances which ignore the architecture of the plays and substitute instant gratification for the pleasures of a coherent reading which could still do justice to the contradictions of the work.

Declan Donnellan's productions for Cheek by Jowl seem, on the whole, to have been able to tread a fine balance between a modernist and popular approach whilst still retaining respect for the text. Kenneth Branagh's Renaissance Company was set up to dive away from the director-dictatorship that actors like Simon Callow and Branagh feel have dominated the past twenty years of British theatre, and it has seen productions directed by the likes of Judi Dench. The company has perhaps erred on the side of taking too many liberties but has still come up with a refreshing and invigorating *Twelfth Night*. Michael Bogdanov and Michael Pennington's English Shakespeare Company's history cycles, too, have found a way of escaping from the hide-bound, with a *Henry V* that adopts a World War I, war-weary irreverence, whilst Anthony Quayle's Compass touring company steers a fairly traditional line.

Despite the director-dominated atmosphere of the ▷ RSC, at its best, its productions are still hard to beat and its record bears witness to a solid stream of productions that have acquired a legendary stamp – from the early 1960s Peter Hall/John Barton history plays, ▷ Brook's landmark *King Lear* and *A Midsummer Night's Dream* (though even he had a slump with his last ▷ RSC production *Antony and Cleopatra*), to John Barton's many textually subtle interpretations (a marvellous *Much Ado About Nothing* with Judi Dench and Donald Sinden, and his classic *Troilus and Cressida* with Ian Holm and Dorothy Tutin). Trevor Nunn, Terry Hands, Adrian Noble, Bill Alexander have all had their share of successes and failures – Noble's *Henry V* with Kenneth Branagh, and Bill Alexander's *Merry Wives of Windsor*, Hand's *Much Ado* with Derek Jacobi, and Nunn's cycle of the Roman history plays have all carved out a piece of theatrical history. With the exception, however, of the late Buzz Goodbody, and until Deborah Warner's arrival, women as directors of Shakespeare at Stratford have been conspicuous by their absence. At the ▷ National Theatre, Peter Hall's mid-life *Antony and Cleopatra*, with Anthony Hopkins and Judi Dench, received rave attention but seemed like a recall of the 1960s. In the summer of 1988, Temba's Alby James also produced a Cuban-set *Romeo and Juliet* which augurs well for some new multi-racial interpretative slants.

SHANGE, Ntozake [1948–]

American dramatist

Plays include:

***for colored girls who have considered suicide when the rainbow is enuf* (1974), *Where the Mississippi Meets the Amazon* (1977), *A Photograph: A Study of Cruelty* (1977), *Spell No 7* (1978), *A Photograph: Lovers-in-Motion* (1979), *Boogie Woogie Landscapes* (1980), *A Daughter's Geography* (1981), *It Hasn't Always Been This Way* (1981), *Savannahland* (1981), *Bocas* (1982), *Betsey Brown* (reading; 1982 and, with Emily Mann, full production; 1986), *The Jazz Life* (1984), *Take Off From A Forced Landing* (1984), *Okra to Greens* (1985), *Riding The Moon in Texas* (1986), *Three Views of Mt. Fuji* (1987), *Daddy Say: Bronc-Bustin' Aint Ladylike* (1986)**

Books include:

***Sassafrass, Cypress and Indigo* (1983), *Betsy Brown* (1985), *A Daughter's Geography* (book of poetry; 1983)**

Creator of one of the longest running shows in Broadway history – *for colored girls who have considered suicide when the rainbow is enuf*, Ntozake Shange is Alice Walker, Toni Morrison, and

TRY THESE:
▷Pam Gems' *Piaf* for a play whose colloquial language (cockney) had similar problems of understanding when it made the transatlantic crossing to the USA; George Wolfe's *The Colored Museum*, Kalamu Ya Salaam's *Black Love Song No 1* are bitter satires on the theme of black stereotypes; American black playwright, Adrienne Kennedy's *A Lesson in Dead Language* deals with young women's education through a vivid, almost grotesque

Maya Angelou for the stage, all rolled into one. Also Ph.D. professor, artist-in-residence, author of over twenty-five stage productions, several novels and books of poetry, Shange would probably see all of them as part of the same process, whilst firmly rejecting the term 'playwright' as irrelevant to the way she sees the relationship of language to the realities of being a black woman.

Shange is a polemicist as well as being a poetic/political writer in the best sense of the personal-is-political school of feminist writing, and her 'choreopoems', as she calls them, are as hard-hitting about the male chauvinism of black males as they are about racial oppression (for which she has been roundly attacked in the States, as was Alice Walker for taking a similar line in *The Color Purple*).

Language for Shange represents resistance but for her, music and dance are equally integral to the realities of expressing black life on stage. Ironically, it is the song-and-dance image that has formed the consistent stereotype of the black community through musicals and song – black entertainers like Fats Waller, ▷ musicals such as *Bubbling Brown Sugar* or *Ain't Misbehavin'* – and which Shange so forcefully attacks in *Spell No 7* (premiered in Britain by the Women's Playhouse Trust in 1985).

Shange has undoubtedly brought a new dimension to the theatre, though the two productions of her works in Britain (*for colored girls. . .and Spell No 7*) have not travelled as well as they might, partly due perhaps to the difficulties of transplanting cultural references and colloquialisms to another clime. Some too, have found her dialogue too purple-prosed and rhetorical, her anger too insistent, the structure of the pieces too loose. Certainly her use of language is luscious, imagistic, tumbling with energy, and the 'choreopoems', like a revue, string together various techniques – poems, anecdotes, satirical sketches, all telling stories and requiring a surrounding vitality in song and dance to contextualise them. Greatly influenced by the women's movement and California's radical women's presses, (*for colored girls. . .* actually started out as a handful of Shange's poems in a Berkeley bar, before developing, with songs added, into the Broadway hit), both shows contain shattering accounts of racial humiliations and pain but balance the anger and images of individual victims with communal celebration and pride. *For colored girls. . .*, is almost a consciousness-raising account of growing into womanhood in which each actress takes on a colour of the rainbow, recounts experiences (often traumatic), swops characters, intersperses it with dance, becomes a member of the Greek-like chorus, culminating, after an horrific account of infanticide, in a recognition of their common history as black women. *Spell No 7* is a more bitter, supremely ironic comment on images, internalised self-hatred (wish fulfillment fantasies of wanting to be white) and the stereotyping of black entertainers. Set in a New York bar with 'resting' actors, and headed by the magician Lou – a Mr Interlocutor figure – who offers to change his casts' black skins into white, this cabaretesque tapestry ranges from the deeply ironic (casting failures because 'the skin isn't black enough') to the outright inhumane (Southern lynching mobs).

Dynamic theatre – and conscience-pricking to boot – Shange's plays allow no compromises and go to the heart of being black and female. Despite the difficulties her experimentation in form brings up, British theatre needs voices such as hers.

visual image; many recent musicals have used the black woman as victim as their central theme including *Blues in the Night* (with Carol Woods) and the musical biography of Billie Holliday, *Lady Day* (with Dee Dee Bridgewater); ▷Brian Friel's *Translations* is also concerned with the use of language as cultural imperialism; ▷Lorraine Hansberry for a contrasting black playwright, thirty years earlier; ▷Jackie Rudet's *Basin* for a British expression of black women's shared history, and Jackie Kay's *Chiaroscuro*.

SHAPIRO, Jacqui [1961–]
British dramatist

Plays include:

***Family Entertainment* (1981), *Thicker Than Water* (1981), *I'm Not a Bloody Automaton You Know!* (1982) *Sharon's Journey* (1981); *One of Us* (1983), *Up The Garden Path* (1983), *Trade Secrets* (1984), *Dead Romantic* (1984), *Three's a Crowd* (1985), *Dance Gazer* (1985), *How Odd of God* (1986), *Winter in the Morning* (1988)**

Though Shapiro once confessed she had been writing ever since she could remember, and had several one-act plays and monologues performed whilst at Manchester University, it was her first major play, *One of Us*, that brought her into more public prominence. Winner of a Yorkshire Television award in the 1983

TRY THESE:
▷Harwant Bains' *The Fighting Kite* gives another image of the young Asian woman's bid for independence; ▷Sue Townsend's *The Great Celestial Cow* looks at cross-cultural pressures on Asian women in Britain; ▷Sharman Macdonald for more female adolescent growing pains; ▷Sarah Daniels

National Student Drama Festival this one-woman monologue that took on racism as seen through the eyes of a Brummy Asian girl brought out descriptions like 'a gem of a piece', 'beady-eyed satire combined with whacky surrealism'. Performed with great panache by Feroza Syal at the Soho Poly, it is notable for its sharp social observation about people, their prejudices and the pressures imposed on a young Asian girl battling for independence – spry, funny and tragic all at the same time.

Trade Secrets, for the ▷ Women's Theatre Group, tackles pornography and violence and an imagined world without men, but its fragmentary structure and characterisations leaves something to be desired; *Dead Romantic* (a Soho Poly commission) is, however, a snappy comedy of recognisable 'ideological' angsts getting in the way of physiological lust! The recent *Winter in the Morning*, taken from Janina Bauman's horrific account of life for Polish Jews under the Nazis in the Warsaw Ghetto, succeeds best in the way it translates its adolescents' yearnings to the stage and as a reminder of the distortion of human values under extreme conditions. The cabaret-within-a-play, caricaturing Hitler and money-grabbing Ghetto Jews alike, is more problematical. Shapiro's adaptation of *Little Dorrit* has successfully toured nationwide (by the Avon Touring Theatre) and she is working on a commission for Manchester's Library Theatre to celebrate the Jewish community's bi-centenary.

Masterpieces is *the* rad fem play on pornography and violence; Siren's *Curfew* dealt more surreally with a world without men; ▷Clare McIntyre's *Low Level Panic* and ▷Winsome Pinnock's *Picture Palace* contrast romantic dreams and marketed images with more frightening day-to-day realities; ▷Terry Johnson's *Unsuitable for Adults*, Jack Klaff's *Cuddles* and ▷Pam Gems' *Loving Women* deal with the difficulties of feminism and heterosexual tangles; ▷Barry Collins' *Judgement* looks at the corruption of human values under extreme pressures.

SHARED EXPERIENCE

British touring company

Shared Experience is a touring company with a high reputation. Founded in 1975 by ▷ Mike Alfreds, its first productions were a trilogy of plays based on stories from the Arabian Nights, followed by a four-evening adaptation of Dickens' *Bleak House*, then two shows collectively created by the company (*Science Fictions* and *Gothic Horrors*), and then an inventive production of *Cymbeline*. This sort of variety has followed ever since, at the rate of about one show per year, and the company has toured widely, both in Britain and to international theatre festivals. Their strength lies in the central importance given to the actors, and in their distinctive line in narrative theatre and minimalist productions. The early improvised plays used clown techniques, and often involved the audience in discussion of what was going on. Since then they have generally based their work on texts, sometimes ▷ Chekhov or ▷ Shakespeare or ▷ Genet, sometimes neglected European classics (▷ Marivaux' *False Admissions* and *Successful Strategies*, Ruzzante's *Comedy without a Title*, ▷ Gogol's *Marriage*); but their most distinctive work has been their adaptations of novels (Waugh's *A Handful of Dust*, Richardson's *Pamela*, *Bleak House*, and most recently their first 'West End' success, Zola's *Nana*, misleadingly sold by the critics as a bawdy romp). In these, the actors move freely from narrative to impersonation, swap characters and sexes, and create scenery and props by mime or suggestion; the acting is free, powerful and yet can vary considerably from night to night. The adaptations have generally been prepared by Mike Alfreds (though *Pamela* was written by Fidelis Morgan and Giles Havergal and *Nana* by Olwen Wymark) who also directed most of the company's productions until 1987, when he left them for the ▷ National Theatre. Since then Nancy Meckler has become the new Artistic Director, and the company is now ensconced in the converted Soho Laundry in London.

TRY THESE:
▷Mike Alfreds; ▷Peter Brook for experimentation and an actor-centred theatre; ▷Cheek by Jowl, a smaller touring company more dependent on its director but with some of the same aims.

SHAW, George Bernard [1856–1950]

Irish dramatist, critic

Plays include:

Widower's Houses* (1892), *Arms and the Man* (1894), *Candida* (1897), *The Devil's Disciple* (1897), *The Man of Destiny* (1897), *You Never Can Tell* (1899), *Captain Brassbound's Conversion* (1900), *Mrs Warren's Profession* (1902), *The Admirable Bashville* (1902), *How He Lied to Her Husband* (1904), *John Bull's Other Island

TRY THESE:
▷Oscar Wilde, born the same year as Shaw, also of Anglo-Irish parents, for a shared background and a very different approach to theatre; ▷Strindberg was also a major figure for

(1904), The Philanderer (1905), Caesar and Cleopatra (1907), Man and Superman (1905), Passion, Poison and Petrification (1905), Major Barbara (1905), The Doctor's Dilemma (1906) The Interlude at the Playhouse (1907), Getting Married (1908), The Shewing Up of Blanco Posnet (1909), Press Cuttings (1909), Misalliance (1910), The Dark Lady of the Sonnets (1910), Fanny's First Play (1911), Overruled (1912), Androcles and the Lion (1913), Pygmalion (1913), Great Catherine (1913), The Music Cure (1914), The Inca of Perusalem (1916), Augustus Does His Bit (1917) O'Flaherty VC (1917), Annajanska, the Bolshevik Empress (1918), Heartbreak House (1920), Back to Methuselah (1922), Saint Joan (1923), The Glimpse of Reality (1927), The Fascinating Foundling (1928), The Apple Cart (1929), Too True to Be Good (1932), On the Rocks (1933), Village Wooing (1934), The Six of Calais (1934), The Simpleton of the Unexpected Isles (1935) The Millionairess (1936), Cymbeline Refinished (1937), Geneva (1938), In Good King Charles's Golden Days (1939), Buoyant Billions (1948), Far Fetched Fables (1950), Why She Would Not (1957)

Films include:

Pygmalion (1938), Major Barbara (1941), Caesar and Cleopatra (1946)

George Bernard Shaw, among the most widely produced of playwrights, and prolific man-of-letters (he published major essays on ▷ Ibsen and Wagner as well as many on political and artistic issues of the day), won the Nobel Prize for literature in 1925, and refused a peerage and OBE on principle. An active Socialist for most of his life, he was a leading member of the Fabian Society, a co-founder with Sidney and Beatrice Webb of the *New Statesman*, helped to establish the London School of Economics, and was a leading figure in the campaign for a ▷ National Theatre.

Born in Dublin of Anglo-Irish parents, Shaw worked briefly in an estate agent's office before moving to London in 1876 to work for the Edison telephone company. He became a music critic and also reviewed books and the visual arts, before moving into drama criticism for the *Saturday Review*, producing some of the wittiest and wisest reviews ever of theatre. Through his reviewing Shaw gained a thorough awareness of the forms of contemporary theatre which informs his own writings: *Heartbreak House* and *Major Barbara* play with the conventions of dramatic form, while *Passion, Poison and Petrification* and *The Fascinating Foundling* are direct pastiches of contemporary commercial West End theatre writing. His first critical and commercial success came with *Arms and the Man*, a comedy with a moral; a contemporary reviewer described Shaw as 'the most humourously extravagant paradoxer in London' (no mean praise, since ▷ Oscar Wilde was a contemporary contender for the title). Besides their inventiveness and wit, Shaw's plays consistently dealt with controversial and often taboo subjects; in 1893 *Mrs Warren's Profession* (her profession is not respectable) was banned by the Lord Chamberlain, and was not produced until 1925 (the year in which Shaw's Nobel prize had unequivocally established him as a Grand Old Man of the British theatre). *Candida* was written as a response to ▷ Ibsen's *A Doll's House*, and Ibsen's philosophy of naturalistic theatre became an informing influence on Shaw's work. Ibsen's exploration of non-realist forms in *Peer Gynt* was also influential: *Back to Methuselah* demonstrates the mix of fantasy, allegory and historical breadth that is an important aspect of Shaw's later (and less often produced) writings.

Man and Superman established Shaw as one of the most important of contemporary dramatists, and initiated a period of Shaw's most popular (both then and now) plays: *Major Barbara, Pygmalion, Saint Joan* and *Heartbreak House*. Shaw was very much involved with the staging of his plays; his stage directions are thorough and copious, and each play has a substantial preface. Many of his plays have been filmed, and he was alive to supervise the productions of three. Shaw is perhaps most widely known through the musical version of *Pygmalion*, which with the

Shaw, in championing a theatre of ideas; Shaw appears as a character in ▷Hugh Whitemore's play *The Best of Friends*; ▷John McGrath is beginning to rival Shaw in the amount of plays he has produced, and shares his commitment to using dramatic form for socialist ideas; ▷Brecht, whose *The Good Person of Szechwan*, like *Major Barbara*, explores the interdependence of charity and capitalism; ▷Trevor Griffiths is another dramatist who uses and extends contemporary dramatic forms to socialist ends; ▷Edward Bond ▷Howard Brenton and ▷Howard Barker tend to be more formally innovative; ▷Karim Alrawi's *A Child in the Heart* and Jonathan Falla's *Topokana Martyr's Day* are contemporary examples of plays which confront the paradoxes of charity in relation to the Third World.

libretto of Alan Jay Lerner became *My Fair Lady*; *Arms and the Man* also became a musical, as *The Chocolate Soldier.*

It is often claimed that Shavian theatre sacrifices dramatic effect and characterisation for the sake of ideas, but with the hindsight of post-Brechtian theatre, Shaw can be seen as an innovator in bringing a challenging theatre of ideas to the West End and to theatres all over the world. The skill that Shaw always demonstrates with paradox becomes in his most successful plays dialectical drama.

Major Barbara
Major Barbara is a play which explores the nature of charity and wealth; Shaw revised it in 1941 for a film version. Subtitled a 'discussion in three acts', the play puts contemporary debates about poverty on stage, and subjects them to dramatic investigation. The first act appears to be a standard 'drawing room comedy', as Lady Britomart and her son Stephen display conventional wit and discuss the marriages of the family daughters; the appearance of a long lost father completes the apparent conventional melodrama. However, Major Barbara, one of the daughters, is a Major in the Salvation Army, committed to the battle against poverty, while her father, Undershaft, is an arms manufacturer and a staunch defender of capitalism. In the next act, the curtain rises on a Salvation Army housing shelter (a real challenge to contemporary West End theatre audiences used to drawing room comedy), and the play confronts Barbara with the fact that her concept of 'charity' rests on a capitalist system. Undershaft demonstrates that he financially supports the shelter, and that it is funded from the profits of breweries; a paradox that overturns the Salvation Army principle of teetotalism. In the final act Barbara and her academic lover Cusins confront Undershaft in a debate about the nature of poverty. Their debate is not a simple one, each employs unexpected arguments, and Undershaft effectively wins. Barbara finally comes to the realisation that her philosophy of faith, hope and charity depends upon the capitalism espoused by Undershaft, and accepts his patronage. The questions raised by the play remain unanswered, however: while Barbara may accept Undershaft, the audience is reminded that his philosophy of a charity made possible by wealth and profit is based on his manufacture of lethal weaponry. *Major Barbara* demonstrates that concepts of 'morality', 'liberty' and 'redemption' can only be abstractions in the face of poverty, and that what is necessary is an economic system based on the principle, as Shaw says: 'to each according to their needs, from each according to their means.' While the play was very much written in response to contemporary topical debates about poverty, its arguments still have potency, particularly in the context of Thatcher's Britain.

SHAWN, Wallace [1943–]
American dramatist

Plays include:
Our Late Night (1975), A Thought In Three Parts (1977), Marie and Bruce (1979), The Hotel Play (1981), My Dinner With André (with André Gregory; 1981), Aunt Dan and Lemon (1985)

Films include:
My Dinner with André, Louis Malle's stunning 1982 adaptation

Although celebrity-spotters know him as that whiny-voiced little man who seems to have bit parts in every other film, Wally Shawn has quietly developed into one of America's most unpredictable and subversive dramatists since he started writing plays in 1971. Whether epic (*The Hotel Play*) or intimate (*My Dinner With André*), seemingly straightforward or sinuously ironic, Shawn's plays get under the skin in a way audiences may not even realise until several days after the event. Often premiered in London at the Royal Court, they may move on to Joe Papp's Public Theatre off-Broadway, where, during the run of *Aunt Dan and Lemon*, New Yorkers could be found nightly arguing whether Shawn himself *agreed* with the play's ostensibly pro-fascist stance. His targets are the nightmarishness of domesticity – the

TRY THESE:
▷David Mamet and, in a superficially lighter vein, ▷Jules Feiffer for rather more cutthroat dissections of the American psyche than people expect from US writers; ▷Strindberg and ▷Edward Albee (especially *Who's Afraid of Virginia Woolf?*) for images of the marital malaise; ▷Michael Frayn's *Benefactors* for examinations of the underside of idealism; ▷Spalding Gray for powerful monologues that catch the jangling, frayed nerve ends of our societies.

couple who can't stop firing invective at one another in his one-act *Marie and Bruce* – as well as hypocrisy disguised as doing-good, and the ceaseless quest for meaning in a society hellbent on its own extinction. Unfortunately, his ideas often exceed his craft, and none of his plays has yet found the shape to make them truly ignite; indeed, their shapelessness often seems to be part of the point. If he can wed his imagination to a stricter control of form, he might come up with the seismic blast of a play which he has so far promised but never delivered.

As an actor, Shawn has appeared both in his own plays (he replaced John Heard to take on the role of Lemon's father in *Aunt Dan*) and in such movies as *Manhattan*, *Simon*, *Starting Over*, *All That Jazz*, *The Princess Bride*, *Prick Up Your Ears* (in which he played ▷ Joe Orton's biographer, John Lahr), and *The Moderns*.

Aunt Dan and Lemon

Overlong yet underwritten, at once wordy and evasive, *Aunt Dan* is a fascinating jumble of a drama about the relationship between a charismatic American don at Oxford, Aunt Dan, and the sickly young Leonora (Lemon) whom she befriends. A lifelong voyeur whose seemingly calm exterior belies a moral blankness inside, Lemon invites the audience into her sickroom only to lead us into a disquieting diatribe against the cult of compassion, in which the Nazis' extermination of the Jews is seen as a mere extension of our annihilation of cockroaches. The tone of the play is its most elusive aspect, and Shawn gives his actors and his director wide room to manoeuvre. Still, the writing itself remains maddeningly opaque; this is a dark treatise on pathology that can't quite illuminate the troubled and troubling people at its core.

SHELLEY, Percy Bysshe [1792–1822]

English radical and poet

Plays include:

***The Cenci* (1819)**

The Romantic poet cast several of his works in dramatic form but only *The Cenci* seems ever to have been performed and that long after his death. Turned down by Covent Garden when originally submitted for production, it was eventually given a private staging by the Shelley Society at the Grand Theatre, Islington, in 1886. A five-act drama in sub-Shakespearean style, it retells a true story Shelley had heard in Rome; Beatrice Cenci is raped by her father, an establishment figure protected by Church and society, and eventually murders him. Its theme of incest was probably a reason why it was not staged for so long. Although it is not a great play it is much better than Byron's or Tennyson's attempts at writing for the stage and occasional revivals, such as the Bristol Old Vic production seen at the Almeida in 1985, demonstrate its theatrical vitality.

TRY THESE:

For modern verse plays see ▷T. S. Eliot and ▷Christopher Fry; ▷Howard Brenton's *Bloody Poetry* and ▷Ann Jellicoe's *Shelley* for plays about Shelley; ▷Artaud's is the most famous production of *The Cenci*; Shelley's dramaturgy was much influenced by the Renaissance dramatists – ▷John Ford's *'Tis Pity She's a Whore* is probably the most famous Renaissance treatment of incest; for contemporary treatments of incest see ▷Barry Reckord's *X* and ▷Michel Tremblay's *Bonjour, Bonjour*; for a black American feminist version, see Adrienne Kennedy's surreal account, *A Rat's Mass*.

SHEPARD, Sam [1943–]

American dramatist and actor

Plays include:

***Cowboy* (1964), *The Rock Garden* (1964), *La Turista* (1967), *The Tooth of Crime* (1972), *Curse of the Starving Class* (1978), *Buried Child* (1978), *Suicide In B-Flat* (1978), *Seduced* (1979), *True West* (1980), *Fool For Love* (1983), *A Lie of the Mind* (1986); numerous one-act plays; and *Cowboy Mouth* (with Patti Smith; 1971),**

TRY THESE:

▷Harold Pinter, ▷David Mamet for their juxtaposition of violent spoken encounters with equally violent and abrupt silences; Lyle Kessler (*Orphans*) and the ▷Steppenwolf

Nightwalk **(with ▷ Megan Terry and ▷ Jean-Claude Van Itallie; 1973),** ***Tongues*** **(with Joseph Chaikin; 1978)**

Films include:

Paris, Texas **(1984),** ***Fool For Love*** **(1985),** ***Far North*** **(1988), also directed** ***The Tourist Guide***

Is Sam Shepard the pre-eminent dramatic observer of the American myth, or the greatest exemplar of it? Whatever one's stance, the Illinois-born playwright has achieved a near-legendary status through a combination of his commanding laconicism and more than two decades of plays which defy classification as they move from the overtly fantastical (some of his early one-act plays) to long, piercing reveries about families rent asunder (*A Lie of the Mind*). The most successful American playwright never to have had a work produced on Broadway, Shepard eschews the tidy dramatics and often pat psychology that make Broadway hits, and his plays tend to take place in the American equivalent of the Outback, far from the East Coast swells. His track record off-Broadway and in London, though, has been exemplary; indeed, his *Tooth of Crime*, an intriguing 'style war' between two rock musicians, Hoss and Crow, was written during Shepard's London residency (at the Bush) in the early 1970s.

Many of his middle-period plays mix comic absurdism with ▷ Pinter-style game-playing; his Pulitzer Prize-winning *Buried Child* takes the form of a homecoming, as a man and his girlfriend return to the family farm in Illinois. In *True West*, two brothers in a Southern California suburb squabble and swap identities, while taking potshots at American myth-making, both Hollywood-style and otherwise. *A Lie of the Mind* posits two families, one in California, the other in Montana, separated by a mileage that is spiritual not spatial. 'I don't think it's worth doing anything unless it's personal,' Shepard says, and despite his increasing fame as a film star and matinee idol, his work shows no signs of accommodating itself to the mob he has never courted.

Shepard has also appeared as a screen actor in *Days of Heaven*, *Resurrection*, *The Right Stuff*, *Raggedy Man*, *Fool For Love*, *Baby Boom*, and – opposite his wife, Jessica Lange – *Frances*, *Country*, *Crimes of the Heart*, and *Far North.*

Fool For Love

'You're gonna erase me,' May tells her former lover Eddie when they re-encounter one another in a motel room on the edge of the Mojave Desert, and Shepard's play is about exactly that – the threat of emotional erasure generated by a love so combustible that it doesn't know its own limits. A long-running success off-Broadway and a West End transfer from the ▷ National Theatre, the four-character drama set in Shepard's favoured terrain, the American southwest, epitomises this playwright's method: at once violent and oblique, highly charged and digressive. The play has been described both as a *Phedra* on amphetamines and a visceral but ultimately empty vehicle for actors. Whatever one's response, there's no denying Shepard's ability to elicit a charge from his re-examination of the ethos of the American cowboy, as the romantically ravaged Eddie lassoes bedposts instead of the woman with whom he should have never become entangled.

Theatre Company of Chicago for other plays, and theatre companies, which seem to take Shepard's high-energy immediacy as their starting-point; ▷Strindberg's *Miss Julie* for another study of explosive sexual attraction, also ▷Botho Strauss' *The Tourist Guide.*

SHERIDAN, Richard Brinsley [1751–1815]

Irish dramatist, theatre manager and politician

Plays include:

The Rivals **(1775),** ***St Patrick's Day; or, the Scheming Lieutenant*** **(1775),** ***The Duenna*** **(comic opera; 1775),** ***A Trip to Scarborough*** **(1777),** ***The School for Scandal*** **(1777),** ***The Critic; or, a Tragedy Rehearsed*** **(1779),** ***Pizarro*** **(1799)**

Son of a Dublin actor-manager and a playwright-novelist, Sheridan was sent to Harrow and intended for a career at the Bar, but his elopement and marriage to Elizabeth Linley brought him need of money and led to him writing *The Rivals*, based on his observation of society at Bath and his own experiences. His plots are fast moving and his dialogue witty and though without the sexual explicitness of Restoration dramatists, his plays have much in common with their comedy of manners. Although his

TRY THESE:

▷G.B. Shaw's *Pygmalion* offers some parallels between Professor Higgins and Sir Peter learning to accept a lively young woman; ▷Farquhar shows society, earlier in the century, visiting the provinces; ▷Aphra Behn's *The Lucky Chance* and ▷William Wycherley's *The Country Wife* for an earlier and more robust treatment of

characters often have identifying names in the tradition of ▷ Jonson – Snake, or Lady Sneerwell (in *The School for Scandal*) for instance – they are nevertheless rounded creations rather than mere caricatures. They include the famous Mrs Malaprop (in *The Rivals*). *The Critic* is a burlesque of the contemporary stage which has not lost its point and is occasionally revived, while *The Rivals* and *The School for Scandal* have won a permanent place in the repertoire. Sheridan's most popular work in his own times was *Pizarro*, a spectacular reworking of a German play.

Sheridan bought David Garrick's share of Drury Lane in 1776 and managed the theatre for over twenty years, though after becoming a Member of Parliament in 1780 he devoted most of his writing skills to speeches in the House. He rebuilt Drury Lane in 1794 but the theatre burned down in 1809. Sheridan watched from an inn opposite, remarking: 'Can not a man take a glass of wine by his own fireside?' He became more and more beset by money troubles and when he died in Savile Row in 1815 there were bailiffs at the door.

town/country conflicts; ▷Goldsmith's *She Stoops to Conquer* for a contemporary version; ▷Tom Stoppard's *The Real Inspector Hound* is a modern play about critics.

The School for Scandal

Undoubtedly his finest work, this play presents the arrival from the country of Lady Teazle, a naive young wife, and her exposure to, and education in, London Society, against a background of intrigue and a parallel plot concerning an inheritance involving virtuous and corrupt brothers. The 'screen scene' in which her much older husband, Sir Peter, discovers Lady Teazle in hiding must rank with the Malvolio letter scene as amongst the finest in English comedy.

SHERMAN, Martin [1938–]

American dramatist

Plays include:

***Passing By* (1972), *Cracks* (1973), *Bent* (1977), *Messiah* (1981), *When She Danced* (1984), *A Madhouse in Goa* (1987)**

Born in Philadelphia, and educated at Boston University, Sherman was resident playwright at Playwrights' Horizons in New York from 1976–77 before coming to England where his *Passing By* was one of half a dozen plays in the 1975 lunchtime season of gay plays put on by Ed Berman at the Almost Free. Sherman is probably best known however for *Bent*, a play about the Nazi persecution of homosexuals, one of the plays that arose out of ▷ Gay Sweatshop's production of *As Time Goes By* which also looked at homosexual persecution in three different periods.

Bent subsequently turned up at the Royal Court and on Broadway and with some star names – Ian McKellen and Tom Bell in Britain, Richard Gere and briefly Michael York on Broadway – scored considerable success. It has also gone on to be performed all over the world.

His two follow-up plays have been less well received: *Messiah*, a parable of redemption set in 1665 Poland in the period following the Cossacks' massacre, and *When She Danced* the story of dancer Isadora Duncan's marriage to the Russian Sergei Esenin in 1923 Paris. A writer with a style that mixes the florid and spare – sometimes an uncomfortable combination – two of the early plays, *Passing By*, a pre-AIDS play dealing with illness and the support men can give to each other, and *Cracks*, are included in Methuen's Gay Plays series, edited by ▷ Michael Wilcox.

Bent

One of the early plays to show gays in a sympathetic and unsensationalistic light, *Bent* used two quite distinct styles: a first half of a *Boys in the Band* type bitchery and a second act set in Dachau with a Beckettian-type duologue between the central character, the tormented Max, and his lover, Horst. This may be partly due to the fact that though ostensibly set in the 1940s, the play is informed by and exudes a 1970s Gay Liberation consciousness and is therefore as much concerned with issues of changing personal politics as it is with historical perspective. Two exchanges also stand out; Max's scene with his elderly, discreet Uncle Freddie and, later, the verbally arrived-at orgasm between the two incarcerated men.

TRY THESE:

▷Drew Griffiths and ▷Noël Greig for *As Time Goes By*; also ▷Greig's *Angels Descend On Paris* for a different treatment of homosexuals under Nazi repression; ▷Manuel Puig's *Kiss of the Spider Woman* for its exploration of homosexuality in a South American political and prison setting; ▷Lanford Wilson, ▷Harvey Fierstein, ▷Larry Kramer, William Hoffman and Neil Bell as other American playwrights who write unabashedly gay plays; ▷Hugh Whitemore's *Breaking the Code* for homosexuality British-style during World War II; *Cabaret*, for glimpses of pre-War gay politics in Germany, ▷Genet's *Deathwatch*, for another treatment of prison and homosexuality.

SHERRIFF, R.C. (Robert Cedric) [1896–1975]
British dramatist and novelist

Plays include:
***Journey's End* (1928), *Badger's Green* (1930), *St Helena* (1935), *Miss Mabel* (1948), *Home at Seven* (1950)**

Films include:
The Dam Busters, Mrs Miniver*, and *Goodbye, Mr Chips

Sherriff is virtually a one-play author, though his other plays were competent Saturday Night Theatre fodder, and he had a long and lucrative career as a Hollywood scriptwriter. *Journey's End* was first put on as a Sunday night production by the Stage Society (with the little-known Laurence Olivier playing Captain Dennis Stanhope), and in spite of doubts about the commercial prospects of a realistic play about World War I, it ran and ran (though without Olivier, who had gone into *Beau Geste* instead). The tension between the public school ethos (which the play accepts) and the grinding horror of trench warfare at its worst, produces one of the 'strongest' plays ever written, and it works surprisingly well whenever revived. It is frequently put on by amateur groups, in spite of the problems inherent in making a dug-out collapse at the end (see Michael Green, *The Art of Coarse Acting*) and was revived again in London in April 1988 with Jason Connery and Nicky Henson as the two young captains.

TRY THESE:
▷Sean O'Casey's *The Silver Tassie* for a very different Expressionist treatment of the war zone; none of the other 'war plays' of the late 1920s seems likely to be revivable, but ▷Willis Hall's *The Long and the Short and the Tall* and ▷Terence Rattigan's *Flare Path* deal with World War II; ▷Noël Greig's *Poppies* is a fiercely pacifist play, seen from a gay perspective; the crop of post-Falklands plays, by ▷Tony Marchant, ▷Louise Page, ▷Robert Holman (*Making Noise Quietly*) and Greg Cullen, all make their anti-war points in various ways; Theatre Workshop's *Oh What a Lovely War*, remains *the* World War I testament.

SHIRLEY, James [1596–1666]
English Renaissance dramatist

Plays include:
***The Traitor* (1631), *Hyde Park* (1632), *The Gamester* (1633), *The Cardinal* (1641)**

Like Heywood, Shirley owes his current theatrical status to the ▷ RSC's Swan theatre and its policy of producing forgotten but lively plays by ▷ Shakespeare's near contemporaries, in his case *Hyde Park*, which appears not to have been staged for some 300 years before the 1987 revival. In his own time, after leaving the Anglican priesthood on his conversion to Catholicism, Shirley was a popular and prolific dramatist but his work has suffered in the general theatrical neglect of the plays of this period. *The Traitor* and *The Cardinal* are very much in the revenge tragedy tradition with plots reminiscent of ▷ Kyd, ▷ Shakespeare, ▷ Tourneur, ▷ Webster and ▷ Middleton; the comedies are very much concerned with contemporary manners and London life, using locations, characters and themes that are more familiar to us in their post-Restoration forms. *Hyde Park* proved to be stageworthy and it would be interesting to see *The Gamester* with its double bed trick in which a man pays off gambling debts by allowing the winner to take his place in bed with the woman he was about to commit adultery with; his wife later informs him that she has taken the other woman's place, but it all turns out not to have happened and decorum of a kind is maintained.

TRY THESE:
For the comedies to ▷Jonson and ▷Middleton, ▷Behn, ▷Etherege and ▷Wycherley as immediate predecessors and successors; the other forgotten dramatists of the pre Civil War period are Richard Brome and William Davenant; ▷Shakespeare uses the bed-trick in both *Measure for Measure* and *All's Well that Ends Well*; and ▷Middleton and ▷Rowley use the same device in their tragedy *The Changeling.*

SIMON, Neil [1927–]
American dramatist

Plays include:
Come Blow Your Horn* (with his brother Danny; 1961), *Little Me* (book of the musical; 1962), *Barefoot In the Park* (1963), *The Odd Couple* (1965), *Sweet Charity* (book of the musical; 1966), *The Star-Spangled Girl* (1966), *Plaza Suite* (1968), *Promises, Promises* (book of the musical; 1968), *The Last of the Red Hot Lovers* (1969), *The Gingerbread Lady* (1970), *The Prisoner of

TRY THESE:
▷Eugene O'Neill and ▷Tennessee Williams for earlier, harder-edged views of families, and ▷Arthur Miller's *Death of A Salesman* for the prototype of the father in *Brighton Beach*; ▷Wendy

***Second Avenue* (1971), *The Sunshine Boys* (1972), *The Good Doctor* (1973), *God's Favorite* (1974), *California Suite* (1976), *Chapter Two* (1977), *They're Playing Our Song* (1979), *I Ought To Be In Pictures* (1980), *Fools* (1981), *Brighton Beach Memoirs* (1983), *Biloxi Blues* (1985), *The Odd Couple* (revised; 1985), *Broadway Bound* (1986), *Jake's Women* (1988)**

Films include:

in addition to adaptations of almost all his plays, original scripts include *The Out-of-Towners* (1970), *The Heartbreak Kid* (1972), *Murder By Death* (1976), *The Goodbye Girl* (1977), *The Cheap Detective* (1978), *Only When I Laugh* (1981), *Max Dugan Returns* (1983), *The Slugger's Wife* (1985)

The most successful living American playwright, the New York-born Simon is also, unsurprisingly, the only living American playwright to have a Broadway theatre named after him. After beginning as a television sketch writer for Phil Silvers and, briefly, Tallulah Bankhead, Simon has written roughly one play or musical libretto a year since the early 1960s, and almost all have been commercial – if not critical – successes. (*The Good Doctor*, adapted from eleven ▷ Chekhov tales, was the rare example of the opposite.) Steeped in snappy repartee and New York Jewish one-liners, Simon has been, often rightly, criticised for sacrificing psychological truth to the convenient punch line and glossing over difficult situations (alcoholism in *The Gingerbread Lady*, a widower's bereavement in *Chapter Two*) in time for a tidy final curtain. His recent autobiographical trilogy, spanning three alliteratively-titled plays, has attempted to rectify that, but each has its soft and sentimental patches as well as, it must be said, its charms.

Brighton Beach Memoirs

This is the play in which the old Neil Simon can be said to give way to the new, and the first in Simon's tri-partite portrait of himself as a young man that also includes *Biloxi Blues* and *Broadway Bound*. 'The world doesn't survive without families,' announces Kate, the mother in the play, and Simon gives us an extended family of seven eking out a living in the Brighton Beach section of Brooklyn on the eve of World War II. Fifteen-year-old Eugene, a chirpy adolescent discovering baseball, girls, and writing, is clearly Simon's alter ego, but more interesting are the adults – his mother, father, and spinsterish Aunt Blanche – all of whom are written in warm, rich hues. The play is undoubtedly cosy – O'Neill, Simon is not – but at its best it's an evocative memory play, as pleasing as a faded family snapshot you've had for years.

Wasserstein as a younger Jewish humorist; ▷Alan Ayckbourn mostly for contrast; ▷Sharman Macdonald for scenes of adolescents growing up; ▷Marguerite Duras for plays about memory of a more elliptical kind; ▷Athol Fugard for the formation of the artist as a young man.

SIMPSON, N.F. (Norman Frederick) [1919–]

British dramatist

Plays include:

***A Resounding Tinkle* (1957), *The Hole* (1958), *One Way Pendulum* (1959), *The Cresta Run* (1965), *Was He Anyone?* (1972)**

N.F. Simpson was first a bank clerk and then an English teacher in adult education; in 1957 he won third prize in *The Observer* play-writing competition with *A Resounding Tinkle*, and went on to considerable success at the Royal Court in its great days. He has perhaps suffered from being over-analysed as an Absurd dramatist and classed as less 'serious' than ▷ Ionesco; however, his plays are beginning to be revived (eg *One Way Pendulum* by Jonathan Miller at the Old Vic, 1988). His logical paradoxes and flow of verbal invention are ultimately more like ▷ Gilbert and Lewis Carroll than ▷ Ionesco. It is difficult to forget Arthur Groomkirby in *One Way Pendulum*, expounding his utterly convincing reasons for having to train these weighing machines to sing the Hallelujah Chorus so that he could take them to the North Pole and melt the ice around it, but it is probably a mistake to go through Simpson's work for profound thoughts about the desperation of the Human Condition.

TRY THESE:

▷Ionesco for word-play and surreal situations, with the qualification above; ▷Alfred Jarry and (more politically inclined) ▷Snoo Wilson for similar approaches to theatre.

SMITH, Dodie [1895–]
British dramatist, novelist

Plays include:

***Autumn Crocus* (1931), *Service* (1932), *Bonnet over the Windmill* (1937), *Dear Octopus* (1938), *I Capture the Castle* (1954)**

Dodie Smith is probably most remembered for her children's novels *A Hundred and One Dalmations* (later made into a Disney film) and *I Captured the Castle*, which was itself to become a stage play. Nonetheless, she was one of the most fashionable playwrights of her generation, and her influence still firmly hovers over the West End. Her first professionally produced play was *Autumn Crocus*, a Tyrolean Romance, and her most successful was *Dear Octopus*. Though now rarely peformed (*Dear Octopus* does sometimes surface) Dodie Smith's work typifies the notion of the 'well-made play' for the West End. Her plays are domestic, if sophisticated, comedies in three acts, delivered with a certain wit and charm. As the drama of the 1930s comes up for reassessment her work may well be due for a revival at any moment.

Dear Octopus
Described by Dodie Smith in her autobiography as 'a play of lamplight, candlelight, firelight, sunset deepening into twilight. . .a play of youth and age', the Octopus of the title is the family, brought together for a Golden Wedding celebration. John Gielgud played the romantic hero in the first production.

TRY THESE:
For other 'well-made plays' see ▷Lillian Hellman, ▷Terence Rattigan, ▷Galsworthy, ▷Alan Ayckbourn; her contemporaries include ▷J.B. Priestley; see also ▷Enid Bagnold and ▷N.C. Hunter for similar approaches.

SOPHOCLES [496–406 BC]
Greek dramatist

Surviving plays include:

***Ajax* (c 442), *Antigone* (c 441), *Oedipus the King* (c 429), *Philoctetes* (c 409), *Oedipus at Colonus* (406), *Women of Trachis* (date unknown), *Electra* (date unknown)**

Sophocles is credited with the introduction of a third actor to Greek drama, thus widening the possibilities of the dramatic conflict; also with introducing those mysterious revolving scenic devices, the *periaktoi*. He is said to have won eighteen prizes at the Festival of Dionysus, and to have written over a hundred plays altogether. Aristotle based his account of tragedy in *The Poetics* on Sophocles, thus influencing his successors for centuries, and Dorothy Sayers claimed him as the originator of the detective story. He was also influential in the development of psychoanalysis.

Oedipus the King
This story of the stranger who becomes King of Thebes by solving the riddle of the Sphinx and marrying the widow of the late king, only to find, after relentlessly interrogating one man after another, that the sins which have brought the plague to Thebes are his own, and that he has killed his own father and married his mother, has one of the most tightly knit and relentless plots in the history of drama. The power of the dialogue may be lost in translation, but the impeccable construction means that the play is effective in any language. The most famous production is probably Laurence Olivier's double of *Oedipus Rex* and ▷ Sheridan's *The Critic* in 1945, but Cocteau's high-camp version, *The Infernal Machine*, had a sudden and unexpected revival in Simon Callow's 1986 Lyric Hammersmith production with Maggie Smith's extraordinary tragi-comic cocktail queen, Jocasta.

TRY THESE:
▷Aristophanes, ▷Euripides, ▷Aeschylus and Menander for surviving Greek plays; a series of French modernisations – ▷Anouilh for updating *Antigone* to deal with the theme of collaboration in wartime France, ▷Giraudoux for a version of *Electra*, ▷Cocteau for a version of the Oedipus story; the Living Theatre for an idiosyncratic use of the Antigone story; ▷Robert Wilson for a version of *Oedipus at Colonus*.

SOYINKA, Wole (Arkinwande Oluwole) [1934–]
Nigerian dramatist, novelist, poet

Plays include:

The Swamp Dwellers* (1958), *The Lion and the Jewel* (1959), *The Invention* (1959), *A Dance of the Forests* (1960), *The Trial of Brother Jero* (1960), *Camwood on the Leaves* (1960), *The Strong Breed* (1964), *Kongi's Harvest* (1964), *The Road* (1965), *Madmen and

TRY THESE:
▷Edward Bond, ▷Ann Jellicoe, ▷Arnold Wesker were also members of George Devine's Writer's group, set up at the Royal Court in 1958; Yemi Ajibade is

***Specialists* (1970), *Jero's Metamorphosis* (1973), *The Bacchae: A Communion Rite* (from ▷ Euripides; 1973), *Death and the King's Horseman* (1975)**

Soyinka was born in Western Nigeria and studied at the University of Ibadan and the University of Leeds. He spent several years after graduation in London, a period when he was closely associated with the Royal Court; between 1958 and 1959 he read plays for them. Soyinka became a member of the Writer's group which was instituted at the Court by George Devine and led by William Gaskill and Keith Johnstone, and the Court put on the first production of a Soyinka play (*The Invention*) in 1959 as a Sunday Night performance, directed by Soyinka himself.

Soyinka returned to Ibadan as a Research Fellow in Drama in 1960 and went on to become a powerful and influential figure in African theatre. In 1967 he was arrested for alleged activities in support of Biafra by the Federal Government, and held at Kaduna Prison as a political prisoner for two years. On his release, Soyinka became Director of the Drama School at the University of Ibadan, and later Research Professor. He has continued to work in Nigeria, although he has travelled internationally with his writing; *Madmen and Specialists* was first staged at a Playwrights Conference at the Eugene O'Neill Centre in the USA; Soyinka was an Overseas Fellow at Churchill College, Cambridge, in 1973, a year in which he wrote *Death and the King's Horseman*. Since 1975, he has been Professor of Comparative Literature at Ife. He was founder of the 1960 Masks Theatre, and a founding director of the Orisun Theatre.

Soyinka's work over the past twenty years has largely been based in Africa, and it bas been hard to find in Britain, although *The Road* was produced at the Theatre Royal Stratford East in 1965 and the ▷ National Theatre presented the commissioned *The Bacchae* in 1973. Even the Royal Court, which was so important in encouraging and championing Soyinka's early writing, has not imported his more recent work.

Soyinka is also a significant figure in African literature for his poetry and novels, has contributed to Nigerian radio and television, and was awarded the Nobel Prize for Literature in 1986.

The Lion and the Jewel

The Lion and the Jewel is Soyinka's best-known play in Britain, mainly because of its production at the Royal Court in 1966. A comedy which explores life in a traditional Nigerian village, the play employs dance and mime, music and folklore; elements which were to become an important part of Soyinka's theatrical practice.

another Nigerian playwright, whose *Fingers Only* is set in a small Nigerian town and was presented by ▷Black Theatre Co-op; ▷Maureen Duffy also draws on ▷Euripides' *The Bacchae* for her *Rites*.

STANISLAVSKI, Konstantin [1865–1938]

Russian director, actor, teacher

Writings include:

***My Life in Art* (1924), *An Actor Prepares* (1926) *Stanislavski Rehearses 'Othello'* (1948) *Building a Character* (1950)**

Stanislavski is probably the most influential figure on performance and acting in Western theatre, his methods still form the basis of much British drama school training and he was the informing principle of Lee Strasberg's enormously influential Actor's Studio in America, which trained such diverse performers as Marilyn Monroe, Shelley Winters and Marlon Brando.

Stanislavski was born in Moscow and began in the theatre working with amateur companies He was much influenced by the company formed by the Duke of Saxe-Meiningen, which is usually regarded as the first in which an ensemble of actors developed productions under the auspices of a director. As he says in *My Life in Art*: 'I was always looking for something new, both in the inner work of the actor, in the work of the producer and in the principles of stage production'. He went on to become the founder of the Moscow Arts Theatre with Vladimir Nemirovich-Danchenko, and developed his ideas with a regular company of actors. After their first tour to Germany, Stanislav-

TRY THESE:

Much of what ▷Brecht has to say about acting in *The Messingkauf Diaglogues* is a direct rebuff to Stanislavskian methods; ▷Joan Littlewood was influenced by Stanislavski and by Brecht; see ▷Mike Leigh for the use of improvisation to create plays.

ski went on a holiday in Finland, where he resolved to set down his findings about acting methods, and to construct a theory of dramatic technique. He felt that the principles of acting developed by actors, directors and teachers had never been organised, and thus he devised a 'system'. The Stanislavskian 'Method' proposed training and rehearsal for the actor in which the actor 'became the part', and lived it not only on stage, but in preparation for performance. The principle was that the actor should explore all aspects of the character, often through improvisation: their history, attitudes and behaviour outside the frame and events of the play should be as much a part of the actor's knowledge as the lines and responses in the play. The aim was to acquire what Stanislavski termed 'inner realism', to 'be' rather than to 'do' a character. His system is based on two main parts; inner and outer work of actors on themselves and the inner and outer work of the actor on the part. Unfortunately only part of Stanislavski's theories was available in translation for many years and led to an overemphasis on the 'inner' element of the Method.

With the Moscow Arts Theatre, Stanislavski began to apply his methods to their productions, training and rehearsal. His direction of ▷ Chekhov's *The Seagull* both established Chekhov as a great playwright, and introduced the Stanislavskian method to world theatre.

STEPPENWOLF THEATRE COMPANY

American regional theatre company

Key productions include:

***The Caretaker* (Chicago, 1979; New York, 1986), *Balm In Gilead* (Chicago, 1980; New York, 1984), *True West* (Chicago and New York, 1982), *And A Nightingale Sang* (Chicago, 1982; New York, 1983), *Orphans* (Chicago and New York, 1985; London, 1986), *Lydie Breeze* (Chicago, 1986; Australia, 1987), *Born Yesterday* (Chicago, 1988)**

Founded as a fully fledged theatrical institution in 1976, this non-profit company stands at the forefront of the prospering regional theatre movement in the USA and has helped establish Chicago as America's leading theatre city after New York. Manhattan, however, remains the media hub, and both Steppenwolf and various of their alumni (John Malkovich, Joan Allen, Kevin Anderson) gained widespread attention after they started transferring productions to New York in 1982 with ▷ Sam Shepard's *True West* followed by *And A Nightingale Sang*, *Balm In Gilead*, *Orphans*, *The Caretaker*, and *Educating Rita*. In April 1986, Steppenwolf's brand of high-voltage kineticism came to London, when Lyle Kessler's *Orphans* – a frenzied pastiche of ▷ Sam Shepard and ▷ Harold Pinter about two orphaned brothers in Philadelphia who kidnap a middle-aged businessman – opened at Hampstead and then transferred to the Apollo, with Albert Finney acclimatising himself well to the visceral performance style of his two Steppenwolf colleagues.

Style is the key with this company, and *Orphans*, saturated in the music of Pat Metheny and his keyboardist Lyle Mays, epitomised the kind of Steppenwolf evening for which few British companies have an equivalent – rock-drenched, high-energy stagings which are at their best allied to scripts of equal muscle (as in *Balm In Gilead*, ▷ Lanford Wilson's galvanic 1964 play set in an all-night coffee shop). But their success with playwrights as diverse as ▷ Athol Fugard (*A Lesson From Aloes*), ▷ Chekhov (*Three Sisters*), and ▷ C.P. Taylor (*And A Nightingale Sang*) offers testimony to an interest in the world repertory that links Steppenwolf with the ensemble companies whose traditions they aim to perpetuate: the ▷ RSC and the Moscow Arts Theatre. With an annual budget of $1.7 million, an artistic advisory board which includes Warren Beatty, Cher, Meryl Streep, and ▷ David Rabe, and an artistic director – Robert Falls – formerly of Chicago's no less esteemed ▷ Wisdom Bridge Theatre, Steppenwolf's continued high profile seems assured.

TRY THESE:
▷Wisdom Bridge and ▷Negro Ensemble Company for other successful institutions; ▷Sam Shepard for a playwright whose raw, rough poetry is peculiarly appropriate to Steppenwolf's style; Lynn Siefert (*Coyote Ugly*, *Little Egypt*) and Lyle Kessler (*Orphans*) for Shepard imitators who have done well at Steppenwolf; ▷American Theatres for general discussion of the non-profit arena.

STOPPARD, Tom [1937–]
Czech-born British dramatist

Plays include:
***A Walk on the Water* (television 1963, staged 1964; revised as *The Preservation of George Riley*, 1964, and as *Enter a Free Man*, 1968) *'M' is for Moon Among Other Things* (1964), *The Dissolution of Dominic Boot* (1964, radio), *The Gamblers* (1965), *Rosencrantz and Guildenstern are Dead* (1966), *Albert's Bridge* (1967, radio), *The Real Inspector Hound* (1968), *If You're Glad I'll be Frank* (1969), *After Magritte* (1970), *Where are They Now?* (1970, radio), *Dogg's Our Pet* (1971), *Jumpers* (1972), *Artist Descending a Staircase* (1973, radio), *Travesties* (1974), *Dirty Linen* (1976), *New-found-land* (1976), *Every Good Boy Deserves Favour* (1977), *Night and Day* (1978), *Dogg's Hamlet, Cahoot's Macbeth* (1979), *The Real Thing* (1982), *Hapgood* (1988)**

Adaptations include:
***Tango* (1968; from ▷ Slawomir Mrozek), *The House of Bernarda Alba* (1973; from ▷ Lorca), *Undiscovered Country* (1980; from ▷ Schnitzler) *On the Razzle* (1981; from ▷ Nestroy, *Rough Crossing* (1984; from ▷ Molnar's *Play at the Castle*, also known as *The Play's the Thing*), *Largo Desolato* (1987; from Vacláv Havel)**

Television includes:
***A Walk on the Water* (1963), *A Separate Peace* (1966), *Teeth* (1967), *Another Moon Called Earth* (1977), *Neutral Ground* (1968), *Boundaries* (1975), *Three Men in a Boat* (from Jerome K. Jerome 1975), *Professional Foul* (1977), *Squaring the Circle* (1984)**

Stoppard is among the most fashionable of contemporary playwrights; 'Stoppardian' is now used as a term for the display of verbal wit and intellectual games. His work is always full of verbal fireworks, intellectual references and literary jokes. Most of his plays are constructed around elaborate conceits; *Jumpers* puts a philosophical discussion of logic together with a troupe of acrobats; *Every Good Boy Deserves Favour* has a full scale orchestra on stage in a play about Soviet dissidents. His most recent play, *Hapgood*, relates the complexities of spying and double agents to nuclear physics. This method of highly improbable juxtaposition owes a lot to Surrealism, and, in *After Magritte*, Stoppard wrote a play around the elements of a Magritte painting (umbrellas, bowler hats, skies, etc) located in a suburban household.

Born in Czechoslovakia, Stoppard was brought up in Singapore, and moved to England in 1946. He began writing as a journalist in Bristol, and became involved in drama through his theatre reviewing. Very much influenced by ▷ John Osborne's *Look Back in Anger*, and recognising that in the late 1950s: 'The theatre was suddenly the place to be', he resigned his job and moved to London, in a period at which the new influences of European and Absurdist theatre were hitting the London stage. His first plays were written for radio and television, but it was *Rosencrantz and Guildernstern are Dead* which first brought him to attention. The play, a sideways look at *Hamlet* from the perspective of two minor characters, intercuts their discussions while off-stage in *Hamlet*, with scenes and events from Shakespeare's play. First produced at the ▷ Edinburgh Festival, it was taken up by the National Theatre and staged in London to wide acclaim. In the 1970s, Stoppard was involved with Ed Berman and the Interaction Group, with whom he developed *Dogg's Our Pet*, and the West End success *Dirty Linen*. His more recent work has largely gone straight to the West End. *The Real Thing* successfully transferred to Broadway. He maintains a relationship with the ▷ RSC (who presented *Every Good Boy Deserves Favour*) and the ▷ National (for whom he wrote a version of a ▷ Nestroy play, *On the Razzle*).

His television plays *Squaring the Circle* (about Solidarity and the Polish trade unionist, Lech Walesa) and *Professional Foul* are both set in Eastern Europe, and take up the questions of political dissidence under Communism which he raised in *Every Good Boy Deserves Favour*.

TRY THESE:
▷Ionesco for logic games; ▷Beckett's *Waiting for Godot* is drawn on heavily for *Rosencrantz and Guildenstern are Dead*; ▷Pirandello and ▷Ayckbourn for theatrical games; ▷David Pownall's *Master Class* for another look at Russian musical totalitarianism.

Travesties

Travesties is based on the actual historical oddity that Lenin, Tristan Tzara, the Dadaist poet, and James Joyce must have been in Geneva in the same period. The events of the play and imagined meeting of the three are recounted by a minor British consular official whose major memory of the time is that he played a minor part in an amateur production of *The Importance of Being Earnest*. The three historical figures are thus cast into characters from *The Importance of Being Earnest*, and their work and influence is intercut with scenes from Wilde's play. The comedy of *Travesties* does very much depend on the recognition of the literary references, audiences for the play do tend to have an air of self-congratulation for getting the jokes, but it is (unlike some of Stoppard's other work) more than an exercise in displays of intellectual wit. It is too a poignant study of the self-aggrandisement of the consul, and a suggestive exploration of memory, and of versions of historical events.

STOREY, David [1933–]

British dramatist, novelist

Plays include:

The Restoration of Arnold Middleton **(1966),** ***In Celebration*** **(1969),** ***The Contractor*** **(1969),** ***Home*** **(1970),** ***The Changing Room*** **(1971),** ***Cromwell*** **(1973),** ***The Farm*** **(1973),** ***Life Class*** **(1974),** ***Mother's Day*** **(1976),** ***Sisters*** **(1978),** ***Early Days*** **(1980),** ***Phoenix*** **(1984)**

Novels include:

This Sporting Life **(1960; later filmed, director Lindsay Anderson),** ***Flight into Camden*** **(1960),** ***Radcliffe*** **(1963),** ***Pasmore*** **(1972),** ***A Temporary Life*** **(1973),** ***Saville*** **(1977),** ***A Prodigal Child*** **(1982),** ***Present Times*** **(1984)**

Storey, the son of a Wakefield miner, is one of the generation of Northern working-class writers who emerged into what was known at the time as the second wave of new dramatists (following the first wave of the *Look Back in Anger* generation). Storey was trained at Wakefield School of Art, and later at the Slade (an experience he draws on in his play *Life Class*). He then worked at a number of jobs, including a stint as a professional rugby palyer (an experience he draws on in *This Sporting Life* and *The Changing Room*). He began writing as a novelist with *This Sporting Life*,and went on to become one of the most commercially successful of the Royal Court 'house writers'. Storey is perhaps the best known exponent of contemporary slice of life kind of drama. His plays are concerned with (almost exclusively) men at work and a recurrent device is the progression of work in real time over the course of the play; the building of a tent in *The Contractor*, a rugby match (with complete team) in *The Changing Room*.

Storey's first play, *The Restoration of Arnold Middleton* written in 1958, was disinterred for production by Lindsay Anderson during the filming of *This Sporting Life* in 1960. According to Storey, the play was not even typed at that point. After a number of rejections, it was finally taken up by the Traverse Theatre in Edinburgh where it was an immediate success, and transferred to the Royal Court. Originally scheduled for a two week run at the Court, it was extended and transferred to the West End; Harold Hobson (among the most influential critics of the time) hailed the play as the most important new drama since ▷ John Osborne's *Look Back in Anger*.

At the Royal Court, the professional partnership between Anderson and Storey was confirmed (in line with George Devine's policy of marrying writers and directors) with the production of *In Celebration*. Anderson went on to direct *The Contractor*, *Home* and *The Changing Room* at the Court, and all transferred to the West End.

TRY THESE:

▷David Mercer whose career followed a similar trajectory and who also trained at the Wakefield Art School; ▷David Williamson's *The Club*, ▷John Godber's *Up'N'Under* and ▷Louise Page's *Golden Girls* for the sporting life; ▷Harold Pinter's *No Man's Land* for an example of a play with similar ambiguity; ▷Edgar White's *The Boot Dance* is also set in a mental hospital; also Dale Wasserman's *One Flew over the Cuckoo's Nest*, ▷Dürrenmatt's *The Physicists*, ▷Peter Weiss' *Marat/Sade*.

Home

In this atypical play Storey explores an encounter between four elderly people in a set of a table and four chairs. Neither this nor the dialogue give many clues as to the context; according to John Gielgud (whose first appearance at the Royal Court was in this play) the text intrigued 'but also somewhat mystified me'.

Storey has said 'Halfway through the writing I discovered it was taking place in a lunatic asylum'. The play was given a taut production by Lindsay Anderson; the original cast comprised Gielgud, Ralph Richardson Mona Washbourne and Dandy Nichols – whose presence lent considerable weight to Storey's status as a major writer. With music by Alan Price, and designs by the Court's Jocelyn Herbert, the first production was a classy affair.

STRAUSS, Botho [1945–]

West German dramatist, poet, novelist, translator, drama critic

Plays include:

***Die Hypochonder* (*The Hypochondriacs*; 1972), *Bekannte Gesichte, gemischte Gefühle* (*Familiar Faces*), *Gross und Klein* (*Great and Small*; 1978), *Kaldeway Farce* (1982), *The Park* (1983), *Tourist Guide* (1986).**

Strauss is one of West Germany's most prodigiously talented men-of-letters. A contemporary of film-maker Rainer Werner Fassbinder, and Austrian playwright Peter Handke, his disenchantment with modern society and anti-naturalistic style seem to have frequently been misunderstood in Britain (though in Germany, he is hailed as a considerable talent, not least for the work he has done as adaptor/translator with the Schaubühne's director Peter Stein). In Britain, *Great and Small*, the story of Lotte, the rejected wife turned bag-lady who embarks on an epic and losing battle for love and affection, *Tourist Guide*, a reworking of timeless themes about intellect versus feeling, and the destructive power of erotic love, and *The Park, A Midsummer Night's Dream* misanthropically updated, and adventurously staged by Sheffield's Crucible theatre in February 1988, have been greeted with less than general enthusiasm. Perhaps the German sensibility does not travel well, or something has been lost in translation. Either way, Strauss remains an elusive, potent European voice railing against contemporary urban society and its selfish materialism.

TRY THESE:
For another image of the female encountering society, see ▷Timberlake Wertenbaker's *The Grace of Mary Traverse*; ▷Strindberg's *Miss Julie* and ▷Sam Shepard's *Fool For Love* for other themes of erotic love; ▷Willy Russell's *Educating Rita* for passion and intellect; for bleakness see ▷Beckett.

Great and Small

Great and Small became a *cause célèbre* in 1983 when it emptied theatres on its regional tour, though London critics received it slightly more sympathetically. Five hours long (even in the drastically cut English version) Lotte's sometimes surreal encounters in the wastelands of urban alienation and isolation (directed by Keith Hack with Glenda Jackson in the central role) seemed in itself to alienate audiences, though in Michael Billington's memorable words, Strauss' female Candide is like 'a tail-wagging puppy, always waiting to be stroked and never able to understand why she gets a kick instead'.

STRINDBERG, August [1849–1912]

Swedish dramatist, novelist, poet, essayist

Plays include:

***Hermione* (1869), *The Travels of Lucky Per* (1882), *The Father* (1887), *Miss Julie* (1888), *Creditors* (1888), *To Damascus* (trilogy; 1898–1901) *The Stronger* (1890) *Playing with Fire* (1892), *Advent* (1898), *Gustaf Vasa* (1899), *Erik XIV* (1899), *Easter* (1900), *The Dance of Death* (1900), *A Dream Play* (1902), *Swan White* (1902), *The Ghost Sonata* (1907), *The Storm* (1907), *The Burnt Lot* (1907)**

Strindberg was enormously prolific; in forty years of writing he wrote more than sixty plays and several volumes of autobiography; his collected writings (outside the plays) run to over fifty volumes.

Strindberg's dramatic imagination is immensely powerful. Although his plays comprise historical drama, fairy tale, fantasy and symbolism he is most associated with a claustrophobic world of embittered relationships, repressions and embattled psyches. The experience of many of his plays can be like watching a dramatisation of one of Freud's case studies; their preoc-

TRY THESE:
The Wanderings of Lucky Per echoes ▷Ibsen's *Peer Gynt* – Ibsen's naturalist dramas opened a way forward for Strindberg; ▷G.B. Shaw was much affected by Strindberg's new 'theatre of ideas', and cross-class sexual attraction is a mainspring of *Arms and the Man*; ▷Genet is among the writers to have exploited the form of dream and fantasy drama that Strindberg forged and both ▷Expressionism and ▷Theatre of the

cupations with sexuality, irrationality and with the family as a site of struggle are more than open to Freudian interpretation.

Born in Stockholm, Strindberg studied medicine and worked as an actor, a journalist and a librarian. His three marriages all ended in divorce, and he held a great bitterness towards women which he explores over and over again in his plays. Throughout his life Strindberg was beset by periods of insanity (he would probably now have been diagnosed a manic depressive), an experience he wrote about in his painful autobiography, *A Madman's Defence*.

He began writing as a very young man; his first plays were historical dramas and rural fairy tales, both preoccupations he explored throughout his writing life. His historical plays, however, take their events as dramatic frames from which to draw metaphors which explore issues of power. In 1882 he wrote the fairy play *The Travels of Lucky Per* which moved him towards an exploration of fantasy.

Strindberg was much influenced by Zola's espousal of a 'naturalism' in art. *The Father, Miss Julie, Creditors* and *The Stronger*, all plays which explore sexuality and power, are a significant part of the naturalist enterprise, although Strindberg has his own particular version of naturalism; which edges very close to symbolism; the plays are full of symbolic images and props, their situations fraught with symbolic resonance.

After *Miss Julie* Strindberg wrote a set of naturalist plays, which confirmed his reputation in Europe. *Creditors, The Stronger* and *Playing With Fire* all present a struggle of wills; in *The Stronger*, two women confront one another, but only one speaks, with the growing realisation that the woman she is addressing is the source of her own husband's infidelity. The 'psycho-dramas' of this period were developed into full scale fantasy plays in Strindberg's late work. *A Dream Play* and *The Road to Damascus* eschew any attempt at realism, in order to explore a form in which, in Strindberg's words: 'imagination spins and weaves new patterns: a mixture of memories, experiences, unfettered fancies, absurdities and improvisation'.

Although Strindberg has often been cast as a virulent misogynist (and his writings are indeed full of scathing accounts of women), he is so obsessed with questions of power and gender that his plays are very open to feminist readings.

Miss Julie

An extraordinary play about power, sex and class set on a Midsummer's Eve in the kitchen of a nobleman's house. As the evening winds on, the daughter of the house Julie seduces the man-servant Jean, and they resolve to run away together. The play charts the shifts in their power relations. Julie begins with all the cards because of her social position, but once she has given herself sexually, she is lost and her class power means nothing in the face of Jean's sexual power. She appeals to Jean, who urges her to kill herself and the play ends with Julie leaving the stage, with the clear intent of suicide. Jean is left to face the class power of Julie's father. According to Strindberg, the play conformed to his development of new forms, in its pattern of 'three art-forms', 'the monologue, the mime and the ballet'. The ballet occurs at the moment of the consummation: a group of peasants sing a Midsummer's Eve drinking song, and point up the class positions that are being negotiated in the offstage bedroom. Jean's fiancée, the servant Kristin, opens the play with a mime of her domestic duties, in which the class difference with Julie is established.

Absurd can be seen as owing a great deal to Strindberg; ▷Shakespeare's *A Midsummer Night's Dream* also deals with Midsummer sexual attraction; ▷Botho Strauss' *The Tourist Guide* is a bleak modern meditation on the destructiveness of obsessive sexual attraction; Fassbinder's *The Bitter Tears of Petra von Kant*, is in the tradition of Strindberg's obsession with power games in sexual attraction.

SYNGE, J.M. (John Millington) [1871–1909]

Irish dramatist

Plays include:

***In the Shadow of the Glen* (1903), *Riders to the Sea* (1904), *The Well of the Saints* (1905), *The Playboy of the Western World* (1907), *The Tinker's Wedding* (1909), *Deidre of the Sorrows* (1910)**

Synge played a significant part in the creation of the Abbey Theatre with ▷ Yeats and ▷ Lady Gregory, both as manager and as dramatist. His plays are centred on the life and beliefs of Irish peasant communities in the west and in the Aran Islands,

TRY THESE:

▷Mustapha Matura's *Playboy of the West Indies* is a sparkling adaptation of the play to the Caribbean; ▷Sean O'Casey's dramatisation of the urban Irish in *The Plough and the Stars* also caused a riot at the Abbey Theatre; *Playboy* is a comic

which he visited on ▷ Yeats' advice, but there is also a strong underpinning from Christian and Classical sources. Synge's most famous play is *The Playboy of the Western World*, partly because of the riots associated with its first production but mainly because of its assured handling of its tragi-comic theme. The contrast between 'a callous story and a dirty deed' lies at the heart of the different reactions to Christy's two apparent parricides, one safely performed far away and glamorised in the telling, the other done in full view of the community, both on stage and in the audience. With the loss of Christy, Pegeen Mike is left to the humdrum spirit-sapping of her previous existence and our responses are divided: Christy and his father are reconciled and Christy has matured, which suggests comedy; Pegeen Mike is left trapped and aware of her loss, which suggest self-knowledge purchased at almost tragic cost.

reworking of the Oedipus story, as is ▷Edward Bond's *Saved*; the Orcadian George Mackay Brown's *The Stormwatchers* is reminiscent in tone and subject matter of *Riders to the Sea*; ▷Caryl Churchill's *Fen* includes a version of the story that provides the plot of *The Shadow of the Glen*.

TALLY, Ted [1952–]

American dramatist

Plays include:

***Terra Nova* (1977), *Night Mail and Other Sketches* (1977), *Word of Mouth* (1978), *Hooters* (1978), *Coming Attractions* (1980), *Little Footsteps* (1986)**

A Yale graduate who has, in turn, taught playwriting at the Yale Drama School, Tally made his reputation early on with *Terra Nova*, a fascinating historically-based drama which seems to bear little thematic or stylistic relation to his subsequent works. Set in 1911–12, the play tells the true story of Englishman Robert Scott's race to the Antarctic against Roald Amundsen, the Norwegian. But the play charts more a metaphysical than a physical contest, as Tally displays an unusual historical and temporal breadth. Few people would associate that play with the author of *Hooters*, a four-character comedy about sexual competition on a Cape Cod beach, distinguished by repeated use of the defamatory 'jerkwad!' Most recently, Tally has turned to contemporary satire on society (*Coming Attractions* strikes out at media manipulation) and the family (the targets in *Little Footsteps* are domestic). While both plays are deftly written, each seems a bit *easy*, and one wishes Tally a return to the challenges he earlier posed himself.

TRY THESE:
▷Jules Feiffer as an elder statesman satirist, and Jonathan Reynolds, James Lapine and ▷Christopher Durang (all veterans of the off-Broadway theatre Playwrights' Horizons, where Tally's last two plays were premiered), as a newer breed working in the same bright, deliberately comic book-like style; ▷Terence Rattigan's *Ross* (about T. E. Lawrence) and *Bequest to the Nation* (Nelson and Lady Hamilton) and ▷Howard Brenton's *Scott of the Antarctic* are other plays about 'heroes'; see also ▷Barry Collins' *The Ice Chimney* for its climbing anti-hero, Maurice Wilson.

TARA ARTS

British Asian theatre company

Tara Arts, the first professional Asian company to be formed in Britain was set up in 1976 in response to the murder of an Asian youth in Southall, London. Since then Tara have set out to chart the difficult path of the British Asian experience, by using classical Indian texts and original ones in English. Under director Jatinder Verma, who has been with the company since the beginning and has adapted many of the Indian texts, their aim has been not only to explore the traditions of their own many faceted culture but to examine that culture and the issues as it emerges within the Asian community in Britain. So while some of their forty-odd productions have been based on traditional texts – like their inaugural production *Sacrifice* (1977) adapted from a text by Rabindrath Tagore, a good many others have been community based and emerged through research and discussion with various local communities.

Tara have made a particular speciality of devising plays from work in schools, *Fuse* (1978), their first original production, was a sharp, funny account of the early school experiences of a young recently-arrived Asian, developed from discussions with local Asian youth in Tooting, south London, where Tara are based; *Chili in Your Eyes* (1984), another slice of local life looking at racial discrimination emerged from a Newham residency.

TRY THESE:
For other writers on the Asian experience in Britain, see ▷Hanif Kureishi, ▷Karim Alrawi; for Farrukh Dhondy, see ▷Black Theatre Co-operative; see also ▷Asian Theatre; ▷Black Theatre Forum.

They have also investigated other subjects, such as mental illness, sexual relations, and disaffected youth.

One of the hallmarks of Tara's work, however, is their manner of production. The journey to find their own voice and means of expressing it has led Tara into exploring various theatrical forms and styles. At one time, through writer/journalist Naseem Khan (then running Minorities Arts Advisory Service), they enlisted the support of Gerald Chapman, one of the directors of the Royal Court's Youth Theatre who encouraged them to explore and develop in a variety of ways and Western techniques; he also wrote *Fuse* and *Playing with Fire* which looked at unwanted pregnancy. In 1988 too, they have taken on the services of Carib Theatre director Anton Philips to direct a modern Indian classic, *Hayavadana*, written in 1968 by Girish Karnad.

Tara's unique style has developed gradually, away from its early, westernised agit-prop stance and exploration of contemporary Asian experiences into a wider investigation of Asian cultural roots, blending East and West, with an inventiveness and energy that has become their trademark – Western naturalism on one side, dance, musical drama, folk and mythical traditions on the other. One of Tara's most successful recent productions for example, is *Little Clay Cart*, taken from an eighth-century Sanskrit play about a prostitute who falls in love with a recently destitute merchant. Combining a wry Brechtian commentary with aspects of vaudeville knockabout and a stylised traditional treatment of the Indian parable, for many commentators it confirmed Tara and Verma's achievement in forging a distinctive new style. Further evidence of this emerged too in *Vanavasa* (*Exile in the Forest*). Based on an epic from the *Mahabharata*, the production was a joint venture between Tara and Calicut University Little Theatre in Kerala, south India, in which both companies spent time in each other's communities. The production, a parable connected to the subject of loss of homeland and re-settlement again mixed two traditions. Highly visual, (and particularly well lit by Paul Armstrong), Calicut brought superb standards of musicianship and martial arts to the enterprise. Some of Tara's other productions include: *Ancestral Voices* (1983) by D. Tony Clarke about the elderly view of being Asian in Britain, seen through the eyes of four youths; *The Lion's Raj* (1982) also by D. Tony Clark, looking at Gandhi and his relevance to the Asian community today; *Scenes in the Life Of. . .* (1982), by David Sulkin, a hard-hitting account, again based on improvisations, about racism, seen through Asian eyes; *Sapno kay Ruup* (*Shape of Dreams*; 1982), a sharp, satiric view of Britain from Asian women, produced in collaboration with students from the Croydon English Language Scheme; *Inkalaab 1919* about the massacre of a crowd of Indians in Amritsar by General Dyer of the British-Indian Army.

After initial funding difficulties, Tara, who also tour round the country and abroad, now have their own performance space – the Tara Arts Centre in south London which has become a focus for the Asian community.

TAYLOR, C.P. (Cecil) [1929–1981]

British dramatist

Plays include:

***Blaydon Races* (1962), *Allergy* (1966), *Bread and Butter* (1966), *Lies About Vietnam* (1969), *The Black and White Minstrels* (1972), *You Are My Hearts' Delight* (1973), *Gynt* (1973), *Schippel* (1974; from Sternheim; later known as *The Plumber's Progress*), *Bandits* (1976), *Walter* (1977), *Ophelia* (1977), *Some Enchanted Evening* (1977), *Peter Pan and Emily* (1977), *And a Nightingale Sang* (1978), *Withdrawal Symptoms* (1978), *Peter Pan Man* (1979; originally as *Cleverness of Us*, 1971), *Bring Me Sunshine, Bring Me Smiles* (1980; as *The Saints Go Marching In*), *Good* (1981)**

Taylor's premature death only months after the initial success of the ▷ RSC production of *Good*, robbed the British theatre

TRY THESE:
▷Peter Nichols' *Poppy* covers similar imperial ground to *Withdrawal Symptoms*, but more noisily and with less certainty of tone; ▷David Pownall's *Master Class* and ▷Tom Stoppard's *Every Good Boy Deserves Favour* also examine the relationship between totalitarianism and music; ▷Peter Barnes' *Laughter* is

of an extraordinarily versatile and talented dramatist who had been grossly undervalued in his lifetime. Born in Glasgow, but long time resident in the Northeast, Taylor wrote some fifty plays for virtually every type of theatre – from the local village to the West End, via ▷ community theatre, television and the ▷ RSC. Much of his work, from his first play to his last, included music, and his wry imagination and capacity for what ▷ Brecht called 'complex seeing' is exemplified in *Ophelia*, which is *Hamlet* from Ophelia's viewpoint, or *Withdrawal Symptoms* which parallels its heroine's drug withdrawal treatment with the pangs of withdrawal from empire. ▷ J. M. Barrie was the inspiration for *Peter Pan Man* and *Peter Pan and Emily* in which Peter Pan becomes involved with a Newcastle working-class family. It is typical of the paradoxical nature of Taylor's career, and of the split in theatre-going audiences, that the majority of those who went to see Harry Secombe in the re-titled *The Plumber's Progress* and the majority of those who went to see Good would have been extremely unlikely to recognise him as the author of both plays.

Good
Taylor's last play was notable for its willingness to confront the banality of evil in its study of its protagonist's gradual drift into Nazism through all the daily minor compromises, adjustments and accommodations which take him from being an emotional advocate of euthanasia in his fiction to advising on giving the Final Solution a caring façade. We can see the terrible seductive power of Nazism as something which offers the protagonist (given a fine performance by Alan Howard in the original RSC production) the possibility of a fixed position in a sea of moral uncertainties and doubts. The idea that public postures have the configuration of private derangements achieves a memorable form: throughout the play he is haunted by snatches of music, so that the discovery that the prisoners' band which greets him at Auschwitz is real represents his complete surrender to the inverted logic of the Third Reich.

another Auschwitz 'comedy'; *And a Nightingale Sang* covers similar wartime working-class territory to ▷Stephen Lowe's *Touched*; ▷David Edgar's *Destiny* is another study of fascism, British style.

TAYLOR, Tom [1817–80]
British dramatist

Plays include:
Masks and Faces (1852; with Charles Reade), _To Oblige Benson_ (1854), _Still Waters Run Deep_ (1855), _Our American Cousin_ (1858), _The Overland Route_ (1860), _The Ticket-of-Leave Man_ (1863), _New Men and Old Acres_ (1869)

Taylor was a Professor of English at London University, a civil servant and, in later years, editor of *Punch*. He wrote over seventy plays, few of which are now performed. *Our American Cousin* and its star part, Lord Dundreary, might be worth reviving, but the unfortunate connection with President Lincoln probably still militates against it.

The Ticket-of-Leave Man
Although *The Ticket-of-Leave Man* is by no means the best of Victorian melodramas (why doesn't someone revive Henry Arthur Jones' *The Silver King*?), it is for some reason the most frequently performed on the London stage. This is possibly because of its apparent social message about the problems of the rehabilitation of a man with a prison record, although the issue is completely fudged because our hero did not commit the crime in the first place. There is some unusual interest in the fact that the villain has the same problem, but the real attraction is Hawkshaw, the detective, and his mastery of disguise. (The ▷ National Theatre's production in 1981 was pedestrian, but a better production at the Theatre Royal, Stratford in 1987 had Tom Watt – Lofty in *East Enders* – as a sweet faced, honest hero, Bob Brierly.)

TRY THESE:
▷Boucicault, for nineteenth-century melodrama; ▷John Galsworthy's *Justice*, for a more realistic picture of the effects of prison.

TEMBA
British theatre company

Key productions include:

TRY THESE:
Nigel Moffatt, ▷Debbie Horsfield, ▷Mustapha Matura,

Attie Kubyane (on crate) and Ewen Cummins in Temba Theatre Company's production of ***Woza Albert*** by Percy Mtwa, Mbongeni Ngema and Barney Simon, directed by Alby James in 1986.

***Temba* (by Alton Kumalo; 1972), *The Dutchman* (by ▷ Leroi Jones; 1974), *The Blood Knot* (by ▷ Athol Fugard (1976), *Black Slaves, White Chains* and *More, More* (by ▷ Mustapha Matura; 1977), *Sizwe Bansi is Dead* (by ▷ Athol Fugard/John Kani/Winston Ntshona; 1977), *The Boot Dance* (by ▷ Edgar White; 1984), *Scrape Off the Black* (by ▷ Tunde Ikoli (1985), *Pantomime* (by ▷ Derek Walcott (1985), *All You Deserve* (by ▷ Debbie Horsfield; 1985), *Basin* (by ▷ Jacqueline Rudet; 1985), *Mamma Decemba* (by Nigel Moffatt; 1985), *The Pirate Princess* (by Barbara Gloudon; 1986), *Woza Albert* (by Percy Mtwa, Mbongeni Nigema and Barney Simon; (1986), *Black Love Songs* (consisting of *Herbert III* by Ted Shine; *Black Love Song No 1* by Kalamu Ya Salaam, 1987)**

Temba is a Zulu word meaning hope, and Temba was set up in 1972 by actors Alton Kumalo and Oscar James (then with the ▷ RSC at Stratford) in the hope of placing black theatre in the mainstream of British theatre. Now the longest running black theatre company in the country, Temba have survived many vicissitudes to establish themselves as one of the country's leading black theatre companies with a range of plays, reflecting not only British but black American and African life.

Under Kumalo's direction in the early years, they introduced a steady stream of premieres by home grown and the best of foreign writers such as American ▷ Leroi Jones' impressive *The Dutchman*, in which the political content for Kumalo was pre-eminent, exemplified in the work of Kumalo himself, and ▷ Mustapha Matura's *Black Slaves, White Chains*. Racism also, of course, was the primary theme of the important productions to have come out of South Africa in the past ten years some of which Temba have presented such as *Sizwe Bansi Is Dead, The Blood Knot, The Island* and *Woza Albert.*

Since 1984, the director of Temba has been Alby James, who in a changing financial climate is now moving Temba away from its more radical stance towards a more mainstream position. His model is the USA's highly successful black dance company, the Dance Theatre of Harlem. To survive, argues James, Temba, who have been resident at Leicester's Haymarket Theatre for the past few years, must provide theatre for their largely white audiences as well as exploring black roots. One of their major aims is to make bridges between black and white cultures, with an equal emphasis on high artistic standards.

Since 1984, Temba have presented ▷ Tunde Ikoli's *Scrape Off the Black*, ▷ Debbie Horsfield's *All You Deserve,* ▷ Nigel Moffatt's *Mamma Decemba* and Barbara Gloudon's *The Pirate Princess* which have all reflected a multi-racial approach.

In 1987–8 Temba set out on a further new direction with a four-month spring residency at the Young Vic which included not only premieres by a new young black British writer, Derrick Cameron on a Cain and Abel theme, *Black Sheep* but also the premiere of a double-bill of new American plays *Black Love Songs* in which Kalamu Ya Salaam's *Black Love Song No 1* stood out as another excitingly theatrical study in cultural oppression along the lines of George C. Wolfe's *The Colored Museum. You Can't Stop the Revolution* by Saira Essa, a coloured South African, presented by Temba and performed by Durban's Upstairs Theatre Company was another example of anti-apartheid resistance, culled from interviews with the women and children of Soweto, transformed into thrilling drama. Mfundi Vundla's *A Visitor to the Veldt* was an over-simplistic but moving attempt to explore black diaspora which has the questionable distinction of containing, in by now a long line of cathartic outpourings, one of the most horrific stage accounts relating to atrocities committed by American soldiers in Vietnam.

James' 1988 production of *Romeo and Juliet* set in nineteenth-century Cuba with a Caribbean and Latin-American backdrop confirms the new direction that James sees the company taking which will see more British-rooted classics explored through a black perspective, as well as a cultivation of

▷Jacqueline Rudet, ▷Tunde Ikoli, ▷Athol Fugard, ▷Leroi Jones; see also ▷Black Theatre; Black Theatre Co-operative; other treatments of Vietnam include Emily Mann's *Still Life*, and the Vietnam Veterans' *Tracers*; for another British black writer see ▷Caryl Phillips.

new British black writers. Future commissions include a Caribbean musical from Felix Cross, and a new rap piece from Benjamin Zephaniah.

TERRY, Megan [1932–]
American, writer, director

Plays include:
***Calm Down Mother* (1964), *Hothouse* (1964; produced 1974), *Ex-Miss Copper Queen on a Set of Pills* (1964), *Keep Tightly Closed in a Cool Dry Place* (1964), *Comings and Goings* (1966), *Viet Rock* (1966), *The Gloaming, Oh My Darling* (1966), *Nightwalk* (1973; with ▷ Sam Shepard and ▷ Jean-Claude Van Itallie), *Approaching Simone* (1974), *Babes in the Bighouse* (1974), *American Kings English for Queens* (1978), *Attempted Rescue on Avenue b* (1979)**

Hailed by American critic Helene Keyssar as the 'mother of American feminist drama', Terry, who has written over fifty plays, is, sadly almost unknown in Britain. One of the major contributors to Joe Chaikin's Open Theatre in the late 1960s and early 1970s, she made her name with the American public with the now famous anti-'Nam musical *Viet Rock* (the first *ever* rock musical), in a double bill with Open Theatre colleague ▷ Jean Claude Van Itallie's *America Hurrah*. The production made history, partly because of its anti-war stance, but also for the style of its presentation, which built on Chaikin's improvisational group work and Terry's favoured 'transformation' techniques – a way of looking at women's lives and theatre technique that informs much of her work.

Her concerns have ranged over a wide spectrum of issues covering sexism, violence, the materialism of American society but the excitement of her work has been both in the way she uses words (Keyssar describes it as similar to ▷ Beckett, 'every word on stage a gesture'), and in the physical and theatrical immediacy of her *mise-en-scène*; sudden Brechtian changes of tempo, visual metaphors; satiric parodies culled from popular culture; lots of music (again often satirising familiar cultural references); gender swopping (in *Babes in the Bighouse* and in *Viet Rock* Terry used male actors to interpret females roles and vice versa).

Since 1970, she has been writer-in-residence at the Omaha Magic Theatre in Nebraska with Jo Ann Schmidman. Of her remarkable output, only the one-act plays *Calm Down Mother* (described as the first American feminist drama; an inter-weaving look at three women's lives) and *Keep Tightly Closed* have been performed in Britain.

For some enterprising women's theatre group a revival of any of Terry's works might repay exhilarating dividends. A triple bill of the two one-acters mentioned above with *Ex-Miss Copper Queen on a Set of Pills* certainly deserves further investigation. So too would *Babes in the Bighouse*, about women in prison (one of the big successes at OMT), or the equally challenging *Approaching Simone* (about the remarkable life of French philosopher Simone Weil who committed suicide by starving herself to death).

TRY THESE:
▷Caryl Churchill's *Cloud Nine*, ▷Susan Yankowitz's *Slaughterhouse* for gender-bending; ▷Clean Break for other images of women in prison; ▷Pam Gems' *Dusa, Fish, Stas and Vi*, ▷Maureen Duffy's *Rites* for collections of women; for American anti-war images, see Emily Mann's *Still Life*, James Duff's *The War At Home*, the Vietnam Vets Ensemble's *Tracers*.

TERSON, Peter [1932–]
British dramatist

Plays include:
***The Mighty Reservoy* (1964), *Zigger Zagger* (1967), *Mooney and His Caravans* (1968; TV version 1966), *The Apprentices* (1968), *Spring-heeled Jack* (1970), *The 1861 Whitby Lifeboat Disaster* (1971), *But Fred, Freud is Dead* (1972), *Cul de Sac* (1978), *Strippers* (1984)**

A working-class Geordie, Terson trained as a teacher after National Service and taught games for ten years, while collecting rejection slips for his early plays. In 1964 *A Night to Make the*

TRY THESE:
▷David Rudkin, especially in *Afore Night Come*, has also recorded the brooding menace behind the tranquility of rural Worcestershire; ▷John Byrne's *The Slab Boys* follows the problems of the developing adolescent

Angels Weep, began a close association with Peter Cheesman and his Stoke Victoria Theatre-in-the-round. Since then his output has been prolific (sixteen plays for Stoke alone in the following ten years) for both theatre and television. Equally at home with a two-hander, such as *Mooney and His Caravans* or *The Mighty Reservoy*, and the large casts of the National Youth Theatre, for whom he has written extensively, his plays often show an allegorical opposition of traditional or rural life and 'progress', but his greatest characteristic is the fluency of his dialogue and his ear for working-class speech. In his plays for the National Youth Theatre Terson has shown the ability to respond to ideas and individual talents coming from the company to rapidly create new material. His earliest plays, set in the Vale of Evesham, where he then lived, all have an air of menace. *The Mighty Reservoy* charts the relationship of the keeper of a new reservoir and a more educated, town-bred visitor who is drowned in Act Three but whose spirit apparently returns to warn the drunken keeper of a crack in the reservoir. The reservoir becomes a dark obsession for the characters and several critics have described their relationship with it as 'Lawrencian'. Many later plays reflect the style developed at Stoke for local documentary drama, including narration and rapid changes of locale. *Strippers*, a provocative examination of the downside of Thatcherism which shows working-class women taking to stripping as a response to the economic collapse of the North East, raises as many questions about the way to present female exploitation as it answers about sexism and male double standards.

Zigger Zagger
His first play for the National Youth Theatre, *Zigger Zagger* brought both Terson and the NYT to public notice and is still his best known work. A football crowd on the terraces surrounds the action played out before it of the dead-end prospects of a football-mad teenager. Naturalistic scenes are framed by songs and interjections from the terraces but these reinforce the overall content rather than providing a Brechtian alienation, though the criticism of a society which presents such no-hope prospects is implicit. Full of vitality, it eschews any false sentiment and is as objectively critical of working-class parents and soccer stars as it is of probation officers and the establishment.

in a tale about apprentices; see also ▷Barry Reckord's *Skyvers* for educational critique; ▷Kay Adshead, in *Thatcher's Women*, and Julia Schofield, in *Love On the Plastic*, have also investigated the relationship between Thatcherism, unemployment in the North, and the sexual exploitation of women; see also ▷Debbie Horsfield for a football trilogy based around four female football fans.

THEATRE-IN-THE-ROUND

This is the name given to a performance when the acting area occupies a central position with audience on all sides of it. An alternative name is arena theatre, or arena staging, though confusingly this has been used to describe a stage which projects into the audience and is only partly surrounded by them, as in John English's Arena Theatre Company, which pioneered this kind of staging in Britain in the 1940s.

▷ Artaud was already proposing this kind of theatre in the 1920s (though his work was not published until 1938) and by the mid-1930s 'in-the-round' was already one of the audience-actor configurations being used by the Realistic Theatre in Moscow.

In Britain the development of this form of staging owed much to Stephen Joseph, who first created a temporary theatre in one of London University's halls of residence and then made a permanent base in Scarborough in 1956, where the theatre is now named after him. The Victoria Theatre, Stoke-on-Trent, and the Royal Exchange, Manchester, are major British theatres-in-the-round, but many studio theatres, such as the ▷ National Theatre's Cottesloe, are sometimes used in this form. In most cases the seating rises in banks above the stage level so that everyone can see well.

Settings for in-the-round productions are not necessarily circular in shape and are carefully designed to create an appropriate atmosphere and indication of location without obscuring the view of any section of the audience; appropriate furniture can often make important points. However, this does not preclude spectacle – as in productions such as *Moby Dick* at Manchester, where the rigging and deck of Ahab's ship were transformed into the heaving body of the whale. The smaller theatres, with only two or three rows of seating, create what Glen Hughes called a feeling of 'being *in* the play', and although this may not be so strong in a larger auditorium the focus of concentration of the audience around the acting space greatly increases the link between actor and audience. In the early days of the form, directors often kept the action irritatingly fluid so that no part of the audience saw an actor's back for long. With confidence, it was realised that this was not necessary and, with the exception of minute and subtle gestures that can only be seen from one side, there is no need for special echoing or duplication. Audiences take in the whole scene and learn through body language and reactions from other characters, even when they cannot see a face. When it is essential that a single actor address the whole audience, positions outside the central area at the head of gangways can be usefully dominant.

Anyone who has never been to a performance where they can see other members of the audience across the stage may take a few minutes to adjust to the situation, but most people find an in-the-round performance more involving than one on a proscenium stage. Since the audience sits on all sides there are no 'best seats', though people may have preferences as to whether they like to sit right next to the acting space or further back.

THEATRE OF BLACK WOMEN

British theatre company

Key productions include:

Short, one-woman shows: *Tiger Teeth Clenched Not to Bite* (1983; by Bernardine Evaristo), *Hey Brown Girl* (1983; by Patricia Hilaire), *Chameleon* (1983; by Paulette Randall)
***Silhouette* (1984; by Evaristo and Hilaire *Pyeyucca* (1985; by Hilaire and Evaristo), *Chiaroscuro* (1986; by ▷ Jackie Kay, *Miss Quashie and the Tiger's Tail* (1987; by Gabriela and Jean Pearse), *The Cripple* (1987; by Ruth Harris), *The Children* (1987; by Ruth Harris)**

Theatre of Black Women is an excitingly innovative black women's theatre company (the first to be formed in Britain), founded in 1982 by Bernardine Evaristo, Patricia Hilaire and Paulette Randall, three young writers and friends who had been at the Rose Bruford College together and had also taken part in the Royal Court's Young Black Writers Festival. Set up to redress a balance they felt to be lacking in the positive representation of black women in British theatre, their early plays are explorations of what if feels like to be young, black and female in modern Britain. This is allied to a search for cultural roots in which they have often successfully dug back into the past to find links with ancestral voices (as in *Silhouette* and *Pyeyucca*) to make positive statements about continuity and cultural identity. One of their most important productions is ▷ Jackie Kay's *Chiaroscuro*, a loosely structured – one reviewer called it 'a cat's cradle' – *mélange* of music, dance and flashback, exploring the conflicts and prejudices as well as support of two lots of women friends, as they come to terms with themselves, their sexuality (revealing some deep-seated homophobia), their cultural histories, and each other.

Their work has shown a particular political commitment to counteracting the dreaded 'isms' – heterosexism, racism, and sexism – but recently has shown a slight change of direction. Ruth Harris' one woman play *The Cripple*, the true story of a remarkable Jamaican woman, crippled since birth, and performed by actress T.M. Murphy with extraordinary dedication and bravura, said much about the unquenchable spirit of human nature in the face of unimaginable adversity. Harris' *The Children*, by contrast, opens out once again into a multi-racial journey into the world of spirit mediums.

TRY THESE:
▷Graeae for a company which also over-rides disability; ▷Bernard Pomerance's *The Elephant Man* shows spiritual beauty within a physically broken body; see also ▷Gay Sweatshop for a company which started out with similar aims of redressing the imbalance of theatre images; ▷Jackie Rudet's *Money To Live* as a contemporary image of being young, black and female in Britain; ▷Winsome Pinnock for a more recent view; ▷Tasha Fairbank's *Up For Demolition* uses ancestral predecessors as positive images for the future; see also ▷Black Theatre Forum, ▷Black Theatre.

THOMAS, Dylan [1914–1953]

British poet

TRY THESE:
▷Artaud, whose life has also become

Radio play:
Under Milk Wood (1954)

Anglo-Welsh poet Dylan Thomas was born in Swansea, and wrote his poetry while living precariously at Laugharne and in London, earning money from articles, broadcasts and film scripts, and eventually from lecture tours in the USA on one of which he died.

Under Milk Wood is probably the most famous radio play in English (well, Anglo-Welsh), but it has very little plot and very little conflict. It is more of a descriptive piece, opulently written and often very funny, about the inhabitants of Llaregub, that Platonic ideal of a Welsh coastal village, read by two narrators and a series of actors, mostly in monologue. There have been several attempts to produce it as a stage play, starting in 1956, but it resists this treatment: the most recent version was at the Greenwich Theatre in 1986, when the critics generally agreed it would have been better heard and not seen. Theatre Clwyd brought to London's King's Head in 1983 an affectionate adaptation of some of Thomas' early semi-autobiographical stories, *Portrait of the Artist as a Young Dog* (1940), which have some fine overripe pictures of his relatives and acquaintances, but are too static to gain much from being put on stage. Brian Abbott's *Milk Wood Blues*, at the Lyric Hammersmith in 1987, featured Thomas losing the original manuscript of *Under Milk Wood* on a Soho pub crawl (with interventions from Douglas Cleverdon and from Big Bill Broonzy and his guitar), but tended to become just an ingenious *Portrait of the Artist as a Drunken Poet*.

mythical and a matter for plays; ▷Emlyn Williams, *The Druid's Rest*, for another relentlessly picturesque view of the Welsh; ▷Thornton Wilder's *Our Town* does the same for middle America; ▷Jim Cartwright's *Road*, has been called a 'radicalised *Under Milk Wood* for the 1980s'; for other ways of using monologues, see ▷Michel Tremblay.

THRILLERS

Excitement is an essential element of theatre, and the thriller genre exploits the excitement of suspense and our pleasure at being vicariously frightened – often, but not always, thrillers involve a murder story. The Elizabethan *Arden of Faversham* or ▷ Webster's *Duchess of Malfi* are thrillers in their way, as are a number of nineteenth-century melodramas like *The Vampire*, while the French school of *grand guignol* certainly set out to horrify, but the modern notion of a thriller has become inextricably linked with that of the detective story. That does not make every detective story a thriller – the crime must almost certainly be murder, and the circumstances that either the murder is still to be committed or further murders are to be expected. The audience may already know the murderer's identity while the characters remain oblivious of the danger of their situation – the suspense lies in whether they will find out in time to be able to outwit him or her.

Wilkie Collins (1824–89) seems to have been the inventor of the modern crime novel and his fifteen plays include dramatisations of his famous novels *The Moonstone* and *The Woman in White*. Thrillers like Bayard Veiller's *The Thirteenth Chair*, in which Mrs Patrick Campbell had a success in 1917, became a popular feature of twentieth-century theatre. Edgar Wallace (1875–1932) made a speciality of the thriller and detective drama with plays such as *The Ringer*, *The Case of the Frightened Lady*, and *On the Spot* (revived at Watford and in the West End in 1984) and later ▷ Agatha Christie, either with her own plays or adaptations by other writers such as Frank Vosper's *Love from a Stranger*, came to dominate the genre. Among the best from other hands have been *Ten Minute Alibi* by Anthony Armstrong (1933), in which the audience is on the side of the murderer who has seen the perfect alibi in a dream; Patrick Hamilton's *Rope* (1929) – another 'perfect murder' story – and *Gaslight* (1939), successfully revived by Sue Todd Derby in 1987; and ▷ Emlyn Williams' *Night Must Fall* (1935).

The failure of a recent West End revival of the Williams' play suggests that, however well plotted, the social background to some pre-war plays may alienate them from modern audiences. However, Frederick Knott's *Dial M for Murder* and *Wait Until Dark* seem to indicate that thrillers have lost none of their attraction. More recently Tudor Gates' *Who Saw Him Die*, with its underworld background, and Ira Levin's *Deathtrap*, with its homosexual twist, have added to the genre.

▷ Anthony Shaffer's *Sleuth* is both a successful thriller and a parody on the form, an even more successful one than ▷ Tom Stoppard's spoof *The Real Inspector Hound*. The comedy thriller, such as Joseph Kesselring's *Arsenic and Old Lace,* is perhaps an easier subject for revival.

TOURNEUR, Cyril [c 1575–1626]

English Renaissance dramatist

Plays include:

***The Revenger's Tragedy* (1606; attributed to Tourneur 1656), *The Atheist's Tragedy* (1610)**

There is now considerable scholarly doubt about the 1656 attribution of *The Revenger's Tragedy* to Tourneur, with ▷ Middleton being the favoured alternative author, in which case Tourneur becomes even more of a shadowy figure. He was in the service of the Cecil family and died after being put ashore from a returning naval expedition to Cadiz. To add posthumous insult to injury, the manuscript of another play was lost in the eighteenth century, when it was used by a cook, apparently to line a pie dish, a fate it shared with a number of other unique manuscripts. *The Atheist's Tragedy* has been described as 'hilarious', particularly in view of the fact that the protagonist D'Amville has to accidentally brain himself as he attempts to execute the hero; it is not likely to become a staple of the contemporary theatre, although its stylistic diversity and changes of mood might be successfully tackled by an adventurous company. *The Revenger's Tragedy*, authorship controversy notwithstanding, has had several productions in Britain and America since 1965 when it was revived professionally at the Pitlochry festival. The most memorable production was Trevor Nunn's 1966 ▷ RSC revival which made Alan Howard a star and gave full weight to the play's satirical theatricality. Most of the conventional elements of revenge tragedy are here: the long delayed revenge, rape, the skull of a dead woman used to poison the man responsible for her death, incest and the culminating masque which leads to multiple deaths. But there is also a strong sense both of the corruption of the world of *Realpolitik* and of the corruption of the revenger who has to move in that world to achieve revenge.

TRY THESE:
Most Renaissance dramatists used revenge plots and malcontent figures – ▷Shakespeare's *Hamlet* is the most famous example of both, but ▷Kyd's *The Spanish Tragedy* started the vogue for revenge and there are notable examples in ▷Chapman, ▷Ford, ▷Marston, ▷Middleton, ▷Shakespeare (*Titus Andronicus*) and ▷Webster; amongst contemporary dramatists ▷Peter Barnes has a gift for the wittily macabre that recalls Tourneur.

TOWNSEND, Sue [1946–]

British dramatist and novelist

Plays include:

***Womberang* (1979), *The Ghost of Daniel Lambert* (1981), *Dayroom* (1981), *Bazaar and Rummage* (1983), *Captain Christmas and the Evil Adults* (1982), *Groping For Words* (1983; revised as *Are You Sitting Comfortably*, 1983), *The Great Celestial Cow* (1984), *The Secret Diary of Adrian Mole aged 13¾*(1984)**

Television includes:

***Adrian Mole* (1985), *The Growing Pains of Adrian Mole* (1987)**

Best-known as the creator of Adrian Mole this phenomenal success has tended to over-shadow the fact that Townsend, suburban lower-middle-class mother of four, ex-hot dog stall and garage forecourt manager, youth club worker and one-time Thames television writer-in-residence at Leicester's Phoenix Theatre, has more than schoolboy strings to her bow.

Townsend writes with a droll, down-to-earth kind of humour that now and again takes on a surreal and surprisingly angry edge – as in *Womberang*, a comic-vitriolic swipe at the bureaucratic inadequacies of the NHS set in the normally stock situation of a hospital waiting-room, with its wonderfully vituperative working-class rebel, Rita Onions. *Groping for Words* also sets up the unprepossessing sit-com of an evening class in adult literacy, but turns it, with warmth and humanity, into quite a grim political warning about the link between illiteracy, frustration and the pent-up anger of society's underclass. *The Great Celestial Cow*, a fantasy-carnival for ▷ Joint Stock based on Townsend's observations of the Asian community in her home town of Leicester, and intended to break down the stereotype of the 'passive' Asian woman, unfortunately was too broad for some, and ended up inadvertently reinforcing the images it was sup-

TRY THESE:
For school-oriented views of adolescence see ▷Mary O'Malley's *Once a Catholic* and Denise Deegan's *Daisy Pulls It Off;* ▷Harwant Bains' *The Fighting Kite* explores a young man's dual identity as a British Asian; few plays have advanced the disjunction of the Asian woman from her roots, but ▷Hanif Kureishi's *Borderline* covers some of the ground and ▷Jacqui Shapiro's monologue, *One of Us*, comes even closer; for contrasting hospital images, see ▷Louise Page's *Tissue* and ▷Tony Marchant's *Raspberry*; ▷Peter Nichols' *The National Health* for a much more expanded and satirical account of the NHS; see also ▷Asian Theatre.

posed to be cracking. *The Secret Diary of Adrian Mole aged 13¾* (which started out life as an unsolicited radio script, then became a best-selling book before becoming a musical and a television series) and its sequel *The Growing Pains of Adrian Mole* will probably remain Townsend's enduring legacy. Of Mole, her spotty adolescent who turns his consistently cool eye on the antics of adult passion, Townsend wrote, somewhat prophetically: 'I wanted to put down what it was like for a certain type of person in 1981 – a class of person that's now deserting the Labour Party – and get it all down in detail because things are changing.'

TRAVERS, Ben [1886–1980]
British novelist and dramatist

Plays include:

***The Dippers* (1922), *The Three Graces* (1924), *A Cuckoo in the Nest* (1925), *Rookery Nook* (1926), *Thark* (1927), *Mischief* (1928), *Plunder* (1928), *A Cup of Kindness* (1929), *A Night Like This* (1930), *Turkey Time* (1931), *Dirty Work* (1932), *A Bit of a Test* (1933), *Chastity, My Brother* (1936), *O Mistress Mine* (1936), *Banana Ridge* (1938), *Spotted Dick* (1940), *She Follows Me About* (1945), *Outrageous Fortune* (1947), *Runaway Victory* (1949), *Wild Horses* (1952), *Corkers End* (1968), *The Bed Before Yesterday* (1975)**

Travers' first plays were adaptations of his own novels but from 1925–1933 he became the 'house dramatist' for the Aldwych Theatre, London, with a succession of meticulously constructed farces written to exploit the talents of actor-manager Tom Walls (hero), Ralph Lynn (hero's friend), Robertson Hare (hen-pecked husband), Winifred Shotter (heroine) and Mary Brough (Amazonian female). These farces preserve the proprieties and restore the status quo – though, as in *Plunder* for instance, that may include an acceptance of corruption and duplicity. Their tension comes from fear of scandal and the conflict between the outbreak of sexuality and its suppression. On the page they present numerous appalling bad jokes, puns and non-sequiturs which can only be hilarious if played with conviction and precise timing. Creating vehicles for the same team does make his characters somewhat predictable, but his plots are inventive, within the basic requirements of farce. Travers himself considered ▷ Feydeau's type of farce far too mechanical and that everything should be absolutely true to life – though today it now seems a rather stylised 1930s kind of reality!

In his last play, *The Bed Before Yesterday*, liberated from the Lord Chamberlain's censoring hand, he made explicit what had previously had to be conveyed implicity. A prude, put off sex by her first bridal night and having survived two marriages without it, finds herself an impoverished widower to marry for company. Intrigued by hearing other women describe sexual passion she then demands it – and gets totally turned on! Though a relatively slight piece, it encapsulates a whole cycle of sexual experience from puritan rejection, through intriguement, experiment, awakening and infidelity, to final conjugal conviviality – and presents it from the woman's point of view.

TRY THESE:
▷Feydeau and ▷Labiche as the acknowledged masters of French farce; English farce is itself the subject of ▷Michael Frayn's *Noises Off*; ▷Joe Orton's *Loot* and *What the Butler Saw* owe much to Travers; Ray Cooney is the contemporary master of English farce, which finds its comic drama from heterosexual sexual intrigues, infidelities and the questionable homosexual jibe.

TREMBLAY, Michel [1942–]
French Canadian dramatist

Plays include:

***Le Train* (*The Train*; 1964); *Les belles-soeurs* (*The Sisters-in-law*; 1965); *La Duchesse de Langeais* (*The Duchess of Langeais*; 1969), *A Toi pour toujours, ta Marie-Lou* (*Forever Yours, Marie-Lou*; 1971); *Hosanna* (1973), *Hello, là, bonjour*, or *Bonjour, Bonjour* (*Hello, There, Hello*; 1974); *Sainte Carmen de la Main* (*Carmen of the Boulevards*; 1976), *Damneé Manon, Sacrèe Sandra* (*Sandra/Manon*; 1977), *L'Impromptu d'Outremont* (*The Impromptu of Outremont*; 1980), *Les anciennes odeurs* (*Remember Me*; 1981), *Albertine in Five Times* (1984), *Le Vrai Monde?* (*Real World*; 1986)**

French Canadian Michel Tremblay is by now one of Canada's

TRY THESE:
Monologues have become a popular technique in modern naturalistic drama – ▷Jim Cartwright's *Road*, ▷Clare McIntyre's *Low Level Panic*, ▷Nick Ward's *Apart from George* are just a few of the recent plays which have utilised it effectively to express internalised thoughts; Robert Patrick's *Kennedy's Children*

most exportable assets as well as one of its most acclaimed sons at home. A prolific novelist as well as playwright, he was brought up in a working-class family in Montreal's impoverished East End, a fact which reflects itself over and over again in his plays. Reminiscent of ▷ Tennessee Williams in his domestic and female obsessions (not surprisingly Tremblay has translated several plays of Williams), Tremblay's heightened, voluptuous prose style, absorption with guilt, sexual fantasy and homosexuality also recalls ▷ Jean Genet and at his best is as exciting, though without the misogyny. The arrival of *Sandra/Manon* at the Traverse in 1984 during the ▷ Edinburgh Festival confirmed this. A taut two-hander about ecstasy, sacred and profane, *Sandra/Manon* is the last in a cycle of plays developed from *The Sisters-in-law* dealing with three sisters: Marie Lou in *Forever Yours, Marie-Lou* (considered Tremblay's masterpiece); her older sister Carmen in *Saint Carmen of the Boulevard*, and finally the younger sister Manon.

Of the other plays, *Hosanna,* (Birmingham Rep and Half Moon) is about a homosexual couple who finally come to terms with their own natures. *Forever Yours*, produced at Leicester Haymarket in 1979 focusses on a worker who murders his wife and then commits suicide himself, whilst *Johnny Mangano and his Astonishing Dogs*, seen briefly at the Lyric Hammersmith in 1982 shows the interdependence of a couple of bickering cabaret/variety artists. *Bonjour, Bonjour,* a typical Tremblay hot-house of familial discord and repression, is an uncomfortable treatment of incest whose main focus is the effect of four sisters on a returning brother.

Albertine in Five Times

Albertine in Five Times, seemingly structurally daring in its multi-faceted view of one woman ageing from thirty to seventy (and played by five different actresses) shows Tremblay at his best and worst. A lyrical and sensitive essay in guilt, its picture of oppressed but also oppressing womanhood is a recurring motif in Tremblay's work as a mother recalls and berates herself for past sins to do with her children (son is put into a mental hospital, daughter takes an overdose). Essentially built around a number of monologues which translate her thoughts and memories, Tremblay's strength is his dialogue, his interweaving and creation of character intense and often thrilling. But the lack of action in his plays, as in this one which recalls things done in the past, often leads some reviewers to regard his plays as more appropriate to the radio. From a feminist viewpoint, too, Tremblay's picture of women remains troublingly victim-bound, pessimistically trapped in some eternal cycle of determinism.

also uses monologues in a multi-faceted way; ▷Shakespeare got there sooner, of course, and his soliloquies in such plays as *Richard III*, *Hamlet*, *Macbeth* are the perfect vehicle for contrasting the levels of action – the inner thoughts of the protagonist and what is going on, on-stage; for more plays on incest, see ▷Barry Reckord's *X*; for plays with back-stage theatre as their setting, see ▷Ronald Harwood's *The Dresser*, ▷Jacki Holborough's *Dreams of San Francisco*; for three sisters see ▷Shakespeare's *King Lear* and ▷Chekhov's *Three Sisters*.

TRIANA, José [1933–]
Cuban dramatist

Plays include:

***El Major General*, (*The Major General*; 1956), *Medea En El Espaio*, (*Medea in the Mirror*; 1960), *El Parque de la Fraternidad*, (*Fraternity Park*; 1961), *La Casa Ariendo*, (*The Burning House*; 1962), *La Muerte del Neque*, (*The Death of Neque*; 1963), *La Noche de los Asesinos* (produced as *The Criminals* in London in 1967), *Worlds Apart* (1986)**

Poems include:

***De la Madera de Los Suenos* (1958), *Revolico en el Campo de Maret* (1971)**

A Cuban playwright who has lived in Paris since 1979, José Triana is known in Britain for two plays – *The Criminals* and *Worlds Apart* – produced by the ▷ RSC over a twenty-year period. An impressionistic drama about three children who may or may not have murdered their parents. *The Criminals* was the first Cuban play to be seen in this country, and its raw, violent mix of reality and fantasy shocked some observers; others took its ▷ Genet-like theatrics metaphorically, drawing an implicit analogy between familial oppression and that of the state. In *Worlds Apart*, set in Cuba between 1894 and 1913, a sprawling family saga unfolds against the background of political upheaval. With his interest in incident-filled family yarns told in a discursive, dream-like

TRY THESE:
▷Genet, ▷Lorca, and (more recently) ▷Wendy Kesselman's *My Sister In this House* for often violent enactments of social ritual, both in and outside the family ▷Jack Gelber's *The Cuban Thing* and ▷Howard Sackler's *Goodbye, Fidel* for American treatments of a country in tumult.

fashion, Triana recalls great Latin American novelists like Marquez and Borges more than his playwrighting peers, although the sagas can get bogged down in *Dallas*-style soap operatics at the expense of dramatic finesse.

TURGENEV, Ivan Sergeivich [1818–83]

Russian anarchist and dramatist

Plays include:

***The Bachelor* (1849), *A Poor Gentleman* (1851), *A Month in the Country* (written 1850; performed 1872)**

Stage adaptations also exist of his novels:

***Rudin* (adapted by Denis Caslon), *Fathers and Sons* (adapted by ▷ Brian Friel)**

Born the son of an impoverished nobleman in Orel, central Russia, Turgenev is one of the great nineteenth-century masters of psychological realism, on a par with Flaubert and George Eliot, and the pre-eminent forbear of ▷ Chekhov, who would further refine Turgenev's incisive sense of character. He travelled extensively through Europe, befriending many of the leading writers of his time. Apart from several early short plays and two full-length plays unknown in this country, Turgenev's stage reputation rests on *A Month in the Country*, a romantic drama about an idle provincial wife who falls in love with her son's tutor. In 1987, the ▷ National Theatre attempted to add to Turgenev's dramatic corpus with ▷ Brian Friel's stage adaptation of *Fathers and Sons*, but the production was done in by highly variable acting and Carl Toms' ugly wood-dominated set.

A Month in the Country

One of the most frequently revived Russian plays after the work of ▷ Chekhov, this play bears many similarities to that other master playwright. The story of the indolent Natalya's infatuation with her son's tutor, the play is also – like *The Cherry Orchard* – a portrait of a shifting society, emblematised both in the Trofimov-like tutor, Belyaev (a spiritual cousin to the celebrated nihilist, Bazarov, in *Fathers and Sons*), and in Natalya's Lopakhin-like husband, Islayev, with his triple interest in the forces of progress, mechanisation, and the psychology of the workers. A languid witness to romantic evasions in which she participates and a world in flux in which she does not, Natalya herself recalls Yelyena from *Uncle Vanya*, and the play has proven a fine showcase for both Ingrid Bergman in London and Tammy Grimes in New York.

TRY THESE:
▷Chekhov and ▷Gorki for later Russian playwrights who offer both acute insights into character and varying degrees of political comment on Russian society on the eve of change; ▷Goldoni's *Villeggiatura* trilogy, ▷Peter Shaffer's *Five Finger Exercise*, and (for a musical bent) Stephen Sondheim's *A Little Night Music* for comparable depictions of romantic goings-on in a country setting.

VANBRUGH, John [1664–1726]

English dramatist, soldier and architect

Plays include:

***The Relapse* (1696), *The Provoked Wife* (1697)**

Vanbrugh's adventurous life included several spells as a soldier, a stay in the Bastille after being arrested in France as a spy, an attempt at theatrical mangagement, and designing Blenheim Palace amongst other great houses. He also found time to adapt plays from the French (including several by ▷ Molière) and finished two of his own. *The Relapse* takes over the characters from Colley Cibber's *Love's Last Shift* and deploys them in a complicated intrigue plot involving town/country contrasts, secret marriages, impersonation and mistaken identity. Although the continued success of both plays probably owes as much to their farcical elements (the humiliation of and satire at the expense of the aptly named Lord Foppington in *The Relapse* and the transvestite antics of Sir John Brute in *The Provoked Wife*), perhaps their most interesting feature is the presentation of unhappily married couples in which the faithful wife resists the temptations of a potential lover. In a period when divorce was practically non-existent Vanbrugh's refusal to adopt the mix and match 'happy' ending solution favoured by some of his contemporaries leaves his comedies curiously unresolved. There is an open ended realism about his endings which suggests that they are resting points rather than conclusions. It probably also ought to be said that in the first version of *The Provoked Wife* Sir John wore a clerical costume rather than women's clothing for his drunken frolics; the scenes were probably altered in response to complaints about their disrespect to religion, but they are anyway more thematically appropriate in their revised form.

TRY THESE:
Vanbrugh's comedies can be compared instructively with those of the other writers of Restoration comedy, ▷Aphra Behn, ▷Congreve, ▷Etherege, ▷Farquhar, ▷Otway and ▷Wycherley and with later exponents of comedy of manners such as ▷Goldsmith, ▷Sheridan, ▷Oscar Wilde, Noël Coward, ▷Doug Lucie; ▷Alan Ayckbourn's pictures of marriage are reminiscent in some ways of Vanbrugh; ▷Pinero's *The Magistrate* offers another pillar of society in court as a result of drunken misdeeds.

VAN ITALLIE, Jean-Claude [1936–]

Belgian-born, American dramatist

Plays include:

***War* (1963), *Almost Like Being* (1964), *I'm Really Here* (1964), *The Hunter and the Bird* (1964), *Where Is De Queen* (1965), *Motel* (1965), *Interview* (1966), *America Hurrah* (1966), *The Girl and the Soldier* (1967), *The Serpent: A Ceremony* (1968), *Take A Deep Breath* (1969), *Photographs: Mary and Howard* (1969), *Eat Cake* (1971), *The King of the United States* (1973), *Nightwalk* (with ▷ Megan Terry and ▷ Sam Shepard; 1973), *A Fable* (1975), *Bag Lady* (1979), *The Tibetan Book of the Dead* (1983), *The Traveller* (1987). Translations and adaptations include: ▷ Chekhov's *The Seagull* (1973), *The Cherry Orchard* (1977), *Three Sisters* (1979), and *Uncle Vanya* (1980), as well as ▷ Euripides' *Medea* (1979)**

Once a central figure in the off-Broadway explosion of the 1960s (his 1966 trilogy of social alienation, *America Hurrah*, is still considered one of the key works of the decade), Jean-Claude Van Itallie is better known of late for his ▷ Chekhov translations, notably his version of *The Cherry Orchard* which was used in Andrei Serban's celebrated 1977 production at New York's Lincoln

TRY THESE:
▷Megan Terry for another playwright influenced by Joseph Chaikin's Open Theatre; ▷Lorca and ▷Wole Soyinka for emphasis on theatre as ritual; Rochelle Owens's *Futz* for a seminal American play of the 1960s along the lines of *America Hurrah*; ▷De Filippo's *Ducking Out*, ▷Julia Kearsley's *Under the Web* and ▷Arthur Kopit's *Wings* for plays featuring stroke victims.

Center. Elsewhere, Van Itallie has experimented with breaking down the expected form and structure of drama eschewing conventions of plot in favour of archetypal situations (the story of the Garden of Eden and temptation in *The Serpent*) or anarchic satire (*Eat Cake*, a brief but telling assault on American consumerism). Recently, his original works have become more pedestrian: his forty-five minute monologue *Bag Lady* never gets inside its peripatetic character's head, and his most recent play, *The Traveller*, based on the stroke and aphasia of his friend and former colleague Joseph Chaikin, sacrifices hoped-for lyricism to obvious dramaturgy. As is often the case with Van Itallie, the play offers – upon examination – less than meets the eye. Nonetheless, for many, *The Traveller* proved a poignant experience.

VINAVER, Michel [1927–]
French dramatist and novelist

Plays include:

***Aujourd'hui ou Les Coréens* (1956; *The Koreans*), *Iphigénie Hotel* (1960), *Par-dessus bord* (*Overboard*; 1972), *Les Travaux et les Jours* (*A Smile on the End of the Line*; 1979), *Chamber Theatre* consists of *Dissident, il va sans dire* –*Dissident, Goes Without Saying* – and *Nina, c'est autre chose* – *Nina, It's Different*; 1978)**

TRY THESE:
See ▷Kroetz for the 'théâtre du quotidien' (theatre of everyday life), but his political commitment is more overt.

Michel Vinaver (whose real name is Michel Grinberg) is one of the most important contemporary French playwrights. He began as a novelist, but has concentrated on plays since 1955, except for a long gap in the 1960s when his work for the Gillette company came first (they never seem to have found out about his second life, and their reactions to his unflattering pictures of international companies are not recorded). His first play *The Koreans* was put on by Roger Planchon in 1956, and shows alternately a group of French soldiers and some Korean villagers, with the events of the war reported and distanced; his second, *Iphigénie Hotel*, similarly shows the coming to power of de Gaulle unreliably transmitted by radio to a group of tourists cut off in a hotel in Mycenae. Planchon also put on *Overboard*, his first play after the twelve-year gap, an epic treatment of the fortunes of a toilet roll company, shown from multiple viewpoints, with hilarious juxtaposing of various styles of discourse. Vinaver is now a full-time playwright, and his later plays tend to show the lives and work of ordinary people, often employed in a big company, with the main events that affect them happening off stage. His plays are neither didactic nor naturalistic. The seemingly banal snatches of dialogue overlap and fragment, and the complex interweaving becomes clearer in performance than on the page. He says he regards theatre as 'a way of making the familiar very strange'.

A Smile on the End of the Line
The play is set in the Customer Service Department of the Cosson Company, a small firm that has made coffee grinders for over a hundred years; we meet three secretaries (female), an office manager, and an older blue-collar craftsman (male), and their overlapping dialogue of unrelated scraps of everyday conversation forms a pattern that intertwines the politics of the business and the lives of the characters. All the main events take place offstage, as the firm is taken over and the after-sales service replaced by computers and standard letters. Sam Walters' careful production at the Orange Tree in 1987 was the first appearance of a Vinaver play in England.

WALCOTT, Derek [1932–]
St Lucian dramatist

Plays include:

***Ti-Jean and His Brothers* (1957), *Dream on Monkey Mountain* (1967), *The Joker of Seville* (1974; from Tirso de Molina), *O Babylon!* (1976), *Pantomime* (1977; produced 1987), *Remembrance* (1977; produced London 1987), *Beef No Chicken* (1982), *The Isle is Full of Noises* (1982), *To Die for Grenada* (1986)**

Walcott is one of the Caribbean's most important playwrights and men-of-letters. His output includes several volumes of poetry, the latest of which, *Collected Poems (1948–1984)* won him the *Los Angeles Times* book prize. However, so far only four of his nearly three dozen plays have been seen in Britain: *Dream on Monkey Mountain*; *Remembrance*; *Pantomime* and *O Babylon!*. The fact that Walcott's work has reached these shores at all must largely be due to the personal drive and initiative of director Yvonne Brewster. She worked with Walcott at the Trinidad Theatre Workshop, which he founded in 1959 (he moved to Trinidad after graduating from the University of Jamaica) to produce his own work as well as other Caribbean and foreign plays. Brewster has directed at least two of the plays – *Pantomime* and *O Babylon!* – whilst *Remembrance* was part of the 1987 Black Theatre season in London. His work has also been produced regularly in the USA by the ▷ Negro Ensemble Company, Joe Papp's New York Shakespeare Festival Theatre, as well as Yale Repertory (he is currently teaching at Boston University),

Walcott's plays, as with those of other Caribbean writers, are an attempt to find ways and means of expressing the richness of their cultural legacies. Rhythms of speech are important, so too is the use of music, ritual, myth, and drumming. *Dream on Monkey Mountain* is regarded as a West Indian classic, an allegory about myth and history; *Remembrance* is a smaller scale study of the legacies of colonialism, focused on the character of Albert Perez Jordan, teacher and fantasist. It is an affectionate, almost sentimental portrait of a far from sympathetic character irrevocably influenced by British rule (especially literature and war-time experiences) but left behind by time – a sort of epitaph to a dying breed. *O Babylon!*, on the other hand, is a hymn to Rastafarianism that takes a hefty, ironical swipe at cracking capitalism, Kingston style, with additional music by Galt MacDermot of *Hair* fame.

Pantomime

This is probably Walcott's most accessible play and certainly one of his most popular. A neat twist on the Robinson Crusoe theme, Walcott's white master and black servant prepare a play to greet the tourists coming to visit the island of Tobago, but with the white hotel-owner and one-time actor playing Man Friday. The device reaps a rich comic harvest in its own right, as well as gleefully giving vent to some painful historical taboos for the black community about colour, gait and language. Indeed, one of its most enthusiastic receptions has been in Cardiff, where the implications about holding on to language were hugely appreciated by Welsh-language supporters in the audience.

TRY THESE:

▷Brian Friel's *Translations* for another play about language as an instrument of invasion; ▷Ntozake Shange, who also sees language as a symbol of oppression; ▷Caryl Phillips' *The Shelter* is another, less successful version of the Robinson Crusoe theme; ▷Mustapha Matura's transplanted *Three Sisters*, *Trinidad Sisters*, is a poignant portrayal of British imperial legacies; Rastafarianism is the consciousness behind ▷Edgar White's *Lament for Rastafari*; ▷Michael Hastings' *The Emperor* sees Haile Selassie in a rather different light; ▷Edgar White's *The Nine Night*, Felix Cross and David Simon's *Blues for Railton*, Felix Cross' *Mass Carib and* Dennis Scott's *Echo in the Bone* all use ritual to greater or lesser effect, Scott and Cross also with graphic references to slavery; Earl Lovelace's Trinidad-set *The New Hardware Store* is an implicit attack on capitalism (the oppressed reproducing oppressive lifestyles) though a social comedy.

WANDOR, Michelene

British dramatist, poet, fiction writer and theoretician

Plays include:

***The Day After Yesterday* (1972), *Spilt Milk* (1972), *To Die Among Friends* (1974), *Penthesilea* (1977; from ▷ Kleist), The Old Wives' Tale (1977), *Care and Control* (1977; scripted for ▷ Gay Sweatshop), *Floorshow* (1977; with ▷ Caryl Churchill, ▷ Bryony Lavery and David Bradford), *Whores D'Oeuvres* (1978), *Scissors* (1978), *AID Thy Neighbour* (1978), *Correspondence* (radio 1978; staged 1979), *Aurora Leigh* (1979; from Elizabeth Barrett Browning), *The Blind Goddess* (1981; from Toller), *The Wandering Jew* (1987; with ▷ Mike Alfreds, from Eugene Sue)**

Michelene Wandor's unique position is well summed up by Helene Keyssar: 'More than any single figure, Wandor is responsible for articulating and supporting the interaction of feminism, theatre, socialism and gay liberation in Britain.' Active in the reborn women's movement from its earliest days – *The Day After Yesterday* attacks the sexism of the Miss World contest, *Care and Control* is about the issue of lesbian mothers having custody of their children – Wandor has made significant contributions at both the theoretical and the practical level, as one of the few theatre practitioners with a strong academic background. As editor of the first four volumes of the Methuen anthologies of *Plays by Women*, she has made a significant body of women's dramatic writing available to those who were unable to see the plays in their first productions and as author of *Understudies* and *Carry on Understudies*, she has documented and analysed the undervalued contribution of women to the contemporary theatre.

A prolific radio dramatist, she has never achieved comparable critical success in the theatre: the ▷ National Theatre production of *The Wandering Jew* lasted for over five hours and, despite ▷ Mike Alfreds' acknowledged gifts with novel adaptations and Wandor's successful radio adaptations of Dostoyevsky, Austen and H.G. Wells, the general view was that the novel simply was not up to it. *Aurora Leigh* is a fine adaptation of Elizabeth Barrett Browning's verse novel that deserves a wider audience, and some of the earlier work, such as *Whores D'Oeuvres*, a fantasy about two prostitutes stranded on a makeshift raft on the Thames after a freak storm, is well worth reviving as more than a historical curiosity. It is probably worth pointing out that *AID Thy Neighbour* is an attempt at a comedy about contemporary attitudes to the family focused on the question of Artificial Insemination by Donor, not a play about AIDS.

TRY THESE:
see ▷Adaptations and Adapters, and ▷Shared Experience for more on adaptations; ▷Monstrous Regiment and Mrs Worthington's Daughters have staged Wandor's work; see also ▷Women in Theatre, ▷Lesbian Theatre, ▷Gay Sweatshop, ▷Women Dramatists for more on the issues Wandor confronts in her theoretical as well as her theatrical writings; ▷Sarah Daniels' *Neaptide* for another lesbian custody case; ▷Kay Adshead's *Thatcher's Women* for a recent play about prostitution.

WASSERSTEIN, Wendy [1950–]

American dramatist

Plays include:

***Any Woman Can't* (1973), *When Dinah Shore Ruled the Earth* (with ▷ Christopher Durang; 1975), *Montpelier Pizzazz* (1976), *Uncommon Women and Others* (1978), *Isn't It Romantic?* (1981; revised 1983), *Tender Offer* (1983), *Miami* (1986), *The Heidi Chronicles* (1988); she also adapted *Man in a Case* from the ▷ Chekhov short story (part of the 1986 anthology *Orchards*)**

The Zeitgeist of the Jewish family comes under primarily comic assault in the work of Wendy Wasserstein, a graduate of Harvard and the Yale Drama School whose work has been under-represented in Britain because of the catch-all explanation that 'it's too New York' (meaning 'too Jewish'?). Certainly, those in search of a distaff *Common Pursuit* could do worse than compare ▷ Simon Gray's Oxbridge milieu with the Radcliffe ladies who gather to reminisce in *Uncommon Women and Others*, Wasserstein's biggest commerical hit to date. Adapted for television, the

TRY THESE:
▷Neil Simon as America's most successful Jewish comic playwright; ▷Christopher Durang, ▷Albert Innaurato, A.R. Gurney as other Playwrights' Horizons authors who write often about family pressures; ▷Chekhov for point-scoring without pretension; ▷Caryl Churchill's *Top Girls*, ▷Nell Dunn's *Steaming* for a gathering of women; Clare Booth Luce's *The Women*; and for contrast

play was followed up by *Isn't It Romantic?*, the story of the friendship between a twenty-eight-year-old Jewish *mensch* named Janie Blumberg and the elegant WASP, Harriet Cornwall. Revised in 1983 in a fuller, more emotionally complete version, the comedy was a financial and critical success for Playwrights' Horizons, the off-Broadway venue where the new production originated. That same venue hosted her 1986 musical-in-progress *Miami*, about a Long Island family on holiday in Florida in 1959 and, specifically, the maturation of their young artist-visionary son. At her best, Wasserstein writes warm but incisive dialogue that casts a critical eye on her characters without ever demeaning them; at her worst, she succumbs to cultural stereotypes she can't always send up or, as in her one-act comedy about estrangement, *Tender Offer*, succumbs to a case of the cutes.

▷Pam Gems' *Dusa, Fish, Stas and Vi.*

WATERHOUSE, Keith

see HALL, Willis

WEBSTER, John [c 1580–c 1632]

English Renaissance dramatist

Plays include:
***The White Devil* (1612), *The Duchess of Malfi* (1613)**

Webster, the son of a London coachmaker, had a legal training which may explain the number of trial scenes in his plays, and he probably wasn't a full-time professional dramatist. Although he did write plays about London life, his reputation rests on the two revenge tragedies set in Italy which bear out ▷ T.S. Eliot's remark that he 'was much possessed by death/And saw the skull beneath the skin'. This emphasis on corruption and death – in *The Duchess of Malfi* the Cardinal's mistress dies after kissing a poisoned Bible –still encourages some people to side with ▷ George Bernard Shaw, who described Webster as the 'Tussaud laureate'. *The White Devil* and *The Duchess of Malfi*, both based on Italian history, are characterised by lavish use of violent and macabre deaths, adultery, dumb shows and apparitions; but they bring a new emphasis to the presentation of the tragic female protagonist since their central figures are victims of events rather than initiators of them, sacrifices to the power of patriarchy who pay the price for stepping out of line.

The Duchess of Malfi
The bare bones of the plot might seem to support the charge that Webster was simply out to give his audience a quick thrill through gruesome effects and sensational plotting. After all, the widowed Duchess makes a secret second marriage to her steward Antonio, thus incurring the wrath of her two corrupt brothers, Ferdinand and the Cardinal, who engineer plots to torment her and destroy the marriage, with the result being a final body count of ten. Not only is the number of deaths high even by the generous standards of the Renaissance but there is a heady mix of mistaken murders, dances of madmen, tableaux of wax dummies, apparently severed hands and lycanthropy to go with it. But throughout the play there is a sense of the Duchess and Antonio as 'ordinary' people attempting to make sense of and to live 'normal' lives in a world which has no fixed positions or moral absolutes, in which good intentions are no salvation, and from whose absurdity there is no escape. Even in a bad production the play has the virtues of good melodrama, but in a brilliant one, such as Adrian Noble's 1980 production for the Manchester Royal Exchange with Helen Mirren as the Duchess, Pete Postlethwaite as Antonio, Mike Gwilym as Ferdinand, Julian Curry as the Cardinal and Bob Hoskins as the malcontent Bosola who does most of the dirty work, the play's resolute refusal to be bowed by corruption and pervasive evil emerges very clearly.

TRY THESE:
Plays by ▷Samuel Beckett and ▷Edward Bond for that curious sense of an optimism that refuses to be bowed by the harshness of life; plays by other Renaissance dramatists, particularly ▷Chapman, ▷Ford, ▷Marlowe, ▷Marston, ▷Middleton and ▷Shakespeare (especially *Measure for Measure* where Isabella is confronted by a similar atmosphere of changing moral absolutes) for the use of Machiavellian villains, revenge plots and malcontents; ▷Brecht's *Galileo* and ▷Hochhüth's *The Representative* for questionable cardinals.

WEDEKIND, Frank [1864–1918]
German dramatist

Plays include:

***Spring Awakening* (1891), *The Earth Spirit* (1895), *The Marquis of Keith* (1900), *Pandora's Box* (1903)**

Wedekind's first play, *Spring Awakening*, was immediately controversial, both by its theme – adolescent sexuality and adult repression – and its anti-naturalistic style. His later plays continued to concern themselves with sex and society, and Wedekind was widely regarded as a scandalous libertine and anarchist. In fact, his work is very much concerned with morality, and his later work has a strongly religious flavour.

Wedekind had a profound effect on the development of twentieth-century German drama. It is fair to regard him as an originator of ▷ Expressionism: his deliberate use of non-naturalistic and symbolic devices, his exaggerated and caricatured characterisation, and his deployment of ▷ music hall and ▷ cabaret technique, clearly influencing Toller, Kaiser, and ▷ Brecht.

His plays display a major preoccupation with the clash between the irresistable force of Life – most strongly experienced as sex – and the immovable object of bourgeois hypocrisy and 'respectability'. In *Spring Awakening* the adults prefer the destruction of their children to a public admission of the facts of life, in the so-called 'Lulu' plays – *The Earth Spirit and Pandora's Box* – Lulu destroys a series of representative bourgeois males through her uninhibited but essentially innocent enjoyment of sex before her death at the hands of a madman. The power of Wedekind's writing is such that his plays continue to disturb and shock. They were still being refused a performing licence in Britain in the 1960s.

Spring Awakening

Stiefel, a fourteen-year old boy, commits suicide rather than face his parents after failure at school. His diaries are found to contain a graphic account of sex written by another boy, Gabor. Horrified respectability expels Gabor from school for possessing this knowledge, and then sends him to a reformatory when his innocent and childishly ignorant girlfriend is found to be pregnant. The girl's mother forces her to have an abortion, and she dies as a result. Escaping from the reformatory, Gabor grieves over her grave and is confronted with Stiefel's ghost, exhorting him to join the other children in death. A strangely positive conclusion is reached, however, by the intervention of a mysterious figure who convinces Gabor that he must not abandon life.

TRY THESE:
Wedekind's personal quarrel with the Naturalistic dramatist Gerhart Hauptmann played a part in his reaction against Naturalism; ▷Strindberg was another major precursor of Expressionism; Wedekind's frankness about sex parallels ▷Ibsen's equally controversial (in its time) frankness; Wedekind influenced Surrealism and the Theatre of the Absurd; ▷Peter Barnes' *The Ruling Class* has parallels with the 'Lulu' plays, ▷Howard Brenton's *Romans in Britain* scandalised the moral majority with its naked buggery, intended as a metaphor for imperialism; ▷Bond's *Saved* still shocks with its baby-battering violence, again a device used by the playwright to show the dehumanising effects of capitalism.

WEISS, Peter Ulrich [1916–82]
Czechoslovakian-born Swedish painter, novelist, director and dramatist

Plays include:

***The Persecution and Assassination of Jean-Paul Marat as Performed by the Inmates of the Asylum of Charenton under the Direction of the Marquis de Sade* (1964), *The Investigation* (1965), *The Tower* (1967), *Discourse on the War in Vietnam* (1968), *Song of the Lusitanian Bogey* (1968), *How Mr Mockingpott was Relieved of his Sufferings* (1968), *The Insurance* (1969), *Trotsky in Exile* (1971), *Holderlin* (1971)**

Born in Czechoslovakia of German parents and resident in Sweden from 1939, Weiss was an intensely political writer with a considerable range. *The Investigation* is a documentary based on the 1964 War Crimes Trial at Frankfurt, *The Insurance* a surrealist allegory, *Song of the Lusitanian Bogey* a record of an uprising in Angola and its suppression by the Portuguese. His work often attracted controversy – attempts to suppress *Discourse on the War in Vietnam* in Berlin, outrage at *Marat/Sade* (as his first play is frequently called) in London – but no one could deny that his plays have a strong theatrical power as well as a forceful message.

Marat/Sade, which brought him an international reputation through the historic ▷ Artaud-influenced 1964 ▷ RSC production

TRY THESE:
▷Büchner's *Danton's Death*; ▷Mnouchkine's *1789*, ▷Pam Gems' *The Danton Affair* are all treatments of the French Revolution; ▷Hochhüth is concerned with similar issues, especially in *The Representative*; the American ▷Wooster Group is one of the few companies still attempting political, social and physical theatre on a comparable scale; see also ▷Robert Wilson; ▷Peter Brook.

by ▷ Peter Brook (a *tour de théâtre* difficult to match), is exactly what the full title describes. In an introduction ▷ Brook says: 'Everything about [the play] is designed to crack the spectator on the jaw, then douse him with ice-cold water, then force him intelligently to assess what has happened to him, then give him a kick in the balls, then bring him to his senses again.' Brook's production gave one little chance to come back to one's senses but the play does include a variety of arguments about revolutionary violence and an ironic picture of the revolution tamed by the new Empire but very likely to re-emerge.

WERTENBAKER, Timberlake

Anglo-French-American dramatist, now resident in Britain.

Plays include:

The Third (1980), _Case to Answer_ (1980), _Breaking Through_ (1980), _New Anatomies_ (1981), _Inside Out_ (1982), _Home Leave_ (1982), _Abel's Sister_ (with Yvonne Bourcier; 1984), _The Grace of Mary Traverse_ (1985), _The Love of a Nightingale_ (1988), _Our Country's Good_ (loosely based on Thoman Keneally's _The Playmaker_; 1988)

Translations include:

False Admissions and _Successful Strategies_ (from ▷ Marivaux; 1983), _La Dispute_ (from ▷ Marivaux; 1987), _Leocadia_ (from ▷ Anouilh; 1986), _Mephisto_ (from ▷ Ariane Mnouchkine; 1986), _The House of Bernarda Alba_ (from ▷ Lorca; 1987), _Pelleas and Melisande_ (from Maeterlinck; 1988)

Wertenbaker, brought up in the Basque country, has been hailed as 'the most successful translator of ▷ Marivaux in the present age, if not ever' (Michael Ratcliffe for *The Observer*), for the two productions she did as writer-in-residence for ▷ Shared Experience: *False Admissions* and *Successful Strategies*. *Abel's Sister* and *The Grace of Mary Traverse*, her two most recent plays for the Royal Court (where she was also writer-in-residence), equally show an intelligence willing to take stylistic and philosophical chances. *Abel's Sister* (co-written with the disabled Yvonne Bourcier) is quite remarkable for its insights into both physical disability – an extraordinary performance from Linda Bassett of honesty and spikiness in the face of disability since birth – and, through its attendant characters of Vietnam veteran and young jaundiced radicals, emotional and spiritual disability. *The Grace of Mary Traverse*, on the other hand, is a picaresque eighteenth-century gallop with Faustian undertones – what price knowledge? – but also, and primarily, an exploration of the possibilities for women when they step outside their own environment. Wertenbaker had already engaged with this topic in *New Anatomies*, a sprawling, ambitious account of two rebellious women who broke the conventions of gender by dressing in male attire: the nineteenth-century explorer Isabelle Eberhardt and the music hall performer Vesta Tilley. Wertenbaker's two 1988 commissions, *Our Country's Good* and *The Love of a Nightingale* confirm her growing stature as one of Britain's most challenging and intellectually stimulating female playwrights.

TRY THESE:
For women in male clothes, ▷Shakespeare's *Twelfth Night* and *The Merchant of Venice*, ▷Middleton and ▷Dekker's *The Roaring Girl*; for 'history' plays with contemporary parallels, ▷Howard Barker's *Victory* and *The Castle*; ▷Goethe's *Faust* for the philosophical knot; for images of disability, see ▷Graeae, ▷Theatre of Black Women's *The Cripple* and ▷Peter Nichols' *Day in the Death of Joe Egg*, ▷Phil Young's *Crystal Clear* and ▷Mark Medoff's *Children of a Lesser God*.

WESKER, Arnold [1932–]

British dramatist

Plays include:

Chicken Soup with Barley (1958), _Roots_ (1959), _I'm Talking About Jerusalem_ (1960) (these three plays forming _The Wesker Trilogy_), _The Kitchen_ (1959), _Chips with Everything_ (1962), _The Nottingham Captain_ (1962), _Menace_ (1963), _Their Very Own and Golden City_ (1965), _The Four Seasons_ (1965), _The Friends_ (1970), _The Old Ones_ (1972), _The Wedding Feast_ (from Dostoevski; 1974) _The Journalists_ (1975), _Love Letters on Blue Paper_

TRY THESE:
▷John Osborne as the first of the generation of 'Angry Young Men'; John McGrath also forged alliances with the labour and Trade Union movements and generated labour support for the arts; ▷Harold Pinter and

Janet McTeer (right) as Mary Traverse, dwarfed beneath Candis Cook's arching set in Timberlake Wertenbaker's ***The Grace Of Mary Traverse***, directed by Danny Boyd, Royal Court, 1985.

(1976), *The Merchant* (from *The Merchant of Venice*; 1977), *Caritas* (1981), *One More Ride on the Merry Go Round* (1981, produced 1985), *Sullied Hands* (1981, produced 1984), *Mothers* (1982), *Annie Wobbler* (1983), *Whatever Happened to Betty Lemon* (1986)

In a 1958 magazine photograph, Wesker is shown with ▷ Harold Pinter, ▷ John Mortimer, ▷ N.F. Simpson and ▷ Ann Jellicoe as an exponent of the 'New Wave Drama'. With Osborne, he was regarded as one of the Angry Young Men in the 1950s, and his work seen to exemplify a 'new realism'.

Born in Stepney, the son of Jewish emigrés, Wesker worked as a furniture maker's apprentice, as a carpenter's mate, plumber's mate, farm labourer and bookseller's assistant and for four years after National Service in the Royal Air Force he worked as a pastry cook, an experience he draws on in *Chicken Soup with Barley* and *The Kitchen*. In 1956 he took a film course and began writing film scripts and for the theatre.

Much of his early writing is very autobiographical, ▷ John Arden has termed it 'autobiography in documentary style'; *The Wesker Trilogy* is firmly set in an East End world of the Jewish family. The Royal Court took up Wesker's first play, *Chicken Soup with Barley*, after its first production at the Belgrade Theatre, Coventry, and the next two plays of the trilogy, *Roots* and *I'm Talking about Jerusalem* followed the same production path. All were directed by John Dexter, whose contributions very much affected their final versions. The trilogy was performed in its entirety at the Royal Court in 1960, and Wesker first presented *The Kitchen* as a Sunday night production at the Court in 1959. In *Chips With Everything* Wesker began to move away from a strictly naturalist form, and employed folk and popular song, a device he was to pursue in his later plays. Wesker's more recent work has tended to move away from the broad chronology and canvases of his earlier work. In *Caritas* he explores the phenomenon of a fourteenth-century woman anchorite (a religious mystic and recluse) who literally walls herself up in a cathedral wall. *Annie Wobbler* and *Mothers* take the form of dramatic monologue.

Wesker has been active in the labour movement, he was briefly jailed for his anti nuclear activities. In 1961 he campaigned to Trade Union groups in a bid to enlist support for a centre for popular arts. This led to the establishment of Centre 42. In 1964 Wesker acquired the Round House in London's Chalk Farm, and based the centre there with support from the Trade Union movement and the Labour government where it became a focus for radical theatre until Centre 42 was dissolved in 1971.

Wesker share an East End Jewish background; ▷Robert Bolt was imprisoned with Wesker for their anti-nuclear protest, and was a fellow member of the Committee of 100; ▷John Arden, for a while also shared their pacificism; see ▷Debbie Horsfield for a contemporary writer who has written a trilogy – on young women and football; ▷Michel Tremblay uses monologue techniques in *Albertine in Five Times*; ▷Shelagh Delaney's *A Taste of Honey* and ▷David Storey were other exponents of social realism; ▷Andrea Dunbar, ▷Jim Cartwright, some of ▷Karim Alrawi, and ▷Tony Marchant are modern equivalents.

Chicken Soup with Barley
Chicken Soup with Barley is the first of *The Wesker Trilogy*. It charts the experience of the Kahns, a Jewish family in the East End over twenty years, beginning in 1936 with the threat of Moseley's Blackshirts, and ending with the 1956 Soviet invasion of Hungary. These events are experienced from within a domestic world; the play traces the decline of the family, a group of people who come to stand for the disillusion of the post-war generations, as their hopes for the future turn to a loss of faith. The play was enormously influential. The Wesker Trilogy uses a form of social realism to depict working-class life. In the last play of the trilogy, *I'm Talking about Jerusalem*, Wesker returns to the Kahn family; the Jerusalem of the title represents the hopes of the future in the face of the failure of socialist idealism, (a reference to the call 'Next Year in Jerusalem!' of the Passover ritual).

WHITE, Edgar [1947–]
Caribbean dramatist, born in Monserrat

Plays include:
Little Orfeo's Lay (1972), The Black Women (1977), Masada (1978), Lament for Rastafari (1979), Trinity (1981), The Nine Night (1983), Redemption Song (1984), The Boot Dance (1984), Moon Dance Night (1987)

Poet, dramatist, Edgar White studied at City College in New York and has had many plays produced there, including five by Joe Papp's Shakespeare Festival Theatre: *The Mummer's Play* (1970),

TRY THESE:
The Nine Night bears strong similarities to American Steve Carter's *Eden*; Derek Walcott's *Oh Babylon* is a rock hymn to Rastafarianism; Felix Cross and David Simon's *Blues for Railton* is one of the most successful, if

The Wonderfule Yeare (1970), *Seigsmundo's Tricycle* (1971), *La Gente* (1973), and *Les Femmes Noires* (or *The Black Ladies*; 1974).

He first came to Britain in the 1960s and later on was involved with the seminal gathering of black actors, musicians and directors at the Keskidee Centre (founded by Oscar Abrahams) in north London, one of two places (The Factory in west London was the other) which for a short time were centres where specifically black and Caribbean plays were performed. Of the plays produced in Britain, many of them are concerned with the question of identity, and, like many West Indians writing of their experiences of living in Britain, with disillusionment. White writes particularly of the quest for roots back in the Caribbean with a mixture of dry humour, sorrow and sometimes dreamy romanticism; his plays invariably introduce elements of mysticism and ritual into realistic settings as well as frequent references to Rastafarianism.

Two of White's most popular plays, *The Nine Night*, revived in January 1988 by Double Edge company, and *Redemption Song*, both deal with the return and disillusionment of the exile as does *Moon Dance* presented in the 1987 Black Theatre Season at the Arts Theatre in London. In *Redemption Song*, a richly ironic title in itself, Legion, a young dreamer and poet returns home to claim his inheritance after his father's death, only to find he is as much of an outcast there as he was in Britain. Legion is in limboland and, as White has written, stands for a generation of young immigrants, brought to Britain when small, but as adults, lost and rejected by both cultures. White tends to concentrate, though by no means exclusively, on the experiences of males; *Moon Dance* which focused on a smart, urbanised black woman from London returning to the Caribbean for a holiday seemed more like caricature. However, this is an aspect of White's writing, and of other black writers generally, which can provoke a variety of responses from outrage to guffaws of instantaneous identification, depending on the cultural background of the audience.

The Nine Night

The Nine Night (it refers to a Jamaican funeral ritual used to help a troubled soul pass to paradise) opens and closes this domestic comedy that highlights the disillusionment of those who came to Britain regarding themselves as British and Britain as 'the mother country' until they started to live here. In the central figure of Hamon, the troubled spirit – 'a Black Alf Garnett only with some brains' (John Connor, *City Limits*) – on the eve of returning to the Caribbean with his son, White has created a character rich in comic pretensions as well as pathos (loss of illusions is also mirrored in loss of power in the home). His fanatical love of cricket – there is a wonderful scene where Hamon and his old friend drunkenly recreate the first West Indies Test victory over England – symbolises a whole generation cast of mind and old 'adopted' values in conflict with the harsher ones of contemporary England. His son, brought up in England, prefers football to cricket.

not *the* most successful marrying of the Caribbean past and British present – great music, riotously funny yet a pungent analysis of 'disillusionment' through the break-up of a Brixton couple's marriage: Dennis Scott's impressively wide-ranging exploration of black history and oppression *An Echo in the Bone* also uses the ritual of the Nine Night; ▷Mustapha Matura, ▷Caryl Phillips, and ▷Nigel Moffatt have all written plays dealing with disillusionment; ▷Trevor Rhone also tends to use caricature; for cultural contrast; see also ▷Ayckbourn and for more images of patriarchy in retreat, De Filippo's *Ducking Out*; see also ▷Black Theatre.

WHITEHEAD, Ted (Edward Anthony) [1933–]
British dramatist

Plays include:

***The Foursome* (1971), *Alpha Beta* (1972), *The Sea Anchor* (1974), *(Old Flames* (1975), *Mecca* (1977), *The Man Who Fell in Love with His Wife* (1984)**

Whitehead worked in various manual jobs, in advertising and as a teacher, before becoming a full-time writer in 1971 when he was resident dramatist at the Royal Court. His television adaptations of Fay Weldon's *The Life and Loves of a She-Devil* (1987) and of ▷ Strindberg's *Dance of Death* (1984) are indicative of his dominant interest in sexual politics, particularly of the obsessive kind. His work is always closely observed and often comic, but there is an edge of uneasiness to the comedy as his characters engage in mating rituals and other games. In *The Foursome* he charts a brief sexual relationship between two couples and in *The Sea Anchor* the emphasis is on promiscuity and the nature of marriage. *Alpha Beta*, a raw battle of the sexes and a misogynistic tirade against marriage, has had a sudden spate of revivals (on its first showing, it had a blistering outing with Billie Whitelaw and Albert Finney as the warring couple). His most

TRY THESE:
▷Euripides' *The Bacchae* for women eating men; ▷Caryl Churchill's *Top Girls* for another all-female meal that also worried some critics; ▷Strindberg, generally, for sexual politics; ▷Ibsen's *A Doll's House* for an earlier strained marriage; ▷Willy Russell's *Stags and Hens* for another version of contemporary mating rituals; ▷Jacqui Shapiro's *Dead Romantic*, Jack Klaff's *Cuddles* have been more recent

recent stage play, *The Man Who Fell in Love with His Wife*, is a revised version of his 1980 television play *Sweet Nothings*, in which a man becomes obsessed with what his wife is doing when she goes to work outside the home after twenty years of childcare and domesticity; the result is that she rediscovers herself and he crumbles into pathological jealousy.

Old Flames
Most of Whitehead's stage work is naturalistic in tone and texture, and he puts this to good use in *Old Flames* which develops from a comedy of manners opening, with a man being put out to find that the woman who has invited him to dinner has also invited his ex-wives and his mother, into a kind of gothic farce as he discovers he is the menu. After the interval, and the dinner, the women sit around talking freely about their lives to one another in a way that is still rare in drama. Inevitably, the static nature and almost monologue quality of the second act has given rise to cries of lack of dramatic interaction, but the value placed on women's discourse is more than adequate compensation.

examinations in the sexual politics arena.

WHITEMORE, Hugh [1936–]
British dramatist

Plays include:
***Stevie* (1977), *Pack of Lies* (1983), *Breaking the Code* (1986), *The Best of Friends* (1988)**

A list of Hugh Whitemore's stage plays gives little indication of his versatility or distinguished career as a television and film writer – with such credits as the screenplay for *84 Charing Cross Road*, a Writers Guild award for a television adaptation of *Cider with Rosie* (1971) and *Country Matters* (1972), as well as a clutch of television drama series. His stage plays, not surprisingly, show an equal craftsmanship, like an old Chippendale, with the same attention to detail. His portrayal of the Palmers Green poet Stevie Smith (*Stevie*) was as much a pinpointing of the minutiae of suburban claustrophobia as the makings of a poet (portrayed with brittle resignation by Glenda Jackson, but made touchingly poignant by Mona Washbourne in one of the last performances she gave before her death, as the irritating but fragile mum). In *Pack of Lies*, suburbia again sets the scene for a microscopic examination of emotional destruction, with the Jacksons, who befriended and then betrayed the Portland Spy case spies, the Krogers. In *Breaking the Code*, about Enigma code-breaker and homosexual Alan Turing, ideas of loyalty and national expediency are again explored alongside homosexuality. His most recent play, *The Best of Friends*, a celebration of friendship, dramatising the correspondence between ▷ G.B. Shaw, Sir Sydney Cockerell and the Abbess of Stanbrook in Worcester, seems to have been an exercise in elegance with a glittery cast including Sir John Gielgud. Both *Pack of Lies* and *Breaking the Code* have successfully transferred to Broadway (with Derek Jacobi repeating his much praised role as Turing).

Pack of Lies
Set in 1961 with the Portland Spy case as its background, Whitemore chose to focus not so much on the Krogers as the way the suburban couple, the Jacksons, were drawn into a web of deceit by MI6, and the effect on them. A subtle study in the pain of betrayal, of conflicting loyalties between friends and country, and of how the lives of ordinary people can be ruthlessly destroyed, it breathed new life into the old soap opera form and became a compelling drama, particularly in the hands of Judi Dench and a bespectacled and cardiganned Michael Williams. *Pack of Lies* started out as a television play and was also turned into an American television film (1986) (with Ellen Burstyn, Alan Bates and Teri Garr).

TRY THESE:
▷Simon Gray, ▷Julian Mitchell also specialise in the 'well-made' play and deal in loyalties and things British; ▷Alan Bennett's *The Old Country* for a theme of betrayal and homosexuality; for images of ageing mothers, see ▷Julia Kearsley's *Under the Web*, ▷Ayshe Raif's *Fail/Safe*; Laclos' *Les Liaisons Dangereuses* (adapted by ▷Christopher Hampton) is entirely based on letters but, on the whole, dramatised letters have been less frequent than anthologies, which over the years have formed the basis of solo performances about specific poets and writers (eg ▷Oscar Wilde in Michael McLiammoir's *The Importance of Being Oscar* in the 1960s; Michael Pennington's *Anton Chekhov* in 1984).

WHITING, John [1917–63]
British dramatist

Plays include:
Conditions of Agreement* (1948), *A Penny For A Song* (1951; revised 1962), *Saint's Day* (1953), *Marching Song

TRY THESE:
▷Robert Bolt's *A Man For All Seasons*, ▷Arthur Miller's *The Crucible* for contrast; ▷Edward Bond

(1954), *The Gates of Summer* (1956), *The Devils* (1961); and staged posthumously, *Conditions of Agreement* (1965), *No More A-Roving* (1975)

Television includes:

***A Walk In the Desert* (1960; based on *Conditions of Agreement*)**

His death from cancer at forty-five cut tragically short one of the most intriguing playwriting careers of the post-war period, as John Whiting, who began his career as a RADA-trained actor, showed a facility for both gentle comedies of character (*Penny For A Song*, last revived by the ▷ RSC in 1986) and large-scale and brutal tragedy (*The Devils*, revived there a year earlier). In between came *Saint's Day*, about an eighty-three-year-old poet, Paul Southman, at odds with the literary society that has scorned him, and *Marching Song*, a story of political disaffection filtered through the individual tale of one Rupert Foster, a war criminal invited to commit suicide by the chancellor of a newly powerless country (Britain?). In 1987, the Orange Tree, Richmond, revived *No More A-Roving*, earning renewed acclaim for an early comedy premiered posthumously. None of his plays, except for *The Devils*, was particularly well reviewed during his life, and the intriguing characters of *Penny For A Song* –in which an English coastal community awaits a Napoleonic invasion – only began to be appreciated following a 1962 revival, one year before his death.

The Devils

The Devils, commissioned by Peter Hall for the ▷ RSC at the Aldwych, established Whiting as a major dramatist capable of a Jacobean richness of language and bold, often shocking stage imagery. Based on Aldous Huxley's *The Devils of Loudun*, the play tells of the supposed 'possession' of a group of nuns in a seventeenth-century French priory. Sister Jeanne, a hunchback abbess, succumbs to an infectious hysteria, and leads the accusations against the lecherous priest, Grandier, that he is in league with the devil. The play is richly baroque in language, epic in scope, and a 1985 ▷ RSC revival at the Pit, with Estelle Kohler, faced one substantial hurdle from the start: a space much too small for the majesties of the text. A 1971 film adaptation by Ken Russell, starring Vanessa Redgrave and Oliver Reed, was expectedly over the top.

(especially *Lear* and *The War Plays*) and ▷Howard Barker for the hair-raising intensity of the images and the elevated prose; ▷Jean Anouilh, ▷Rolf Hochhüth's *Soldiers* for studies in disillusionment akin to *Marching Song*.

WILCOX, Michael [1943–]
British dramatist

Plays include:

***The Atom Bomb Project* (1975), *Grimm Tales* (1975), *Roar Like Spears* (1975), *Phantom of the Fells* (1977), *The Blacketts of Bright Street* (1977), *Pioneers* (1977), *Dekka and Dava* (1978), *Rents* (1979), *Accounts* (1981), *Lent* (1983), *78 Revolutions* (1984), *Massage* (1986)**

Wilcox, a former teacher who lives in Northumberland, is probably best known for his plays about the gay community, although he has also tackled nuclear (in both the atomic and family senses) themes in *The Atom Bomb Project*, and reassessed folk tales in *Grimm Tales* and *Dekka and Dava*, which is a Newcastle version of *Hansel and Gretel*. His initial breakthrough came with *Rents*, a study of Edinburgh rent boys in which the staccato, episodic presentation represents the fragmented nature of their lives. He followed this with *Accounts*, in which the homosexual theme is only one element in an altogether gentler account of both literal and figurative balancing the books, in an English hill farming family in the Scottish Borders, which was successfully filmed by Channel Four. *Lent* is similarly gentle on the surface, with its picture of a boy spending his Easter holiday virtually alone in his prep school, although under the surface Michael Billington detected a lament for the Peter Pan-like inability of British men to mature fully. In *78 Revolutions* Wilcox used two Americans attempting to record singers in the Russian Imperial Opera in the early days of recording as a means of investigating various kinds of cultural clash, but the enterprise turned into something more like an illustrated recital and lecture on the technicalities of

TRY THESE:
Wilcox acknowledges ▷C.P. Taylor's influence on him and there are similarities between their interests in, for example, Peter Pan and retelling old stories; ▷Stewart Parker's *Spokesong* shares *Massage*'s bicycle shop setting; ▷David Pownall's *Master Class* and ▷Tom Stoppard's *Every Good Boy Deserves Favour* also deal with the theme of music in Russia; ▷C.P. Taylor's *Good* uses music in its investigation of Nazism; Wilcox's *Phantom of the Fells* is a reworking of ▷J.M. Synge's *In the Shadow of the Glen*; for rather different versions of schooldays, see

recording. More controversial is *Massage*, in which Wilcox tackles questions of paedophilia. Wilcox also edits Methuen's *Gay Play* volumes.

▷Julian Mitchell's *Another Country* and Denise Deegan's *Daisy Pulls It Off*; see also ▷Gay Sweatshop; ▷David Rudkin for another version of *Hansel and Gretel*.

WILDE, Oscar Fingal O'Flahertie Wills [1854–1900]

Irish dramatist, poet, essayist, novelist

Plays include:

***Vera* (1882), *The Duchess of Padua* (1891), *Lady Windermere's Fan* (1892), *A Woman of No Importance* (1893), *An Ideal Husband* (1895), *The Importance of Being Earnest* (1895), *Salomé* (1896)**

Wilde's father was an ear surgeon, his mother an Irish nationalist who wrote political pamphlets and poetry. A graduate of Trinity College Dublin and later Oxford University he emerged from both as a brilliant scholar and had his first book of poetry published in 1881. With Walter Pater Wilde became a focal point for the Aesthetic movement, popularising Pater's gospel of 'the ecstasy of beauty'. ▷ Gilbert and Sullivan parodied his style in *Patience* with their portrayal of Bunthorne, a 'very, very sensitive young man', waving a lily. He produced his first play *Vera* in New York, which flopped; *The Duchess of Padua*, a verse drama, produced in New York in 1891, was no more successful but the 1892 London production of *Lady Windermere's Fan* was acclaimed and established Wilde as the darling of *fin de siècle* London. *A Woman of No Importance* and *An Ideal Husband* confirmed Wilde's position. His reputation was however precarious; celebrated for his social dramas and comedies, his novel *The Picture of Dorian Gray* was branded as 'immoral', his play *Salomé* banned by the Lord Chamberlain; the first night of his most successful play *The Importance of Being Earnest* was the evening on which the Marquess of Queensberry, father of his lover Lord Alfred Douglas, accused Wilde of being a sodomite. Arrested and tried for homosexuality, Wilde was sentenced to the maximum penalty of two years hard labour. While in prison he wrote *De Profundis* and his major poem, *The Ballad of Reading Gaol*. Released in 1897, a declared bankrupt, he moved to France where he lived until his death in Paris from meningitis.

The Importance of Being Earnest

Subtitled 'A Trivial Comedy for Serious People' Wilde's last major play has been described as 'the wittiest comedy in the English language'. Structurally, the play is a brilliant inversion and extension of theatrical conventions, with the elements of farce and melodrama thrown together to the point of absurdity. The plot of mistaken identity, long lost brothers, frustrated romance and foundlings, is couched in the sophisticated and urbane wit of contemporary London society. According to Max Beerbohm: 'the fun depends on what the characters say, rather than on what they do; they speak a kind of beautiful nonsense, the language of high comedy, twisted into fantasy'. For ▷ Shaw, however, 'three acts of studied triviality, however brilliant, are too much.'

TRY THESE:
▷Joe Orton, ▷Alan Bennett and ▷Noël Coward share with Wilde a camp wit and a sardonic awareness of the hypocrisies of conventional society manners; the elegant wit of Wilde's comedy owes a great deal to the eighteenth-century comedy of manners, (writers such as ▷Congreve, ▷Goldsmith and ▷Sheridan); see also ▷Tom Stoppard who takes *The Importance of Being Earnest* as the structure for his play *Travesties*.

WILDER, Thornton [1897–1975]

American dramatist

Plays include:

***The Trumpet Shall Sound* (1927), *The Long Christmas Dinner* (1931), *Pulman Car Hiawatha* (1931), *The Happy Journey to Trenton and Camden* (1931), *Our Town* (1938), *The Merchant of Yonkers* (1938), *The Skin of Our Teeth* (1942), *The Matchmaker* (1954; revised version of *The Merchant of Yonkers*), *A Life in the Sun* (1955), *Three Plays for Bleecker Street* (1962); adaptations include *Lucrece* (1932; from Obey's *Le Viol de Lucrece*, and ▷ Ibsen's *A Doll's House* (1937)**

TRY THESE:
▷Chekhov, ▷Lanford Wilson (especially *The Rimers of Eldritch* and his narrative use of Matt in *Tally's Folley*) and ▷Dylan Thomas' *Under Milk Wood* for ensemble pieces strongly allied to a sense of place and a similarly gentle yet tough-minded tone;

Films:

***Our Town* (1940), *Shadow of a Doubt* (1943; in collaboration with Sally Benson and Alma Reville)**

A three-time Pulitzer Prize-winner, Wilder paints an often Chekovian picture of small-town American life, finding in the minutiae of experience the electrically charged matter of drama. Often mistaken as bland and cosy, Wilder can be surprisingly subversive both in form and content, and – as with ▷ Chekhov – pain never lies far outside the borders of any of his scenes. In *The Long Christmas Dinner*, for example, a family gathering slowly reveals its darker shades until the would-be festivity has an air of melancholy more akin to James Joyce's *The Dead* than, even, comparable scenes in ▷ Neil Simon's *Brighton Beach Memoirs*. Catastrophe defines the human experience in *The Skin of Our Teeth*, a play which sees the history of mankind as a litany of encounters with chaos. Even the celebrated *Our Town* finds some sadness in its pastoral landscape. Wilder was, however, capable of a great laugh and in *The Matchmaker*, which inspired the legendary musical *Hello, Dolly!*, he wrote a classic farce about a woman who becomes engaged to the same penny-pinching man she has been trying to match up with somebody else.

▷Mark Medoff and ▷Sam Shepard for modern, often absurdist variants on Wilder's small-town reveries; A.R. Gurney's *The Dining Room* as a 1970s WASP update of *The Long Christmas Dinner*; ▷Jim Cartwright's *Road* for a lethal contemporary British version of *Our Town*; ▷Alan Ayckbourn's *The Norman Conquest* trilogy for another cataclysmic account of Christmas dinner; *The Matchmaker* and ▷Stoppard's *On the Razzle* are ultimately derived from John Oxenford's *A Day Well Spent* and ▷Johann Nestroy's *Einen Jux Will er Sich Machen*.

Our Town

Beginning in Grover's Corners, New Hampshire, on a determinedly ordinary day in 1901, Wilder's Pulitzer Prize-winning play is one of the most often produced – and, perhaps, misunderstood – American plays in America, where it is seen as the theatrical equivalent of apple pie by people who overlook its depth. Embracing fourteen years over its prologue and three acts, the play is an exalted chronicle of the everyday – Wilder's attempt, as he puts it, 'to find a value above all price for the smallest events of our daily life'. Those events may be small, but they are significant, and Wilder takes a scalpel to human psychology in a way that restores an often lacking immediacy to matters of love and loss. Innovative in form, the play is both abstract and utterly realistic, with its use of a Stage Manager to act as narrator and chorus, and the inexorable progression of its three acts, entitled 'anti-illusionary', 'love and marriage', and 'death'. The story is about two families, the Webbs and the Gibbses, but it's Everyfamily, of course, as well – this is *our* town – Wilder makes clear, and his incisive and loving play is both the quintessential comment on Americana and the perfect by-product of it. A Broadway musical – entitled *Grover's Corners*, and written by the men who wrote *The Fantasticks* – has been kicking around American regional theatre for years but has yet to open in New York.

WILLIAMS, (George) Emlyn [1905–1987]

British dramatist, stage and film actor, and director

Plays include:

***A Murder Has Been Arranged* (1930), *The Late Christopher Bean* (1933; from Sidney Howard's 1932 play of the same name, itself a version of René Fauchois' 1932 hit *Prenez Garde à la Peinture*), *Spring 1600* (1934), *Night Must Fall* (1935), *The Corn is Green* (1938), *The Light of Heart* (1940), *The Druid's Rest* (1944), *The Wind of Heaven* (1945)**

Night Must Fall, a 'psychological thriller' – about the cheerful pageboy with a head in his hatbox, and the old lady in the wheelchair whom he doesn't quite murder – was successfully revived at Greenwich in 1986. It still has a good deal of theatrical force, and is the only play by Welsh-born Williams that is likely to wear well – except perhaps his genial comedy of Welsh public house life, *The Druid's Rest*, which is full of affectionately drawn Welsh characters of the kind he was brought up with. His other plays, including the more famous *The Corn is Green*, are marred by being too 'well-made' and too sentimental (Deborah Kerr's genteel revival at the Old Vic in 1985 showed this only too clearly; though it might still work if the schoolmistress were played as a battleaxe, as it was by Sybil Thorndike). His two volumes of autobiography, *George* (1961) and *Emlyn* (1970), give

TRY THESE:

▷Terence Rattigan for well-crafted plays partly based on autobiographical material; ▷Agatha Christie for thrillers; see also ▷Thrillers.

as vivid a picture of life in North Wales, Oxford, and the London theatre of the 1920s and 1930s as one is likely to find, and could be effectively dramatised, perhaps as a one-man show of the kind that he himself did so well.

WILLIAMS, Heathcote [1941–]
British dramatist

Plays include:
***The Local Stigmatic* (1965), *AC/DC* (1970), *Hancock's Last Half-Hour* (1977), *The Immortalist* (1977), *At It* (1982; part of *Breach of the Peace*)**

Williams is one of the key figures of the counter-cultural landscape as the Founding Editor of *Suck* and the author of *AC/DC*, which was greeted as 'seminal to the seventies'. Williams' work is generally concerned with individuals at the margins of existence in a world that is hostile to the individual and to non conformism in any form. Much of *AC/DC* now seems trapped in a kind of period aspic with its two schizophrenics and three hippies, its relentless energy and its linguistic violence, though it is itself critical of the ways in which hippiedom had become another form of conventional behaviour; the attack on 'psychic capitalism', the way in which the media set a conformist and coercive mindscape, is still as relevant as ever but the contemporary theatre has moved on to more detailed analyses of the ways agendas are set. *Hancock's Last Half Hour* is likely to be revived more frequently, not only because it offers a fine part for an actor but because its meditation on the nature of the self, the relationship between performers and their audiences, the role of the media in creating and destroying individuals, and the meaning of comedy and of fame is more readily accessible. Williams' 1964 book *The Speakers*, about Speakers' Corner in Hyde Park where individuals put forward often bizarre socio-politico-religious theories to whoever will listen, was successfully dramatised by ▷ Joint Stock.

TRY THESE:
▷Snoo Wilson for works not entirely dissimilar to *AC/DC*; ▷Artaud for a highly physical idea of theatre; Bill Gaskill compared Williams to ▷Congreve on the strength of *AC/DC*; *Hancock's Last Half Hour* is one of many theatrical meditations on the role of the performer and of comedy, including Colin Bennett's *Hancock's Finest Hour*, ▷Trevor Griffiths' *Comedians* and ▷John Osborne's *The Entertainer*; *The Local Stigmatic* is reminiscent of early ▷Pinter and ▷Albee's *The Zoo Story*.

WILLIAMS, Nigel [1948–]
British dramatist, novelist and screenwriter

Plays include:
***Double Talk* (1976), *Class Enemy* (1978), *Easy Street* (1979), *Sugar and Spice* (1980), *Line 'Em* (1980), *Trial Run* (1980), *WCPC* (1982), *The Adventures of Jasper Ridley* (1982), *My Brother's Keeper* (1985), *Country Dancing* (1986)**

A versatile writer who has won awards for his fiction, has translated ▷ Genet, and works for the BBC, Williams made his initial impact as a gritty presenter of claustrophobic urban tensions in the classroom drama *Class Enemy* but has branched out into political farce (*WCPC*) and analysis of myth-making and the cooption of the past in *Country Dancing*. Society has already given up on Williams's group of streetwise teenagers in *Class Enemy* as they mark time at school but he reveals the mixture of individual needs and aspirations beneath their surface of malcontent bravado. The bleakness of this world is continued into the sexual politics of *Sugar and Spice*, the racial politics of *Trial Run*, and the confrontation between pickets and the army in *Line 'Em*. There is more comedy in *WCPC* and *The Adventures of Jasper Ridley* but it remains based on a firm sense of the absurd waste and endemic corruption of society, even if the use of cartoon techniques and caricature sometimes give rise to accusations of being patronising: in *WCPC* a straight policeman's mission to arrest cottaging gays spirals into farce, as first he discovers his sergeant in highly suspicious circumstances and is then frustrated in his attempts to bring him to 'justice' by the discovery that virtually everyone else in the force is involved in a gay conspiracy; Jasper Ridley is a picaresque hero in the Candide mould whose adventures include being sponsored by Prince Charles as Unemployed Young Person of the Year. In *My Brother's Keeper* we have family tensions at a dying old actor's bedside and in *Country Dancing* Williams examines the folk song collector Cecil Sharp as he gathers songs from an old man just before World

TRY THESE:
▷Debbie Horsfield, ▷Hanif Kureishi, Michael Mahoney, and ▷Barrie Keeffe for images of contemporary urban life ▷C.P. Taylor's *Good*, ▷David Pownall's *Master Class*, ▷Tom Stoppard's *Every Good Boy Deserves Favour* for other variations on the musical theme; ▷Eugene O'Neill's *Long Day's Journey into Night*, ▷Tunde Ikoli's *Scrape Off the Black*, ▷Catherine Hayes' *Skirmishes* for combative siblings; ▷Timberlake Wertenbaker's *The Grace of Mary Traverse* for contemporary female picaresque: ▷Peter Flannery's *Our Friends in the North* and ▷G. F. Newman's *Operation Bad Apple* for peculiar police procedures; for pickets and the army see ▷John Arden's

War I, using Sharp's antiquarian interests to make points about the function of song and the need to reclaim the past from myths which reduce its contradictions and sentimentalise its hardships.

Serjeant Musgrave's Dance; see also ▷Joe Orton's *Loot* for realism spiralling off into farce.

WILLIAMS, Tennessee (Thomas Lanier) [1911–1983]

American dramatist

Plays include:

***Battle of Angels* (1940), *The Glass Menagerie* (1944), *A Streetcar Named Desire* (1947), *Summer and Smoke* (1948), *The Rose Tattoo* (1951), *Camino Real* (1953), *Cat On A Hot Tin Roof* (1955), *27 Wagons Full Of Cotton* (1955), *Orpheus Descending* (1957), *Sweet Bird of Youth* (1959), *Period of Adjustment* (1960), *Night of the Iguana* (1961), *The Milk Train Doesn't Stop Here Anymore* (1962), *The Seven Descents Of Myrtle* (1968), *Small Craft Warnings* (1972), *Outcry* (1973), *Red Devil Battery Sign* (1975), *Vieux Carré* (1977), *A Lovely Sunday for Crève Coeur* (1979), *Clothes For A Summer Hotel* (1980), *Something Cloudy Something Clear* (1981)**

Books include:

***The Roman Spring of Mrs Stone* (novel 1950; later filmed), *Moise and the World of Reason* (novel 1975), *Memoirs* (autobiographical)**

Films include:

***Baby Doll* (1956; Williams' only original film script, although almost all of his major plays were made into films)**

The Mississippi-born son of a travelling salesman who – to quote from *The Glass Menagerie* – 'fell in love with long distance', Williams turned his own poignant life into the material for some of the most rending and luminous plays of our time. His father was cool, remote, and given to calling him 'Miss Nancy'; his mother an unstable rector's daughter; and his sister Rose the victim of a lobotomy in 1937. After a nervous collapse himself at age twenty-three, Williams, a homosexual, spent much of his life in various stages of ill health, and he frequently wrote about people (often women) on the brink of a breakdown – most memorably, Blanche du Bois, in *A Streetcar Named Desire*, but also Zelda Fitzgerald in his late play *Clothes For A Summer Hotel*. After repeated critical acclaim on Broadway for over two decades, Williams' fortunes turned sour in the late 1970s and 1980s as play after play met poor receptions only to turn up (often) to better notices in the West End. His key themes are the physical ravages of time and the emotional ravages of deceit, and his plays often pit the sexes against one another on a continuum of regret in which both ravages take their toll: Blanche and Stanley in *A Streetcar Named Desire*, the alcoholic Brick and his wife Maggie the Cat in *Cat On A Hot Tin Roof*, the fading actress Princess Kosmonopolis and her young gigolo Chance Wayne in *Sweet Bird of Youth*. Critics often complained that his later plays were pale shadows of the earlier ones, leaving Williams the ironic embodiment of his own theme – a man victimised by memories of an earlier, more productive time.

TRY THESE:
There is barely an American playwright alive who has not been touched by Tennessee Williams; ▷Lanford Wilson and ▷August Wilson for their compassionate, graceful looks at often blighted lives; ▷Sam Shepard for his dissections of the peculiar landscape of the American family; and, amongst non-Americans, South Africa's ▷Athol Fugard, for his similarly sustained use of metaphor – he uses images of flames and candles in *Road To Mecca* the way Williams does in *The Glass Menagerie*.

The Glass Menagerie

A four-character work set in St Louis, this early memory play is an almost perfect miniature, which distils Williams' gifts for transmuting autobiography into art. A talkative domineering mother, Amanda Wingfield, runs roughshod over her shy daughter, Laura, and her rebellious son, Tom. In an effort to kindle a romance for Laura, she invites to dinner one of Tom's workmates, Jim, The Gentleman Caller, only to watch her well-intentioned plans fall to pieces as cruelly as the glass figurine in the menagerie of the title. Written with a fragile delicacy, the play not only offers a haunting portrait of the playwright as a young man – the would-be poet Tom, who seeks solace in the cinema and bursts with dreams of 'the moon' – but also a quartet of superb parts that have been cornerstones of many actors' careers, from (as Amanda) the legendary Laurette Taylor at its premiere to Jessica

Tandy and Constance Cummings, and (as Tom) a wonderfully mercurial and passionate John Malkovich in Paul Newman's 1987 movie.

A Streetcar Named Desire
The play that brought Williams his first Pulitzer Prize (the second was for *Cat On A Hot Tin Roof* eight years later), *Streetcar* shows the playwright at his sweatiest and most fevered best. The neurasthenic Blanche arrives in the 'Belle Reve' quarter of New Orleans to stay with her sister Stella, only to enter into a fraught battle of attraction and repulsion with Stella's bestial husband Stanley. A woman in need of constant pampering, Blanche has her illusions shaken by Stanley, who in turn feels his domestic territory to be at risk. A lyrical plunge into emotional territory that wipes both the characters and the audience out, the play ends as a showdown between two wounded, deceptively strong-willed souls, who find that the promised Elysian Fields where Stella lives hide a landmine of sorrow and pain.

WILLIAMSON, David [1942–]
Australian dramatist

Plays include:
> ***The Coming of Stork* (1970), *The Removalists* (1971), *Don's Party* (1971), *Jugglers Three* (1972), *What If You Died Tomorrow* (1973), *The Department* (1974), *A Handful of Friends* (1976), *The Club* (1977, also known as *Players* and *The Team*), *Travelling North* (1979), *Celluloid Heroes* (1980), *The Perfectionist* (1982), *Sons of Cain* (1985), *Emerald City* (1987)**

Williamson's plays are mainly dissections of Australian society that cast a sceptical eye on what he has described as its 'conformist philistine, sexist, and aggressive' aspects. For non-Australian audiences the danger is to assume that Williamson's studies are purely naturalistic, thus fuelling anti-Australian prejudice, for Australian audiences there is the danger that the delight of recognition may obscure the social criticism; in both cases these are the classic dangers of a socially aware comic drama. Williamson has tackled many significant topics from the roots of violence in *The Removalists*, through the fading dreams of youth in *Don's Party* to role swapping in an 'open' marriage in *The Perfectionist*. The British reception of *Sons of Cain* was perhaps typical: there was virtually unanimous praise for Max Cullen as a crusading newspaper editor, coupled with the usual journalists' refusal to admit any similarity between their own newspapers and the stage presentation of journalism and, more significantly, a rather dismissive attitude to a major Australian political scandal that formed the basis of the play on the grounds that it was parochial. *Emerald City*, his most recent play to appear in Britain, is an examination of the vexed relationship between popular appeal and artistic integrity; although Williamson appears to come down on the side of integrity at the expense of popularity the popular success of his own high quality screenplays for *Gallipoli* (1981) and *The Year of Living Dangerously* (1983) suggests that another view is not untenable.

TRY THESE:
▷Doug Lucie for contemporary dissections of British manners; ▷David Storey's *The Changing Room* for a view of rugby league comparable to *The Club's* view of Australian Rules football; ▷Ron Hutchinson's *Rat in the Skull* for an analysis of police behaviour offering interesting parallels with *The Removalists*; ▷Thomas Babe's *Buried Inside Extra* for a contemporary American play about journalism, Stephen Wakelam's *Deadlines* and ▷Howard Brenton and ▷David Hare's *Pravda* for recent British thoughts on the subject; see ▷Dario Fo and ▷Franca Rame's *The Open Couple* for a different treatment of an 'open' marriage; for another Australian performer/writer see ▷Robyn Archer.

WILSON, August [1945–]
American dramatist

Plays include:
> ***Ma Rainey's Black Bottom* (1984), *Fences* (1985), *Joe Turner's Come and Gone* (1986), *The Piano Lesson* (1987)**

A black American playwright born in Pittsburgh but living in St Paul, Minnesota, Wilson has rapidly established himself in a short space of time as a key American dramatist in the tradition of ▷ Lorraine Hansberry and ▷ James Baldwin but capable, in addition, of the sustained lyricism of ▷ Tennessee Williams. Having begun his career as a poet, Wilson writes distinctively eloquent and passionate waves of speech that subordinate conventional exposition to a sheer pleasure in the richness of language.

TRY THESE:
▷Tennessee Williams and ▷Lanford Wilson for dramatic lyricism; ▷Lorraine Hansberry and ▷James Baldwin for earlier comparable treatments of black domestic life; ▷Arthur Miller for examinations of the American dream gone sour; ▷Mustapha Matura, ▷Hanif Kureishi for social acclimatisation.

Intriguingly, he is planning a cycle of plays about black American life in the twentieth century – one play for each decade – to constitute the sort of major dramatic statement which would be a natural for subsidised companies in Britain. To date, all his plays have been directed by Lloyd Richards, dean of the Yale Drama School and artistic director of the Yale Repertory Theatre in New Haven, Connecticut. The two men hit the critical and financial big time on Broadway in 1987 with *Fences*, a family drama set in the Pittsburgh inner city in 1957 in the period before the civil rights movement of the 1960s brought America's festering racial tensions to the boil. *Joe Turner's Come and Gone*, set in a Pittsburgh boarding-house, links the experiences of black Africans and their American descendants.

Ma Rainey's Black Bottom
Although *Fences* is enjoying a longer Broadway run and has been bought for the screen by Eddie Murphy, *Ma Rainey's Black Bottom*, Wilsons' first play, still seems to be his best. Set in a Chicago recording studio in 1927, the play is a piercing look at American racism and bigotry – not just white-against-black but, significantly, black-against-black – coupled with snatches of American blues music that reflect on and recapitulate the drama. Despite having her name in the title, the legendary Ma Rainey herself is a secondary figure in the play; central to it are the four musicians in her band – Slow Drag, Levee, Toledo, and Cutler – who weave a tale of beauty and pain perfectly in keeping with the power of the music which they perform.

WILSON, Lanford [1937–]
American dramatist

Plays include:

***Balm In Gilead* (1965), *The Sand Castle* (1965), *The Rimers of Eldritch* (1966), *Lemon Sky* (1970), *Serenading Louie* (1970), *The Great Nebula In Orion* (1972), *The Family Continues* (1972), *The Hot-1 Baltimore* (1973), *The Mound Builders* (1975), *Brontosaurus* (1977), *Fifth of July* (1978), *Talley's Folly* (1979), *Thymus Vulgaris* (1981), *A Tale Told* (1981), *Talley and Son* (1985), *A Betrothal* (1986), *Burn This* (1987), *A Poster of the Cosmos* (1988); the libretto for Lee Hoiby's opera *Summer and Smoke* (1971); translations include ▷ Chekhov's *Three Sisters* (1984)**

A leading American writer for over twenty years, Lanford Wilson is an inextricable part of the history of off-Broadway. Born in Lebanon, Missouri, where many of his plays are set, Wilson moved to New York's Greenwich Village in 1962 and had his earliest one-act plays produced at the now-defunct Caffe Cino off-off-Broadway. In 1965, he and director Marshall Mason collaborated on *Balm In Gilead*, an exhilarating tapestry of New York low-life set in an all-night coffee shop; their partnership not only led to the founding of Circle Repertory Theatre off-Broadway – long Wilson's authorial base – but to a sustained partnership that has seen thirty-eight productions of eighteen Wilson plays over twenty-two years. A writer with a Chekhovian sense of human fallibility and compassion, Wilson is best known for his trilogy of works spanning thirty-three years in the various generations of the Talley family in Lebanon, Missouri, and two further plays are planned to complete an ambitious historical tapesty which will be known, collectively, as *The Wars In Lebanon*. Two plays so far have been seen in London: *A Betrothal*, which had its world premiere in the summer of 1987 at The Man in The Moon Theatre, and the second play of the trilogy, *Talley's Folly*, which had its London premiere in 1982 with Jonathan Pryce and Hayley Mills. A sharp clever two-hander about Matt Friedman's courtship of young Sally Talley in 1944, it won Wilson the 1980 Pulitzer Prize, but the first one, *Fifth of July*, is the most resonant. The third, the deliberately old-fashioned *A Tale Told*, has been revised to the newly titled *Talley and Son*. Wilson has also written well on topics beyond the Talley's Midwest farm: his underrated *Angels Fall*, set on a New Mexico mission, is one of the most piercing, yet unpolemical plays to date on the subject of nuclear fall-out. His 1987 *Burn This* is an affecting, if overwritten, piece about the

TRY THESE:
▷Chekhov for comic rue tempered with wisdom; ▷Athol Fugard for particular emphasis on human charity and redemption; ▷August Wilson for another American playwright who uses story-telling to good advantage in his plays; ▷Howard Brenton's *The Genius*, ▷Nick Darke's *The Body*, ▷Robert Holman's *The Overgrown Path* for British plays on the nuclear issue; Emily Mann's *Still Life* for the effects of Vietnam on life at home, ▷Noël Greig's *Poppies* and Philip Osment's *This Island's Mine* for British counterparts where the gay issue is a part of the general action.

relationship between a grief-stricken dancer and the volatile brother of her deceased lover.

Fifth of July

A homosexual who lost his legs in Vietnam might seem an unlikely figure to put at the centre of a comedy, but Wilson accomplishes the unexpected in *Fifth of July*, set on the day after American Independence Day in 1977. Ken Talley, the paraplegic schoolteacher who may or may not sell the Talley farmhouse, dominates this often rending, humane comedy about loss, acceptance, and maturation – a *Cherry Orchard* re-written for the post-1960s generation, with a casual acceptance of gay life that is gratefully free of cliché. The play has robust supporting roles (the singer Gwen is so strongly written that she can unbalance poorly directed productions), all put to the service of its author's keen-eyed sense of grace. Life may be painful or sad, but our best hope – this play tells us – is to make our own individual peaces and move on.

WILSON, Robert [1941–]

American avant-garde performer/director

Key productions include:

> ***The King of Spain* (1969), *Deafman Glance* (1970), *KA MOUNTAIN AND GUARDenia Terrace* (1972), *The Life and Times of Joseph Stalin* (1973), *A Letter For Queen Victoria* (1974), *The $ Value of Man* (1975), *Einstein On the Beach* (1976), *I Was Sitting on My Patio This Guy Appeared I Thought I Was Hallucinating* (1978; with Lucinda Childs), *Death Destruction and Detroit* (1979), *The CIVIL warS* (1983), *Death Destruction and Detroit II* (1986), *Hamletmachine* (1986; after Heiner Müller)**

TRY THESE: ▷Shakespeare and ▷Beckett; Peter Stein and Peter Sellars for contrast; also ▷Lee Breuer and the ▷Wooster Group for shared histories; Jan Fabre for a European equivalent.

Texas-born and trained as a painter and an architect, Robert Wilson is arguably the leading director of the American avant-garde. He works both in opera houses in Italy (he directed *Salomé* at La Scala) and on the London fringe (his *Hamletmachine* was seen at the Almeida), at New York's trendy Brooklyn Academy of Music and at the Schaubühne in West Berlin. Though potentially limited in scope and appeal, his work has reached a wide audience: like some of his collaborators, notably Laurie Anderson and David Byrne, Wilson has transmuted heightened aestheticism into the stuff out of which media celebrities are made.

Interested in the language of visual signs and signals, Wilson has an ambivalent relationship with scripted texts, claiming that they are incorporated only to be destroyed; for him, texts are interesting for their ambient significance, for providing what he calls 'the weather, the atmosphere' of the occasion. His evenings can be long – *The Life and Times of Joseph Stalin*, with a cast of fourteen, ran twelve hours; *KA MOUNTAIN AND GUARDenia Terrace* for 168 hours (a full week!) – but their rigours frequently fascinate, and few who saw *Einstein On the Beach*, his million-dollar project set to continuous music by Philip Glass, failed to be hypnotised by the seductive rhythms and repetitions throughout its five hours. As he has aged, both his chosen venues and his running-times have become more conventional, perhaps reflecting financial frustrations that have, for example, kept his ambitious project *The CIVIL warS* from reaching completion, despite its being considered for the 1985 Pulitzer Prize for Drama. Whatever the reason, Wilson's non-narrative theatre of free-association has had an indelible effect on theatrical form and function on both sides of the Atlantic.

Hamletmachine

Seen at the Almeida in 1987 as the lone British stop on a European tour, this 1986 piece serves to crystallise the Wilson experience. There's only one major difference – it's atypically short. At two hours without an interval, the play is a disturbing, often corrosive expansion upon East German playwright Heiner Müller's 1977 six-page version of ▷ Shakespeare's *Hamlet*, and the production bespeaks Wilson's interest in what theatre evokes rather than what it means: the repeated sight of characters scratching their heads could serve to tease audience members searching for ready explication. References abound both to Ingmar

Bergman and to ▷ Beckett, as well as to Hamlet's problem – the curse of rationalism – in a society marked by revolution, genocide, and the human potential for bestiality. The staging, at once deliberate and provocative, highly cerebral yet immediate, captures the Wilsonian paradox: theatre full of import and meaning which is best approached in a fluid, non-academic manner.

WILSON, Snoo [Andrew] [1948–]

British dramatist and director

Plays include:

***Pericles* (1970), *Pignight* (1971), *Blow Job* (1971), *Lay By* (1971; with ▷ Howard Brenton, ▷ Brian Clark, ▷ Trevor Griffiths, ▷ David Hare, ▷ Stephen Poliakoff, Hugh Stoddart), *Boswell and Johnson on the Shores of the Eternal Sea* (1972), *England's Ireland* (1972, with ▷ Howard Brenton, Tony Bicât, ▷ Brian Clark, ▷ David Edgar, ▷ Francis Fuchs, ▷ David Hare), *The Pleasure Principle* (1973), *Vampire* (1973), *The Beast* (1974; revised version as *The Number of the Beast*, 1982), *The Everest Hotel* (1975), *Soul of the White Ant* (1976), *England-England* (1977), *The Glad Hand* (1978), *A Greenish Man* (1978), *Flaming Bodies* (1979), *Spaceache* (1980), *Our Lord of Lynchville* (1983), *Loving Reno* (1983), *The Grass Widow* (1983), *More Light* (1987)**

After writing and directing with Portable Theatre, Wilson worked as a script editor for the BBC and as a resident dramatist with the ▷ RSC but, unlike his Portable contemporaries ▷ David Hare and ▷ Howard Brenton, he has never developed a sustained relationship with one of the major institutions. This probably relates to his eclectic and anarchic approach which, at its best, can juxtapose apparently discrete material and produce a theatrically exciting and spectacular event but can also lead to turgid self absorption and a lack of disciplined writing. Wilson's interest in the occult, magic, politics, fantasy, and all the paraphernalia of the counter-culture leads to, for example, Jung, Freud, Enoch Powell and a talking ox in *Vampire*; gorillas emerging from 'a huge eyeball in the corner of the theatre' to enact a character's subconscious impulses in *The Pleasure Principle*; a fascist sailing an oil tanker to the Bermuda Triangle in the hope of entering a time warp to encounter the Antichrist in a previous manifestation during the Wyoming cowboy strike of 1886; and ectoplasm, karma, piranha fish and marijuana in *The Grass Widow*. The occultist Aleister Crowley inevitably attracted Wilson's attention in *The Beast*; three girls sing from the top of Mount Everest to save the world from Communism in *The Everest Hotel*; a magician has an incestuous relationship with his daughter in *Loving Reno*; Jerry Falwell attempts to convert the Jews in *Our Lord of Lynchville*; a car crashes through a window in *Flaming Bodies*; and a Pope dreams that Giordano Bruno asked ▷ Shakespeare to revise *Il Candelaio* in *More Light* (presumably this may not be unrelated to Wilson's own aborted verstion of *Il Candelaio* for the ▷ RSC). Some of this may work well, some of it may leave you cold and it can be a close run thing between the two depending on the production and your own personal taste.

TRY THESE:
▷Heathcote Williams' *AC/DC* is another example of early 1970s counter-cultural play making; ▷Barry Reckord's *X* is another modern treatment of incest; the extravagant imaginative quality of Wilson's work is generally reminiscent of ▷Peter Barnes, and *The Everest Hotel* of ▷N. F. Simpson's *One Way Pendulum*; Wilson has been described as a poltical absurdist – the link would be with ▷Jarry, ▷Genet and ▷Ionesco rather than ▷Beckett.

WISDOM BRIDGE THEATRE COMPANY,

American regional theatre

Started in the summer of 1974, with $2,700 dollars by a young actor named David Beaird, this small storefront Chicago theatre has gone on to become one of the premier off-LOOP (ie fringe) companies in a city that rivals New York for its abundance of theatres. Less interested in getting its productions to New York than their more high-profile Chicago cousin, the ▷ Steppenwolf company, Wisdom Bridge nonetheless has helped define the potentially explosive, kinetic style of performance now associated with the cultural capital of the Midwest. This energy was felt in Britain in 1985, when *In the Belly of the Beast* – director Robert Falls' adaptation of prisoner Jack Henry Abbott's letters

TRY THESE:
▷American Theatres for general discussion of the non-profit scene; ▷Steppenwolf and ▷Negro Ensemble Company) for other important venues; for other plays on the brutalisation of prison, see ▷Tom McGrath and Jimmy Boyle's *The*

to Norman Mailer – brought its portrait of a man unhinged to Glasgow and London.

The 196-seat theatre – with an annual budget of $1.4 million and a subscriber base of around 10,000 – mounts four productions a year, for eight weeks each: both classics (for example *A Streetcar Named Desire*, ▷ Clifford Odets' *Awake and Sing*) and new works by dramatists such as ▷ Tina Howe, John Olive and Donald Freed; and both American and British plays (Stephen Jeffreys' adaptation of Dickens' *Hard Times*, for example). Film actors have returned to the theatre to recharge their batteries – Aidan Quinn in *Hamlet*, Brian Dennehy in *Rat In the Skull*. In November 1987, Robert Falls stepped down as artistic director after a decade, to move laterally to Chicago's Goodman Theatre, and Richard E.T. White took over.

Hardman, ▷Brendan Behan's *The Quare Fellow*.

WODEHOUSE, P.G. (Pelham Greville) [1881–1975]
British humorous novelist, librettist and autobiographer

TRY THESE:
▷musicals

Libretti include:

Miss Springtime* (1916), *Have a Heart* (1917), *Oh, Boy!* (1917), *The Cabaret Girl* (1922), *Oh, Kay!* (1926), and one song (*Bill*) in *Showboat

In partnership with Guy Bolton, Wodehouse wrote the book and lyrics of many of the most successful American ▷ musicals of the 1910s and 20s; in 1917 he had five shows running on Broadway at the same time, mostly with music by Jerome Kern. They are revived from time to time (more for the music than the words). He adapted very few of his novels or stories for the stage, and none of the most Wodehousian ones (eg *Leave It To Psmith* (1930) rather than Wooster and Jeeves); subsequent attempts to do so have generally proved the soundness of his judgment. Andrew Lloyd Webber's only real failure to date has been his musical version of *Jeeves*, though there have been successful one-man shows such as *Jeeves Takes Charge* (1981 and revived again in 1987 very successfully with Edward Duke). More modern styles of adaptation may solve the problem, and we may yet see Gussie Fink-Nottle's Speech Day oration to the boys of Market Snodsbury Grammar School before the horrified gaze of Bertie Wooster. . .

WOMEN DRAMATISTS [women writers pre 1945]

TRY THESE:
▷Medieval Drama for more on Hroswitha; ▷adaptations for female novelists/poets in stage adaptations; ▷Agatha Christie, ▷Lillian Hellman, ▷Susan Glaspell, ▷Dodie Smith, ▷Enid Bagnold as better known dramatists of previous generations; see also ▷Women in Theatre.

Although there have been women dramatists working regularly and successfully in the professional theatre since the late seventeenth century their work has tended to be marginalised, neglected and disparaged to a far greater extent than that of their male contemporaries, both by their contemporaries and by posterity. ▷ Aphra Behn, the Restoration dramatist, is the classic example of a woman whose personal and artistic reputation was subject to male attack in her own day and has been attacked almost continually since from a variety of mutually contradictory moral and artistic positions whereas her male contemporaries have suffered far less. But Behn is at least visible, partly because Virginia Woolf's championing of her made her an obvious starting point for a theatrical reclamation of plays by women, while other women authors languish in, at best, footnotes and scholarly limbo. The actress Fidelis Morgan has played an important part in reclaiming women dramatists with her book *The Female Wits* (Virago, 1981), which made texts of plays by Behn, Catherine Trotter (1679–1749), Delarivière Manley (c 1667–1724), Mary Pix (c 1666–1709) and Susannah Centlivre (c 1669–1723) readily available to the general public. One practical result of the interest generated by the book was Annie Castledine's respectfully received 1987 Derby Playhouse production of Pix's *The Innocent Mistress* in an adaptation by Elizabeth Rothschild. No one has yet tried anything by the late seventeenth-century Duchess of Newcastle and most late eighteenth and nineteenth-century women writers still languish unperformed, although so too, it must be added in all fairness, do most male writers of those periods. Hannah Cowley (1743–1809), a contemporary of ▷ Sheridan and ▷ Goldsmith, wrote comedies which were regarded as among the best of their day. Elizabeth Inchbald (1753–

1821) was another highly competent dramatist whose comedies could be worth revival. The campaign for women's voting rights at the beginning of the twentieth century led to a considerable number of essentially agit-prop plays, often performed at suffrage meetings, some of which have been revived very effectively in recent years, particularly by Sidewalk Theatre Company and by Mrs Worthington's Daughers (a company with a commitment to staging plays by women from the past). Among the short plays, Inez Bensusan's *The Apple* is a fine exposé of double standards and Evelyn Glover's *A Chat with Mrs Chicky* neatly reverses assumptions that the middle-class woman knows best. Among the longer plays *Votes for Women* (1907) by the actress/novelist Elizabeth Robins, best known as an early champion of ▷ Ibsen, stands comparison with ▷ Granville Barker in its handling of sexual politics and has a fine scene set on the edges of a Trafalgar Square Suffrage meeting where public and personal issues are entwined in a way reminiscent of the second act of ▷ Sean O'Casey's *The Plough and the Stars. How the Vote Was Won*, by Cicely Hamilton and Christopher St John is a farce which extends the argument that women did not need the vote because men looked after them to its logical extreme; as more and more female relatives descend on the male householders of Britain to be 'looked after' so the men become more and more convinced of the need for female suffrage. Hamilton and St John (whose real name was Christabel Marshall) were also involved with Edith Craig (daughter of Ellen Terry) in the 1914 staging of Hroswitha's *Paphnutius* in St John's translation. The significance of Craig's pioneering work in the theatre has been greatly undervalued; as ▷ G. B. Shaw said, 'Gordon Craig [her brother Edward] has made himself the most famous producer in Europe by dint of never producing anything, while Edith Craig remains the most obscure by dint of producing everything'. Githa Sowerby's *Rutherford and Son*, produced by Craig in 1912 was revived successfully by Mrs. Worthington's Daughters in 1980, but there has so far been no interest in reviving the 1933 *Richard of Bordeaux* by Gordon Daviot (better known under another pseudonym, Josephine Tey) or anything by the mid-century dramatist Clemence Dane (pseudonym of Winifred Ashton).

WOMEN IN THEATRE

Why a 'ghetto' entry for women in theatre? The answer is not hard to guess. Women and the way they work in the theatre tend to be invisible; that is to say, although women make up over 50 per cent of audiences, and certainly a good deal more in terms of working personnel, women as writers or as directors in positions of power in large companies tend to get ignored. This is not just another feminist bellyache, but a fact borne out in studies carried out in the past few years by two organisations: the Conference of Women Theatre Directors and Administrators, and the Women's Playhouse Trust.

Of course, women as writers have made their mark; ▷ Aphra Behn, ▷ Caryl Churchill, ▷ Sarah Daniels, ▷ Ann Devlin, ▷ Maureen Duffy, ▷ Tasha Fairbanks, ▷ Berta Freistadt, ▷ Pam Gems, ▷ Bryony Lavery, ▷ Deborah Levy, ▷ Sharman Macdonald, ▷ Louise Page, ▷ Ayshe Raif and ▷ Timberlake Wertenbaker, amongst others, are there to prove it. However, they are only the tip of the much larger iceberg which has to do with the way women have often chosen to work, how plays have emerged through feminism and working collectively, and, at another level, power structures in society at large and theatre in particular.

Some of the entries in this book reflect that collective collaboration (a method, of course, not exclusive to women only), but there are many more women's groups whose work has entertained, puzzled, infuriated, thrilled, and drawn energetic comment. Women continue to bring their political commitment to their creativity with varying degrees of success (right-on ideologies do not always good theatre make!) but where the two

TRY THESE:
▷Lesbian Theatre; ▷Cabaret; ▷Performance Art; ▷Theatre of Black Women; ▷Gay Sweatshop; ▷Women Dramatists; the two studies mentioned in this entry are *The Status of Women in the British Theatre, 1982–1983* commissioned by Sue Parrish (published by the Conference of Women Theatre Directors and Administrators in 1984), and *What Share of the Cake?* by Caroline Gardiner (published by the Women's Playhouse Trust in 1987).

merge – as in the Nancy Sweet and Catherine Carnie adaptation of Dumas' *Camille* – then sparks fly. Burnt Bridges' City exposé *Deals*, too, was a lesson in group continuity finally paying off, though their production was inevitably much overshadowed by ▷ Caryl Churchill's higher-profiled and admittedly brilliant verse treatment in *Serious Money*. There have also been groups set up for a specific purpose such as Spare Tyre, initially triggered by Susie Orbach's book *Fat Is A Feminist Issue*, who have brought a light-hearted revue type approach to the very serious subjects of compulsive eating, women's images and their social construction. Sensible Footwear, equally, have made a name for themselves as a sharp feminist performance group, and Scarlet Harlets, as a performance-oriented feminist group with a highly physical style and organic approach to their material (they have used acrobatics, clowning, puppets and even fire-eating) in shows which have particularly concentrated on the nature of violence to women, in relation to psychiatric treatment (*We Who Were The Beautiful*) and rape (*Broken Circle*), self-affirmation (*Out of Bounds*) and female sexuality and fantasies, *Appetite of the Mind*.

Other visually oriented groups with a fine track record include Siren, the lesbian feminist group whose radical feminism has been matched with a similarly daring visual style, humour and imagination, particularly in *From the Divine* (a post-Falklands attack on jingoism and the macho war mentality) and PULP (a high camp lesbian thriller which dived into the murky waters of the thriller genre to explore identity, betrayal, fantasy, glamour and sleeze).

ReSisters, another feminist group, which started off specifically looking at self-defence, has tackled such issues as women's refuges (*The Refuge Show*), women in the miners strike (the remarkable *About Face* compiled from original research in the Nottinghamshire and Derbyshire coalfields by Cordelia Ditton, in which she also played all thirty parts – including a jazz band and a police horse), and their latest, *Women-in-Law*, with a sparkling script by newcomer April de Angelis, again works off the thriller genre to take another look at women and violence.

Feminist polemics has not necessarily meant tedium (though sometimes it has) and groups such as the wacky and wonderful (and alas no more) Cunning Stunts showed a much appreciated anarchic strain; so too did Beril and the Perils. The lesbian duos of Parker & Klein and, recently, Donna & Kebab have touched a common vein of rebellion and hilarity. At the upmarket end, Fascinating Aida are a cabaret trio of immense mainstream popularity, whose musicianship is beyond question and whose humour needs only more radical bite to make them superb. The Raving Beauties, too, have also cornered a market with their combination of poetry, music and prose.

Mentioning such visually oriented groups as Tessa Schneideman's always challenging Loose Change company, or the sadly now defunct groupings of Hesitate and Demonstrate, Natasha Morgan's That's Not It, Jude Alderson's irregular Sadista Sisters, or the dazzling American group Split Britches can still only give a glimmer of the activity that has poured out on the fringe over the past ten years or so. All this is a far cry from the early Women's Company and the landmark Women's Theatre Festival set up in the spring of 1973, out of which grew so many initiatives and the writers, directors and performers who have gone on to form the backbone of so much women's creativity, including ▷ Monstrous Regiment and the ▷ Women's Theatre Group. That festival also included the highly influential *Voices* by Susan Griffin – a stream-of-consciousness monologue of five different women's lives directed by Kate Crutchley, who as director at the Oval House has been a steadfast supporter of women's work – and *The Three Marias*, a dramatised reading of the true story of three Portuguese feminists imprisoned for their anti-Catholic views.

To what extent has all this activity affected the theatrical landscape in Britain? It has to be admitted – little. To go back to the beginning, women as creators are still in the minority. There are some women directors of regional theatres: Clare Venables in Sheffield, Annie Castledine and Sue Todd in Derby, Sue Dunderdale at Greenwich – and where there are women, there is a likelihood of women as writers being further encouraged (although the Royal Court under Max Stafford-Clark has certainly done its bit in encouraging young women writers, if not necessarily doing much to sustain them). But it was out of a sense of frustration with the larger companies such as the ▷ RSC and ▷ National Theatre resolutely withholding opportunities and power that a number of women got together in the early 1980s to form the Women's Playhouse Trust in the hope of securing a building that would place women and their work in the mainstream. Sadly, this has not happened, though the WPT set the ▷ Aphra Behn revival going with *The Lucky Chance*, commissioned a Christmas reworking of *Beauty and the Beast* from ▷ Louise Page, and presented the British premier of ▷ Ntozake Shange's *Spell No 7*. Despite formidable fundraising attempts, and a series of important workshops, WPT remain brick and mortarless at time of writing in April 1988. Discussions of how and why plays by women do or do not emerge must, we fear, await another time and place.

WOMEN'S THEATRE GROUP,

British Theatre company

Key productions include:

Hot Spot (by Eileen Fairweather and ▷ Melissa Murray; 1978), _The Wild Bunch_ (by ▷ Bryony Lavery; 1979), _Breaking Through_ (by ▷ Timberlake Wertenbaker, 1980), _The Soap Opera_ (by ▷ Donna Franceschild; 1979), _Better a Live Pompey Than a Dead Cyril_ (devised by ▷ Clare McIntyre and Stephanie Nunn, 1980), _New Anatomies_ (by ▷ Timberlake Wertenbaker; 1981) _Trade Secrets_ (by ▷ Jacqui Shapiro; 1984) _Pax_ (by ▷ Deborah Levy; 1984), _Witchcraze_ (by ▷ Bryony Lavery; 1985), _Our Lady_ (by ▷ Deborah Levy; 1986) _Lear's Daughters_ (written by the company with Elaine Feinstein; 1987), _Picture Palace_ (by ▷ Winsome Pinnock; 1988)

The oldest women's theatre group in the country, it emerged from a larger gathering called the Women's Company in 1974 as a feminist styled group whose major aim was to look at the female situation in a political and social context, and to reach new audiences. Their first shows were devised and this has remained a cornerstone of their work, as has working collectively and commissioning new work.

Women's Theatre Group have had their ups and downs but some of their most successful productions have also been positively breath-catching, intellectually stretching and risky in the best sense. Early plays directed at teenagers about contraception (*My Mother Says*; 1974) and finding a job after leaving school (*Work to Role*; 1975) used a kind of agit-prop technique to put over factual information and make feminist points about solidarity between women and the importance of communication. These are fairly constant themes best exemplified in *Dear Girl* (devised by Tierl Thompson and Libby Mason in 1983), a lengthy but quite remarkably moving piece about women's friendship, constructed from the letters and diaries of four women at the turn of the century. Women and writing is also the subject of another of their early pieces, *Better a Live Pompey Than a Dead Cyril* about poet Stevie Smith.

Comradeship recurs in *The Soap Opera* by Donna Franceschild, a naturalistic consciousness raising piece in which women shared their experiences when locked in a launderette; and in a simpler way with *Double Vision*, a delightful and honest account of the sexual relationship and personal/political differences of two young women.

Women's Theatre Group have also tackled women in historical terms from several different angles: *New Anatomies*, by ▷ Timberlake Wertenbaker, used the story of nineteenth-century explorer Isabelle Eberhardt who dressed as a man and Vesta Tilley, to make points about women breaking free from

TRY THESE:

▷Bryony Lavery's *Origins of the Species* also focuses on the transmission of history/information through a female line; see also ▷Wendy Kesselman's *I Love You, I Love You Not*, and ▷Christina Reid's *Tea in a China Cup* which highlight that process in terms of attitudes; for women exploring their lives in a confined space, see ▷Nell Dunn's *Steaming* and for contrast; ▷Maureen Duffy's *Rites*, and for an updated version, Penny O'Connor's *Dig Volley Spike* which uses women together to examine the thorny question of the difference between assertiveness and aggressiveness; for groups who have also worked collectively see ▷Monstrous Regiment; ▷Women in Theatre, ▷Joint Stock, ▷Black Theatre Co-op, ▷Theatre of Black Women.

convention; *Love and Dissent*, about the Russian Alexandra Kollontai, had problems in mixing past with present in its study of her relationship to her daughter and to her political work; *Time Pieces* reclaimed some personal history, using the technique of a photo album, told by an aunt to her younger niece – a relationship of older to younger woman passing on information that runs deeply through much of the group's work. *Anywhere to Anywhere*, about women pilots in World War II was another naturalistic account of women's hidden history, but perhaps one of the most remarkable history-sifting pieces remains the densely evocative, *Pax* by ▷ Deborah Levy, in which the surrealist and intellectual heights of the script were equally matched by Sue Todd and Anna Furse's production, shimmering with ancient female archetypes. In 1987, the group also came up with *Lear's Daughters*, a marvellously bracing and imaginative production, told with child-like simplicity, which said a good deal about an enormous number of issues to do with women as wives and mothers, carers, social conditions, and patriarchy.

WOOD, Charles [1932–]

British dramatist

Plays include:

***Cockade* (1963), *Don't Make Me Laugh* (1965), *Meals On Wheels* (1965), *Fill the Stage with Happy Hours* (1966), *Dingo* (1967), *H: or Monologues at Front of Burning Cities* (1969), *Welfare* (1970), *Veterans* (1972), *Jingo* (1975), *Has 'Washington' Legs?* (1978), *Red Star* (1984), *Across From the Garden of Allah* (1986)**

Films include:

Richard Lester's *The Knack* (1965), *Help!* (1965), *How I Won the War* (1967), *The Charge of the Light Brigade* (1968), and Tony Palmer's epic *Wagner* (1984), *Tumbledown* (1987).

Blackly comic views of the military and of filmmaking dominate the plays of Charles Wood, who began his career as a stage manager and designer, largely for ▷ Joan Littlewood. Wood spent five years in the army in the 1950s, and the experience doubtless facilitated the writing of plays like *Dingo*, a satirical piece set in a German prisoner-of-war camp and focusing on two World War II heroes, and *Jingo*, set amongst the British army in Singapore in 1941. Survivors of film sets are heroes of a sort, too, and Wood has often written about the art form where he made most of his money. Many of his screenplays have turned out to be classics: *Veterans*, which starred two great theatrical Sirs, John Gielgud and John Mills, focuses on two seasoned actors on the Turkey location shoot of a film; and *Has 'Washington' Legs?* is a satire about a film being made of the American Revolution. His most recent plays have been poorly received – the Russian-set *Red Star*, seen at the ▷ RSC, and the West End comedy, *Across From the Garden of Allah*, a piece of anti-Hollywood bile that merely recycles better, similar treatments from novelists like Evelyn Waugh and Nathaniel West. The 1988 BBC screening of *Tumbledown* excited a political controversy over the treatment of a young officer badly wounded in the Falklands.

TRY THESE:
▷Beckett, for the speech rhythms of plays like *Dingo;* ▷Clifford Odets, ▷Kaufman and ▷Hart, ▷David Rabe's *Hurlyburly*, and ▷Nick Darke's *The Oven Glove Murders* for comic and/or bilious treatments of Hollywood and the film industry; ▷Anthony Minghella's *Made in Bangkok* for examinations of the Englishman abroad; ▷Willis Hall's *The Long and the Short and the Tall* and ▷Peter Nichols' *Privates on Parade* for contrasting accounts of the British army in World War II; ▷Louise Page's *Falkland Sound/Voces de Malvinas* for another view of the Falklands War.

WOOSTER GROUP, THE

leading American avant-garde troupe

Key productions include:

***Sakonnet Point* (1975), *Rumstick Road* (1977), *Nayatt School* (1978), *Point Judith (An Epilog)* (1979), *Route 1 & 9* (1981), *L.S.D. (. . .Just the High Points)* (1984), *The Road To Immortality, Parts 1 & 2, The Temptation of St. Anthony* (1987)**

A non-profit theatrical collective founded in 1975. The Wooster Group is an ongoing ensemble devoted to a living repertory. It began as an outgrowth of Richard Schechner's Performance Group, an avant-garde company itself started in New York in

TRY THESE:
▷Spalding Gray, ▷Lee Breuer, ▷Robert Wilson for individuals who have helped shape and define the American avant-garde, ▷Arthur Miller for contrast; Impact Theatre, Lumiere and Son for British analogues; ▷Ionesco, ▷Alfred Jarry for playwrights

1970 which was devoted to blurring the boundaries between life and art, the observer and the observed, form and content, space and time. Heavily steeped in the ideology of environmental theatre and, particularly, Grotowski, the Performance Group eventually splintered, leaving former members ▷ Spalding Gray and Elizabeth LeCompte to launch the Wooster Group at the 150-seat Performing Garage in SoHo along with four other erstwhile collaborators (but not Schechner). Gray is now an acclaimed solo artist known internationally, but the Wooster Group gave him his start, premiering his monologues *Sex and Death to the Age of 14* and *Booze, Cars, and College Girls*, among others.

Studies in the rudiments of consciousness and of meaning, Wooster Group productions throw the burden of narrative sense on the observer, and many on-lookers resent and resist the prismatic nature of pieces where sounds and images are as important as the text. Source works are essential to the company, but they are frequently subverted or abstracted in a way not always to the originator's liking – ▷ Arthur Miller, for example, made his displeasure known with the Wooster Group's usage of *The Crucible* when he attempted to halt their 1984 production of *L.S.D. (. . .Just the High Points).*

The Road To Immortality, Part Two
This is a trilogy made up of *Route 1 & 9*, *L.S.D. (. . .Just the High Points)*, and *The Temptation of St. Anthony.* The second part is the section best-known in Britain, because of its 1986 engagements in Edinburgh, Cardiff, and the Riverside Studios, London. Timothy Leary, Allen Ginsberg, Jack Kerouac, and G. Gordon Liddy are among the names and characters invoked during this impressionistic, fragmentary account of 1960s drug culture. Arthur Miller's legal threats against their co-option of passages from *The Crucible* meant various passages had to be changed or deleted. The cast sit at a table as at a high-tech Last Supper, giving us a decade Dada-ist style in a splintered, collage-like fashion which is moving to some, muddled to others.

offering comparable theatrical dislocation.

WRIGHT, Nicholas [1940–]
South Africa-born British dramatist

Plays include:

***Changing Lines* (1968), *Treetops* (1978), *The Gorky Brigade* (1979), *One Fine Day* (1980), *The Crimes of Vautrin* (1983), *The Custom of the Country* (1983), *The Desert Air* (1984), *Mrs Klein* (1988); he also adapted ▷ Pirandello's *Six Characters In Search of An Author* (1987)**

Presently in charge of new writing at the ▷ National Theatre, the South Africa-born Wright began his career as an actor and director before turning to playwriting in 1968 with *Changing Lines* at the Royal Court, where he worked as a casting director and – in 1976–7 – as joint artistic director. In his six original plays since then, he has shown an impressive command of history and period, without finding that one fusion of form and content that might make his writing ignite. *Treetops*, set in Cape Town, draws upon his childhood as the youngest of three boys to emigrate from South Africa; and the African continent figures as well in *One Fine Day* (set on an East African coffee plantation), *The Custom of the Country* (racial acculturation in Johannesburg in the 1890s), and *The Desert Air* (a wartime satire set mostly in Cairo in 1942). *The Gorky Brigade* shifts the scene to Russia following the 1917 Revolution, and *The Crimes of Vautrin* –adapted from Balzac's *Splendeurs et Misères des Courtesans* – uses Paris in the 1830s to strike an anti-Thatcherite critique of a society worshipful of money and power. Wright's strengths are his intellectual curiosity and range; his weaknesses, a tendency towards overlength and caricature (for example, the opportunistic Colonel Gore in *Desert Air*).

TRY THESE:
Many plays by expatriated South Africans, including Michael Picardie's *The Cape Orchard*, Yana Stajno's *Salt River*, ▷Ronald Harwood's *Tramway Road*; ▷David Hare (especially *Plenty*) for the vagaries of British colonialism; Olwen Wymark's *Nana* as an adapted nineteenth-century French novel used to lash out at Britain today; also ▷Nick Darke's *Ting Tang Mine*, ▷David Edgar's *Entertaining Strangers* for use of nineteenth-century contexts to comment on Thatcherite Britain.

WYCHERLEY, William [1640–1716]
English Restoration dramatist
Plays include:
***Love in a Wood* (1671), *The Gentleman Dancing Master* (1672), *The Country Wife* (1675), *The Plain Dealer* (1676)**

Wycherley trained in the law but never practised, inherited one of Charles II's mistresses, married the Countess of Drogheda for her money and ended up in prison for her debts before settling down to burnish his literary reputation, which, however, rests on his plays and not on the verse to which he devoted the last thirty years of his life. The plays, robust, sexually explicit and satirical, are fine examples of what the term 'Restoration Comedy' has come to mean with their emphasis on the interrelationship of money, sex and power. But the really interesting point about Wycherley is that there is no obvious fixed authorial position for the audience to adopt. Wycherley used to be condemned, as many satirists are, for recommending the behaviour he presents in his plays; then he was praised for his celebratory presentation of a society in which the streetwise achieved their ends at the expense of those who failed to match their pretensions; now he seems to be a writer aware of the glitter and attractions of the life he presents but also aware of the void beneath. This comes over very clearly in *The Country Wife*, where the central character Horner is both hero and victim of the strategy which allows him unlimited sexual access to allegedly modest women but also condemns him to exhaustion as a provider of production line orgasms, particularly in the scene where a number of women exhaust Horner's supply of what is euphemistically called china.

TRY THESE:
▷Molière's *Le Misanthrope* is a distant source for *The Plain Dealer*; there are similarities between Wycherley's work and the comedies of ▷Jonson as well as other Restoration comic writers such as ▷Aphra Behn, ▷William Congreve and ▷George Etherege; other writers of comedy of manners, such as ▷Goldsmith, ▷Sheridan, ▷Oscar Wilde, ▷Noël Coward, ▷Doug Lucie; Wycherley's analysis of sex, class and power is reminiscent of ▷Joe Orton, and to a lesser extent, later ▷Alan Ayckbourn; ▷Edward Bond's *Restoration* uses conventions and themes derived from the practice of Restoration writers to make modern points.

YANKOWITZ, Susan [1941–]
American dramatist

Plays include:
***Terminal* (1969), *Transplant* (1971), *Sideshow* (1971), *Slaughterhouse Play* (1971), *Boxes* (1972), *Acts of Love* (1973), *Wooden Nickels* (1973), *American Piece* (1974), *Still Life* (1977), *True Romances* (1978), *Qui Est Anna Marx* (1978), *Baby* (1983), *A Knife in the Heart* (1983), *Taking Liberties* (1986), *Alarms* (1987), *Monk's Revenge* (1988)**

New Jersey born Yankowitz was an original member of Joe Chaikin's Open Theatre, one of the most influential groups in America's breakaway avant-garde theatre movment of the 1960s and 1970s, where company-created, physically intensive, performer-centred styles of theatre held sway. Yankowitz collaborated on several texts with Chaikin (also with the Omaha Magic Theatre), though *Terminal*, an extraordinary and clinical exploration on the subject of death and morality – which according to John Lahr had the therapeutic effect of 'sending audiences away thirsting for life' – is perhaps one of her best known. Equally, the notorious, *Slaughterhouse Play*, written for Joe Papps' Public Theatre, has been seen as one of the more grotesque theatrical visions of society, with its central visual metaphor of butchered slabs of meat and slaughterhouse atmosphere where white men go to sell black genitals as prize meat. Thus far, however, British audiences have had a slightly more tame, though no less controversial, introduction to Yankowitz's work with *Alarms*, written and prompted by the appalling implications of the Chernobyl disaster of 1987. Presented by ▷ Monstrous Regiment, this part-surreal thriller (with more than a touch of Karen Silkwood paranoias), part-passionate anti-nuclear polemic, caught the agony of trying to raise alarms that fall on stony ears (the central figure is an obstetrician, a contemporary Cassandra, who falls foul of her lover and authority in her quest), but the play itself somehow seemed still-born. Despite this unpropitious start to Yankowitz's connections with British theatre, her stage and television track record (her American television credits include a teleplay on Charlotte Perkins Gilman, author of *The Yellow Wallpaper*, and a documentary on Sylvia Plath) as well as a screenplay of her novel *Silent Witness* would suggest that there is much to be reaped from further acquaintance with her work.

TRY THESE:
See Vladimir Gubaryev's extraordinary post-Chernobyl play, *Sarcophagus*; Cordelia Ditton and Maggie Ford's *The Day the Sheep Turned Pink* for another post-Chernobyl, documentary-style look at nuclear power, though it was initiated *prior to* Chernobyl; ▷Deborah Levy's *Clam* is another anti-nuclear/sexual politics play; ▷Stephen Lowe's *Keeping Body and Soul Together*, for other feminist images of grotesquerie, see black American Adrienne Kennedy's *A Rat's Mass*, *A Lesson in Dead Language* and *Funnyhouse of a Negro*; ▷Caryl Churchill's *Owners* and American feminist playwright Myrna Lamb's *The Butcher's Shop* for other slaughterhouse images; ▷Megan Terry also has close connections with Omaha Magic Theatre.

YEATS, W[illiam] B[utler] [1865–1939]
Irish poet, dramatist, theatre manager and politician

Plays include:
The Countess Kathleen* (1892), *The Land of Heart's Desire* (1894), *The Shadowy Waters* (1900), *Diarmuid and Grania* (1901; with George Moore), *Cathleen ni Houlihan* (1902), *The Pot of Broth* (1902), *Where There is Nothing* (1902; revised version with ▷ Lady Gregory as *The Unicorn from the Stars*, 1907), *The Hour Glass* (1903), *The King's Threshold* (1903), *On Bailie's Strand* (1904), *Deidre* (1906), *The Golden Helmet* (1908; revised version as *The Green Helmet*, 1910), *At the Hawk's Well* (1916), *The Dreaming of the Bones* (1919), *The Only

TRY THESE:
▷J. M. Synge and ▷Sean O'Casey were originally staged at the Abbey under Yeats' aegis; ▷T. S. Eliot wrote the other most successful twentieth-century verse drama – *Sweeney Agonistes* is particularly interesting to compare with Yeats; ▷Melissa

***Jealousy of Emer* (1919), *The Player Queen* (1919), *Calvary* (1921), *King Oedipus* (1926), *Oedipus at Colonus* (1927), *The Resurrection* (1934), *Fighting the Waves* (1929), *The Words Upon the Window Pane* (1934), *The Herne's Egg* (1938), *A Full Moon in March* (1938), *The King of the Great Clock Tower* (1938), *Purgatory* (1938), *The Death of Cuchulain* (1939)**

As well as being one of the great poets of the twentieth century, Yeats played a major part in establishing the modern Irish professional theatre through his managerial work at the Abbey and wrote throughout his life a series of mainly short plays, usually in verse, which are stylisticaly innovative, blending symbolist, oriental and Irish elements to create an art which, in his own words, does its work 'by suggestion, not by direct statement, a complexity of rhythm, colour, gesture, not space-pervading like the intellect but a memory and a prophecy'. Irish legend provides the material for most of the plays from the early personifications of Ireland in the figure of Cathleen ni Houlihan to his final play, *The Death of Cuchulain*, which is the culmination of a lifelong interest in the Red Branch cycle of folk tales. His concern for the supernatural also finds an outlet in the seance of *The Words Upon the Window Pane*, his play about Jonathan Swift. In many ways Yeats' interest in non-naturalistic use of sound, music, masks and colours anticipates much of the ▷ performance art of the present but outside Ireland he is seldom produced professionally. The Cuchulain plays have been performed as a cycle and they offer a tempting proposition to an adventurous director in view of the success of ▷ Peter Brook's *The Mahabharata.*

Murray's *The Crooked Scythe* is a verse drama about the Black Death. American Maxwell Anderson's verse dramas were popular in the 1930s and 40s, especially *Mary Stuart*.

YOUNG, Phil [1949–]
British director and dramatist

Plays include:

***Crystal Clear* (1983), *Kissing God* (1985), *Torpedoes in the Jacuzzi* (1987)**

After winning the ▷ RSC Buzz Goodbody Award for Best Director at the National Student Drama Festival in 1976, Young went on to a career as a director in a variety of theatres including Leeds Playhouse, Leicester Haymarket and Croydon Warehouse. In 1983 he devised *Crystal Clear* through improvisation and workshops with a small group of actors. This play won an *Evening Standard* most promising playwright award. Since then he has worked on other projects in a similar style.

Crystal Clear
The play uses a naturalistic form to convey an intense and, at times, distressingly intimate sense of pressure, as Richard, an art dealer with diabetes, falls victim to the abrupt onset of blindness. Ironically, he is having a love-affair with Thomasina, who is blind. Their gentle and genuinely touching relationship is highlighted by visits from Richard's ex-lover Jane, who, after trying unsuccessfuly to maintain her previous place in his life, attempts to help him after his blindness. He drives her away, only to discover that Thomasina now rejects him, despite her feelings for him. In this way the defensive layers of politeness and passive acceptance which conceal the awful realities of life for the blind are stripped away to reveal the agony and desperation which lie beneath.

TRY THESE:
Mark Medoff's *Children of a Lesser God* is a similarly honest account of deafness and its effects on personal relationships; ▷Brian Clark's *Whose Life Is It Anyway* raises painful questions, comically, on terminal illness, responsibility and dignity; ▷Jean-Claude Van Itallie's *The Traveller* deals with aphasia (inability to make sense of words) with equal passion as well as beauty; see also ▷Graeae for other images of disability.

ACKNOWLEDGMENTS

The authors would like to thank the many people without whose help and co-operation this book could not have been compiled. Especial thanks are due to: Mrs Foster at the British Theatre Association's reference library for her invaluable help in research; to Ian Herbert's *London Theatre Record* and his personal generosity in answering numerous queries; to all the agents (and some of the playwrights themselves) who supplied information, sometimes at very short notice; to innumerable press officers in various theatres and theatre companies, from the National, to the Bush and especially Mavis at the Drill Hall; to *City Limits* for innumerable facilities; to the following for enlightening conversations — Yvonne Brewster, Luke Dixon, Jonathan Lamede, Alan Pope, Sue Sanders, Lyn Gardner, Ros Asquith. Many thanks also go to Naseem Khan for supplying the entry on Asian Theatre, and to Stephanie King, Wendy Wheeler, Kerry Shale and Ursula Philips.

FURTHER READING

There are a vast number of books on theatre ranging from do-it-yourself manuals to theoretical works and studies of individual authors and directors. This list is made up of some of the books we found useful in writing this guide, both reference works and studies of specific topics which offer in depth coverage of individual issues.

Antonin Artaud, *The Theatre and its Double,* Calder, 1970
Eric Bentley (ed), *Theory of the Modern Stage,* Penguin, 1968
C. W. E. Bigsby (ed), *Contemporary English Drama,* Arnold, 1981
Gerald Bordman, *The Oxford Companion to American Theatre,* Oxford University Press, 1984
Edward Braun, *The Director and the Stage from Naturalism to Grotowski,* Methuen, 1982
Peter Brook, *The Empty Space,* Penguin, 1983
Peter Brook, *The Shifting Point,* Methuen, 1988
Simon Callow, *Being an Actor,* Methuen 1984, Penguin, 1985
Sandy Craig (ed), *Dreams and Deconstructions; Alternative Theatre in Britain,* Amber Lane, 1980
John Gassner and Edward Quin, *Reader's Encyclopedia of World Drama,* Methuen, 1970
Phyllis Hartnoll (ed), *The Oxford Companion to the Theatre,* Oxford University Press, originally 1951, 4th ed 1983
Catherine Itzin, *Stages in the Revolution,* Methuen, 1980
Catherine Itzin, *Directory of Playwrights, Directors, Designers 1,* John Offord, 1983
Helene Keyssar, *Feminist Theatre,* Macmillan, 1984
Helen and Richard Leacroft, *Theatre and Playhouse,* Methuen, 1984
David Ian Rabey, *British and Irish Political Drama in the Twentieth Century,* Macmillan, 1986
Constantin Stanislavski, *Creating a Role,* Bles, 1963
J. L. Styan, *Drama, Stage and Audience,* Cambridge University Press, 1975
J. L. Styan, *Modern Drama in Theory and Practice,* 3 vols, Cambridge University Press, 1981
William Tydeman, *The Theatre in the Middle Ages,* Cambridge University Press, 1978
James Vinson (ed), *Contemporary Dramatists,* Macmillan, 1982
Michelene Wandor, *Carry on Understudies,* RKP, 1986
Michelene Wandor, *Look Back in Gender,* Methuen, 1987
John Willett (ed), *Brecht on Theatre,* Methuen, 1969

CONTRIBUTORS

Trevor R. **GRIFFITHS** is currently Chair of the Department of Language and Literature at the Polytechnic of North London where he teaches drama on the MA in Modern Drama Studies and to undergraduates; he has reviewed theatre for *City Limits, The Scotsman* and the *Glasgow Herald*; while lecturing at Strathclyde University he played a prominent part in the award winning Strathclyde Theatre Group; he is currently Chair of the touring theatre company Foco Novo; his previous books are *Stagecraft* and the *Longman Guide to Shakespeare Quotations* (with Trevor A. Joscelyne).

Aeschylus
Albee
Ardrey
Aristophanes
Arnott
Barker
Beaumont
Bill
Brenton
Byrne
Chapman
Churchill
Congreve
Corrie
Dekker
Druid
Drury
Dryden
Eliot
England
Etherege
Euripides
Expressionism
Fagon
Field Day
Flannery
Fletcher
Foco Novo
Ford
Glaspell
Goldsmith
Gooch
Hare
Heywood, T.
Hill, E.
Hutchinson
Ikoli
Jonson
Johnson, T.
Kureishi
Kyd
Lowe
Lucie
Marlowe
Marston
Massinger
Matura
Medieval drama
Middleton
Mikron
Morrison
O'Brien
O'Casey
Paines Plough
Pollock
Pownall
Red Shift
Rowley
Saunders
Schofield
Shakespeare
Shirley
Synge
Taylor, C. P.
Tourneur
Vanbrugh
Wandor
Webster
Whitehead
Williams, H.
Williams, N.
Williamson
Wilson, S.
Wilcox
Women Dramatists
Wycherley
Yeats

Carole **WODDIS** is a freelance journalist, former theatre co-editor and regular theatre reviewer with *City Limits*. She has had articles and reviews published in all of the major theatre magazines and journals in Britain as well as the *Guardian* and *New Statesman*. She also worked in theatre for a number of years as a publicist (with the RSC, the National Theatre, the Round House).

Abbensetts
Abbott
Adshead
Age Exchange
Alfreds
Alrawi
Anouilh
Archer
Arden
Bains
Behn
Black Theatre
Black Theatre Forum
Black Theatre Co-op
Blood Group
Cartwright
Charabanc
Clean Break
Collins
Community Theatre
Craze
Daniels
D'Arcy
De Angelis
De Filippo
Delaney
Devlin
Duffy
Dunn
Ellis
English
Fairbanks
Finnegan
Franceschild
Freistadt
Gay Theatre
Gay Sweatshop
Gems, P.
Graeae
Greig
Griffiths, D.
Hansberry
Hayes
Heggie
Hellman
Holborough
Horsfield
Kay
Kearsley
Kesselman
Lavery
Lesbian Theatre
LIFT
Luckham
Macdonald, S.
Marchant
McIntyre
Monstrous Regiment
Moffatt
Mornin
Motton
Murray
New Playwriting
O'Malley

Page
Phillips
Pinnock
Raif
Rame
Reid
Rhone
Rudet
Shange
Shapiro
Strauss
Tara Arts
Temba
Terry
Theatre of Black Women
Townsend
Tremblay
Wertenbaker
Whitemore
Women in Theatre
Women's Theatre Group
Yankowitz
Walcott
White

Alastair **CORDING** is a professional actor. He has a Ph.D. from Glasgow University. He has taught there and at Strathclyde University, where for a number of years he was Assistant Director of the University Drama Centre.

Büchner
Campbell
Dürrenmatt
Gorki
Handke
Joint Stock
Mayakovsky
McGrath, T.
Parker
Pirandello
Poliakoff
Wedekind
Young

Eileen **E. COTTIS** is Senior Lecturer in French and co-founder of, and former Course Tutor for, the MA in Modern Drama Studies at the Polytechnic of North London. She is a committee member of the Society for Theatre Research and a member of the International Federation for Theatre Research, and has written on French and English nineteenth-century theatre.

Adamov
Adaptations and Adapters
Arrabal
Artaud
Barrie
Beaumarchais
Brook
Bubble Theatre Company
Bulgakov
Calderon de la Barca
Cheek by Jowl
Cixous
Claudel
Corneille
Dumas fils
Duras
Eveling
Farce/Light Comedy
Feydeau
Fo
Galsworthy
Garrick
Gatti
Gilbert
Giraudoux
Glasgow Citizens' Theatre
Goethe
Granville Barker
Grass
Gregory
Havel
Hochhuth
Horvath
Ionesco
Jarry
Kleist
Kroetz
Labiche
Lessing
Luke
Machiavelli
Manchester
Marowitz
Mnouchkine
Molière
Mrozek
Music Hall/Variety
Nestroy
Ostrovsky
Performance Art
Pinero
Pub/Café Theatre
Racine
Sartre
Schiller
Schnitzler
Seneca
Shared Experience
Sherriff
Simpson
Sophocles
Taylor
Thomas
de Vega Carpio
Vinaver
Williams, E.
Wodehouse

Howard **LOXTON** was an actor and stage manager in repertory and the West End before becoming a writer and editor and although he is also the author of a number of books on historical and natural history subjects theatre remains his greatest enthusiasm. Recent publications include an introduction to theatre for young readers and he is currently completing a book on promenade performances.

Arbuzov
Auden and Isherwood
Bagnold
Barnes
Behan
Bennett
Berliner Ensemble
Betti
Bolt
Boucicault
Bridie
Capek
Carroll
Christie
Clark, B.
Dyer
English Stage Company
Farquhar
Fry
Fugard
Gay
Genet
Gill
Gogol
Goldoni
Gray, Simon
Harwood
Home, W. Douglas
Hopkins
Hunter
Jellicoe
John, E.
Kemp
Kops
Lan
LIFT
Littlewood
Marcus
Maugham
Mitchell, J.
Molnar
Orton
Otway
Pantomime
Priestley
Promenade Performances
Puig
Rattigan
Reckord
Rudkin
Russell
Shaffer, A.
Shelley
Sheridan
Terson
Theatre in the Round
Thrillers
Travers
Waterhouse and Hall
Weiss

Deborah **PHILIPS** teaches Literature and Women's Studies. She once worked for Ray Cooney Productions. She was a co-founder of *Women's Review* and has written for *The Stage* and *City Limits*.

Ayckbourn	Edgar	Lorca	Shaw
Beckett	Edinburgh Festival	McGrath, J.	Smith, D.
Berkoff	Frayn	Mortimer	Soyinka
Bond	Frisch	National Theatre	Stanislavski
Brecht	Godber	Nichols	Stoppard
Brook	Griffiths, T.	One Person Shows	Storey
Cabaret	Hampton	Osborne	Strindberg
Chekhov	Hastings	Pinter	Wesker
Delaney	Ibsen	RSC	Wilde
Dunbar	Leigh	7:84	

Matt **WOLF** is the London theatre critic for The Associated Press and *The Wall Street Journal* (Europe) and has free-lanced regularly for *City Limits, Harpers & Queen,* and *The Spectator* since he arrived in Britain from New York in September, 1983. In America, he is a frequent contributor to *The Chicago Tribune* and *American Theatre Magazine.*

American Theatres	Henley	Minghella	Steppenwolf Theatre Company
Babe	Holman	Musicals	Talley
Baldwin	Howe	Negro Ensemble Company	Triana
Baraka	Hughes, D.	Nelson	Turgenev
Barry	Inge	Norman	Van Itallie
Bernard	Innaurato	Odets	Wasserstein
Bleasdale	Kaufman and Hart	O'Neill	Whiting
Breuer	Keeffe	Owens	Wilder
Coward	Kilroy	Pomerance	Williams, T.
Darke	Kopit	Rabe	Wilson, A.
Dear	Kramer	Sackler	Wilson, L.
Durang	Leonard	Schisgal	Wilson, R.
Feiffer	Linney	Shaffer, P.	Wisdom Bridge
Fierstein	Mamet	Shawn	Wood
Gelber	Medoff	Shepard	Wooster Group
Gems, J.	Mercer	Simon	Wright
Gray, Spalding	Miller		
Hecht and MacArthur			

INDEX

Numbers in bold indicate main entries

D

F

G

I

L

O

U

V

X

Y

Z